THE
ANNALS OF CLONMACNOISE

BEING

ANNALS OF IRELAND

FROM

THE EARLIEST PERIOD TO A.D. 1408

TRANSLATED INTO ENGLISH A.D. 1627

BY CONELL MAGEOGHAGAN

AND NOW FOR THE FIRST TIME PRINTED

EDITED BY

THE REV. DENIS MURPHY, S.J.

LL. D., M. R. I. A.

VICE-PRESIDENT OF THE ROYAL SOCIETY OF ANTIQUARIES
OF IRELAND

DUBLIN
PRINTED AT THE UNIVERSITY PRESS
FOR THE ROYAL SOCIETY OF ANTIQUARIES OF IRELAND

1896

THIS COPY IS PRINTED FOR

FRANCIS EDMUND CURREY, J.P.,

FELLOW OF THE ROYAL SOCIETY OF ANTIQUARIES OF IRELAN

Editor's Preface.

THESE ANNALS have, in later times at least, usually gone by the name of the 'Annals of Clonmacnoise.' In the book itself there is nothing to show why it should be called by this name. No doubt it gives a special prominence to the history of those parts of the country on both sides of the Shannon bordering on Clonmacnoise, as Teaffa, Meath, Brawnie, Ferkeall, Annaly, Roscommon, Hymany, Moylorg, and to the families inhabiting them, the MaGeoghagans, O'Melaghlens, O'Molloys, O'Feralls, O'Conors, McDermots, O'Kellys, O'Roircks; and indeed the chief value of these Annals arises from the historical details given of these districts and families which are not found to the same extent elsewhere. Frequent mention is made of St. Queran, who was not only the founder of Clonmacnoise, but the patron saint of the men of Connaught, as we know from the 'Saltair na Rann'; whereas few of the other Irish Saints are mentioned and only in a passing way, if we except St. Ruadhan of Lorrha, and St. Columkille, founder of Durrow, both of which places are in the neighbourhood of Clonmacnoise. In the Censura of the Guardian of the Franciscan Convent of Donegal, prefixed to O'Donovan's edition of the 'Annals of the Four Masters,' mention is made, among the books from which extracts were made by the authors of that work, of the 'Book of Clonmacnoise.' O'Donovan thinks the reference is to the book that now goes by that name; not so O'Curry, who believes they are entirely different books, for the reason that the work used by the Four Masters came down but to the year 1227, whereas this one ends with the year 1408.

Nor is there any clue to the author's name throughout the work. He is said to be 'an authentic author and worthy prelate of the Church, that would say nothing but the truth,' 'a great Latinist and Scholler,' yet 'he could not get his penn to name the Kings of England or other foraigne countryes by their proper names but by such Irish names as he pleased to devise out of his own head.' He was Irish too, if we judge from his sympathies shown by 'the reproachful wordes which he layeth down in the ould books and which he declared of an evil will he did beare towards William Burk,' commonly known as William Fitz Adelm, and which the translator will not insert in his translation 'because they were uttered by the author for the disgrace of soe worthy and noble a man as William Burk was.' Nearly all the Irish writers agree with the author of these Annals in their estimate of William Fitz Adelm; indeed the passage in the 'Annals of the Four Masters,' referring to his death, seems to be but a transcript of this passage. Giraldus' estimate of him, almost equal in incisiveness and terseness to Sallust's character of Catiline, is well known; but then Giraldus is hardly to be relied on when he commends any one of his own relatives or censures those with whom he was not connected by blood.

The original work was in Irish. The translator more than once refers to 'the ould Irish book out of which he wrote,' 'to the ould Irish book which he translates, out of which many leaves were lost or stolen,' 'to certain years that are missing in mine ould Booke.' And even the whole of the book is not given by the translator: 'the ould Irish book by longe lying shutt and unused, I could hardly read, and left places that I could not read because they were altogether grown illegible and put out'; and he asks to be excused 'for not naming the King's deputies and Englishmen therein contained by their right names, for I goe by the words of the ould booke and not by my owen invention.'

The original was supposed to be in the possession of the family of Sir Richard Nagle some fifty years ago, a descendant, by his mother's side, of the translator. There was a belief that it contained certain facts tending to their discredit, which that family did not wish to have made known, and for this reason they would not allow it to be examined; but perhaps this unwillingness arose from a desire to keep secure possession of what was looked on by some members of them as a family relic.

These Annals begin with the Creation and end with the year 1408. The translator points out that several parts of the original work are missing, as from 1182 to 1199, and again from 1290 to 1299, and he shows how such books were destroyed, not merely by the chronicles being burnt by the Danes, 'but by taylors being suffered to cutt the leaves of the said books (which their auncestors held in great accoumpt), and sliece them in long peeces to make theire measures off.'

To show the value set on this book by students of Irish history, we need but mention two facts: first, that it was one of the works which the Irish Archæological Society intended to publish ; second, that very copious extracts have been made from it by O'Donovan to illustrate the text of the "Annals of the Four Masters."

The translator was Conell, or Conla, MaGeoghagan, of Lismoyne, Co. Westmeath, who, O'Clery, in his preface to the 'Succession of the Kings,' says, 'prized and preserved the ancient monuments of our ancestors, one who was the industrious collecting Bee of everything that belongs to the honour and history of the descendants of Milesius and of Lughaidh, son of Ith, both lay and ecclesiastical, so far as he could find them.' He dedicated this translation to his brother Terence Coghlan, whose family was among the last to uphold and practise the old Irish tribal customs. It was finished April 20th, 1627, in the 'Castle of Leyeuachan,' or Lemanaghan, the remains of which still exist six miles south-west of Clara, in the King's County. The original manuscript of MaGeoghagan's translation is lost, but there are several copies of it, one in the British Museum, another in the Library of Trinity College, catalogued F. 3,19, both made by Tadhg O'Daly. The latter is that from which this book has been printed. It was made in 1684. The copyist goes somewhat out of his way to censure both the author and the translator for their partiality to the descendants of Heremon, the Hy Neill, to the prejudice of those of Heber, the McCarthys, O'Briens, and their co-relatives of the south.

Of the translation O'Curry says :—'It is written in the quaint style of the Elizabethan period, but by a man who seems to have well understood the value of the original Gaedhlic phraseology, and rendered it every justice, as far as we can determine in the absence of the original.' The copyist's introduction will remind the reader of the pompous style of composition in use among the hedge-schoolmasters half a century ago. I have printed the whole just as it stands in O'Daly's copy. The orthography is such as will lead no one astray, and if an editor begins to 'improve' on such things, it is not easy to know where to stop.

The thanks of the Royal Society of Antiquaries of Ireland are due to the Board of Trinity College, who kindly permitted a copy to be made of their manuscript for the purpose of printing this book.

D. M.

NEW YEAR'S DAY, 1896.

Contents.

	PAGE
EDITOR'S PREFACE,	v
COPYIST'S PREFACE,	3
TRANSLATOR'S PREFACE,	7
ANNALS OF CLONMACNOISE,	10
INDEX,	329

THE
ANNALS OF CLONMACNOISE.

A Booke

Contayning all the Inhabitants of Irel[d] since the creaõn of the World untill the Conquest of ye eng: WHEREIN is shewed all the K[s] of Clanna Neuie Firvolge Twathy Dedanan & the sons of Miletus of spaine. Translated out of Irish into English faithfully and well agreeing to the History de captionibus Hiberniæ[1] Historia Magna[2], & other authentick Authors. Partly Discouering the yeares of the raignes of the s[d] K[s]. wth the manner of theire governm[ts] & alsoe the deaths of Diuers saints of this Kingdome as dyed in these seuerall raignes wth the Tyranicall rule & Gouernment of the Danes for 219 Years.

A brief Catalogue of all the K[s] of the seuerall races after the comeing of S[t] Patrick until Donnogh mc Bryan carried the crown to Roome, & of the K[s] that raigned after untill the tyme of the conquest of the english in the 20 yeare of the raigne of Rory O'Connor, Monarch of Ireld.

Alsoe of certaine things hapened in this kingdome after the conquest of the english untill the sixt yeare of the raigne of King Henry the fourth in the yeare of our Lord god 1408.

Leigteoṗ ṗgṁoḃneoṗ ṗgiaṁġlan ṗgaġta,
Sgṗeaptṗa na Sgol ḋo ṗgṗúḃ ṗé
Ag ṗin ḋuit ṗailltean a ṗaiḋḃṗeiṗ
Naṗ ḋog ḋo lucht ainḃṗoṗ hé[3].

Taḋg ó'Ḋalaḋh.

---

[1] *C. Hiberniæ.*—i.e. The *Leabhar Gabhála*, or *Book of Invasions*, compiled by the O'Clerys in 1630. O'Curry's *MS. Materials*, p. 168.

[2] *H. Magna.*—i.e., The *Seanchus Mír. Ibid.*, p. 16.

[3] hé.—'Illustrious, choice reader, writer, he searched the writings of the schools. Here he sets forth his treasures before thee as the ignorant do not conceive.' Tadhg O'Daly.

To the courteous ingenious pregn^t and juditious
Reader:

I haue presumed (Courteous reader) to premonish you of some both preposterous mistakes used by the translator in this booke in Immitacõn (haply) of the prototypon or primitiue whence it was extracted and Deriued, for he being reputed a curious crittick & a good Chronicler, as certainly he professed himselfe to be & therefore noeways ignor^t of the right antiquitie & just Lotacõn of the sons of Miletus of Spaine, through this voluntary Mistake, procliuity, or partiall Inclinacõn to Heremon (of whom he Descended), the youngest sonne of the s^d Miletus except Herenan & Dissonant to his scientificall knowledg), hath promiscuously & unjustly (though in way of a two late Colourable excuse he Demonstrates not onely a recantation, but alsoe himselfe to be a kind of ambedexter, neutralist or indifferant party) delt wth Heber the while in Postponeinge not only the scept and ffamilies Descended of him, but also Heber himselfe after the said Heremon and his scepts & families in all or most places of this booke, & because that either in auoyding of the noysome clam^s, Inueterate grudge hatred & malice of certaine knowne persons or in Loathsomeness by alteracõn to Disorder the Industryousnesse of the obliedging Translator I haue inconfusedly and imutablie Transcribed his work, (onely the augmenting of some marginalles for your good, nothing relateing to any dislocacõn & the compileing of a Confuser, yett according to the pages somewhat orderly index, Importunity preventing it from being alphabeticall, Whereby concerning my obliuious omission I must be contented to stand in one predican^t which must be always one of the post with the translator untill my next[1]

. . . .

---

[1] A line of the manuscript has been cut off here by the binder.

skilfull friends in Chronologie I am right sorry—clipœum post vulnera sumo, it is good to be wise by other mens follys, and therefore courteous reader, to the end y^t you should not participate of the cruditie of my Cruelly bleeding wounds or of the voluntariness of the translators mistakes I obtestate before you enter profoundly into the perusall of this booke y^t you be Indifferently possessed by assurance of Hebers Refulgent antecedency & priority in antiquity of life and Death privious Determinaçõn & end thereof in maintenance of his & his successors theire just right & lawfull prerogatives. and least excecated Ignorance, obstinacy violent elation, partiall, resolute proteruity, or else the odiousness of your . . . . to atribute Heber and his said scepts theire just dues should diuert you from . . . .

with my postulated request: for your bett^r encouragm^t to comply, &c.

To the worthy and of Great expectacōn young gentleman Mr. Terenc Coghlan his Brother Connell maGeoghagan wisheth long health w^{TH} good success in all his affaires.

AMONG all the worthy & memorable Deeds of K. Bryan Borowe sometime K. of this Kingdome, this is not of the least accoumpt, y^t after he had shaken off the Intollarable Yoake & Bondage wherew^{th} this land was cruelly tortured & harried by the Danes & Normans for the space of 219 yeares that they bore sway, & receaved tribute of the Inhabitants in Generall, & though they nor none of them euer had the name of K. or Monarch of the land yet they had that power as they executed what they pleased & behaued themselves soe cruell and pagan-like as well towards the eclesiasticall as Temporalls of the K.dome, that they broke downe theire churches and razed them to theire very foundations and burnt theire books of Cronicles & prayers to the end that there should be no memory left to theire posterityes & all Learninge should be quite forgotten, the said K. Bryan seeing into what rudenesse the kingdome was fallen, after settinge himselfe in the quite Governm^t thereof, & restored each one to his auntient Patrimony, repayred theire Churches and houses of religion, he caused open schoole to be kept in the seuerall parrishes to Instruct theire youth, which by the s^d Long warrs were growne rude and altogether illiterate, he assembled together all the nobility of the K.dome as well spirituall as temporall to Cashell in Mounster, & caused them to compose a booke contayning all the Inhabitants, euents and scepts that lived in this land from the first peopleing, Inhabitacon and Discouery thereof after the creacon of the world untill that present, which booke they caused to be called by the name of the psalter of Cashell[1], signed it wth his owen hands together wth the hands of the K^s. of the five provinces, & alsoe wth the hands of all the Bushops and prelates of the K.dome, caused seuerall coppyes thereof to be given to the K^s of the provinces, wth straight Charge, that there should be noe credit giuen to any other Chronicles thenceforth, but should be held as false, Disannulled & quite forbiden for ever. Since wch time there were many septs in ye k.dome that liued by it, & whose profession was to Chronicle and keep in memory the state of the K.dome as well for the time past present & to come, & now because they cañot enjoy that respect & gaine by their said profession as heretofore they and theire auncestors receaved they set naught by the s^d knowledg, neglect their Bookes, and choose rather to put their children to learne eng: than their own native Language, in soe much that some of them suffer Taylors to cutt the leaves of the said Books (which their auncestors held in great accoumpt, & sliece them in long peeces to make theire measures[2] off) that the posterities are like to fall into meere Ignorance of any things hapened before theire tyme.

Ireland in ould time, in the raigne of the s^d K. Bryan & before was well stored with learned men and colledges that people came from all partes of Christendome to learne therein, and among all other nations that came thither there was none soe much made of nor respected with the Irish as was the english & Welshmen, to whome they gave severall Collages to Dwell and Learne In, as to the

---

[1] *Psalter of Cashell.*—The author is usually said to have been Cormac MacCullenan, king of Munster and bishop of Cashel. There is in the Bodleian library a copy of some parts of it made in 1454 for MacRichard Butler. O'Curry's *MS. Materials*, p. 19. Keating often makes mention of it in his *H. of Ireland.*

[2] *Measures.*—See Wilde's *Lough Corrib*, p. 202.

englishmen a collage in the towne of Mayo[1] in Coñaught, wch to this day is called Mayo of the english, & to the Welshmen the town of Gallen[2] in the K^s County, wch is likewise called Gallen of the Welchmen or Wales, from whence these said twoo nations haue brought theire charactors, espetially the eng: saxons as by confering the old saxons Characters to the Irish (wch the Irish neuer change) you shall find little or no Difference at all.

The earnest Desire I understand you haue to know these things made me to undertake the translating of the ould Irish booke for you, wch by longe lying shutt & unused I could hardly read and left places, that I could not read because they were altogether growne illegible & put out; & if this my simple Labour shall any way pleasure you I shall hould myselfe thorough recompensed & my payne well Imployed, wch for your owene Reading I have done, & not for the reading of any other Curious fellow that would rather carp at my Phrace, then take any Delight in the History & In the meane time I bid you heartyly farewell. from Leyeuanchan[3] the Twentyeth of Aprill Año Dñi 1627.

Y^r very Loveing Brother

CONELL MA GEOGHAGAN.

---

[1] *Mayo* —Six miles west of Claremorris, Co. Mayo It was called Mayo of the English, as it was founded for English monks who had come with St. Colman from Lindisfarne. An account of its foundation as well as of the monastery of Inisboffin, off the south-west coast of Mayo, will be found in Bede's *Historia Eccles. Anglorum*, IV 4, and in the Most Rev. Dr. Healy's *Ireland's Ancient Schools and Scholars*, p. 526.

[2] *Gallen.*—Near Ferbane, King's Co. A monastery was erected here by St Mochanog in 492. Archdall's *Monasticon*, p. 396.

[3] *Leyeuanchan* — Now Lemanaghan. The castle of the Mageoghagans is still standing, close by are the remains of the ancient church of St. Manchan.

The names of the severall authors wch I have taken for this booke

Saint Colum Kill¹, sainte bohine², Collogh O'More³ Esqr, Venerable Bede, Eoghye O'Flannagan⁴ arch dean of Ardmach and Clonfiachna, Gillernew Mac Conn ne mboght, archpriest of Clonuckenos, Keilachar Mac Coñ als Gorman, Eusebius Marcellinus⁵, McOylyne O'Mulchonrye⁶ and Tanaige O'Mulconrye, 2 professed Chroniclers.

MEMORANDUM.

from Adam untill the Deluge there were yeares	1656
from the Deludge untill Abrahams tyme -	0292
from Abr. untill the Departing out of egypt -	0500
from the Departing out of Egypt untill the building of the temple of Sollomon	0480
from the building of the Temple untill the Captiuity in Babylon	0410
from the returne from the Captiuity untill the Machabees Tyme,	0432
from the Machabees tyme untill Herods, &c. -	0134

---

¹ *St. Colum Kill.*—The only works of his are the account of the miracles of St. Patrick and some poems and prophecies.

² *St. Bohine.*—He wrote a *Life of St. Columkille* and some prophecies. He succeeded St. C. as abbot of Iona. O'Reilly's *Irish Writers*, p. xl.

³ *C. O'More.*—He is not mentioned either by O'Reilly or O'Curry. Keating often gives him as an authority

⁴ *E. O'Flannagan.*—He is mentioned in the *Leabhar na hUidhri* as one of the authors from whose works Flann of Monasterboice composed a tract on the pagan cemeteries of Ireland. None of his works have come down to us. See O'Curry's *MS. Materials*, p. 138.

⁵ *Eusebius Marcellinus.* — His chief historical works are his *Ecclesiastical History*, up to A.D. 324, and his *Chronicon*, containing chronological tables from the Creation to the 20th year of Constantine's reign.

⁶ *M. O'Mulchonrye* —The *Annals of the O'Mulchonrys* was one of the books from which the Four Masters compiled their *Annals*. Two of the name assisted in the compilation of this latter work.

ADAM in the 130 yeare of his age Begatt Seth, and afterwards Adam Liued 800 yeares & in all he liued 930 yeares. Seth in the 105th yeare of his age Begatt Enos, and liued afterwards 137 yeares. Enos in the 90th yeare of his adge Begatt Cainan and liued after his Birth 815 yeares. Cainan in the 70th yeare of his age Begatt Malalle and liued himself after 840 yeares. Malalele in the 65th yeare of his age Begatt Jareth and liued after 830 yeares. Jareth in the 62nd yeare of his adge begatt Enoche and liued after 800 yeares. Enoche in the 65th yeare of his age Begatt Methusalem, after whose Byrth He Waked with God. Methusalem in the age of 187 years Begatt Lamech and liued himself after 782 yeares. Lamech in the yeare of his adge 182 Begat Noeh and liued after 595 yeares. This yeare of Lamech's age came the woman called Cesarea[1] or Keassar accompanied onely with three men and 50 Women to this Land which was the first habitacōn of Ireland, though others say yt this land was first Discouered and found by three fisher men[2] who were sayleing in these parts of the world, and Because they made noe Residence in the Land I will make noe mention of them.

The 3 men that came with the said Keassar were called Layerie, Bethe, and ffintan. Leyerie after 7 years continuance in the Land Dyed, and was the first that ever Dyed in Ireland of whome Ardleyren[3] (where he dyed and was entered) tooke the name. Beth Dyed at the mount called Sliew Beth[4]. Fintan survived and was Drowned

---

One branch of the family were hereditary ollamhs of the O'Conors, another of the O'Briens. The *Annals F. M.* say, 'Mailin, the most highly respected and honoured of all the poets of his time,' died in 1441. Tanaige, his son, died in 1446.

[1] *Cesarea.*—For the bardic account of C. and her companions, see O'Grady's *H. of Ireland*, pp. 72-81.

[2] *Fisher men.*—See Keating's *H. of Ireland*, p. 61.

[3] *Ardleyren.*—O'Donovan thinks this is Ardamine, five miles southwest of Gorey, Co. Wexford, where there is a curious moat.

[4] *Sliew Beth.*—Twelve miles north of Clones, Co. Monaghan. The *Annals F. M.* say he was buried under a carn. There is a townland here called Carn Mor.

where the Generall flood did ouertake him. Keassar Died at Keassra[1] in Connaught and soe euery of the 50 women were Drowned where each of them was ouertaken as my Author Eochy O'Flannigan Reporteth, whoe giueth no credit to that ffabulous tale of many that giue out that fintan Liued in Ireland before the fflood, shunned himselfe from the violence thereof In a caue at Lochdeirke untill the flood was past and then after liued[2] in the Kingdom for many Hundred years, wch is a thing contrary to Holy Scripture wch sayeth that all the world was Drowned in the Generall fflood saueing Noech and his 3 sonnes Sam, Cham, and Japhett with their 4 wives.

This Keassar was neace unto Noeh, his Brothers Daughter. A Little before The flood the Arke was made, and in the 600 yeare of Noeh's age came the flood, wch is the first age of the world, from Adam to the fflood and Contayneth 1656 yeares, and according to the 70 Interpreters of the Hebrews 2242.

The second age is from the flood to Abraham and contayneth [292 yeares, or as the Interpreters aforesaid vizt. the 70 Interpreters of the Hebrews 940.]

Noeh haveing but 3 sonnes as aforesaid, Gaue them three parts of the world, that is to say to Shem Asia, to Cham Africa, and to Jaffet Europa. and because Miletus of Spaine and his nephew Lauthus (of whom all Ireishmen and Ireishscotishmen are Descended) came from the Race of Japhett, I will Discourse of him and leaue to speake of his 2 other Brothers Shem and Cham as Impertinent to the thing I haue in hand, saue onely that I Intend to speake a Little of the Monarches of the Assirians, Medes, Gretians, and Romans as the occasion of my History shall Require;

Ireland long time after the flood lay wast untill about the Yeare after the Creation of the World 1969 and after the flood 313 yeares in the 21 year of the age of the Patriarck

---

[1] *Keassra.*—On the Boyle river.
[2] *Lived.*—So, too, the *Leabhar na hUidhri* says he survived the deluge and lived to the coming of St. Patrick. Keating's *H. of Ireland,* p. 69.

Abraham and alsoe in the 1st yeare of the Raigne of Semiramis then monarches of the world in Assiria.

Bartholeme a Gretian Born of Morea and his 3 sonns Rowrye, Slaynge, and Laughlen fleeing out of Greece for Murderinge his one father & mother execrablie to help one of his friends and kindsmen to the Gouernment of that Kingdom landed in Ireland with such as followed him about the 17th of May in the same yeare and there continued with such as Descended of him 269 yeares, whereof he gouerned himself 30 years after all which time spent all that then Remayned aliue of them to the number of 9008 persons from the first Monday in May untill the next Monday after Dyed of a suden Infection upon the playnes of Moynealta[1]. It was called Moynealta[1], Because all the foule in the kingdome for the most parte Gathered themselves there to shunn themselves.

At his coming into Ireland hee found but three laughs and nyne Rivers in the Kingdom, The laughs were called Laugh Luymnin[2], Laugh Forareawan[3], and Finlogh[4] in Connacht. The Rivers were called the Liffie or Rurhagh, Lye[5], Moye, Slygeagh[6], Sayuer[7], Bwaise[8], Banne, Mayowne[9], and Finn.

In his time he Diuided Ireland into foure parts, one to each of his 3 sonns and the 4th to himselfe, and for that Ireland was then all couered with woods, hee and his sones made manye plaines by cutting Down the woods wch after did turn the contry to great good, and was the only thinge worthe the memory that was don in that second Inhabitation of Ireland, Dureinge wch time of 269 yeares, that is to say

---

[1] *Moynealta.*—*i.e.* the plain of the birds, extending from Howth to Tallaght.

[2] *Laugh Luymnin.*—The ancient name of the Shannon from Limerick to the sea.

[3] *Forareawan.*—Near Sliabhmish, Co. Kerry.

[4] *Finlogh.*— In Erris, county of Mayo.

[5] *Lye.*—The Lee, that flows through Cork.

[6] *Slygeagh.* — Now the Gitley, which flows through Sligo.

[7] *Sayuer.*—The ancient name of the river Erne.

[8] *Bwaise.*—The Bush, which falls into the sea near the Giant's Causeway.

[9] *Mayowne.*—The Mourne.

from the 12th of Semiramis Raigne to the 33rd of Baleus the second there Raigned in Assiria Being the first monarch and Monarch 8 Monarches wch was first begun by Nibroth sonn of Chus, who was son of Cham, who was sonne of Noeh.

Ireland after the death of Bartholeme and his People was 30 yeares waste and desolate dureinge which time Assiria was Gouerned by too Monarches, that is to say, Baleus Secundus, 19 yeares, and Altades, 11 yeares.

Culloch O'More sayeth that it was wast but the said 30 yeares onely; the first of the before Recited monarchs was Semaramis who Rayned 30 yeares, Sameas Nimas 38 yeares, Arius 30 yeares, Araleus 40 yeares, Baleus 30, Armarkes 30, Bellochus 30 and Baleus Tertius 33 yeares.

HERE ENDETH THE SECOND INHABITACŌN OF IRELAND AND FOLLOWETH THE THIRD, WHICH IS OF CLANNA NEVYE AND FFIRVOLGE.

In the Later end of the Raigne of the said Altades, came Neuie Mc Agamemnon with his foure sonns Into Ireland out of Greece, his sonnes names alsoe were Sdarne, Jaruanell, the prophett, Fergus Leahdearg, who had a son called Brittan the Balde, of whome all Welchmen are Descended, and Anynn wch people Ruled Ireland 382 yeares. During wch time there Gouerned in Assiria 13 Monarches wch were Altades 21 yeares, Mamillus 30, Spartus 40, Ascatades 41, Amintas 45, Belochas Junior 52, Belopares 30, Sphereus 20, Mancaleus 30, Mamillus 30, Lamprides 32, Sorares 20, and Lampares 18.

Starna McNevie fought a Greate Battle in Dalriada against Conyn(ge) McFewer 7 yeares after their comeing. Conyngs tower was besieged both by sea and land with 60000 men, that is to say 30000 by sea And soe many more by land, and in the end was Gotten by ffomores And destroyed. These ffomeres were a sept Descended from Cham the sonn of Noeh, that there liued by pyracy and spoyle of other nations and were in those days very troblesom to the whole world. Many Laughs and Rivers broke out in their time. Many playnes were by them made, by cutting down the woodes, and Diging the Rootes of the trees, Alsoe they erected manye Rathes, these were the only thinges of marke Don by y^t sept of Clann Nevye. In the End after longe strife and continuall vexeation such as were of most account of them were Driuen out of the country by the said troblesom sept of ffomores and went Back againe to Greece where they continued the space of 50 yeares or thereabouts. Dureinge wch time of 50 yeares there Raigned in Assiria two Monarches wch were Lampares 12 yeares, and Pannias 38 yeares. At the end of wch time they being overlayed by the exactions of the Gretians, and Desirous alsoe to recouer theire naturall contry which at the first they did quitly posses without strife or Interuption, and soe did Enioy the same for the space of 37 yeares after under the rule of nine Kings. This sept were called ffiruolge, there were 5 Brothers that were theire Chieftaines, the sonnes of Dela m^c Loich that first Diuided Ireland into fiue partes. 1. Slane theire eldest brother had the prouince of Leynster for his part, wch contayneth from Inuer Colpe, y^t is to say where the River of Boyne Intereth into the sea now called in Irish Drocheda[1], to the meetinge of the 3 Waters by Waterfoord where the Three Rivers Syure, ffeoir[2], and Barrow doe meete and run together into the sea. 2. Gann the second brothers parte was South Munster which is a prouince extending from that place to Bealaghconglaissy[3]. 3. Seangan the third Brothers part was from Belachconglaissy to Rose De Hoileagh, now called Limbricke, wch is the prouince of North Munster. 4. Geanann the fourth Brother had the prouince of Conaught contayneing from Limbricke to Easroe[4]. 5. And Rorye the 5th Brother and youngest had from Easroe aforesaid to Inver Colpe wch is the prouince of Ulster. The sayd fiue prouinces

---

[1] *Drocheda.*—i.e. *drochet atha,* the bridge of the ford.

[2] *ffeoir.*—i e. the Nore, an ffeoir.

[3] *Bealaghconglaissy.* — Keating says it was 'at Cork.'

[4] *Easroe.*—Now Ballyshannon.

are Diuided into 33 Countyes. The whole kingdom Containeth 184 Cantredes, and each cantred a hundred townes[1].

First Lynster contayneth 31 Cantreds wch are Diuided into eight Countyes. Both the prouinces of Munster seauenty cantreds which are but seauen counteyes.

Connaught 30 cantredes, six Countyes. Ulster 35 Cantredes which are 6 Countyes, and Meath eighteen Cantreds which are 2 Countyes and counted to be the 11th part of the Kingdom and for the goodness thereof was reserued alwayes for the maintanance of the monarch, and which was annexed by Kinge Twahall Teaghtwar[2] to the King's Royall seat of Taragh.

After makeing of which Diuision Slane theire said elder Brother by the Consent and election of his other 4 Brothers was chosen King, and was the first King that euer absolutely ruled in Ireland. There were 9 Kings of them one after another whose names ensue: Slane Raigned 1 yeare, Rowry Raigned 2 years, Gann and his brother Geanann jointly Raigned 4 yeares, Seangan Raigned 5 yeares, Fiagha Keannnan Raigned 5 yeares, Rional als Riongall Raigned 6 yeares, Foyngen Raigned 4 yeares, and Eochy m^cEirck 10 yeares. Dureinge the saide ten yeares Raigne of the saide last Kinge Eochy m^cEircke there was noe Raine in Ireland, notwithstanding there was aboundance of graine and fruite and was the Last Kinge of that septe called ffirvolge and upon them came in the people called Twathy De Dannan out of Greece too, Being a Braunch of the same stock that ffirvolge were of and were kinsmen. Dureinge the time of ffirvolge, which was 37 yeares, there Raigned in Assiria 3 monarchs to witt Pannias 7 yeares, Sosarmus nineteen yeares and Mitreus 11 yeares. Twany de danaan after they had spent much tyme abroad in learneinge nigromancy Magicke, and other Diobolicall artes wherein they were exceedingely well skilled, and in these Dayes accounted the Cheefest in the

---

[1] *Townes.*—*i.e.* townlands.
[2] *Twahall Teaghtwar.*—He was ardrigh from A.D. 76 to 106. More about him later.

world in that profession, Landed in the west part of Connaught. ffirvolge hearinge of theire comeing made towards them, and meeting them in a greate plaine called Moytoyrey¹ in Connaught, fought wth them, where ffirvolge was ouerthrone and one Hundred thousand of them slaine with theire said King Eochy m^cEirche², which was the greatest slaughter that euer was hard of in Ireland at one meetinge.

HERE ENDETH THE 3RD INHABITATION OF IRELAND
AND FOLLOWETH THE FOURTH
WHICH IS OF TWANY DE DANANN.

The Contry being thus conquered by Twany de Danann one Newae was theire first kinge and lost his Arme in that greate Battle of Maytory³, wh^{ch} by the coning skill of his surgion and goldsmith whose names were Dyan Kight and Credyn, which were Passing skilfull in theire profession, as it did well apeare by the wonderfull cure they did, for they made a siluer hand and put on theire King which serued for all Interprises and purposes, and thereof he was called Nwae with the siluer hand. Dureinge the time his hand was in cure (which was 7 yeares) his kinsman Breasse was king, but he being well Recouered of his hurt was againe King of Ireland, and others to the number of 9 Kinges of that sept all whose names Doth follow :

Breasse Raigned 7 yeares. Nwaey Raigned 20 yeares and was then slaine in Moyetorye in the battle aforesaid by ffomerie where ffomeries themselves for the most parte was slaine, and such of them as made escape from that Danger were quite Driven out of the whole Kingdom 27 yeares after

---

¹ *Moytoyrey.*—Near Cong. See Wilde's *Lough Corrib*, p. 217.

² *E. m^cEirche*—He is supposed to be buried under the carn on the hill of Killowen. There are many other sepulchral monuments in the neighbourhood.

³ *Maytory.*—Called northern M. It lies between Loughs Arrow and Allen.

the first Battle. After Breasse succeeded Loway Keyhleann (of whome Iniskihlean tooke the name) and Raigned 40 yeares. Andagha Raigned 80 yeares. Dealvoye Raigned 13 yeares. Fiagha mᶜDealvoye Raigned 10 yeares. mᶜKoyll Raigned 10 yeares. mᶜKight Raigned tenn yeares, and mᶜGreny 10 yeares. These last 3 beinge 3 Brothers, the sonns of Kearmad Milvoyle were marryed to 3 sisters the Daughters of Fiagha mᶜDealvoye, whose Daughters names were Banva, Foala, and Ere; now for that the said three Brothers did in some sorte square about the Gouernment of the kingdom, there was order taken by their friends that the Eldest Brother should Raigne for the first yeare, the second for the second yeare, and the 3ʳᵈ the third yeare, and soe each of the Brothers took his turne of the Gouernment in that manner, with this promise Between them, that when any of the Brothers should be Kinge that then the Realm for that yeare should be called after the Kinge for the time Beinge his wifes name. By meanes whereof Banva, Foela and Ere are the names of Ireland euer since the 8 sonns of Miletus of Spaine came and conquered the whole Land, whose comming you shall understand soone in the Insueinge Discourse.

But before I speake of them, It is fitt that I shall put the Reader in Remembrance as some of our Antiquarists affirme, that about this time Paris of Troye ravished and tooke away Hellen the wife of Menelaus In his one absence, & by the greate mediation and Intercession of Menelaus the peeres of Greece followed wᵗʰ a greate Army and continued 10 yeares wares with the Troyans, where in a certaine Cessation & truse made by the said partyes a certaine souldier named Alea[1] being vacant and Idle invented Dice and tables to pass away the wearisomeness of the tyme, of whome the Dice took the name. Alsoe aboute this tyme the art of medicine was first found by Apollo, or as others affirme, by his sonn Aestulapius. Orpheus of thratia the Inuentor of musike and cheefe Musistion of the Gretians florished about this Tyme.

---

[1] *Alea.*—The Latin for dice, dice-playing

The Annals of Clonmacnoise. 19

Haueinge thus Digressed from my History I will now Returne where I left the same.

Long before this Time Neale or Nioule m^cFenius ffearsy ancester of Clanna Miley from Scithia came to Egypt and there liued under the Gouernment of Pharao, and when the Israelhtes were in Discord with the Egiptians they landed at the place neare the Read Sea called Capacyront. This Neale came to converse with them and to know whoe they were that Landed in that place. Then Aaron the High Priest of the Jewes told him that they were Jewes, and how his Brother Moyses by the Helpe of God Brought diuers pleagues on the Egyptians for theire abuses &c. Then Neale and Earon falling into more friendly familiarity & Conuersation together, Neale asked him whether the Israelites had any victuals, whereunto Earon Replied & told him that they had but very little, for they came then from the Captivity and Bondage of the Egytians, soe as it were Impossible for them to haue but little sustenance. You shall command whatsoeuer I haue, said Neale & shall haue wheat and wine at y^r pleasure. Whereupon Aaron repayred to the camp of the Isaraelites, and tould his brother Moyses & the rest of the courteous entertainment offered by the said Neale to them, whereof they were exceeding glad and went to the house of the said Neale, where they were wonderfully well used to their own Contentment. It was their Chance the same night that a snake did Runn ouer the partes of the Body of a Child that was in the House whose name was Gathelus, sonn of the said Neale for which the childe was extreame sicke. The snake left markes euerywhere on his Body where it was toched, thereupon the childs said ffather procured him to be Brought to Moyses, who after long praying touched his sores with a Rod (wherewith he made a way through the Red sea) and immediately the Child was Restored to his perfect and former health, and with all Moyses said by way of a prophesye that God was pleased that noe snake or other venemous worme would euer after annoye or hurt that child or any of his posteritye and that no venomous Beast should neuer Dwell in the contry where the Issue and offspring of the Child would live, prophesied alsoe that there should many Kings, Princes, Saints and just men Descend of that child, which is the cause (as some are of opinion) that venemous beasts are not seen in this kingdome, others say that there was an Infinite number of them there untill the comeing of St. Patricke, and that they were bannished here hence, by his prayers.

After all which past Neale conplayned to the Isaraellites how odious he would groe with Pharao for using any friendship with the Israellites. Moyses, Aaron, and the rest Requested Neale with his whole familie and followers to goe with them, and that if God did please to giue them the promised land they would giue him a good share thereof, & use him thenceforward no worse then one of themselues, or if he pleased to bark with them they would prouide some place for him on the seas Remote from the power of pharao, where he might quitely Remaine untill he had seen the finall end Between the Egyptians and the Isaraelites. Then they apoynted 3000 souldiers under Neale with command as admirall of theire fleete. Neale sayled Back to the place where the Egiptians were Drowned in the Red Sea, where he found certainely that pharao himself, together with 60,000 footmen and 50,000 horsemen were Droned soe as there escaped none of the said number undrowned but one man whose name was Fasteus. Neale seeinge the Death of Pharao and his armye sheaked off all his feare and Determined to stay thenceforth in the Kingdome and to possese his share thereof for him and his posteritye for euer, soon after Neale Dyed, his sonne Gathelus succeeded in his place, whoe accordinglye possessed the same until he Dyed and had issue Essrue, sonn of the said Gathelus, which Essre had alsoe a sonne called Srue who was sonn of Neale. Neale mac Fenius Farcy was son of Baath, whoe was son of Magog, whoe was sonn of Japhett, whoe was sonn of Noeh, whoe was sonn of Lameth, whoe was sonn of Methusalem, whoe was sonn of Enoch, whoe was sonn of Jaruett, whoe was sonn of Malalecle,

The Annals of Clonmacnoise.

whoe was sonn of Cainan, whoe was sonn of Enos, whoe was sonn of Seth, whoe was sonn of Adam.

About this Tyme these ensueinge laughs did first break out & spring, Lough da Keigh[1], Laugh Grayne[2], laugh Kymy[3], laugh Bway[4], laugh Baye[5], Logh Finmeay,[6] and Laugh Raigh[7].

Labdon Raigned ouer the Isaraelites 8 yeares, the 3rd yeare of whose Raigne Troy was taken and Priamus killed. This Labdon being dead the Iseraelites serued the Phylistins for 40 yeares, he was of the tribe of Ephraim. Ascanius Aenææ filius Raigned 39 yeares and founded the Cytty Alba longa. Sampson sonne of Manue was Judith[8] of the people 20 yeares. he was of the tribe of Dann.

OF THE COMEING OF THE SONNS OF MILETUS OF SPAINE TO THIS KINGDOM: OF THE OUERTHROE THEY GAVE TO TWANY DE DANAN. OF THE JOYNT RAIGNE & DIUISION OF IRELAND BETWEEN THE TWO BROTHERS HERMON & HEBER, & HOW THEY SQUARED AMONGUE THEMSELVES, AND CONSEQUENTLY HOW HERMINN SLEW HEBER AND RAIGNED HIMSELFE AS SOLE MONARCH OF THE KINGDOM.

The most part of our Ireish Cronacles agree that the sonns of Miletus came to this land in the beginning of the destruction of Troy, & that Hermon and Heber sons of the said Miletus Raigned together joyntly when Agamemnon with his Gretians came to that Destruction. The occation of

---

[1] *L. da Keigh.*—The ancient name of Waterford harbour.

[2] *L. Grayne.*—Now L. Graney, ten miles S E of Gort, Co. Galway.

[3] *L. Kymy* —Now L. Hackett, in the barony of Clare Galway.

[4] *L. Bway* —Now L. Baa, near the village of Castleplunkett, Co. Roscommon.

[5] *L Baye.*—Perhaps Lough Beagh in Donegal.

[6] *L. Finmeay.*— Now Garadice Lough, in the barony of Carrigallen, Co. Donegal

[7] *L. Riagh.*—Near Loughrea, Co. Galway.

[8] *Judith.* — *Recte* Judge : see *Judges*, xv. 20.

theire coming is as followeth. In the yeare after the flood 1245 being about the 12th yeare of the Raigne of Dauid king of Isarael & Judea, Gallo the sonn of Billus king of Scithia after surnamed Miletus of spaine for his manye and great exployets, heareing of the great wars wch the Egyptians held then with theire neighbouring contryes, being before in some Displeasure at home for the strife that grew Between him and his Kinsman for the kingdom of Scithia & being alsoe himself much given to warr, ambitious of honour & Desirous to encrease his name (as the manner of his contry was) passed out of Scithia with a number of his friendes, kinsmen & ffollowers into Egypt, where he was no sooner ariued then well entertained by the Egyptians, & in short time after did soe well aquite himself in theire seruice, that he was made Generall of theire armies & withall married the Daughter of Symedes then the Greatest prince in Egypt or Pharao as they did then commonly call theire monarch, his other Daughter was after married to Solomon, King of Jerusalem. This Symedes or Symenides by other authors is called alsoe Silagh & became soe great & mighty, that he had in his army 1200 chariots, 60,000 Horses, and 400,000 footmen.

After the Death of king Solomon & alsoe after the Departure of Gallo out of Egipt he entred with the same into the city of Jerusalem, Ransacked the cittye spoiled the Jews, & carried away all their Treasure & Jewells with him into Egipt. Some few years before this was don, when Galle saw that his father-in-law was quiete at home and could command his neybours abroad, & after that Dwelt in Egypt 6 years or somewhat more, he tooke leaue of his friendes there and wth a number of his Depend^{ts} did pass on Towards Parthia & encamped at the foot of a great Hill (which for good lookes sake he called after his wife's name Scota, at lenth after a long & wearisome jorney; when he had been tossed too and froe for the space of 2 years he was wind-driuen into Portugall 126 years after that king seased to rule that kingdom; Gargoris, surnamed Meliola for his skill in making of Hony being the last of them. Spaine was Diuided into prouences amongst the princes thereof, soe it was much the sooner Brought under by Gallo who in less than one yeare ouerthrew the Spaniards in sundry fights, and cheefly in 3 great batles, after which victoryes, his wife Scota, Pharao his Daughter dyed. You are to understand (to make the History more manifest) that Gallo was thrice married; first in Scithia to Seang Rifflar his Daughter, a great Prince in Scithia, by whome he had two sonns Begotten in Scithia which were called Don and Heragh Feura. Secondly to Scota Pharao's Daughter (as is afore said) by whome he had alsoe 4 sonns borne unto him in Egipt, that is to say Heber the white, Avirgin, Ire, and Colp with the sword; thirdly to Savia, the Daughter of Nicicorus, then the cheefest of Spaine, by whom he had likewise 2 sonnes which were Borne in Spaine, wch were called Heremon and Herenan, and by that marriage he had great quiteness in Spaine all his lifetime after.

In process of time being well multiplied in numbers, he Remoued some of his company into Biscaie, then called Colteberia, where they did Edifie Brigantia and aded thereto a great Tower that was named of the builder Breons Tower[1], for soe Galloes grandfather was called Breowen, & soone after some of them came into Ireland, which hapened upon this ocation. Ithus mcBreowyn, sonn of him that built this Tower above mentioned, and uncle to the said Miletus, was Reputed for a wise learned and Great traueller, hearing of the good success his kinsmen had in Spaine, followed them thither. Being met & after great joy made on either side upon ocation of ffurther speech, told them of the manners and ffassions of sundry nations that he had seen, and more ouer told them that there was an Island that stood north East of Spaine of good Report as he alledged, which if he had once seen & taken notice of he would euer after live at home with his kinsmen, set up his Rest, and take such partes as they

---

[1] *Breons Tower.*—A detailed description of it will be found in *The Ancient Lighthouse of Corunna*, by Rev. Dr. Todd; it is also mentioned in Wilde's *Voyage to Madeira*, 1. 13.

had, upon this, within fewer Dayes after he made Ready for Ireland, went forward in his Jorny, and after his landing he made towardes the three Kings of Ireland, that were the Brothers married to the three sisters whereof I haue made mention before and lay them at Oleagh Neyde[1] and were at variance for the goodes, treasures, and jewells, that then theire father-in-law and late predecessor King Fiagha m^cDealvoy left after him, which was a great thing in these days. When Ithus came in the presence of the said Kings he was very friendly & courteously entertained, & much made of by them, he to Requite their kind fauours, told them againe in a louing manner that they ought not to Disagree in any sort, for any worldly Ritches, being Brothers & friendes, as they were, and espetially in soe much that God Dealt so bountifully with them in sending them the Great Ritches they had in hand and such good soyle that yealdeth such abundance of all good Things meet for their sustenance of man, as wheat, Hony, fish, and foule, not onely suffitiently for theire one maintenance, But alsoe plentifull for the Relieueing of many of the nib^rs, Being therewith all very temperate of itselfe & right meet for men to liue in at ease.

These words were soe carefully marked by the Brothers, and struck such feare into them that as soone as Ithus tooke his leaue of them they sent certaine of theire friends priuily to murther him by the way, as he Passed on towards his ship, thinking by that foule fact to preu^t the worse, If he or any other by his means & instigation would couet soe good a Contry as he took theires to be, & soe in time troble them for their one, when noe such thing had been looked for or meant. Ithus in that manner was ouertaken, grieuiously wounded and the most part of his men slaine. The place where this murther was committed to this day is named Moynithe[2] which is to say, Ithus his plaine, and at lenth with such of

---

[1] *Oleagh Neyde.*—Keating says it was in the confines of Ulster. *H. of Ireland*, p. 122.

[2] *Moynithe.*—The plain along the river Finn, in the barony of Raphoe, Co. Donegal.

his men as were left him aliue, he gott him a shipbord all
Bloody as he was, and soe sailing towards Spaine he Dyed
by the way, when the ship landed his dead Corps was brought
all mangled as it was before his Kinsmen, whoe upon the
Report made by his men of their ill usage in Ireland took
the mater uery Grieueously and presently swore the Reuenge
thereof; when they had thoroughly consulted of the cause,
they agreed of all hands to make ready for Ireland, & soe
leaueing Gallo well settled in Spaine 40 of the chiefest of them
in 30 shipps made towards Ireland, Galloes 8 sons being of
the number, and the greatest in authoritye & Reputacōn : but
being come towards the shore about the 17th of May 2934 and
the year before the birth of our Sauiour Jesus Christ the sonn
of God 1029 as Collogh O'More setteth forth who was a uery
worthy Gentleman and a Great searcher of antiquities, but
Philip O'Sulivan[1] in his printed book Dedicated to Phillip the
4th, King of Spaine, sayeth that they came in the yeare
before the birth of our Saviour 1342 which is from this present
year 1627 the number of 2966 yeares, Laestheness being then
the 33rd monarch of the Assirians, they were kept of a long
time from Landing for Twathy de Danan that were then
Ruler of Ireland did use such witchcrafts, sorcerye, and other
magick arts and Incantations that thereby they Did procure
such tempest, stormes, and continuall contrary winds, that
Diuers of the principle of them as Donn, Ire, and fferanan,
three of the Brothers, were lost & Drowned, wth others of the
best sort to the number of 100 besides Gentlewomen, Gentlemen, & others of less Reckoning. Some say that Donn
was Drowned at a place in the Weast called Teahdoyne[2] or
Don his house. They alsoe say that the picts heareing of y[e]
great number of widowes in Ireland, came & married the
Relict widows of the said Drowned persons & couenanted
with the sons of Miletus that if they had failed Issue male,

---

[1] *O'Sulivan.—Historiæ Catho-
licæ Hiberniæ Compendium*, t. i.,
l. iii., c. i.

[2] *Teahdoyne.*—Keating says this
was somewhere near the cliffs of
Skellig, in west Kerry.

y^t then the ofspring of Miletus should inherit theire Contry, which accordingly came to pass after a long space, for in Defect of their Issue one fergus[1], the king of Ireland's son, was sent ouer into Scotland & was Inuested as King thereof, they were called Picts of a certain oyntment they used to paint theire faces wth all; their land in English is called pictland[2], in Irish cnocha cpucneach.

After the Landing of the sonns of Miletus & Receaveing such Losses, they made forwardes towardes Taylten[3] where they were met with Tawthy de Danan & fought with them & after a cruell and bloody Bataile which lasted almost from morning untill night twathy De Danan were ouerthrone to theire utter Destruction, where m^{c}Quoill, m^{c}Keght and m^{c}Grenie theire 3 Kings with their three wivs Ery, Fodla, and Banva were slaine.

This people Twathy de Danann were most notable Magisians and would work wonderfull things thereby; when they pleased, they would they would troble Both sea and Land, darken Both sonn and Moone at theire pleasures. They did frame a great broade stone which they called Lya Fail[4], or the stone of Ireland, by theire art and placed the same at Tarragh, which by Enchantment had this property: when anyone was borne to whome to be a King of Ireland was predestinated, as soone as the party soe Borne stood upon this stone forthwith the stone would giue such a shouting noyse that it was hard from sea to sea, throughout the whole Kingdom, which presently would satisfie the party standing on the stone, and all the Rest of his future fortune to the

---

[1] *Fergus.*—Surnamed Mor. He was son of Erc, son of Eochaidh Muinreamhair. He and his brothers went to Scotland about the year 506 of our era. See Adamnan's *Life of St. Columba*, edited by Reeves, p. 433.

[2] *Pictland.*—On the origin of the name and the history of the Picts, see Nennius, *Historia Britonum*, published by the Irish Archæological Society, p. 121.

[3] *Tayllen.*—Now Teltown, midway between Navan and Trim. See Wilde's *Boyne and Blackwater*, p. 149.

[4] *Lya Fail.*—See Petrie's *History and Antiquities of Tara*, p. 159, in *Transactions of the R.I.A.*, vol. xviii. He says it is still at Tara.

The Annals of Clonmacnoise.

Right of the Crowen, this stone remained a long time in the King of Ireland's pallace of Taragh, whereon many Kings and Queens were crowned untill it was sent ouer into Scotland by the King of Ireland with his sonn ffergus, who was created the first King of Scotland on that stone, and for a long time after all the Kings of Scotland receaued theire Crownes thereon untill the time of King Edward the first, King of England, whoe tooke the same as a Monument from thence into England in the wares between him and Scotchmen & placed it in Westminster abby, where many a King of England haue been likewise Crowned thereupon, & is to be seen there amongst other monum[ts] this day.

These Twathy de Danan ruled in Ireland for the space of 197 years, under the Gouernment of 9 Kings, During w[ch] time there Gouerned in Assiria seuen Emperors or Monarchs, to witt Mitreus 15 yeares, Tulanes or Tantanes 22 yeares, Tarileus 40 yeares, Thineus 30 yeares, Dercilus 40 yeares, Euphalus 30, and Loasthenes 12 yeares.

Soon after this Conquest made by the sonns of Miletus theire Kinsmen and friendes, they Diuided the whole Kingdome amongue themselues in manner as followeth: But first before they landed in this land, Tea the daughter of Louthus, that was wife of Heremon, Desired one Request of her husband & kinsmen, wh[ch] they accordingly Granted, w[ch] was, that the place shee would most like of in the kingdom should be for euer after called after or by her name, And that the place soe called should be euer after the principle seat of her Posteritie to liue in, and upon their landing she chose Leytrym[1] which is since that time called Taragh, where the Kings pallace stood for many yeares after, and which she caused to be called Tea-mur, mur in Irish is a town or pallace in English, and being joined to Tea maketh it to be the town, pallace, & house of Tea. The

---

[1] *Leytrym* — For an account of the former names of Tara and on the origin of its present name, see the extracts from the ancient writers Amergin and Fintan, which are given *Ibid.*, p. 129.

south part was for 6 of them, whereof Heber the white, Louthus sonn of Ithus, Ehan m⁰Vga, Un m⁰Uga, Chahir, & fulmann were the number. The north part was allotted for 7 of them, who were Aeremon, Ebrick m⁰Ire, Avirgin, Goisdean, Seaga, Sorge, and Souarge. Heber the white was king of the south, and Heremon king of the north.

Within one year after this Diuision by the procurement and seting on of theire wives that fell at Debate for some places allotted to them as theire share of the said Diuision as Droym-tinyn[1] and Droym Bethi[2] faught a great Battle at Argedrosse[3] als Gessil[4] where Heber the white was slaine, and on the other side Gosdean, Seaga, and Sorge, then Heremon himself was king of all the kingdome alone, and was the first of Clanne Mille and 19th king of Ireland; he made two kingly rathes, the one named Rathonie[5] in the land of Kwalann and Rathbehie[6] over the riuer of Feoire. He made Crwachan or Criowhan Skeihuell[7] King of Dowrancha⁸ King of Lynster; he sufered the 4 sonnes of Heber to enjoy the 2 kingdomes or prouences[9] of Both the Monsters whose names were Ere, Orba, Ferone, and Feagna. He allowed the kingdome of Connaught to Un m⁰Uga, and the kingdome of Ulster to Ebricke m⁰Ir. This last Diuision of Kingdomes was made the 13th year of Laesthenes monarch of Assiria. In the time of Heremon Donsovarke[10] and Donkearmna[11] with a number of such other places of

---

[1] *Droym-tinyn.*— The ridge of hills between Castlelyons, Co. Cork, and the south side of Dungarvan bay.

[2] *Droym Bethi.*—Near Loughrea

[3] *Argedrosse.*—On the Nore, two miles below Ballyragget

[4] *Gessil.*—Midway between Portarlington and Tullamore.

[5] *Rathonie.* — Rathdown, Co. Wicklow; the territory was formerly called Cualan

[6] *Rathbehie.* — In the parish of the same name, in the barony of Galmoy, Co. Kilkenny. The rath is still in existence.

[7] *Skeihuell.*—He joined the Milesians on their landing and helped them to defeat the Britons. See Keating's *H. of Ireland*, p. 150.

[8] *Dowrancha.*—A tribe of the Firbolgs, usually called Damnonii.

[9] *Prouences.—i.e.* Desmond and Ormond. The district called Thomond, *i.e.* North Munster, formerly belonged to Connaught

[10] *Donsovarke* — Now Dunseverick, three miles east of the Giant's Causeway.

[11] *Donkearmna* — A fort on the Old Head of Kinsale.

note were made by himself and his people. In his time there was a Battle fought between Avirgin and Cahire at Cowle Cahire[1], where Cahire was slaine. The Riuers of Brosnagh, Suck, and Eihnie[2] did first break out and some laughs to the number of six. There was another Battle fought between Heremon and Avirgin where Avirgin was slaine at Bile Tanna[3] and fought another called the Battle of Comar[4], where Un m°Uga, Ean, & Ehan were slaine, and when Heremon was King of all Ireland and victoriously Raigned 14 yeares, Dyed at Argedrosse and was with great and solmne funerals buried at Rathebehie on the riuer of Feoire. He had Issue 4 sonns, but before I proceed any further I will Laye Down unto you the severall septs Decended of Heremon especially the cheefest of them, and then after the septs of Heber, Ire, and Lauthus, to the end the Reader may know them.

O'Neale of Tyrone, o'Donell, o'Moyledory[5] o'Doherty, o'Cahan, macLaghlen, o'Donnoyle and o'Boyle are the o'Neals of the north. o'Melaghlen, o'Kelly Brey[6], o'Mulloye, Mageoghagann, o'Ffox, magauley, o'Byrne, o'Sheile, maCarhon, o'Mullanna with Divers others are the o'Neals of the West. O'Connor Donn, o'Connor Roe, and o'Connor Sligo, o'Roirk, o'Reylie, Magmahon, o'Madden, maGwier, o'Kelly of Imainie, o'Neaghtin, m°Kiegan, m°Donnell of Scotland, and others are Descended of Heremon, but not of the o'Neals but of other collatterall kinsmen. Also macMurrogh of Lynster, o'Connor of Affalie, macGillepatrick, o'Broyne, o'Toole, o'Doynn, o'Dempsye, o'Colgan, o'Heredin, o'Nolan, o'feilan, and others are of the said

---

[1] *Cowle Cahire.* — The name is now obsolete.

[2] *Eihnie.*—The Inny, which falls into the north-eastern angle of Lough Ree.

[3] *Bile Tanna.*—Probably Billywood, in the parish of Moynalty, Co. Meath.

[4] *Comar*. — Now Kilcomeragh, near the hill of Usneagh.

[5] *o'Moyledory.*—They were chieftains of Tyrconnell in the ninth and tenth centuries. The name is now extinct.

[6] *Brey.* — The plain between Dublin and Louth, called Magh Breagh and Bregia. See *Annals F. M.*, ii. 879.

Descent. The scepts of Ire, son of Miletus, are Magenis Viscount of Ivhagh, o'Ferall, o'More, magranell[1], o'Connor of Corcomroe, o'Connor Kiery, macartan &c. The scepts of Heber the white: Macarthy, o'Brian, Mainemarye[2], macochlan, o'Kenedy, o'Gartie[3], o'Harie, macMahon, o'Hiffernan, maCrathe, m^{c}Brian, o'Harlagh, o'Finallan, o'Dea, some say that Powers[4], Eustaces[5], and Plunketts[6], are of the said sept. o'Keruell[7] too whoe should not be forgotten. The scepts of Lauthus, sonn of Ithus: o'Heiraisscoll, o'Coffie, o'Flynn, Maglannchye of Dartry[8] and others &c.

Hauing treated of the Raigne of Heremon, it is necessary that I Relate unto you whoe suceeded him in the kingdom. The three eldest sonns of Heremon, Moynie, Layne, and Lwyne were kings joyntly after theire said father and Diuided the kingdome into three partes among themselves, & soe Rayned together for three years. Moyne dyed at Crwachan[9] in Connaught, Layne and Lwyne were slain by the 4 sons of Heber the white, wh^{ch} were called by the names as before Recited.

Ere, Orba, Ferone and Feargna, sonns of Heber the white, when they had slaine the said joynte kings, succeeded themselues in the Gouernment of the Kingdome & Raigned but one quarter of a yeare when they were all slaine by Iriell the prophett, Youngest sonn of King Heremon, in the Battle of Ardlaura[10].

---

[1] *Magrannell.*—Now anglicised Reynolds.

[2] *Mainemarye.*—Mac Namara of Co. Clare.

[3] *o'Gartie.* — *i. e.* O'Fogarty of Elyogarty, in Co. Tipperary.

[4] *Powers.*—This family is descended from one of the first Anglo-Norman settlers in this country.

[5] *Eustaces.*—The origin of this family is very uncertain. We have discussed the subject in the *Journal of the Co. Kildare Archæological Society* for 1893.

[6] *Plunketts.*—They are usually supposed to be of Danish descent

[7] *o'Keruell.*—Of Ely O'Carroll, which included the south-west of King's Co. and a part of Tipperary.

[8] *Dartry.*—A barony in the west of Co. Monaghan.

[9] *Crwachan.*—Now Rathcroghan, midway between Elphin and Boyle, Co. Roscommon. This was one of the ancient palaces of the Kings of Connaught, and later their burialplace See a description of it by O'Donovan in *Annals F.M.*, iii. 204.

[10] *Ardlaura.* — *i. e.* Ardleyren. See *antea*, p. 11.

Iriell the prophet afterwardes succeeded as king, whoe did cut down and make smooth 12 plaines, to witt, Moyrched[1], Moyelly[2], Moylawra[3], &c. He made alsoe seven principle rathes. He fought a Battle at Ardanmaith[4], where Sorge mᶜDuff was slaine, another at Teanmay[5], where Eochy Eigeann, king of Fomoraghes, was likewise slaine, and the third alsoe he fought at Loghanmoye[6], where Loway, Roch mᶜMaffias was slaine, and Dyed himself at Moymwaye[7] when he had Raigned 10 years.

Ethrial his sonn succeeded him and made seven playnes that is to say Mayessil[8], &c. He was slaine in the battle of Rocean[9] by Convoyle or Convallo mᶜHeber the white, after he Rayned 10 years.

Convallo or Convoyle mᶜHeber was the first absolute king of Ireland of yᵉ Munster men. He did overthrow the sept of Heremon in 25 batles, and at lenth was slaine himself in the battle of Eawyn-Vacha[10]; he raigned 20 years and was slain by Tygernwas the sonn of king Erial aforesaid.

Tigernwas was king of the kingdome. He overthrew the offspring of Heber the white in 27 Battles within one yeare, whereof the field of Clonkwase[11] in the conty of Teffa[12], the battle of Kille[13] where Rochork mᶜGollann was slaine, the

---

[1] *Moyrched.*—Morett, near Maryborough.

[2] *Moyelly.*—In the parish of Kilmanaghan, King's Co.

[3] *Moylawra.*—Perhaps Moygara, in the barony of Coolavin, Co. Sligo.

[4] *Ardanmaith.*—The name is now obsolete.

[5] *Teanmay.*—Obsolete.

[6] *Loghanmoye.*—Perhaps Loughmoe, midway between Thurles and Templemore.

[7] *Moymwaye.*—i. e. Maghmuaide, Knockmoy, six miles S. of Tuam.

[8] *Mayessil.*—The plain through which the Aele, now the Blackwater, flows, it rises in Virginia Lake, Co. Cavan, and falls into the Boyne, at Navan.

[9] *Rocean.*—Perhaps Magh Reighne, in Ossory. See *Annals F.M*, i. 860.

[10] *Eawyn-Vacha.*—Emania, or the Navan fort, of which more later.

[11] *Clonkwase.*—Now Cloncoose, in the barony of Granard, Co. Longford.

[12] *Teffa.*—The ancient name of Longford and the western half of Westmeath.

[13] *Kille.*—Or Elne, the district between the rivers Bann and Bush, in Co. Antrim.

battle of Commor[1], the ouerthrow of Kliew[2], where ffearagh (of whome Carnefery tooke the name) was slaine with the Rest of the battles which were very long and tedious to particularize, in soe much that almost he mad an end of the scept of Heber and Besides his fortunate and lucky success in Battles he was the first that caused standing cupes to be made, the Refining of gold & silver, & procured his goldsmith that dwelt near the Lyffie (named Ighdonn) to make gold & silver pines to put in men & womens garments about theire neckes, and alsoe was the first that ever found the Dyeing of coulered[3] cloathes in Ireland. Many famous laughs and pooles sprung in his tyme, as Lough Foyle, Lough Sileann[4], &c. He Dyed a famous, victorious, and worthy king when he had Raigned 30 years.

Cearmna finn and his Brother Sovarke the sonns of Ebrick m^cIre were the first kings of Ireland that euer Raigned of the house of Ulster[5]. They Divided the whole kingdome amongst themselves in 2 parts. One of them Dwelt in Doncearmna, the other at Donsovarke; the one was king of the south, and the other king of the north, wch Division Remayned soe for the space of 100 years. King Kearmna fought a field where Eochie Edgohagh was slaine and was himself soone after slain by Eochie Fewerglass, king of Fomaraghes when they had nobly raigned 20 years.

Eochie Fewerglass son of king Convallo tooke upon him the Government of the kingdom, he Broke[6] 7 Battles upon his enemies, that is to say the overthroe of Lwacherdea[7] and the field of Dorymlehan[8] where Smirgol was slaine, with 5 other fields, he was 12 yeares king and then was killed by Fiagha Lawrynne.

Fiagha Lawrynne was then king, he gave Divers overthroes

---

[1] *Commor*.—O'Donovan has not identified this place, the name being a common one.
[2] *Khew*.—Obsolete.
[3] *Coulered*.—Purple, blue, and green. *Annals F. M.*, i. 43, and Keating, *H. of Ireland*, p. 155.
[4] *L. Sileann*.—L. Sheelin, on the borders of Cavan and Longford.
[5] *Ulster*.—i.e of the descendants of Ir, son of Milesius.
[6] *Broke*—An Irish idiom.
[7] *Lwacherdea*.—Slieve Lougher, N.E. of Castleisland, Co. Kerry.
[8] *Dorymlehan*.—Drumlahan, in Co. Cavan.

to the sept of Heber and amongst the rest that of Gathly[1] is not to be forgotten where mᶜFevis mᶜEochy Fewerglasse was killed, another where Laugh Eirne stands now, which soon after Broke out. In this tyme the river Lawryane[2] did first break out of whome he took that surname. He Raigned 8 yeares, and at last was slaine by Eochy Momo of the scept of Heber, of whome Munster was called or named.

Eochy Momo raigned 10 years and was slain by Enos Olmoye.[3]

Enos Olmoye was king and a valiant one. Strangers made many Invasions in his time, but he coragiouslie withstood and Drove them out with the cost of theire Bloods and lives by giueing them many bloody ouerthroes and covered Divers fields with heapes of theire slaughtered Bodies, that underneath they could scarcely get Buriall for them, he was of the scept of Heremon and was slaine by Enna Argheagh, whoe was of the scept of Heber when he had rayned 6 years.

Enna Argheagh was king and was the first king that caused silver Targets to be made in this land and Bestowed abundance of them bountifully on his friends and nobilities in generall. He raigned 24 years and was slain by Rogheaghty mᶜMoyne.

Roheaghty Raigned 11 years & then was slain by Sednie Art of the house of Ulster.

Seadna Art Raigned 18 yeares & was slaine filthily and unnaturally by his one sonn Fiagha Finnsgohagh.

Fiagha Finnscohagh succeeded his father and was surnamed ffiñsgohagh of the abundance of white flowers[4] that was in his tyme; and was slaine by his one trusty friend, Mownemon. The ould Irish proverb fell out truly with him, that inasmuch as he unaturally killed his one father, another in whome he Reposed fatherly trust should kill him. He Raigned 24 years.

---

[1] *Gathly.*—Gayly, in the barony of Iraghtyconor, Co Kerry
[2] *Lawryane* —O'D conjectures this was the Cashen river, Co Kerry
[3] *Olmoye.*—i e. of the Great Swine, or the Great Destroyer.
[4] *Flowers.*—These flowers were found full of wine, so that the wine was squeezed into bright vessels. *Annals F. M.*, i. 53.

Mownemon was the first king that ever Divised goldin chains fit to be worn about men's neckes and Rings to be put on theire fingers, which was then in great use, he raigned five yeares and then Died. He was of the sept of Munster.

Aldergoid his son succeeded him, in his tyme rings of gold were much used on men and women's fingers in this Realme; he was slaine by Allow Fodla[1] of the house of Ulster after he had Raigned 9 yeares.

Allow Fodla of the house of Ulster was king of Ireland & of him Ulster tooke the name. He was the first king of this land that euer kept the Great feast at tarragh called Feis[2] Tarach which feast was kept once a yeare, whereunto all the kings friends and Dutifull subjects came yearly and such as came not were taken for the kings enemies, and to be prosecuted by the law & sword as undutifull to the state. This king was soe well learned and soe much given to the favor of Learning that he builded a faire pallace at Tarrach, onely for the learned sort of this Realm to Dwell in, at his own peculiar cost & charges, of whome he was soe much againe beloved and Reverenced that ever after his house stocke and family were by them in theire Rimes and Poems preferred before any others of their equalls of the Irish nation; alsoe at Divers Times after when the nobilitie of Ireland had proclaimed ye utter abollishinge and Bannishing[3] of poets out of the land they were protected & maintained from tyme to tyme by the Issue of this king, as on a time one Moyle Cova,[4] king of Ulster, who was of his Discent, kept and maintained in his one house for the space of a whole year the number of 360 Irish poets; 6 of his Children succeeded him one after another

---

[1] *Allow Fodla* —Usually written Ollamh Fodhla, *i. e.* chief poet of Ireland. See Keating's *H. of Ireland*, p. 160.

[2] *Feis*.—'This was the great convocation of the men of Erin, and which was continued by the Kings of Erin from that down every third year, to preserve the laws and rules, and to purify the history of Erin, and counted in the Saltair of Tara, that is, the Book of the Ardrigh of Erin.' M'Firbis, in O'Curry's *MS. Materials*, p. 218,

[3] *Bannishing*.—See the Introd. to vol. v. of the *Ossianic Society's publications*, Keating's *H. of Ireland*, p. 370, and Adamnan's *L. of St Columba*, p. 79 n.

[4] *M. Cova*.—He was slain in 646.

The Annals of Clonmacnoise.

as kings of this land without any other comeing betwixt them, which good never hapned to noe other before him. He Died at Taragh a famous king rich learned wise, and generally well beloved of all men, and Raigned 40 years. His right name was Collawyn.

Fineaghty his eldest sonn succeeded him, he was soe called of the aboundance of snow that fell in his time, & then Dyed in Moyniss[1] in Ulster, when he raigned 20 yeares.

His brother Slanoll was king after him, During whose Raigne the kingdom was free from all manner of sickness. It is unknowen to any of what he Dyed, but dyed quietly in his bed, & after that he Remained 5 years Buried. His body did not rot, consume, or change collour, he raigned 26 years.

Geye Ollogagh, king Ollowe his third son, raigned after his said Brother. Observers of antiquity affirm of him that the Conversations of his subjects in general in his tyme was as sweet Harmonye to one another as any musicke, because they liued together in such amitye, concord, and attonem^t amongst themselves that there was noe Discord or strife heard to groe between them for any cause whatsoever. He founded Doncowole Sivrille now called (for avoiding of bawdiness) Kellis, he raigned 18 years.

Fiagha 4th son of king Ollow was the next king that succeeded after his said Brother & raigned 8 yeares, he was a good king, though I cannot recoumpt any notable thing that happened in his time.

Bearngal m^{c}Geye, Grandchild of the said king Ollow, was king 12 years, in his time there was continuall warres which brought great scarsitye of victuals throughout the whole Kingdome, he was slaine by his one cousin germond Olleal, king Slanols sonn.

Oillell was king 15 yeares and then was slaine by Siorna m^{c}Deyn of the sept of Heremon, whoe was he that violently tooke the Government of the septer of this land from the sept of Ulster.

---

[1] *Moyniss.*—The barony of Lecale, Co. Down

Siorna (after slayning thus the king) was king himselfe, in whose time Lawgire m{c}Lowagh brought in Fomoraghs into Ireland. King Siorna went to meet them at the Bogg of trogy in Kyonnaghta[1] with all the forces of the Kingdome, where a cruell Battle was fought between them with such vehemensy that almost both sides perrished therein, with ouerlabouring themselves & especially the Irish nation with theire king alsoe. Loway & Kisarme king of the Fomoraches were slaine, others write that king Siorna was slain by Rohaghty Roha m{c}Roayne, when he had Raigned 21 years, it is alsoe reported of him that he liued an outlawe one 100 years together before he was king and that onely against the Ulstermen.

Rohaghty was the first king that ever used coaches wth 4 Horses in Ireland. He raigned 7 years and at last was burnt by wild fier[2] at Dunsovarkie. He was a very good king.

Elim Olfinsneaghty was king for one yeare, he was soe called because it raigned snow continually that yeare. he was slaine by Giallcha m{c}Oillealla Olcloin.

When first Giallcha was made king he tooke hostage of every of the chiefs of the 5 provinces. He raigned tyrannically 9 years, and was in the end slain by Art Imleagh of the sept of Heber.

Art Imleagh was king and builded 7 Downes or paleces for himselfe to Dwell in them to Recreate himself. After 6 years raigning he was slain by Nowafinfaile.

Nowafinnfaile of the sept of Heremon was K. and was slaine by Breasry sonn of K. Art Inleagh after he had reigned 13 years.

Breasry raigned king 10 yeares, in whose time Fomory came again into Ireland; but he overthrew them in many batles and did quite expell them out of the kingdome. He Dyed at Carne anlwayne[3] and was much Lamented in generall

Eochy Ophagh, captaine of the former kings Guard, he

---

[1] *Kyonnaghta* —Perhaps K. Breagh, in ancient Meath.
[2] *Wild fier.*—i.e. lightning.
[3] *Carne anlwayne.*—Not identified.

was of Corkelaye,[1] usurped the kingdom & name of king thereof after the former kings death and obtained the same but one year. There was great faintness generally ouer all the whole kingdom once euery month during that year, and was slain by Finn m^cBraha.

Finn was king 20 years and was then slaine by Sedna Anerie, son of king Breasry.

This Seadna was a worthy noble king and the first that Rewarded men with cattle in Ireland, many other good things he did, he raigned 14 yeares and was then slain by Symon Breachus.

Symon Breachus als Breake, was king 6 yeares and was then slain by Dwagh the foster son of Dea; he was of the sept of Heremon.

Dwagh raigned 8 yeares and was then slain by Moriegh Balgragh. Kimboy m^cFinton in his time was king of Ulster, which was about 450 years before the Incarnation.

Morieagh raigned but one yeare when he was slaine by Enna the red, sonn of king Dwagh.

Enna reigned 5 yeares and then Dyed at Shevemis wth many of his people.

Loway his son was king and raigned 5 yeares and was then slaine by Syrelaw m^cFinn.

Sirelaw was king, & was so called because he had such long handes that when he would stand or be a horseback he could without stooping reach to the ground, and was slaine by Eochye Fiemoyne and by his brother Conynge.

These 2 brothers Eochy & Conynge raigned jointly 5 years, the kingdom of the north part was king Conynge's share, and of the south part king Eochies proportion. King Eogye was slaine by Loway mac Eochy na Keasse, uaıp cheap.

Lowaye reigned 4 yeares.

Conynge Begeglagh Raigned 7 yeares, he was soe called because he was never knowen to be afraid in his life & was at last slain by Art m^cLowaye.

---

[1] *Corkelaye.*—*i.e.* of the race of Lughaidh, son of Ith, son of Breogan.   See *Miscellany of the Celtic Society*, p. 2.

Art sonn of king Loway raigned 6 years and was slaine by Dwagh Layer.

Oilleall the sonn of K. Art succeeded his father in the kingdome and after he had raigned 9 yeares, he was slaine by Argedwar Fiagh & Dwagh mᶜFiaghy with their partakers.

There was a battle fought between Argedwar and Fiagh where argedwar was ouerthrone, another they fought at Breauie[1] where Fiagha was slaine by Eochy mᶜOillealla Finn, Dwagh Iagragh with the progeny of Heremonn did gather all theire forces together and Drew Argedwar to soe narow a plunge that he was Driven to goe to sea 7 yeares, During which time Eochy mᶜOillealla Finn was king. At last Argedwar & Dwagh accorded and made peace & friendship; Then joyning theire forces together they came unknowen to the king upon him. The king being then at the feare of Cnockany,[2] where they slew the king with many of the nobilityes of Munster, and raigned but 7 years as aforesaid.

Argedwar succeeded him and was a valiant king. He raigned 26 yeares and then was slaine by Dwagh Lagragh and by Loway Laye.

Dwagh then after reigned 10 years & was slaine by Loway.

Loway was K. 4 yeares and was slaine by Hugh Roe macBayorne of the house of Ulster.

Hugh Roe was king 7 years Dihorba mᶜDimaine of Usneagh in Westmeath then called Meath was K. 7 years & Kimboy mᶜFintan of Eawinn Macha 7 years These three being of the House of Ulster raigned together, at this time Eawinn Macha and Ardmach were first founded by one Macha that was Daughter to the sᵈ K. Hugh Roe, which happened after this manner:

There were 3 kings of Ireland at once. All were kinsmen, Hugh, Dihorba, and Kymboye aforesaid, and because they liued together in some contention for the kingdome, for theire

---

[1] *Breauie* —There are two places of this name, one in Co. Donegal, the other in Co. Mayo.

[2] *Cnockany* — Near Bruff, Co. Limerick. See Keating's *H. of Ireland*, p. 253.

better peace and security there was order taken for theire agreement in theire Government that each of them should rule 7 years orderly one after another without Impediment of any of the rest, & for making good the same, there were 7 magisians, 7 poets, and 7 Lords of the principal of the Ulster nobilitie chosen out to see that agreement firmly kept, the magisians by theire art to work against him that the same agreement would break what they could, the poets to chide and scould at them in their Rhimes & writings with as great a Disgrace as they might Invent, which was a thing in these days much feared[1] by the Irish nation, and the seven principal lords to follow & prosecute the violator with fier & sword. But all this was not necessary for the preservation of theire agreement for they did agree without any square at all, untill at last K. Hugh Roe was drowned in Easroe (of whome that easse or falling of the water took the name[2]) leaueing no issue behind him but one only daughter named Macha Mongroe (in Irish Macha wth the red tresses of haire). She soone after her father's Death chalenged her father's part of the kingdome due unto her by as her proper Right, which was denied her by king Dihorba & king Nymboye saying that it was unfit that a woman should Govern the kingdom where the issue male had not failed, and that it was never seen before. Whereupon she challenged them both to give to yeeld her battle, wch they were redy to doe and did accordingly where K. Kimboy was ourthrone, & K. Dihorba slaine. Then shee took upon her the Governm^t as Queen & behaved herselfe very honorably untill K. Dihorba's 5 sons named Beaha, Brasse, Beaaghah, Wallagh, and Borbeasse, being nobly given challenged theire fathers part of the K gdom as Queen Macha did before, wch she Denied them and said as shee got their Right by the sword they should not haue theirs but by the sword too : wh^{ch} as soone as they knew they Gathered together their forces

---

[1] *Feared.*—On the satire (*aer*) in use among the bards, see O'Donovan's preface to O'Daly's *T. of Ireland*, and *Ware's Antiquities*, ii. 136.

[2] *Name.*—He was buried in the mound over the cataract, which from him was called Sith Aodha, now Mullaghnashee.

and fought a strong batle against her, where they were put to flight and after all Driven to the wilderness of Conaught for theire Reliefe & safety. Soon after that overthrow given she married king Kymboy being her own neare kinsman and of the contrary faction, after wch marriage she Disguised herself like a poor woman all alone (when shee understood that king Dihorbas sonns went to Conaught to seek them out) & followed, and whom she at last found in a wild and Desert wood in ye west of Conaught all alone, none with them but themselves, siting by a fire, and as it should seem mightily afraid, Dressing a wild bore for theire sustenance. When she came near seeing her a poore woman (as shee shewed to be) they Desired her to come neare them and enquireing of her many things & newes, such as she could tell without offence, which shee in a suptile manner Did, and after long-talk & speeches the eldest of them looking very earnestly on her and having better view of her, said to the rest of his Brothers, that she was a very faire woman well eyed & limed, and that he would needs use her carnally, & with that carried her presently aside from them, where he began to abuse her; & when she found him there all alone, she took a hard gripp upon him and Gaue him a fall, and neuer suffered him to rise until shee did bynd him fast enough both hand and foot by meere strength, and soe left him there and came herselfe where the rest of the Bretheren were, after leaveing him close corded in a Bush. They Inquired where she left the man that went with her into the wood. He is (said shee) ashamed to shewe his face before you after committing soe vile a fact as to abuse himself wth a poore old & beggarly woman. Let him be nothing ashamed (said they) for we will do the same act as he Did, she seemed to be sorry thereat, and went with the first of them a contrary way & used him as shee did the first, and soe the rest after one another and when they were bound then shee Brought them to one place, & conveighed them to a friends house of hers, that was hard by, and from that brought them to Ulster, all the best sort desired to put them to Death presently as malefactors and offenders of the kingdome, but the Queen s^d it would not be soe, for it was (said shee) against the Royalty of a prince and the Laws of armes that men of their condition should be put to death, but yett (said she) they must for theire offences committed build for me the Rath of Eawyn[1] Macha as a Ransome reproachful for them to pay & convenient for me too take, which place shall be called after my one name and shall be always the Royall seat of the kings of Ulster, which work was presently taken in hand by the said prisoners, & for the speedier finishing thereof, she compelled the Munstermen to help them, & at last was finnished with wonderfull Celerity, and in the same shee & the kings of Ulster her successors kept their pallace and place of Residence for the space of 855 years after. It was built 450 years before the birth of Jesus Christ and was rased and broken down again for spight to Clanna Rorie by the three brothers the three Collaes sonns of Eochy Dowlen, who was sonn of king Carbry Liffechar. Her husband king Cymboye died 7 yeares before this Queen, and she Ruled the land with .Discretion, liberality, & severity as her occasions did Require, was in the end slaine by Roheaghty Rihdearg and was much commended for her noble mind, virtue, and courage.

Roheaghty Rihdearg was a good king and after he had reigned 9 years he was Diservedly slaine by Owgany More, son of king Eochie Bway whoe in and from his childhood was nourished and well fostered by King Cymboye & Queen Macha, as well as if he had been theire one naturall child The manner in those dayes was to bring up noblemens children, especially theire friends, in princes and great men's houses, & for ever after would call them fosters[2] and love them as well as theire own natural father.

Owgany More was K. after he had reuenged the death of

---

[1] *Eawyn Macha.*—See Keating's *H. of Ireland*, p. 182, and Reeves' *Ancient Churches of Armagh*, p. 37.
[2] *Fosters.*—On the custom among Celtic peoples of fostering, see Davis' *Discovery*, &c., p. 179. The Brehon Laws enter into great details about the duties of fosterers to those in their charge.

Queen Macha by killing K. Roheaghty. Some of our antiquarists affirm in their old writeings that this king Conquered all the land to the tirrhian sea.[1] He married Cesarea the king of frances Daughter with very great pomp & Royaltie & had by her 25 children, that is to say 22 sonns & 3 daughters, he Divided Ireland into 25 parts among them, a part to each of them, which Division Continued 300 years after, untill the kings of the provinces almost quenched the Remembrance thereof, vizt. to his son Cowhagh Koylebry was alotted the Country of Brey, where the lordship of Taragh stood, to Cowhagh Minn Mooreheyvmye,[2] to Loygery Lorcke the lands about the river of Liffie, to Foyldio Mayfea,[3] to Narne Mamemoye,[4] to Fergus Reyne,[5] to Narb Moynarb,[6] to Carrey Moyargedrosse, to Tarry Moytar,[7] to Triah Triagharney,[8] to Syn Lwacherdea, to Bard Cloncork,[9] to Fergus Knoy the land of Desyes in Munster, to Orb Orney,[10] to Moyne Moynemoye, to Sanv Moysainue now commonly called Meath, to Moriegh Male, Clieu Maile,[11] to Eachye Seolmoy,[12] to Lahra Laharna, to Marka a part of Meath which was reserved from Sanv, to Lowey Loyney,[13] to Carbry the land of Corran.[14] These were the names of the sonns with their posterities proportions. To the Daughters alsoe were allotted as theire shares these ensuing lands, which the K. was pleased to give them towardes their preferments, because he had but a few of them: first to princesse Alvie Moyneailve,[15] to Ife or Eva

---

[1] *Tirrhian sea.*—The Mediterranean.
[2] *Mooreheyvmye.*—Muirtheimhne, the plain between Drogheda and Dundalk.
[3] *Mayfea*—In the barony of Forth, Co. Carlow.
[4] *Mamemoye.*—Near Loughrea, Co. Galway.
[5] *Reyne.*—In the barony of Kells, Co. Kilkenny.
[6] *Moynarb.*—In the barony of Crannagh, Co. Kilkenny.
[7] *Moytar.*—Perhaps Moytra, Co. Longford.
[8] *Triagharney.*—Obsolete.
[9] *Cloncork.*—In the western part of Co. Limerick.
[10] *Orney.*—*recte* Aidhne, the district included in the present diocese of Kilmacduagh.
[11] *C. Maile.*—O'Malley's Country, along Clew Bay, Co. Mayo.
[12] *Seolmoy.*—Now the barony of Clare, Co. Galway.
[13] *Loyney*—Maghline, Co. Antrim.
[14] *Corran.*—A barony in County Sligo.
[15] *Moyneailve.*—A plain in the southern part of Co. Kildare.

Moye Ife,[1] and to Morisk Moymoriske,[2] the most part of which lands since the time of this diuision lost their old names and assumed these many Hundred yeares other names by which they are now knowen. Although the king had soe many children yet he none of this number that had issue male, but 2 only, which were Cowhagh Kolebrey and Lagery lorck, he raigned 30 yeares, one of the noblest and worthyest kings that ever governed this land before him. He was of the sept of Heremon and was slain by his one half brother Banncha m^cMorehea in the Contry of Breawye.[3]

Of Cowhagh Koylebrey, K. Owganes sonn, are Decended 4 principall houses, that is to say, Colman of whome the O Meleaghlyns and Hugh Slain the O'Kellyes of Brey, Conell & Owen, of whome the earles of Tyrone & tyreconnell, besides many other great houses in Meath, Ulster, Connaught, & kingdom of Scotland, wch to avoid prolixity I omit to Recount, between wch 4 Houses the Crowen of Ireland remained for the most part *in Diebus illis* untill the Conquest of Ireland by K. Henry the second, king of England.

About this tyme the monarch of the Assirians was Destroyed by Arbatus & translated ouer to the Meaths.[4] But to our history againe. After king Owgany succeeded his sonn in ye Kingdom named Lagery lorck & was king 16 years, and last was slaine by his one Brother Covhagh. Alsoe the said Cowhagh slew oilille Anye son of the said Lagery. After which foule fact done Lawry Longseagh, grand child of K. Owgany & sonn of Logery lorck was banished by him, who Remained many yeares beyond seas, seeking to bring foraigners to invade this land, & in the end after long Banishment, his great Uncle the K. of Ireland made friendship wth him and bestowed upon him & his heires for ever ye province of Leinster, since which time there hath ever been mortall hatred, strife, & Debate between those of the provinces of Connaught, Ulster, & Leynster, the one Desend-

---

[1] *Moye Ife.*—In South Tipperary.
[2] *Moymoriske.* — Murrisk is a barony in the south-west of Co. Mayo.
[3] *Breawye.*—Magh Breagh. See *antea*, p. 29.
[4] *Meaths.*—*Recte* Medes.

ing of K. Cowhagh, & the other of his Brother K. Lagery lorck. K. Cowhagh was Invited to a feast by his s^d nephew Lawry, and there was treacherously burnt together with 30 Irish princes in his one house. After he had raigned 17 years King Cowhagh little regarded the Irish proverb which is, that one should never trust a Reconciled adversary; this murther was Committed on the Barrow side at a place called Dinrye[1] or Beanrye and Diuers of the nobility were murthered there as aforesaid. Some say that the City of Roome was first founded about the beginning of this precedent Ks. Raigne; alsoe Finn McBaicke reigned then in Eawinn Mach as K. of Ulster.

Lawry Loyngseagh after thus murthering his uncle succeeded as K. of the kingdom, the province of Leinster took the name of him, for in the time of his Banishment he brought Diuers forriners into this land that were armed wth a kind of weapons wch they brought wth them like pikes or speares wch in Irish were called layny,[2] & were neuer before used in Ireland, of whome the leinster men took the name, and soe did Leinster itselfe; he raigned 14 yeares & was slaine by Melge son of king Couhagh. Connor Moyle m^cfuhie raigned then K. of Ulster twelve years.

Melge was king 12 years and was slain by m^cCorb. logh Meilge[3] tooke the name of him.

McCorb was king 6 years & was slaine by Enos ollow, about this time was borne that famous Poet of the Romans Virgill in a village called Anais not far from Mantua.

Enos was 7 years K. and at last was slaine by Irero, sonn of King Meilge, Neere about this tyme Pompeius was ouercome by Julius Cesar and driven to take his flight into Egypt.

After King Enos suceeded as K. Irero, who raigned 6 yeares, & was slaine by Fear Corb

---

[1] *Dinrye*—A short distance below Leighlin Bridge, on the western bank of the Barrow. A large moat still remains there

[2] *Layny*.—Laighean, a spear.

The termination "ster" is supposed to be Danish. The former name of the province was Gailian

[3] *L. Meilge*—Now L. Melvin, in the north of Co. Leitrim.

Fear Corb was K. 7 yeares, and was slaine by Conlye Keywe[1] ats the fine, sonne of Irero.

Conlye succeeded in the Government of the kingdom 4 yeares and then quitely Dyed in hes Pallace of Tarragh.

Oillill his sonn succeeded next in the government of the Kingdom and Raigned 25 years & at last was slaine by Adamar.

Adamar was K. 5 yeares, & was slain by Eochy Altleahan.[2]

Eochy was king 7 yeares & was slaine by ffergus Fortawyle.[3]

ffergus was king 12 yeares & was slaine by Enos Twyrmeagh[4] at Taragh.

Enos succeeded & was a very good king. He left issue 2 Goodly and noble sonnes Enna Aynagh & Fiagha Firvara, the most part of the Kings of Ireland Decended of his son Enosa, & the kings of Scotland for the most part Desended of Fiagha, soe as the great houses in both those kingdoms Derive their pedigrees from them, he was of the sept of Heremon & Raigned 32 years & then Dyed quietly at Taragh in his bed.

Conell Collawragh[5] raigned 5 years & was slain by Nia Sedawyn[6].

Nia was K. 7 years & was slaine by Enna Ayneagh.[7]

Enna Ayneagh succeeded him (being next unto him) as K. of the Realm & reigned 10 years, & was slaine by Criowhann Cosgragh.[8]

Criowhann was K. 4 yeares, & was slaine by Rowry m^cSitrick auncestor of the Clanna Rowrys, as of Magenyes, o'fferall, o More &c.

---

[1] *Keywe.*—*i.e.* caomh, beautiful.
[2] *Altleahan.*—*i e.* of the broad house.
[3] *Fortawyle.*—*i e.* the strong.
[4] *Twyrmeagh.*—*i. e* the prolific. *Ogygia*, p. 264. Keating gives a different reason for the name. *H of Ireland*, p 193.
[5] *Collawragh.*—*i.e* pillar-like.
[6] *Sedawyn.*—Because in his time the does (*seadha*) gave milk like the cows, through the incantations of his mother.
[7] *Ayneagh.* — *i. e* the hospitable.
[8] *Cosgragh.*—*i.e.* the victorious, for he was successful in every battle which he fought.

Rowrye raigned 70 years, Of him are Desended many great houses In this kingdom & in Scotland. There were many K. of that house & were the Right aunciently Ulster men, & were in those Days accoumpted second to none in the kingdom. The three cheef houses in Ireland were Conn, Araye, & Owen, I mean of the Irish Nobility, that is to say the house of Cashell in Munster, the house of Crwacha in Connaught, and Eawyn Macha in Ulster. Between which 3 houses the Crown of Ireland Rested a great while. Rowry Dyed at Argedgryne[1] after many great acts were don by him, & was of Great fame for his long & peaceable Government, he had issue 4 sonns vidzt., Congall Claringneagh[2] Breasall Bodivo, Ross, and Ita.

Ionamar was the K. wch succeeded Rowry, he raigned 3 yeares & was slaine by Breasall m^cRowry als Breassall Bodivo.[3]

Breasall was K. 10 years, in his time there was such a merren of Cowes in this land as there were noe more (then) left alive but one bull and one Heifer in the whole kingdom, which Bull & heifer lived in a place called Gleann Sawasge,[4] he was slaine by Loway Lwange, son of king Ionamar aforementioned. Some say that the monarchy of the Romans began about this seasonn, & that Julius Cæsar after that he had Conquered the Gales and Brittans was their first Emperour, & made the Brittans stypendiaries, since whose raigne there hath been Emperors wth them.

Loway m^cIonamar raigned 15 yeares, & was slaine by Congal Claringneagh.

Congal succeeded Loway in the kingdom, he did many notable acts of Chivalrye as there are Great volumbes of history written of his hardiness & manhood. He was slaine by Dwagh Dalta Dea when he had Raigned 15 years.

---

[1] *Argedgryne.*—In the barony of Farney, Co. Monaghan.
[2] *Claringneagh.*—*i.e.* the flat-faced
[3] *Bodivo.*—This word refers to the mortality of kine. Keating, *H. of Ireland*, p. 195.
[4] *G. Sawasge.*—*i.e.* the heifer's glen, in Co. Kerry. See *Annals F M.*, 1. 86.

Dwagh Dalta Dea[1] succeeded him, he raigned 7 years & During his raigne behaved himselfe uprightly & justly, & was slaine by Faghtna Fahagh.[2] About this time Julius Cesar was murthered in the Senate with Bodkins[3] by Brutus and Cassius.

Faghtna Fahagh was K. 24 yeares and was slaine by Eochy Feyleagh. Some of our writers affirm that our Saviour Jesus Christ, the onely Begotten sonn of God almighty, was borne of the spotless Virgin Mary about the 16th year of this kings raigne, & that then Connor, sonn of ye said king Faghtna was king of Ulster, Oillill McRoss king of Connaught, Finnell mcRosse k. of Leinster, Cowry mcDary was king of one of the Munsters, and Eochy McLughta was king of the other province of Munster.

Eochy Feyleagh[4] was king 12 years & then Dyed at Taragh, he was father to yt famous (but not altogether for Goodness) woman Meaw Crwachan[5] & to 4 other Daughters, as to Clehra of Munster, Ailby, Eihyn &c. But the lady Meaw was of Greater Report then the rest because of her great boldness, Buty, & stout manlyness in Giving of battles, insatiable Lust, her father allowed her for her portion the province of Connaught, & shee being thereof possesed grew soe Insolent and shameless that shee made an oath never to marry wth anyone whatsoever that would be stayned wth any of these 3 Defects and Imperfections as she accoumpted them vidzt wth jealousy for any Letchery that she should committ, wth unmanliness or Imbecillitie, soe as the party could not be soe bould as to undertake any adventure whatsoever were it never soe Dificult, & Lastly she would neuer marry with anyone that feared any man liveing.

---

[1] *Dalta Dea.—i. e.* fosterer of Deaghadh, his younger brother. *Ibid.* p. 196. O'Flaherty gives another origin of the name.

[2] *Fahagh.—i.e.* the discreet.

[3] *Bodkins.—i.e.* small daggers.

[4] *Feyleagh.—i. e.* the sigher, because of his continual sorrow for the loss of his two sons who were slain at the battle of Drumcriadh. *Ibid.*, p. 197.

[5] *M. Crwachan.*—So called from Rathcroghan, where her father built a residence for her. An account of her death will be found *Ibid.*, p. 214.

Eochie Oireaw[1] was the next K. & Brother to the former K.; raigned 15 years & was then slaine & burnt by lightning fire from heaven.

Edersgel More succeeded, he raigned 5 years, and was then slaine by Nuada Noaght.

Nuada Noaght[2] was the next K. after Edresgell. He Raigned half a year & was slain by conry mᶜEdersgell in the battle of Cliah in the Country of Idrona.[3]

Conary was K. 60 years & was burnt by Anckell, K. of Wales, his sonn by night in Brwyne da Dearg.[4]

Jesus Christ was crucified in his time, but some of the antiquarists afirm that our Saviour Jesus Christ was borne in the Raigne of K. Eochy Feyleagh, & not in the reign of Faghna fathagh & crucified by Tiberius Cæsar in the raigne of Edersgall, K. of Ireland.

It is thought that the nobility of Ireland obtained their libertie afterwards from the progeny of Vaghan more, Cosgragh mᶜConnor raigned K. of Ulster 3 years. Cowchoullen[5] the Heroicke champion of Ireland and Heber his wife Dyed. The Champion was killed by the sons of Calletin of Connaught in the 27th yeare of his age. The Report goes that he killed a Ravenous and uenemous Dogg[6] when he was but the age of 7 years & was alsoe but of the age of 17 years when he surpassed all the Champions in Ireland in the Disention between them for the famous prey called in Irish tane Boe Cwailgne.[7]

---

[1] *E. Oireaw.*—So called from *uir*, a grave, he being the first who introduced the custom of burying the dead in graves dug in the earth. *Ibid.*, p. 225.

[2] *N. Noaght*—*i.e.* Snow-white, from the colour of his skin.

[3] *Idrona.*—A territory in the west of Co. Carlow, now forming two baronies.

[4] *B. da Dearg.*—On the river Dodder. The name is still retained in Boher-na-Breena.

[5] *Cowchoullen.*—He was a native of Ulster. Tigernach in his *Annals* calls him fortissimus heros Scotorum. He was killed at the battle of Muirtheimhne in Louth. See O'Curry's *MS. Materials*, p. 37.

[6] *Dogg.*—Cuchullin, *i.e.* the dog of Culann, artificer of King Conor MᶜNessa. His first name was Sesanta.

[7] *Tane Boe Cwailgne.*—For an account of this, one of the most important works of our ancient literature, see O'Curry's *MS. Materials*, p. 33.

Loway Srewdearg[1] suceeded K. Conary in the kingdom, he raigned 25 yeares & dyed of a Conceat he tooke of the death of his wife Queen Dervorgill. St. Peeter the Apostle, after he founded the Church of Antioch came to Rome about this time to Expell Symon Magus thereout, & there held his sea Apostolike 25 years untill in the Last yeare of Nero he was hanged wth his feet upwardes & head Downward, also St Paul was beheaded. Iriell Glunwar son of Conell Kearneagh raigned king of Ulster this time. Also Marchus the Evangelist befor the Death of St. Peeter wrote his booke of the Holy Evangelist, & sent it to St. Peeter to Alexandria, & was ordayned Bishop of that Place by Saint Peeter.

Connor Auraroe[2] was K. next to K. Loway & was slain by Criohann m'Loway and raigned but one year. Anacletus was Pope 20 years.

Criowhan Raigned 16 years, it is Reported that he was brought by a Fairy Lady into her pallace, where after great Entertainment bestowed upon him & after they tooke their pleasure of one another by carnall knowledge shee Bestowed a gilted Coate wth a sume of Gold[3] on him as a token of love & soone after Dyed. St. Andrew was Crusified about the fourth year of this K.'s raigne, & alsoe St. Philip the Apostle was likewise Crucified & stoned to Death in the citty of Herapolim in Phrigia.

Càrbry Kinncatt[4] succeeded as K. of Ireland, a man whose birth[5] is unknowne, therefore thought to be of mean parentage

---

[1] *Srewdearg.*—*i.e.* of the red circles, which surrounded his neck and body.

[2] *Auraroe.*—*i.e.* of the red eyebrows.

[3] *Gold.* — The *Annals F. M.* enumerate many precious articles which he brought from the famous expedition on which he had gone. The story of the *Echtradh* was well known. No copy of it is now in existence. See O'Curry's *MS. Materials*, p. 589.

[4] *Kinncatt.*—*i.e.* Cathead. He was placed on the throne by a rising of the Aitheach Tuatha, or democracy, who had been enslaved by the Milesian nobles. This rising and the slaughter of the nobles are described at length in O'Clery's *Leahbar Gabhála* and in Keating's *H. of Ireland*, p 229.

[5] *Birth.*—Keating says he was descended from one of those who came to Ireland with Lawry Loinseach. *Ibid*, p. 229.

to Govern the kingdom & subjects, his Ears were like a Kats eares, of which he tooke the name. He raigned 5 years and then Dyed. He hated noble men & their decents. About this time Mary Magdalen Dyed in the yeare of our Lord from the Incarnation 63. Domitian, the son of Vespation the Emperour was soe eloquent in speaking he needed noe advocate or oratour to set forth his cause but himself, & made poesyes in Greek & lating, he was held to be soe virtuous that of all the People in general he was called *amor et delitium humani generis*, he made the amphitheaters of Rome & slew 500 wild beasts in them

Feraagh Feaghtnagh[1] succeeded king Carbry, he raigned 22 yeares, & then Dyed.

Fiagha Finn of whom Dalviagha is called reigned 3 years and was slain by Fiagha Finnolay about the yeare of our Lord 95.

Fiagha Finnolay was king 7 yeares & was then slaine by Elym m^cConragh. The s^d Fiagha was of the sept of Heremon.

Elym was K.[2] 20 yeares & was slaine by Twahal Teaghtwar[3] sonn of king Fiagha Finnolay & was left fatherless in his mothers wombe, shee being the K. of Scotlands daughter, who soone after her husbands death fled secretly into Scotland, where she was Delivered of a goodly sonne called Twahall, whoe was by her brought up in all princely qualities untill he was 20 years old, at wch time he came into Ireland accompanyed wth his said mother & few others of his friends, where after his landing in this kingdom one Fiachra Cassan and others euil contented with their estates to the number of 800 chosen men mett him and Presently saluted him as K. of the Realm, & soe went forward with the said Company & fought a battle against K. Elym & was therein slaine by the said Twahall. Hee Discomfitted the Ulstermen

---

[1] *Feaghtnagh* —*i.e.* the just. In his reign lived the famous judge Morann, styled of the collar. *Ibid.*, p. 227

[2] *King.*—He, too, was placed on the throne by the Aiteach Tuatha. He was descended from Ir.

[3] *Teaghtwar.*—*i.e.* the plentiful, from the prosperous state of the country during his reign.

in 30 battles, the Connaught men in 28 battles, the Leinster men in 38 & the Monster men in 37, beheaded the kings of of the five provinces, and tooke a part from each of the provinces which he aded together & thereof composed the Contry called Meath,[1] consisting now of 2 Countyes vidz^{t} the Countys of East meath & West meath, wch was alwayes Reserved for the maintenance of the Monarch of Irelands table untill after the Death of Neallus Magnus, als Neale of the 9 hostages, K. of Ireland, Meath among the Rest was Divided among the sonnes of ye said Neale; In which division Meath was allotted to Connell m^{c}Neale, auncestor of the o'Melachlins & o'Kellyes of Brey, & to Fiagha. Conell was the first K. of Meath by the name of K. of Meath, to whome succeeded Fiagha auncestor of the Magoghegans and o'Molloyes, whoe Raigned 28 years & Dyed at Carne fiagha,[2] of whome Kinaliagh (which is Mageoghegans contry and the teritory of fercall[3]) took the name, after the death of which Connell succeeded as K. of Meath the number of 47 kings until the Death of Connor o'Melaghlin by the handes of Morrogh m^{c}flynn O'Melaghlin in the year of our Lord 1073, as by a Cathalogue of their names in Irish meeter may apeare to the Reader with the yeares of every of them in their scueral raignes.

There were 16 kings of Ireland desended of the said Connell, that is to say 7 kings of the sept of Colman, of whome are Clann Colman,[4] and nine kings of the sept of Hugh Slane,[5] whose names shall be Remembered in their Right places when wee come to make mention of them, as the matter of the History wee have in hand shall require. And fearing that the reader would take advantage of me for not naming the Popes in

---

[1] *Meath.*—Keating says it bore this name from the time of Nemedius, but it was only in King Tuathal's time it became distinct from the other provinces. He gives two derivations of the name. *Ibid.*, p. 55.

[2] *Carne fiagha.*—In the parish of Convy, Co. Westmeath.

[3] *Fercall.*—The territory now included in the baronies of Eglish, Ballycowan, and Ballybritt, King's Co.

[4] *Clann Colman.*—The tribe name of the O'Melaghlins.

[5] *Hugh Slane.*—He was ardrigh from A.D. 595 to 600.

their sucessions, for mine excuse I say that the ould Irish book out of wch I writt this is soe ouertorne & rent that the Characters of the very letters are quite lost in some places, soe as I must be content to translate what I can Read, and undertake that the succession of the monarchs is truely translated & agreed upon by all the Irish Cronicles of the K dom. Here I find that St. John the apostle & Evangelist in the 78th year after the passion of our Saviour Jesus Christ & 98 of his own age Dyed at Ephesus. Pope Clement with an anchor tyed to his neck throne into the sea by the Emperor Trajan.

Butt now let us Returne to our History, When K. Twahall was thus established in the quiet Possession of the Crowen & kingdom, & had brought the whole K. dom into his subjection, he kept the Great feast of Taragh Called feis Tawra,[1] whereunto all the nobility of Ireland men & women yonge & ould came, & after banqueting the K. being merry among his nobles wth a Company of chosen men for the purpose, enjoined all the nobility & caused them to sweare by the sonne & moone, and all other oathes which they then had in use, never to gainsay himself nor any of his posterity, or that would linally suceed him in the government of Ireland, & to Disclaime all theire one tytles & Interests unto the premisses for euer, as long as the land of Ireland would be Compass'd with the seas, & that none of them or any of them would make claim to the Crowen or any of their heires and posterityes, notwithstanding their Rights thereunto were as Good as his, soe as if their posterityes had then after Groon more potent & of Greater abilitie than his, notwithstanding their potency they should he quite excluded from the tyme of that oath for euer from claiming any (Right) or title thereunto, & that they should suffer him & his heirs & successors quitely to enjoy the Crowen for euer, & doe him and them all services due to a king, which oath was duely & voluntarily sworn by them & every one of them one after another.

---

[1] *Feis Tawra.* — See Petrie's *Antiquities of Tara*, p. 31, and Keating's *History of Ireland*, p. 235.

The Annals of Clonmacnoise.

At that time Eochye Anchean was K. of Leinster & was suiter to one of the K. of Irelands daughters named Darynna, whose request was presently Granted, whereupon the marriage after the heathen manner was concluded with such Royalty as belonged to their greatness. Soon after the said marriaage the K. of Leinster brought her to his own house of Naase, & when the nobility of Leinster saw theire Dutchess soe Deformed they were very grieveous at it, Reprehending theire K. for making such a Choyse, the K. of Ireland having a fayrer Daughter & better nurtured & brought up. At which Reprehension & mistaking the K. was very sorry & said y[t] he would goe back to the K. & crave his other Daughter in marriaage, and withall would mak his Majestie believe, that his other Daughter was Dead; w[ch] he accordingly told & did, whereupon the K. Immediately Granted his other Daughter to the said K. Eochye, wth he accordingly married & brought home to his house of Naase afores[d].

When Darinna saw her sister ffyher (for soe shee was called) come upon her in that nature, shee of very spight, jealousy, & shame Dyed out of hand, Because shee conceaved soe much sorrow thereat, soone after when the heavy newes of his Daughters Death & his own Deceipt came to the kings eares, he was much Grieved, & gathered together all his Royall army & forces, with whome the king in his one person marched towards Leinster to be Revenged on them, the Leinstermen seeing themselves unable to Resist the K[s] power & fearing to be held as traytors to the Crowen, did advise their K. to submitt themselves to the K. of Irelands clemency & submissively to Cry for mercy at his hands, w[ch] he at their Request did, whereupon the K. of Ireland well Pondering or weighing the Grievousness of that fact ordered that the king of Leinster & all the Inhabitants of that province for the time being for euer should henceforth yield & pay yearly to himselfe, his heires, and successors for ever in Recompense of the s[d] offence the number of 150 Cowes, 150 Hoggs, 150 Couerlets or peeces of Cloth to couer beds withall, 150 Cauldrons, wth 2 passing Great Cauldrons consisting in Breath & Deepness five fists for the kings one Brewing, 150 Couples of men & women in servitude to Draw water on their backes for the said Brewing, together with 150 maides with the K. of Leinsters one Daughter in the like Bondage & servitude. All which was accordingly paid yearly to the s^d king Twahall & his sucessors for the time being for the space of about 500 years until K Fineaghty ffleacagh his time, who for the Great Reverence he bore to St Moling[1] Lauchra (a man famous for holiness of life) at his request in a learned sermon he made in the s^d K Fyneaghties presence, of the unjustness of y^t taction, was content of his Bounty and devotion to the said Saint to Remitt it for euer after, this was paid by ye Leinstermen for & dureing the raignes of 40 kings & monarchs of Ireland from the yeare of the Incarnation of our Lord 134 to the year of the said sermon 693 which fine in the Irish tongue was called Borohua,[2] which as soone as it was taken up, and Divided into three partes, whereof one was to the Connaught men, & another to those of Uriell,[3] & the third to the K. of Taragh and sept of the O'Neals, because the said three tribes or septs among whome the said Borohua was Divided were Dessended of the said K. Twahall, & when K. Twahall had raigned 30 years he was slaine by Male m^{c}Rochrye, king of Ulster, at Dalnary[4] in Ulster.

Male was K 4 yeares & was slaine by Felim Reaghtwar, the former kings sonn, in Reuenge of the Death of his father. Galen the famous phisitian florished in Rome about this time.

ffelym Reaghtwar[5] suceeded in the Government of the

---

[1] *St. Moling.*—He lived in the 7th century. He founded Techmoling, now St. Mullin's, on the Barrow, and was buried there A Life of him is in the *Liber Kilkenniensis* in Marsh's Library, Dublin.

[2] *Borohua*—i e. cow-tribute See Keating's *H. of Ireland*, p.237. An ancient tract on the B. has been lately published in *Silva Gaedelica*, by S O'Grady.

[3] *Uriell.*—*i.e.* Oirghilla, for this clan used fetters of gold to bind their hostages. *The Book of Rights*, p 140 This territory included the present counties of Louth, Armagh, and Monaghan

[4] *Dalnary* —i e. Dalaradia, a district in East Ulster, extending from Newry to Sliabh Mish in Co Antrim

[5] *Reaghtwar* —i e the lawful, his decisions and those of his judges being strictly in accord with the ancient law of retaliation; others say because he instituted in its place the system of eric or fine to be paid to the injured party or his relatives

kingdom, in whose time there was Great war between Munster & Leinster, Derghine being the K. of Mounster & Cowcorb m^cMoycorb K. of Leinster, the Munstermen gott from the Leinstermen from the borders of Leinster to a little foord neere the hill of Mullamaisden[1] called Athantrosdan. The Leinstermen were then very bare, by Reason of the yearly payment of the Great taction of the Borowa beforementioned, & therefore they could not of themselves wthstand the Great Power of the Munstermen, whereby their K. was constrained to have Recourse to the K. of Irelands Court, and there submissively to crave his ayd, where he Remayned 3 monthes together, humbly beeseeching the K. (whose loyall subjects they did acknowledg to bee) not to Remember the offences of their predecessors but presently to succour and ayd them against the wrongfull Invasions and daly Incursions of the Munstermen, being in his Royallty bound for their Defence because he was their naturall leidge, Lord, & K., and they his Dutifull subjects, wherefore they pittifully Craved his assistance, that in the mean time under the shelter of his wings they might come to their own againe.

Whereupon the K. & Councell Delibraly considering how the cause stood & with the mature advice of all his nobility, thought fitt the K. of Leinster and leinster men should be instantly ayded, & the speedier to perform the same to send K. felyms one second sonn & the king of Ulsters sonn named Lowaye Lysie & Eochye Finn m^cfelym (this lowaye lysie was sonn of Liseagh leanmore) wth all the kings forces wth the K. of Lynster against the Munstermen who were already possessed of the best part thereof, the king of Leinster Covenanted wth the K. of Ireland's sonn And wth the K. of Ulsters y^t if they would Recover all that was in the Munstermen's hands of his lands & Drive them out by force of arms & withstand their forces still, he & his heires would

---

[1] *Mullamaisden.*—Now Mullaghmast, 5 miles N.E. of Athy, Co. Kildare. An account of the massacre of three or four hundred of the Irish of Offaly and Leix, which took place here in 1577, will be found in O'Donovan's notes to *The Annals F. M.*, ad ann.

make Good to them & their heires all that was then possessed by the Munstermen wch was from the Borders of Munster to the foorde of Athantrosdan afores^d wth many other privileges from the K. of Leynster to them & their heirs perpetually, & for performance thereof the K. of Leynster & all those y^t were with him did solmnly sweare before the K. of Ireland at his pallace at Taragh as well in their own Behalves as alsoe in the behalfe of their posterityes to make the Premisses Good for euer to the said Eochy & Lowaye and their heirs in perpetual, which was presently inrolled in the King of Ireland who reigned at Taragh. When these Conditions were soe strongly sworne & confirmed Eochy & Lowaye Lysie marched on with 7000 Ulstermen in Loway's company, & 3000 Meath & Connaught men in Eochye's Company who wth all Celerity came upon the Monstermen at Athrosda, where they asayled them at unewares and gave them a Great overthrow, the Munstermen thinking to Recover their Disgrace Gathered all their forces together againe and mett theire Enemies at Athy, where they were likewise Discomfitted, the Munstermen were alsoe overthrone at Leack Riada[1] in Lease[2] & at Athlayen[3] (which is a foorde on the River limitting Leinster from Munster, & after these Great overthrows the Munstermen were quite Driven out of Leinster; Eochy Finn & Loway had then these Contryes y^t were then possessed by them which were there afore called by the names of both the fohertyes[4] & the seven ould Leases,[5] which countryes were ever since possessed by the said Eochy & Loway, their

---

[1] *L. Riada.*—This name is obsolete.

[2] *Lease*—The territory now included in the south-east of Queen's County. It belonged to the O'Mores The residence of the chief of the tribe was on the Rock of Dunamaise, five miles east of Maryborough.

[3] *Athlayen.*—The name is obsolete.

[4] *Fohertyes.*—The barony of Forth in Co. Carlow, and the district of Fotharta airthir Liffe in Co. Kildare.

[5] *Seven ould Leases.*—i.e. the seven tribes of Leix. In the reign of Queen Mary they were driven from their native territory and transplanted to North Kerry, where many families bearing these names are now found. See O'Sullevan's *Hist. Cath. Iber.*, p. 92.

The Annals of Clonmacnoise. 57

Issues and Posterityes, o'Nolan, o'ffoylan,[1] o'Broyan,[2] etc. are of the issue of Eochy, o'More, o'Dowlen &c. are of the sept of Loway; when king felym had raigned 10 yeares he dyed & was a very good king.

Cahire More succeeded in the kingdom. This is the comon ancestor[3] of the most part of the Irishry of Leinster as of m^{c}Morrogh, o'Connor of offaly,[4] o'Dempsie, o'Doyne,[5] &c., and Raigned but 5 yeares when he was slaine by the hardy hand of Conn Cedchahagh; for K. Cahire having taken upon him the Gouernment of the kingdom, after the death of king felym, Conn Cedchahagh the sonn of K. Felym, Being brought up in princely Education, as well in the knowledg of letters as alsoe in feats of arms & chivalry by Conell, K. of Connaught wth whome he was soe well fostered & Brought up from his childhood as became the sonn of soe Great a monarch, untill on a day a Magition, one that liued in king Felym's Court came to Crwachan where young Prince Conn was Hurling amongue other children, the Magitian knowing him by the figure of his father, seeing how childishly he was given, drew neare him and wept Bitterly, saying, little wottest thou (child) what king Cahire doth how hee taketh & usurpeth unto himself the Revenewes of the Crowen due to y^r fathers son together with the Borrow of ye women & maids of Leinster wch of right did alsoe Belong to you: which when Prince Conn heard, he threw away the hurley he had in his hand and Repayred to his said foster-father & tould him of the wordes of the Magitian, & that he would Rather venture his life to Recover his right, then to sufer Cahire to enjoye it, What Child, content yourself, you are not Come to that Ripeness of yeares, as to undertake to war against the K., & therefore I shall Desire you to stay wth me untill you groe to

---

[1] *O'ffoylan*—Now Phelan.
[2] *O'Broyan.*—O'Brien or O'Byrne.
[3] *Ancestor.*—See Keating's *H. of Ireland*, p. 242, for an account of Cahire More's sons and their descendants.
[4] *Offaly.*—This territory included the baronies of east and west Offaly in Co. Kildare, of Portnahinch and Tinnehinch in Queen's Co., and that part of King's Co. comprised in the dioceses of Kildare and Leighlin. *Top. Poems*, L.
[5] *o'Doyne.*—*i e.* O'Dunn.

be of greater Perfection & of maturer judgment to Gouern yourself in the prosecution of y^r right: and when Connell saw that his persuasions did little auaile wth Prince Conn, he with his whole Power & forces of Connaught came wth him against king Cahyre & Gaue him a Battle near the river of Boyn where king Cahires army was ouerthrone, and K. Cahire himself slain and Buried neare the river of Boyne.

Conn Kedcahagh having thus slaine K. Cahire, he succeeded himself, & was more famous then any of his auncestors for his many victoryes & Good Government, he was called Conn Kedcahagh of a 100 battles Given by him in his time, he is the Common auncestor for the most part of the north of Ireland except the Clanna Rowries and the sept of Lauthus, son of Ithus. He had 3 goodly sonnes, Conly, Crienna, & Artemar, and three daughters, Moyne, Saw, & Sarad; Saw was married to the K. of Munster, by whom shee had many sonns, as the auncestors of the Macarthyes, o'Bryans, o'Kervells, o'Mahons, & divers others of the west part of Ireland, By wch meanes they have Gotten themselves to that selected & Choyse name much used by the Irish poets at the time of their Comendations and prayses called Sile Sawa wch is as much in English as the Issue of Saw.

Owen More ats Moynod[1] warred upon him a long time, he was king of Munster & was soe strong that he brought the K. to Divide with him & to allow him as his share from Esker-Riada,[2] beginning at Dublin whereupon the high street is sett, & extending to Athkleyh Mearye[3] in thomond, Owen's share was of ye south wch of him took the name Lehmoye[4] or Moyes half in Deale, K. Conn's share stood of the north of the said Eisker, wch of him was likewise Called leagh Conn or Conns halfe in Deale, & doe retaine these names since.

The division of Ireland stood for one year untill Owen More als Moynod, being well ayded by his Brother in law

---

[1] *Moynod*—i.e. Mogh Nuadhat On the origin of this name see *The Battle of Magh Leana*, p. 5.
[2] *Esker-Riada.*—A line of gravel hills extending from Dublin due west.
[3] *A. Mearye.*—Now Clarenbridge at the east end of Galway Bay.
[4] *Lehmoye.*—i.e. leith Mogha.

the king of Spains sonn and a Great army of the Spaniards, picked ocation to quarrell & fall out with the K. for the Costomes of the shiping of Dublin alleging that there came more shipps of K. Conn's side then of his side, and that he would needs have the Custome in common between them, which K. Conn refused, whereupon they were Insenced mightily against one another, & met with their Great armies on the playnes & heath of Moylen[1] in the territory of Fercall, where the army of Owen More was overthrone, himself & Fergus the king of Spaines sonn slaine & afterwards buried in two little Hillockes, now to be seen on the said plains which as some say are the tombs of the said Owen and Fergus. The K. having thus slaine & vanquished his enemies, he raigned peaceably & quietly 20 years wth great increase & plenty of all good things among his subjects throughout the whole kingdom, soe as all in general had noe want untill the kings Brother Eochie Finn before mentioned and Fiagha Swyn seeing the K. had 3 Goodly sonns Art, Connly and Crionna, which were like to inheritt the Crowen after their fathers death sent Private message to Tiprady Tyreagh sonne of king Mall m^{c}Rochrye whoe was slaine by felym Reaghtwar the said king Conn's father as before is specified. Whereupon the said Tybrady with a very willing hart came up to Taragh accompanied wth certaine other malefactors, asaulted the king of unewares and wilfully killed him on Tuesday the 20th of October in Anno 172 in the 100 yeare of the kings age as he was makeing Great Preparation towards the great Feast of Taragh called feis Taragh, wch yearly on Hollantide and for certaine dayes after was held.

Conary Kew, K. Conn's sonn in law was next king, he raigned 8 years, & was slain by Nevy m^{c}Srawgynn.

Art Enear m^{c}Conn succeeded next, & raigned 24 yeares, & was slain by Loway m^{c}Conn in the Battle of Moymucroyve.[2]

---

[1] *Moylen* — Moyleana in the parish of Tullamore, King's Co. See *The Battle of Magh Leana*, edited by O'Curry.

[2] *Moymucroyve.*—Near Athenry, Co. Galway.

Loway was K. 18 years and was slaine by Fergus m'Canyne.

Fergus Dowdedagh was king one yeare and was slaine by Cormack m°Art.

Cormack was obsolutely the best king that euer Raigned in Ireland before himselfe. He wrote a Book, entitled Princely Institutions, which in Irish is called Teagasg Ri (ceaṡaŗṡ ŗí)¹, which Booke Contaynes as Goodly precepts and morall Documents as euer Cato or Aristotle did euer write, he was wise, Learned, valiant, & mild, not Given causelesly to be bloody as many of his auncestors were, hee Raigned magestically and magnifitiently² 23 yeares or as som others write 40 years, in the 90th yeare of his age Dyed. He was the first that euer believed in God³ in this K.dome, & because he Refused to adore the Golden Calfe wch was then worshyped as God & for saying that he would sooner worship the artificer that made the Golden Calfe than the Golden Calfe itselfe, & that the Goldsmithe was a worthyer Creature then itt, and therefore Rather to be adored, for which the Priest of the Golden Calfe being heavily Displeased wrought such meanes by the K. as he made a Salmon bone stick fast in his throat untill it choked him, & soe Dyed in one of the K.'s mannor houses called the house of Cleiteagh⁴ near the River of Boyne.

Eochie Gunnall Raigned one yeare & was then slaine by Loway.

Carbrye Liffeachair,⁵ sonn to K. Cormack (to whome he Dedicated his book of Princely Institution) succeeded Eochy & raigned 17 years, others say that he raigned 26 years, & was slaine at Gawra⁶ in a battle called the Battle of Gowra,

---

¹ *Teagasg Ri.*—A copy of it is found in *The Book of Ballymote.* He wrote *The Psalter of Tara* also.

² *Magnifitiently.*—See the account of his reign from *The Book of Cuchongbhail* in O'Curry's *MS. Materials,* p. 44, and Keating's *H. of Ireland,* pp. 262-269.

³ *Believed in God.*—A curious legend of his skull being baptised by St. Columba is told in O'Donnell's *Irish Life* of the Saint.

⁴ *Cleiteagh.* — Near Stackallen bridge, on the south side of the Boyne.

⁵ *Liffeachair.*—So called because he was fostered near the Liffey.

⁶ *Gawra.*—Near Tara. See *Transactions of the Ossianic Society,* I. 68.

this is about the Incarnation of our Lord 267, neere about which time the three sonns of king Carbrey killed the valiant champion of Leinster called Enos Gaybwaifeagh nephew to king Conn Kedcahagh for killing 2 base sonns of K. Cormack & puting his eye out. Alsoe Euticianus Byshopp of Roome was martyred to Death & was Buried in the church yard of Calixtus, after that himselfe, with his one proper hands, had buried 313 martyres.

Alsoe Finn m'Coyle[1] als O'Boysgne the great Hunter, Cheef head of all the Ks. forces in Ireland and Defender of the kingdom from foraine invaders was Beheaded[2] by Aihleagh m^cDurgrean and by the sonns of Wirgrean of the lordship of Lwyne[3] of Tarah at Athbrea on the river of Boyne. This Finn had under his leading 7 Great Cohorts[4] of very huge & tall biggness. None was excepted into any of the Cohorts untill he had Learned out the 12 Irish Books of poetry & could say them without booke, if the Party to be excepted would Defend himself with his targett & sword from 9 throwes of Dartes of 9 of the Company that would stand but 9 Ridges from him at distance, and either cut the Darts with his sword or Receave them all on his targett without Bleeding on him he would be accepted, otherwise not, if the party running through the thickest woods of Ireland were overtaken by any of the seven Cohorts they all pursueing him with all their might & maine he would not be taken of them in their

---

[1] *Finn m^cCoyle.*—'It is quite a mistake,' says O'Curry, 'to suppose him to have been a merely mythical character. Much that has been narrated of his exploits is, no doubt, apocryphal enough; but Finn himself is an undoubtedly historical personage; and that he existed about the time at which his appearance is recorded in the annals, is as certain as that Julius Cæsar lived and ruled at the time stated on the authority of the Roman historians.' *MS. Materials*, p. 304.

[2] *Beheaded.*—An ancient poem says he was killed at Achleagh by a fisherman with a fishing-gaff, in order to obtain for himself everlasting fame by killing one so illustrious.

[3] *Lwyne.* Donough Patrick near Teltown is said by Colgan to be in their territory. *Trias Thaum*, p. 130

[4] *Cohorts.*—Called from him the Fianna Eirion. See an account of them in Keating's *H. of Ireland*, p. 280, and of the ancient literature narrating their exploits in O'Curry's *MS. Materials*, p. 299.

Company. But if he had out-Runned them all without loss of any haire of his head, without Breaking any ould stick under his feet & leping ouer any tree y^t he should meet, as high as the top of his head without Impediment, and stooping under a tree as low as his knee & taking a thorne out of his foot (if it should chance to be in) with his naile without Impediment of his Running; all which if he had Don, he would be excepted as one of the Company, otherwise not, this Finn his Dwelling place was Allon[1] in Leinster, he had many sonns & Daughters as Ossyn[2] mac Finn, Aydan m'Finn, &c. hee had another Dwelling town called Moyelly in Meath, wch is now called Foxes contrey, he was very Learned, wise, & a Great Prophett. He prophesyed[3] of the coming of the Englishmen into this land, with many other things.

The Fothyes[4] Raigned one year Equally together, Fothey Cairpheagh was slaine by Fothey Argheagh, & himself after in the Olorb.[5] These Fothies were none of the blood Royal

Fiagha Scraptine,[6] sonn of king Carbry Liffeacharr, tooke upon him the Government after these Fothyes, hee raigned 18 years & was slaine by his own neare kinsmen the three Callaes in the battle of Duffcomar.[7] St. George was martired to Death about this time & within 30 days after 7000 Christians did suffer martirdom. King Fiagha Straptine ouerthrew the

---

[1] *Allon.*—The hill of Allen, Co. Kildare.

[2] *Ossyn* —He survived the defeat of the Fianna Eirionn at Gaura It was thought that after the battle he was spirited away to the fabulous Tir na og and reappeared on earth at St Patrick's coming Two poems in the *Book of Leinster* are attributed to him, in one of which he gives an account of the battle of Gaura, when his son Oscar and Cairbre Liffeachair fell by each other's hands. See O'Curry's *MS. Materials*, p 304, and *Transactions of the Ossianic Society*, i. 32.

[3] *Prophesyed.* — See O'Curry's *MS. Materials*, p 395 He says this so-called prophecy was fabricated at the close of the 16th century.

[4] *Fothyes* — i. e. the Fothadhs They were sons of Macon, who defeated King Art at Moymucroye.

[5] *Olorb* —The river Larne in Co. Antrim.

[6] *Scraptine.*—So called from the frequent lightning storms during his reign

[7] *Duffcomar* —The confluence of the Boyne and Blackwater.

Leinstermen in 3 Battles, that is to say, at Slieve Twa¹ the battle of Smeyrtire² & battle of Kyerway,³ alsoe he Discomfitted them in the Battle of Dublin.

Colla Wais,⁴ grandchild of king Carbry Liffechair, vidz᷑ son of Eochie Dowlen who was sonn of the said king Carbry, was K. 4 years & was then Banished into Scotland⁵ by Moreagh Tyreagh (king Fiagha Scraptine his son) Colla Wais had two other Brothers Colla da Krioch and Colla Meann. Of Colla Wais are Desended the mᶜDonnells of Scotland with many other Irish-Scotish men. Colla Meann had little or no issue at all, & of Colla da Krioch there are Divers septs as the Maghmahones, Magwyres, O'Kellies of Imany, O'Maddens, O'Neaghtyns, the mᶜEgan elder than Madden or Neaghten. Near about this time or soon after in the year of our Lord 319 St. Martyn Bishopp of Turren or towers in France, & uncle of St. Patrick of Ireland was born.

Moreagh Tyreagh after he had Banished king Colla Wais into Scotland & his brothers with 300 men only in their Company raigned 13 yeares & was slain by Cayluoth mᶜCrouvarie of the house of Ulster.

Cayluoth was king but one year when he was slain by Eochy Moymean.

Eochy Moymean raigned 8 years and was called Moymean in English Moystmidle, because he was much troubled with the flux of the Belly.

St. Patrick in this kings Raigne was brought Captive to this land, where he remayned 7 years after in servitude with the K. of Dalnary in Ulster until he had Redeemed himselfe⁶ with the gould which Victor the angel shewed him in the Digging hole of the Swine wᶜʰ St. Patrick then kept. Neer after this time St. Anthony the Monk Dyed in the 100th year of his age. Amongst few of the kings of this K. dome this K died

---

¹ *Slieve Twa.*—Near Ardara, Co. Donegal.
² *Smeyrtire.*—Not identified
³ *Kyerway.*—Not identified
⁴ *C. Wais.*—*i.e.* the noble. See Keating's *H of Ireland*, p 298.
⁵ *Scotland*—Their mother was Oilean, daughter of the King of S
⁶ *Redeemed himselfe.*—See *Trias Thaum.*, p. 120.

quitely in his bed in Taragh leaving behind him 4 sonnes,[1] Bryan of whome the o'Connors of Connaght, the o'Royrckes, the o'Reylies; Fergus of whom o'Fearghusa and many other septs in Connaught; Fiaghra of whom the o'Dowdyes, o'Fleyns, o'Seaghnoseyes; Neal the yongest & best of them all, of whome the o'Nealls of the West & North are desended, & had more sonnes above these 4.

Criowhann was K. 26 yeares & was then slain by his own sister Monyfinn Daughter of Fyr, Shee was wife to the former K. & thinking to Get the K. dom to one of her own sonns, shee Gave a Potion mingled with Poyson to her one Brother king Criowhann, & fell out quite contrary to her intent[2] and expectation, for after the K.'s Death the kingdom & Crowen came to the hands of Neale the youngest sonn of K. Eochy, whose mother shee was not. St. Martyn Bishop of Turren or Towers in France and flourished there with many miracles about the year 360.

Nealus Magnus als Neal Noygiallagh in English Neal of the 9 hostages, Because he had the hostages of 9 kingdomes, was K. about this time and raigned 19 yeares, was slain wth an arrow by one of his own army called Eochy m[c]Enna kinnsealy,[3] K. of Leinster, at the Tirrhian sea. His body was brought to this kingdome and entered with great sorrow, he had 14 sonns, Owen of whome o'Neales, the three Macswines, o'Cahan, Maclaughlin &c, Conall Golban of whome o'Donell, o'Dochorty &c, Conell Criowhann of whome the o'Melaghlins, &c Manie M[c]Neal of whome o'Fox, Magawley, o'Bryne, o'Dowgennann, o'Mulchonry &c; Enna, of whome o'Brennan &c; Fiagha of whome Mageoghegans & o'Mulloyes &c; of these 14 sonnes there had issue but 8.

Dahye m[c]Fiachra nephew to king Neal was king 26 yeares

---

[1] *Sonnes*—See the Genealogical Table of the descendants of Eochaidh M. in *Tribes and Customs of Hy Fiachrach*, p. 477.

[2] *Intent.*—To recommend the draught to him, she tasted it and died of the poison which it contained.

[3] *Kinnsealy.*—He had been banished to Scotland by Nial, and joined the army as a volunteer in the hope of finding an opportunity of avenging himself. He effected his purpose when the army reached the Loire. See Keating's *H. of Ireland*, p. 321.

next after king Neale. He dyed at the hills of y⁰ Alpes by a thunderbolt or Lightning.¹

Lagery, sonn of king Neale, succeeded after his Cossen Germon, to the former king & in the 4th year² of this kings Raigne St Patrick the apostle of Ireland, &c was sent ouer by Commission of Pope Calestine whoe was the 43rd Pope of Roome, to convert the land from paganism to Christianity; But he did not Land heare untill after the Death of Cælestine in the first yeare of Sixtus his successor, in the 9th year of the raigne of Theodosius the yonger in Anno Domini 425 (432² Rather).

By St. Patrick Ardmacha was Edified & made the Metropolitan Sea of Ireland, together with all other Bushop seas in the K. dome in such convenient Places as he thought fitt. Because all the former Ks were all heathens, I will write their ensuing kings apart from them. All the heathen K.'s y⁵ ever governed this land from the beginning of the world until the coming of Saint Patrick in number were 136, whereof 9 were of Clanna Nevie, 9 other kings of Twaha de Danann, & the rest of Clanna Miletus or of the issue of Miletus. Some writers say that St. James Zebedius ye apostle came to this land: others say that Palladius Bushop was sent there by Pope Cælestine befor St. Patrick but he had not such good success,³ for the Conversion of this land as St. Patrick had, for he converted to faith but 5 parishes onely wch were in Leinster, & as he was Returning to Roome from Ireland Dyed⁴ in his voyage in Pictland. St. Patrick the Archbishop knowing thereof and being in his minority in Ireland, was sent over for their conversion againe, whereof K. Lagery had intelligence by his

---

¹ *Lightning*—A detailed account of the manner of his death is given in *Leabhar na hUidhri*, fol. 35. O'Donovan gives a translation of it in *The Tribes, &c, of Hy Fiachrach*, p. 19. He was buried at Rathcroghan See Petrie's *Eccles. Arch of Ireland*, p. 104.

² 432.—This is the date most commonly given by Irish writers for his coming to Ireland. Pope Celestine died 13th July, 432.

³ *Success*.—He built three churches only, Ellfine, not identified, Donard Cillfinte, and Teach Romaind.

⁴ *Dyed*.— Some say at Fordun, others at Lanforgund in Perthshire. See Todd's *Life of St. Patrick*, p. 299. His feast was kept in the Scottish Church on the 6th of July.

Magitians y^t were familiar with the Devill, that St Patrick would come into the K. dom, & withall they made the K. believe that all the subjects & Inhabitants would be Ruled by him, he would be a means to Destroy and subvert the Gouernment of the K. dom & succession, & bring all into a Confusion, the king being a plain dealing credilous & easy man of beleefe Gave Credit thereuntoe & Commanded that such a man (speaking of St. Patrick) should not be suffered to land in the kingdom & that noe body should give Creditt to his wordes & Doctrine, whereupon the most part of the subjects of the kingdom were vigilant that he should not land upon their Landes, & at last St Patrick came in at ye Coast of Wickloa in Leinster, where he was strongly Resisted by the K. of Leinster, who was son-in-law to K. Lagery; St Patrick attempting to come ashore, one of the subjects of Leinster in the Resistance they made ag^t St Patrick Landing, strock Manton (one of the clergymen y^t were with St Patrick on the teeth & took 4 of his teeth away) with a troe of a stone that he made him toothless, for Mantan in Irish is as much as toothless in English. Whereupon St Patrick & his clergy cursed the haven soe as from that time to this day there is little or noe fish caught there.[1]

St Patrick after his landing thought best to have his first Recourse to the K of Dalnary in Ulster, with whome he was in servitude as before. But the king of Dalnary understanding thereof & consulting with his Deuill what was best to doe (for Deuills in those dayes were conversant with men) whoe advised him, that it were better & more Worthyer for him to burne himself in his own house than to be Ruled by one that was his own bondman before. The K. listning to the wordes of the Deuills put his jewels about him, & in the midst of the house was burnt,[2] together with all his movables wch St. Patrick seeing, amongst other voyages he tooke in Ireland, he went to the kings pallace of Taragh[3] where K. Lagery was. The K. by

---

[1] *There.*—Killmantan is the Irish name of the town of Wicklow.

[2] *Burnt.*—See *Trias Th.*, p. 125.

[3] *Taragh.*—*Ibid.*, p. 74.

his magitian (that was familier with the Deuill) knowing of yᵉ saints coming, made one of his men (named Cronnmoyle) to lay himself dead on the ground in the St's passage with his face & head all besprinkled with Blood, & a woman under his head (to make the Saint believe at the time of his passage by that the party was dead, and that she would soe tell him, & withall desire him to Revive him from the Dead to the end the party would make noe answer to the St's calling, & that thenceforwards there should be no Creditt given him). Whereupon St. Patrick aproaching the kings Pallace, & passing by the supposed dead, asked the woman what ailed the dead man. She tould him that he Dyed of a fall he gott & prayed him if his prayers were of any force, that he might be the mean to Revive him to life again, & St. Patrick asked the mans name and being told thereof, knowing by Divine inspiration of the falsehood of the matter, Called him & prayed God that all should fall out ill with this man according to his Disert. When yᵉ woman stirred him this way & that way shee could not make him stir, & was found stark Dead[1] by the miracles of St Patrick.

Then after he asked the king to Receave Baptism of him & become a Christian, which the king absolutely Refused & Compared his magitians with St Patrick, saying that they cou'd work more wonders than hee, & therefore worthier to be Believed, & after long comparisons between them in presence of all the people St. Patrick ouercame the Magitians & by the help & power of God ended boisterous Whirlewyndes & Earthquakes to terrifie the king and people to the end by terrour to make them believe, notwithstanding all which the K. was so obstinate that he would not Receave Baptism, but faynedly[2] by mouth onely untill at Last the Queen[3] being

---

[1] *Dead.*—His name was Murenus. Colgan says this pretended sleep of his gave rise to an Irish proverb.—*Ibid.*, p. 91.

[2] *Faynedly.*—It is very doubtful whether Lagery was ever a believer in Christianity.—See Petrie's *Antiquities of Tara*, p. 145

[3] *Queen.*—Aillinn, daughter of Aengus mac Nadfraich, king of Munster, whom St Patrick later baptized at Cashel.

much terified by these strange sights tould the St. that the K. was ready to Receave baptism; but the St. knowing that this was for Dissimulation & fear cursed the K. and his posterity for ever, & humbly besought God of his Infinite power that none of that Kings Posterity should euer after inheritt the Crowen of Ireland. The Queen hearing the curse prayed the St. that it might stand with his pleasure to auert that curse & that it might not light on the issue[1] then in her womb, to whom he Replyed & said that he was content that it should soe stand with Gods Pleasure, that the s^d curse might not fall upon the issue[1] then in her womb, untill the Issue had Deserved it by speaking or Doing something against St. Patrick.

Now wee will leave speaking of K. Lagery untill we come to the place where wee ought to make mention of him; & follow St. Patrick to Dublin[2] where he was receaved by the Senate & people thereof wth great Reverence & welcome, to whom hee promised (after they receaved Baptism of him) that masses & mattins with holy orders would remaine & be in that towen for ever; and after many & inumerable miracles don by him, as were too long to Resite the Hundreth part of them, he Dyed in the 123 yeare of his age; others say he liued not long, but my authour whose written booke of him is no less than 300 yeares written, sayeth that his age was noe less. Some say he was a Welshman, others a frenchman of Brittanie in france. Butt howsoever he was Desended of Brutus, as by his genelogy is set forth in his booke shall apeare to anyone that shall be Desirous to know the truth. Hee was borne in a village called Taburna neer Emptor[3] Town in the south of England. The ffrenchman sayes that he was of his Country, the Scottchman affirmeth him to be

---

[1] *Issue.*—This was Lughaidh, who succeeded to the throne twenty years after his father died

[2] *Dublin.*—At this time it was but a small village, 'pagus exiguus.' *Trias Thaum*, p. 90.

[3] *Emptor* —St. Fiacc of Sletty, in his metrical *Life*, says 'Genair Patraic i Nemthur', and the B. of Armagh 'Qui (i e pater ejus) fuit vico Bannavem Taberniae.' See Todd's *Life of St Patrick*, p. 355.

of his K. dome, & the Englishman claimeth him to be an Englishman; for my part it is not my meaning to giue a verdict against any right either of them may have in soe noble a prelate in a matter Disputable & undiscussed whom I know each of them would esteem that soe Ritch a Jewell as St. Patrick was would be a Great loss upon soe slight a evidence as I can shew.[1]

425.—Now I intend to lay down the K[s] of Ireland, the K[s] of Scotland, the K[s] of the 5 Provinces & the K[s] of the County of Ossory y[t] Lived in the time of one raigne since the time of the Coming of St. Patrick untill the coming of K. Bryan Borowa ut Sequitur. Lagerie before the coming of St Patrick did raigne but 4 yeares and at that time Moneagh Mwindearge was K. of Ulster, Criocohann m^cEnna was king of Lynster. Enos m^cNaofreigh K, of Mounster, and Dwaghgaly K. of Connaught. The first Indiction Romane beginneth Anno 433. Secundinus[2] als Seachnall Patron of Donsoghlyn[3] nephew of St. Patrick & Auxilius[4] were sent hither by the pope to help the Conversion of this land. The Chronicles of Ireland were Renewed this yeare. St. Bridgett the Virgin was borne[5] about this time in Anno 425. Joanes Cassianus[6] died. Manie m^cNeale Noygiallagh auncestor to those of the land of Teaffie died.

427.—Xixtus, Pope of Rome & raigned 8 yeares & 18

---

[1] *Shew.*—The birthplace of St. Patrick has given rise to much controversy. The more commonly received opinion now is that he was born at Dumbarton, on the Firth of Clyde. The question will be found discussed in O'Hanlon's *Lives of the Irish Saints*, iii. 436, and Todd's *Life of St Patrick*, p. 355.

[2] *Secundinus.*—He wrote a hymn in honour of St. Patrick, beginning: 'Audite omnes.' See the *Book of Hymns*, published by the I. A. S., p. 11. His feast was on Nov. 11th.

[3] *Donsoghlyn.*—12 miles S.W. of Trim.

[4] *Auxilius.*—He was uterine brother of St. Secundinus. He founded Killashee (cella Auxilii), near Naas, Co. Kildare. His feast was on September 16th. See the *Journal of Co. Kildare Arch. Soc.* for 1892, p. 13.

[5] *Borne.*—At Faughart, 4 miles north of Dundalk.

[6] *Cassianus.*—He was abbot of a monastery near Marseilles. His name is introduced here probably on account of his connexion with Lerins, where St. Patrick is said to have lived for a time.

days when hee Died. Pope Leo was ordayned the 46 or 47 to succeed, by whom St Patrick was approved in the Catholique Religion and by the rest of the Popes of Roome that succeeded in his time, & then after florished in the heat of Christian Religion in this land. Nahie[1] m^cFiaghra of Ulster died in anno 427. The battle of Fevin in which Carhinn m^rCorlvoy m^cNeale was slaine. Some say y^t this man was a Pict. Secundinus in the 75 yeare of his age dyed. Hee was a son of Colmana, sister of St Patrick. There were 3 long shipps carried, wherein there were 7 Saxons of whome Hingist & Orsa were Captines of the Saxons of Hingest or King of England and were Receaved and obeyed by Vertiger K. of Brittans 450. The Councell of Calcedo[2] consisting of 630 Bushopps was about this time in anno 445. 451. The Resurection of Our Lord was celebrated the 8 of the Calends of May by the Pelagion heresie. The Brittans were much trobled by certain fiench Bishopes therein, the Brittains Requireing aid of the Pope of Roome were sent for their ayd & Defence of their faith Germanuss[3] Altiodorensis Bishopp & Bushopp Lupus, who confirmed their faith by worde, examples, & miracles. The picts made great warrs wth the Brittaines then which was likewise annihilated by Divine Providence for the Brittans chosed as their Governour of their armies against the Picts Lupus, who did ouercome their enemies not with the sound of trumpet or Drum, nor force of armes, but the singing of Alleluia[4] making it sound in the very skies, that thereby the said Bishopes ouercame their enemies & returned home wth victory to Ravenna was with Great Reverence & honor Receaved by K. Valentinian & Placida his wife, whose body being after dead was carried with an honorable com-

---

[1] *Nahie.*—Or Dathi. This must be the same person who is mentioned at p. 65, *antea*, for the *Annals F. M.* give 428 as the year of King Dathi's death by lightning at Shabh Ealpa.

[2] *Calcedo.*—A city on the Asiatic side of the Bosphorus. A General Council was held here in 451 to condemn the errors of Eutyches.

[3] *Germanuss.*—B. of Auxerre His first visit with St. Lupus was in 429. See an account of it in Newman's *Lives of the English Saints,* ix. 138.

[4] *Alleluia.*—*Ibid*, p. 154.

The Annals of Clonmacnoise. 71

pany to Altiodorensis. King Lagerius fought a battle wth the Leinstermen, wherein the Leinstermen Got the worst. The Great Feast of Taragh called ꝼeıꞅ Ceaṁpac was made this yeare by K Lagery. Enna m^cCathfie Dyed. Martianus the Emperour Dyed.

449.—Pope Leo raigned 17 years. Drust m^cErb, K. of Pictland, Died. The Lynstermen fought the battle of Athdara[1] against K. Lagery wherein K. Lagery himselfe was taken Captiue & his army altogether overthrone, but the K. was enlarged upon his oath[2] by the sunn and moone (which was solemnly sworn by him) to restore them their cowes.

454.—Auxilius of Liffie Bushop Dyed. Now Pope Leo dyed in the 25th year of his Popedome, one month and 13 days, to whome succeeded Hillarius. The battle of Ardcorran[3] was Given by the Leinstermen to K. Lagery, wherein Crewhan was slaine. K. Lagery Died an evill Death. Some say he sunck down in the earth between the 2 hills[4] neere the River of Liffie called Irland & Scotland, but the most part agree that hee was stroken Dead at a place called Taw Caissi by the wind & sunn for forswearing himselfe to the leinstermen for the Restitution[5] of the Cowes which he was sworn to perform at the time of his Captivity. He Dyed about the year 458.

After the death of king Laygery Aillill Molt began his raigne, during whose raigne & the raigne of the former K. which was for 43 yeares there Raigned in Ulster 3 K^s namely Moreagh Kewe Cerall and Eochy m^cMorey. There Raigned in Munster two K^s Enos & ffeylim 20 yeares after the Battaile

---

[1] *Athdara.*—On the Barrow, in the plain of Magh Ailbe. So an ancient Irish tract. The name is now obsolete.

[2] *Oath.*—See the form of it in Petrie's *H. of Tara,* p. 34.

[3] *Ardcorran.*—The name is obsolete.

[4] *Hills.*—So *Leabhar na h Uidhri*, fol. 117; it adds: 'He was interred on Tara with his face turned southwards upon the men of Leinster, as fighting with them, for he was the enemy of the Leinster men during his lifetime.' *Ibid.* The hills are supposed to be Dunmurry and the Hill of Allen.

[5] *Restitution* —More properly, because he raided Leinster, though he had sworn very solemnly not to demand the borumha from the inhabitants.

of ockie[1] where Aillill Molt was slaine. The sonns of Erck went over into Scotland anno 498 qui est anno 478, 20 sed so 483-15. Hillarius Pope dyed, to whom succeeded Simplicius Pope. The Cytty of Ravenna was quite Destroyed by an Earthquake. Dureing the raignes of the said Kings, that is to say the raign of King Leway m'Lagery, K. Mortagh, K. Twahall Moylegarve, and K. Dermott there Raigned in Scotland five Kings who were Dawangart, Fergus (whom I should first name), Enos, Convallo, sonn of Dawangart, and Gawran his other sonn, Dureing which time there Raigned in Ulster 4 kings vidz[t] Eochy m'Conley, ffearga, Deman & Broydan m'Carill. In Mounster their Reigned 3 kings Eochy, Criowhan, & Scanlan; in Connaught alsoe there Rayned 5 kings vidz[t]. Owen vell Oillill, fitz Owen vel Dwagh Teangowa Eochy Tyrncharna, and fearadagh m'Rossa. Benignus[2] the Bishop dyed 468. Iserninus[3] bishopp died 469. King Ollill Molt made the Great feast of Tarag, called feis taragh, the second Booty that the Saxons tooke from out of Ireland. Docus Bushopp of the Brittans dyed. Brandon[4] Bushopp of Ardmagh dyed. Conell Criowhan m'Neale, auncestor of y[e] o'Melaghlyns died. Earlahy,[5] third Bushop of Ardmagh, dyed.

482.—Simplicius Pope dyed to home succeeded Pope Felix.

487.—When King Aillill Molt had thus raigned 20 years Loway m'Lagerie with his Partakers (which were long to number) as Mortagh m'Earcka and Fergus Ker(bel) m'Connell Criowhan chalenged him to the field, where the

---

[1] *Ockie.*—Colgan says it was near Tara *Trias Thaum.*, p 565.

[2] *Benignus.*—He succeeded St. Patrick in the See of Armagh, which he occupied from 455 to 465 He is said to have compiled the *Book of Rights* See Introd., p. ii His feast was celebrated on November 9th.

[3] *Iserninus.*—He came to Ireland with Auxilius to aid St. Patrick, and founded the church of Kilcullen in Co. Kildare See *Trias Thaum.*, p. 19.

[4] *Brandon* —This is a mistake, as Earlahy was the immediate successor of Benignus

[5] *Earlahy* He is called in the *Annals F. M* Iarlathe, and is not to be confounded with St. Jarlath of Tuam See Ware's *Bishops*, p. 34

King was slain in yᵉ battle of Oicke. Then began the raign of Loway son of king Lagery and reagned 25 years. The battaille of Granie¹ where Moriertagh mᶜErcka had the victory. There was another battaile of Granie¹ between the Lynstermen themselves fought, where Fynncha king of o'Keansly² was slaine, and Carbry had the victory. Bushopp Moyle³ died in Ardacha. St. Kineann⁴ of Dowliag Dowleeke⁵ to whome St. Patrick gave his one booke of the Holy Euangelist dyed. The Bishopp mᶜCaille⁶ dyed. The sixth of yᵉ Ides of October, the battle of Killosny⁷ in Moyffea was fought wherein Enos mᶜNadfreagh, king of Mounster, and his wife Eihny Wahagh daughter of Criowhan mᶜEnna Kinsealy was slaine, also Illan mᶜDowlan his brother. Aillill Eaghie Gwyneagh and Mortaugh mᶜEcka prince of Oilegh were victors. St. Patrick the apostle and archbishopp dyed⁸ in yᵉ 123ʳᵈ yeare of his age the 16ᵗʰ day of the Calends of Aprill. Felix, Pope dyed, to whom succeeded Gelatius pope Cwymka mᶜCathmoa, bishop of Lusk,⁹ dyed. Gelasius pope dyed. Anastatius pope was ordained Pope in his place. The battle of Sleawyn in Westmeath was giuen by Carbry mᶜNeale where the Leinster men were discomfited. Mocheus¹⁰ of Indroym¹¹ in Ulster, dyed.

---

¹ *Granie.* — Now Graney, near Castledermot, Co. Kildare.

² *O'Keansly.* — Hy Kinsellagh, which included not only the present diocese of Ferns, but also a part of Co Carlow It had its name from Enna Kinsella, King of Leinster in the 4th century.

³ *Moyle* —*i.e.* Mel, a disciple of St Patrick and first bishop of Ardagh. His feast is on February 5th.

⁴ *Kineann* —His feast is on the 24th of November.

⁵ *Dowleeke.*—In Meath, 7 miles S.W. of Drogheda.

⁶ *McCaille.*—He was Bishop of Cruachan Bri Eile, *i.e.* Croghan, in King's Co. He gave the veil to St. Brigid. His feast was kept on the 25th of April.

⁷ *Killosny.*—*i.e.* the church of the lamentations, now Kelliston, in the barony of Forth, Co. Carlow.

⁸ *Dyed .*— At Saul, near Downpatrick. He was buried at Downpatrick. On the year of his death, and his age when he died, see O'Hanlon's *Lives of the Irish Saints,* iii. 795.

⁹ *Lusk.*—See D'Alton's *History of Co. Dublin,* p. 414.

¹⁰ *Mocheus.*—He was a disciple of St. Patrick. See *Trias Thaum.,* p 14.

¹¹ *Indroym.*—Now Island Mahee in Strangford Lough.

497.—Bushopp Cormack Inderny Cowarb[1] of St. Patrick, died.

501.—Anastatius pope died in anno 501. [498] Symmachus raigned pope 15 yeares. Carbry m'Neale gave the battle of Kynnailve[2] to Leinstermen. The battle of Seaisse[3] was Given by Moriertagh mac Earka to Dwagh Keangowa, king of Connaught, where Dwagh was slain. Fergus More mac earka, with Certaine Ulstermen held part of Brittaine where the said Fergus Remayned until he dyed.

504.—The battle of Inne[4] fought against the Leinstermen & Illann m'Dowenlenge, where Moriertagh m'Earka had the victory. Bishopp Iver[5] Dyed the 9th of the Calends of May in the 30rd yeare of his age. Coarban, Bushopp of Fearta Coarban,[6] dyed 501. Aidan m'Gawran, K. of Scotland fought a battle in the Isle of Man.

509.—Brwidy m'Milcon K. of Pictland, & Dawangort m'Nissie, K. of Scotland, Dyed-foede hiec erratum est.[7] Fiacha m'Neale of whom Kinalagh decended fought a battle at freawynn in Westmeath, where fiacha was victor Loway m'Lagery K. of Ireland, as he was walking in the fieldes, saw a chaple that was Dedicated to St. Patrick, & said this is the Church of the Clerk that Prophisied that none of my father's posterity should inherit the Crowen of Ireland, he is false and in saying soe, sudainly there Came a thunder-bolt from heaven w[ch] lighted upon the kings head & struck him starck Dead, this was at a place called Achy forcha.[8] Thus St.

---

[1] *Cowarb.*—The word is used here not in its original sense, steward of the church property, but successor.

[2] *Kynnailve.*—Probably a hill in Magh Ailbe in the south of Kildare.

[3] *Seaisse.*—The Seaghais or Boyle river

[4] *Inne* In Crioch Ua nGabhla, a territory in the southern part of Co. Kildare.

[5] *Iver.*—Ibhar, the patron of Beg Erin, an island near Wexford, where he founded a monastery and school. His feast was kept on 23rd April.

See *Ireland's Ancient Schools*, p. 136.

[6] *Coarban.* — Near Tara. See Lanigan's *Eccl. Hist. of Ireland*, i. 419

[7] *Erratum est.*—'This is a great mistake.' These words evidently were inserted by O'Daly. On B. M'Melcon see Reeves' *Adamnan*, p. 150.

[8] *Achy forcha.*—Colgan says this was in the territory now included in the baronies of Slane. *Trias Thaum.*, p. 172.

Patricks words were fullfilled in this king; none of his posterity (thoughe he was the eldest son of King Neallus Magnus) neuer enjoyed the Crowen since, nor never shall. Moriertagh Mac Earcka was the next K. and raigned 24 years. Mᶜ Nisie aïs Enos Bushopp of Conrye[1] dyed, whose fathers name was ffobreagh and mothers name Cnesy, of whom he was called mᶜCnessye. Broyn, bushopp of Cashell,[2] dyed, rather bishop of Cuill-iro, in Sligo Contry. Earck, bushopp of Slane, dyed in the 90th yeare of his age.

515.—The nativity of Querainn the carpenters sonn in Anno 515. Symachus Pope dyed, to whom succeeded Hormista, who raigned 9 years, as Marcellinus declareth. The Battle of Dromdeargye[3] was fought by ffiagh mᶜNeale in which he Recouered Usneagh[4] to be of the land of Kynaleagh, where Foilge Merrye was ouercome.

516.—Duffagh abbott of Ardmach dyed. Darearca of Kill in Slievgowlyn[5] dyed.

518.—S. Congallus of Beanchor[6] was borne this yeare.

519.—The nativity of Saint Kenny or Canicus of Eachybo.[7] In the province of Dardany there was a horrible earthquake in so much that 24 Castles were fallen down in one moment by it. Anastatius the Emperor dyed of a sudaine & unprovided death of a Thunderbolt which by Gods providence was sent him for the favour he did bear to the Eutitian Heretickes & persecuted the Catholiques. Justinus senior raigned Emperour 8 years. Conly,[8] Bishop of Kildare,

---

[1] *Conrye.*—The See of Connor in Ulster.

[2] *Cashell.*—These words are added in a different hand. It is in the south-west of the barony of Carbury.

[3] *Dromdeargye.*—Not identified.

[4] *Usneagh.*—A hill in the parish of Killare, Co. Westmeath. Here the five provinces met. See Keating's *History of Ireland,* p. 54.

[5] *Slievgowlyn.*—Slieve Gullion, in Co. Armagh. The church is now called Killeavy.

[6] *Beanchor.*—Now Bangor, on the south side of Belfast Lough. On St. Congall and Bangor, see Healy's *Ireland's Ancient Schools,* p. 367. Hardly a trace of this once famous monastery remains.

[7] *Eachybo.*—Aghaboe, 8 miles west of Abbeyleix, Queen's Co. This saint transferred his see later to Kilkenny. See Graves' *History of St. Canice's Cathedral,* p. 14.

[8] *Conly.*—See Comerford's *Dioceses of Kildare and Leighlin,* i. 9. His feast is on May 3rd.

dyed. The battle of Delna in Drombrey,[1] wherein Ardgall mᶜConnell and Criowhan mᶜNeale was slaine; Colga Moclothe mᶜCowynn mᶜfelym & king Moriertaigh had the victory, was fought Boyhin mᶜBroynn, dyed. St. Culumbkill was borne this yeare. He was born the night that St. Boyhinn dyed. They were of one family, & both of the families of the O'Donells of Tyr Connell as may appeare by St. Columb's genealogie as Columbkill was sonn of felym who was son of fergus Ceannada, whoe was son of Connell Culban, whoe was son of Neale of the 9 hostages &c. We will leave to speak here of St Columb, until we come to make mention of him at the yeare of his Death. St. Boghinn was his cozen germond,[2] errat.

522.—Beoy,[3] bishopp of Ardkarna,[4] dyed. Ailhill abbott of Ardmacha, dyed. Hormista Pope dyed, to whom succeeded Johanes Pope 53 years, whoe comeing to Constantinople Restored a blind man to his sight in the presence of all men, at the gate called Aurea. Saint Bridgett the virgin, in the 27th or as others say the 70th year only of her age dyed. This St. was of noble decent.[5] Shee was of Leinster, Descended of Eochy ffinn (of whom I had made mention before) who was brother to king Conn Kedcatagh as may apeare thus: St Bridgett was daughter of Duffagh, who was sonn of Dreivne, who was sonn of Breasall, who was son of Deine, who was sonn of Conly, who was sonn of Artkir who was sonn of Carbry Nia, who was sonn of Cormacke, who was sonn of Enos who was sonn of Eocha fynn aforesᵈ, who was sonn of K. felym Reaghtwar and Brother of king Conn Kedcahagh. Illan mᶜDunleng, K. of Lynster, dyed. Saint

---

[1] *Drombrey.*—The northern part of Meath, adjoining Cavan.

[2] *Cozen germond.*—He was the son of Brennan; C. was son of Feidhlimidh, both sons of Fergus Ceanfoda. The word 'errat,' 'he makes a mistake,' has reference to the time of Baithin's death, which was 600. He succeeded St. C. as abbot of Iona, and survived him three years.

[3] *Beoy.*—Colgan gives his *Life* on the 8th of March, *Acta SS.*, p. 562.

[4] *Ardkarna.*—Four miles east of Boyle.

[5] *Decent.*—See O'Hanlon's *Lives of the Irish Saints*, ii. 11, where this question is discussed fully. The relationship of Columba and Brigid will be found in Todd's *Life of St Patrick*, p. 252.

Ailve[1] Dyed. Benedictus the monk flourished in the Mount of Cassina in all manner of vertue & Good life, & whom St Gregory the pope hath numbered among other Sts in the Book of Dialogues. ffelix pope raigned 4 years 2 months & 14 Dayes.

529.—Keybann Brick was born this year. The battle of Kynneagh[2] & the battle of Sye[3] was Given by K. Moriertagh against the Leinster men, where the king had the victory. Dionitius this year wrote the Pascall Cyrcle beginning at the year of our Lords Incarnation, 532, wch the year of Diocletian 218 after the consulship of Lampades and Orestes, wch yeare alsoe Justinianus divulged his Chronicles of the world. Pope Felix dyed. The battle of Evlyne[4] was fought by K. Mortaugh together with these Ensuing battles, vidz^t the battle of Moyalve against Leinstermen, the battle of Ayne[5] against Connaughtmen, the battle of Allon & Kynneigh against Leinstermen and the Destruction of Kliagh[6] in one yeare. Bonifacius Pope raigned two years & 26 days. King Moriertagh having had prosperous success as well before he came to the Crowne as after against these that Rebelled against him, he was at last Drowned in a kyve of wine in one of his own mannor-houses called Cleitagh neare the river of Boyne by a fayrie woman that burnt the house over the K's head on Hollantide night, the K. thinking to save his life from burning entred the kyve of wine which was soe high that the K. could not keep himselfe for Depth for he was soe fifteen foot high as is laid Down in a Certaine book of his life and Death. This is the End of king Moriertagh who was both burnt, Drowned, & killed together through his own folly in trusting to this woman Contrary to the advice of St. Carneagh.[7]

---

[1] *S. Ailve*—First bishop of Emly. His feast is on September 12th. See Healy's *Ireland's Ancient Schools*, p 131.

[2] *Kynneagh*—O'D says it is in the Co Kildare, adjoining Wicklow.

[3] *Sye*.—Or Athsighe, now Assy, in the barony of Deece, Co. Meath.

[4] *Evlyne*.—The Slieve Phelim mountains, in Co Tipperary.

[5] *Ayne*.—Hy Fiachrach Aidhne, a territory in the S E of Co Galway, conterminous with the diocese of Kilmacduagh.

[6] *Kliagh*—In the barony of Idrone, Co Carlow

[7] *St. Carneagh*.—Of Dulane, Co. Meath.

535—Twahal Moyle Garve began his raigne & raigned 11 years He was sonn of Cormack Keigh, who was sonn of Carbry who was sonn of Neale of the nine Hostages He caused Dermot m^cKeruell to live in Exile & in Desert places because he Claimed to have Right to ye Crowen. St. Moychey,[1] Disciple of St. Patrick & Patron of Louth,[2] dyed the 16th of the Calends of September, himselfe writeth in his Epistle thus: Mocheus peccator & presbiter Sancti Patricy Discipulus in Domino salutem &c whose age at the time of his death was 300 years & 3 days Bonifatius Pope Dyed, to whom succeeded Mercorius, who raigned 2 years 4 months & 6 dayes. The battle of Lwachra[3] between the two Invers by K. Twahall was fought on Kyannaght[4]. Marcellinus hath brought his chronicles thereunto.

536.—Aillill, abbott of Ardmach, dyed. The nativity of Saint Boyhinn,[5] scholar of Saint Columbkill.

539—Mercorius Pope dyed. Agapicus succeeded eleven months & eight Dayes The battle of Kleynlogh[6] was fought where Maney m^cKervil was slaine maintaining the liberties of o'Mayne[7] in Connaught, & Goivneann of ffiachra Ayney was victor. Cowgall Mac Dawangort, K. of Scotland in the 35th year of his raigne, dyed.

543—Bread was very scarce this yeare. Silverius Pope raigned one year 5 months & 11 Days & Dyed. The nativity of Pope Gregory Nean Bishop dyed. Pope Vigilius by birth a Romane raigned 17 years & 9 months and 22 days, dyed at Siracusa & was buried in Via Salaria, as Venerable Beda recounteth.

---

[1] *St Moychey.*—See *Annals F M.*, i. 135. Lanigan shows how the error about his reputed great age arose *Eccl. H. of Ireland*, i. 310

[2] *Louth*—See Healy's *Ireland's Ancient Schools*, p 126.

[3] *Lwachra.*—At Cluan Ailbe, in the barony of Upper Duleek, Co. Meath.

[4] *Kyannaght.*—The territory of K Breagh included the baronies of Upper and Lower Duleek

[5] *Boyhinn*—See p. 10, *antea*

[6] *Kleynlogh.*—In Cinel Aedha, i.e. in Hy Fiachrach Aidhne

[7] *o'Mayne.*—Hy Many, a district which included the present baronies of Athlone, in Co Roscommon, and the baronies of Ballymoe, Tiaquin, Killian, and Kilconnell, in Co. Galway It was inhabited by the O'Keilys and O'Maddens See the *Tribes and Customs of Hymany*, edited by O'Donovan

546.—The was a great mortality wch was called Irish Blefeth,¹ of which Disease Clarineagh ats Berchann,² who is supposed to be called in English Merlyn³ dyed. Ailve Seanchwa⁴ o'Naillealla dyed.

547.—The battle of Tortan⁵ against Leinster men, where m°Ercka sonn of Ailill Molt was slaine, was fought this yeare. The Battle of Slygeagh where Owen Bell, K. of Connaught, was slaine; and Fergus & Donell the two sonns of m°Ercka finnire m°Sedna & Nynny m°Divagh were victors. Lugedus, Bishop of Connery, dyed.

King Twahal hauing proclaimed throughout the whole K. dom the banishment of Dermot m°Kervel (as before is specified) with a great Reward to him y^t would bring him his hart, the said Dermot for feare of his life lived in the deserts of Cluonvicknose (then called Ardtibra) and meeting with the abbot St. Kieran in the place where the Church of Clonvickenose now standes, who was but newly come thither to live or dwell from Inis Angin⁶ & having noe house or place to Reside & dwell in, the said Dermot Gave him his assistance to make a house there, & in thrusting down in the earth one of the peeces of the timber or wattles of the house, the s^d Dermot took St. Queran's hand⁷ & did put it ouer his one head or hand in sign of Reverence to the St., whereupon the saint Humbly besaught God of his great Goodness that by that time to-morrow ensuing that the hands of Dermot might have superiority over all Ireland, which fell out as the St. Requested, for Mulmorry OHargedy, foster-brother of

---

¹ *Blefeth.*—See the *Census of Ireland for 1851*, pt. v. vol. i. p. 416.

² *Berchann.*—Called also Mobi Clairineagh, *i.e.* of the flat face. He was founder of the monastery of Glasnevin. His feast is on October 12th. See Reeves' *Adamnan*, lxii.

³ *Merlyn.*—A famous enchanter. It is not easy to see what connexion could be between him and St. Mobi.

⁴ *Seanchwa.* — Shancoe, in the barony of Tirerril, Co. Sligo. This church is mentioned in *Trias Thaum.*, p. 134.

⁵ *Tortan.*—Near Ardbraccan, Co. Meath.

⁶ *I Angin.*—In Lough Ree, now called Hare Island.

⁷ *Hand.*—This event is commemorated in the carving of one of the crosses of Clonmacnoise. *See* Introduction.

Dermott, seeing in what perplexity the nobleman was in, besaught him that hee might be pleased to lend him his black horse, & that hee would make his Repaire to Greally da Phill,[1] where he hard K. Twahall to have a meeting with som of his nobles, & there would present him a whelps hart on a speares head, instead of Dermots hart, and soe by that means gett access to the K. whom he would kill out of hand & by the help & swiftness of the horse saue his one life whether they would or noe. Dermott listing to the wordes of his foster-brother, was amongst two extremityes, loth to refuse him & far more loth to lend it him, fearing hee should miscarry & be killed, but between both he Granted him his Request, whereupon hee prepared himselfe & went as he was Resolved, mounted on the s^d black horse, a hart besprinkled with blood on his speare, to the place where he hard the K. to bee; the K. & people seeing him come in that manner supposed it was Dermotts hart that was to be presented by the man that rode in post hast; the whole multitude gave him way to the K., & when he came within reach to the king as though to Tender him the hart, he gaue the K. such a deadly Bloe of his speare, that the K. Instantly fell dowen Dead in the midst of his people, whereupon the man was besett on all sides & at last taken & killed, soe as speady news came to Dermot, who Incontinently went to Tarach, & there was crowned K. as St Queran Prayed & Prophesied before.

Dermot m^{c}Cervell began his raigne Immediately after king Twahal was killed, & raigned 20 years from the beginning of the raigne of K. Dermot to the death of Hugh m^{c}Ainnreagh 36 years, dureing which time there raigned in Ireland the number of 7 kings, vidz^t Donell, ffergus, Boydann, Eochy, Boydann, Ainmire, and Hugh his sonn. There raigned also in Scotland 2 kings Connall m^{c}Cowgall & Hugh m^{c}Gawran. There Raigned likewise in the province of Ulster 2 kings David m^{c}Connell and Hugh Duff m^{c}Swynie,

---

[1] *G da Phill.*—O'Donovan says this place was on the Liffey, in Co. Kildare.

in Leinster there raigned 2 K⁸, Colman & Hugh, in Ossery two K⁸ Colman & Ceanfoyla, & in Mounster 4 K⁸ raigned, ffelym, Hugh, Garvey, & Auley, & in like manner in the province of Connaught there Raigned 2 K⁸, that is to say Moylecahy & Hugh.

Dermot was not aboue 7 months K. when St. Queran dyed in Clonvickenose when he Dwelt therein but seven months before in the 33 year of his age, the 9th of September. His fathers name was Beoy, a Connaught man & a carpenter. His mother Darerca, of the issue of Corck m^{c}ffergus m^{c}Roy of the Clanna Rowryes, he in his Childhood liued with his father & mother in Templevickinloyhe in Kinaleagh[1] until a theef of the Contry of Affaly stole the one cow they had, wch being found, hee forsooke together with his father & mother the said place of the stealth fearing of further Inconvenience; he in the mean time earnestly Intreated his parents that they would please to give him the Cow, that he might goe to school to Clonard[2] to Bushopp Finnann, where St. Columbkill, Columb (M^c) Criowhann,[3] Colman[4] of Lynnealae, St. Boyhinn, & Divers others were at school, which his parents Denyed, whereupon he resolved to goe thither as poore as he was without any maintenance in the world. The Cow followed him thither with her calfe, & being more Given to the care of his learning than to the keeping of the Cowes, having none to keep the Calfe from the Cowe, Did but draw a strick of his batt between the Calfe & Cow, the Cow could not thenceforth come noe nearer the Calf then to the strick, nor the Calf to the Cow, soe as there needed noe servant to keep them one from

---

[1] *Kinaleagh.*—Perhaps L. Kineel, near Abbeylara, Co. Longford.

[2] *Clonard.*—Ten miles S W. of Trim. See an account of this famous school and its founder in Healy's *Ireland's Ancient Schools*, p. 188 St. Finnian's feast is December 12th

[3] *Columb McCriowhann.* — Of Terryglass, on the western shore of Lough Derg, in the barony of Lower Ormond, Co. Tipperary. His feast is December 13th. See Lanigan's *Eccl. H*, ii. 71.

[4] *Colman.*—Called C. Ela. Hence the name of the monastery, which is situated two miles S.W of Tullamore, King's Co., and at the same distance from St. Carthach's monastery of Rahan His feast is on September 26th.

another but the strik. But wt doe I speak of his miracles which are soe innumerable as would fill a whole volume, which was a rare thing in anyone of his age, when he was Dying he desired his monkes, that they would bury his body in the little Church of Clonnvickenos & stop the doore thereof with stones & let nobody haue access thereunto until his companion Keyngynn or Keyvinn had come, which they accordingly did, But St. Keyvinn dwelling at Gleanndalock in Leinster then, it was reveled to him of the death of his deare & loueing Companion St. Queran, whereupon he came sudainly to Cluonvicknose & finding the moncks & servants of St. Queran in their sorrowful & sad Dumpes after the Death of their said lord & Master, he asked them of the Cause of their sadness, they were soe heartless for Greef as they gaue noe answer & at last fearing he would grow angry, they tould him St Queran was dead & byried, & ordered or ordayned the place of his buriall should be kept without access untill his Coming, the stones being taken out of the doore, St. Kevinn entred, to whom St. Queran apeared & remayned Conversing together for 24 hours, as is very confidently Laid Down in the Life of St Queran, & afterwards St Kevin Departed to the place of his one abiding, left St. Querin buried in the said little Church of Clonvickenois.

But K. Dermot most of all men Grieved for his death in soe much yt he grew Deaf & could not heare the Causes of his subjects, by reason of the heauiness & troblesomnes of his braines. St. Columb Kill[1] being then Banished into Scotland, K. Dermot made his repaire to him, to the end he might work som meanes by miracles for the recouery of his health & hearing & withall tould St. Columb how he assembled all the Phisitians of Ireland & that they could not help him, Then said St. Columb mine advise unto you is to make your Repaire to Clonvickenois to the place where yr Ghostly father & friend Saint Queran is Buried, & there to put a little of the earth of his grave or of himselfe in your Ears, wch is the

---

[1] *St. Columb Kill.*—On his so-called banishment by St. Molaise, see Reeves *Adamnan*, lxxiv. and p. 247.

medisine wch I think to be most auaileable to help you, the K. having receaved the said instructions of St. Columb took his Journey Imediately to Clonvicknose & finding Enoy Mac Eloysie (who was abott of the place after St Queran) absent he spoke to Loway then Parish priest of Clonvickenois & tould him of St. Columbs Instructions unto him whereupon Priest Loway and K. Dermott fasted & watched that night in the little Church where St. Queran was buried, & the next morning the priest took the bell¹ that he had (named then the white bell) & mingled part of the Clay of St. Queran therein with Holywater & put the same in the kings eares, and Imediately the K. had as Good hearing as any in the kingdom, & the whole sickness & trobles of his braines ceased at that Instant, which made the K. to say, ᵻꞅ ꞃ꞉ᵹꞅᵹꞇᵹꞇ ᵹꞃ ꞃ꞉ ꞁ꞉ ᵹꞃ ꞁ꞉ ᵹꞃ ᵹꞁ꞉ᵹ ꞈ꞉ꞅꞀꞁ, wch is as much to say in English, as the Bell did doe us a miraculous Turn, which bell Saint Lowna convoyded with him to the church of ffoyrie² where he remayned afterwardes. K. Dermott bestowed great Gifts of Lands on Clonvicknois in honour of St. Queran for the Recouery of his health.

550 —The prophet Bey m^cDe began to prophisie anno 550. He prophisied that lords would loose their Chiefries & seignories, & that men of Little estate & lands would loose their lands, because they should be thought little, & lastly, there should come Great mortality of men which would begin in ffanid³ in Ulster, Called the sweep⁴ of Fanaid. The battle of Cowle Conery⁵ in Keara was fought, in which Aillill Molt Invanna, K. of Connaught, & Hugh Fortawill, his brother, were slaine. Fergus & Donell, the two sonns of m,Earcka were victors. The Great Pestelence called the Boy Connell⁶

---

¹ *Bell.*—On the use of bells in ancient times in Ireland see Reeves' *Memoir of St. Patrick's Bell.*

² *ffoyrie.*—Perhaps Fore, in the barony of this name in Co. Westmeath.

³ *ffanid.*—The north-east of the barony of Kilmacrenan, Co. Donegal. It belonged to the M'Swinys in ancient times.

⁴ *Sweep* —The *Felire of Aengus* speaks of this plague under August 29th, the feast of the Beheading of St. John Baptist.

⁵ *C. Conery.*—The name is not known in the barony of Ceara or Carra, Co. Mayo.

⁶ *B. Connell.*—It seems to have

began, of which these saints Dyed Finnya m`Wihealla of Clonard, Columb m`Criowhan, Columb of Innis Kealtra,¹ Sincheall² m`Kean Keanaynaynn Abbott of Killeachie Dromata, and macTayle³ of Killcullyn who was otherwise called Owen m`Corcrann. Fohagh m`Conell dyed Ahagh m`Conlay, K. of Ulster, of whom Iveahagh⁴ is called, dyed. Biag m`Dee,⁵ the prophett, Dyed. Crowhan m`Briwyn, K. of Teaffa, dyed. The Nativity of Saint Mowlua.⁶

552.—This year there grew a sickness called the Sawthrust.⁷ Caffie m`effergossa bishop of Achy Conn⁸ in the 150th year of his age Dyed. Pope Vigilius dyed. Pelagius, a Roman by birth, succeeded as pope 11 yeares and 8 dayes.

561.—The nativity of Caeman⁹ of Leymore in Connaught. Fiacha o'Huiday, K. of Ulster, was killed in the battle of Dromkleichy¹⁰ by Deman m`Carill and by the oNeahaghes of Nardo ¹¹ Nisan¹² the leaper Dyed. Colman More sonne of K. Dermott was killed in his Coach by Duff Slatt O'Freana. The abbey of Beanchoir in Ulster was founded this year

---

been a sort of jaundice See *Census of 1851*, pt v vol 1 p 415

¹ *Innis Kealtra* —Now Holy Island, in Lough Derg, 10 miles N. of Killaloe, Co. Clare. St Colum is here put by mistake for St Caimin, the founder of I See Keating, *H. of Ireland*, p 357

² *Sincheall* —There were two saints of this name, both of the same monastery The elder, who founded Killachie, now Killeigh, in the barony of Geashil, King's Co , is meant here His feast is on March 26th. See Colgan's *Acta SS* , p 747

³ *MacTayle* —O'Donovan conjectures he was patron of St Michael le Pole in Dublin *Annals F. M.*, ii. 638

⁴ *Iveahagh* The baronies of Upper and Lower Iveagh, forming the western portion of Co. Down.

⁵ *B m`Dee* —On his prophecies

see O'Curry's *MS Materials*, p 399

⁶ *Mowlua* —The founder of Clonfert Molua, in Ossory. His feast is on August 4th.

⁷ *Sawthrust* —Some sort of cutaneous disease.

⁸ *Achy Conn.*—Now Aughnakilly, in the barony of Kilconway, Co Antrim.

⁹ *Caeman.*—Usually called Mochaemog, the name given him by St Ita. His church was at Leamokevogue, near Two-mile-Borris, Co Tipperary. His feast is on March 13th. See Colgan's *Acta SS* , p 589

¹⁰ *Dromkleichy* —O'Donovan conjectures Kilclief, Co. Down.

¹¹ *Nardo* —Of the Ardes, a district in the east of the same county.

¹² *Nisan* — Of Mungret, near Limerick His feast is on July 25th He is known as the leper.

563.—St. Brandon[1] abbot founded the church of Clonfert. The assention of St Brandon Birr to the skyes in his Chariot or Coach. King Dermott to mak manifest unto his subjects of the K dom his magnificience apointed a sergiant[2] named Backlaure wth a speare to Travaile through the kingdom wth power to break such doores of the nobilities as he should find narow in such manner as the speare could enter into the house thwartwayes or in the breadth of the doores. The sargeant travailing to & fro' with his Directions putting in execution the kings pleasure in that behalfe by breaking of either side of such Doors as he could find unfitt for that purpose, untill at last he came to the house of one Hugh Gwary in Imaine in Connaught, where being desired by those of the house to enter in the absence of the said Hugh, the sargiant said, he could not bring in his speare as he ought. Noe, s^d they of the house, wee will break the doores of either side & make it in such manner as you may bring in your speare as you Desire, which they accordingly did, the sargiant haveing the Doores broken, entred & feasted with them, & soone after Hugh Gawrie came to the towen & seeing his Doore broken he asked who broke it, & being tould that it was Backlaure the K^s sergiant he entered the house in a Rage, & without much adoe Killed the sargiant presently and tooke his flight himself to Roadanus[3] abbot of Lohra[4] who was his mothers Brother, thinking for his sanctitye & meanes, to secure himselfe from the K^s furie for killing his sargiant.

Rodanus sent his said nephew to the K. of Wales, who was his well-wisher, & one in whome hee reposed Great Trust. The K. of Ireland hearing of the killing of his sargiant by Hugh Gwarey, caused narrow search to be made for him, & understanding that he was sent to the K. of Wales, wrote to

---

[1] *St. Brandon.*—The first-mentioned here is known as the Mariner; his feast is on May 16th. The feast of St. B. of Birr is on November 29th. See Healy's *Ireland's Ancient Schools*, pp. 210 and 522

[2] *Sergiant*—*i e.* a steward. The Irish word was probably *maor*.

[3] *Roadanus.*—His feast is on April 15th.

[4] *Lohra.*—In the barony of Lower Ormond, Co. Tipperary. A monastery for Dominicans was founded here in 1269 by Walter De Burgo, Earl of Ulster. See *Hibernia Dominicana*, p. 274.

him, that he should send him back, or Refusing soe to do, that he w^(th) all his forces would go ouer to him, & Destroy his K. dom, & Remaine there untill he had found Hugh Gwary, which the K. of Wales perseaving sent him back to Roadanus the abbott againe; When king Dermott understood how he was sent ouer he prepared to come to Lohra w^(th) a few of his guard & in his coach came to Lohra afores^d, & sent one of his men to know where Hugh Gawry was. The man looked about him & could see none but Roadanus, that sate in his accustomed chaire or seat where he did used to say his prayers, under whose feet or neer adjoyning he Caused a hole to be made in ye floore, for Hugh Gwary to rest in, whereoff no body had knowledg but Roadanus himselfe & one more that carried him his meat at the Times of Refections. The K. seeing the man brought him no tydings, he entred himselfe & was Confident; Roadanus being Inquired of the place where Hugh Gawrey was, would not lye but tell truth as was his Custom, the K. accordingly entred & saluted him with harch salutations of Bitter & pinching words, such as were unfitt to be spoken to such a holy and virtuous man, saying that it did not belong to one of his Coat to shelter or keep in his house one that Committed such a fact as to kill his sargiant y^t was Imployed in the execution of his Instructions, & prayed that there might be noe abbott or monk to succeed him in his place in Lothra. By God's grace, s^d Roadanus, there shall be abbots & monkes for euer, & there shall be no K^s Dwelling in Tarach from henceforward, when they had thus bitterly spoken, the king asked where Hugh Gawry was, I know not where he is said Roadanus if he be not where you stand, for soe he was indeed Right under the K^s feet. The K. thinking he spoke in jest departed, and being out of the house thought with himselfe, that the holy man spoke truth & that Hugh Gwarey was under the place where he stood, & sent one of his men in again with a pick-ax to Digg the place & to bring him out by force. As soon as the man came to the place, he struck the earth with the pick-axe, his hands Lost all their strength on the sudaine in such manner as the party could not lift the pick-axe from the Ground, then he cryed mercy & Besaught Roadanus his forgiueness & Remission wth his benediction which Rodanus accordingly gave him & kept the man thenceforth with him in the habitt of a monke, the K. seeing him not Returning entred himselfe & caused the hole to be digged where he found Hugh Gwarrie, whom he carried Prisoner to tarach

Roadanus seeing himself violently abused & bereft of his kinsman sent for others of the Church & followed the K. to Tarrach, & there craved Hugh Gawry of the K., which he absolutely Refused; After supper the K with the nobles of his court & prelates of the Church went to bed, & about midnight the K. being heauiely asleep, dreamed that he saw a Great Tree that Rooted Deeply in the earth, whose lofty top & braunches were soe high & broad that they came neere the Cloudes of heaven & that he saw 150 men about the tree, with 150 broad mouthed sharp axes cutting the tree, & when it was cut when it fell to the earth the Great noyse it made at the time of the falling thereof awaked the K. out of his sleep, wch Dream was Construed, Interpreted, & expounded thus, that this Great Tree thus strongly Rooted in the earth, & branches abroad, that it Retched to the very firmament, was the K whose power was over all Ireland and that the 150 men with sharp axes cutting the tree were these prelates saying the 150 Psalms of Dauid, that would cut him from the very Rootes of his Destructions & fall for euer. When the morning came the K^s nobles & prelates arose, and after the Clergyman had done with their prayers they besaught the K. again to enlarge unto them Hugh Gwairye, which he did as absolutely refuse as hee did before, and then Roadanus & a Bushop that was with him tooke their bells that they had, wch they rung hardly, & cursed the K. & place, and prayed God, that no K. or Q. ever after would or could Dwell in Tarach, & that it should be waste for euer wth out Court or Pallace, as it fell out[1] accordingly K Dermot himself nor his successors

---

[1] *Fell out.*—Though the Ardrighs did not dwell there, they were called Kings of Tara, to distinguish them from the provincial kings

kings of Ireland cou'd never Dwell in Tarach since the time of that curse but every one of the kings chose himself such a place as in his own Discression he thought fittest & most Convenient for him to Dwell &c as Moyleseaghlyn more, Donasgiah,[1] Brian Bowrowey, Kincory[2] &c. Roadanus being thus Refused he tendered a ransom of 30 Horses, which the K. was contented to accept, & soe granted him Hugh Gwairye.

Gawran sonn of Dawangart K. of Scotland dyed. The Scottish men were put to flight by Brwydy m^{c}Milcon K. of Picts. Cornan m^{c}Eahagh Tyrmcarna was killed by K. Dermot. The battle of Cowle Innsyn[3] was given by Hugh m^{c}Brenynn K. of Teaffa to K. Dermot. The sayleing of St Columb Kill to Scotland in the 42nd yeare of his age.

563.—The O'Neales gave the battle of Moneyderg[4] to the Picts, where they killed 7 of their kings, together with Hugh Brecke. Aydan o'ffighragh Dyed.

569.—King Dermot was slaine by Hugh Duff m^{c}Swyne at Rathbeg,[5] whose body was entred in Conrie & head brought to Clonvicnose, as he requested himselfe. This K. Dermott had issue three noble & goodly sonns, Hugh Slane who was auncestor to nine K^s of Ireland, Colman More who was auncestor to 7 K^s of Ireland, of whom Clann Colman tooke the name, and Colman Begg, he was son to Fergus Keruel, who was son to Conall Criowhan, who was sonn of Neale of the 9 Hostages.

Donell, Fergus, Boyan Eochye, & Anmine were K^s jointly seven years and after them Boydan m^{c}Anynnea raigned one yeare. Eochy succeeded half a yeare, & was slaine by Cronan m^{c}Tygernye. Saint Brandon of Birr dyed anno Dño 569. The battle of Gawra Liffee was Given by the Leinstermen,

---

[1] *Donasgiah.*—On the western bank of Lough Ennell.

[2] *Kincory.* — At Killaloe, Co. Clare. The palace extended from where the Catholic church now stands to the river side near the weir. See Frost's *History of Clare*, p. 176, and White's *H of the Dalcassian Clans*, p. 9.

[3] *Cowle Innsyn.*—Not identified.

[4] *Moneyderg.* — Reeves conjectures Moneymore, Co. Derry.

[5] *Rathbeg.*—In the parish of Donegore, Co Antrim.

where Fergus & K. Donall were victors. Dawyn m⁽Dawyn Daweargid dyed. Joannes by birth a Romane Raigned pope 12 yeares 11 months & 26 dayes. Deman m⁽Carrill was killed by the Baghlayhes of Barney or Roaring boys of Boren. Aynmire m⁽Setna joynt K. was slain by fergus m⁽Nellyne which ffergus was soon after slaine by Hugh m⁽Ainmireagh. Eonoye m⁽Eioysie second abott of Clonvicknoise dyed, successor and next abbot after St. Queran. From the death of St. Patrick to this time were 100 yeares. Mayneann bishop of Clonfert died. Carbry m⁽Criowhan king of Munster did Give a battle to Colman Beg son of K. Dermott, where Carboy was victor. The battle of Talo & fartalo, the names of 2 fields between Elie & Ossorie, which is between Clonfertt Molwa & Sayer[1] where ffiachra m⁽Boydon was victor. Conell[2] son of Cowgall that gave the Island of Hugh[3] to Columb kill dyed in the 16th year of his reign of Dalriaty. Brenaynn m⁽Briwyn, K. of the land of Teaffa, died. Diseases of the Leaprosie did abound and knobbes this year.

579. St. Brandon of Clonfert died 577 16 maii vell 583.

580. Echtgen, Bishop of Clonfada Boghan,[4] dyed. The Departing of Ulstermen from Eawyn. Vinianus Bishop nephew to ffiacha Dyed. Benedictus by birth a Romane sate 4 years 1 monthe & 29 dayes. The battle of Drom m⁽Eircke[5] was Given, where Colga m⁽Donell m⁽Murtough was slaine and Hugh m⁽Aynmreagh was victor. Ceannath K of the Picts dyed. Boyhan m⁽Carill K. of Ulster dyed. The Battle of the Isle of man was given by Aydan. m⁽Gawran was victor.

584.—Brwydie m⁽Milchon, K. of Pictland Dyed Feradgh m⁽Dwagh K of ossery was killed by his one men. Pelagius by birth a Romane sate 10 yeares 10 months and 10 dayes.

587.—Pope Gregory sent to the Brittanes for their con-

---

[1] *Sayer* —Now Seir Kieran, four miles east of Birr.

[2] *Conell* —He was king of the Dalriada of North Britain. *Annals F. M*, i. 209.

[3] *Hugh* —*i.e.* Iona. On the various forms of this name see Reeves' *Adamnan*, p. 258.

[4] *C Boghan*.—Now Clonfad, in the barony of Farbill, Co. Westmeath.

[5] *D. m⁽Eircke.*—Not identified.

version to the Catholique faith, St. Augustine, Militus, & John with Divers other monks, who had Good success for the Conversion of England. Fergus B. of Dromleahglaissy,[1] who founded kill Brian Dyed. m⁀cNissie an Ulsterman third abbot of Clonvicknoise, Died. In the 16th yeare of his place Hugh m⁀cSwinie K. of Moynmoye dyed. Boyhan m⁀cNynnea m⁀cDwagh m⁀cConel Gulban, K. of Taragh, was killed Comyn m⁀cColman and Comyn m⁀cLyvren killed him by the provocation and setting on of Colman Begg, sonn of K Dermot. Ainmyre m⁀cSedna was king three years and was then slaine by ffergus m⁀cNelline In his time flourished in this kingdom Enna o'Loingsye,[2] a famous Learned and most virtuous scholar. Hugh m⁀cAinmyreagh succeeded in the kingdom & Reigned 25 years. In his time the meeting was between him and Aidan m⁀cGawran,[3] K. of Scotland in Dromkehaire[4] with Divers of the nobility both spirituall & Temporall of Ireland & Scotland, in their Company for Deciding the Controversie between the said kings for the Teritory and Lordship of Dalriada. St Columb Kill and St Bohyn were then present at that meeting. The battle of Bealaghatha was fought, where Colman Begg sonn of K. Dermot was slaine. I take the place to be called Belanaha neere Mollingare, he was slaine by K. Hugh. David m⁀cCarill Died. Carlan[5] B. of Ardmach dyed Senagh B. of Clonard dyed. The conversion of Constantine to Our Lord. There was great frost this yeare.—*Anal. Ulst.*

---

[1] *Dromleahglaissy.* — Downpatrick. The Dun within which was the dwelling of Celtchar, one of the Red Branch Knights, is still standing to the north of the cathedral. See Reeves' *Antiquities of Down,* &c., p. 141.

[2] *Enna o'Loingsye.* — Neither O'Reilly nor O'Curry makes any mention of his writings.

[3] *A. m⁀cGawran.*—He was inaugurated by St Columba in 574 king of the Dalriada They had settled in Scotland, and wanted to refuse all subjection to the Irish monarch. It was decided that they were bound to go on hostings with the men of Erin, but not to pay tribute to them. See *Leahbar na hUidhri*, fol. 9, and Reeves' *Adamnan*, pp. 92 and 403.

[4] *Dromkehaire.*—i.e Drumceat, now called the Mullagh, near Newtownlimavaddy, Co. Derry. See Keating's *H. of Ireland*, p. 370.

[5] *Carlan.*—He occupied the see for ten years. See Ware's *Bishops*, p. 38.

588.—Hugh Duff mᶜSwyny K. of Dalnary, that killed K. Dermot mᶜKervel, was slaine. Bushop Hugh mᶜBrick¹ Died. This is St Hugh (as some think it) B of Lyncolne in England; but I am of a contrary (opinion), for Hugh B. of Lincolne² was of the order of Carthusians & this other Hugh was many yeares before St. Bruno, (the founder of that order,) was borne. Bushop Hugh mac Bricke is Desended of ffiacha mᶜNeale of the 9 Hostages as may apear thus: Bishop Hugh was sonn of Bricke, who was sonn of Cormack, who was sonn of Criowhan, who was sonn of Carbry, who was son of the sᵈ ffiagha. Hugh mᶜBrenaynn, K. of the country of Teaffa that granted Dorow³ to St. Columb Kill, dyed. The same yeare there was much frost and winde. St. David of Kilmoney⁴ Dyed.

589.—ffelym mᶜTygerny, K. of Mounster, dyed. The Battle of Leihrye⁵ was fought by K. Aidan of Scotland.

590.—The Battle of Moyeoghter⁶ over Cloncury westward was fought by Branduffe mᶜEaghagh against the O'Neales. Lowy of Lismore⁷ Dyed. The nativity of Comyn Foda. Enos Magawley Died. Gregory by birth a Romane begotten of Gordiamus raigned 13 yeares 3 months & 10 days. Seanchan mᶜColman more was killed.

Saint Columb Kill Dyed⁸ on Whitsunday ieve the 5ᵗʰ of the Ides of June in the Island of Hugh in the 35ᵗʰ year of his pilgrimage in Scotland, & banished thither & in the 77 yeare of his age, as he was saying his prayers in the Church of that

---

¹ *H. mᶜBrick.*—Founder of Killare, Co. Westmeath. He is venerated at Shevelague, Co. Donegal. His feast is on February 28th. See Colgan's *Acta SS.*, p. 418.

² *Hugh B. of Lincolne.*—He died in the year 1200.

³ *Dorow.*—Four miles N of Tullamore, King's Co. Of the monastery founded by St. Columba nothing remains. A cross and holy well are close by its site. See Reeves' *Adamnan*, p. 23.

⁴ *D. of Kilmoney.*—He is mentioned in the notice of St. Molua in the *Martyrology of Donegal*.

⁵ *Leihrye.*—Not identified.

⁶ *Moyeoghter.*—A plain in north Kildare.

⁷ *Lismore.*—In Co Waterford. St. Carthach, after leaving Rahan, built a monastery here about 633. See Colgan's *Acta SS.*, p. 539

⁸ *Dyed*—On the date of his death see Reeves' *Adamnan*, pp. 182 and 309.

Isle with all his monkes about him, & was entred¹ in the place where the aby of Dowen is (before the aby² was founded by Sʳ Joⁿ Coursey) where St. Patrick & St. Bridgett were buried before. St. Columb, as I said before, was of the o'Neales³ of Tyrr Connell and was prophisied to come by St. Patrick 100 yeares before his birth, as he was baptizing Connell mᶜNeale & ffergus his son, St. Patrick held both his hands over the heades of the said Connell and ffergus & kept his hands⁴ longer over the head of ffergus than he Did over the head of Connell, whereat Connell being somewhat moued asked St. Patrick the question why he held his hand longer ouer the head of ffergus than over his head, to whom St. Patrick answerd that there should descend of ffergus one for sanctity of Life & hospitality would proue a very Good man, whose name would be Columb Kill, wᶜʰ came to pass accordingly Moyty,⁵ the ould priest before mentioned, prophisied of his coming, alsoe Movie Clarineagh did the like prophisie wᵗʰ many others. Eihny⁶ St. Columb kills mother, Dreamed⁷ when she was bigg with child & St. Columb Kill in her womb, that one Gave her a great Coverlett that Reatched from the North of Ireland to York in England, wherein all Colours seemed to be soe fairley dyed as could be, & saw a man in shining Cloaths take the same from her & conveyed it up to the Cloudes of heaven, which procured Great sorrow in her; be nothing sad (said the partie) You ought rather to solace & jocund then sad for the exposition of this Coverlet soe far reaching is that you shall be Delivered of a sonn whose Christian Documents shall reach everywhere in these kingdoms of Ireland & Scotland. Shee dreamed another vision, that the fowle of the ayre carried her entreales into

---

¹ *Entred*—He was buried at Iona, sometime in the 8th century his remains were brought to Ireland, to save them from being seized by the Danes. *Ibid.*, p 312

² *Aby*—The reference is to the Abbey of Inis, founded for Cistercians in 1180.

³ *o'Neales*—He was fourth in descent from Niall of the Nine Hostages.

⁴ *Hands*—See Colgan's *Trias Thaum.*, pp. 145 and 192.

⁵ *Moyty*—Not identified.

⁶ *Eihny.*—She was descended from Cathaoir mor. See Reeves' *Adamnan*, p. 163.

⁷ *Dreamed.*—*Ibid.*, p. 190.

the skies, & Dispearsed them in every place in Ireland & Scotland; which she presaged herself that shee would beare a sonn whose instruction & sermons in the Catholique faith would be throughout the Realmes of Ireland and Scotland Hee was borne the 17th of the Ides of December on Thursday in a place called Gortann,[1] & as soon as he was borne he was brought to that venerable & worthy priest Crwinneachan m^{c}Kellaghan, who christened[2] him by the name of Columb, to whom God by an angel Revealed, & desired him to norrish & foster him, & not to trust him to none else & alsoe to keepe him to Learning, which the Priest accordingly did.

When he came to age to be put to schoole he went to schoole to ffynann of Moybile[3] where he had Good success in his learning, from thence he went to schoole to German,[4] and after he remained a while there he Departed & went to St. ffynan to Clonard. There was a course held among them at Clonard, that the schollers should by Turns Grind their corn wth a queran Dayly, & when it came to St. Columbes turne to take that work in hand, then an angel did handle it for him, wch was signe that he was in Greater Estimation with God then the rest of the schollers, which were many in number. It was shewed to St. ffinann that two sonns did apeare and shew their Rayes in Clonard, the one shewed like gould, the other like silver. The golden sunn seemed to shine in the north, which give light to Ireland & Scotland of the north, which St. ffinan expounded to be St. Columb, The other of the Colour of silver apeared neare the riuer of Synan that it gave light to the midst of Ireland, which St. ffynan did likewise expound to be St. Queran, who would shine there wth the vertues of his good life. from Clonard he went to Movie Clarineagh, where he Remained but a fortnight.

---

[1] *Gortann.*—Now Gartan, ten miles W. of Letterkenny, Co Donegal

[2] *Christened*—The tradition is that he was baptized at Temple Douglas, a little to the west of Gartan.

[3] *ff. of Moybile.*—See Healy's *Ancient Schools*, p. 244. Moville is a mile to the north of Newtownards, Co Down. St. Finnian died in 589. His feast is on September 10th.

[4] *German.*—Or Gemman, a Christian bard. See Reeves' *Adamnan*, p. 187

Cainneagh[1] & Cowgall with Divers others were there, & as they were conversing together one of the Clergy enquired what thing each of the scholars were most Desireous to have in his Church that would be Dedicated to him. St. Queran s[d], I had rather have the [church] full of monkes & Religious persons to help to say mattins and even song. Cainneach said I had rather to have my church full of good books to leave to my Posterity for their Instructions. I had rather, said Cowgall, to have my body full of diseases & pains & the bodyes of my Convent, that they and I might be subject to the spirritt, & Lastly St. Columb said that hee had rather have his church full of Gould and Silver to found & build churches & houses of religion & to adore the Relicks & shrines of Saints that they might be in the Greater Reverence with Posteritys. Then said Movie (ats Merlinn) I gather & prognosticate unto you that the successor of St. Columb shall be the rightest of any of you all in Ireland & Scotland.

Hee Departed from thence & made his Repaire to K. Hugh m[c]Ainmereagh (to whom Saint Columb was a neere kinsman[2]) and dwelt then at Dirry. When St. Columb was come to the Kings Court, the king of his great bounty and affection he did bear to St. Columb for his affirmityes sake Graunted & Dedicated unto him the Town of Dery[3] with the appurtenances; Soon after St. Columb sent some of his monkes & people to the ajacent or adjoining woodes to cutt wattles for to build a House there to Dwell in, who being met with y[e] Lord of the wood Did speak some Distastefull wordes to them for coming thither without his Lisense, whereof his People gave St. Columb intelligence, whereupon he gave som of his servants the seed of beare to be carried to the oner of the wood in satisfaction of the watlings and timber, & withal wished the servants to bid the partie to sow the Beare in the earth notwithstanding the time was past midsummer then,

---

[1] *Cainneagh.*—Canice, patron of Kilkenny His feast is on September 11th.

[2] *Kinsman.*—Hugh's father and C. were the children of brothers.

[3] *Dery.*—For an account of Derry see *The Ordnance Survey of the Parish of Templemore*, p. 18.

whereof the owner Greatfully excepted & sowed ye beare accordingly, & was sooner reaped than any other beare whatsoever. He went from thence to Rathboth,[1] where he founded a church also, in which he revived the Carpenter[2] from death which was drowned in the milpond of that Town, & being for a while Dwelling in that Town, a Great houskeeper had plowing, and one of his Plowmen wanted a sock & had noe smith near him. he called the Plowman to stretch forth his hands, wh{ch} being donn he blessed the mans hands, & from thence foorth the man was as skilfull a smith as any in the kingdom & better too. from thence he Repaired to the K. of Teaffa Hugh M{c}Brenaynn to preach to him, who gave him the place where the church of Dorew stands. He was presented in Dorow with sour apples which by his Prayers he converted to be sweet apples. From thence he went to Hugh Slane,[3] who Dwelt then at Kells,[4] wch Town was held by the O'Neales of the West, to be the seat & Dwelling place of the Prince & next heire to the Crowen, which town was freely Granted to St. Columb & his successors for ever after. There was a great Tall Oake neere adjoining the town under which St Columb did accustom to Dwell, wch oak was seen of late yeares untill it was fallen by a Great blast of wind. One of the townsmen seeing it lay prostrate on the earth took the bark thereof & put it on leather to Tann it, whereof he put a paire of shooes on his feet, & as soon as they were on Imediately the party was Infected with leprosie from top to toe, & thereof Dyed.

He wrote 300 bookes[5] wth his one hand. They were all new Testaments, left a book to each of his Churches in the

---

[1] *Rathboth.*—Now Raphoe, seven miles W. of Lifford, Co. Donegal. It gives its name to a barony and to the diocese.

[2] *Carpenter.*—See *Trias Thaum.*, p. 399.

[3] *Hugh Slane.*—See Keating's *H. of Ireland*, p. 392.

[4] *Kells.*—In the north-west of Co. Meath. St. Columb's house, or oratory, is still standing. There is a round tower here and three ancient crosses. See Reeves' *Adamnan*, p. 278.

[5] *Bookes.*—One of these is supposed to be the Book of Kells, one of the finest existing specimens of the art of illuminating. It belongs to Trinity College, Dublin.

Kingdome, which Bookes have a strange property which is that if they or any of them had sunck to the bottom of the Deepest waters they would not lose one letter, signe, or character of them, wch I have seen partly myselfe of that book of them which is at Dorow[1] in the K^s County, for I saw the Ignorant man that had the same in his Custody, when sickness came upon cattle, for their Remedy putt water on the booke & suffered it to rest there a while & saw alsoe cattle returne thereby to their former or pristin state & the book to receave no loss. When St Columb had gone thus over all Ireland preaching & teaching the word of God, he Determined to take his course to foraine Contryes to do the like in England, Scotland, & Wales, & in the 42nd year of his age went to Scotland accompanied with 20 Bushops,[2] 40 Priests, 30 Deacons, & 50 learned scholers, where he remayned 34 yeares until he died as before is Demonstrated and discoursed.

The Reader may perceave by St. Columbs pedigree that he is not a Scotch man as Thos Dempster[3] untruly reported, nor St Bridgett.[4] What better testimony can be had then to Derive their Linial Degrees from their auncestors (whoe were knowen to be of the marrow of the meer Irish blood) the one of the families and Discent of Conell m^cNeale the other the race of Eochy ffinn, K. Felym Reaghtwar's son. But now to our History again.

The battle of Kirkynn in Scotland was fought where the sons of king Aidan namely Bryan Dowangart, Eahagh ffinn, and Arthur were slaine & K. Aidan himselfe overcome. The Battle of Slieve Kava[5] in Mounster where Fiagha m^cBoydonn

---

[1] *Dorow* —This MS. also belongs to Trinity College.

[2] *Bushops* —These only accompanied him to the shore when he was about to embark. See O'Hanlon's *Lives*, &c., vi. 371.

[3] *Dempster* —In several works published by him he claimed as Scotch many of our Irish saints, hence he has got the name of hagioclept, or saint-stealer. See O'Hanlon's *Lives of the Irish Saints*, i. xxxvi.

[4] *Bridgett*.—Her descent from Feidhlimidh, ardrigh from 164 to 174, is given in Todd's *Life of St. Patrick*, p. 252.

[5] *Slieve Kava*.—The Knockmeldown Mountains, on the northern boundary of the baronies of Cosh-

of Ulster was victor was alsoe fought. Tiprady m'Calgie died. St. Bohynn abbott of Hugh in the 66th year of his age died. The battle of Dunbolge[1] was fought [where] Branduff m'Eahagh with his Leinstermen were killed, K. Hugh m'Ainmereagh K. of Ireland & Beag m'Kwawagh king of Uriall with divers other princes & noblemen.

Colman Rivea & Hugh Slane raigned joyntly seven years. There were 43 years from the death of king Hugh m'Ainmereagh to Donell m'Earcka, during which time there raigned in Ireland 7 K^s, vidzt., Colman, Hugh Slane, Hugh Orineagh, Moylekova, Swyne Meann, and Donell. There Raigned in Scotland four kings, Eochy Boye, Connad Kearr, Fearchair m'Donogh & Donell, there raigned in Ulster four kings Fiaghna m'Boydan, Fiaghna, Congall and Donogh. In leinster 3 K^s Branduff m'Eahagh, Renan, Criowhan, Kwalann, & ffaylann In ossorie 3 K^s Scanlan m'Kinley, Twaymsnawa & ffoylcha & in ye province of Mounster Cahal, Failve, Curaw, & Moynagh m'ffinyny, & lastly in the province of Connaught there Raigned ffwadagh, Colmann m'Cobheye, & Ragall (of whom the oKellyes) m'Fwadagh Aliter abbot of Clonuisknois Dyed. Garnat King of the Picts died. The Saxons Receaved the Catholique faith.

599—Canneagh of Aghaboe named St. Kenny in the 84th yeare of his age died.

603—The battle between King Aidan and the Saxons was fought, where Aidan had the victory and Canfrith, brother of King Ethelfrith was slain by the hands of Moyleawa m'Boylan. Swyne m'Colman was killed by K Hugh Slaneat at the Riuer called Swaniou.[2] Cowgall[3] abbot of Beanchor in the 90th year of his age and in the fiftieth year of

---

more and Coshbride, Co. Waterford

[1] *Dunbolge*.— Now Dunboyke, near Hollywood, Co. Wicklow. Hugh m'A had gone to demand the borumha from the Leinstermen. See an account of the battle in *Annals F M*, 1 218.

[2] *Swaniou*.—Lough Sewdy, midway between Athlone and Mullingar.

[3] *Cowgall*—See *Ancient Irish Schools*, &c , p 364, and Lanigan's *Eccl. H. of Ireland*, ii 60 His feast is on May 10th. The *Annals F. M*, give 600 as the year of his death.

his abbotship & 3 months Dyed. The battle of Sleawyn[1] in Meath was given, where K. Colman Rivea was victor & Conall Chowe sonn of king Hugh mᶜAinmireagh put to flight. Saint ffintan[2] of Cloneyneagh[3] Dyed. Saint Sineall,[4] B. of Moyvile Dyed. K. Colman Rivea[5] was killed by one of his one near kinsmen named Lochan Dalmanna and alsoe K. Hugh Slane was likewise killed by one Conell Guthvinn mᶜSwynie.

601.—Hugh Rone prince of Affaily & Hugh Boy prince of Imaine were killed the same Day by the self same man.

604.—ffocas the Emperor raigned 8 years. St Beagny[6] Abbot of Beanchor died. King Aidan of Scotland dyed in the 34th yeare of his Raigne and in the 78th year of his age. The 2nd year of the raigne of the Emperor ffocas, Gregory Pope died. Sabinianus, a thuscan by birth raigned Pope two yeares fiue months & 9 dayes. Sillane mᶜComyn abbott of Beanchor died. Aidan the Anchorite Died, & Moyleowa m Boydan & Colgan Dolene mᶜFiaghna, all Dyed.

THE END OF THE CHRONICLES OF EUSEBIUS.

Saint Colman Eala mᶜWihealla in the 56th year of his age died. Nemon abbott of Lismore Dyed. Hugh Orineagh raigned seven yeares and then Dyed. Moyle Cova succeeded next & raigned fiue yeares. The battle of Ova[7] was given, where Conell Loybrey mᶜHugh Slane was killed by Enos mᶜColman. Heraclius raigned 16 years. Anastatius, a Persian monck, suffered noble matrydom for Christ. He

---

[1] *Sleawyn.*—Now Slewen, near Mullingar.

[2] *ffintan*—A contemporary of St. Columkille, and the teacher of many of the Irish Saints. See *Ancient Irish Schools*, p. 398.

[3] *Cloneyneagh.*—Four miles S.W of Maryborough. It is said there were seven churches here.

[4] *Sineall.*—His feast is on 28th February. See Colgan's *Acta SS.*, p. 424.

[5] *C. Rivea.*—He was king jointly with Aedh Slaine

[6] *S. Beagny*—Perhaps St. Beagna, abbot of Bangor, whose feast is on August 22nd.

[7] *Ova.*—Now obsolete —See *Annals F. M.*, i. 31, for the origin of this name.

was born in Persia and there learned Magick art of his father, and being afterwards taken by certaine christians did relinquish his former manner of living, and desirous to recave baptism came to Jerusalem, and entered into religion in the monastery of Saint Anastatius but four miles distant from Jerusalem, and afterwards was by Acoranen king of Persia together with 70 martyres beheaded. This is about the time that in Ireland they had some doubts for observing the Feast of Easter[1] and wrote their letters of Pope Honorius, and were resolved by his successor Severinus, whereunto they willingly agreed. The death of Fintan mac Intrewe abbot of Beanchor was this year.

613.—The battle of Carleil or Carlegion, where Folinn m'Conan, king of the Brittans, was killed by Ethalfrid, who haveing the victory, Died himselfe instantly.

617.—Lucall, brother of Saint Queran, Died. Folva Foda, abbot of Clonvicknoise, dyed. A starr was seen the seventh houre of the Day this year. King Moyle Cova was slain in Sliewe Twa by Swynie Meann. Swynie reigned 15 years. This yeare came in pilgrimage to Clonvicknose one Gormon, and remayned there a yeare and fasted there that yeare on bread & water of ffinyns well. He is auncestor to m'Conn na mbocht and Moynter Gorman, and died in Clone aforesaid. Beanchor was burnt in Ulster.

614.—Isiodorus chronicles endeth this yeare, which is the 5th yeare of the raigne of the Emperour Heraclius & in the 4th yeare of the raigne of the most Religious prince Sesibutus. There are from the Creation of the World to this fifth year of Heraclius 5814 years. Coygenus or Keuinus[2] of Gleanda-Locha (he was fellow of Saint Queran) Died in the 120 yeare of his age. Cowgall Bushop & Owen Bushop of Ardsrathy[3] died. Liber abbott of Eochy bo of Kenny, dyed. Sillan of Moibille, and Finnin m·ffiachra, died. Hugh Beannan Died.

---

[1] *Easter.*—See Lanigan's *Eccl. H. of Ireland*, ii. 388, and *Irish Eccl. Record*, xii. 65.

[2] *Keuinus.*—His feast is on June 3rd. See O'Hanlon's *Lives* &c.,

vi. 28. On the Antiquities of Glendalough see Petrie's *Eccl Arch.*, p. 168

[3] *Ardstrathy.*— Now Ardstraw, near Newtown Stewart, Co. Tyrone.

Seanagh Garve, abbot of Clonfert, dyed. Enos, sonn of Colman More, was killed and was called K. of the O'Neales. This time the church of Tory[1] in the North was founded and finished.

624.—m^cLasre abbot of Ardmach Died. Ronan m^cColman & Colman Stellan, died & were hurt by Failve fflannfivay. The Baptizing of Etayn m^cElly who first Receaved faith in the religion of the Saxons.

627.—Mongan m^cFiaghna a uery well spoken man, & much given to the wooeing of women, was killed by one Bicor, a Welchman, with a stone. Cahal m^cHugh king of Mounster, died. Saint Mayochus[2] of fferns Died The battle of Leheid-mynd[3] was fought, where Fiaghna m^cDemayne called Fiaghna m^cBoydan K. of Dalnary was killed, and in revenge thereof those of Dalriada chalenged Fiaghna m^cDemanye & killed him in the battle of Corrann by the handes of Conard Kearc. The battle of Carnferagh, where Failve fflynn had the victory, and Gwyare[4] Aynie took his flight, Conell m^cMoyle Duff prince of Imainy, Moyledoynn, Moylecalgie, & Moylebressal with many other nobles were slaine, was fought this yeare. The vision of Saint Fursie[5] was seen The battle of Bwilg Lwatha where Bwilg Lwatha himself was slain and ffoylann m^cColman had the victory. Columban m^cLardan abbott of Clonvicknoiss, died. The Wasting and Destroying of Leinster by Donall m^cHugh. Donall m^cHugh succeeded next K. of this land & Raigned 30 yeares, he got 2 victoryes of his enemies by name, the battle of Sattynn[6] & the battle Moyroth.[7] There were 105 yeares from the death of K.

---

[1] *Tory*.—An island off the north-west coast of Donegal. St. Columkille founded a church here.

[2] *Mayochus*.—Called Mogue, i e Mo Acd og. See *Annals F. M.*, i. 247.

[3] *Leheid-mynd*. O'Donovan says there are several places of this name in Co. Cork.

[4] *Gwyare*.—King of Hy Fiachrach Aidhne, then named the Hospitable

See *Transactions of the Ossianic Society*, v 32.

[5] *Fursie*.—His feast is on January 16th See Colgan's *Acta SS.*, p. 75, O'Hanlon's *Lives* &c., i. 222, and Bede's *Eccl. Hist.*, iii 19.

[6] *Sattynn*.—The name is obsolete.

[7] *Moyroth*.—Now Moira, in the barony of Lower Iveagh, Co. Down See *The Battle of Magh-Rath*, edited by the I A. S.

Donell to the death of K. Hugh Allen. During which time there raigned in Ireland 14 kings, namely Conell, Cellagh, Blathmac, Dermot, Seachnassach, Ceanfoyly, Finaghtye, Loynseagh, Congall Kymnajor, Fergall m̅Moyledoyne, Fagarthagh, Flaihvertagh m̅Loyngsy, and Hugh Allen. There Raigned in Scotland Eight kings, vidz^t Conell, Donnogh, Dongh, Ferall, Eochy, Ceallagh, Eoghy. In the midst of whose Raigne, Hugh Allen K. of Ireland was killed, as shall be declared when occation shall serve. There Raigned in Ulster 7 kings, that is to say Moyle Cova, Congall, Blathmac, Beaghvarchye, Cowkowran, Hugh Royne, & Cahasagh.

There Raigned in Leinster seven kings alsoe, which were Bran, Ccallagh, Morieagh, ffylan, Bran, and Morieagh mac Mourrough. There raigned likewise in Ossory seven kings, Cowkearky, ffoylan, ffeann, Oillill, Ceallach, Anmcha, & Twamsnawa. There raigned likewise in Connaught 10 kings, vizt. Laighnen, Gwairy, Keanfoily, Cahal, Ferall, Morieagh, Ceallagh, Inreaghtagh m̅Donogh, Inreaghtagh, and Donell m̅Cahall the 10th. The battle of ffeawyne wherein Moylekeigh m̅Seannoile, K. of the Picts was killed; Many of Dalriada were killed, as Connall Kearr their prince, the nephewes of Aidan were killed, Rigallan m̅Conyng and Failve m̅Eahagh & offrick m̅Alfrithe prince of the Saxons with many of his nobles, were likewise killed. Eahagh boye, sonne of King Aydan of Scotland, in the 20th year of his raigne died a°. regni 15 vel. 16, xti 621.

630.—The battle of Leahtairve^1 was fought between the two families of Kynelvickearka^2 and Kinell fferay,^{3} where Moylefihre was slaine & Ernany m̅Fiaghna had the victory. Bryan Duff macMoyle Cova was killed. Elli king of Saxons Died. Movie m̅Wiheally Died. The battle of Etwynn son of K. Elly that raigned king over all the Saxons, wherein Acathlon K. of the Brittans was overcome, was fought.

---

^{1} *Leahtairve*—Not identified.

^{2} *Kynelvickearka*.—The descendants of Earc, daughter of Lorne, who was married to Muiredach, son of Eoghan. See Reeves' *Adamnan*, p. 387.

^{3} *K. fferay*.—A tribe inhabiting the barony of Clogher, Co. Tyrone.

632.—Cenay mᶜLachtren king of the Picts died.

634 —The battle between Acathlon and Anfrith was fought, who therein was beheaded, and Oswald son of Ethalfrith, had the victory. The battle of Idris K. of the Brittans, wherein he lost himselfe, was also fought. The battle of Athgoan[1] near the Liffee where Criowhann Enna mᶜSeny, K. of Leynster, was slain. ffailan mᶜColman, Connell mᶜSwynie, K. of Meath, & failve flaynn K. of Mounster had the victorie. More[2] queen of Mounster and surnamed More of Mounster died. The killing of the 2 sonnes of K. Hugh Slane, Congall prince of Brey of whom the o'Conynges discended, & Aillill the Harper ancestor of Sile Dluhy by the hand of Conell Mac Swyny at Logh Treahan neare ffrenayne in Westmeath. Segene abbot of Hugh, founded the church of Rachran.[3] The Saxons made Great assemblies against K. Oswold. Conell mᶜSwyny K of Meath was slain by Dermot mᶜHugh Slane, or rather by Moyleowa mᶜfforanany. Fintann[4] of Tymonna & Ernany mᶜCressine Died the 12ᵗʰ of the calends of Nouember The battle of Cowle Keallan[5] was fought where Dermot mᶜHugh Slane killed Moyleowa mᶜEnos and his brother Colga. The banishment of Saint Mochuda[6] out of Rahinn[7] to Lismore Mochodda in Easter holly days.

637.—The death of Mochudda of Rahin in the Ides of May 14 May. Cronan Mac Oloye, abbot of Clonvicknois died. Duchna of Balla[8] died. The death of Downsy, wife of King Donell and Queen of Ireland.

---

[1] *Athgoan.* — Perhaps Athgoe, near Saggart, Co. Dublin.

[2] *More.* — She was the wife of Finghin, king of Munster, ancestor of the O'Sullivans.

[3] *Rachran.* — Now Rathlin, off the coast of Antrim.

[4] *Fintann.*—An account of him is given in Adamnan's *Life of St. Columba*, p. 18. His feast is on October 21st. Tymonna, now Taghmon, is seven miles west of Wexford.

[5] *C. Keallan.*—Not identified.

[6] *St. Mochuda.*—Called also Carthach. See Keating's *H. of Ireland*, p. 394, and *Ancient I. Schools*, p. 447.

[7] *Rahinn.* — Five miles W. of Tullamore, King's Co. The remains of the monastery are described in Petrie's *Eccl. Arch.*, p. 242.

[8] *Balla.*—In the barony of Claremorris, Co. Mayo. St. Mochua founded a monastery here in the beginning of the 7th century. His feast is on March 30th. See his Life in Colgan's *Acta SS.*, p. 791.

638.—The battle of King Oswalde against King Pantha, wherein Oswald was slain. Cridan died at Indroym, and Hugh Duffe Abbot of Kildare. Dalasse Mac Winge Abbot of Leighlin¹ Died. Ailleall mᶜHugh Royne, died.

639.—Theodorus Pope florished. Moyle Doyne mᶜColman was killed. Saint David² of Inverdoile Died. Constantine the sonn of Heraclius Emperour raigned six months. Donell mᶜHugh K. of Ireland died in Ardfahie³ in the latter end of January anno 641. 64½.

642—Aillell mEolman chief of the race of King Lagery was killed. The battle of Osu against Roman & the Brittainies was fought this yeare   Constantine the son of the Emperour Constantine raigned 28 yeares. Ceallagh & Congall Keyle mMoyle Cova, were the next kings of Ireland & raigned 22 years. Cronann bishop of Indroym Died. Scanlan More mᶜKean foyle, K. of Ossory, Died. Cwanach mᶜCailcín K. of fearny⁴ Died. Saint Mocheus of Indroym died. Foradruyn the son of Beag mᶜBrinyn or Cwanagh Prince of Mackwaises⁵ died. Lochyne, sonn of finnie K. of the Picts, died. uaiṗle, in English Gentle, Daughter of Swynie mʳColman K. of Meath, Queen of Leinster, (she was wife of foylan king of Leinster) Died. Maclaisre abbot of Beanchor died. Beda the venerable monk of England was born this year. Martyn the Pope florished now. Rogally mᶜTreadagh, K. of Connaught, was deadly wounded and killed by one Moylebridey o'Mothlann. Of this K. Ragally issued the o'Rellyes.⁶

The battle of Cornie Conell⁷ in the feast of Pentecost was given by Dermot mᶜHugh Slane, and goeing to meet with his

---

and O'Hanlon's *Lives* &c., iii. 1016.

¹ *Leighlin.*—In the barony of Idrone, Co. Carlow.

² *Saint David.*—St. Dagan, of I. in East Leinster, whose feast is on Sept. 13. See *Mart of Donegal*, p. 247.

³ *Ardfahie.*—In the barony of Tirhugh, Co. Donegal.

⁴ *fearny.*—Now the barony of Farney, Co. Monaghan.

⁵ *Mackwaises.*—Now the barony of Moygoish, Co. Westmeath.

⁶ *o'Rellyes.*—A marginal note of the transcriber says he was not their ancestor.

⁷ *Cornie Conell.* — O'Donovan conjectures this is Ballyconnell, near Gort.

enemies went to Clonvickenois to make his Devotion to Saint Queran, was met by the Abbot, Prelates, & clergie of Clone in procession, where they prayed God & Saint Queran to giue him the victory over his enemies, which God Granted at their Requests, for he had the victory & slew Cwan, K. of Mounster, & Cwan m'Connell K. of Figinty,[1] & soe giving the faile to his enemies Returned to Clonvicknois againe to congratulate the Clergie, by whose Intercession he gained the victory & bestowed on them for ever Toymnercke with the appurtenances now called Liavanchan in honor of God & Saint Queran, to be held free from and without any Charge in the world, In soe much that the king of Meathe might not thenceforth challenge a Draught of water thereout by way of any charges. Saint Mochevogus of Leithmore in Connaught Died. The battle of Ossve against Pantha, in which Pantha with 20 K[s]. were slaine anno 625.

647.—Ceallagh sonn of Donel Breck, died. Cronan[2] of Moyvile died.

648—Blathmack m'Aidan, B. of England, dyed. this is St. Aidan,[3] B. of Lindisfarn. The two sonnes of Hugh Slane Donogh & Conell were killed by the Leinstermen in the mill of Oran called Molen Oran near Molengare.

649.—Segeni[4] abbot of Hugh died. Longe, abbot of Clonvicknois died. Manchinus abbot of Menadrochatt,[5] died. Vitalianus Pope florished this time. fferith m'Foholan & Octlarge m'Fogith K. of Picts Died.

650—The battle of Connaught wherein Marcan m'Dawayn Prince of Imanie in the province of Connaught was slaine & Ceanfoyle m'Colgan and Moynagh m'Bwyhy had the upper hand.

651—Moyledoy M'Swyne K. of Meath Died. Colman B.

---

[1] *Figinty.*—Ui Fidhgeinte, the portion of Co. Limerick west of the river Maigue.

[2] *Cronan.*—The feast of this saint is on August 7th.

[3] *St. Aidan.*—This sentence is written in a different hand from the rest. On St A. See Reeves' *Adamnan*, p. 340.

[4] *Segeni.*—Fifth abbot of Iona, which he governed from 623 to 652. His feast is August 12th.

[5] *Menadrochatt.*—Mondrehid, six miles E. of Roscrea.

mᶜVihelly & Ossyny ffoda 2 abbots of Clonard, died in one yeare. Dachra Lwachra abbot of ffernes died. Fergus sonn of king Donell and ffergus son of Ragally, were killed and Hugh Bethra mᶜComyne. Saint Furse died in France in a town called Pariena.¹ He was of Clanna Rowry.

652.—The battle of Pantha K. of the Saxons was fought against Ossve where Pantha himselfe together with 30 kings were slaine and Ossve victor.

653.—Aihgean abbot of Tirdaglasse² and Cailkine of Lohra died. Saint Ultann³ son of O'Connor Died the 3ʳᵈ of the Nones of September. Swyne mᶜCwoihre abbot of Hugh Died. Tolorchan mᶜAnfrith K. of the Picts died. Conchayune of Killsleyve⁴ died.

654.—Ceallach mᶜMoyle Cova Died, and Ceallagh mᶜSarayne abbot of Othna more⁵ Died. Saint Mochwa mᶜLowaine died.

655.—Dymma B. of Conrye, Comyn B. of Indrym, Sillan B. of Daiwinis⁶ and Donogh son of king Hugh Slane, died. Hodibeis,⁷ King of France, died.

656—Finian mᶜRivea B. died, Colman of Glanndalogha died, & Daniel of Kingary⁸ died. Eaghagh mᶜBlathmack son of K. Hugh Slane died. Conell Cronndawna Died. Eoanan mᶜTwahallam, died. ffoylan K. of Ossorie was killed by the Leinstermen Aillill mᶜDonogh mᶜHugh Slane Died.

657.—Comyn Abbot & Bishop of Ardmach Died. Conyng ODaynt abbot of Imleagh Iver⁹ died. Comyn came to Ireland this year. Magopoc mᶜIlawa died.

658.—Comyn ffoda¹⁰ in the 72ⁿᵈ year of his age died. St.

---

¹ *Pariena.*—Peronne, near Amiens, in the department of Somme, France.

² *Tirdaglasse.*—Now Terryglas, in the barony of Lower Ormonde, Co. Tipperary, founded in the first half of the 6th century.

³ *St Ultann.*—Called of Ardbraccan, Co Meath. His feast is on September 4th.

⁴ *Killsleyve.*—Now Killeavy, near Newry, Co. Armagh.

⁵ *Othna more.*—Now Fahan, on the east side of Lough Swilly.

⁶ *Daiwinis.*—Devenish, near Enniskillen, where there is a round tower.

⁷ *Hodibeis.*—Clovis II., who died in 655.

⁸ *Kingary.*— Kingarth in Bute. His feast is on February 18th.

⁹ *I. Iver.*—*i.e.* Iubair, of the yew, now Emly, in Co. Tipperary.

¹⁰ *Comyn ffoda.*—*i e.* the tall, of Iniscealtra. His feast is on March 24th. See Colgan, *Acta SS.*, p. 746.

Saran m⸱Cridan died. Moyle Dwyn son of Hugh Beannan died. The battle of o'Gawyn[1] at Kincorbadan where Conyng m⸱Knoyle m⸱Hugh Slane was killed and Ultann m⸱Ernany K. of Kynnaghty in which battle king Blakimack was quite overthrown by the army of Dermot m⸱Hugh Slane and Ouchawe m⸱Sarann were the chiefe actors. Moynagh m⸱Finyn, king of Mounster, died. Scanlan abbot of Louthe died.

The General Councel of Constantinople was held under Pope Agatho and Constantine the king, and was the 6th universall Synod consisting of 150 Bushops, which there resided together. The first General Councel was the Nicene in the Citty of Bithinia, where there was a congregation of 318 ffathers in the time of Pope Julius against Arius in the presence of Prince Constantine. The second in Constantinople of 150 ffathers against the Heresies of Macedonius and Eudoxius in the time of Damasus Pope and Prince Gratian, where Nector was ordayned B. of that Citty. The third in Ephesus of 200 ffathers against Nestorius B. of Augusta under Pope Celestine and Theodosius. The fourth under Pope Leo in Calcedon consisting of 630 ffathers, in the time of Martian against Utices prelate of ye Manichees. The fifth was at Constantinople in the time of Pope Vigilius in the presence of Justinian against Theodorus and all his hereticks.

Beag m⸱Fergus and Connell Clogagh died. Gwayre Ainie died.

659.—Gartnayt son of Donall king of Picts, Donall m⸱Twahallan and Twohall m⸱Morgan, Died. Segain m⸱Ikwid, abbot of Beanchor, Died. Twenoc abbot of Fernes, Dearky and Dimma 2 Bishopps died.

664.—There was great darkness in the 9th hour of the day in the month of May in the calends and the firmament seemed to burn the same summer with extream heat. There was great mortality[2] through the whole kingdom which began in

---

[1] *o'Gawyn.*—Not identified.

[2] *Mortality.*—This was the Buidhe Conaill, a sort of jaundice; two-thirds of the inhabitants of Ireland perished by it. Bede says it ravaged England too. *Eccl. Hist.*, iv. 14. A century before it had ravaged this country. See p. 83, *antea*, and *Census of I. for 1851*, p. 49.

The Annals of Clonmacnoise.

Moyith the first of August this yeare Kearnagh Sota sonn of Dermott m^cHugh Slane died thereof. There was a great earthquake in Brittanie. Cowgan m^cCuthenna Bearagh, abbot of Beanchor, died thereof From the death of Saint Patrick to this mortality were 203 yeares. The mortality continued still. Dermott McHugh Slane and Blathmacke the two joynt kings of Ireland dyed thereof, Alsoe Moyle Breasaile m^cMoyldoin and Ultan m^cIchonga dyed thereof who was abbot of Clonard. Also Saint Fehyn[1] of Fower. Aleran[2] the witty, Ronan m^cBeraye, Moyledoye m^cFenin, and Cronan Mac Silny died. Cowgan Mather m^cCahall, king of Mounster died. Blathmack king of Teaffa died Enos of Ulster and Saint Manchan of Leith Manchan together with many other princes bishops and abbots died of the said pestilence, and because the Coworkes of Saint Manchan say that he was a Welshman and came to this kingdom at once with Saint Patrick, I thought good here to sett downe his pedegree to disprove their allegations. Manchan was son of Failve who was son of Angine, who was son of Boganie, who was son of Connell Gulban, the ancestor of ODonell, as is confidently laid down among the genealogies of the saints of Ireland. Colman Casse abbott of Clonvicknois dyed. Comynie abbott of the same died likewise. Seachnassach son of king Blathmack began his reign and was king 5 yeares.

662.—Ailleall Flanneassa who was son of Donell who was son of Hugh Mac Ammereagh died. Moyle Keith m^cScanalt king of the Picts and Moyledeyne m^cScan, prince of the race of Carbry, died Eochie Jarlaly, king of Picts died. Ceallagh McGwayre died. The battle of Feirst[3] between the Ulstermen and the Picts was fought, where Cahasagh McLorkynie was slaine. Bohyn, abbot of Beanchor, died.

663.—Foylan Mac Colman king of Leinster died. There was a great mortality whereof 4 abbotts died one after

---

[1] *Saint Fehyn.*—See his *Life* in Colgan's *Acta SS*, p. 130, and O'Hanlon's *Lives*, 1 356.

[2] *Aleran*—He is author of the fourth *Life of St. Patrick* in Colgan's *Trias Thaum.*, p. 35.

[3] *Feirst.—i e.* Belfeirste, the mouth of the ford, now Belfast.

another this yeare, namely Bearagh, Comynye, Columb, and Aidan.

664.—Branynn m׳Moyle Oghtray king of the Desies of Mounster, was killed. The sailing of Bishop Colman with the relicks of the Saints to the Island of Innish-Bofinny,[1] where he founded a church.

665 —Comyn the white abbot of Hugh, Critan abbott of Beanchor, and Mochwa abbott of Beanchor, died all. Moyledwyne, the son of Moynagh, was killed.

666.—The race of Gartnayt of Pictland returned to Ireland. Branynn, the son of Moylefohorty, was killed. Donogh the nephew of Ronan, died.

667.—Ossve the son of king Ethelfrith, king of Saxans, died. King Seachnassagh in the beginning of winter was killed by Duffe Doyne prince of the race of Carbry in the kings Pallace of Taragh.

668.—Ardmagh and Tailtean were burnt. Ceanfoyle M׳Blathmack raigned seven years. Dregtus was expelled out of the kingdom, Bangor[2] in England was burnt.

669.—Justinus the younger reigned tenn yeares. Dawangort m׳Donell Brick king of Dalriada, was killed. The sailing of Failve,[3] abbott of Hugh into Ireland. Moylelonge was burnt. Congall Keannfoda, king of Ulster, was killed by one Beagbrwich.

670.—The Moone was turned into a sanguine collor this year.

671 —The battle given by K Kynfoyle against ffinsneaghty where finsneaghty had the victory. Noeh m׳Daniell died. The son of king Pantha died, alsoe Finnaghty slew K. Kinnfoyle.

672.—Fynnaghty Fleagh was K. 20 yeares, this ffinnaghty at the Request of Moling Lwachrawe forgave[4] the Leinstermen

---

[1] *I. Bofinny* —See p 9, *antea*.

[2] *Bangor*. — In Carnarvonshire, North Wales.

[3] *Failve* —Eighth abbot of Iona. He presided over it from 669 to 679. His feast is on March 2nd. See

Acta SS., p. 719.

[4] *Forgave*.—See Keating's *H of Ireland*, p. 239, for an account of the manner in which the Saint obtained the remission of this tribute.

the Borowe. Colman Bishopp of Inis bofynne & ffynian arannan Dyed.

673.—There was a comet & a star of great brightness seen in ye months of September & October. The Leinstermen gave a battle to K ffineaghty in a place hard by Loghgagawar,[1] where K. Finnaghty was victor. Beagan Reymynn Dyed in the Isleland of Wales.

674.—Colgan m^cFalve fflyn K. of Munster Died. Darchill m^cCuyletty. B. of Gleandalogha, Died. Coman B. and Moyledoyer Bishop, Died. Twaymsnawa K of Ossory Died Drostus, sonn of Donell, Dyed. The Battle of Calathros[2] was given, where Donell Breark was vanquished. ffealvy abbott of Hugh died. Cleaufoile the wise Died.

675.—Colman abbot of Beanchor died. Finnawla, K. of Leinster was killed Cahall m^cRagally Died. The battle of the Saxons was given, where Almon son of K Ossve was slaine. There Raigned a kind of a Great Leprosie in Ireland this yeare called the pox in Irish bolgagh. Conell m^cDonnogh was killed in Kyntire.

676.—Seachnassach m^cArueay & Conyng m^cConoyle was killed Cinnfoyle m^cColgann king of Connaught died.

677.—The battle of Rathmore[3] was given against the Brittans where Cahasagh m^cMoyledoyn, K. of Picts & Ultan m^cDicholla were slaine. Swynie m^cMoyleowa, Prince bushop of Corcke Died. Justinian for his falshood was banished by his Empyre and compelled to flie into Pontus. Leo raigned 3 years.

678.—Here beginneth the mortality of Children. Colman abbott of Clonvicknois died.

679.—Manie, abbot of Indroym, Died. Loaghneaagh was turned into blood this yeare.

680 —There was an extreame great winde and earthquake in Ireland The Saxons, the plains of Moyebrey with Divers churches wasted[4] & Destroyed in the month of June, for the alliance of the Irish with the Brittaines.

---

[1] *Loghgagawar* — Lagore, near Dunshaughlin, Co. Meath

[2] *Calathros* —Reeves conjectures Calros on the north side of the Forth

[3] *Rathmore.* —In the parish of Dounegore, Co. Antrim.

[4] *Wasted* —This expedition, undertaken against the Irish, 'who

681.—Danell Breack mᶜEahagh Boye was slaine by Henery king of Brittons, in the battle of Strathkaron (Sṗaıc coṗṁaıc). Foriron abbot of Clonvickenois, died.

682.—Adawnanus brought 60 captives[1] to Ireland.

683.—Segine Bishop of Ardmagh died. Canon son of Gartnaitt entred into Religion.

684.—King Fynsneaghty Returned into Ireland from his pilgrimage Cahasagh mᶜDonell Breack Died. ffeareagh mᶜTwahallan died.

685.—Congall K. of Mounster, Doneagha mᶜorckdy, Ailleall mᶜDongaile, K. of Picts, and Eilny mᶜScannaile, were killed. Bran mᶜConell K. of Lynster Dyed. Gnahnat abbesse of Kildare died.

686 —Cornan mᶜCowcaylne abbot of Beanchor, Died. Theodorus B. of Brittaine Died. Fihellagh mᶜfflyn prince of Imanie, died

687 —The moone was of sanguine Colour the eve of the nativity of St Martin.

688 —Dyrath bushop of Fernes and Bran nephew to ffoylan, king of Leinster Dyed The sonn of Pantha was challenged to battle. There was a battle between the Leinstermen and those of Ossery, wherein ffoylchor o'Moyloyer was slaine. It raigned Blood in Leinster this yeare. Butter was turned into the colour of blood, & a wolf was seene and heard speak with humane voyce.

689.—Cronan Beag abbot of Clonvickenois, Died.

690.—K. ffinaghty was killed by Hugh mᶜDluhye son of Aileall who was sonn of Hugh Slane at a place called Greallaghtollye[2] and Prince Breassall the Kˢ sonn Mynn Beaireann abbot of Achabo Died Loyngseagh mᶜEnos began his raign and was K. 8 yeares

---

were always most friendly to the nation of the Angles,' is said by Bede to have been punished by the death of King Sigfrid and the defeat of his army by the Picts in the following year. *Hist Eccl.*, iv 26.

[1] *Captives.*— Taken during the expedition. A. was the author of *The Life of St. Columba,* and sixth abbot of Iona See Reeves *Adamnan,* xlv.

[2] *Greallaghtollye.*—Perhaps Girley, near Kells.

691.—Fingvyne K. of Munster Died. Lochne meann abbot of Kildare died. Comyne of Moyorne Died

692.—Moling[1] lwachra, a man for whose holiness & saintity K. ffinaghty Remitted the great taction of the Borowe to ye Leinstermen Died. The Brittaines & Ulstermen wasted & Destroyed the lands of Morheyvne.

693.—The battle between the Saxons & Picts where the son of Bernith, who was called Bregghtra was slaine. fforanan abbot of Kildare Died

694 —Phillippicus Raigned one year & 6 months   A great morren of cowes throughout all England

695.—The same morren of cowes came into Ireland next year & begann in Moyhrea in Teaffa. Hugh O'Sleivtyne anchorite Dyed. There was such famyne and scarcity in Ireland for three years together, that men & women did eat one another for want Conell m^cSuyne K. of the Desies,[2] died.

696.—Anastatius raigned three years & took captive Phillippus and did put out his eyes. Aillill, king of Mounster, Dyed.

697.—Moriegh of Moy Je[3] (of whom seeley Morie in Connaght) Died. Irgaliagh o'Conyng was slaine by the Brittaines. ffeldova of Cloghar Died.

698.—The battle of Moygullyn was fought between Ulster and Brittans where the sonn of Ragainn the adversary of the Church of God was slaine and Ulstermen victors

699.—King Loyngseach with his three sons named Artchall, Connaghtagh, and fflanngearg were slaine in the battle of Corann, the fourth of the ides of July the 6th houre of Saturday.

700.—Adawnanus abbot of Hugh in ye 78th yeare of his

---

[1] *Moling.*—He was called Luachra, *i e.* of Luachair His feast was on June 17th.

[2] *Desies.*— The Deisi were first settled in Meath. About the beginning of our era they were driven from thence, and settled in the present counties of Waterford and Tipperary. Four baronies in these two counties take their names from them

[3] *Moy Je*—The plain lying between Elphin, Roscommon, Strokestown, and Castlereagh. It has its name from a Tuatha de Danaan chief Aoi, son of Allguba.

age died,¹ of whom Syonan² in Kinleagh is named in Irish Siui Aoamnán which is as much in English as the seat of Adawnan, but noe Church land as I take it. Alfrith sonn of Ossve, the prudent K. of the Saxons died.

701.—Leo Pope Raigned 9 yeares. Congall Ceanmayor raigned king of Ireland 19 years & Died of a sudden sickness Feargall mᶜMoyledoyne raigned 11 yeares, & was slaine by Murrough mᶜBroyn in the battle of Allon³ in Leinster.

710.—This year venerable Bede finnished his Chronicles Boyhan Bishupp of Inisbofinne died. Cormack mᶜAllella, K. of Mounster, was slaine in battle. Folorg the sonn of Drost, was fast bound by his one brother king Neaghtin. Seachnassach Prince of Imanie, Died. This yeare there were certain pilgrimes killed by the Mounstermen vidzᵗ. Claringneach with all his family.

711.—There was a shineing and extreame cleare night in harvest.

712. Ceallagh Cwalann, K. of Leinster, Died. Flann ffeaula, abbot of Ardmach, died. Killin, Bishop and abbot of ffernes, Died. Murragh mᶜBrayn with a great army went to Cashell.

713.—Osrith, son of king Alfrith, king of Saxons was killed. Foyliow⁴ sate in the seat of St Columbkill in the 74ᵗʰ year of his age. Calitigernus of Cloneois abbot, died.

715.—It reigned a shower of honey on Ohinmbig,⁵ a shower of Money on Ohinmore, and a shower of Blood upon the ffosses of Leinster, for which cause Neal Frossach who then was borne was called Neal Frossac.⁶

716.—All Lynster was five times wasted and preid in one yeare by yᵉ O'Neales.

---

¹ *Died.*—The precise year of his death is 704. See Reeves' *Adamnan*, lvii.

² *Syonan.* — A townland in the barony of Moycashel, Co Westmeath.

³ *Allon*—This battle is said later to have taken place in 720. See an account of it in Keating's *H. of Ireland*, p 407.

⁴ *Foyliow.*—He was 12th abbot of Iona. See Reeves'*Adamnan*, p. 381.

⁵ *Ohinmbig*—i e Fahan, on the east shore of Lough Swilly.

⁶ *Frossac.*—i. e. of the showers He became ardrigh in 782.

The Annals of Clonmacnoise.

717.—Sinagh of Innis Clothrann[1] died. ffohartagh mac Neale raigned one yeare & was killed by Kynoye mac Irgally in the battle of Kyndealgan[2]; but before K. Fohartagh began his reign, the battle of Allone before mentioned was fought wherein king fferall was slaine by the Leinstermen on friday the third of the Ides of December in the yeare of our Lord 720. King fferall had in his army 21,000 men well armed & the Lynstermen 9,000. These are they that were slaine in the K's side in that battle. first fferall himselfe with 160 of his guard, Conell Meann prince of the race of Carbry, fforbosagh prince of the race of Bowyne,[3] fferall OHaylyeaghty, fferall m^cEahagh Leawna, prince of Tawnye ; Conallagh m^cConyng ; Eigneach m^cColgan, prince of the Narhirs[4]; Cowdenagh m^cFeaghragh, Morgies mac Conell ; Leahayegh m^cConcarad ; Edgen O'Mathgna; Anmcharad m^cConcharad; Niva Mac Oirck, prince of ye Orcades ; the ten nephews of Moylefithry, these were the O'Neales of the North, the O'Neales of the West and South were those that were slain in the said battle Flann m^cRogellye, Aillill m^cfferay ; Hugh Leinster o'Kearnie, Swynne m^cKonolaye, Nia Mac Cormack, Duff Dakrich m^cDuffe, Da Inver, Aillell Ma Conill Graint, Ilaiheawil m^cDeuchte & Fergus oHeoaine, all which number were slaine. There were nine that flyed[5] in the ayre, as if they were winged fowle, and soe saved their lives. Of both armyes there were slain but 7000 both king's guard and all.

722.—Connleas abbot of Clonvicknois, Died. Neaghtin K. of the Picts entred into Religion, & Drust succeeded him in the kingdom. Colman Wamagh scribe of Ardmach, died.

723.—Rubinn chief scribe of Mounster Died ; & the sonn of Brogaine of Tehille[6] who was a Great Preacher & Divine, died.

---

[1] *Innis Clothrann.*—An island in Lough Ree, 15 miles north of Athlone.
[2] *Kyndealgan.*—Not identified.
[3] *Bowyne.*—Bogaine, a territory lying between Loughs Foyle and Swilly.
[4] *Narhirs.*—Orior in the S.E. of Co. Armagh.
[5] *Flyed* —'Nine was the number that fled with panic and lunacy from the battle.' *Annals F. M.*, ad ann. 718.
[6] *Tehille.*—Near Clonmacnoise.

724.—Alchon abbot of Clonarde died. Connell m‘Mowday was crowned with martyrdome. Murrogh m‘Brain king of Lynster Died. Duff Damver m‘Conolay, K. of Picts, was killed.

725 —The battle of Moynid Krewe was fought between the Picts themselves, where Enos was victor and many of Elphines side slain. There was another battle between them neare the castle of Credy, where it was a pitifull spectakle to behould K. Elphinus take his flight and ye most part of his army yeald themselves to the mercy of their enemies: Eolbeck the son of Moydan and the rest of the nobles & People of the Picts turned their backes to Elphinus and did receave Neaghtinn the son of Derills as king into the K. dome again. Donell m‘Ceallay king of Connaught Died.

726.—Egbricht the champion of Christ died on the feast day of Easter. Faghtna m‘ffolaghtaine abbot of Clonfert of St. Brandon died. The battle of Dromadery was fought in the kingdom of ye Picts between Drust & Enos king of the Picts, where Drust was slain the 12th of the Kallends of August.

HERE ENDS[1] THE CRONOCLES OF BEDE.

727.—The Returne of the Reliques of Adawanus to Ireland in the month of October. Anchon, the scribe of Kildare, Died The sonn of Concumba scribe of Clonvicknois died.

728 —The battle between the Picts and Dalriada, where the Picts was overcome was fought. There was a battle between the sonn of Enos and the son of Congus, where Brudeus vanquished Tolorg flying.

729 —Flann o'Colla abbot of Clonvicknois, Died. The battle of Connaught was fought wherein Moriegh m^cInreaghty, Bushop of Moye[2] of the English, was slaine. Garalt died. Ceallagh the daughter of Dunnough, a good and bountifull Queen, died. Tymnen of Kilgarad, a Religious and virtuous man, died. Ferdonagh, scribe of Armagh, Died, Neaghten

---

[1] *Ends.*—The last entry in Bede's *Eccl. Hist.* is Ann. 731.

[2] *B. of Moye.*—*i.e.* of Mayo of the English. See p. 9, *antea*.

m'Derilly Died. Sevdan, the Daughter of Corck, abbess of Kildare, died. Konolagh of Castle Cnock died.

730.—Fergus brought an army out of Dalriada into Inis Owen in Ulster, upon whom there was great slaughter made, amongst whom Connor, son of Locheny and Branchowe the son of Bran were slaine and many others Drowned in the river of Banne. The nativity of Donough m'Donell. There was a cow seen in Deilginis this yeare (myne author Reporteth to have had conference with Divers that did eat of her milk & butter) which was formed with one body one neck and two hynder parts with two Tayles and 6 feet.

731.—Talorg m'Cougusa was bound by his one brother & presented and sent to the Picts, who cast him into the water and drowned him. Tionoye raigned 5 years & was slaine in a battle by Flaithvertagh & Donell. Flaithvertagh Raigned seven years and died at Ardmagh[1].

734.—Hugh Allan raigned 9 years. There was 132 years between ye death of king Hugh Allan & the death of K. Hugh ffinleich. During which time there Raigned in Ireland 8 kings which were fferall, Neale ffrasagh, Hughornye, Donnogh, Coñor m'Donnogh, Neale Glunduffe, Moyleseaghlynn, and Hugh ffinliah. There raigned in Scotland 26 kings vidz^t. Dungall, Alpine, Moriegh, Conell, Conell, Enos, ffergus, Eochy, Donell, Constantine, Owen, Alpine, Owen Kymboye, Fiachna, Eochy, ffomaltagh, Carcall, Moylebressal, Morieagh Madadan, Leathlovar, Ainvith, Eochagann, Eremon, ffiaghna m^{e}Heremon, Moriegh, & Ahagh. There raigned in Leinster 13 kings, vidz^t. Ceallagh, Rory, Bran, Fynaghty, Morieagh, Ceallagh, Bran, Rwarck, Dunlenn, Twahall, Dunnlenn, and Daniell. There Raigned alsoe in Ossery, seven kings Dungall, ffoylan, Moyldeyn, ffergall, Dunlen, Karvell and ffiaghna. There reigned during the said space in Mounster nine kings, Artry, ffeylim, Moyldwyn, olchovar, Algenan, Moylegula, Ceanfoyla, Donnogh, and Duffelaghtna. There raigned in Connaught 18 kings vidz^t., Cahall, Hugh Balb, Fergus Oilill, Dowmreaght, Donnogh, Lahry, Tiprady,

---
[1] *Ardmagh.*—He became a monk there. *Annals F. M.*, ad ann. 729.

fflathry, Ardgall, Muries, Dermott, Cahall mᶜMorgissa, Murrogh, ffynaghty, ffergus mᶜEothy, and Connor mᶜTeige. There are 138 yeares from the Death of king Hugh ffinleih to the Death of king Bryan Borowe that was killed by the Danes in the battle of Clontarfe. During which time there raigned in Ireland 6 kings viz. Flann mᶜMoyleseaghlynn, Neale Glunduffe, Congallagh, Donnell, Moyleseaghlynn mᶜDonell, & king Bryan.

There was a Dragon both huge & ugly to behould this harvest seen, and a great Thunder heard after him in the firmament.

734. This yeare venerable Beda Died in the 88th yeare of his age and was called the Sage of all England.

733.—Enos mᶜffergos K. of Picts wasted the Region of Dalriada or Redshankes, tooke Dunatt and burnt Cregg & bound the 2 sonnes of Sealuy with coardes Dungall and fferaagh. A little while after Brudeus the son of Enos who was son of Cron Moyle mᶜColgann abbot of Lusk, Died. ffergus died.

734.—The work done in Upercroossann was sunck in the Debth of the sea & certaine sea-fareinge men to the number of 22. Convall or Conmoyle O'Locheny, abbot of Clonvicnois, Died. The lawes[1] & Constitutions made by St. Patrick were caused to be put in execution by king Hugh Allan.

735.—ffaylan oBroyn king of Leinster Died of a sudden & Immature death little thought of before. Tola mᶜDonnogh, B. of Clonard, the worthy champion of Jesus Christ Died The battle of Athseany[2] in the 14th day of the Calends of September was cruelly & bloodyly fought by the O'Neales & the Leinstermen, where the 2 Kˢ heades of the two Armyes, did soe roughly aproch to one another that K. Hugh Allan

---

[1] *Lawes.*—'About this time there was an interview between Hugh Allan, King of Ireland, and Cathal, King of Munster, at Tirda Glass, in Ormond, where, among other debates, they consulted what methods should be used to advance the revenue of St. Patrick throughout the kingdom, and they established a particular law for that purpose.' Keating, *H. of Ireland*, p. 409.

[2] *Athseany.*—Now Ballyshannon, Co. Kildare, five miles S. E. of old Kilcullen.

K. of Ireland & Hugh mᶜColgan K. of Leinster, whereof the one was sore hurt & lived after, the other with a Deadly Blow lost his head from his shoulders, the o'Neales with their king behaved themselves soe valiantly in the pursuit of their enemies & killed them soe fast in such a manner as they made Great Heapes in the field of their Carcasses, soe as none or very few of the Leinstermen escaped to bring Tydings home to their friends. In this Battle the two joynt kings of Leinster Hugh mᶜColgan & Bran Beag mᶜMurchowe, Fergus mᶜMoynaye & Dawdachrich, the Lordes of ffoharte, mᶜo'Kelly mᶜTreyn fiangallach oMoyleaghlin the 2 sons of fflann o'Konoly, Ealgach O'Moyleoyer & many others which my authour omitteth to Relate for brevity sake, were slaine, and sayeth that this was the Greatest slaughter of a long time seen in Ireland.

Cahall mᶜffynguyne prepared a Great army & went to Leinster & brought Hostages from Bran Brick mᶜMurchow with many rich Bootyes.

736.—Fergus Glutt Prince of the race of Icova with the spittle of men & witchcraft died. Sawhyn of Clonbrony[1] virgin died.

737.—Donell entred into Religion. fforbosach mᶜAileala, K. of Ossery, was killed. O'Haillealla, lord of Kinaleagh, was killed. Duff Davoreann abbot of Tower, Died. Ceallagh abbot of Clonvickenois, Died. Saint Brayn of Linneally[2] dyed.

738.—Conly king of Teaffa Dyed. Morogh mᶜfferall mᶜMoyledoyn, was killed.

739.—Kyneleagh & Delvyn were spoiled by Ossory. Cahall macffiinguyne, king of Mounster, & fflann ffeorna prince of Corcomroe, Dyed. Dachwa mᶜDavid Anchorite Died. Conyng mᶜAwley prince of Kynnaghta[3] was strangled by king Hugh Allan. Hugh Balire, K. of Connaught, died. Affrick, abbess of Kildare, died.

---

[1] *Clonbrony*—In the barony of Granard, Co. Longford. Her feast is kept on December 19th.

[2] *Linneally*.—Near Tullamore, founded by St. Colman Elo about 600.

[3] *Kynnaghta*.—There were two territories of this name, one in Meath, the other in Co. Derry.

740.—The laws and constitutions of O'Swanye[1] of Rahyne were established by the king and subjects. Donell Raigned 20 yeares & then Dyed. Laygnen m'Doneanny, abbot of Sayer[2] in Elly was killed. The Lawes & Rules of good life ordayned by St. Queran & St. Brandon were caused to be put in execution in Connaught by ffergus m'Keally K. of that Province.

744.—There was a strange thing seen in Ulster in the time of fiaghna m'Hugh Royne K. of Ulster, & the time of Eahagh m'Breassall, Prince of Neathagh, or Iveagh of Ulster, which was this: The seas haue put a whale a shore in that Contry, in whose head there were three teeth of Gould, every of the teeth weighed fiue ounces, & for the strangeness of the thing there was one of the teeth brought to Beanchor, & there laid on ye Alter for a wonder which remained there for a long space.

741.—fforannan, abbot of Clonard, Died. Comynge o.Mooney abbot of Loyre Lere[3] Died. m'Nideferty, abbot of Tehilly, Died.

742.—Cormack Bishop of Athrumni[4] Died. There was Drogons seen in the skyes. Saran, abbot of Beanchor, Died.

743.—Coman[5] the Religious Dyed. ffiachra m'Garvan of Meath was drowned in Loghre.

74?.—There was snow this yeare of wonderfull Greatness that there was in no man's memory such seen. In so much that the cattle of Ireland for the most part Died, after which ensuing Great & unaccustomed Drowth in the world. The Rules of O'Swany of Rahin were established in Leigh Coynn[6] or Con's half in Deale. There were shipes seen in the skyes with their men this yeare.

---

[1] *O'Swanye.*—He founded a monastery in the place from which St Carthach had been driven two centuries before. His feast is on October 1st.

[2] *Sayer.*—Now Seir Kieran, midway between Roscrea and Birr, founded by St. Ciaran of Ossory.

[3] *Loyre Lere.*—On the east side of Lough Ennell, Co Westmeath.

[4] *Athrumni.*—Now Trim in Co. Meath.

[5] *Coman.*—Founder of the monastery of Roscommon according to Colgan. *Acta SS.*, p. 791. His feast is on December 26th.

[6] *Leigh Coynn.*—*i.e.* the northern half of Ireland. See p. 48, *antea*.

745.—Conell, abbot of Twaym Greny,[1] Died. Breassall m Colgan abbot of ffernes, died.

746.—Swarlagh B. of ffower,[2] died The battle of Ocky between the Picts & Brittans was fought where Talorgan m'ffergus, brother of K. Enos, was slaine. Cahall Moynmoyne, prince of Imainie, Died.

747 —Cwangus abbot of Leihmore[3] in Connaught died fflann oCongoghe, Prince of Offaily, Died. Colman of the Welshmen, abbot of Slaine, Died. Furseus abbot of Leakyn[4] in Meath & Moyle Imorchor Bishop of Achroym O'Maynye,[5] died.

748.—Dicolla m⸱Menedi abbot of Inis Morye,[6] Dyed. ffiachra o'Macnya, abbot of Clonfert, died.

749.—Lucritt abbot of Clonvickenois, Died. The Rules of St Columbkill were established in Meath by king Donell. Scanlagh m'Clonbayren died. Furseus of Eacha m'Neyrck[7] dyed. The Moone was of sanguine colour. Twaliah the daughter of Cahall & Queen of Leinster died.

750.—Longseach m'fflaithverty prince of the Race of Tirrconnell, Died. Abel of Athomna[8] dyed.

751.—Clonvickenose was burnt the 12th of the kalends of Aprill. Suanus[9] als Fimoyne O'Swanaye of Rahin died.

752.—Fergus m⸱Keallay K. of Connought Dyed. The

---

[1] *T. Greny.*—Now Tomgraney, on the western shore of Lough Derg. Petrie gives a description of a church and round tower erected there by Brian Boroimhe, in *Eccl. Arch.*, pp. 277, 380.

[2] *ffower.*—A monastery founded by St. Fechin about 650. See *Ibid.*, p 174, and Colgan's *Diocese of Meath*, 1. 64.

[3] *Leihmore.*—Near Borris, in the barony of Eliogarty, Co. Tipperary, founded by St. Mochaemog, who died in 655. His feast was on March 13th.

[4] *Leakyn.*—Four miles south of Rathowen, Co Westmeath, founded by St. Cruimin about 650. His feast was on June 28th

[5] *A. O'Maynye*.—Now Aughrim, 7 miles south-west of Ballinasloe, Co. Galway.

[6] *I. Morye.*—Off the north-west coast of Sligo. A monastery was founded here by St. Molaise. His feast is on August 12th. There are here ruins of several small churches which are described in the *Journal of the R. S. of Antiquaries* for 1885, p. 175.

[7] *E. m⸱Neyrck.*—Now Assylin, near Boyle

[8] *Athomna.*—O'Donovan suggests Portumna on the Shannon.

[9] *Suanus.*—In the *Annals of Ulster* he is called Nepos Suanaich.

shippwrack was this yeare of Delvyn Nwagat (which is between the river of Suck and Synenn) on Logh Rye against[1] theire Capitaine Dymsach. Ethelbald, K. of England, Dyed.

753.—Cumascach prince of Affayly, was killed by Moyledwyn m‘Hugh Beanan K. of Mounster. The Rules of Saint Sagnus[2] were yett observed.

754.—Slane abbot of Louth died. Cahal K. of o'Keansealy, Elpin of Glassnayen & ffivagh of Killalga,[3] all Dyed. Martha abbess of Kildare, Dyed. The battle of Dromrovay[4] fought between the o'Fiachras and the o'Briwynes, where Teag m‘Mordevor & three o'Kellyes were slaine viz[t] Cathrannagh, Caffye, and Ardvronn Ailleall o'Donchowe had the victory. Mac Moriey o'Morgan, K. of Leinster, Dyed. Gorman Coworb of St. Mocht of Lowth died, in Pilgrimage at Clonvicknois.

755.—Enos, K. of Scotland, dyed. Cosedge, abbot of Louth, dyed.

756.—Moriegh o'Broyne, K. of Leinster, died. There was great scarcity of victualls this yeare & abundance of all manner of the fruites of trees. Algnio m‘Gnoy the second next abbot of Clonard, dyed. There was a field fought between Clonvickenois and the Inhabitants of Birr in a place called in Irish Moyne koysse Blaie.[5] Eghtigin B. was killed by a Priest at St. Bridget's alter in Kildare, as he was celebrating of mass, which is the Reason that since that time a Priest is prohibited to celebrate mass in Kildare in the presence of a Bushopp

757.—Enos m‘Fergus, K of Pictland, Dyed.

758.—Cormack, abbot of Clonvicknois, Died. ffearlio, the sonn of a Smith, abbot of Conrie[6] in Meath, Died. Fogartagh

---

[1] *Against* —*The Annals F. M* have ' with their lord.'

[2] *Sagnus* —I find no mention of him either in the *Mart of D.* or in Colgan's works.

[3] *Killalga*.—Kildalkey, five miles south of Athboy, Co Meath. There was a church here dedicated to St. Dympna, whose feast is on May 15th

[4] *Dromrovay*.—In the parish of Breaffy, barony of Carra, Co. Mayo.

[5] *Moyne koysse Blaie*.—Not identified.

[6] *Conrie*.—Now Kilcomeragh, in the barony of Moycashel, Co. Westmeath. A church was erected here by St. Colman His feast was on September 25th.

Prince of Elye, Died. Swyne, abbot of Clonfert, Died. King Donell was the first K. of Ireland of Clann Colman or o'Melaghlynes & Dyed[1] quitly in his Deathsbed the 12th of the kalends of December in the year of our Lord God 759.

759.—Nealle Frassagh, son of K. fferall, began his reign immediately after the Death of K. Donell, & raigned seven years. There was Great famine throughout all the kingdome in the beginning of his raigne, In soe much that the K. himself had very little to live upon, & being then accompanied with seven godly Bishops, fell upon their knees, where the king very pitifully before them all besaught God of his Infinite Grace & Mercy, if his wrath otherwise could not be appeased, Before he saw the Destruction of so many thousands of his subjects & friends that then were helpless of releefe, & Ready to Perrish, to take him to himself, otherwise to send him & them some Releefe for maintenance of his service, which request was noe sooner made then a Great shower of Silver fell from heaven, whereat the K. Greatly Rejoyced, and yett (said he) This is not the thing that can Deliuer us from this famine & eminent Danger, with that he fell to his Prayers againe; then a second shower of heavenly honey fell, & then the K. said with Great thanksgiving as before, wth that ye third shower fell of pure wheat, which covered all the fields over that like was never seen before, soe that there was such plenty & aboundance of wheat, that it was thought y^t it was able to maintaine manye kingdomes. Then the K. & the seven Bushopes gave great thanks to the Lord. There was a Great Battle fought between the familyes of Dorow & Clonvicknois at Argamoyne, where Dermott Duff m^{c}Donell was killed. There was exceeding great drought this yeare. Aileall o'Donchow, king of Connaught, Died. Donnogh, sonn of K. Donell Gave a Battle to the families of the O'Dowlies in ffertulagh.[2] Moll king of England entred into Religion. Flaithvertagh m^{c}Loyngsy,

---

[1] *Dyed.*—The *Annals of Ulster* give 762 as the date of his death. The *Annals F.M.* agree with our author.

[2] *ffertulagh.*—Now a barony in the S.E of Co. Westmeath. See *The Book of Rights*, p. 180.

K. of Tara died in the habbitt of a Religious man. ffollawyn m'Conchongailt, K. of Meath, was willfully murthered.

760.—The Battle of Carnfiaghy[1] was fought between the 2 sonns of K. Donell, Donnogh & Murrough, and after slaughter in either side made, Murrogh was putt to fflight. A Battle fought between those of Meath & the Inhabitants of Moybrey where Moyleowa m'Tayhill & Dongall m'Dereth were killed.

761.—ffear-Dachrich, abbot of Ardmach, Died. Glandibar, abbot of Lathreagh Broyne,[2] Died. The Lawes of St. Patrick were established by the K. Duffeinreaght, K. of Connaught, Died of a sanguine flux. Neale K. of Meath Died.

762.—Murgaill m'Nynnea, abbot of Rachrynn, Died. There Raigned famine & many Diseases in this kingdome untill they were suckoured by the prayers of K. Neale & his Bushopes as before.

763.—Donnogh sonn of K. Donnell & second monarch of y'e O'Melaghlynns succeeded after K. Neale. Moriertagh sonn of K. Donell, King of Meath, died. Gorman, the daughter of Hugh m'fflynn, died.

764.—Beag m'Conley, prince of Teaffa, Dyed. Moyleyghen abbot of Cloneyneagh, Died.

765.—The rules of St. Queran & St. Aidan were Practized in the three thirds of Connaught, whereof the 2 Brenyes[3] & Analey, the Countes of Leytrym, Longford, & Cavan were one third part, called y'e rough third part of Connaught.

766.—Aidan, B. of Mayo of the Saxons, Dyed. Moynagh m'Colman, abbot of Slane & ffobrey, Dyed. Donnagh, K. of Connaught, Dyed.

767.—Seanchan, abbot of Imlcach, Dyed. Ernagh m'Ehinn, abbott of Leihlyn, & fforannan, B. & Scribe of Treoide,[4] Dyed.

768.—Queran, the Deuout, of Beladoyn,[5] Died.

---

[1] *Carnfiaghy.*—Now Carn, in the barony of Moycashel in the same county.

[2] *L. Broyne.*—Now Lara Brien, near Maynooth.

[3] *Brenyes.*—i.e. B O'Rourke, Co. Leitrim, and B. O'Reilly, Co. Cavan.

[4] *Treoide.*—Trevet, in the barony of Skreen, Co. Meath.

[5] *Beladoyn.*—Now Disert Kieran, near Kells. The feast of the Saint is on June 14th.

769.—Colman Abbot of Clonvicknois died, Ceallagh Murchow, K. of Leinster, Died. Moyle Kovay o'Mooney Died. Myne author sayeth that K. Neale ffrossagh & Hugh ffynn K. of Dalriada or Red shankes, Died this yeare.

770.—Flathry m'Donell, K. of Connaught, Dyed. There raigned many diseases in Ireland this yeare. A great Morren of Cowes came over the whole kingdom, called the Moylegarow.

771.—There was a battle in Calah[1] between King Donough & Conolagh, in which Conolagh m^{c}Comyn prince of Moybrey, Cwana m^{c}Eigny, Donnogh m^{c}Allene, Prince of Mogornn, and Dermot m^{c}Clothny with many other nobles, were slaine. Anfceally, abbot of Coinre & Lynnealla, Died. Sith-math abbesse of Clonboreann,[2] died. ffinan, abbot of Cloneois, Died.

772.—ffulartach, B. of Clonard, Died. Monann m^{c}Cormacke, abbott of St. Fursens his Place[3] in france, died, & fflathy, K. of Connaught, Died. The Murren of the Cowes in Ireland still continued, & which was worse Greate scarcity & penurie of victuals amongue men continued. Kildare was burnt the 4th of the Ides of June. The Pope rained over all the kingdome. K. Donnogh brought an armie to ye North & took hostages of Donell m^{c}Hugh K. of the North. There was a Battle fought between the Mounstermen, where fferall m^{c}Elay Prince of Desmond, was slaine, and Breassall of Bearry was victor. fforbasach m^{c}Moyle Tola, abbot of Roscomman, Died.

773.—Alpinn, K. of ye Picts, Died. The ffight of Rwaragh from the upper part of Oycke, & Carbrey m^{c}Loygnen with the 2 Races of the Leinstermen whome K. Donnogh Pursued with his forces, & wasted their Landes, & confines & Burnt the Churches. Murgeall m^{c}Reaghtaioratt & m^{c}Nya m^{c}Cormack were killed by the Leinstermen & of the Leinstermen

---

[1] *Calah.*—There is a place of this name in the barony of Kilconnell, Co. Galway.

[2] *Clonboreann.* — On the west bank of the Shannon, nearly opposite Clonmacnois. The foundress was St. Cairech, a sister of St. Enda of Aran.

[3] *Place.*—*i.e.* Peronne. See p. 105, *antea.*

the 2 sonns of Kynadon, Anlon & Bran, were killed. Faruley the Daughter of Conly Prince of Moyteaffa, abbesse of Clwainbronaye, died. Augustin of Beanchor, & Sedragh m{c}Sobarchinn, & Nadarcha the Sadge died. There was a Great Convocation in the K{s} pallace of Taragh of the o'Neales and Leinstermen & also of the clergie to decide their long-continued controversies, where there was a Reverent assembly of many worthy, Reverent & Venerable anchorites and scribes, of all which assembly Dowlittye[1] was ye cheefest. Scannall, abbot of Kilkenny, Died.

778.—There was a Great fray in Ardmach on shrouetide, where Conolagh m{c}Conoy Died. Seannchan, abbott of Imleagh, Onagh abbott of Lismore, Seirgall O'Daingne, abbott of Clonfert Molwa, Duffinreaght m{c}ffergus, abbot of fferness, Algna B. of Ardbreachan,[2] Moyneagh O'Mooney, abbott of Loghtere, ffaghtnagh, abbot of ffower, and Ailvran o'Lugdadan, abbott of Clondalcann,[3] Sayrgus o'Cahaille ye sadge, & ffergus m{c}Cahall, K. of Dalriada or Redshankes, all Died. There was a battle given at ye River of Rie[4] by the Inhabitants of Moybrey to Leinstermen, where the Leinstermen had the victory. This was the first of November in the year of the Margent Quoted, which ouerthrow was Prophysied by the wordes Ar, fier, rigi, jugi.

To the end that the Reader may not be ignorant of Moybrea & of the Inhabitants thereof, I will in a few wordes shew the boundes thereof and to whome it was allotted. Dermott m{c}Kervell K. of Ireland, of whome mention was made in this History, had issue Hugh Slane, Colman More, & Colman Beagg. To the Race of Hugh was allotted this Moybrey extending from Dublin at Bealaghbricke westerlie of Kelles, & from the hille of Houth to the mount of Slieve Fwagde[5] in

---

[1] *Dowlittye.*—There was an abbot of Finglas of this name whose death is given in *Annals F. M.* under 791, and here under 793.

[2] *Ardbreachan.* — Now Ardbracan, near Navan.

[3] *Clondalcann.*—Four miles W. of Dublin. There is here a round tower in perfect preservation.

[4] *Rie.*—Now the Rye water, which falls into the Liffey at Leixlip.

[5] *S. Fwagde.* — Perhaps Slieve Fuaidh, in the barony of Upper Fews, Co. Armagh.

Ulster. There raigned of K. Hugh his race as monarchies of this kingdome nine kings as shall be shewed when I come to the Place where Remembrance ought to be made of them. There were many other Princes of Mobrey besides the said kings, & behaved themselves as becommed them, & because they were nearer the Invasions of the Land then other septs, they were sooner Bannished & Brought lower then others. The o'Kellyes of Brey was the chiefe name of that Race, though it hath manye other names of by-septs, which for brevityes sake I omitt to particulate, they are brought soe low now a Dayes that the best of the Chroniclers In the kingdom are ignorant of their disents, though the o'Kellyes are soe common every where that it is unknown whether the Disperst partyes in Ireland of them be of the familie of o'Kellyes of Connaught or Brey, that (scarcely) one of the same familie knoweth not the name of his one great-Grandfather, & are Turned to be meere churles & poore laboring men, soe as scarce there is a few or noe parishes in the kingdome but hath some one or other of those Kellyes in it, I meane of Brey.

To Colman the other sonn of K. Dermot was alsoe allotted Claynn Colman, of whome there hath been seven Monarches in Ireland, beside the kingdome of Meath that they held still for many hundred yeares as superiours thereof, theire Power was latter then the o'Kellyes because they were farther from Invassions, Bloodshed, & Banishments then ye others. Yett their one malignant mindes towards theire one Bloode, theire Contentions, & Debates with one another was the occation of theire overthrow. Moyeteaffa whereof is often mention made is the contry & Landes where the Race of Many mcNeale were Resident. ffoxes country Callrie, Brawnye, Cwoicky lands in the county of Longford as Moghrea, &c.

779.—Twilleliah, the daughter of Murrogh, abbesse of Cloncuiffyne,[1] died. Querann of Tymonna,[2] died.

---

[1] *Cloncuiffyne.*—Clonguffin, in the parish of Rathcore, Co. Meath. It was founded by St. Fintinna.

[2] *Tymonna.*—There are two places of this name, one in Co. Westmeath, the other in Co. Wexford.

780.—Donell mcfflothnia, Prince of Affailie, was killed in Clonconor, in Gessell. Mayo of the English, Ardmach, & the abby of Clonbronay were burnt with horrible fier on Saturday night in the fourth of the nones of August. Moynagh o'Mooney prince of Imacwais & mcfflathnya abbott of Clonfert, Dyed

781.—Rochnia, abbott of Clonvicknois, Died. Queran abbot of Rathmoyeanye¹ & Tymmonna, Conell mac Cronnmoyle, abbot of Luslann or Lusk, died. fflann B., one of the Sadges & abbot of Iniskoynedea,² was poysoned to death

782.—Moylechraich mcDonnell abbot of Killcullen,³ and scribe of Killnamannagh,⁴ Died. Elbrig, abbess of Clonbronagh, died.

783.—Tipraide mcTeige, K. of Connaught, died. Sneriagall, abbot of Clonvicknois, Died. There was a Generall Disease in the kingdom this yeare called the Kawagh.⁵ There was a battle fought between K. Donnogh and the race of K. Hugh Slane, wherein Fiaghra mcCahell the two nephews of Conyng and Dermott were slain. Moylecomar abbott of Gleandalogha, died

784.—Lergus o'ffiachayn the sadge of Kellmaynam,⁶ Rouartagh mcMooneye, spenser⁷ of Slane and abbot of Fobrie, and Morieagh mcCahall abbot of Kildare, Died, and Lomhwhile,⁸ B. of Kildare, Died. There was a Battle fought between the Race of Owen and Conell, wherein Moyledwynn mcHugh

---

¹ *Rathmoyeanye* — O'D. thinks this is Routh, near Manor Cunningham, in Co Donegal.

² *Iniskoynedea.* — Iniskeen, ten miles W. of Dundalk A monastery was here so early as the beginning of the 6th century.

³ *Kilcullen.* Old Kilcullen, in Co. Kildare, where there is a round tower and an ancient cross.

⁴ *Killnamannagh.* — Ten miles W. of Kilkenny. A monastery was founded here about the middle of the 6th century by St. Natalis. His feast is on July 31. See Colgan's *Acta SS.*, p. 169.

⁵ *Kawagh.*—Some kind of cutaneous disease.

⁶ *Kellmaynam.*—In the western suburb of Dublin, founded by St. Maighnan It was afterwards a priory of Knights Templars, and later of the Knights of St John. The site is now occupied by the Royal Hospital.

⁷ *Spenser.* — This official was called the cellarer in later times

⁸ *Lomhwhile.*—He was bishop of K from 747 to 785. See Ware's *Bishops*, p 382.

Allen had the victory & Hugh Mundearg was putt to flight Duff Davareann abbot of Clonard made his visitations in the Parrishes of Mounster.

785.—Columb m‘ffoylgussa, B. of Lothra, died. The Rules of St. Queran were Practized in Connaught.

786.—The Battle of Cleiteagh between Hugh Orney the 2 Races of Connell & Owen, where the families of Connell were vanquished & Donell escaped, was fought this yeare. The Relickes of St. Patrick were taken by force at a certaine faire.

787.—Fighna, K. of Ulster, died. There was a great slaughter of Ulstermen by the Redshanckes or Dalriada, Sayrbrey, abbott of Clonvickenois, died. Awley, prince of o'Manie, Died.

788 —Moylerwayn Tawlaghty & Aidan of Rahin Died. Dowdaleah abbott of Ardmach, Died.

790 —The Rules of St. Coman were Practized & putt in execution in the three partes of Connaught, & the lawes of Ailve of Imleagh in Mounster. Kynnaye m^cCumusky, abbot of Dorowe, Died. Artry m^cCahall was ordayned K. of Mounster. Moyle Tola abbott of Lareagh Bryen Dyed.

791.—Arraghtagh o'Fielan, abbott of Ardmach, Dyed & Adfiath[1] B of the same in one night. Thomas abbott of Beanchor & Joseph o'Kearny abbott of Clonvickenois, Died. Cathnia o'Gwary abbott of Tuam Grenie, & Lerveanvan, abbesse of Cluonbardann[2] Died. K. Donnogh sent an army to assist the Lynstermen against the Mounstermen. All the Islands of Brittaine were wasted & much troubled by the Danes; this was theire first footing in England.

792.—Bran king of Leinster & his wife Eihnie Daughter of Donell of Mieth, Queen of Leinster, died. Rachrynn was burnt by the Danes. Moniagh, abbott of Clonfert Molwa died.

793.—Dowlitter (of whome I have spoken before[3]) abbott of

---

[1] *Adfiath.* — He occupied the See of Armagh for one year only. *Ibid.*, p. 42.

[2] *Cluonbardann.* — Clonburren. See p. 123, *antea*

[3] *Before.*—At p. 124

ffinglasse, & olchovar m`<sup>c</sup>`Eyrck, sonn of fflann, K. of Mounster, B anchorite and scribe, died. Osfa, a good K. of England Died, whoe was soueraigne over the rest of the K^s of England.

794.—Donnogh, K. of Taragh & Ireland, with his brother Inreaghtagh Died the 6th day after the kalends of February anno Dni 794 Hugh Ornye succeeded K. Donnogh & Raigned 27 yeares. In the Beginning of his raign, he wasted & spoyled all Meath for noe other cause but because they stuck to the o'Melaghlynns, which were his Predecessors in the government.

795.—The island of St. Patrick[1] was burnt by the Danes, they taxed ye Landes with great taxtions, they took the Reliques of St. Dochonna[2] & made many Invassions to this kindome & tooke many rich & great bootyes, as well from Ireland as from Scotland.

798.—Befaile, the daughter of Cahall, & wife of K. Donnogh & Queen of Ireland, Died in Anno Domini 798.

799.—Moriegh m^{c}Donnell king of Meath, Died. Hugh K. of Ireland, came with a Great armye to Meath & Divided it into 2 Partes, whereof he Gave one part to Connor, sonn of K. Donnogh, & the other part to his brother Ailill fferall m^{c}Anmcha, K of Ossory, died. Eugenell, Daughter of K. Donnogh, Queen of Ireland, Died. Loghriagh[3] was destroyed by Morgies.[4]

800.—The battle of Rouaye Connell[5] between the 2 sonns of K Donnogh, where Aillell was slain, and Connor victor, was fought. m^{c}Laysre, the Excellent of Inismorye, Died.

801.—Donell m^{c}Hugh K. of the North, Died. K. Hugh wasted Leinster twice in one month, took away all their preyes and Bootyes. Kynoy king of Leinster Died. There was such horrible & Great Thunder the next after St.

---

[1] *I. of St. Patrick.*—Near Skerries, Co. Dublin.

[2] *St. Dochonna.*—He was Bishop of Connor, and died in 725. See Ware's *Bishops*, p. 218.

[3] *Loghriagh.*—Loughrea, in south Galway.

[4] *Morgies.*—In the *Annals F.M.*, under the date 803, he is said to be the son of Tomaltach, a Connaught chief.

[5] *R. Connell.*—Now Rowe, in the barony of Rathconrath, Co Westmeath.

The Annals of Clonmacnoise.

Patrickes day that it putt assunder[1] 1010 men between Corck Baeskynn[2] & the land about it. The sea Divided an Ileand there in three partes ; the seas & sands thereof Did couer the earth neare it. Laygery, prince of Desmond, Died.

802.—ffine abbesse of Killdare, Died. K. Hugh with a Great armye went to Donkuare[3] & divided Leinster into 2 partes, between the 2 Morieghs, vidz^t. Moriegh m^cRiuaragh & Moriegh m^cBroyne. Mortaugh m^cDongaile prince of Brenie, Died.

803 —There was a great pestilence all ouer the kingdome this yeare. Gormgall m^cDynaye, abbott of Armach & Cloneois,[4] Died. Congall abbott of Slane, sonn of Moonagh, a virgin from his birth, died. Loicheach a Doctor of divinity of Beanchor, Died. There was 68 of the familie of Hugh of St. Columb Kill, slain by the Danes. Flaithnia m^cKinoy K. of Affalie was killed in Rathangann.[5]

804.—Connraih m^cDuffdaleah abbott of Ardmach, Died of a sudden death. There was a new church founded in Kells in honour of St. Columb Kill. Hillarius, anchorite & scribe of Loghne,[6] Died. The Danes burnt Inismoriey & invaded Roscomman.

805.—Torbagh scribe & abbott of Ardmach he was of the o'Kellyes of Breye, Died. Finnsneaghty m^cKeallay K. of Leinster Died in Kildare. Toighigh o'Tigernie, abbott of Ardmach, Died.

806.—ffynnban abbesse of Clonbronay, Dyed. There was a battle fought between the families of o'Keanseallyes, where Ceallagh m^cDungaill was slain.

---

[1] *Assunder.*—The island is now called Mutton Island. See Frost's *H. of Clare*, p. 145.

[2] *C. Baeskynn.*—A territory in south-west of Clare, including the baronies of Clonderlaw, Moyarta, and Ibrican.

[3] *Donkuare.*—Rathcore, near Enfield, Co. Meath.

[4] *Cloneois.*—In Co Monaghan. A monastery was founded here by St Tigernach in the beginning of the 6th century.

[5] *Rathangann.* — Seven miles N.W. of the town of Kildare.

[6] *Loghne.*—The *Annals F.M.*, have Lochre, near the present Roscrea. This was the famous 'Insula Viventium,' now Monahincha, of which Giraldus speaks, *Topog. Hib*, d. ii c iii. The church is still standing.

807.—Gwairy, abbott of Glanndalogha, Died. Cathnia, abbott of Dowlyke, & Tigernagh founder of the church of Derymelly,[1] abbott of Killachy, died.

808.—Dyman Ara, Anchorite of all Mounster, Died a happy death. There was a Great slaughter of the Deanes in Ulster Blathmac o'Mardivoe, abbott of Dorow, Died.

809.—They of Iarhar Connaught made a Great slaughter. Mounstermen made a Great slaughter of the Danes Couhagh abbot of Saye Died.

810.—There was a Great slaughter of these of Iarhar Connaught by the Danes againe. Charles the great, K. of France, and Emperour of all Europe, died.

813.—Cahassagh of Killitte,[2] Dyed. Gromflath, abbesse of Clonbarrenn, Dyed.

814.—There was a Battle fought between Cahall mᶜDunlinge and those of Tymmonna of the one side against the familye of ffarnes where there were 400 of Lay & Churchmen slaine. The families of St. Colme[3] went to Taragh, & there excommunicated K. Hugh wᵗʰ bells, Bookes, & Candles. Conchongeall K. of Leinster died.

815.—Mortagh mᶜBraine, halfe or K. of halfe Leinster, Dyed. Add three years hence to bring in the right yeare as 815 is 818 and 816 is 819 &c. A battle was fought in Delvin Nuadatt, where the o'Kellyes of o'Manie with their prince were overthrone. This Delvin Lyeth between the rivers of Synnen & Suck.

816.—All Leinster was Distroyed & wasted by K. Hugh of Glendalogha. King Hugh sonn of K. Neale ffrassagh Died at the foorde[4] of the two virtues or two miracles Áṫh uá Feaṗc. Connor mᶜDonnogh, third monarch of the o'Melaghlyns, begann his raigne & governed this Land 14 yeares. ffelym mᶜCriowhhainn began to Raigne in the province of Mounster in the pallace of Cashell.

---

[1] *Derymelly.*—In the parish of Rosinver, Co. Leitrim. St. Tigernach built a monastery here for his mother Melle.

[2] *Killitte.*—Now Killeedy, i.e. the church of St. Ita, five miles S. of Newcastle, Co. Limerick. Some parts of the monastery are still standing.

[3] *St. Colme.*—i e Columkille.

[4] *Foorde.*—Not identified.

The Annals of Clonmacnoise. 131

818.—Conulf, king of the Saxons, Died. Ceanfogla, Ceanfogla m^{c}Rwamann Bishop, scribe, anchorite, and abbott of Trym,[1] Dyed. King Conner brought an armye to the mounte called Sliew ffwaide in Ulster & Distroyed & wasted all the Landes & Countryes from thence to Eawynn Macha. Beighrenne[2] & Darensie[3] to Eawynn by the Danes was spoyled.

819.—There was such froste this yeare y^t all the Laughes, pooles & Riuers of Ireland were soe dryed upp & frozen, y^t steed & all manner of cattle might pass on them without Danger. Murrogh m^{c}Moyledwynn with the o'Neales of the North came to Ardbrachann, where they were mett wth those of the countryes of Moybrey with the Race of Hugh Slane, whose Cheefe was Dermott, & they were Joynt partakers with him against K. Connor. St. Garuan[4] flourished this time. The Ileand of Corck and Inisdoicble[5] was spoyled & Ransackt by Danes.

820.—ffelym m^{c}Criowhann, K. of Mounster Caused to be put in practice through that Province the rule and constitutions of St Patrick. Murcha m^{c}Moyledynn (Before mentioned) was Deposed by Neal m^{c}Hugh, & the Race of Owen m^{c}Neale The Danes invaded the Church of Beanchor. Gallen of the Welshmen was altogether Burnt by Phelym m^{c}Criowhayne bouth houses, Church & Sanctuaries. fflannsug m^{c}Loyngsy, abbott of Armach, Died.

821.—Beanchor was spoiled & Ransackt by the Danes together with St. Cowgalls church yard. Fynnachan m^{c}Cosgrye, Prince of Brawyn,[6] Died.

822.—There was an ouerthrow of the Deanes at Moynis

---

[1] *Trym* —A monastery is said to have been founded here by St. Patrick in 432 See Todd's *St. Patrick*, p. 257.

[2] *Beighrenne*.—An island in the north of Wexford Harbour. St. Ibar founded a monastic school here.

[3] *Darensie*.—An island in Wexford Harbour.

[4] *St. Garuan.*—The *Mart. of Donegal* gives eight of this name. It is not possible to decide which of them is referred to here.

[5] *Inisdoicble.* — The *Mart. of Donegal* describes it as between Hy Kinseallagh and the Decies. p. 187.

[6] *Brawyn*.—Breaghmhoine, now the barony of Brawny, Co. Westmeath.

by the Ulstermen. Artry m^cConnor, K. of Connaught, caused to be established the Lawes of St. Patrick in and throughout the thirds of Connaught. Blathmac m^cfflaynn was martured by the Danes in the island of Hugh.

823.—Dermott m^cNeale prince of the Southe of Moybrey, Died. The sonn of Longseagh, abbott of Ardmach, Died. Delvyn Beathra was burnt by K. Phelym.

824.—Owen Mainisdreagh was overcome & put out of Ardmach by Artry m·Connor & Comaskagh m^cCahaill. There was a meeting between K. Connor and Phelym att Byrre. Owen Manisdreach againe was Restored by the clergie to the abbottshipp of Ardmagh.

825.—Moriegh m^cRwaragh K. of Leinster died. There was an overthrow given to the Danes by the Keansealies[1] & those of Tymonna.

826.—Ceruall m^cFinnaghty, Prince of Deloyn Beathry, Died. Aidan O'Connuaye, scribe of Dorow, Died. Dermott abbott of Hugh went to Scotland & conveighed with him the Relickes[2] of St. Columb Kill. There was a great ouerthrow given to Connaughtmen by Meathmen, where there were many slaine.

827.—ffoyrye was burnt by ffelym m^cCriowhayn in Delvyn. Swyny m^cffarny, abbott for 2 months in Ardmagh, Died. Shiell m^cfferay, abbott of Kildare, Died. Mortean of Kildare died.

828.—Dermott abbott Returned into Ireland againe & brought the said Relickes of St. Colume. Morean, abbesse of Kildare, Died. ffelym m^cCriowhayn with the forces of Mounster and Leinster came to ffynore[3] to destroy, prey, and spoyle Moyebrey. The landes about the Liffie were preyed & spoiled by K. Connor o'Melaghlin.

829.—The first outrages & spoyles committed by the Danes in Ardmach was this year, & Ransacked these ensuing

---

[1] *Keansealies.*—The inhabitants of the country included now in great part in the diocese of Ferns. They derive their name from Enna Kinseallagh, king of Leinster in the 4th century.

[2] *Relickes.*—On the various translations of the relics of St. C., see Reeves' *Adamnan*, p. 312.

[3] *ffynore.*—Fennor, near Slane.

churches, Louth, Mucksnawe,[1] oaMeith,[2] Droym mꞏawley,[3] and Divers other Religious houses were by them most Pagan-like Ransacked. Alsoe the Relicks of St. aDawnanus was outragiously taken from Twahall mꞏfferaye out of Downagh Moyen[4] by the Danes, & with the like outrage they spoyled Rathlowrie[5] and Conrye in Ulster.

830.—Cinaye mꞏArtragh K. of Dalaray in the north was killed by his one men. Lisse-more was Ransackt by the Danes. ffelym mꞏCrewhynn Burnt, spoyled, & preyed the lands belonging to St. Queran called Termynlands & Deluyn Bethra three times. Ceallach mꞏBran K. of Leinster, preyed Kildare Artry, K. of Connaught[6] died. Connor mꞏDonnogh O'Melaghlin, K. of Taragh & Ireland, Died this year.

The Danes intending the fool conquest of Ireland, continued theire invassion in Ireland from time to tyme, useing all manner of crueltyes euer untill the latter end of king Brian Borowes raigne, by whome they were either Drowned or slaine in the Battle of Clontarfe, where himselfe alsoe was slaine, & the Danes quite overthrone & expelled out of the kingdome. They were most troblesome to this land, & continued putting their crueltyes in execution, 219 years during the Raignes of 12 kings, & still the natives, by all means Possible, withstood them during that time. Diuers great fleetes & armyes of them arriued in Ireland, one after another, under the leading of sundry Great & valiant Captaines as Awus, Lir, Fatha, Turgesius, Imer, Dowgeann, Imar of Limbrick, Swanchean, Griffin a herauld, ffynn, Crioslagh, Albord Roe, Torbert o'Duffe, Tor, Wasbagh, Gotman, Allgot, Turkill, Trevan, Cossar, Crouantyne, Boyvinn, Beisson, the

---

[1] *Mucksnawe.*—Mucknoe, a parish in Co Monaghan, including the town of Castleblaney.

[2] *Oa Meith*—A district in Co. Monaghan See *Book of Rights*, p. 148.

[3] *Droym mꞏawley.*—i. e. D. mic Ua Blae, which was somewhere in the barony of Upper or Lower Slane. St. Sedna was its patron; his feast was in March. See Colgan's *Acta SS.*, p 569.

[4] *D. Moyen.*—In the barony of Farney, Co. Monaghan. *Ibid.*, p.424.

[5] *Rathlowrie.* — Now Maghera, Co Derry.

[6] *K. of Connaught.*—A marginal note by O'Daly says . 'This A. was not king of C., but bishop of Armagh, as anno 824 *supra.*'

Read Daughter, Tormyn mᶜKeilebaron, Robert Moylann, Walter English, Goshlyn, Tahamore, Brught, & Awley K. of Denmark & K. of the Land in Ireland called Fingall, Ossill, and the sonnes of Imer, Ranell o'Hemer, Costry Hemer Ottyre Earle, and Altyre Duff earle. The aforesaid Captaines & other armyes Did ouerrunn all Ireland to utter Destruction allmost to Both sides. The Irishmen striuing to Defend theire Patrimony & Liberties which themselues & their forefathers enjoyed, the Danes as a most barbarous, Riotous, Proud Tyranicall & ungodly people of Infidles to conquer them, & after conquering them using them much worse than the Turks doe the Christians now a Dayes; useing theire cruelty with all the Spight and Tyranny that could be Devised. There was noe Province, Contry, Teritory, Citty, or Principall towen or Good village that had not a Governour of the Danes to oversee it, and that by the name of soeveraigne or Lord Dane, which commanded the Place wherein he executed his charge in as ample manner as if he had been lord and absolute king thereof. As many women as they coud Lay hands upon, noble or ignoble, young or ould, married or unmarried, whatsoever birth or adge they were of, were by them abused most beastly, and filthily, and such of them as they liked best, were by them sent over seas into their one countryes there to be kept by them to use theire unlawfull lusts. They had another Custome that the cheefe Governour of them should have the bestowinge . . . .

. . . .
. . . .
. . . .

. . . .

There was noe creature Living from the smallest chicken to the Greatest and full growen beast,[1] but paid a yearly Tribute to theire K., noe not soe much as the youngest infant newly borne, but paid a noble in gold or silver or the nose[2] from the

---

[1] *Beast.*—See *Wars of the Gaedhil*, p. 49, and Keating's *H. of Ireland*, p. 426.

[2] *Nose.*—*Wars of the Gaedhil*, Introd. ciii., and p. 51, on the nature of this tax.

bare bone. If the owner of the house where a Deane would lodge, had noe more in the world to live upon but one milch cowe for the maintenance of himselfe and his familie, he was compelled presently to kill her to make the Dane good cheere, if it were not otherwise Redeemed with money or some other good Thing to his Likeing. The howses of religion generally throughout the whole K.dome were by them turned to be Brothell houses, stables, & houses of easment. Yea, the sacred alters of God, that saints had in great Reverence were broken, abused & cast down by them most scornfully,[1] Paganlike and wickedly, to the great Grief of all Christian people. The great Tamberlane, called the scorge of God, could not be compared to them for Cruelty, Couetousness, & Insolency.

Neale Caille son of king Hugh Orney began his reign after the Death of K. Connor, and raigned 16 yeares. After whose Raigne the most part of the kings that were in Ireland, untill K. Bryan Borowes tyme had no great Profitt by it but the bare name, yet they had kings of their own that paid intolerable tribute to the Danes. King Neale & Murrogh of Ulster gave an overthrow to the Danes of Derycalgie.[2]

830.—Clondalkan was preyed, & spoyl'd by the Danes. Ceallagh mᶜBran gave an overthrow to the clergy of Kildare within their one house, where there were manye & an infinite number of them slaine on Saint John's day in harvest.[3] Felym mᶜCriowhaine killed & made a great slaughter upon the clergy of Clonvickenois & burnt & consumed with fier all Clonvickenois to the very Doore of the church, & did the like with the clergy of Dorow to theire very Doore also. Dermott mᶜTomalty king of Connaught died. Owen Manisdreagh[4] abbott of Ardmach and Clonard, and . . . . rick[5] abbesse of

---

[1] *Scornfully.*—For the causes of the hatred of the Christian religion shown by the Danes, see Haliday's *Danish Kingdom of Dublin,* p. 9.

[2] *Derycalgie* — This was the ancient name of Derry. See *Ordnance Survey of the Parish of Templemore,* p. 17.

[3] *St. John's day in harvest.*—The feast of the Beheading of St. John Baptist, August 29th.

[4] *O. Manisdreagh.*—i.e. of Monasterboice, in Louth, where he was lector.

[5] . . . *rick.*—Affrick. See *A. of Ulster,* i. 333.

Kildare died. Ceallagh mᶜBran king of Leinster, and Cynay mᶜConyng prince of Moyvrey, and Dermott mᶜConyng King of Teaffa died. Twachar B. & scribe of Kildare died. Gleandalogha was ransacked & preyed by Danes. Ceallagh mᶜffynnaghty abbott of Killehy died.

832.—King Neale prepared an army & went to Leinster where he ordayned Bran mᶜFoylan king of that province. K. Neale preyed & spoyled all Meath to the house of Moyle Conoge prince of Deluinn Bethra now called mᶜCoghlans contry. Comasgach mᶜEnos abbott of Clonickenois died. Fernes and Clonmore[1] of Moye were ransacked & spoyled by the Danes. Fiegann mᶜTorvie of Louth died in Pilgrimage in Clonvickenois, whose son Owen mᶜTorvey remayned in Clonn aforesaid, of whome issued the familye of Conn mboght & Muintyr Gorman, they are of the O'Kellys of Brey.

833.—Sayrgus o'Kenny abbot of Dorow died. Felym mᶜCriowhayne tooke the church of Kildare on forrannan abbot of Ardmach and substitute of St Patrick & therein committed outrages. The church of Gleandologha was burnt, & the church of Kildare ransacked by the Danes. The Danes upon the nativity of our Lord in the night entred the church of Clonmore Moyoge[2] and there used many crueltyes, killed many of the clergie, & tooke many of them captives. There was abundance of nutts & akornes this year, and were soe plenty that in som places where shalow Brookes runn under the Trees men might goe drye shod, the waters were soe full of them. The Danes this year harried and spoyled all the province of Connaught, and confines thereof outrageously.

834.—A fleet[3] of 60 sailes was on the River of Boyne by the Danes, & another of 60 on the river of Liffie, which two fleetes spoyled & destroyed all the borders of Liffie and Moybrey alltogether. Moybrey gave an overthrow to the

---

[1] *Clonmore.*—In the barony of Ferrard, Co. Louth. It is called of Moy, because it was in Magh Breagh.

[2] *Moyoge.*—*i. e.* Clonmore Maedhog, six miles E. of Tullow, Co. Carlow.

[3] *Fleet*—All our annalists speak of

Danes in Mogorne,[1] where there were 120 of them slaine & killed. The o'Neales gave a great overthrow to the Danes at Inver ne marke,[2] where they were pursueing them from Synan to the sea, and made such slaughter on them, that there was not such heard of in a long space before, but the chiefest Captaine of the Danes escaped. Iniscealtra and all the Islands of Logherny were taken, spoyled and ransacked by the Danes. Clonvickenois and Dauinis were alsoe spoiled by them, & banished out of their howses. Felym m^cCriowhayne made havock and spoile of the race of Carbry Crom.[3] Saxolve, chiefs of the Danes, was killed by those of Kyannaghta. There was an overthrow and slaughter of them at Carneferay,[4] another at Ffear[5] and another at Easrow. The first taking and possession of the Danes in Dublin was this year 834. Cahall m^cMoresse m^cTomallty K. of Connaught, Died.

835.—There was a great meeting between king Neale & Felym m^cCriowhayn, at Clonconrie Tomayne.[6] St. Dochat[7] B. and Anchorite, died. The Danes gave a great battle to the Connaughtmen, where Moyledwyne m^cMorgissa was killed with many others. Brann m^cFoylan K. of Leinstermen Died. Felym m^cCriowhayne went over all Ireland, and was like to depose the king and take the kingdome to himself.

836.—Moriegh m^cEahagh, king of Ulster, was killed by his one brothers Hugh and Enos, and Hugh m^cEahagh, was killed by Mathew m^cMoriey. The Danes made a fforte, and had shipping on Logh Neaagh of purpose and intent to wast and spoyle the north from thence, and did accordingly.

---

this 'fleet,' by which the Danes penetrated into the heart of the country; but under the date 836.

[1] *Mogorne.* — This is probably Mughdorna Breagh, in east Meath.

[2] *Inver ne marke.*—Rath-inver, the mouth of the Bray river. So O'Donovan in note to *Annals F.M.*, 1. 455, but in the index he says it is in Munster.

[3] *C. Crom.*—He was chief of Hy Many in the middle of the 6th century.

[4] *Carneferay.* — Perhaps Carnearny, in the parish of Connor, Co. Antrim. See p 32, *antea*

[5] *Ffear* —O'D conjectures Fearta-fear-feig, on the Boyne, near Slane.

[6] *C. Tomayne.*—Now Cloncurry, in north Kildare.

[7] *St. Dochat.*—In the *A of Ulster* he is said to be of Slane, i 341.

Fearnes and Corcky more[1] were burnt by the Danes. Reaghlawra, abbot of Leih[2] in Connaught, dyed.

837.—Louth was destroyed by the Danes of Loghneagh and lead with them many Bushopps, Prelates, and Priests captives from thence, & killed many others. Flodricus,[3] emperour & king of France, died. Ardmach, the town church & all, was burnt by the Danes. ffelym m'Criowhayn, king of Munster, preyed and spoyled all Meath and Moybrey, and rested at Taragh. Kenny m'Cosgray prince of Brawnie in the country of Teaffa was killed. Joseph of Rossemore, B., scribe, and venerable anchorite Died; he was abbot of Cloneois and other places. Orhanagh[4] B. of Kildare died.

838.—The Danes continued yett in Loghneaagh practizing their wonted courses. They had forte at Lynndwachal,[5] from whence they destroyed all the temple & church lands of the contry of Teaffa. They had another fort at Dublin, from whence they did alsoe destroy the lands of Leinster and of the o'Neales of the South to the mount of Slieue Bloome.[6] Felym m'Criowhaine came with a great armye to Logh Carman alias Weixford, & there was mett with king Neale and another great armye. Cloneyneagh was destroyed by the Danes, and the clergie of Clonard quite Distroyed or banished out of the same, and for the most part killed. St Moyle Dihriv[7] called the Sage, anchorite of Tirrdaglasse died. This St. made many prophesies.

839.—The Danes continued in Dublin this year and the Danes of Lynndwachill preyed and spoyled Clonvickenois, Birre, and Sayer. Morain m'Inreaghty,[8] B. of Clochar was killed by the Danes. There was a fleet of Normans at

---

[1] *Corcky more.*—*i.e.* the great morass, now Cork.

[2] *Leih*—See p. 119, *antea.*

[3] *Flodricus.*—*i. e.* Ludovicus, Louis le Pieux, who died in 840.

[4] *Orhanagh.*—He was bishop of that See from 883 to 840. See Ware's *Bishops*, p. 383.

[5] *Lynndwachal.*—Now Maghera-lin, 5 miles north-west of Dromore, Co. Down.

[6] *S Bloome*—The range of mountains on the north-west boundary of Queen's Co.

[7] *St. Moyle Dihriv.*—He is not mentioned in the *Mart. of Donegal.*

[8] *M. m'Inreaghty.*—The date of his succession to the See is not

Lynnrosa¹ upon the river of Boyne, another at Lynsoleagh² in Ulster, and another at Lyndwachill aforesaid. Keowan abbot of Lyndwachill was both killed and burnt by the Danes, and some of the Irishmen. Disertt Dermott³ was destroyed by the Danes of Keyle Usge.⁴ Dinngall mᶜFerall prince of Ossory died. Kennety⁵ and Clonvickenois were destroyed and burnt by the Danes. Mugron mᶜEnos prince of Affaille died.

840.—Comsowe mᶜDyrero, and Moynagh mᶜSachaday two Bushopps & two anchorites died in one night in Desert Dermott. Fergus mᶜJohie K. of Connaught died. Donchann mᶜMoyletoyly, scribe and anchorite, Died in Italy. Moyle Rony mᶜDonnogh K. of Meath died.

841.—Ronan, abbott of Clonvickenois, died, and Brickny abbott of Lohra. Clonfert was burnt by the Danes of Loghrie. Carbry mᶜCahall king of Leinster died.

842.—Forannan, abbott of Ardmach, was taken⁶ captive by the Danes at Cloncowardy,⁷ together with all his familie, rilickes, & books, and were lead from thence to their shipes in Lymbrick. Dunn Masse⁸ was assaulted & destroyed by the Danes, where they killed Hugh mᶜDuffe, Dachrich, abbott of Tyredaglasse and Cloneynagh, and alsoe there killed Kehernagh mᶜComasgagc, old abbott of Killdare. Turgesius Prince of the Danes, founded a strong force on Loughrie, from whence Connaught and Meath were destroyed, burnt Clonvickenois, Clonfert, Tyrdaglasse, Lothra, and withal theire churches and houses of religion. King Neale gave a great over throw to the Danes in the plaines of Moynith. Donnogh mᶜSolowann

---

known. See Ware's *Bishops*, p. 178.

¹ *Lynnrossa.*—The name of the part of the Boyne near Rosnaree.

² *Lynsoleagh.* — Perhaps Lough Swilly.

³ *D. Dermott.* — Now Castledermot, in Co. Kildare.

⁴ *K. Usge.* — *i.e.* narrow water, between Newry and Warrenpoint.

⁵ *Kennety.*—Ten miles E. of Birr, King's Co.

⁶ *Taken.*—See Keating's *H. o, Ireland*, p. 428.

⁷ *Cloncowardy.* — Now Colman's Well, in the barony of Upper Connello, Co. Limerick. See *Wars of the Gaedhil*, civ.

⁸ *D. Masse.*—Dunamaise, 3 miles E. of Maryborough. Later it was the stronghold of the O'Mores.

and Flann m͏ͨMoyleroyrie were preyed by Moyle Seachlynn m͏ͨMoyleroye and afterwards drowned him. The Danes of Dublin founded a forte at Clondewer[1] and spoyled Lis-Keilleachie[2] and executed martiredom therein upon Nwadat m͏ͨSegenye. Bressall m͏ͨAngne, abbot of Killnamannagh, died.

843.—Cahall m͏ͨAillella K. of Munster and Ferdoronagh the sage and venerable scribe of Ardmach, died. This yeare king Nealle Kailly died at Kallen[3] in Mounster. All the Termynlands belonging to St. Queran were preyed and spoyled by Felym m͏ͨCriowhainn without respect of place, saint, or shrine.

844.—After his returne to Munster ye next year, he was avertaken by a great disease of the flux of the belly, which happened in this wise. As king felym (soone after his return into Mounster) was takeing his rest in his bed, St. Queran apeared to him with his habitt and bachall, or pastorall stafe, & there gave him a push of his Bachall in his belly whereof he tooke his disease and ocation of Death, and notwithstanding his great iregularity and great desire of spoyle he was of sum numbered among the scribes & anchorites of Ireland. He died of the flux aforesaid A° 847.

847.—Moylseaghlinn m͏ͨMoyleronie of the race of the o'Melaghlinns of Meath, suceeded after K. Neale in the kingdom, and raigned 17 years. Olchover king of Cashell did overthrow the Danes in a battle in Mounster, where he slew 1200 of their best men.

848.—King Moyleseaghlin did overthrow them in the battle of ffarcha.[4] ffarannan and Dermott were Primates of Armach in his time one after another. King Moyleseaghlin

---

[1] *Clondewer.*—It is written in the *Annals F. M.*, cluana an Dobhair There is a parish called Tubber, near Clara, King's Co.

[2] *Lis-Keilleachie.*—Now Killeagh, 5 miles S of Tullamore. See p. 84, antea.

[3] *Kallen.*—Now Callan, 12 miles south-west of Kilkenny The province of Munster extended formerly to Gowran. See Keating's *H. of Ireland*, p. 59.

[4] *ffarcha.*—Farach, near Skreen, Co. Meath.

Died in the 2nd of the kalends of December anno Domini 859.

863.—Hugh Finliah of the Clanna Neales of the North succeeded and raigned 14 years, & at last died at Driwymkoylinn.[1] In this king's time it Raigned blood. Fehyn was primate[2] of Armach. Because I shall not let slipp that Great and nottable act done by Moyleseaghlin m^cMoyleronie unrelated, you shall know that upon som occation given by the Munstermen hee prepared a huge army and went to Mounster, and there in one day burnt all the countreys therein, which was in the 11th year of his reign.

862.—Hugh m^cNeale, king of Ireland, did put out the eyes of Lorcan m^cCahill, king of Meath. Awley prince of the Danes killed Connor m^cDonnogh king of half Meath. Owen Britt,[3] B. of Kildare, scribe, anchorite, and a venerable worthy old man of the age well nigh of 116 years, died. Kearmott m^cCahassy, cheefe of Corckbaskyn, was put to Death by the Danes.

863.—There was an eclipse of the sun and moone in January this year. Keallagh m^cAilealla abbot of Kildare and Hugh, died in Pictland. The Welshmen were banished by the Saxons from out theire one contry this yeare. Machenie,[4] Bushop of Leighlynn, died.

864.—Awley and Hushe, the 2 princes of the Danes with all their forces went to Pictland and there spoyled the contry and brought from thence hostages in sign of subjection A.D. 871. King Hugh assaulted a fort the Danes had in Orear Anoghlae between Tire Owen and Dalnarie,[5] and from thence tooke all theire Jewels, cattle, and goodes, together with a great number of their captives, and also made a great slaughter upon them to the number of 240 of theire heades were taken.

---

[1] *Driwymkoylinn.* — Drumiskin, near Castlebellingham, Co. Louth.

[2] *Primate.*—From 852 to 874. So Ware, *Bishops*, p. 45.

[3] *O. Britt.*—He seems to have occupied the See from 840 to 862.

Ibid., p 383.

[4] *Machenie.*—It is not known how long he was Bishop.

[5] *Dalnarie.*—This tribe inhabited south Antrim and a great part of Down.

865.—Moyledwin mᶜHugh Prince of Aileagh died among the clergie after that he had entered religion, of a long and grievous disease. Rovartagh of ffynglas, B. and Scribe, and Conell of Killskry,[1] B. died. Cosgrach of Tehille, scribe and anchorite, Cormack o'Liahan, B. and anchorite, and Egechar, abbot of Coynrey and Lyneally, died. Husey, third prince of the Danes, was murthered by his owen bretheren. There was a battle fought at York in England between the Saxons and Danes, where Allie king of the north Saxons was slaine. Donawley[2] at Clondalkan was burnt and destroyed, Goyheynie o'More and Moylekearan mᶜRonane took with them 100 heads of the cheefest Danes dwelling there.

866.—Ceallagh mᶜComaski, abbot of Fower, a sage and witty young man, died. Cormac, abbot of Clonvickenos died. Daniel abbot of Gleandalogha and Keyman mᶜDalye, abbot of Dowleeke, died. King Hugh o'Connor mᶜTeige King of Connaught, gave a great battle to the o'Neales of Moybrey, Leinstermen, and Danes, where Flann mᶜConying prince of all Moybrey, and Dermott mᶜEbergell, prince of Loghggwar with many of the Danes were slaine.

867.—Moylekieran mᶜRonan, a hardy Champion of the west of Ireland, & a great destroyer and resister of the Danes, was killed. Awley burnt Ardmach and therein burnt 1000 persons and tooke captives with a great booty. Dubtactus alias Duffagh mᶜMoyletoylye, the most learned Doctor and Latinizer of all Europe died.

868.—Swarleagh, B., anchorite, and abbot of Clonard, a famous and learned doctor of divinity died. King Hugh distroyed and wasted all Leinster from Dublin to Gowrann. Dalagh mᶜMortaugh (of whom Sile Daly[3]) prince of Tire Connell was killed by some of his owen Race. Dermot mᶜDermott killed one before the King's gate in Armagh. Geran mᶜDichosta, abbot of Sayer, Dermott,

---

[1] *Killskry.*—Kilskeer, six miles south-west of Kells, Co. Meath.

[2] *Donawley.*—A little to the east of Clondalkin. A small Anglo-Norman castle stands on the site.

[3] *S. Daly*—Dalach was eighth in descent from Conall Gulban. By this name the O'Donnells were designated. See the *Life of Hugh Roe O'Donnell*, xii.

abbott of ffearnes, Domdahoile, abbot of Leyhmore Mochoeuoy in Clonvey in Connaught, and Moyledor, anchorite and abbot of Dawinis, died. Moyleseaghlin mᶜNeale, king of half Moybrey, was treacherously killed by a Dane called Uwlfie.

869.—Donell mᶜMoregan, K. of Leinster, died. Cahallann mᶜCarbry prince of Affalie died. Scannall,[1] B. of Kildare, died.

870.—Tuylelaidh, abbesse of Kildare, died the 4th of the Ides of January, the 10th of the Moone. There was a child born at Crewlasragh this yeare, who was heard to call upon God by distinct wordes saying good God in Irish, being but of the age of two months. Moriegh mᶜBroym K. of Leinster and abbot of Kildare, died. Fiaghna, king of Ulster, was killed by some of his owen familie. Kildare was preyed and spoyled by the Danes, and from thence took Swynie mᶜDuff davorean, the old abbot with 280 of his clergie and familie captives with them.

871.—Moylemorey a learned poett and the best historiographer of Ireland died. Aidann mᶜReaghtay abbott of Roscere died. Saint Moylerrwayn abbot of Dysart Dermot, Killeaghie, and Tihellie, died. He prophesied many things. The Connaughtmen committed a great slaughter upon the Danes of Lymbrick. Colga mᶜConnagann abbot of Kynnetty, the best and elegantest Poet in the kingdome, and their cheefest chronicler, died.

872.—Moylecova abbot of Ardmach, Cowchongalt, abbot of Clonard, and Donnogh mᶜDuffdavoreann, king of Cashell, died.

888.—The Danes of Dublin gave a great overthrow to Flann mᶜMoyleseaghlyn where Hugh mᶜConnor, K. of Connaught, Lergus mᶜCronenn B. of Kildare, Donnogh mᶜMoyledwyn, abbott of Kyllealga, and many other noble men were unfortunately slain. Juffrie mᶜIwer, Prince of the Normans, was unhappiliy murthered by his owen brother.

---

[1] *Scannall.*—He was bishop from 880 to 884. There is a saint of this name in the *Mart. of Donegal*, whose feast is on June 27th.

897.—Flann m‘Moyleseaghlyn (of the o'Melaghlins of Meath) succeeded king and raigned 33 years. Hee had all the pledges and hostages of Ireland, which hee did lett goe at his pleasure, & tooke again by force. Lann, daughter of Dongalie, was then king of Osseryes mothers name, and Kennydy m‘Goyhinn lord of the contry of Lease. This same Kennedy broke dowen Donn Awley beside Dublyn (Awley himself being the cheefest Dane in Ireland and then dwelling within that town) now it is called Clondalkan; hee killed many of his men and chased himselfe to the citty of Dublin. There was a great overthrow given to the Munstermen at Beallaghmowna,¹ (by those of Leih Conn and Leinstermen Anno 900, where Cormack m‘Cuilleanann king of Mounster, and arch-bishop of Cashell was pittifully slaine by the hands of a cowheard. Fohortagh m‘Swyny prince of Kerry and Cork, Ceallagh m‘Kervill prince of Ossery, Ailleall m‘Owen, prince of Corck, Mullmory prince of Rathlim, and Mullmory, prince of Kierry Lwachra,² were therein slaine. Flann m‘Moyleseaghlinn, king of Taragh, Cearvell m‘Moregan king of Leinster, and Cahall m‘Connor, king of Connaught, were victors.

901.—Cervell m‘Moregan, king of Leinster, and Cahall m‘Connor were deceitfully killed. It is thought that he was so killed by Murtagh O'Neale Anno Dni 909 by Danes. O'Leihlovar prince of Dalnarie died. Rwadan B. of Lusk died. m‘Rwaragh king of Brittans, died. King Flann and Colman Conelleie this yeare founded the church in Clonvickenos called the church of the kings.

902.—King Flann accompanied with the princes of Ireland, his owen sonns, gaue a great battle to the Breniemen, wherein were slain Flann m‘Tyrnie, prince of the Brenie, with many other noblemen of his side. Wallaghan m‘Cahall prince of Affalie was killed. A strange thing fell out this year, which was two sunns had their courses

---

¹ *B. Mowna.*—Three miles N. of Carlow. A detailed account of the battle will be found in Keating's *H. of Ireland*, p. 441.

² *K. Lwachra.* — The district about Castleisland.

together through out the space of one day which was in the pride¹ of the Nones of May.

903.—Fohartagh mᶜKelly prince of o'MacWais, died. Dowlen mᶜCarbry, king of Leinster, died. Donnell sonn of king Hugh prince of Aileagh, died.

904.—Cearnachann mᶜDowlegen comitted great outrages in Armach, took one of the house captive to the poole beside Armach called Loch Kirre, there killed the captive, soon after Neale mᶜHugh (surnamed Neale Glunduff) took the said Kearnachan and drowned him in the same logh for abuseing the town dedicated to St. Patrick. Edulfe King of the north Saxons died. King Flann died at Kinneigh of the familie of Cloone on Sunday the 8th of the Calends of June Anno Dni 912. Some say he raigned 36 years, others say 33 onely.

905.—Neale mᶜHugh gave a battle to the Connaughtmen, where Moylecloiche mᶜConnor with a great many Connaughtmen were slain. Moilmarie, daughter of king Kenneth mᶜAlpin, king of Scotland, died. Neale Glunduffe was king three years and was married to the lady Gormphley, daughter to king Flann, who was a very faire, vertuous, and learned damozell, was first married to Cormack mᶜo'Cuillennann king of Mounster, secondly to king Neale, by whome she had issue a sonn called prince Donell who was drowned, upon whose death she made many pittifull and learned dittyes in Irish, and lastly shee was married to Kervell mᶜMoregan king of Leinster, after all which royall marriages she begged from doore to doore, forsaken of all her friends and allies, and glad to be relieved by her inferiours.

910.—Flathvertagh raigned king of Cashell. There came new supplyes of Danes this year and landed at Waterford. Enos mᶜFlaynn mᶜMoyleseaghlim prince of Ireland died an immature death. Donell mᶜHugh prince of Aileagh died. Corck, Lismore, and Achaboe were spoiled preyed and ransacked by the Danes. Cobfath daughter of Duffe Dowen, abbesse of Kildaré, died. Moylebarryn priest of Clonvickenos died. Anoroit mᶜRwaragh king of Brittons died.

---

¹ *Pride.*—*i. e.* pridie, the day before.

917.—The faire¹ of Tailten was renewed by king Neale. King Neale accompanied with all the forces of Ireland, Meath, and Moybrey, went to Mounster where he lost diuers of his armye, amongue whome Doncwan mᶜFlannagan prince of the land of Teaffa, was accompted. Dublin was taken by the Danes, in despight of the king and all his forces. Moreann, daughter of Swart, abbesse of Kildare, died on Monday the 6ᵗʰ of the Calends of May. Adalvleih Queen of the Saxons died. Eihinge, daughter of king Hugh mᶜNeale Queen of Moybrey, & More daughter of Kervell mᶜDongaille died penitently. She was Queen of Leinster. Hugh mᶜFlinn o'Melaghlyn, had his eyes put out by his owne brother, Donnogh m'Flynn.

915.—This yeare the great battle² of Dublin was fought by king Neale Glunduff³ accompained with all his forces of the one side, and Himer and Sitrick with all theire Danes of the other side, where king Neale himself, prince Connor o'Melaghlyn, Hugh mᶜEoghagan king of Ulster, Moylemihil mᶜFlannagan prince of Moybrey, Moylecriny o'Donsynay prince of Uriell, Moylecrivie mᶜToylegen prince of Torlann, Ceallagh mᶜFogorty, prince of the South of Brey, Heremon mᶜKinnedy prince of the race of Manic mᶜNeale, with many other great captives were slaine.

916.—Donnogh mᶜFflyn of the o'Melaghlin's of Meath began his raigne this year Anno Domini 916 and reigned twenty five years. This king gave a battle to the Danes where there was such a slaughter committed on them that the one halfe of the Danish army was not left alive, there was never such a massacre of them before in Ireland, in which great conflict Moriertagh mᶜTiernie one of the kings nobles

---

¹*Faire.*—In the *Annals of Ulster*, under the date 872, it is said that 'the fair of T. was not celebrated without just cause, a thing we have not heard to have occurred from ancient times.'

²*Battle.*—It took place at Kilmashog, near Rathfarnham. In the *Annals F.M.* the date of it is given October 15th. See Keating's *H. of Ireland*, p. 453. A large cromlech marks the grave of some of the chieftains who fell in this battle. *Wars of the Gaedhil*, &c., xci.

³*Glunduff.*—i.e. of the black knee.

The Annals of Clonmacnoise. 147

was cruelly wounded and thereof died. Kelles was altogether ransacked and spoyled by the Danes and raced down the church thereof. Finchar abbot of Dowleeke, and Scanall m⁰Gorman sage, abbot and scribe of Rossecre, Died. Cormack m⁰Cuilleannann[1] bushop of Lesmore and king of the Desies was killed by his owen familie. St. Queran[2] abbot of Dawinis died. This is not St. Queran of Clone.

917.—King Donnogh killed his owen brother Donell, who was elected to be his successor in the kingdom. Moonagh m⁰Sheil abbot of Beanchor, the best scribe of all Ireland, died. There reigned a great plague in Ireland this yeare. Godfrey o'Himar[3] was elected by the Danes of Dublin to be theire king, whoe imediately spoiled and ransacked Armach.

918.—Teig m⁰Faylan king of the West of Leinster died. flannagan o'Riagan abbot of Killdare, and prince of Leinster died. Moylepoyle m⁰Ailleall Bishopp, best scribe and anchorite of all Leihkoyn, died. King Donnogh went with an army to Connaught where in the wilderness of Athlone hee lost divers of his army and Kenny m⁰Connor, king of Affallie. Indreaghtagh m⁰Connor, prince of Connaught died. The Danes of Limbrick spoiled and ransacked Clonvickenos and from thence they went on Logh Rie and preyed all the Ilands thereof. Fingonie o'Molloy king of Fearkeall, died.

919.—Ligach, daughter of king Flann m⁰Moyleseaghlyn, queen of Moyvrey died, and was buried in Clonvickenose. Dowlitter priest of Ardmach was killed by the Danes. Dedimus o'Foirvhen tanaised abbott[4] of Clonvickenos died.

920.—Two hundred of the Danes were drowned in Logh Rowrie.[5] The Danes made residence on Loghrie by whom Eghtigern m⁰fflancha prince of Brawnie was killed. Lorckan m⁰Donnough, prince of Moybrey, died. Cahall m⁰Connor and

---

[1] *C. m⁰Cuilleannann.*—A detailed account of his reign will be found in Keating's *H. of Ireland,* p. 439.
[2] *St. Queran.* — The *Mart. of Donegal* makes no mention of him.
[3] *G. o'Himar.*—He was slain by his brother Godfrey during an excursion into Gaul. See Haliday's *Scand. H. of Dublin,* p 46.
[4] *Tanaised a.*—i. e. appointed in the abbot's lifetime to succeed him.
[5] *L. Rowrie.*—The bay of Dundrum, Co. Down.

Edward king of Saxons died. Donnell m^cCahall prince of Connaught was killed by his own brother. ffoylan m^cMurtagh or Morey, K. of Leinster was taken by the Danes, and lead captive together with his sonns.

921.—Colman m^cAillealla abbot of Clonvickenos and Clonard, a sage doctor, died in his old age. Donsovarke was preyed by the Danes of Loghewan,[1] Kildare by the Danes of Waterford and againe by the Danes of Dublin the the same year. Mortaugh son of king Neale Glunduff, made a great slaughter of the Danes where Aludon son of Godfrey, Awfer, and Harold together with 800 Danes were killed. Downacha m^cLagerye, prince of Farkeall, died. Moylseaghlin m^cMoylronie, arch prince of Taragh died.

922.—Moylbrigitt m^cTornayn[2] or substitude Cowarb of St. Patrick and of St. Columbkill and chiefe head of the Devout of Ireland died. Sittrick o'Himer,[3] prince of the new & old Danes, died. The Danes of Dulbin departed from Ireland. The faire of Tailten was held by king Donnogh, & Mortaugh m^cNeale. MyAuthor sayeth of Mortaugh that he was Membrüm Iniquüm Mobediens Capíti iníquo. Cyndealvan m^cMoylcron prince of the race of K. Lagerius, died, of whome the sept of Moyntyr Keyndelan. Maceilgi with the sons of Sittrick tooke Dublyn on Godfrey. Colen m^cCeally prince of Ossorie, Died. Tormair[4] m^cAlchi king of Denmarck (is reported to goe to hell with his pains) as he deserved.

923.—Bohine abbot of Byrre died. Morgeall daughter of King Flann mac Moyleseaghlinn died & old & rich woman. Kildare was ransacked by the sonn of Godfrey of Waterford, and from thence brought many captives.

924.—Twahall m^cOenagann bushopp of Dowleeke and Lusk, sergeant[5] of St. Patrick, died. Cayneagh daughter of

---

[1] *L. Cwan.*—Strangford Lough.

[2] *M. McTornayn.*—He occupied the See of Armagh from 885 to 927. See Ware's *Bishops*, p. 46.

[3] *S. o'Himer.*— In the *Annals F. M.* he is called lord of the Dublighoill and Finnghoill. n. 617.

[4] *Tormair.*—Or Tomar. See his descent in *Wars of the Gaedhil*, &c., p. 266. He plundered and burnt Clonmacnoise. *Annals F.M.*, ii. 609.

[5] *Sergeant.*—The word is *maor*, which is usually translated steward, i.e. manager of the temporals.

Connannann, queen of Ireland and wife of king Donnogh o'Melaghlynn died penitently. Dermott mac Kervall king of Ossery died. Inreaghtagh mᶜCahallaine prince of Lecale died. Donogh mᶜBrenan, priest of Kildare, died. Virgill abbot of Tyrdaglass, Keyly mᶜScannall cowarb of Beanchor, and Cowgall died happilye in Pilgrimage.

925.—The Connaughtmen committed a great slaughter on the Danes of Logheirusean.[1] The Danes of Lymbrick resided at Moyreyne.[2] Forolve prince of the Danes arrived at Loghneaagh. Nwa, bushop of Glandalogcha, and Moylekevyn abbot of Tymochwa,[3] died.

926.—The Danes of Lymbrick resided on Loghrie. Onchowe priest of Kildare died. Godfrey went to Ossery to bannish Himar from Moyerayney. Crommoyle[4] B. of Kildare, Ceanfoyle mᶜLorcan, cowarb of Cloneois & Clochor, and bran mᶜColman abbot of Rossecrea, died.

927.—Fortulfe Asalftand was killed by these of Dalnarye & by prince Moriertagh mᶜNeale. Swyne abbott of Lynnlere, Ferdownagh mᶜfflanagan abbot of Clonard, Twagarta abbott of Keyndea[5] and Moyngall mᶜBeacan abbot of Dromclewe, Died a good and happy death. Enos mᶜAngussa cheefe poet of Ireland died. Dowlih mᶜSealvay abbott of Tymoling,[6] & Lector of Gleandalogha, died.

928 —Seachnassagh, priest of Dorowe, Died. Adalstan king of Saxons preyed & spoyled the kingdom of Scotland to Edenburrogh, & yett the Scottishmen compelled him to return without any great victory. Adulf mᶜEtulfe king of North Saxons died. The Danes of Loghernie preyed and spoyled all Ireland, both temporall and spirituall land without respight of person, age, or sex, untill they came to Logh-

---

[1] *Logheirusean*. — L. Oirbsen, now L. Corrib, in Co. Galway.

[2] *Moyreyne*.—A plain in Ossory, the limits of which are not known.

[3] *Tymochwa*.—Now Timahoe, 7 miles north - east of Abbeyleix, Queen's Co

[4] *Crommoyle*.—He occupied this

See from 920 to 929.

[5] *Keyndea*.—Perhaps Kinnetty.

[6] *Tymoling*—i. e. St. Moling's house, now St. Mullin's on the Barrow, 7 miles north of New Ross. There are remains of several ancient buildings here. See the *Journal of the R. S. A. I.* for 1892, p. 377

gawney.¹ M°Godfrey preyed Armach on St Martyns eve from Logh Cwan. Mathew m°Hugh with the forces of the five provinces, and Awley m°Godfrey with the Danes of Ireland, preyed spoyled and made havock of all places, untill they came to Slieve Beacha,² where they were mett by prince Moriertagh m°Neale who in a conflict slewe 1200 of them, besides the captives hee tooke. The Barde of Boyne³ (cheefe of all Ireland for poetry) was killed by O'Neachagh of Ulster.

929.—The Danes of Lymbrick preyed & spoyled all Connought to Moylerge⁴ of the North and to Bowgna⁵ of the East. Godfrey, king of Danes, died a filthy & ill-favoured Death.

930.—Cormack m°Mooney abbot of Achyboe, m°Leanna abbot of Imleagh-Iver, and Leihmore, were slain by these of Eoganaght.⁶ Cynay m°Corbry king of o'Keansealie, was killed by night, by the Danes of Waxford. The 2 abbotts and worthy successors of St. Patrick in Ardmach, Joseph, and Moylepatrick, the 2 sages of Ireland, Bushops,⁷ anchorites and scribes, died. Clonvickenose was preyed by the Danes of Dublin and also it was sacrilegiously Robbed, afterwardes by Ceallaghan, king of Cashell, and his Monstermen. The Danes of Logherney arrived at Loghric on Christmas night, Awley Keanchyreagh, and there remained seven months preying and spoiling the borders of Connaught called Moyenoye. King Donnough m°Flynn burnt all Dublin.

931.—The Danes of Loghric, arrived at Dublin. Awley with all the Danes of Dublin and north part of Ireland

---

¹ *Loghgawney.*—Now L. Gawna in the barony of Granard, Co. Longford

² *S. Beacha.*—On the boundary of Fermanagh and Monaghan.

³ *Barde of Boyne.*—The Annals F M., too, give him this title, but do not mention his name.

⁴ *Moylerge.*—Moylurg, now called the Plains of Boyle.

⁵ *Bowgna.*—A mountainous district included in the barony of north Ballintobber, Co. Roscommon.

⁶ *Eoganaght.*—i e the descendants of Eogan, eldest son of Oiholl Olum, the M'Carthys, the O'Sullivans, &c. The residence of the king was Cashel.

⁷ *Bushops.*—Joseph, who occupied the See of Armagh from 927 to 936, and Maelpatrick, who held it for one year only. See Ware's *Bishops*, p. 48.

departed and went over seas. The Danes that departed from Dublin arrived in England, & by the help of the Danes of that kingdom, they gave battle to the Saxons on the plaines of othlyn, where there was a great slaughter of Normans and Danes, among which these ensueing captaines were slaine, vizt. Sithfrey and Oísle ye 2 sones of Sithrick, Galey, Awley ffroit, and Moylemorrey the sonn of Cosse Warce, Moyle Isa, Gebeachan king of the Islands, Ceallagh prince of Scottland with 30000 together with 800 captives about Awley m^{c}Godfrey, and abbot of Arick m^{c}Brith, Iloa Deck, Imar, the king of Denmarks owen son with 4000 souldiers in his guard were all slaine. Conyng m^{c}Nealle Glunduffe Died.

932.—Connor m^{c}Moylekeyne king of Affalie and his two sonns were killed by Lorcan m^{c}Foylan. Killkolyn[1] was preyed by the Danes, and led 1000 captives from thence.

933.—Adulston king of England Dyed. The sunn for one day apeared like blood untill noone the next day. Aileagh was taken by the Danes on Mourtaugh m^{c}Neale and himselfe taken therein untill he made a good escape from them as it was God's will. Ceallachan of Cashell with his Mounstermen and Danes harryed and spoyled all Meath to Clonard. Congalagh m^{c}Moylemihie gave an overthrow to that part of Leinstermen called Gallenges,[2] where 80 persons were slaine. King Donnogh o'Melaghlyn and Mourtaugh m^{c}Neale went over all Munster and Leinster and took their hostages. Harald o'Hymer king of the Danes of Lymbrick was killed in Connaught at Ratheyney.[3] Neale m^{c}Ferall prince of Aileagh was killed by Mortaugh m^{c}Neale. fflann, daughter of king Donnogh, queen of Aileagh, died. Moylemartan o'Skellan Lector of Leithlynn,[4] died. Ceallaghan of Cashell made a great slaughter on those of Ossorie. Awley Cwaran

---

[1] *Killkolyn.*—*i.e.* Kilcullen. See p. 126, *antea.*

[2] *Gallenges.*—There were several districts of Leinster so called. In the *Annals of Ulster* the names of Gailenga mor and Gailenga beg are given, *i.e.* Morgallion in Meath, and the district immediately north of Dublin.

[3] *Ratheyney.*—Not identified.

[4] *Leithlynn.*—Now Old Leighlin, Co. Carlow.

came to Yorck, and Blackare mᶜGodfrey arrived in Dublin to govern the Danes.

934.—There was such Drouth and Ise over loghs & the waters of Ireland this yeare that the Danes went to Inis Moghty[1] upon Ice & spoyled and ransacked the same. Mortaugh mᶜNeale with the forces of the North went to Ossery and Desies and preyed them. Awley mᶜGodfrey king of Danes died. Ceallaghan[2] of Cashell and his Mounstermen gave an overthrow to the Desies, and slew of them 2000. They of Affalie, and Kynaleagh killed 1200 Danes. Orlath daughter of Kennedy mᶜLorcan was queen of Ireland this time. Mortaugh mᶜNeale with the kings forces went to Cashell and there took Ceallaghan (that unruly kinge of Mounster that partaked with Danes) prisoner, and lead him and all the hostages of Mounster and the other provinces of Ireland with him, & Delivered them all into the hands of king Donnogh mᶜMelaghlin.

935.—Donnogh B. of Clonvickenose died. ffoylan mᶜMoreay, king of Leinster died of a bruse he receaved of a fall. Idvall mᶜAnoroit prince of Brittons, was killed by the Saxons. The 2 sons of Lorcan mᶜDonnogh were killed by Congalach mᶜMoylemihi. Blacaire mᶜGodfry with the Danes of Dublin robed and spoiled Clonvicknose. Donlaith daughter of Moylemihie and sister of king Congalagh, died. Donleithglasse[3] was spoiled by the sonn of Randalfe the Dane, whoe within a weeke after was killed by Mathew, kinge of Ulster. Liahmore in Connaght this yeare the one halfe thereof next the water, was granted to Clonvickenois.

936.—Lambert B. of Killmayne[4] died, they of Leihcale made a great slaughter of the Danes of Logh Cwann. Mortaugh mᶜNeale upon Shrove-tide sonday at Athfirdia[5] was

---

[1] *I. Moghty.*—Now Inishmot, in the barony of Slane, Co. Meath. There are remains of the old church of St. Mochta here.

[2] *Ceallaghan.*—He was ancestor of the M‘Carthys, O'Callaghans, &c. His death is set down in the Annals F.M. under the date 952

[3] *Donleithglasse.* — Now Downpatrick.

[4] *Killmayne.*—Now a barony in south Mayo.

[5] *Athfirdia.*—Now Ardee in Co. Louth. On the origin of the name see O'Curry's *MS. Materials*, p.39, and Joyce's *Names of Places*, i. 118.

killed in Battle by the Danes of Dublin. This Mortaugh was son of king Neale Glunduffe, king of Ireland, and was surnamed Moriertagh na Gochall Croickeann, which is as much to say in English as Murtaugh of the lether Coates,[1] which name was given him upon this occasion. Gormphley (of whome mention is made before) Queen of Ireland and wife to Neale Glunduffe after that king Neale was slain in the battle of Dublin by Danes and Leinster men, the king of Leinster . . . . conveighed to his house of Naase there to be kept as a monument to keep tablemen in. After the death of king Neale, queen Gormpley married tne king of Leinster, whose name was Kearvall mᶜMoregan, and upon a time as the king Leinster and queen Gormpley were playing of tables in Naas aforesaid . . . .
. . . .
. . . .

Whereupon she begott somewhat interiorly grieved, concealed her griefe for a time, and sent privately to Mortaugh mᶜNeale, who came with a company of Lusty and choice Ulstermen, clad themselves with cowhides, and lay in the king of Lynsters parcke at Naas neare his pallace in their hides like cowes, to the end that the king upon sight of them, would take them for cowes, the king after he had gotten out of his bedd looked out of the windowe of his pallace, and seeing soe many cowes lye couchant in his park, as Mortagh brought men out Ulster or the North to be Revenged, and thinking they had layne there all night, hee fell in a rage, and went himself among the cowes, and was miserably killed. Mortaugh and his Ulstermen carried his bones with them to the north, and there artificially caused to be made a payer of tables of the said kings bones, which for a very long time after was kept as a monument in the king of Ulsters house, and of

---

[1] *M. of the lether Coates.*—An account of his excursion to the north will be found in *The Circuit* *of Ireland*, edited by O'Donovan for the Irish Archæological Society in 1841.

these cowhides Mortaugh was ever after during his life named, Mortaugh of the Leathercoates.¹

937.—Flann m'fflynn Prince of Leinster died. Ceallaghan of Cashell fought Kennedy m°Lorcan, (this is Bryan Borowes father) in the plains of Moydwyne,² where there was a great many of Kennedyes side slaine. Iwayre m°Moylegann, Priest of Clonvickenois, Died. Dublin was ransackt and spoyled by Congalagh m°Moylemihie, these of Moybrey and Broen m°Moylemorriey with his Leinstermen, and in burning Dublin they killed forty hundred Danes, that made resistance to keepe the forte, and took away all their jeweles, goods, and hangings. Downagh, king of Ireland, died. The king of the Danes was killed by the Saxons at Yorke. Congallagh m°Moylemihie Raigned 20 years. Enos m°Donnogh king of Meath died. Blacairey was banished from Dublin and Awley succeeded him to the government. o'Cannann³ prince of Tireconnell went to Moybrey, and there lost some of his forces. There were two lightning pillars seene in the firmament this yeare for the space of a senight before Allhollantide, which shined soe bright, that they gaue light to this whole climate. King Congallagh took hostages of all Connaught this year. Areaghtagh m'Anfie, cheefe of Calric,⁴ was killed.

941.—Awargin m'Kynaye king of Affalie, Died. Ettymon, king of the Saxons, was killed by his own familie.

942 —There was contention seen to be between the foule of the seas and the foule of the land at Clonvickenois, where there was a great slaughter of Crowes of one side.

943.—Blacaire m'Imer, king of the Normans, was killed by king Congallagh and a thousand Danes, and upwards with him were slaine alsoe. Ainmere o'Kahallaine, abbott of Clonvickenois and of Leackan⁵ in Meath, Died in his old age.

---

¹ *Leathercoates.*—On the origin of this name see *ibid.*, p. 14.

² *Moydwyne.*—Not identified.

³ *O'Cannann.*—These and the O'Muldorys were chiefs of Tirconnell, and were succeeded by the O'Donnells. See the Introduction to the *Life of Hugh Roe O'Donnell*, xix.

⁴ *Calric.*—Several districts were so called.

⁵ *Leackan.*—Low Leckin, in the barony of Corkaree, Co. Westmeath. It was founded by St. Cruimin,

Gormphly daughter of king Flann mᶜMoyleseaghlyn and Queen of Ireland Died of a long and grieveous wound which happened in this manner. Shee dreamed that she sawe king Neale Glunduffe, whereupon she gott up and sate in her bedd to behould him, whome hee for anger would forsake and leave the chamber, and as hee was departing in that angry motion (as shee thought) shee gave a snatch after him, thinking to have taken him by the mantle, to keep him with her, and fell upon one of the beddstickes of the bedd that it pearsed her brest, eaven to her very hart, which received no cure untill she Died thereof. Colman mᶜMoyle Patrick archDeane of Slane was slaine by the Danes. The Danes brought a great prey from Dromrahie,[1] and burnt the church thereof, and also killed 170 men therein.

944.—Flaithvertaugh, son of Mortaugh, mᶜNeale prince of Aileagh, was slain by Tireconell. Donnel mᶜFynn prince of Leinster, died.

945.—Donnogh mᶜDonell o'Melaghlin prince of Taragh was killed by his owen Brothers. Hoell mᶜCahall king of Wales, died. Scathyne, archdeane of Dorowe, died. The steeple of Slane was burnt by the Danes, which was full of worthy men, and relicks of Saints, with Keyneachar, Lector of Slane. The battle of Moynebrokan,[2] was fought this year betweene the Danes of the one side and king Congallagh and Irish men of the other side where Godfrey cheefe of the Danes was put to flight, and 6000 of his army slaine, and Rowrie o'Canan was alsoe slaine therein. Donogh mᶜDonnell king of halfe Meath died. Cormack o'Haielealla arch-Deane, of Killcollyn, Died. K. Congallagh preyed west Mounster and in pursuit of the prey hee killed the two sonns of Kennedy mᶜLorckan, named Eghtygerne and Donnaganis.

964.—Beag mᶜDonncwan, king of Teaffa, and Kennedy mᶜLorckan died. This Kennedy was cheefe of all Dalgaisse.[3]

---

about the middle of the 7th century; his festival was June 28th.

[1] *Dromrahie.*—Colgan says this is the diocese of Achonry, but he

does not determine its position further.

[2] *Moynebrokan.*—Not identified.

[3] *Dalgaisse.*—i.e. the descendants

Godfrey mᶜSittricke with the Danes of Dublin preyed and spoyled Kells, Downaghpatrick,¹ Ardbrackan, Tullean,² Disart Queran, and Killskryre with many other churches, and tooke from them about 3000 captives with many rich bootyes of gold, silver, and cloathes, which God soone after did revenge on them. Awley was king of Yorck for a year after. King Congallagh granted that freedome to Clonard that there should never after be cess or press or other charge thereupon.

947.—Connor mᶜDonell o'Mellaghlin, Constantine mᶜHugh, king of Scottland, and ffeardownagh o'Mooney abbot of Clonvickenos died. The pox (which the Irishmen called then Dolor Gentilium) ran over all Ireland this yeare.

948.—Malcolme mᶜDonell king of Scotland died. Dermot mᶜThorpa, abbot of Lismore, died. Clonvickenos was preyed by the Mounstermen and Danes. Eihne daughter of Ferall, Queene of Ireland and wife of king Congallagh, died.

949.—Ceallaghan king of Cashell, Reaghtaury, abbott of Killeachie and fflanagan mᶜAlchon cowarb of mᶜNissy³ and of Colman Eala, died. Neale Tolairy, lord of Machair Cwickny now called the barronie of Killkenny,⁴ Died. Karne Itolarge at the side of Loghrie took the name of this man. Sayer was preyed by Mounstermen.

950.—Enos mᶜConloingsie arch-Deane of Moyvile and Enos mᶜMoylebryde arch-Dean of Dowleeke died. Downagh mᶜEgertay (of the o'Kellyes of Brey) B of Clonvickenos died.

951.—King Congallagh king of Ireland was slain by the Leinstermen and Danes of Dublin, at the Liffieside together with divers of his nobles, as Hugh mᶜAichie, king of Teaffa, Mathew mᶜHugh mᶜMoylemihye the kings nephewe, and

---

of Cas, son of Olioll Olum, from whom Brian Boroimhe was 20th in descent.

¹ *Downaghpatrick.* — Midway between Navan and Kells.

² *Tullean* —Perhaps Tullavin in Co. Cavan.

³ *MᶜNissy.*—i e. Connor, which was founded by St Mac Nissi, a disciple of St. Patrick. His feast was December 3rd. See *Annals of Ulster*, 1. 473

⁴ *Killkenny.*—i.e Kilkenny West, in Co. Westmeath.

prince Cormack m⸲Cahallaine with divers others. Moylefohartie king of Munster died, and Moylecolumb o'Cananann prince of Tireconnell died. Donnell o'Neale succeeded king Congallagh and raigned 25 years. In his time there were two great fieldes fought, the one is called the battle of Killmoney,[1] the other the battle of Bealayleaghta,[2] where Mulmoye or Mulloye king of Munster was killed, and the Danes discomfitted by Bryen Borowe, after which battle Meath remayned wast and Desolate for the space of 5 yeares and without a king.

952.—Tandy m⸲Gwyer cowarb of Cowgall was killed by the Danes. Twahall m⸲Awgaire, king of Leinster, Died.

953.—Clonvickenois was preyed by Mounstermen. Dowdavorean m⸲Donell, king of Cashell, was killed by one of his owne people. Donnell m⸲Moylemoray king of Affalie died. Moonach m⸲Cormack abbot of Lismore, and Moonagh, Archdeane of Lothra, Died.

954.—King Donnell m⸲Mortaugh of the Lether coates went to Dalnarie and took hostages of Clanna Rowryes.

955.—There was a great Dearth of cattle this year, and many diseases genenrally raigned over all Ireland by reason of the great frost and snow, which procured the Intemperature of the ayre.

956.—Flathvertagh m⸲Connor prince of Aileagh made a great prey in Dalnarye, and ransackt Conrey[3] & was overtaken by the inhabitants of that country and killed by his 2 brothers Teige and Conn with many others. Iwulfe king of Scotland died. Enos o'Moyledorie prince of Tireconell was killed. Mowgroyn o'Molloy prince of Fearkeall died. Clonvickenois was preyed by those of Ossery.

957.—Godfrey m⸲Awley m⸲Godfrey a very fair and handsome man died. King Donnell brought shiping on Logh Innill. Dowhagh of Disert Kyeran a very merry and jocund

---

[1] *Killmoney.* — There are two places of this name, one in Meath, the other in Westmeath.

[2] *Bealayleaghta.* — Near Macroom, Co. Cork. But see *Annals F.M.*, ii. 705.

[3] *Conrey.* — Now Killcomeragh, near the hill of Usneagh.

fellow died. Donnogh mᶜCeallachan, king of Cashell was killed. fferall o'Roirck was king of Connought this time. Ferall gaue an ouerthrow to the Mounstermen, in a place between Clonvickenois and Clonfert, neare the river of Synann, called the field of Rattynie, where there were many slaine and immediately after fferall preyed and spoyled all the race of Dalgaisse.

958.—Kildare was preyed by the Danes of Dublin and tooke many captives, and were put to their Ransome.

970.—Inis Cahie[1] was taken by Bryan mᶜKennedy upon the Danes of Limbrick, that is to say Imer and his two sonnes, Awley and Dowgeann. Awley mᶜIllulfe king of Scotland was killed by Kynay mᶜColme. Noyman of Inis Cahie died. Moylerwanie god o'Melaghlyn prince of Ireland was treacherously slaine.

971.—The scrine of Adawnanus[2] was preyed and spoiled by Donnell o'Neale. Bryan mᶜKennedy and Moylemoye his brother fought a battle against one another where Moylemoye was discomfitted and slaine. The Danes of Dublyn gave the battle of Bithlynn[3] to the Leinstermen where Awgary mᶜTwahaile king of Leinster was killed, and Moreigh mᶜRyan prince of o'Keanseallye and Congallagh mᶜFlinn prince of Ley[4] and Riched with many others were alsoe slaine.

972.—Flann o'Moylemihie Lector of Clonvickenois died. Morean daughter of king Congalagh, abesse of Kildare died. Donnell Cloin, king of Leinster, was taken prisoner by the Danes of Dublin.

973.—Donnell o'Neale king of Ireland, after long pennance died in Ardmach and thereof was called Donell of Ardmach, because he resided at Armach a long time to doe pennance.

974.—Moyleseaghlyn mᶜDonell tooke upon him the kingdome and raigned 23 years. The first act hee did was

---

[1] *I. Cahie.*—Now Scattery Island, at the mouth of the Shannon.
[2] *Adawnanus.*—i.e. St. Adamnan, author of the *Life of St Columba.*
See Reeves' *Adamnan*, lxiii.
[3] *Bithlynn.* — Now Belan, near Athy.
[4] *Ley.*—Near Portarlington.

that hee challended the Danes to battle and gave them the battle of Taragh where the Danes were quite overthrone, and Randulphe m{c}Awley and Conawill m{c}Gillearrie with many other Danes were therein slaine. After which overthrow, king Moylseaghlin prepared together a great armye accompanied with Eachie m{c}Ardgar king of Ulster, went into the partes of Fingale[1] and there remayned three nights and three days (which was the place of greatest strength with the Danes then) untill he compelled the Danes and the rest of Ireland to yeeld him hostages, & afterwards proclaimed that as many of the Irish nation as lived in cervitude, and bondage with the Danes (which was at that time a very great number) should pressently pass over without Ransome and live freely in their own countryes, according to theire wonted manner, which was forthwith obeyed without contradiction, amongst which Prisoners Donell Kloen king of Leinster was forced to be sett at libertie and also procured from the Danes, that the o'Neales of the West shou'd have free libertyes from the river of Synan to the sea without Disturbance of Dane or other person whatesoeuer. Awley m{c}Sitricke king of the Danes of Dublin went a pilgrimage to the Island of Hugh in Scottland and there after pennance Died.

975.—St. Ancha[2] B. of Kildare Died an old and holy man.

976.—Dalgaisse was preyed altogether by king Moyleseachlin and hewed down the great tree of Moyeayre[3] in spight of them.

977.—King Moylseachlin & Glen Iarn[4] m{c}Awley gave a battle to Donell Kloen, king of Leinster, and to Iver of Waterford, where many of Donell Kloen's side were both drowned and killed, as Patrick m{c}Iver and many others. Gleandalogha was preyed by the Danes of Dublin. All

---

[1] *Fingale.*—The territory along the coast to the north of Dublin.

[2] *Ancha* —He occupied the See from 965 to 975.

[3] *Moyeayre* —Now Moyre, near Tulla, Co. Clare. The O'Briens were inaugurated under this tree. See Mr. T. J. Westropp's account of this place in *The Journal of R.S.A.* for 1891, p. 463, and *Annals F M*, ii. 715.

[4] *G. Iarn* —i.e. the iron-kneed.

Leinster to the sea was preyed and destroyed by king Moyleseaghlyn. Donell Kloen did putt out the eyes of Gillekeyvyn m‘Kenneye.

978.—Donell Kloen king of Leinster was killed by Hugh m‘Neghtigerne of the o'Kinsealyes. Hugh o'Dowdy,[1] king of the north of Connaught, Died. The three sons of Kervell m‘Lorckan preyed the Termynland of St. Kevyn and were killed themselves immediately the same day together by the miracles of St. Kevynn. Donell m‘Lorckan king of Leinster was killed by the o'Keansealyes.

979.—King Moylseachlin preyed and wasted all Connaught, destroyed theire Islands and fortes, and alsoe killed and made havock of theire cheeftaines and noblemen. Ferall m‘Lorckan prince of Kenaleagh was killed.

980.—More daughter of Donnog m‘Keally Queen of Ireland, Died. Moylekyeran o'Mayney was cruelly tortured and martyred to death by the Danes of Dublin, he was Cowarb of St. Columbe Kill.

981.—St. Ceallagh[2] the virgin died this yeare. This yeare began the morren of Cowes called in Ireland the Moylegarie (Maolgarb). There was such boysterous windes this yeare, that it fell dowen many turretts, and among the rest it fell down violently the steeple of Louth, and other steeples. St. Dunstan arch-Bushopp of England died. Donnogh o'Broyne cowarb of St. Keyeran of Clonvickenois, a holy and Devoute anchorite, died in pilgrimage in Ardmach.

982.—Gluniarn[3] king of the Danes was unhappilly killed by a base churell of his one called Colvan. Godfrey son of Harold king of Inis-gall was killed by the king of Dalriada or Readshankes. King Moyleseachlin gave the battle[4] of

---

[1] *H. o'Dowdie.*—See an account of this family in O'Donovan's edition of *The Tribes of Hy Fiachrach*, p. 343. They take their name from Dubhda, 12th in descent from Eochaidh Muighmheadhoin. Their territory was the district now included in the barony of Tireragh, Co. Sligo.

[2] *St. Ceallagh.*—See O'Hanlon's *Lives of the Irish Saints*, iv. 5.

[3] *Gluniarn.*—He and Maelseachlin, king of Ireland at that time, were born of the same mother. See Haliday's *Scandanavian K. of Dublin*, p 77.

[4] *Battle.*—This was probably the battle of Drum da Moighi mentioned

Dublin to the Danes, where an infinite number of them were slaine, and tooke the forte of Dublin where hee remayned three-score nights, that hee made the Danes that they drank noe other drink dureing the said space but the saltish water of the seas untill they were driuen at last to yeald to king Moyleseachlin his one desire dureing his raigne, which was an ounce of Gold out of every garden and craft in Dublin yearly at Christmas to the king, his heirs and successors for ever.

983.—Erard mᶜCoyssie[1] cheef poet of Moyleseachlin and all Ireland died in Clonvickenois very penitently. This man for his devotion to God and St Queran had his residence in Clonvickenois, to the end he might be near the church dayly to hear mass, and upon a night there appeared an Angle unto him that reprehended him for dwelling soe neere the place, and told him that the paces of his journey comeing and goeing to heare mass dayly would be measured by God, and accordingly yeelded him recompence for his paines, & from thence foorth mᶜCoyssie removed his house a good distance from Clonvickenois to a place among boggs to this day called the place of mᶜCossyes house, from which hee did use daily to repaire to Clonvickenois to heare mass as he was wardned before by the angle. Before mᶜCossye fell to these devotions king Moyleseaghlyn of his great bounty and favour to learning and learned men bestowed the revenewes of the Crown of Ireland for one yeare upon mᶜCossye, who enjoyed it accordingly, and at the yeares end when the king would have the said revenewes to himselfe mᶜCossye said that hee would never suffer the king from thenceforth to have any part of the royaltyes or profits, but would keep all to himselfe whether the king would or noe or lose his life in Defence thereof. Whereupon the king challenged mᶜCossye to fight on horseback, which mᶜCossye consented willingly to doe, though hee knew himself unable to resist the valourous and incomparrable hardy hand of king Moyleseachlin, whoe was computed to be

---

by Keating, *H. of Ireland*, p. 436. is given in O'Reilly's *Irish Writers*,
[1] *Mᶜ Coyssie*.—A list of his poems p. lxix

the best horseman generally in those partes of Europe, for king Moyleseachlins delight was to ride a horse that was never broken, handled, or riden untill the age of 7 years, which hee could soe exactly ride as any other man could ride an old tame and gentle horse. Notwithstanding all which m^cCossye was of such hope that the king of his favour of poetry and learning would never draw his blood, which did imbolden and incourage him to combat with the king, and being a horseback m^cCossye well provided with horse and armour and the king only with a good horse & a staffe without a head, fell eagerly to the encounter, m^cCossye desireous to kill the king, to the end he might enjoy the Revenewes without contradiction; the king coningly defended himself with nimble avoydings and turnings of his horse, feared to hurte m^cCossye unttill at last with his skillfulness and good horsemanship hee vanquished m^cCossye and enjoyed his kingdom and revenewes thereof ever after untill Bryan Borowe & his Mounstermen tooke the same from him. Hugh o'Moyledorye prince of Tire Connell Died. King Moyleseaghlyn gave a great ouerthrow called the ouerthrow of Fordroyne[1] where Daniell m^cLurckan prince of Muskery[2] & many others were slaine.

984.—Donnogh o'Konoly Prince of Taragh and next heire of the crown was willfully killed by those of Cloynn Colman, and Connor mack Kervell. The Island of Logh Kynne,[3] was by a great whirlwinde sonk on a sudaine, that there appeared but 30 feet thereof unsunkt.

985 —King Moyleseachlin with an army went into Connaught, and from thence brought many captives and rich boottyes, such as none of his predecessors neuer brought. During the time the king was occupied in Connaught Bryan Borowe with his Munstermen came to Meath and there wasted, & Destroyed all places untill they came to Logh Innill, where the kings house was, in soe much that they left not cow,

---

[1] *Fordroyne.*—Not identified.
[2] *Muskery.*—M. Tire, now the baronies of Upper and Lower Ormond, Co Tipperary.
[3] *Logh Kynne.*— Now Lough Hackett, in the barony of Clare, Co. Galway. It is called L Kiney, p. 21, *antea*.

The Annals of Clonmacnoise. 163

beast, or man that they could meet withall untaken, Ravished and taken away.¹

986.—Twahall m^cMoyle Rowa Cowarb of St. ffinian and Mocolmocke,² a man sage and holy, died. Donnogh o'Hughtann lector of Kelles, died. There was great mortallity in St. Querans sea of Clonvickenois. Connor m^cKeruell o'Melaghlin died. Moyleronye o'Kyergie prince of Carbry now called Berminghams Contry,³ died. The two o'Canans were slaine, that is to say, the 2 sonnes of Gillicholme, Donnell & Flathverthagh.

987.—Moylemorie m^cScanlan,⁴ Bishop of Ardmach, died.

988.—King Moyleseachlin burnt and spoyled all the hether Mounster, and overthrew⁵ Bryan Borowe and Munstermen in the field. Hymer raigned in Dublin after Awley. Randolphe was killed by the Leinstermen, Hymer was put to flight, and Gittrick⁶ was king of Dublin in his place. Cynath sonn of Malcolme, king of Scotland, died. Downagh Patrick was preyed by the Danes of Dublin and by Mortagh o'Konolley, but God revenged the same on Murtaugh before the end of the same month by looseing his life. King Moyleseachlin tooke from the Danes of Dublin the sword of Charles with many other Jeweles.

989.—They of Uriell preyed Ardmach, and tooke from thence 2000 cowes, Ardmach was also burnt, both Church houses and steeple, that there was not neuer such a poore spectacle seen in Ireland.

990.—The Scottish men in battle slew theire own king Constantine and many others. Malcolme m^cDonnell king of the North Wales died. Duffigh m^cTagaine priest of Clonvickenoise Died. Rory m^cNeale o'Kannanann prince of Tire Connell died.

---

¹ *Taken away.* — The *Annals F.M.* give a different account of this excursion and say 'he did not take a cow or person,' but went away from thence by secret flight.

² *Mocolmocke.* — There are five saints of this name in the *Mart. of Donegal.*

³ *B.'s Contry.*—The barony of Carbury, in the north-east of Co. Kildare.

⁴ *McScanlan.*—He is mentioned by M'Geoghegan, but not by Ware.

⁵ *Overthrew.*—See O'Donovan's note to *Annals F.M.*, ad ann. 994.

⁶ *Gittrick.*—Or Sittrick.

991.—King Moyleseachlin and Bryan Borowe joyned together, and took hostages of all the Danes of Ireland, and went alsoe to Connaught together, and tooke their hostages and jeweles such as they made choyce of. Duffe dalehe cowarb of St. Patrick and St. Columbkill in the 73 year of his age died, a good devoute sage and holy man. Derie Kalgie was preyed and robbed by the Danes. Gillapatrick mᶜDonnogh king of Ossery, died. King Moyleseachlin preyed and spoyled Moynoye in Connaught.

992.—Donnogh mᶜDonnell, king of Leinster was taken by Sittrick mᶜAwley and held captive. King Moyleseachlin preyed all Leinster. Kildare was destroyed and preyed by the Danes of Dublin. King Moyleseachlin, and Bryan Borowe with a great army went to Gleanmannye[1] where they were encountered by the Danes of Dublin, in which encounter the cheefest Danes of Dublin with theire captaine Herald mᶜAwley and Cwillen mᶜEtigen with many others of theire principalls were slaine,[2] after which slaughter king Moyleseachlin and Brian entred into Dublin and fort thereof and there remained for the space of a senight, and at their departure tooke all the Gold, silver, hanging, and other pretious things that were there with them, burnt the town and broke down the fort, and bannished Sittrick mᶜAwley king of the Danes of Dublin from thence.

993.—Bryan Borowe went with great power to the north, rested a night at Tailten, and from thence went to Ardmach, where hee remayned a senight and offered Tenn pound in gold at the alter at Ardmach, and gott noe hostages of the Ulstermen. O'Donnell prince of Durlesse[3] was killed willfully by Hugh O'Neale prince of Tireone. Hymar of Waterford died. The Danes returned to Dublin againe and yeelded hostages to Bryan Borowe. Flathvertagh o'Kananann, prince of Tire Connell, was killed by some of his own familie.

---

[1] *Gleanmannye*—Near Dunlavin, Co. Wicklow. The date in the *Annals F.M* is 998.

[2] *Slaine* — The *Wars of the Gaedhil* says 17,000 of the best of the foreigners of Ireland were slain in this battle, p. 111.

[3] *Durlesse*.—This was the residence of O'Lynn, chief of Hy Tuirtre, in Antrim. Its site is not known.

Ulgarg o'Kyerga did put out yᵉ eyes of his brother Hugh o'Kyerga. Bryan Borowe with a great army accompanied with the Danes of Dublin went towards Taragh, and sent a troope of Danish horse before them who were met by king Moyleseachlin, and slew them all for the most part at Moybrey and from thence Bryan went to Ffearty Nevie¹ in Moybrey, and after some residence there, returned to his contry of Mounster, without committing any outrage, or contending with any.

994.—They of the borders of Mounster came to the nether part of Meath, and there made a great preye and were overtaken by Enos mᶜCarrhie Calman, who tooke many of theire heades. ffcrall mᶜConyng prince of Aileagh died. Neale o'Roirke was killed by Tire Connell and Hugh o'Neale of Tireowen. Moyle Paile bushopp of Clonvickenois and cowarb of Saint ffechyn died. King Moyleseachlin and Cahall o'Connor of Connaught made a bridge² at Athlone over the Synan. Dermott o'Laghtna prince of the land of Teaffa was killed by some of his owen men. King Moylseaghlyn made a bridge at Athliag³ to the one halfe of the river.⁴

995.—Moylemoye mᶜDowgille prince of Delvin Beathra (now called mᶜCoghlan's country) died. Colume abbot of Imleagh died.

996.—Bryan Borowa tooke the kingdome and government thereof out of the handes of king Moyleseachlin in such manner as I doe not Intend to Relate in this place. Hee was very well worthy of the place and government, and raigned 12 years, the most famous king for his time that ever was before or after him of the Irish nation for manhood, fortune, manners, laws, liberties, religion, and many other good partes,

---

¹ *F. Nevie.* — Feartagh, in the parish of Moynalty. 'This was the first turning of Brian and the Connaughtmen against Maelseachlainn.' *Annals F.M.*, ad ann. 999

² *Bridge.*—The *Annals F.M.* say under that Turlogh O'Connor built three bridges in 1120, at Athlone, Shannon Harbour, and Dunlo. These were probably of wickerwork hurdles. See Haliday's *Scandanavian K. of Dublin*, p. 214.

³ *Athliag.*—Athleague, 7 miles south of the town of Roscommon

⁴ *River.*—The Suck.

hee neuer had his peere amongst them all, though some chroniclers of the kingdome made comparisons[1] between him and Conn Cedcahagh, Conairey more, and king Neale of the nine hostages. Yett hee in regard of the state of the kingdome when hee came to the government thereof was judged to beare the bell away from them all. At his first entry into the kingdom the whole realme was overrunn and overspread by the Danes every where, the churches, abbyes, and other religious howses were by them quite Razed, and Debased, or otherwise turned to vile, base, servile, and abominable uses. Most of all, yea almost all the noblemen, gentlemen and those that were of any account were turned out of theire landes and liveings without any hopes of recovery or future redress; Yea some of the best sort were compelled to servitude and bounden slavery; both human lawe and Godes feare were set aside. In summe, it was strange how men of any fashion could use men as the Danes did use the Irish men at that time. King Bryan Borowa was a meet salve to cure such festred sores, all the phisick in the world could not cure it else, where in a small time he bannished the Danes, made up the churches and religious houses, restored the nobilityes to their auntient patrimonies and possessions, and in fine brought all to a notable reformation. At lenth in the yeare of our Lord God 1007 the 22nd of march being good ffryday hee assembled together all his forces to give battle[2] to the Danes at Clontarffe, and on the other side Brwader Earle of the Island of the Orcades called together and assembled all the Danes of Denmark out of all parts and kingdoms that owed them any service to that place as Generall and captain of the Danes, where there was a bloody battle between them fought at Clontarffe aforesaid. Brwader himself with his thousand men in shirtes of maile were slaine, the rest of his army were both slaine and drowned in the sea. Mulmorrey mᶜMurrogh mᶜffinn king of Leinster and mᶜBrogaroann prince

---

[1] *Comparisons.* — See *Wars of the Gaedhil*, p. 203.
[2] *Battle.* — The best account of this battle will be found *ibid.*, pp. 151-217. See also Keating's *H. of Ireland*, p. 494.

of Affaile that partaked with the Danes with many Leinstermen about them were slaine alsoe in this battle, and of the other side king Bryan Borowa sonn of Kennedy mᶜLorckan then greatest monarch in these partes of Europe, then of the age of 88 years, his nephew Conyng mᶜDon Cwan, prince Murrogh his son then of the age of 63 yeares, were killed, Terence the kings grand-child, then about the age of 15 yeares was found drowned neare the fishing wier of Clontarffe with both his hands fast bounde in the haire of a Danes head, whome he pursued to the sea at the time of the flight of the Danes, Mothlae mᶜDonell mᶜFoylan, prince of the Desies of Mounster, Eachy mᶜDawny, Neale o'Coyne, and Cowdaylye mᶜKennedy, 3 noblemen of the kings bed-chamber, Teig o'Kelly prince of Imanie, Moyleronye o'Hoynn prince of Ayny,[1] Geveannagh mᶜDowagan king of Fearnmoy,[2] mᶜBeachy mᶜMorreaye, Kloen, prince of Kerry Lawchra, Donnell mᶜDermott prince of Corka avaiskin, Scannlan mᶜCahall prince of Eonaght of Loghlyen,[3] and Donnell mᶜEvin mᶜCaynich earle of Dombarr in Scottland, all which noblemen with many others were slaine in that battle, to the great greefe of the whole Realme. The o'Neales[4] forsooke king Brian in this battle and soe did all Connaught except Ferall o'Roirch and o'Ferall. The Leinstermen did not onely forsake him but were the first that opposed themselves against him of the Danes side, onely o'Morey and o'Nolan excepted. Moyleseachlin[5] that was late before king of Ireland (but at that time but king of Meath) all be it hee fought of his side, was his mortall enemie, and therefore for his evill will to king Brian, he was content rather to lose the field then win it.

---

[1] *Ayny.*—Hy Fiachrach Aidhne. See p 77, *antea*. The O'Heynes were chiefs of it.

[2] *Fearnmoy.*—Now Farney, in Co. Monaghan.

[3] *Loghleyn* —Now the Lakes of Killarney. The O'Donoghues were chiefs of this district in later times.

[4] *O'Neales.* — The clan Luighdeach, who took part in the battle, were not the O'Donnells and their co-relations, but the descendants of Lughaidh Mean, king of Thomond. See *Wars of the Gaedhil*, p. 167.

[5] *Moyleseachlin.*—Keating says he took no part in the fight, though present with his forces. *H. of Ireland*, p. 497. See *Annals F. M.*, ii. 776.

Moyleseachlin, after king Bryan was thus slaine, succeeded againe king of Ireland and reigned 8 years, dureing which time hee fought 25 battles both great and small against his enemies, wherein he for the most part had the victory. Donnogh the son of king Bryan Borowe, went with an army to the west of Ireland, and there killed Cahall m^cDonell and took hostages of Donell. Teige sonn of king Bryan, and his brother Donnogh, feel at debate and were against one another in the field where Donnogh had the worst, and Rory m^cDonnagann, prince of Arie,[1] was slaine. Dowlenn m^cTwahall king of Leinster died. Carbry m^cCahall, and Newman O'Seanchin, 2 anchorites, Died. O'Moyledorie prince of Tire Connell, and O'Royrck killed Donnell m^cCahall and destroyed all Connaught and tooke theire hostages.

1008.—Donell m^cDuff Davereann brought an armye to Lymbrick where he was mett and strongly resisted by Teig and Donnogh, the 2 sons of Bryan Borowa with the forces of Thomond, where there was a cruell and bloody battle fought between them, in the end whereof Donell had the worst and lost the field and his life too. o'Neill went with a great armye of Meathmen to Leinster, and spoyled wasted and destroyed all that province all along to Gleandalogha, and killed some of theire gentry. King Moyleseachlin, o'Neale, and o'Moyledorie with theire forces went to Dublin, and burnt all the houses therein from the forte out, and from thence they went to o'Keanseally in Leinster which they preyed, harried, and spoyled, and took Divers captives with them, among whom Congallagh m^cConnor king of Affailie was taken, and Gilla Colme o'Hugh prince of Teaffa. The king accompanied with o'Neale and o'Moyledorie, went all over Leinster, tooke their hostages and constituted Donowan m^cDowlen king of that province. Gillechrest m^cNeale o'Dowley was killed by the king prince of Feartullagh. The son of Randalphe m^cHymer of Waterford was slaine by the o'Liahans of Munster.

---

[1] *Arie.*—Now Arra, a barony in north Tipperary.

The Annals of Clonmacnoise. 169

1009.—King Moyleseaghlin went into Ulster and tooke their hostages. mᶜLiag[1] arch poet of Ireland and one that was in wonderfull favour with king Bryan died; he was named Mortaugh, a very good man. There was a great scarcity of Corne and victuals this yeare in Ireland, in soe much that a hoope was sold for no less than five groates which came (as my author sayeth) to a penny for every barren. Eihne (o'Suartes daughter), abbesse of Kildare died. Connaught men broke downe Killaloe and Kynkorey (king Bryan his mannor house) and tooke away all the goodes therein.

1010.—Munster men preyed and spoyled Inis Clohran and Inis Bofinny. Dermott o Moyletelcha, cowarb of St Cowgall, an old Bushop and learned Scribe died. Enos mᶜCarry Calma prince of Taragh, the joy of Ireland, died. Moriegh Ultagh anchorite of Clonvickenos died.

1011.—Broen mᶜMoilmorrey king of Leinster had his eyes putt out by the deceipt of Sittrick. There apeared this yeare in the Authumne two shining Comets in the firmament, which continued for the space of two weekes. King Moyleseaghlin with a great army went to Ferkeall and Elye,[2] where he tooke a great preye and through the sturdy resistence of the inhabitants of the said countrey in defence of theire preyes and libertys, Donnell o Kindelan, prince of the race of king Lagery, and Cosmy the kings stewarde with many others were slaine. Congallach mᶜMoylemorrey, prince of Leinster, was killed willfully.

1012.—All the Towen of Kildare was burnt by a thunderbolt but one house. Sittrick mᶜAwley of Dublin irreverently and without respect made havock of all the things in the church of Kelles, and killed many within the walles of the said church. The shrine of St Querean was abused by

---

[1] *Mᶜ Liag.*—See O'Reilly's *Irish Writers*, p. lxx, for an account of his works. Hardiman gives one of his poems, *Irish Minstrelsy*, ii. 197, and a fragment of another is in *Wars of the Gaedhil*, p. 95.

[2] *Elye.* — This territory included the present baronies of Clonlisk and Ballybritt in King's Co., and those of Eliogarty and Ikerrin, in Co. Tipperary. The O'Carrolls were chiefs of it.

Donnell mᶜTuloge, who by the miracles of St. Queran was killed within a weeke after. The son of one Caharnagh of o'Cassine¹ in the territory of Thomond, fell upon Donogh mᶜBrian Borow, and gave him a blow in the head and did cutt of his right hand. Donnogh escaped alive, the other was killed in that presence. Molemorey mᶜMoylemoye prince of Delvyn died.

1013.—Murtagh o'Carry Calma tooke Molloye or Moylemoy prince of Ferkeall from out the church of Dorowe and killed him at Moylena² adjoyning to Dorowe. King Moyleseachlin o'Neale, Donnogh mᶜBrian, and Art o Royrck went with theire forces into the province of Connaught, tooke hostages there, and Delivered them into the kings hands. Kildare, Gleandalogha, Clonard, Aron, Swordes, and Clonvickenos were thoroughly burnt by Danes. Ardmach the third of the calends of June was burnt from the one end to the other, save onely the library, all the houses were burnt, the great church steeple, the church of the Sauall,³ the pullpitt or chaire of preaching together with much gold, silver, and books were burnt by the Danes.

1014.—Owgaire mᶜAillealla, king of Leinster gave a great overthrow to the Danes of Dublin at a place called Deirgne Mogoroge⁴ where an infinite number of Danes were slaine. Cowchoylle mᶜDowleyn, prince of Fertullagh, died. There was a shower of wheat in Ossery this yeare. Moylemary daughter of Awley of Dublin Queen of Ireland, and wife to king Moyleseachlin died.

1022.—MᶜKervell, prince of Elye, was killed. Sittrick mᶜIlymer king of Waterford, was killed by these of Ossery. Flann o'Fagan archdean of Dorow, a worthy sage and holy

---

¹ *O'Cassine.*—This was formerly the territory of the MᶜNamaras, including Quin, Tulla, Cloney, Doora, Kilraghtis, Templemaley, Inchicronan, and Kilmurry, in east Clare. See Frost's *H. of Clare*, p. 35.

² *Moylena.*—Two miles west of Tullamore, in King's Co.

³ *Sauall.*—Now Saul, near Downpatrick. This was the church built by St. Patrick. See *Trias Thaum.*, p. 72.

⁴ *D. Mogoroge.*—Delgany, in Co. Wicklow. In the *Annals F.M.*, ii. 799, it is called Derge Mogorog.

man, died. There was a great shower of haile in Summer this yeare the stones whereof were as bigg as crabbes, there was alsoe such thunder and Lightning that it killed an infinite number of cattle everywhere in the kingdome. King Moyleseachlin m^cDonnell m^cDonogh king of all Ireland, haveing thus triumphantly raigned over all Ireland, and his enemies the Danes, died in Croinnis[1] upon Logh Innill neere his house of Doone Sgiath in the 43 yeare of his reigne in the forth of the noones of September, the sunday next before the feast day of St. Queran in the yeare of our Lord 1022. The archbushopp of Ardmach, the cowarb of St. Columbkille and the cowarb of St Queran being present, after hee received the sacrament of extreme Unction, died a good death. This was the last king of Ireland of Irish blood that had crowen. Yett there was seven kings after without a crown before the comeing of the English, as shall be made manifest in the ensueing Discourse.

Now that you may know the kings of the severall races, and how many of them raigned since the comeing of St Patrick the Apostle into this land, which were in number 48 kings Dureing the space of 615 yeares, it shall appeare unto you by this table following :

Saint Patrick came into this land the 4 yeare of the reign of King Lagery, in the yeare of the Incarnation 425 as before is specified. Dureing the raigne of the said 48 kings there Raigned none but the Clanna Neales, except Ailleall Molt of Connaught and Brian Borowa for 12 yeares onely, as may appear by a cathologue of their names. Of the race of king Lagery there raigned but 2 kings vizt. Lagery himself and his son Lauthus or Leway m^cLagery.

Off the of Carbry m^cNeale there reigned but 1 king vizt. Twahall Moylegarve.

Of the race of king Dahye m^cFiaghragh a nephew of king Neale of the 9 hostages there Raigned but one vizt. Aíleall Molt.

---

[1] *Croinnis.* — An island in the north-eastern part of Lough Ennell, a little to the south of Mullingar.

Of the race of Conell Gulban mᶜNeale of Tire Connell there raigned 10 kings vizᵗ. Ainmirre, Boydan, Hugh mᶜAinmireagh, Moylegova, Donell, Connell, Ceallagh, Loyngseagh, Congall, and Flaithvertagh.

Of the race of Owen mᶜNeale of Tyreowen there reigned 16 kings vidzᵗ. Mortaugh, Donell, Fergus, Boydan, Eoghy, Colmanrymy, Hugh Oirneagh, Swyne Mean, Ferall, Hugh Alan, Neale Frassagh, Hugh Ordan, Neale Kaille, Hugh Finlich, Neal Glunduff, and Donell.

Of the sept of Hugh Slane, son of king Dermot mᶜKervell there raigned 9 kings.

Blathmac, Dermott, Seachnassagh, Ceannfoyle, Fionaghta Fleaagh, Fogartagh, Cynath, Congalach mᶜMoylemikie, and their ancestor Hugh Slane himself.

Of the o'Melaghlins of Clann Colman there reigned seven kings vidzᵗ.

Donell, Donnogh, Connor, Moyleseachlin mᶜMoylerwanie, Flann, Donnogh, and Moyleseachlin mac Donell. Of all Mounstermen there Raigned but one King since Ireland was converted to Christianity that had a crown vidzt. Bryan Borowa. Of the race of Conell Criowhan, auncestor of the o'Melachlins, & the sept of Hugh Slane there raigned one King who was ancestor to both the septs of Hugh Slane and Clann Colman, Dermott mac Keruell. Which number of kings may be added together thus,

```
    02 ⎫
    01 ⎪
    01 ⎪
    10 ⎪
    16 ⎬  48 Kings of Irish blood.
    09 ⎪
    07 ⎪
    01 ⎪
     1 ⎪
    ── ⎪
    48 ⎭
```

HEREAFTER FOLLOWETH A DISCOURSE OF THE KINGS OF IRELAND THAT LIVED WITHOUT A CROWN & OF CERTAINE ACCIDENTS HAPPENED IN THEIRE RAIGNES.

After the death of king Moylseaghlin this kingdome was without a king for the space of twenty years : Dureing which time the Realme was gouerned by two learned men, the one called Cwan o'Lochan,[1] a well learned temporall man and cheefe poet of Ireland, the other Corcrann Cleireagh[2] a devout & holy man, that was anchorite of all Ireland, whose most abideing was at Lismore. The land was Governed like a free state, & not like a monarchy by them. There fell a great wonderfull snow at this time before the battle of Sleive Grott.

1023.—There was an Eclipes of the Sunn aboute noon the first of the calends of February. Donell m'Hugh Beag o'Melaghlin K. of halfe Meath was killed by the sonn of Seannan o'Loogan[3] and by those of Lwynie. Donnogh o'Doyne prince of Moybrey was treacherously slaine by the Danes & carried over seas. Teige, son of K. Bryan Borowa, was unaturally delivered[4] by his owen Brother Donnogh to those of Elye o'Karoll, whoe accordingly killed him, as was desired of them by his Brother Donnogh. Leavelin king of Wales, died. Henry,[5] monarch of the world died, and Conrado succeeded him in the monarchy.

1024.—o'Moiledorie gave an overthrow to o'Roirk in Connaught near Corann,[6] where o'Roirck had great loss of his people. M'Neochy[7] of Ulster tooke hostages of the

---

[1] *C. o'Lochan.*—He was a native of Westmeath. The *A. of Ulster* call him the chief poet of Ireland. See O'Curry's *MS. Materials*, p. 9.

[2] *C. Cleireagh*—*i e.* the clerics. See the *Book of Rights*, xlii.

[3] *S. o'Loogan.*—He was chief of Gailenga mora and Linghae, now Morgallen and Lune in Meath.

[4] *Delivered.*—' At the instigation of his own brother.' *Annals F.M.*, ad ann.

[5] *Henry.*—Henry II., Emperor of Germany.

[6] *Corann.*—At Ath na Croise, according to the *A. of Ulster*. The name is now obsolete. C. is now a barony in the south of Co. Sligo.

[7] *M'Neochy*—*i. e.* Niall, son of Eochaidh, King of Uladh.

Danes and caused them to set at liberty theire Irish Captives. Ossery and Leinstermen went to Taylchoynne[1] & Brought a rich booty of Jeweles and prisoners from the Danes. Faghtna lector and priest of Clonvickenos arch dean of Ffynnawragh,[2] abbott of Hugh, arch-dean of Inenen,[3] and abbot of all Ireland died in Room doing pennance. Cwann o'Lochan prince poet of Ireland, a great chronicler, and one to whome for his sufficiencie the causes of Ireland were committed to be examined and ordered, was killed by one of the land of Teaffa, after committing of which evill fact there grew an euill sent and odour of the partye that killed him, so that hee was easily knowen among the rest of the land. His associate Corcran lived yet, and survived him for a time after. Dowslany that was first Priest of Arbrachan and afterwards prime anchorite of Ireland, died.

1025.—Gearrgeala king of Moybrew was both killed and burnt by the South of Moybrey & by Mahon o'Riagan. Flaithvertagh o'Neale with his forces of the north took with him all the captives of Ireland that were with the Danes. Donell God[4] with his forces banished o'Neale over the mount of Sleieve ffwaide. Melaghlin God king of Meath Died at this time.

1026.—Donnogh son of king Brian Borowa with his forces this yeare had all the hostages of Meath, Brey, Danes, Leinstermen, and Ossery to himselfe. Flathvertagh o'Neale, and the sonn of Moyleseachlin m^cMoyleronie with theire forces came to Meath, tooke theire hostages, and upon Ice entred in upon Innis Moghty, which they bereaved of all the Goodes therein. Gearr an Choggan[5] made a great prey upon Downagh or Downsoghlin, & was killed himself with his two brothers the next day, Etigen and Moriegh. Cowdoly

---

[1] *Taylchoynne.*—The Tolka river, which passes by Finglas and Glasnevin.

[2] *Ffynnawragh.*—Kilfenora, 12 miles N.W. of Ennis, Co Clare. It gives its name to a bishop's See.

[3] *Inenen.*—This place is mentioned in the *Annals F M*, under the dates 920 and 1024, but O'Donovan does not identify it

[4] *God.*—*i e.* stammering, lisping, or dumb.

[5] *G an Choggan.*—*i.e.* the short man of the war.

o'Bearrga, killed Awargin o'Morrey king of Lease. Molrony o'Moyledorie went a pillgrimage over seas. Roen prince of Meath gave three great overthrows this yeare vidz^{t.} an overthrow to Meathmen, another to these of Brey, and the third to the Danes of Dublin, hee was of Cloynn Colman. The pavement from the place in Clonvicknois called the Abbess her Garden to the heape of stones of the three Crosses was made by Breassall Conealagh.

1027.—Teige m^cGillepatricke had his eyes putt out by Donnogh m^cGillepatrick. Donnogh m^cBrian with his forces went to Ossery, where the Inhabitants of that Contry gave an overthrow to som of the army of prince Donnogh, killed Gara m^cDownay prince of Silanmchie,[1] Donell m^cScanchan, m^cfflathvertagh prince of Mounster, and Moyleseachlin o'Connor prince of Corcomroe,[2] the two sonns of Cowleannan m^cConnor king and prince of o'Connell,[3] and the 2 sons of Egertagh prince and king of the North of Eognaght of Cashell were alsoe killed. Moylerony o'Moldory died in pilgrimage. Roen o'Melaghlin robbed the shryne[4] of Saint Colume. Richard king of France Died. Sittrick m^cAwley and Donnogh king of Moybrey with their forces came to Meath to Leigh Olav,[5] and Moynevillan,[6] and were mett and strongly oppugned by Roen o'Melaghlin king of Meath whoe gave the Danes the overthrow & killed Donnogh o'Doyn, K. of Moybrey, Gillenesally m^cGillekevin, prince of Ibriwyn,[7] and afterwards the Danes returned and gave a new onsett, & killed Roen king of Meath, with many others.

---

[1] *Silanmchie.*—*i.e.* the O'Maddens, whose territory included the barony of Longford, Co. Galway, and the parish of Lusmagh, in King's County.

[2] *Corcomroe.*—In the north of Co. Clare.

[3] *O'Connell.*—*i. e.* Hy Conaill Gabhra, the barony of Connello, Co. Limerick.

[4] *Shryne.*—Kept at Skreen, Co. Meath. It was brought from Iona in 878, to save it from the Danes. See Reeves' *Adamnan*, p 315.

[5] *Leigh Olav.*—Now Lickblaw, in the barony of Fore, Co. Westmeath.

[6] *Moynevillan.*—Not identified.

[7] *Ibriwyn.*—Called na Sionna; their territory lay on the western bank of the Shannon, to the east of Elphin. See *Annals F. M*, iii. 86, for an account of this district, and the map prefixed to the *Tribes and Customs of Hy Many.*

1037.—Dermott m^cMoylenemo of Leinster, preyed, spoyled, and burnt Lymbrick. Donnogh m^cDowlen king of Leinster had his eyes put out by m'Gillepatrick king of Ossery, and soone after died for grief. It rained much this summer. Conn o'Melaughlin, did putt out the Eyes of Flann o'Melaughlin.

1038.—Flaithvertagh m^cLoingsy, Lector and Bushopp of Clonvickenois, died. Aillealla o'Gair Lector of Dorow, died. The was such an abundance of ackorns this yeare that it fattened the pigges[1] of pigges. There arose great contention and fray between those of Delvin m^cCoghlan & those of Imanie in Clonvickenos on St. Querans Day, and fell twice the same day to fray, in which strife there were slain 33 persons of Imanie.

1039.—The steeple of Clonard fell Dowen to the earth. Donnagh m^cGillepatrick king of Ossery and Leinster Died. Leithmanchan[2] was preyed & spoyled by these of Imanie in revenge of the falling out between those of Imanie and these of Devlin in Clonvickenos before.

1040.—The overthrow of Killdrounan[3] given by the Danes and m^cBrayn to m^cffoylan where m^cffoylan was killed. Corcran anchorite of all Ireland died at Lismore, this is hee that had the hearing of all the cawses of Ireland. Eghtigerne m^cBroyne, prince of Brawnie, Died.

1041.—Dermott m^cMoylenemo[4] was king nine yeares. The kings or cheefe monarchyes of Ireland were reputed to be absolute monarchyes in this manner: If he were of Leah Conn or Cons halfe in Deale, & had one province of Leahmoye or Moah's halfe in Deale at his command, hee was counted to be of suffitient power to be king of Taragh or Ireland, but if the party were of Leahmoye if hee could not command all Leah moye and Taragh and with the loppe thereunto belong-

---

[1] *Pigges*—*i.e.* the pigots or rutlands.
[2] *Leithmanchan.*—See p. 9, *antea.*
[3] *Killdrounan.*—Now obsolete.
[4] *D. m^cMoylenemo.*—He was king of Hy Kinseallagh, and was made king of Leinster by O'Neill, who set aside the son of Maelmordha because his father had aided the Danes at Clontarf.

ing and the province of Ulster or Connaught (if not both) he would not be suffitient to bee king of all. Dermott m^cMoylenemoe could command Leahmoye, Meath, Connaught, and Ulster, therfore by the judgement of all hee was reputed suffitient monarch of the whole. Moylebride o'Moylefin priest died. Moyleronye m^cRoen prince of Taragh was killed by forriners.

1042.—Flann m^cMoyleseachlin God, prince of Ireland, was killed by Connor o'Melaghlyn.

1044.—Clonvicknos was preyed by the Mounstermen in the absence of Donnogh m^cBrian for which Donnogh granted to St. Queran & Clonvickenois perpetuall freedom & for forty Cowes at that present, and gave his malediction to any Mounstermen that would euer after abuse any belonging to St. Queran. Clonvickenois was preyed by the o'Ferals, of whome a certaine poet made this Latin verse:

> Haec urbs horrendis hodie vastata inimicis
> Quae polis ante fuit Scotorum nobile culmen.

For which outrages committed upon the clergie of St. Queran God horribly plagued them, with a strange unknowen disease, that they died soe fast of that infection, that theire townes, howses and Derie[1] places were altogether wast without men or cattle in soe much that at last they were Driuen to graunt in honour of St. Queran the abbye landes of o'Roircks sonne and the 12 best sonnes of all the o'Ferals, and a certaine sum of money for theire maintenance, which was paid by the Pole throughout that country for appeasing the Indignation of the saint conceaved against them.

1045.—Clonard was thrice burnt in one weeke. Cahassagh cowarb of St. Kevyn died. Hymar son of Harold made a great slaughter of Ulstermen in Inispatrick[2] in Rathlyn to the number of 300 of them.

1055.—Gorman a venerable anchorite died. Hugh o'Con-

---

[1] *Derie*.—i e their winterages for cattle, perhaps from the Irish *dair*, an enclosure.

[2] *I. patrick*.—There is also an island of this name near Skerries, Co. Dublin.

nor made a great prey in Meath, called the prey of May. Gillopatricke king of Ossery, died of Greefe.

1056.—Murrogh, prince of Leinster and sonn of king Dermot, made a prey upon the race of Lagery, whoe by them was pursued and a great slaughter made of them, for which cause the Meathmen spoyled and preyed all Leinster, from the mount of Sliew bleanne[1] to Clondalcan adjoyning to Dublin. fflann lector, the best learned, & chronicler in these partes of the World, died. Odor m'fflynn prince of Callrie was killed by Swynie o'Hogan, cowarb of Termyn of St. Foychinn.

1059.—Neale o'Moyledorie, prince of Tire Connell, died. There arose great contention and warres between Meathmen and Leinstermen this yeare that there were many slain of Leinstermens side. Connor o'Melaghlin prince of Taragh gave a great overthrow to Murrogh m'Dermott king of the Danes. There was another overthrow given to the Leinstermen in Dorow the same Day by the miracles of St Columekill.

1060.—They of Ely o'Karoll, and o'fforga[2] came to prey Clonvickenos, and tooke certaine captives from the place called (Crosse na Streaptra) and killed twoo there, a layman and a spirituall. Whereupon the clergie of Clone incensed these of Delvyn Beathra with their king Hugh o'Royrck in theire pursuit, who gave them an overthrowe & quite discomfited them, & killed the prince of o'fforga that before killed the spirituall man, and alsoe brought their captives the next day back againe to the place from whence they were soe conveighed.

1061.—Hugh o'Roirck, prince of Delvyn m'Coghlans contry was treacherously killed. Hugh o'Connor king of Connaught broke dowen the mannorhouse of king Brian Borowo in Kincoro, burnt Killalo, and also did eat the two salmons that were in the kings ffountaine or fishpond, there. Queran, lector of Kelles, died.

1062.—Prince Teige m'Hugh o'Connor was treacherously

---

[1] S. bleanne.—Slieve Bloom.
[2] O'fforga. — This tribe dwelt about Ardcroney, three miles north of Nenagh.

slaine by the o'Flathvertyes. Neale mᶜEochie king of Ulster, and his son, died. Gillaerrie o'Moylemihie a rich young prince of all Ireland, died. Lymbrick was burnt by king Dermott mᶜMoylenemo, and by Terence or Terlagh o'Brien.

1063.—Donnogh mᶜBrian Borowa was king, some say, and was soon deposed again (and went to Rome), to Doe pennance because hee had a hand in the killing of his owen eldest brother Teige mᶜBryan. Hee brought the Crowen[1] of Ireland with him thither, which remained with the Popes untill Pope Adrean gave the same to king Henry the second that conquered Ireland. Donnogh mᶜBrian died in pilgrimage in the abby of St. Stephen the Protomartyre.

1064.—o'Mahon king of Ulster was treacherously slaine.

1065.—There appeared a comet for the space of three nights, which did shine as clear as the moone at the full. Gillebrwitte, prince of the Brenie, was killed, and Orlaith his wife alsoe. Fogartagh ffinn, an anchorite and sage, died at Clonvickenos. There was a battle fought in England between Harolde and the Normans and Saxons this yeare, where there was an overthrow given to the Danes, and a fleet of 17 shipps of them killed. This was William the Conqueror's abby battle.[2]

1066.—Mortagh o'Carhie chiefe poet of Connaught was drowned in Logh Colgan.[3] Celeagher Moyornogh bushopp of Clonvickenos, died. King Dermot mᶜMoylenamo, and Terrence or Terlagh o'Bryen king of Mounster with theire forces went to Connaught, where they were met by Hugh o'Connor king of that province, whoe gave them a fierce battle, where o'Connor Kiery[4] with many others were slain. Soon after the Brenie men gaue battle to the said Hugh, & slew him therein, Hugh mᶜArt o'Roirck had the victory.

1067.—Murogh o'Bryen prince of all Ireland was killed

---

[1] *Crowen* —See Keating's *H. of Ireland*, p. 534.

[2] *Abby battle.* — Battle Abbey, built by William the Conqueror to commemorate the victory of Hastings over Harold, November 14th.

[3] *L. Colgan.*—Perhaps L. Caelan. See *Annals F.M.*, ii. 907.

[4] *O'C. Kiery.*—See an account of this family in notes to the *Annals F. M.*, ii. 891 and 1109, and *King James' Army List*, ii. 325.

by the people of Teaffa for preying them before, whose head was buried in Clonvickenos, and body buried in Dorow. Donnell o'Melaghlyn prince of Ailleagh was killed by his own Brother.

1068.—Cowhagh priest of Killdare, flower of all Leinster, died.

1069 —Murrogh son of king Dermott king of the Danes of Ireland and Leinster under his father died the 21 of November Anno Dni 1070. Murtagh o'Connor of Affalie was blinded by his own brother of both his Eyes. Moyleronye king of Ulster was killed. o'Clohoghan lector of Ardmach and one famous throughout the kingdom, Died. Gillebryde o'Molloy prince of ffearkall died. Dermott mcMoylenamo king of Ireland, Wales, Danes of Dublin, and protector of the honour of Leah Coynn, was killed[1] & mangled by Connor o'Melaghlin king of Meath with many of his nobles, both Irishmen and Danes in the battle of Owa.[2] Dowgill abbesse of Kildare died. Murrogh mcConnor o'Melaghlyn, prince of Meath, did so overcess the family of Moylekyeran mcCon ne mboght in Isillkyeran[3] and the poore of that house, that the steward of that familie was slain by them, for which cause Moyvora[4] was granted to the poore.

1070.—Terlogh als Terrence o'Brian Borowe son of prince Teige mac Brien Borowa succeeded as king next after king Dermot, and raigned full 25 years. Connor o'Melaghlin king of Meath and Leahcoyn was treacherously and filthylie slaine by his own nephew Murrogh mcfflynn. Meath was wasted and destroyed between them. Clonard and Kelles were burnt with their churches in one month. King Terrence o'Brian did violently take from out of the church of Clonvickenos the head of Connor o'Melaghlin, king of Meath, that was

---

[1] *Killed* —'He burned territories and churches, Granard, Fobhar-Feichin, but Feichin slew him face to face.' *Annals F.M.*, ad ann.

[2] *Owa.*—A territory in ancient Meath. The name is now obsolete. The *Annals F.M.* give 1072 as the date of his death.

[3] *Isillkyeran.* — Near Clonmacnoise. It is called later on in these *Annals* the hospital of St. Ciaran.

[4] *Moyvora.*—O'D. suggests Moyvore, in the barony of Rathconrath, Co. Westmeath.

buried therein, and conveighed it to Thomond. A mouse rann out of the head, & went under the king's mantle, & immediately the king for fear fell sick of a sore disease by the miracles of St. Queran, that his haire fell off his head, and was like to dye untill hee restored the said head againe with certaine gould, which was taken upon Good Friday, and sent back the day of the Resurrection next ensuing.

1073.—Cowhagh, abbot of Disert Dermott, died. Downan[1] archbushop of Dubline both of Irish and Danes died. Ardmach with the churches was burnt. Donnogh o'Kelly, prince of Imanie, was killed by his own brother grandchild of Connor o'Kelly, at the island of Logh Keylan.

1074.—Louth with the church was burnt. King Terlagh o'Bryan with a great army of Meathmen, Connaughtmen, Danes, and Leinstermen with all his forces of Mounster and Ossery went to the north of Athfirdie to get hostages of the Ulstermen, & returned from thence without any with a great slaughter and loss[2] of his army in that part. Murtaugh o'Brian, son of king Terlaugh, was constituted king of Dublin and Danes thereof.

1075.—Murtogh m^cfflyn o'Melaghlin that Raigned King of Meath but three days and 3 nights, was killed by Awley m^cMoielan prince of Gailenge in the borders of Leinster. He was killed in the steeple of Kells, and afterwards the said Awley was killed immediately by Melaghlin m^cConnor o'Melaughlin by the miracles of St Columb, who is patron of the place.

1076.—There was great scarcity of victuals this year. The scarcity of victualls continued for this yeare, there was alsoe a great persecution of all the houses of religion belonging to Clonvickenose. The people of Teaffa for envy and Deceipt murdered Murrogh m^cConnor o'Melaghlin. Gillepatrick o'Kiergie prince of Carbry, now called Bremynghams

---

[1] *Downan.*—Donatus O'Hainghly, who occupied the See of Dublin from 1085 to 1095 See Ware's *Bishops*, p. 309.

[2] *Loss.*—The *Annals F.M.* say Terlagh O'Brien was defeated with great loss at Ardmonnan; this name is now obsolete.

contry, died. Moriegh o'Nwaat, auntient and sage of Dorow died. Gormphlath daughter of o'ffohortie Queen of Ireland and wife of king Torlaugh died and bequeathed much cattle and a rich legacie on the church for her soule.

1077.—O'Layhen arch prince of Uriell, Connor o'Brian prince of the eonaght of Cashell, Donell m{{c}}Tiernan prince of the Brenie, and Kearnaghan Gott o'Melaghlin young prince of Meath were all killed this yeare   Ceallach o'Ronow arch poet of Ireland, died. Moylescachlin m{{c}}Connor o'Melaghlin came to Teaffa to a place called Kwasan[1] in Brawnie, and there made a great prey, and tooke captives by the vertue of St. Queran because the inhabitants of Kwasan[1] aforesaid robbed the church of Clonvickenos the presedent yeare.

1078.—The people of Teaffa came to the Termynland of Killeachie[2] in Affalie and preyed and spoyled the whole Termynland, and also killed Gillemorie o'Keyrgie King of Carbrey and the sonn of m{{c}}ffinbarr, chiefe of the o'Giarans or Gerans with many others.

1079.—Gillesynata Magawley prince of Calrie was killed by Moyleseachlin o'Melaghlin for robing or ravishing the goods of the church of Clonvickenos the precedent yeare. Corcke and Kildare were burnt.

1080.—Donell o'Connor young prince of Connaught was killed by his owen Uncle Cahal m{{c}}Hugh o'Connor without any other cause but onely for envy and malice. A great part of Westmeath vidz{{t}} of Delvin, Cwickney[3] and others were slain by Donnell m{{c}}fflynn o'Melaughlin king of Meath on Loghry, and alsoe the houses in the church yard of the nunns of Clonvickenos together with theire church was burnt.

1082.—Donnogh son of Koyleagh o'Roircke accompanied with the East of Connaught, the Carbryes and Galenges, were met by prince Mortaugh o'Brian son of King Terlaugh, whoe

---

[1] *Kwasan.*—Now Coosane, three miles north of Athlone.

[2] *Killeachie*—Now Killeigh in King's Co. See p. 84, *antea*.

[3] *Cwickney.*—The district now comprised in the barony of Kilkenny West, Co. Westmeath ; it was inhabited then by the O'Tolairgs.

was likewise accompanied with the forces of the Danes, Mounster, and Lynster, and killed the said Donnogh in battle, and alsoe Kennedy o'Brian and the sonn of o'Connor of Affalie with many other noble men were killed of the prince side.

1083.—The king fell sick of a grieveous sickness this yeare, and was soe ill therein that all his haire fell off.

1084.—Moyle Issa o'Brothloghann,[1] the ealder and sage of Ireland was soe ingenious and witty, and withall soe well learned that he composed great volumes containing many great Misteryes and new sciences devised by himselfe, died this year. Terlaugh o'Briann king of Ireland in the 25 year of his Raigne died quietly in his bedd, and his son Teige Died the next month. Moileseachlin mac Connor o'Melaghlyn went to Dublin and was encountred & discomfitted by the Danes, where Kyeran o'Cahassie prince of Saithne[2] with the moste part of the land of Lwynie were killed. Teige Sheannagh[3] o'Kaharnie arch-prince of the land of Teaffa was killed together with his sonn Kynath and the chiefe of Montir Thlaman[4] were killed treacherously by Moyleseachlin mᶜConnor o'Melaghlin in revenge of his brother Morrogh mᶜConnor that was slain by Kaharnagh Shennagh; of this Teige Montir Hagan (now called Foxes contrey or the contry of Killcoursey[5]) took the name. Moyleseachlin mᶜConnor king of Meath was soone after slaine by Cahall mᶜMoregan and these of Teaffa in the towen of Ardach. Rory o'Connor king of Connought and the sonn of Art o'Roirck encountred in battle with each other, at last o'Roirck with the most part of his famelye were slain.

1086.—Dowcooley the King of Connaught's daughter & Queen of Mounster died. Lady More daughter of king Terlaugh and Queen of Connaught, wife of Rory o'Connor died.

---

[1] *M. o'Brothloghann.*—His *Life* is given by Colgan, *Acta SS.*, 1. 109.

[2] *Saithne.*—This tribe inhabited Fingal in Meath.

[3] *Sheannagh.*—*i.e.* the fox; the name has been taken as a surname by some branches of this family.

[4] *M. Thlaman.*—*i.e.* O'Muireadhaigh, anglicized Murray.

[5] *Killcoursey.* Now a barony in the north of King's Co.

1087.—Munstermen brought a greater fleet on the river of Synann, and Loghrye, & robbed and took the spoyles of the churches upon the islands of the Lough vidz[t] of Innis Clothran, Innis Bofinne, Innis Angnie, and Cloneawynn,[1] which Rory o'Connor, king of Connought seeing, hee caused to be stopped the foordes on the Synann called Adyrchreach[2] and Rathkrae,[3] to the end they should not be at liberty to pass the said passages at their Returnes, and were driven to turne to Athlone where they were overtaken by Donell m^cfflyn o'Melaghlin, king of Meath, to whose protection they wholly committed themselves, & yeelded all their shippes, barkes, boates, and coyttes[4] alsoe to be disposed off at his pleasure, which hee received and sent safe conduct with them untill they were left in their native place in Mounster. Gillekenny o'fflattyhe prince of Delvyn Beathra was killed by his owen brother Hugh m^cCoghlan. Donnogh m^cDonell Reawar (in English the fatt) king of Leinster, was killed by Connor o'Connor prince of Affalie, and alsoe Donnogh m^cDonnell m^cGillepatrick prince of Osserie, was killed. Isill Kieran or the hospitall of St. Queran was purchased by Cormack m^cCon-na-moght, from Fflayhenn, and Donell m^cfflynn o'Melaghlin of Meath for ever.

1088.—William the Conquerrour Died this yeare, had issue three noble sonns, Robert the Cortois, to whome hee bequeathed all Normandy; Henry Beaucleick, to whome he left the kingdome of England, who is called Henry the first; and William Rufus, to whome hee bequeathed all his treasure. Moriertgh o'Brian son of king Terlaugh o'Bryan succeeded his father and Raigned 11 years. The king came with his forces into Meath, and took a prey there, was overtaken by Donell m^cfflynn, king of Meath, at Moylena[5] in Fercall where many of king Moriertagh's armye were slaine, as Moyleseaghlyn o'Dongaly, the sonn of Conyn o'Dowgin, & the son of Molmory o'Donell, prince of the o'Keanseallyes.

---

[1] *Cloneawynn.* — Now Clonoon, near Athlone.
[2] *Adyrchreach* — Now Insherky, five miles west of Banagher.
[3] *Rathkrae* — Not identified.
[4] *Coyttes.*—From the Irish *cot*, a small boat.
[5] *Moylena.*—See p. 59, *antea*.

1089.—Donsleyve o'Heoghay king of Ulster was killed by Donell mᶜLoghlyn prince of Aileagh. Cynath o'Morrey and Mulronie mᶜConcornye fought hand to hand in the king's house in Cashell and were both slaine. Moyleissa[1] primate of Ardmach died.

1090.—The fleet of Mounster robbed and tooke the spoyles of Clonvickenos. Rowrie o'Connor king of Connought had his Eyes put out most maliciously by fflaithvertagh o'fflahertye and ffogartagh o'ffogarty. Cormack Mainisdreach[2] the sage and learned divine of Ireland died.

1092.—Hugh o'Konoyle dean of the Little chuich of Clonvickenos died. Malcolme king of Scotland was killed by ffrenchmen, whose wife Margarett Queen of Scottland and daughter of the king of England for griefe and sorrow of the kings death died

1094.—All the nobility & forces of Ireland assembled & gathered together at Dublin with king Moriertagh o'Bryan both Munstermen, Leinstermen, and people of Ossorie, Donell mᶜfflynn o'Melaghlin king of Meath, Donnogh o'Heoghie of Ulster and Godfrey of Dublin with ninty shipes. These of the east came to oghterard[3] where they gave a Discomfiture to the Mounstermen, people of Ossery and Leinstermen retracted upon them, & would neither appugne nor hinder the Leinstermen, but went and banished Godfrey out of Dublin, and also deposed Donell king of Meath. Whereupon the deposed king of Meath went to the land of Lwyne and there tooke a prey, being pursued by eastmeath & the king of Mounster's Guard, was slaine among the cowes at Loghlevin[4] by one belonging to himself called mᶜAgenann, & soe this was the end of Donell king of Meath, that was deposed of his kingdome and slaine by his owen people. Connor o'Connor of Affalie king of Leinster was taken

---

[1] *Moyleissa.—i.e.* consecrated to Christ. He was primate from 1065 to 1092. See Ware's *Bishops*, p. 50.

[2] *C. Mainisdreach.*—He was abbot of Monasterboice, 'head of the wisdom and piety of the Gaedhil.' See *Annals F M*, ii. 943.

[3] *Oghterard.*—Near Lyons, Co. Kildare. There is a round tower here, in a very ruinous condition.

[4] *Loghlevin.* — L. Leana, near Foie, Co. Westmeath.

captive by king Moriertagh o'Brian. Clonvickenos was robbed and the spoyles taken by those of Brawny, & the o'Royrcks, on Monday in shrovetide. Dorow was likewise robbed by those of Fercall and Affailie, Clonvickenos was alsoe the same day robbed by the sonn of mᶜCoghlan and Delvyn. King Mortagh o'Brian with his Mounstermen went to Connaught to take hostages and returned from thence without any. The king with an other army came to Dontaise¹ in Meath & divided Meath into too parts between two kings of the o'Melaughlins, vidzᵗ Donnough mᶜMurrogh mᶜfflynn & Connor mᶜMoyleseaghlyn o'Melaghlin. Cowchogry o'Hanvye prince of Fearbill² died. There was a great mortality and pleauge all over Europe this yeare, in soe much that it Depopulated great provinces and contryes, there was not such a pestilence in this Kingdome since the death of the sonns of King Hugh Slane (that died of the Disease called Boye Konneall³) untill this present year, of which disease the ensueing noblemen with infinite numbers of meaner sort died, vidzᵗ, Godfrey king of the Danes of Dublin, and the Islands, Dunchus⁴ archbushop of Dublin, Brehawe o'Manchan, cowarb of Sᵗ Kevyn, Donell Duff o'fferall prince of the borders of Leinster, mᶜInrwise o'Koewan cowarb of Oeny,⁵ the Bushop of Kehernie⁶ cowarb of Moye oge,⁷ Glasdin o'Koyn chiefe judge of Leinster &c. The king and subjects seeing the plague continue with such heat with them, were strucken with great terrour, for appeasing of which plague the Clergie of Ireland thought good to cause all the inhabitants of the kingdome in generall to fast from Wensday to Sunday once every month for the space of one yeare except solmne and great festivall dayes, they alsoe appointed certain prayers to be dayly said. The king, the

---

¹ *Dontaise* —Not identified.

² *Fearbill.*—Now a barony in the south-west of Co. Westmeath.

³ *B. Konneall.*—See pp. 83 and 106, *antea*.

⁴ *Dunchus* —Donat O'Hainghly, already mentioned, p. 181.

⁵ *Oeny.*—Probably St. Enda of Aran.

⁶ *Kehernie.*—Cairbre O'K., who is called Bishop of Ferns in *Annals F. M.*, ii. 951.

⁷ *Moye oge.*—*i.e.* Maedhog, of Ferns.

noblemen, and all the subjects of the kingdome were very benefitiall towards the Church and poore men this yeare, whereby Gods wrath was aswaged. The king of his great bounty gave great immunityes and freedom to churches that were then before charged with Cess and other extraordinarie contry-charges with many other large and bountifull gifts. mᶜCorthean cheef of Delvyn more was slaine by the race of Lagery, after hee was delivered by them to K. Mortaugh for takeing from them three ounces of Gold, 100 cowes, and eight prisoners.

1096.—Awargin o'Morrey died, he was prince of Lease. King Moriertagh with the forces of Leahmoye and Meath with the forces of part of Connaught, went to Ulster of purpose to get hostages, (and returned from thence without bootie or hostages.)

1097.—King Mortaugh o'Brian tooke the spoyles of the people of Teaffa & wasted them this yeare. All Meath was wasted and destroyed bytween Donnogh mᶜMorrogh, and Connor mᶜMoyleseaghlin, both of the o'Melaghlins. Flathvertagh o'fflathverty was killed by one Mathew o'Kwanna for putting out Rory o'Connors eyes; this fflathvertagh was prince of Silemorrey and Ighter Connaught.[1] o'Hart prince of the East of Teaffa killed treacherously (by) Kaharnagh mᶜentynnay alias Fox prince of Teaffa. Douhowly, daughter of Dermot mᶜTeige wife of king Mortaugh and Queen of Ireland, died. Donnogh mᶜMurrogh o'Melaghlin tooke the kingdom and government of Meath upon him. Dervorgill, daughter of Teige mᶜGillepatrick, mother of king Moriertaugh o'Brian and of Teige o'Brian, Queen of Ireland, died this year.

1098.—Donell mᶜDonnogh king of Scotland, was blinded of both his eyes by his owen brother. mᶜLaughlin of Ulster, with his forces preyed the Danes. King Mortaugh with his forces of Ireland went to Easroe in Ulster to get hostages of the North, & returned home without hostages, prey, or booty, with the loss of many of his horses, and

---

[1] *Ighter C.—i. e.* lower C. See Hardiman's *History of Galway*, p. 56.

men in that Jorney. King Mortaugh again accompanied with a great fleet of Danes, arrived in Derry in Ulster, and did noe outrages by the way, & were mett by the sonn of m᷊Laughlin, whoe gave them an overthrow, and made a slaughter upon them.

1100.—There was an assembly of all the subjects of Ireland at Cashell in the presence of king Mortaugh, and in the pressence of Downan archbushopp and Elder of Ireland, with the clergy of the kingdome, where the king of his meer motion and free will graunted to the Church and all devout members thereof such a grant as none of his predecessors the kings of Ireland ever graunted to the church before, which was his cheefest seat, court, and town of Cashell,[1] to be held in common by all spírituall men and women in perpetuum to them and theire successors. King Mortagh with the forces of Munster, Leinster, Ossery, Meath, and Connaught went to Easroe in Inis-Owen in the north, destroyed all the towns, ffortes, and churches of Inis Owen & brake downe the Stone-house that was in Aileagh,[2] and took their hostages, when they went over Fertas Camsa[3] to Ulster, and soe went over all Ireland, in the space of 6 weeks without disturbance, strife, or impediment of any mann. Two companyes of Kerne contended together in Clonvickenose, that is to say Mointir Hagan, and Moyntir Kennay, where in the end Gilleffinn m᷊ m᷊Gillwallachain, chieftaine of Sile Anmchie, was slaine. The Singles of the great church of Clonvickenos and the tower end of the wales of the said church, was Repaired and finnished by fflathvertagh o'Loyngsie, after the work was begun by Cormack m᷊Connemboght, cowarb of St Quæran, though others call it m᷊Dermots church. This year a woman in Mounster was delivered of a cople of chilldren that were joyned together in their bodyes.

---

[1] *Cashell.*—The King of Cashel after that transferred his residence to Limerick. His palace stood on the site now occupied by St. Mary's Cathedral.

[2] *Aileagh.*—In revenge of Kincora, which had been destroyed by the Ulstermen. See p. 169, *antea.*

[3] *Fertas C.*—A ford on the river Bann, near Camus Macosquin.

1104.—Connor o'Melaughlin, king of Taragh, Moybrey, and halfe Meath, was slaine by these of the Breine. Donell m{c}en Gott o'Melaughlin was killed by these of Kinnaleagh. Donnogh o'Melaghlin was Deposed from the kingdom of Meath and betooke himself to the contry of Uriell (Magmahons land), and from thence preyed the most part of east meath. King Mortaugh hearing thereof assembled together a great army, pursued him thither, and did nothing there but burnt some stakes of corn for protecting him in that contry, and afterwards divided Meath in two partes between the two sons of Donnell o'Melaughlin, when Donnogh refused to accept protection of him.

1105.—Donnough o'Melaughlyn was killed by o'Mynnachan of o'm{c}Waise of Meath. Bushopp o'Boyle[1] arch bushop of Ardmach, Moriegh o'Moyledowne[2] bushop of Clonvickenos, Cormack o'Killin, Deane of the house of Clone, and Sittrick m{c}Convaye chief of Sile Ronan, died.

1106.—The family of Kilkeny gave an overthrow to the family of Leighlyn. There grew great contention between the East and West of the contry of Teaffa, where Cynath m{c}Awalgie prince of Calrie with many others, were slaine.

1107.—Cogrich daughter of Unonn, abbesse of Clonbrony, died. o'Karvell, prince of the Eonaght of Loghlein, was killed by his brothers.

1108.—Flathvertagh o'Loyngsy, cowarb of St. Queran and venerable priest of Clonvickenos, died. After the death of king Mortaugh o'Brian Ireland was for som space without a king, untill Terlaugh alias Terence m{c}Rory o'Connor. Terlaugh alias Terence m{c}Rory o'Connor was king for the space of 9 years. Ceallagh[3] was primatt of Ardmach in his time. Connor Maglaghlin with the forces of Ulster

---

[1] *O'Boyle.*—He seems to have been merely a suffragan or assistant bishop to Donald Mac Amalgaidh. See Ware's *Bishops*, p. 51.

[2] *M. o'Moyledowne.*—He is not given by Ware in the list of Bishops of Clonmacnoise.—*Ibid.*, p. 169.

[3] *Ceallagh.*—Better known as Celsus. He was Primate from 1106 to 1129. He died at Ardpatrick, in Co. Limerick, while on a visitation, and was buried at Lismore as he desired. See *Trias Thaum.*, p. 330, and Ware's *Bishops*, p. 53.

came to Meath & burnt the race of Lagerie and the towen of trymme and alsoe burnt two hundred persons and above in the Church of Trymme. Tailty daughter of Morrogh o'Melaghlin wife of King Terlagh and Queen of Ireland, died. The great alter of Clonvickenos was robbed[1] this yeare and many jewells sacrilegiously taken from thence, vidz[t], Kearnaghan[2] of Sollamons Temple, which king Moyle-seaghlin bequeathed to that church, the standing cup of Donnogh m{c}fflynn, the three jewells that king Terlaugh gave to that church, vidz[t] a cup of silver, a guilt cross & another jewell, a silver challice marked with the stamp[3] of the daughter of Rorye o'Connor, and a cup of silver which Keallagh primate of Ardmach bestowed on the church, the clergy of Clone made incessant prayers to God and St. Queran to bee a meane for the Revelation of the party that tooke away the said jewles. Mathon o'Brian, sonn of King Mortaugh died.

1130 —Dermott o'ffallawyn chieftaine of Kloynolagh,[4] and Goll Cuana otherwise named Gillepatrick, cheefe poet of Westmeath, died. The jewles that were stolne from out the church & alter of Clonvickenos were found with one Gille-cowgan, a Dane of Lymbrick, the said Gillecowgan was apprehended by Connor o'Bryan, and by him delivered over to the familie of Clonvicknos, whoe at the time of his araignment confesed openly that he was at Corck, Lismore, and Waterford, expecting for wind to goe ouer seas with the said jewles   All the other passengers and shipes passed with good gales of wynde out of the said townes save only Gillecowgan, & said as soone as he would enter a shipboard any ship hee saw St. Queran with his staffe or bachall

---

[1] *Robbed.*—It has been surmised that the Cup of Ardagh, now in the National Museum, may have been one of the precious objects stolen at this time from Clonmacnoise. See Petrie's *Christian Inscriptions*, ii. 128.

[2] *Kearnaghan.*—Rather *carra-can*, a model

[3] *Stamp.*—With an engraving (*tesc*) by the daughter of R. O'C. *Annals F.M.*, ii. 1033.

[4] *Kloynolagh.* — Clan Uadach, comprising the parish of Camma and Dysart, in the barony of Athlone, Co. Roscommon.

returne the shipp back again untill hee was so taken ; this much he confesseth at the time of the putting him to death by the said familie.

1131.—Connor o'Brian arrived in Meath, seeking to pass through Athlone to get hostages there, after that hee had the hostages of Leinster. Tyernan o'Royrck gave an overthrow to these of Uriell, where Gillaryavagh o'Hoeghea king of Ulster, and o'Krychan prince of Fearnoy and his sonn with many others were slaine. Thomond was preyed by the kings of both the Munsters, by Cormack m‹Carrhie & Connor o'Brien. Moyleseaghlin m‹Murtaugh o'Melaghlin was killed by those of Fearkeall. A thunderbolt burnt the castle of Athlone and the castle of Donleo[1] was burnt by casuall fire. The o'Bryns of Thomond banished the m‹Carthys out of Mounster into Leinster and tooke to themselves the possession and government of Mounster. Donnogh o'Molloy king of Fearkall was killed in captivity by Murrogh o'Melaghlin. Mortagh o'Molloy that succeeded as king of Fearkall, was burnt by the family of Moyntyr Swanym in the church of Rahinn. Mack Randalphe m‹Morey, chief of Montyr Luss[2] was treacherously killed by Tiernan o'Royrck. Cowchonnought o'Daly of Meath, cheefe and arch-poet of Ireland, died.

1132.—Terlagh o'Connor king of Ireland made a wooden bridge over the river of Athliag, and came himself to the land of Teaffa to keep the o'Feralls, where hee was mett by Murrogh o'Melaghlin king of Meath, Tyernan o'Roirck, and Teaffymen with theire forces, and put the king and also Connaughtmen out of the camp, & burnt the place afterwards, and killed divers of the kings armye. King Terlaugh made another wooden bridge over the river of Synen at Athlone, that hee might at his pleasure have access to take the spoyles of Westmeath. Tiernan o'Roirck was deposed of his principality by his owen scept, and again restored thereunto.

---

[1] *Donleo*—It was erected seven years before. It was in the town of Ballinasloe, close to the river.

[2] *M. Luss.*—*i.e.* M. Eolais, a district in the southern part of Co. Leitrim, called also Magh Rein, of which the M‹Rannalls were chiefs.

1133.—Dermott mcMurrogh,[1] king of Leinster, exercised great tyranyes and crueltyes upon the Leinster nobility, hee killed o'Faylan prince of Leinster, and Murrogh o'Twahaile, and did excrably putt out the eyes of Gillemocholmoge[2] king of Kwalannmen,[3] which brought all Leinster under hand. Donnogh o'Connor of Affalie was killed by others of Affallye vidz.[t.] by Clan malirge. Connor o'Bryan went with his forces to Dublin and obtained there of the Danes to be their king. There was a meeting at Usneagh between king Terlaugh o'Connor, and Morrogh o'Moyleaghlin king of Tarragh, where Morrogh yielded hostages to king Terlaugh for Meath and Teaffa, and took hostages of Brenie also. Connor, grand-child of Donnogh o'Melaughlin, was killed in captivity by Morrogh o'Melaughlin, which was soone avenged by God, by taking away Art sonn of the said Melaughlin within a fortnight after. The cowarb of St. Queran was robbed at Clonfinlogh by these of Sile anmchye and Connor mcCoghlan, & the spoyles restored again, by the procurement of prince Connor the kings sonn. King Terlagh o'Connor with the forces of Connaught, Meath, and Brenie came to Mounster, but they returned without hostages & spoyled some corners in Lease and Ossery. Canute, sonn of Sane King of England and Denmark died. Sittrick the Dane preyed & spoyled Ardbreakan & tooke certain captives from thence too. Connor o'Melaughlin king of Meath, took the spoyle and prey of Swordes together with many captives

1134.—Connor mcDermott o'Bryan king of both the provinces of Mounster died at Killaloe. Donnogh mcCarrhie came to Munster, and committed a slaughter on Terlaugh o'Bryan that succeeded the said Connor in the kingdom of Monster. McConrye prince of Delvyn of Tiredalogha,[4] was

[1] *D mcMurrogh.*—He was grandson of Dermot mac Mael na mbo, who from being King of Hy Ceinnscallaigh, became King of Leinster.

[2] *Gillemocholmoge.* — He was chief of the territory which lies between Dublin and Bray.

[3] *Kwalann.* — The present Co. Wicklow.

[4] *Tiredalogha.*—i.e. the land of the two lakes, now the barony of Moycullen, Co. Galway, lying be-

killed by som of his owen familye. Terlaugh o'Connor with the forces of Meath and Brenie went to the provinces of Leinster & Munster to take hostages, had none, but returned without doeing anything worthy of note, save the burning of som cornes in the contryes of Lease and Ossery. The son of Ferall o'Molloye prince of ffearkell was killed by the grand-child of Rory o'Molloy and the familie of Montyr Rodan[1] at Dorow. McOtyr prince of Inis Gall[2] was chosen to be prince of the Danes of Dublin. These of Ormond and Elie tooke a prey from Kynnaleagh.

1135.—Murrogh o'Connor was restored againe to his kingdom of Meath. The abesse of Killdare was forced and taken out of her Cloyesters by Dermott mcMurrogh king of Leinster, and compelled to marie one of the said Dermotts people, at whose takeing he killed one hundred and seventy of the Townesmen and house of the abesse. Cormacke mcCarrhie, and Connor o'Bryan with their forces of Mounster came to Connaught, where they cleared the paces of Rath or Rather Rwabehy[3] & Belfada.[4] They burnt the twoo Corckes, Mogorne[5] and Dunmore,[6] and also killed Cahall mcCahall, prince of Connaught and Gillenewe o'fflynn prince of Sile Moyleroyne.[7] The bridge of Athlone and castle was broken and razed down by Morrogh o'Melaghlin king of Meath. Connor mcMurrogh o'Melaghlin, prince of Meath, was killed by Donnogh mcGillemocholmocke and the Danes of Dublin, for which cause the said mcGillemocholmocke was killed within a weeke after by Meathmen and Hugh

---

tween Lough Corrib and Lough Lurgan, the ancient name of the bay of Galway.

[1] *M. Rodan.* — St. Ruadan of Lorrha.

[2] *I. Gall.* —The Hebrides, off the west coast of Scotland.

[3] *Rwabehy.*—Now Rovehagh, in the parish of Killeely, Co. Galway.

[4] *Belfada.*—This name is not given among the townlands in the Ordnance Survey list.

[5] *Mogorne.* — *i. e.* Dunmogorne, four miles east of Westport, Co. Mayo.

[6] *Dunmore*—Eight miles north of Tuam. The castle is still standing, a short distance from the town.

[7] *S. Moyleroyne.* — The tribe-name of the McDermots of Moylurg, who were descended from Maelruana, 3rd son of Teige an eich gill, king of Connaught from 1014 to 1036.

o'Hugh. There was a meeting of Connor o'Brian, king of Munster, and king Terlaugh o'Connor with all the clergie of Mounster at Avall Keherny,[1] where there was a truce for one yeare confirmed between them. Luske[2] and the contry of Fingall was altogether burnt by Donnell mᶜMurrogh o'Melaghlin in revenge of the killing of his brother Connor o'Melaghlin, prince of Meath. Melaghlin mᶜDermott mᶜMoylenemo and Eochy o'Nolan, king of ffohartye, were killed in a fray by Owgarie o'Twahill and by the o'Tooles of Leinster with a great slaughter of many others. Morrogh o'Harie and his wife, king Terlaugh o'Connors daughter, were killed by Taighleagh o'Harie. Clonvickenos on Easter Sunday was burnt with the church yard of Moriegh o'Duffie & the place called Liscanabbeye. There was a great assembly of Leath moye in Cashell at the consecration of the churche[3] of Cormake mᶜCarhie king of Cashell. They of Ossery gave an overthrow to Dermot mᶜMurrogh, king of Leinster, where Owgarie o'Twoole, chief of the Tooles, was killed. The said Dermott gave an overthrow to those of Ossery, to Conell o'Bryen, and Danes of Waterford, where an infinite number of them were slaine. Morrogh o'Melaghlyn, king of Meath, gave an overthrow to those of Farnoy and killed 215 of them with 10 Cheeftaines. Hugh mᶜCoghlan o'fflatilye, prince of Delvinn Beathra, died. Henrick mᶜWillelan, king of France and Saxonie, died. Conradoe Emperour died. Morrogh o'Melaghlin king of Meath with a fleet of barkes and boates went upon the river Synnen, where the princes of Sile Morey in Connaught came to his house, Connor mᶜTeilagh and the o'Kellyes with their prince Teige o'Kelly, and yealded him hostages as pledges of their fidelity to him.

1136.—Donnell o'Duffie[4] arch Bishopp of Connought and

---

[1] *A. Keherny.*—Near Uisneagh, Co. Westmeath

[2] *Luske.*—Fifteen miles north of Dublin.

[3] *Churche.* — Called Cormac's chapel. For a detailed description of this very beautiful building see Petrie's *Eccl Arch. of Ireland*, p. 284.

[4] *D. O'Duffie.*—He occupied the See of Tuam from 1161 to 1201. See Ware's *Bishops*, p. 603.

cowarb[1] of St. Queran, immediately after celebrating Mass by himself, died and was buried on St. Patricks day at Clonfert, where he died and celebrated the said Masse. Clonard was preyed & the spoyles thereof taken by the Breniemen, they behaved themselves soe exceeding outragious in the takeing of these spoyles, that o'Daly[2] arch Poet of all Ireland, without respect was very irreverently stripped of his cloathes to his naked skinn, & amongst the rest they tooke a sword out of the vestery preserved by St. Finnan himself. Murrogh o'Melaghlin, king of Meath, tooke his own sonn whom he committed to prison for his eavell behaviour and miscarriage of himselfe. Dermott m^{c}Morrogh king of Leinster accompanied with all the forces of the Danes came to Westmeath to be revenged of the o'Melaghlins for theire abuses don to him before, hee was mett by the o'Roircks, o'Kellyes, and those of Uriell of the other side, where they caused m^{c}Murrogh with his Danes and Leinstermen to return without committing any hurtes worthy to be remembred, but only the burning of Ardbrackan. Whereupon they of the East of Meath, went to the o'Foylans[3] and borders of Leinster, burnt and spoyled theire townes without respect to either spirituall or corporall lands. Soone after Dermott m^{c}Murrogh king of the Danes and Leinster, came to the house of Morrogh o'Melaghlin in Clonard, where he made an offer to the said Morrogh of his own service in the field against any one with his forces with as great an army for king Murroghs assistance against any other during the kings pleasure, as long as his occasions required at his owen charges, soe that Morrogh would be pleased to suffer him quitely to enjoye only the Territorys of the o'ffoylans and Affailies without disturbance, which the said Murrogh accepted. Terlaugh o'Connor king of Ireland did put out the eyes of his owen son Hugh, for som haynous

---

[1] *Cowarb.*—Perhaps he had been abbot of Clonmacnoise, or bishop.

[2] *O'Daly.* — O'Reilly says he knows no works of this writer. *Irish Writers*, p. 83.

[3] *o'Foylans.* — They inhabited ancient Ossory. The name, anglicised Phelan and O'Phelan, is still very common throughout the midland counties.

misdemeanors of his. Soirvrechagh[1] o'Kelly, cowarb of Rahin o'Swanay, died.

1137.—There was Boysterous tempestous windes this yeare that it fell dowen many trees, houses, turrets, steeples, and other things, & whirled som of them into the seas. Donnell mᶜMurrogh o'Melaughlin, prince of all Ireland and king of Meath for a time, a very bountifull and noble prince, as free harted as Gwairy of Connaught, was killed by the east of Meath, for being in Rebellion against his father and Meath men. Waterford was besciged by Dermot mᶜMurrogh, king of Leinster, and Connor o'Bryan prince of Dalgaisse, where the Danes had a fleet of 200 shipes at sea, at last they obtayned hostages of the Danes and Donnogh mᶜCarhie, which they brought with them All Connaught from Esroe to the river of Synen, and from Clonvickenos to Eghtgie[2] was wast this year, save Iarhar Connought. More, daughter of King Mortaugh o'Bryan, and wife to Morrogh o'Melaughlin and Queen of Meath, died a very good death at Dorow. Moyle Issa called Crossan ffyn a King and arch-poet of Ireland, in that kind of meeter which is called Crossanaght, died at Clonconrie in Leinster.

1139.—They of the country of Elye, tooke a prey of Fearkeall, after they were sworn friendes to each other by great oathes for the preservation of the peace between them. King Terlaugh tooke his owen son prisoner after that he gave him before upon these oaths and securityes following, vidzᵗ (his owen name was Rory o'Connor that was afterwards king of Ireland) Moriegh o'Duffie arch bishopp with all the laymen and clergie of Connought, Teige o'Bryan, king of Thomond, Tyernann o'Royrck king of the Brienie, & Murrough mᶜGillenenewe o'Fergall, cheeftaine of the Analie. They all both Clergie and Laymen fasted[3] at Rathbrendon[4] to gett the said prince

---

[1] *Soirvrechagh.—i.e.* noble judge. This name, a common one among the MᶜCarthys, is anglicised Justin. See O'Donovan's Introd to *Top Poems.* p. 56

[2] *Eghtgie* —Now Sheve Baughty, on the north-east boundary of Clare.

[3] *Fasted* —See Preface to Reeves' *Adamnan*, liv.

[4] *Rathbrendon.*—Now Rathbrennan, a townland in the parish of Roscommon.

Rory out of the kings hands and could not. Alsoe king Terlaugh took Morrogh o'Melaghlin king of Meath prisoner, after hee agreed with him that each of them would be true to one another, and seeke noe advantage or hinderance of another, these were the oathes and suretyes that were between them of either side for performance of theire said agreement, vidz^t. the alter of St. Querans shrine, Relicks, Norannagh,[1] two prelates of every severall howeses together with Moriegh o'Duffie arch Bishopp of Connaught, primate of Ardmach, the staff of Jesus[2] which St Patrick brought into this kingdom, the coworb of St. ffehin, St. Fehins bell, and the boban[3] of St. Keuin, by all which suretyes and oathes they were bound to each other, not to seeke advantage either by captivity, bynding, or encroaching upon eithers lands, untill apparent occation had apeared to the sureties, & notwithstanding all which Murrogh was taken by king Terlaugh, and kept prisoner for the space of a month, without any breach of his side, untill at last hee was enlarged by the intercession of the said prelates and noblemen that were suretyes for him, whome they sent with safe conduct to Munster. In the meane time king Terlaugh ceased upon the kingdom of Meath into his owen hands and graunted the same to his son Connor o'Connor, which was made by this devise. The king caused to be assembled to Keylke the nobility of Meath and to Bryan of the Brenie, where he aprehended king Murrogh of Meath and took hostages of the rest of Meath which he delivered to his said son, with the possession of the Kingdome of Meath as aforesaid. o'Garmley[4] tooke the Principallity of Tyre Owen to him, was king thereof & Banished there hence the sonn of Neale.

---

[1] *Norannagh.* — O'Donovan thinks this was a crozier ornamented with gold.

[2] *Staff of Jesus.*—Said to have been given to St. Patrick by an angel. It was one of the insignia of the Archbishop of Armagh, as successor of St. Patrick. It was burnt by the Reformers in 1537. See Introd. to *Obits of Christ Church*, viii.

[3] *Boban.*—O'Donovan thinks this was a bell which had belonged to St. Kevin of Glendalough.

[4] *o'Garmley.*—They were chiefs of the district now comprised in the barony of Raphoe, Co. Donegal. See *Annals F.M.*, ii. 1071.

Gilla Enos o'Clowan[1] arch poet of Connaught in the art of Poetry died.

1140.—There raigned strange diseases of biles and patches this yeare in Munster, whereof many died, and among the rest these two noble young men, Bryan mᶜTerlaugh o'Bryan, prince of Munster, and Teige mᶜTerlaugh o'Connor ought not to be forgotten. Connor mᶜTerlaugh o'Connor, prince of Ireland and king of Meath for the space of half a yeare, was killed by o'Dowlyn, king of ffertullagh, because he was unjustly constituted to raigne over Meath, which o'Dowleyn conld never well brooke King Terlaugh granted the government of Westmeath to Donnogh mᶜMorrogh o'Melaghlin, and the government of Eastmeath to Tiernan o'Royrcke and Dermott mᶜMurrogh to be held of the king of Connaught by services of homage and fealty dureing pleasure. Rory o'Connor was enlarged by his father king Terlaugh upon further securityes. There was an agreement of truce made between king Terlaugh and Terlaugh o'Bryan at Tyredaglasse, as the prelates of the church ordained between them. Terlaugh o'Connor king of Ireland came to Meath to constitute a king over them, where he appoynted Donnogh o'Melaughlin king of the weast of Logh Innill and the son of Mortagh o'Melaughlin of the east part of the said Logh. Meathmen gave an erick[2] of four hundred cowes to king Terlagh for killing his son.

1141 —There was a great disease of Biles, potches, and scabbes in Connaught and Munster this year King Terlaugh o'Bryan king of Munster with all his forces came to Leitter Crannagh[3] on the mount of Slieve Bloome to meet with Tyernan o'Roirck in Meath. King Terlagh o'Connor encamped with his forces in Rawaghan[4] in Foxes contry, and sent his son Donell, together with Melaghlin mᶜMurrogh o'Melaghlin, Connor mᶜDonnell o'Bryan, and Dermott

---

[1] *o'Clowan.*—Several ollamhs of this name (O'Clumhain) are mentioned in the *Annals F.M.*

[2] *Erick* —A fine in kind given to the family of the person slain by the murderer or by his tribe.

[3] *L. Crannagh.* —The name is now obsolete.

[4] *Rawaghan.*—Now Killarue, in the barony of Kilcoursey, King's Co.

m‸Cormack m‸Carhie with great and many forces went to Fearkeall to defend Meath, that the said Munstermen should not passe through that contry to anoy Meath, and were mett by the Munstermen in a wood in the west part of that contry, where they killed divers of them, and compelled them to returne to their howses without doeing anything worthy to be remembered. King Terlaugh o'Connor with his forces of Connaught tooke hostages of all Munster, except west Munster, which he left to Terlagh o'Bryan. Munster in old time was divided in five Munsters, vidz^t Ormond, Thuomond, Desmond, Middle Munster, and West Munster. King Terlagh o'Connor this yeare gave the battle of Moynemore[1] on the Munstermen, he was accompanied with Dermott m‸Murrogh and the forces of Ireland, where Murtagh m‸Connor o'Bryan, and an infinite number of the nobility of Munster were slaine, and all Munster brought in subjection to king Terlagh. The hostages of Leinster were sent to Mortagh m‸Neale m‸Loghlyn eaven to his house. John Papirion[2] Cardinall came to this kingdom from the Pope to procure the inhabitants of the land to an amendment of theire lives.

1152.—All Munster was much impoverished by continuall contentions of the maCarthies and o'Bryans contending against one another. King Terlagh o'Connor for appeasing of which contentions went to Munster, and divided that province in two parts between Cormack m‸Carhie, and the o'Bryans, Teige and Terlagh. King Terlaugh accompanied with Murtagh m‸Neale m‸Laughlin came to Meath, which he likewise divided into tooe parts between Murrogh o'Melaghlin, and his son Melaghlin, that is to say, of the West of Clonard to Morrogh, and of the East as farr as Meath extendes to his said sonn. Dermott m‸Murrogh king of Leinster tooke the lady Dervorgill, daughter of the said.

---

[1] *Moynemore.*—In the parish of Emly, Co. Tipperary.

[2] *Papirion.*—The principal object of his coming was to bring the pallia to the four archbishops. *Trias Thaum.,* p. 306, and Lanigan's *Eccl. Hist*, iv 139. See also *Annals F.M.,* ii 1095.

Morrogh o'Melaghlin, and wife of Tyernan o'Royrck, with her cattle with him, and kept her for a long space to satisfie his insatiable, carnall and adulterous lust, shee was procured and enduced thereunto by her unadvised brother Melaghlin for some abuses of her husband Tyernan don before. Henry mᶜDavid, king of Scotland, dyed.

1153.—Murrogh o'Melaghlin king of Meath, bordres of Leinster and Taragh, the cheefest of all Ireland for bounty and hospitallity, died at Dorow in his owen house. Hugh o'Malone, cowarb of St. Queran of Clonvickenos, whoe for his great ritches, charity, and bountyfull hospitallity was called in generall the fountaine of all happiness of Leath Coyne, died. Gillegott o'Kierga,[1] prince of Carbry,[2] was killed at Clonard by Donnogh o'Melaghlin, king of Meath. Donnogh o'Melaghlin was deposed by the Meathmen of his kingdome, and Dermott mᶜDonnell o'Melaghlin put in his stead, who was his owen brother. There was a great Discomfiture of these of Brawnie and Mointer Moyleynna[3] by Hymer mᶜCarhon and the son of o'Conway and these of Mointer Hagan alias Foxes contry. St. Queran was Intercesser to God to give this ouerthrow to these of Brawnie, because they went with their cottes and boates to Clonvicknos and tooke all the swyne and hoggs that the monkes had upon the woodes of Faailt, which the monkes with the shrine of St. Queran followed to the place called Lisan Tosgely,[4] desireing restitution, which was denied them, and by Gods will Brawnye receaved this Disgrace and ouerthrow the next day. King Terlagh mᶜRory o'Connor, monarch of Ireland, a great benefactor of the church and all spirituall men in generall, a man of wonderfull hospitality, and in fine a reliever and cherisher of the poor, died in Donmore, the 13ᵗʰ of the Kalends of June in the 50ᵗʰ year of his reign and

---

[1] *o'Kierga.* — Now anglicized Keary and Carey.

[2] *Carbry.*—Now a barony in the north-west of Co. Kildare.

[3] *M. Moyleynna.*—This tribe inhabited the ancient Cuircne, now the barony of Kilkenny West, Co Westmeath

[4] *Lisan Tosgely.*—i.e the fort of the gospel. The name is now obsolete

the 68th year of his age, after whose death his sonn prince Rory was invested in the government of Connaught as king of that province, untill Mortagh mᶜNeale mᶜLaughlyn ended his raigne, then Rory was promoted to the monarchie of Ireland. Mortagh mᶜNeale was king of Ireland 14 years, he was of the o'Neales of the North. Terlagh o'Bryan, king of Munster, came unto the house of Rory o'Connor, and gave him 12 hostages of the cheefest of Dalgaisse. King Mortagh with this forces went to Leinster, and gave the kingdome and Government thereof or of that province to Dermott mᶜMurrogh for yeelding him hostages of obedience & allegiance. They wasted and spoyled all Ossery without respect of Church or Chaple. Cowley o'Kendalan, prince of the race of Lagery, a nobleman both ready and hasty to put in practice all goodness, as liberall as Gwairie of Connaught, as well spoken as Mongan mᶜffiaghna,[1] was unhappily and treacherously killed by Donnogh mᶜDonnell o'Melaghlin king of Meath, haveing sworne to each other before by these ensueing oathes to be true to one another without effusion of blood, for performance of which oathes the primate of Ardmach was bound to the Popes Legatt, Greman[2] arch Bushopp of Dublyn, the abbott of the monkes of Ireland, the cowarb of St. Queran with his oathes, the staff or bachall of Jesus, the cowarb of St Fechin with his oathes, the cowarb of Saint Columbkill, with his oathes. These oathes were taken before king Mortagh, Donnogh o'Kervell king of Uriell, Tiernan o'Royrck king of the Breine, and Dermott mᶜMorrogh king of Leinster, and the principallest of Meath and Teaffa alsoe, and if there were no such oathes or suretyes, it was a wicked act to kill such a nobleharted man without cause. There was a great convocation of the clergie consisting of 17 Bishopps with the primate of Ireland and Legatte in Tredath this year aboute the consecration of the church[3] of monkes that

---

[1] *M. mᶜffiaghna.* — See p. 100, antea, and O'Curry's *MS Materials*, p. 589.
[2] *Greman.*—Gregory, who occupied the See from 1121 to 1161 See Ware's *Bishops*, p. 311.
[3] *Church.* — Of the Cistercian monastery of Mellifont, founded in

was there in the presence of king Mortagh, Tiernan o'Royrck, Donnogh o'Kervell, & o'Heoghie, where the said Donnogh o'Melaghlin was excommunicated by the clergy, and deposed from the kingdome and principallity of Meath by the kings and said noblemen, and the whole kingdome and government given to his brother Dermott as more worthy thereof. Cowoley m'Dunleyue o'Keoghie, king of Ulster died. m'Dowell steward of Donmore was killed. King Mortagh with his forces went to Leinster, where Dermott m'Murrogh king of Leinster gaue him hostages. They of Affalie, Lease, and Ossery fled into Connaught, the king afterwards with the forces of Leinster went to Desmond, where they had the hostages of that contry, from thence went to those of Dalgaisse whom he banished to Thomond & also did putt som of them to the sword, he also besieged Limbrick, and compelled the Danes to submit themselves to his grace, and to acknowledge him as theire king, & to forsake Terlaugh o'Bryan & also to banish him from out of their jurisdiction, & there divided Munster in two parts between the son of MaCarhie and the son of Donnell o'Bryan, from thence the King came to the plaine of Moyfarcha,[1] tooke the preyes and spoyles of Sileanmchie, killed part of the inhabitants, & gave them an overthrow. They of the Eoganaght of Cashell destroyed and preyed Rosscre and from thence the king came to his house. While these things were a Doing Rory o'Connor king of Connaught went with a great army to Ulster in the absence of King Murtogh, there burnt Iniseany,[2] hewed and did cut downe all the trees in the orchard, and tooke away the preyes and spoyles of Tyreowen to Kwaillie Kyannaghty.[3] Rorie o'Connor with his forces went to Munster, and settled Murtagh o'Bryan in possession as halfe king, or king of halfe Munster, and caused the sonn of Cormack m'Carthy to yeeld hostages into his handes with

---

1142 by O'Carroll, prince of Oriel, at the desire of St. Malachy.

[1] *Moyfarcha.*—In the barony of Ballybritt, King's Co.

[2] *Iniseany.* — Incheny, in the barony of Strabane, Co. Tyrone.

[3] *K Kyannaghty.*—Coolkeenaght, in the parish of Faughan, Co. Derry.

condicion of forfiture of theire lives, if king Mortagh would not come to defend them. The head of Eochie m`c`Lughta that raigned king of Munster at the time of the birth of Christ, (as before[1] is remembered) was this yeare taken out of the earth, where it was buried at Ffynnorey.[2] It was of such wonderfull biggness, as mine Author sayeth, it was as bigg as any cauldron, the greatest goose might easily pass thorow the holes of his eyes, and in the place or hole where the marrowe was towardes his throate a goose might enter.

1158.—Rory o'Connor king of Connaught with his forces went to Leythlyn, where he tooke the hostages of Ossery and Lease, and tooke captive with him m`c`Rath o'More, prince of Lease. Hugh o'Demsy prince of Clanmaliere[3] died. Carbrey o'Kyergie accompanied with Teaffa men, made a retrait upon Dermott o'Melaghlin, deposed him, and putt again Donnogh o'Melaghlin in his former place. Tyernan of Royrick and Dermott followed them to Athmoyne (now called Lismoyne[4]) where they gave them an overthrow, and took great preyes from Sileronan and Moyntyr Kyergie, Carbry was banished to Leinster, and afterwards came to an atonement,[5] and Donnogh was banished into Connaught. Connor m`c`Donnell o'Bryan was taken by Terlaugh o'Bryan, and his little son with him, they both had their eyes put out, notwithstanding there was an agreement made before by them of conditionall peace with suretyes and oathes taken before great prelates of the church. There was a conuocation of all the clergie in Ireland at Breyuick Teige.[6] The bishopps of Connaught with the archbishopp, Hugh o'Nosyn,[7] tooke their jorny to come thither, & as they were passing towards Clonvicknose with

---

[1] *Before*—See p 47.
[2] *Ffynnorey.*—Corofin, Co. Clare
[3] *Clanmaliere.* — The territory along the Barrow, now included in the baronies of Portnahinch and Upper Philipstown.
[4] *Lismoyne.*—A townland in the parish of Ardnurcher, Co. Westmeath.
[5] *Atonement.—i.e.* reconciliation.
[6] *B. Teige.* — Near Trim. The See of Derry was established then, and given to O'Brolchain, successor of St Columba, with control over all the abbeys of Ireland. See *Trias Thaum.*, p. 309.
[7] *H. O'Nosyn.* — He was archbishop of Tuam from 1150 to 1161. He was buried in his own cathedral. See Ware's *Bishops,* p. 604.

2 of the cowarbs of St. Queran in theire company, and as they were comeing to the joysts or wooden bridge over the Syenn at Clonvicknos called Cuir Clwana, they were mett by the Rebell Carpreach[1] the swift and his kearne, whoe killed two laymen, and robbed the clergie, and did not suffer them to goe neerer the said Convocation, for another cause he had himself. There was a great mount of fier seen in the firmament this yeare, westerly of Tea Doynn in Mounster, it was bigger then St. Patricks mount, which dispersed in severall showers of small sparkles of fier without doeing any hurt, this was upon the Eave[2] of St. John in Autumne.

1159.—King Mortagh came to Rowe Connell[3] in Meath, & banished Dermott o'Melaghlin from out of all Meath, and deposed him of his principality, and confirmed Donnogh his brother in the possession thereof. Abbell, anchorite of Ardmach, died. Rory o'Connor and Tyernan tooke their several oathes, to be true to one another in all respects, whereupon they retrayted against Mortagh, king of Ireland and rebelled against him. Rory o'Connor made a wooden[4] bridge at Athlone, that he might have passage to take the spoyles of Meath. The forces of Meath and Teaffa came to Athlone to hinder the makeing of the said bridge with theire king Donnogh o'Melaghlin, and fought with Rory o'Connor, where in the end Hugh o'Connor, Rory o'Connor's son, was sore hurt of an irrecoverable wound, whereof hee died within a weeke after.

1160.—David mcMoyle Colme, king of Scotland, Wales, and the borders of England, the greatest potentate in these parts of Europe, died. Eugenius Tertius, the Pope, and Conrado the emperor of Almayne, died. King Mortagh graunted the kingdome of Meath, from the river of Synen to the seas, to Melaghlin mcMurrogh o'Melaghlen, & the princi-

---

[1] *Carpreach.*—The *Annals F M* say by the soldiers of o'Melaghlin, king of Meath.

[2] *Eave.*—Perhaps the feast of the Beheading of St John the Baptist, August 29th.

[3] *R. Connell.*—Rathconnell, in the parish of Moycashel, Co. Westmeath.

[4] *Wooden.*—A wicker bridge. So *Annals F. M* ad ann.

pallity of the o'Bryuns[1] to Tyernan o'Royrck, tooke their hostages, and returned to his own house. St. Barnard abbott of Claravall[2] died. Melaghlen m⁰Murrogh king of Meath tooke hostages of o'ffielan and of o'ffalie for theire obedience to him.

1161.—o'Clocan, cowarb of St Columkill in Kelles, died. King Mortagh went to Dublin and caused the Danes to submitt themselves to him, and acknowledge him as theire king, and gave them 1200 cowes in their payes, because hee employed them before in divers services.

1162.—Melaghlin m⁰Morrogh o'Melaghlin, king of Meath and of the most part of Leinster in his prime and flourishing estate on the night[3] of St. Bridgett the virgin, died in the house of Dorow. King Mortagh with his forces came to the river of Inneoyn,[4] at the foorde of Dongolman[5] and there tooke the hostages of all the contry of Teaffa, and established Donnogh o'Mellaghlin in the government of Meath as king thereof. Tyernan o'Royrck took prisoner Donnogh o'Keruell king of Uriell and fettered him with irons on his heeles Soone after Godfrey or Geffery o'Relly tooke him away by force from the said Tyernan. The bridge of Athlone was broken and the fort raysed to the earth by Donnogh o'Melaghlin king of Meath. Donnogh m⁰Donnell o'Melaghlin, king of Meath, was killed by Murrogh o'Finnollan king of Delvin More, and by his sonns, for the great and extortious dealings of the said Donnogh continually used against them.

1163.—King Mortagh m⁰Neale went to Tyrebryan,[6] preyed and spoyled that contry, where Dermot m⁰Morrogh king of Leinster came to his house and yeelded him hostages; Rory o'Connor gave him 12 good hostages, he graunted all the

---

[1] *o'Bryuns.*—The tribe-name of the O'Rourkes of Breffny.
[2] *Claravall.*— Clairvaux, in the diocese of Langres, France, a Cistercian abbey founded in 1115. St. Bernard was its first abbot.
[3] *Night*—February 1st.
[4] *Inneoyn*—A river which divides the barony of Kilkenny West from that of Rathconrath, in Co West-meath.
[5] *Dongolman*—In the parish of Ballymore in the latter barony
[6] *Tyrebryan*—Breffny O'Rourke.

province of Leinster to Dermot mᶜMurrogh, hee gave one halfe of Meath to Dermott o'Melaghlin and the other halfe to Rory o'Connor king of Connaught. Beann Artgalie[1] was giuen by Dermott o'Melaghlen king of Meath to God and to St Queran.

1164.—Donnogh mᶜGillepatrick mᶜDonnogh king of Ossery, died. Kill o'Milchon[2] and Rossemide,[3] were freed by Dermott o'Melaghlin, king of Meath from all manner of cess and press for ever in honour of God and Saint Queran. Mortagh was slain by those of Uriell, after whose death Rory o'Connor king of Connaught succeeded in the monarchie. Rory more mᶜTerlagh o'Connor in the English Chronicles is called Rotherick, was the last king of Ireland of Irish blood, and raigned 10 years. Our Irish Chronicles for the most part call those seven and last kings imperfect and defective kings, because they raigned without a crown[4] (as before is mentioned) since the raigne of Bryan Borowe, and Moyleseachlin more o'Melaghlin. In king Rory o'Connors time Dermot mᶜMurrogh ats Keyuanagh was banished from out of the province of Leinster by king Rory, Tyernan o'Royrck, and their partakers in the year of our Lord 1166 for the unjustly taking and keeping of Deruorgill daughter of Murrogh o'Melaghlyn king of Meath, and wife of the said Tyernan o'Royrck, being before for his pride, tyrany, and badd government hated[5] of the Leinstermen themselves, and at last being thereunto compelled by necessity went for England and brought with him from thence Robert king of Stephen's sonne, called Robert Fitzstephen,[6] twenty knights of Englishmen, and 50 archers of Welshmen, with a great armye,

---

[1] *Beann Artgalie.* — Now obsolete.

[2] *K. o'Milchon.* — Now Kilmaelchon, in the parish of Lusmagh, King's Co.

[3] *Rossemide.* — In the barony of Delvin, Co. Westmeath.

[4] *Crown.* — They are called kings 'go fresabhra,' *i.e.* with opposition.

[5] *Hated.* — This, not the abduction of Dervorgill, was the true cause why Dermot was banished. See *Annals F.M.*, iii. 96.

[6] *R. Fitzstephen* — He was the illegitimate son of Stephen De Marisco, Constable of Cardigan, and of Nesta. Fitzstephen and Maurice Fitzgerald were uterine brothers.

& with them and those that joyned with him after his landing here hee preyed and spoyled the territoryes of Ossery and gave the inhabitants a great ouerthrow at Sliew Mairge.[1] King Rory hearing of these things went with his forces to Rathee or Rathouth[2] where he met with Dermot m^cMurrogh, who came to his house, submitted himself, and yeelded king Rory his owen sonn[3] in signe of obedience with other hostages, whereupon king Rory, leaving all Leinster in peace, returned to Connaught.

1167.—Thomas Beckett, Bishopp of Canterburry, was killed without cause and innocently in the abby of Canterburry by Sr William Bretton, St Hugh Morvile, Sr William Tracy, and Sr Reynold fitz Vrse, in English the beares son, 1171. 29th December.

This year Dermott m^cMurrogh brought with him Richard Strongboe,[4] earle of Cheapstowe and Ognie with a great armye of Englishmen, hee was afterwards to make his repaire to the king of England, to king Henry the second, who being ready to go to France to warr with the French king, notwithstanding the matter the king had in hand was of such importance as could not admitt of other trobles, yet he had such regard and pitty to m^cMurrogh, that he sent his favourable letters in his behalfe to Griffin then prince of Wales, & to the Bishopp[5] of St. David, soe that Dermott was soe strongly aided into Ireland, that in short time hee did not onely recover his owne patrimony, but a great deale more then in reason he could make challenge unto, for Dermott as soone as hee was sure of his aid in the beginning of winter came privily before into Ireland, and soe lay close hidden in the abbey of Fearnes, among the monks there, untill Robert Fitzstephen, Raymond De la Grosse, and

---

[1] *Shew Mairge*—Now a barony in the south-east of Queen's Co.

[2] *Rathouth.*—A town in the barony of the same name in the south-east of Meath.

[3] *Sonn.*—This was Conor, who was, according to some writers, put to death by O'Connor. See *Hib. Expug*, l. 10 and 17.

[4] *Strongboe.*—*i. e.* Richard De Claie, Earl of Pembroke and Strigul.

[5] *Bishopp.*— David Fitzgerald, brother of Maurice, bishop of St. David's.

others to the number of 3000 souldiers came over, well furnished with suffitient armour and other necessaryes according to theire promise the next spring in Anno 1166, as before is mentioned. Soone after came Mourise fitz Gerald, then after the earle of Cheapstow, to whome Dermott gave his daughter Ife or Eave[1] in marriage, alsoe Dermott m^cMurrogh in the year of the incarnation 1170 died of an unknown disease,[2] without doing pennance,[3] shrive or Extrem Unction. King Henry hearing of the good success the said englishmen had in Ireland, the kings majesty in his owen person came over, who made a final end of an intire conquest in Ireland, in the year of our Lord God 1173.

FINIS.

---

[1] *Eave.* — Usually called Eva. There is a fine painting by Maclise in our National Gallery of the marriage of Strongbow and Eva.

[2] *Disease.*—'An unsufferable and unknown disease, for he became putrid while living.' *Annals F M.*, ii. 1182.

[3] *Pennance.*—A catalogue of the Kings of Leinster in Trinity College library, quoted by O'Donovan, says 'he died at Ferns after the victory of Unction and penance.' *Ibid.*

FOR YOUR BETTER INSTRUCTION (BROTHER) I WILL SETT YOU DOWNE THREE PEDIGREES OF THE RACES DESCENDED OF THE THREE SONS OF MILETUS THAT HAD ISSUE, AS HEBER THE WHITE, IRE, AND HEREMON. AVERGIN SONNE OF MILETUS HAD NO ISUE AS FARRE AS I CAN GATHER.

The Genealogie of the Lord Randolph earle of Antrim[1] of the race of Heremon.

Randolph is sonne of—		Fergussa	
Sawarle		Eirck	
Alexander		Carhayne	
Eoyn Kahanay		Eirck.	
Eoyn		Eahagh	
Donell Ballagh.		Colla wais	
Eoyn More		Eochy Dowlen	
Eoyn		Carbry Liffeghar	
Enos the Younger		Cormack	
Enos the Great		Art Enear	
Donell (of whom the Family of the MacDonells)	mac	Conn Cedcahagh	mac
		Felym Reaghtwar	
Randolph		Twahall Teachtwar	
Sawarle		Fiaghy Finnolay	
Gillebride		Feray Ffinnaghtny	
Gille adawnayne		Cnowhynn nia nare	
Salamon		Lwiegh Shrewderg sonn of the 3 Eawnais viz[t.] Breasse, Nare, and Lothar theire names	
Meargaye			
Swyne			
Nealgusa			
Manye		Eochye Feylie	
Godfrey		Fynn	
Cathwaye		Roynie Roe	

---

[1] *E. of Antrim.*—The 2nd Earl, who was born in 1609. He took an active part in the war of 1641 as a Royalist, on the Irish side. He died in 1682. See Archdall's *Peerage*, i. 207.

Easawyn Eawna ⎫
Blaheaghty
Beoheaghty
Lawra Lwirck
Enna Aignye
Enossa Twirmeagh of
  Taragh
Eahagh Foltleahan
Ailealla Cassaicklagh
Conley Crwackelgay
Iaranngleo Fathay
Meilge Mollthye
Cowhye Koylbreye
Owynie the great
Eaghye Bwagaye
Dieaghladhrye   ⎬ mac
Fiaghye Tolgaye
Moreaye
Symon Brechus
Aidan Glasse
Nwadad fyn Fayle
Giallchaa
Oillealla Olcheoyn
Iiorna Siorgalye
Deyne
Roheaghtye
Moeyne
Enossa
Fiagha Lawryne
Simyrgwill ⎭

Enuotha ⎫
Tygernvais
Folla
Eithreoile
Iaranngle of Athye
Heremon
Miletus hispanius
Billus
Breowynus
Bratha
Deatha
Archaa
Allayde
Nwadad
Ninnvaille.
Heber Glasse   ⎬ mac
Agnomoynfin
Heber Glunyenn
Lawfynn
Thayde
Tauorne
Eogawyne
Beogawyne
Heber Swift ⎭
Sru mac Esrue.
And soeforth as in the genealogie of Gathelus at Addam remembred on folio 4°.

The Genealogie of the Lord Henrie earle of Thomond[1] of the race of Heber the white, whome I should write first for Antiquities sake of place.

Henry is sonn of		Blayd	
Donnogh who was son of		Tall alias Casse	
Connor		Cassyne	
Donnogh		Cwircke	
Terlagh		Connell Eahtwar	
Teige		Lwyeagh myonn	
Terlagh		Enossa Tyrie	
Bryen		Tirewirb	
Mahon		Moe Corb	
Moriertagh		Cormack Cass	
Teige		Oillealla olwyn	
Connor ne Suidyne		Moa Nwadad	
Donnogh Carbrye		Aloa Neide	
Donnell the great		Deirg	
Mortagh		Deirghyne	
Terlaugh		Enna Moncheoyn	
Dermot	mac	Loch	mac
Terlaugh		Moreay Muchna	
Teige		Eachye Gairve	
Brian Borowa		Dwagh Donn Dalts Dea	
Kinnedy		Carbrey Losckleahan	
Lorcan		Lwyegh Lwyne	
Laghtna		Inamar	
Corcke		Nia Sedawyne	
Anlwan		Agnamayne foltchoeyn	
Mahon		Fearcuirb	
Terlaugh		Moacorb	
Cahal		Cowhye Koew	
Hugh Koew		Roheaghty Rithderg	
Conell		Lwyegh Lwyne	
Eaghy Ballderg		Eaghye	
Carhyn finn		Aillealla Fynn	

[1] *E. of Thomond.*—The 5th Earl. *Ibid.*, ii. 30.

212 The Annals of Clonmacnoise.

Art
Lwyeag Lawdearg
Eaghy Warcheasse
Lwyeagh Iardonn
Enna Derig
Dwagh finn
Sedna Innaríe
Breisry
Art Imlye
Felimie
Roheagty
Rochoeyne
Failve Ilchoraye
Caiss Kedcoyngnye
} mac

Allergoide
Mwynemon
Cassclohie
Irero Arda
Roheaghty
Rossawyn glass
Nwadad Delawe
Eaghie Fewerglass
Convallo
Heber the White
Miletus Hispanius
as in the precedent Gene-
 ologie to Addam.
} mac

The Genealogie of Magenus Vicecount of Ivehaghe.[1]

Arthur is son of
Hugh
Donell oge
Donell more
Hugh
Art
Hugh
Art ne Mangye
Mortaugh Riaganagh
Eachmyle
Rory
Gillecolme
Dowinsye
Hugh Beawar
Flathvertagh
Eaghmyle
} mac

Enos
Eaghmyle
Enos oge
Enos More of whom the
 race of Magenos is
 named
Eldeaa
Laygneyn
Blathmach
Donnell
Connor
Breassall
Fergus
Aidan
Mongayne
Saraynne
} mac

---

[1] *V. of Ivehaghe.*—Arthur Magennis; he was outlawed in 1642, but his outlawry was reversed, and he sat in the parliament of 1689. At the close of the Jacobite war he entered the Austrian service with a battalion of 500 men. See D'Alton's *K. James' Army List*, ii. 732.

Manye		Gillchaa
Fathye		Fiachy finawnus
Conell		Iriell Glunmar
Coylevotha		Conell Kearnagh
Crwyn Bagroye		Awirgin
Eahagh Cova, (of whom O'Heachagh in Ulster is said.)		Caisee
		Cathwaye
		Gioga
Lwyeagh		Rowrye
Rosse		Sittricke
Finchaa		Duffe
Finchaa.	mac	Fomore	mac
Fiacha Araye (of whom Dalnary is said)		Argedwar
		Silelawe, desunt 4 generationes
Enos G.		
Fergus G.		Ollaw Fodla
Tybradye Tyrey		Fiaghy Finsglothy
Breassall brick		Sedna Art
Fiagha		Artry
Kyrb		Ebrick
Mayle		Heber
Rochry		Ire
Cathway		Miletus Hispanus &c

In the year 1170 last mentioned, there was a great Convocation of the clergie of Ireland at Clonfert by commisson from the Pope, for the reformation of certaine abuses of a long time used in Ireland. These were the Bishops and clergy that were in that assemblye, vidz^t o'Twahall[1] arch Bushopp of Dublin and Leynster, Legat of Ireland and Bishop of Meath, Echytygerne m^cMoylekieran Bishop o'Kervell bushopp of Uriell, Cadla o'Duffie archbushopp of Conaught, Cealachar o'Carmeady bushopp of Clonfert, Tomaltagh o'Connor bushopp of Moye Iie, o'Moylefomer B. o'Rwadan Bishop, Abbott of Clonvicknose, cowarb

---

[1] *O'Twahall.*—Laurence. His *Life* has been written by the Rev. John O'Hanlon.

of St. Queran, and the cowarb of Saint Brandon &c, where it was laid down by them by a Constitution that noe layman should have the rule of any Church or Church matters from thence forth, that noe portion Canons should be sought of women theire husbands liveing, that Holy Orders should not be given to bushopp nor Priests sonns, and for example of these their Constitutions, they tooke the livings of seven bushopps that had Bushopricks and were laymen.[1] There was money[2] coyned in Clonvickenos this year. Lorcan o'Twahall archbushopp of Dublin and legat of Ireland died in England.[3]

1180.—The church of the Nunns of Clonvicknos was finished by the lady Dervorgill daughter of Morrogh o'Melaghlen before mentioned this year. Dervaile daughter of o'Melaghlen and wife of Randalphe mᶜCoghlan, mᶜCoghlans sonne, died this year.

1181 —Sir John Coursey returned again to Downe Dalealiglasse, and repaired to his house there. Clonard was well renewed by his own natives being altogether spoyled, razed, and defaced by the Danes and other foreigners before. Dowchauley daughter of o'Roirck queen of Ireland, and wife to Rory o'Connor king of Ireland, died in pennance. Miles Cogan, Raymond de la Grosse, Keannkoylean, and the two sons of Fitz Stephen, were killed by mᶜTyre prince of Imokuylle.[4] There was a great slaughter of Englishmen by the Welshmen this yeare, there were 28 of their chiefest slaine. It is not knowen how many of the inferiour sort because the slaughter was soe great that they could not be numbred. The most part of the Englishmen that were in the north were slaine by Ulstermen this yeare. The steeple of Ardbracan

---

[1] *Laymen* —St. Bernard speaks of this abuse in the Irish Church, and he says eight laymen in succession had taken possession of the temporalities of Armagh. See his *Life of St. Malachy*, ch. 7

[2] *Money* —Ware says a mint was established here by Turlogh O'Connor, in which silver coins were struck. *Antiquities*, p. 204.

[3] *England.*—In the monastery of Eu, in Normandy, November 14th. He was canonized by Pope Honorius III. in 1225.

[4] *Imokuylle.* — Now a barony in the south-west of Co. Cork.

fell this yeare. Donnogh o'Kervell prince of Uriell (who killed king Mortaugh m^cNeale) died.

1182.—William the Conqueror king of England died in Normandy in the yeare of our Lord 1082. William Rufus son of king William the Conqueror succeeded next after his father and raigned 13 years, a great persecutor of the church and at last was by mischance slaine by Sr Walter Tyrrell knight with an arrow at new forrest. Also Henery the first after hee raigned 35 years died in anno 1137, he was surnamed Henry Beauclearck. King Steephen reigned 19 yeares and died in Anno 1155. Henry the second after he raigned king of England 33 years died in Anno 1190, he began his conquest of Ireland about the fourteenth yeare of his raigne of England

There are soe many leaves lost or stolen out of the ould Irish book which I Translate, that I doe not know how to handle it, but to satisfie your request, I will translate such places in the book as I can read, and yett in the mean while I shall entreat you to hold me excused for not nameing the kings deputies and Englishmen therein contained by their right names, for I goe by the words of the ould booke and not by my owen invention, which is soe illfavouredly and confusedly handled, that mine author could not gett his pen to name the Kings of England or other foraigne contryes by their proper names but by such Irish names as he pleased to devise out of his owen head, although he was a great Latinist and Scholler, which I thought fitt to declare for mine owen excuse soe I rest

Yrs assuredly

C. M. G.

1199.—Cahall Crovdearg[1] o'Connor preyed Fouver, upon the followers of Cahall Carragh,[2] where Cahall Carragh slew Moyleguley offichertie prince of the west of Connaught, and

---

[1] *Crovdearg.* — *i. e.* the red-handed. On the origin of this name see *Annals F M.,* iii. 210.

[2] *C. Carragh.*—He was son of Conor Maenmoy, son of Roderic O'Connor, the last ardrigh.

the knight, Grandchild of Donnogh o'Melaghlen, young prince of Meath, and Hugulat mᶜConvey o'Leygachan. Cahall Carragh o'Connor with the forces of William Burk, Mortagh o'Bryen, and Connor Roe o'Bryan, deposed Cahall Crovdearg o'Connor and banished him to the North of Connaught & tooke hostages of all Connaught, they preyed and tooke the spoyles of the Hospittalls of Clonvicknos, Bushoppe and all the churches of Connaught of that voyadge. Richard the first King of England died this year.

1200.—Meiler,¹ and the Englishmen of Leinster came to Clonvicknose to meet with Cahall Carragh o'Connor, where they remained together 2 nights and at last tooke the spoyles of the towen and churches. Rory mᶜDonnsleyve o'Heoghaa king of Ulster, was killed by John De Coursey and his Englishmen. Cadley o'Duffie arch-bushopp of all Connaught died. Cahall Crovdearg o'Connor, o'Neale, and these of Fermanagh, preyed Arteagh² and Varde eallae,³ and at last Cahall departed from his assotiats ill content. Cahall Carragh and William Power overtooke o'Neale and these of Farmannagh and gave them an overthrow where o'Heignye King of Farmannagh with many others were slaine. Cahall Crovdearg o'Connor accompanied with the forces of John De Coursey and Hugh Delacie, passed through Connaught untill they came to Tyrefiaghragh Ainye,⁴ where they were mett by Cahall Carragh o'Connor, with all his Irish and English forces, and were overthrown and pursued to Royndowne⁵ (now called Teagh Eoin or Johns town neer Loghrie) John De Coursey was forsed to take boate when he

---

¹ *Meiler*—FitzHenry, illegitimate son of Henry II and of Nesta. He was made Justiciary the year before.

² *Arteagh* — A district in Co. Roscommon, including the parish of Tibohine. See *Annals F. M.*, iii. 119.

³ *Varde callae.*—Not identified.

⁴ *T. Ainye.*—See p. 77, antea.

⁵ *Royndowne.*—Eight miles west of Athlone, on the western shore of Lough Ree. A considerable part of the castle is still standing. The dun, from which it takes its name, is said to have been erected by Turgesius. A priory of Knights of St. John was founded here in the reign of King John. *Mon Hib.*, p. 617.

came to that place, and his people knew not where to betake themselves for their safety, but only by saileing into the Islands of Loghrie, where an infinite number of them were slaine and drowned. Soone after Cahall Crovdearg was taken deceatfully by the Englishmen of Meath, and by Hugh Delacy the younger and was conveighed to the Castle of the Obber,[1] there to be safely kept, untill he had given them theire pay, which he was content to give in part, and for the rest to give security, by which means he was sett at liberty, and immediately went to Mounster to MaCarthye and Wm Burke. And for John Coursey after slaying of his people, (as before you heard) returned to Ulster again. Some of Meyler Bermingham's people tooke the spoyle of the castle of Ardmurcher,[2] and burnt all the houses of the markett.

1201.—Cahall Crovdearg and William Burke with all theire forces of English and Irishmen came to Connaught, passed from Limerick to Twayme,[3] from thence to Owran,[4] from thence to Oylfyn, from thence to the Carrick of Loghke,[5] from thence to the abbey of Athdalaragh,[6] where the chambers and roomes of that abbey were the lodgings of the armye. Cahall mᶜConnor o'Dermott went to prey the lands of mᶜDermott and was slaine by Teige mᶜConnor Moenmoy there alsoe Cahall Carragh o'Connor king of Conaught came in view of the said forces, to a place called Gurtin Cowle Lwachra,[7] and from thence he came to the skirmish between his forces and them, who finding his people discomfitted and put to flight, was killed himself by the miracles of St. Queran together with Koylle mᶜDermott o'Moylerwayne and many others. Cahall Crovdearge and William Burk after committing these great slaughters went with their

---

[1] *Obber.*—*i.e.* Nobber, ten miles north of Kells. The castle is still standing.

[2] *Ardmurcher.*—Now Horseleap, in the barony of Moycashel, Co. Westmeath.

[3] *Twayme.*—Tuam.

[4] *Owran.*—Oran, in the barony of Ballymoe, Co. Roscommon. See *Mon Hib*, p. 617.

[5] *C of Loghke.*—The residence of the Mᶜडermots of Moylurg in Lough Ce, near Boyle.

[6] *Athdalaragh.*—The Cistercian Abbey of Boyle, founded in 1161, by Maurice O'Duffy.

[7] *G. Cowle Lwachra.*—Now obsolete.

forces to Moynoy¹ and Moylorge, over Donleoy into Moynemoy, from thence to West Connaught, untill they came to Cownge² of St. Fehine, where they then kept theire Easter. At which time William Burk and the sonns of Rory o'Flathvertye privily consulted and conspired together to kill Cahall Crovedearge o'Connor, which God prevented, for they were by great oaths sworne to each other befor which whosoever would break was to be excommunicated with booke, bell and candle. William Burke sent his souldiers to distrain for their payes and wages throughout Connaught, who were soone cut off, for 6 or 700 of them were soone after slain. William Burk afterwards repayred to Lymbrick, and Cahall Crovdearg tooke upon him the name of King of Connaught again. Teige o'Broyne prince of Lwynie in Meath died. Moriegh mᶜNeale ffox o'Kaharnye died William Burk and the sons of Connor tooke a great prey from the clergie and monkes of St Brandon,³ and tooke great spoyles also from the abbott of Malone,⁴ and the bushop of Morican⁵ till they came to the place called Snáṁe ḋa en,⁶ which is as much to say in English as the Swiming of the two birds.

1202.—William Burke and the sons of Connor Meenmay with great and maine forces, about the first of February, came to Connaught, tooke the spoiles of Clonfert, church, town, and all, from thence went to Milick,⁷ tooke the spoyles thereof alsoe, and founded a castle adjoining to the church, from thence William Burke came to the abbey of Cnockmoy⁸

---

¹ *Moynoy*.—*i.e.* Magh Naoi. See p. 111, *antea*, where it is called Moye Je.

² *Cownge*.—*i. e.* Cong, at the northern end of Lough Corrib; founded by St. Fechin in the early part of the 7th century.

³ *St Brandon*.—Perhaps Clonfert, in South Galway, where St B founded a monastery about 560.

⁴ *Malone*.—He was bishop of Clonmacnoise from 1230 to 1236. Very probably he had been a monk at Kilbeggan, for he chose this abbey as his place of burial. See Ware's *Bishops*, p. 170.

⁵ *Morican*.—He was bishop of Clonmacnoise from 1171 to 1213, *Ibid*.

⁶ Snáṁe ḋa en.—The ancient name of that part of the Shannon which lies between Clonmacnoise and Clonburren in Co Roscommon.

⁷ *Milick*.—Five miles south of Clonfert.

⁸ *Cnockmoy*.—Six miles south-east of Tuam; it was founded for Cistercians in 1190 by Cathal O'Connor.

which he preyed and spoyled of all things whatsoever both great and small, and from thence held on marching through Connaught preying and spoileing all places both temporall and spirituall without respect, untill he came to Mayoe of the English where they killed the two sonns of Hugh Dall o'Connor, came also from thence to Cownga of St. ffehin, where he did likewise spoyle the towne and church and stayed for a long space. The Englishmen of Milick and Sile Anmchye accompanied with the 2 families of Moyntyr Kenay, and Moyntyr Milchon came to Clonvicknose upon the feast day of Saint Gregory, preyed and spoyled the church, Sanctuary, and towne of Clonvicknose, the next friday the said company came to Clonvicknose and tooke the like spoyles from thence, and though the first spoyles were much, yett the second were farr greater. Some of Delvin were at the taking of the said spoyles, they took from out of the church the holy vestments, books, chalices, cloth, Linnen, and corn, and all other things they could finger soe that they left the croftes, gardens, and houses of the town wast and voyde, like an empty chaos without any manner of thing but their empty and foot-troden grounds. After doing of which William Burke returned again to Milick, and from thence he marched to Limerick and left a good company to guard the castle of Meelick. The ward seeing William gon they fled by night out of the castle and followed William into the south. Meyler Bremyngham accompanied with the forces of Cahall Crovdearg o'Connor king of Connaught, consisting of a great army of English and Irishmen, marched on till they came to Lymberick, and banished William Burk from out the same and refused to give him one castle[1] there, and caused him to go to England, to the king, and afterwards Meyler, the king of Connaght, and o'Bryan parted with one another, in peaceable and friendly manner, with good attonement and agreement between them, and immediately the king of Connaught broke down the castle of Meelick. There was great scarcity of victualls throughout the whole kingdom of Ireland

---

[1] *One castle.*—A portion of it is still standing in the English town.

this year, that infinite numbers of the meaner sort perished for want, and there was plenty of milk.

1203.—Hugh Delacye brought a great army with him to Ulster into the town of Downe daleithglasse, where he was mett by Sr John Coursey & his forces, where in a long encounter of battle Coursey was overthrowen, his people slain, and himself banished into England.

1204.—William Burk tooke the spoyles of all the churches of Connaught, vidzt. Clonvicknose, Clonfert, Milick, Killbryan,[1] the churches of o'ffiachragh, Twayne, Killeneoene,[2] Killeneoyne,[3] Mayo of the English, Cownga of St ffehin, the abby of Ath-da-laragh, Ailfin, Uaran, Roscommon, with many other churches. God and the patrons of these churches shewed theire miracles upon him that his entrayles and fondament fell from his privie place and it trayled after him even to the very earth, whereof he died, impenitently without shrive or extrem unction or good Buriall in any church in the Kingdom but in a wast town. These and many other reproachful wordes my author layeth down in the ould books, which I was loth to translate because they were uttered by him for the disgrace of soe worthy and noble a man as William Burk was, and left out other his reproachful words which he (as I conceave) rather declared of an evil will he did beare towards the said William than any other just cause. John De Coursey and the Englishmen of Meath fell to great contentions, strifes, and debates among themselves, which at last fell to a deadly warr, to the ruine and destruction of Ulster. John was gon to the contrye of tireowen or tireone. Hugh De Lacy went to England.

1205.—McGoill of Bealykervell prince of Elie was killed by the English. Hugh Delacie the younger took the spoyles of Ardmach, which was soone after revenged upon him by the Saints of Ireland. Gillebrenyn o'Bichollye cowarb of Leithmancan died. Moylekieran o'Kelly of Rahine cowarb of

---

[1] *Killbryan.*—Not identified
[2] *Killeneoene*—Killenen, in the barony of Dunkellin, Co. Galway.
[3] *Killeneoyne.*—Now Kilmaine, a parish and barony in the south of Co. Mayo.

St Suanus in Rahine, died. 47 houses both great and small were burnt about the place called Liseanabby in Clonvicknose. There was an alter of stone made by Melaghlen o'Melaghlen and these of Clonvicknose with the degree thereof in the great church of Clonvicknose aforesaid. Meiler the younger son of Meyler Bermingham besieged Limebrick, and at last tooke the same per force, for which cause there arose great dissention between the English of Meath. In which dissention Cowley mᶜConvey o'Leygaghan was killed by these of Kinnaleagh, he was chief of Sile Ronan[1] with many other hurts done amongst the Englishmen themselves.

1206.—Cahall o'Malone arch Bushop with the o'Neales and Connaught men, died the 8th of February, I mean the 8th of the Ides of February, he for his great riches, hapiness, learning, and many other good partes was held in great reverence, ended his life with a very happy and commendable end at Clonvicknose. Eaght daughter of Rowrie o'Connor king of Connought died. The sonnes of Art o'Melaghlen preyed the town of Baleloghloe,[2] and burnt part thereof, were overtaken by Melaghlen begg o'Melaghlen. Gille Crowherfrey mᶜCarrhon and certaine English forces, were in pursuite that route of Meathmen were discomfitted and putt to flight, killed Mortagh or Morrogh son of Melaghlen begg, Mortaugh mᶜDonnogh Koyle, and alsoe Morrogh mᶜMorrogh o'Kelly was taken. Robert Delacie son of Hugh Delacie, died.

1207.—There arose great warrs in Leinster between the Englishmen there, vidz$^{t.}$ between Meyler and Geffrey March,[3] and also William Marschall,[4] which soon brought all Leinster and Mounster to utter destruction. There arose alsoe the like contention and strife between Meyler and Hugh Delacie that between the said parties the land of Foherties was wasted, preyed and destroyed. The sons of Hugh Delacie

---

[1] *Sile Ronan.*—The tribe-name of the O'Flynns of Co. Roscommon.

[2] *Baleloghloe.*—A village 6 miles east of Athlone, the residence of Magauley, chief of Calry.

[3] *G. March.*—Usually called De Marisco. He was Viceroy in 1216.

[4] *W. Marschall.*—He was son of William M., who married the heiress of Strongbow, and in right of her became Earl of Pembroke and Lord of Leinster.

with the forces of the English of Meath lay seige to the castle of Ardnurcher, and the same continued for the space of five weeks, untill they forsed Meyler to abandon and forsake all the cantred of Kinaleagh from Burr to Killare.[1] An English bushop was sent over into this land by the king of England to govern the land as Deputy thereof, he was Bushop of Norway,[2] and was excommunicated by the Pope together with all Englishmen in England (which excommunication hung over them for the space of two or three yeares, in so much that their churches did not use the sacraments dureing the said time. The English of Meath and Leinster with their forces went to Killaloe to build a castle there, near the Borowe,[3] and were frustrated of their purpose, did neither castle nor other thing worthy of memory, but lost some men and horses in theire jorney, and soe returned to their houses back again. Morieitagh m^cBryen an Tleyve besiedged the castle of Byrre and at last burnt the whole town. The castle of Athronny[4] in Lease was spoyled altogether by the said Mortagh and the sonnes of o'Connor of Connaught, slew many of the inhabitants, and after taking away all the cowes, sheep, harnesses, and other things therein, they burnt the towne. David Breathnagh[5] bushopp of Waterford was killed by o'Foylan of the Desies. The castle of Kenedy, the castle of Burre, and the castle of Lothra, were broken downe and quite destroyed by the said Mortagh o'Bryen. Mortagh o'Donnell o'Bryen prince of Thomond was taken by the Englishmen of Limerick against the wills of 3

---

[1] *Killare.* — Or *Kinclare*. The name is now obsolete It was situated a little to the west of Lismoney.

[2] *Norway* — *Recte* Norwich King John was excommunicated by the Pope for intruding him into the archbishopric of Canterbury. See Lingard's *H. of England*, ii. 221. He was Justiciary from 1210 to 1213. An interesting sketch of this warlike Bishop's career in Ireland is given in Stokes' *Anglo-Norman Church*, p 242.

[3] *Borowe*—Now Balboru, a hill in the neighbourhood of Killaloe. See Mr. T J Westropp's account of Killaloe in the *Journal of the R. S. A.* for 1893, p. 183.

[4] *Athronny*. — Now Ballyroan, 4 miles south of Maryborough.

[5] *Breathnagh* —Angleised Walsh He is mentioned in the *Annals F. M.*, under 1208.

Bushopps by the procurement of his owne brother Donnogh Carbreagh m^cDonnell o'Bryan.

1208 or 9.—The king of England King John, with a great company[1] of men and shipps came into Ireland and landed at Dublin,[2] came from thence to Tibreydultan, called Ardbrackan in Meath, where Cahall Crovdearg o'Connor came to the kings house, banished Walter Delacy out of Meath into England. Whereupon the king and o'Connor with his fleet separated, and went to Carrickffergus, and banished Hugh Delacie from out of Ulster into England. o'Neale came then to the king of Englands house, and departed from him again without hostages or securitie. o'Connor returned to his own house from thence. The king of England lay siege to Carrickffergus, and compelled the warde to leave the same, and put a strong ward of his owne into the same; and from thence the king came to Rath Gwary or Rathgwayrie,[3] o'Connor came again to the kings house and yealded him four hostages vidz^{t.} Connor God o'Hara prince of Lwayne[4] in Connaught, Dermott mac Connor o'Moyleronie, Ffinn o'Carmackan, chieftain of Klyn Kelly, and Torvearan m^cGallgoyle: the king of England soone after went for England and conveighed his hostages with him. The English bushopp before mentioned with the English of Meath and theire forces went to Athlone and there made a castle and bridg. The Englishmen of Munster accompanied with Geffrey March, Thomas Fitz Moris fitz Gerald,[5] and Donnogh Carbreagh o'Bryan with their forces marched through Connaught, till they mett with the said Bushopp (that was Deputy) at Athlone aforesaid, where they constituted and ordained a certain rent to the king of England out of the lands of Ireland in generall as well of the Englishmen as Irishmen.

---

[1] *Company* — Seven hundred ships. *Ibid.*, iii. 162.

[2] *Dublin*—Rather at Waterford.

[3] *Rathgwayrie.* — Rathwire, six miles south-west of Mullingar. De Lacy erected a castle here.

[4] *Lwayne.*—Luigne, the territory now comprised in the diocese of Achonry.

[5] *Fitz Gerald.*—He was third son of Maurice, the first of the family who came to Ireland, and ancestor

1210.—Mortagh Moyneagh mcTerlaugh, tanist or next successor of the kingdome of Connaught, died. The castle of Keyleuskie[1] was made by Gilbert mcCosdealvie; o'Neale came with his forces to the place, caused them to desist from building thereof, killed the builders with the constable of the place called Henry the younger. The English bushopp that was Deputy, and Richard Tuite founded a stone castle in Athlone, wherein there was a tower of stone built, which soon after fell & killed the said Richard Tuite with eight Englishmen more. My author sayeth that this befell by the miracles of St. Queran, of St. Peter and St. Paule, upon whose land the castle was built.

Caiplén cloici do denam ag at Luain la gallaib .i. lap in ngaill-erpoc 7 la Riocapd Deuinid top cloici do denam ip an caiplen, 7 a tuitim co po mapb Riocapd 7 ochtap gall maille pip .i. tpia pertaib Ciapáin Póil 7 Peadaip pa feapann ap a ndeapna an Caipléan pin.[2]

The English bushopp being Deputy went for England, and was excommunicated by the Pope at once with the king, and all the men and women of England, in so much that during the said excommunication there was noe holy orders given, noe mass celebrated, noe christning or Extrem Unction used, or noe ceremonies performed at burialls in any place in England. There was a great convocation of the clergie of Connaught before the bushopp of Twayme, to make constitutions, for the taking away the Termine lands or Cowarb lands, and annexing them to the bushopricks of the diocess where they lay, where the cowarb of St. Patrick, the cowarb of St. Brandon, the cowarb of St. Queran, and the cowarb of St ffechine with many others appeared. Cahall Crovdearg o'Connor fell sick of a great disease, and through the grievousness of his maladie hee lost the use of his feet for a

---

of the Earls of Desmond. See *The Earls of Kildare*, p. 10.

[1] *Keyleuskie.*—i.e. narrow water, near C. Caldwell, Co Fermanagh.

[2] pin —This is but an almost literal Irish translation of the ten lines which immediately precede it.

time, and notwithstanding his sickness Connaght received no great losses, and at last he recovered his health.

1211.—Ranelt daughter of Rowry o'Connor died. The English Bushop came over into this land again and was deputie thereof and went with all the forces of Ireland to Cloneis[1] in the North where he built a castle, the English Bushopp sent certain of the army to Magmahons land to take the preyes of the contry, were overtaken and mett by Magmahon, who slew divers of them about Meyler. Meyler Robert, and Meyler himself and divers of the Englishmen of Leinster, tooke and caused them to leave the prey and horses and gave them many fierce onsetts as well by night as by day from thence forward. The Deputie came from thence to Leinster and sent for the forces of Munster, whoe came accordingly with Donnogh Carbreagh o'Bryan, and marched with all their forces to Killnegrann, in ffercall, now called Killmore, where they were met by Cormack m^cArt o'Melaghlen who discomfitted them, where they left all their cowes, horses, gold, silver, and other things to the said Cormack. Cahall Crovdearg o'Connor went to the Deputies house to Dublin to keep Christmasse with him and returned afterwards to his owen house. Cormack m^cArt o'Melaghlen expelled the Englishmen out of Delvin and gave a great overthrow to a company of Englishmen that were left to defend that contry, in which discomfiture, Robertt Dongomer, their constable and chiefe head was slain together with Gillernew m^cCoghlan the prince of Delvins son.

1212.—Gillebert m^cCosdealvie was killed by o'Heignie by the procurement and setting on of o'Neale. William Pettit[2] died. o'Neall with the forces of the North assaulted the castle of Cloneis afterwards, and took the same and killed all the warde that were therein. Mortagh o'Bryan, Donnell m^cDonnell o'Melaghlen, Cowlen o'Dempsye, and Donnell Clannagh m^cGillepatrick gave an overthrow to Cormack

---

[1] *Cloneis.* — Clones, Co. Monaghan.

[2] *Pettit.*—They were barons palatine of Mullingar. See *Hib. Dom.*, pp. 210 and 264, and D'Alton's *Army List*, ii. 231.

mᶜArt o'Melaghlen, where were killed Gillechrist mᶜMurrogh mᶜCoghlan, and Donslevie mᶜConnor mᶜCoghlan with many others. Donnell mᶜDonnell Bregach[1] o'Melaghlen next in succession of Meath and Irish of Ireland made a jorney to take a prey from Meyler Bermingham, whoe was overtaken by Meyler himself and great forces of both English and Irishmen, who killed the said Donnell with many others with him at the river of Rahan in ffercall. The Englishmen of Meath with their greatest forces tooke their journey to Kilnegrann in Ffercall where they were mett by Cormack mᶜArt o'Melaghlen, and were quite overthrowne by Cormack, with a slaughter of the chiefest and principallest Englishmen in Meath as Ferrus Mersey,[2] the two sons of Leyunie Wanie,[3] and William Howard, with many others of them, that they left all their cattle, both horses and cowes, gould and silver, shirts of maile, & pursued them to the abby of Kilbegan, and the place called Beallaghmonie ne Sirrhidye.[4] Melaghlen mᶜCahall Carragh o'Connor was killed by Jeffrey March of that jorney

1213.—Melaghlen mᶜCoghlan prince of Delvin died in pilgrimage in the abby of Kilbeggan. Cormack mᶜArt o'Melaghlin tooke a great prey from the Towne of Ardnurcher, and the next morrow after tooke the spoyles of the castle of Ardnurcher, and markett of the same, he tooke many other small preys and booties. The said Cormack mᶜArt tooke a prey from the castle of Kinclare,[5] together with the spoiles of the bwane[6] and markett of the said towne, and alsoe killed many of the Englishmen, that they left him 28 horses with 8 other harnished horses and shirts of maile, and burnt many men in the said town, Returned to his own house without loss. All the forces of the English of Ulster, Mounster, Lynster, and Meath, together with all the Irish forces that owed service to

---

[1] *Bregach.* — i.e. liar, or the inhabitant of Bregia.

[2] *F. Mersey.*—i.e. Pierce Mason Annals F. M., ad ann

[3] *L. Wanie.*—The sons of Sleviny. Ibid.

[4] *B. ne Sirrhidye* —Not identified.

[5] *Kinclare.*—A townland in the parish of Ardnurcher.

[6] *Bwane.*—The enclosure round the castle

the king of England throughout all the provinces and parts of Ireland assembled and mett together at the Bridg of Tinnie[1] to assault the said Cormack mᶜArt o'Melaghlen, whom they did alsoe meet at a place then called Clare-athmonce, now called Kilclare adjoining to Lismoyne, and were fought coragiously withall, where four principall men of the said Cormack's armye were slain, as Rory o'Kiergie and others. The english army came from thence to Delvin mᶜCoghlan, and soe to Clonvicknose where they built a castle, also they finished and made the castles of Dorow, Byrre, and Kinnety of that voyage. Moriegh o'Moriean[2] bushopp of Clonvicknose, a very venerable, ould, Learned, and witty man, and one compleat with all the good parts belonging to one of his function, Died. ffinn o'Dempsy and his brother Donogh, were taken by Geffry March most deceiptfully, and conwayed him to Dublin, where he was bound to a horse Taile & soe haled through all the streets and afterwards hanged. Terlagh mᶜCahall Croudearg o'Connor, the king of Connaughts sonn, died in restraint with the Englishmen. Cormack mᶜArt o'Melaghlen went to Athboy, and there devised a stratageme to make the ward to come out of the castle and killed tenn of them immediately, and took all the preyes and spoyles of the towne with him. Soone after he departed the contry and came after a long space into the contry againe, tooke all the spoyles of Melaghlen Begg o'Melaghlen, and killed some of his people, and amongst the rest killed the knight called the son of William Moylyn and tooke the possession of the contry againe in spight of them. Cormack mᶜArt tooke the spoyles of the castle of Smerhie[3] together with all the cowes, horses, and other cattle in the towne, was overtaken and fought withall by the English of the Towne, where the English forces were overthrone, three of their knights slaine with their constable and

---

[1] *Tinnie.* — O'Donovan conjectures this was a wooden bridge on the Brosna or the Silver River. *Annals F M*, iii 183.

[2] *M. o'Moriean.*—The time during which he occupied this See is uncertain. See Ware's *Bishops*, p 170

[3] *Smerhie* — Perhaps Smear, in the barony of Granard, Co Longford.

chiefeman, and Cormack brought himself men and prey home safe and sound.

1214.—Lorcan o'Twahall young prince of Leinster and next successor in the Superiority of that province (if he had lived) was killed by Melaghlen Oge m{c}Melaghlen, and o'Conor of Affailie in Moyne Corne (now called Ballinechowrry[1]) in ffercall. There was a synod[2] of all the clergie and prelates in Christendome in Rome this year before Innocentius 3rd Pope where there appeared foure hundred bushops, eight hundred abbotts, and an inumerable number of other spirituall men, to examine and decide the doubts that then arose among Christians, and to lay down constitutions for their amendment of life for the tyme to come.

1215.—The king of England was deposed by his own subjects and ordained that the French king's sonne should succeed him in the kingdome, and soone after the king of England died. William sonne of Hugh Delacye came from England and tooke upon him the kingdome of Meath and government thereof. Whereupon there arose great contention and warrs between the English of the south of Ireland in generall and him, whereby many Damages and losses of preys and spoyles were sustained by either party. Gillekoewgyn o'Keally was taken in the abby[3] of St. Peter in Athlone, and from thence was convayed to Trymm and there hanged. This man was o'Kelly of Brey. Murrogh o'Molloy prince of ffercall was killed by these of Affalie.

1216.—The busshopp of Conackine[4] called B of Morie[5] died. Melaghlen o'Dempsy was killed by those of ffearkeall and Meylers people. Geffrey March founded a castle[6] at Killaloe, and forced the inhabitants to receive an English Bushop.[7]

---

[1] *Ballinechowrry* —In the parish of Ballymore, Co. Westmeath.

[2] *Synod.*—The fourth General Council of Lateran

[3] *Abby* —Of Cistercians. It stood near the present castle, on the western bank of the river. The date of its foundation is uncertain.

[4] *Conackine.* — Conmaicne, *i. e.* Ardagh.

[5] *B. of Morie.*—*i.e.* Adam O'Murredai. See Ware's *Bishops*, p. 250.

[6] *Castle* —See Mr T J Westropp's account of Killaloe, its ancient palaces, &c., in the *Journal of R. S. A. I* for 1893, p. 190.

[7] *Bushop*—Robert Travers. In

1217.—More, o'Bryens daughter, Cahall Croudarg o'Connors wife, died. King John died this year in the abbey of Swynshed being poysoned by drinking of a cup of ale wherein there was a Toad pricked with a Broach.

1218.—Henry III. began his raign and raigned 65 years. Melaghlin and Rory m^cCoghlan the 2 joynt princes of Delvin died in pillgrimade in the abbey of Kilbeggan. This year was wett, wyndie, and boysterous, with great destruction of corn.

1219.—Walter Delacie and the sone of William Burk came over from England.

1220.—Jacob the Popes Legatt came to Ireland this year, went about all the Kingdom for the reformation of the inhabitants and constituted many wholsome rules for their salvation. Melaghlen m^cMelaghlin Begg o'Melaghlin was drowned in Loghrie. Walter Delacye and the English of Meath with theire forces went to Athliag, where they founded a castle, which they finished almost, whereupon Cahall Croudearg king of Conaught with his forces went to the west of the river of Synen, which the Englishmen seeing them encamped in Calae[1] were strucken with fear, and came to an atonement of truce, the Englishmen returned to their owne houses, and Cahall Crowdearg broke downe the said castle. The two sonns of Mortogh o'Bryan were killed by the englishmen of Munster for taking theire prey before.

1221.—The sone of Gillenenew m^cConn o'Seagnossa tooke a house upon Gillemochoynne o'Cahall prince of Kyneleagh, who killed him after his comeing forth

1222.—Albyn o'Molloye,[2] bushop of ffernes, Died. Hugh Delacye came over from England and took divers spoyles in the east parts of Meath, he was Earle of Ulster. William Delacy and the English of Meath with their forces founded a

---

[1221] he was deprived of the See by the Papal Legate. See Ware's *Bishops*, p 591.

[1] *Calae.*—A district included in the parish of Rathclin, in the west of Co. Longford.

[2] *O'Molloye.*—He held the See of Ferns from 1186 to 1222. He had been abbot of the Cistercian house of Baltinglas. His reply to Giraldus Cambrensis is well known. See Ware's *Bishops*, p. 439.

castle at Loghloygeaghann.¹ The Conaughtmen of the other side came with theire forces to Loghloygeachan, the ward of the said castle came forth to the principals of Conaught and as soone as they were out of the castle, the Conaught men broke the same and soe departed.

1223—Cahall Crovdearg o'Connor, king of Conaught and king of the Irish of Ireland, one that used reverence and Bounty towards the church, one both rich, fortunate and happy,² died in Broyeoll³ in Conaught and Hugh mᶜCahall his son was constituted king of Conaught in his place. William Marshall Deputie of Ireland departed over into England.

1224—Melaghlin mᶜNeale mᶜanteannie alias Ffox o'Caharnie, Died in the flower of his happy estate Donogh mageoghegan was slaine. Hugh o'Neal and Tireowen with theire forces accompanied with Terlaugh o'Connor and his brother, the sonnes of Rory o'Connor with their forces alsoe, wasted and destroyed all Moylorge Artagh and the most part of the contrey of Moynoy. Donn mᶜOyreaghty made a Retrayt upon Hugh o'Connor and afterwards went to o'Neals house. O'Connor returned to the deputies Geffry March his house in Athlone. Whereupon the said Geffry March sent his letters to all the parts of Ireland and assembled together his forces of the five provinces which, being soe assembled and gathered together, the Deputy and o'Connor with their great forces sought to Banish o'Neale with the sons of Rory o'Connor from out of Conaught, pursued them; o'Neale returned home to his owne house and left the sons of Rowrie o'Connor in Conaught, between whom and the forces of the Deputy and o'Connor, all Conaught was wasted upon the Deputys and o'Connors going to Twayme, from Easroe to Clonnicknose, in so much that there was not in all these

---

¹ *Loghloygeaghan*.—The name is now obsolete. It is called Inis Laodachain and Loch L. in the *Annals of Ulster*

² *Happy*—See *Annals F. M.*, iii. 213, and *Annals of Ulster*, ii. 273.

³ *Broyeoll*.—Rather at the Cistercian abbey of Knockmoy, near Tuam. Broyeoll, or Briola, is in Co. Roscommon, little is known of its history. See *Mon. Hib.*, p. 606.

contreys the doore of a church left unburnt, with great slaughters of both partyes. Eachmarkagh mᶜBranan chieftaine of Corckaghlan,[1] was killed. Mories mᶜMurrogh with his brothers, Mahon mᶜConnor Menmoye, Neal o'Teige, Teige mac Gilleroe o'Connor, fflann ffallawyn &c. were all killed. The son of Rory o'Connor left Connaught. Hugh o'Connor took hostages of all the province. Geffry March the Deputie with the most part of the English returned to their howses.

1225.—Moylemorey o'Connor of Affalie was killed at Rosseglassie[2] by Cowlen o'Dempsy. Donum Dei,[3] Bushop of Meath, died.

1226.—Hugh o'Connor king of Connaught went to the English court of Dublin by the compulsary means of the English, they tooke his sonn and daughter as hostages with the hostages of all the principall men of Conaught, upon examining of some criminall causes there objected to the said Hugh, he was found guiltie in their censure and being to be aprehended for the same, a speciall friend[4] of his then within, and of great favour and power with the king of England, did assist Hugh, and by the help of his sword, and strength of his hand, he conuayed Hugh away from them, and soe departed to Conaught in safety. Within a week after the Englishmen kept court in Athlone, whereunto the Conaught men came and tooke captive William March the Deputyes sonne, and two other principall men belonging to him, and alsoe killed a good knight at his takeing. Connor o'Neale mᶜCahernie alias ffox, prince of the contry of Teaffa, a haughty and hardy man for valour, was killed by a rout of Leinstermen that Hugh o'Connor king of Conaught kept defending Clowne Barynn.[5] Henry o'Melaghlen son of the

---

[1] *Corckaghlan.*—In the eastern part of Co. Roscommon. See *Annals F. M.*, iii 358.

[2] *Rosseglassie* —Now Monasterevan, Co. Kildare.

[3] *D. Dei.*—Called by Ware Deodatus. He was Bishop of Meath from 1224 to 1226. See Ware's *Bishops*, p. 142.

[4] *Friend.*—'William Mareschal, his friend, coming in with forces, rescued him, in spite of the English.' *Annals F. M.*, iii 243.

[5] *Clowne Barynn.*—Now Cloonburren, on the western bank of the Shannon, opposite Clonmacnoise.

knight o'Melaghlen, was killed by the Englishmen of Ardnurcher. Murtagh McMelaghlen Begg was also killed by the English. Donnogh ne Maliagh alias Donnogh of the Browe o'Melaghlen, was killed by the English. Mclaghlen o'Connor of Affalie was killed by Cullen o'Dempsie. Gillecolume o'Molloye was killed by o'More. Donnell o'Keruell was killed by the English. Cormack m'Art o'Melaghlen lay at a certaine house at Clonvicknose, where being assaulted himself, his wife, fosterfather and steward, were taken by the English alsoe. Mortagh O'Bryan of Lwyne, Melaghlen o'Daly, Connor m^cDonell with many others of noble and ignoble sort were killed, at last Cormack m'Art redeemed himself and the rest with his money and gould out of theire hands. Geffry March Deputy of Ireland with a great army went to Conaught to expell Hugh o'Connor from out of that province, which he did accordingly, and established the 2 sons of Rory o'Connor named Terlagh and Hugh in the possession and superiority thereof. Hugh o'Connor that was before king of Connaught, returned from Tireconell, into which he was banished by Geffry March, brought with him his wife, sone, and his brother Felym o'Connor, and came to a place in Conaught called Gortyn Cowle Lwachra,[1] out of which place m'Meran his porter fled from him, and betrayed him to the sones of Terlagh o'Connor, whoe came privily to the said Gortyn, without knowledge of the said Hugh; o'Connor knowing them to be then about the house, tooke one of his sons, his brother Ffelym tooke the other sone, and so departed safely, save only that the lady Ranelt, Hugh his wife and daughter of o'fferall, was taken, Mclaghlen m^cllugh m_cBryen o'Connor was killed and the said Ranelt delivered to the Englishmen. The Englishmen immediatly founded a castle in Rindown[2] now called Ceaṡh eoin or John's house neer Loghrie.

1227.—Hugh o'Connor came to an atonement with Geffry March, and was againe restored to his kingdome of Conaught

---

[1] *G. Cowle Lwachra.*—Now obsolete.

[2] *Rindown.*—*i.e.* John's point. See p. 216, *antea*.

by the said Deputy, and being afterwards in the Deputys house was treacherously killed by an Englishman, for which cause the Deputy the next day hanged the Englishman, that killed him for that foul fact. The cause of killing the King of Connaught was, that after the wife of that Englishman that was so hanged by the Deputie had washed his head and body with sweet balls and other things, he to gratifie her for her service, kissed her, which the Englishman seeing for meere jealoussy and for none other cause killed o'Connor presently at unawares. Symon Clifford founded and builded the castle of Rahan o'Swaynie[1] this yeare. This man gave an annuity of 40^d to the pryor of Dorow and Convent. The castle of Athliag was built by Wm Delacie and the English of Meath. Ife the daughter of ⁊eannac, alias fox, died. Clonvicknose was burnt thrice in one quarter of a yeare by the sone of Donnell Bregach o'Melaghlin. They of fferceall gave an overthrow to the sone of Donnell Bregagh and killed many of his people.

1228.—Dermott m^{c}Carhie king of Desmond died. Denis o'More,[2] Bushopp of oilfyn, died.

1230.—Moylemoric o'Moyleoyne abbott of Clonuicknose, a great and worthy house keeper, died. Felym o'Connor, brother of Hugh o'Connor, tooke upon him the name of king of Connaught. Donogh m^{c}Areaghty was killed by ffelym o'Connor and by William Burk in a skirmish at the mount called Sliew Seysie.[3] Hugh o'Neale king of Aileagh, the greatest spoyler of the Churchmen, and churches of Conaught and the onely banisher and extirper of the English, and destroyer of the Irish, died.

1231.—There was a meeting betweene the Lord Deputy and Ffelym and Donnogh Carbreagh o'Bryen at Milick, where Phelym was taken. Donell o'Donnell, with his forces came to Cahall o'Reyly and took his wife forceably from him.

---

[1] *R. o'Swaynie.*—Rahan, in the King's Co. See p. 118, *antea*. Nothing remains of this castle, nor is its site known.

[2] *Denis o'More.* — According to Ware, he resigned his See in 1229, and died in 1231. *Bishops*, p. 628.

[3] *S. Seysie.* — Now the Curlew mountains, to the north of Boyle.

1232.—The castle of Bonagaluie[1] was made by the sone of William Burk. The sone of Neale o'Gormley chieftaine of Kyneal Moan[2] died.

1233.—Hugh m^cRorye o'Connor, king of Conaught, was killed by ffelym o'Connor, together with his brother Donogh more m^cRory, and Hugh Mowneagh m^cRory the same day. The castle of Bonegaluie, and the castle of Kallye[3] were both fallen down by Felym o'Connor. William Delacy, chiefest champion in these parts of Europe, and the hardiest and strongest hand of any Englishman from the Nicene seas to this place, or Irishman, was hurt in a skirmish in the Brenie, came to his house, and there died of the wounde. Charles[4] o'Connor was also wounded the same day, and died thereof. Neale ffox, king of Teaffa land was likewise hurt in the said skirmish, came to his house in like manner, and after receauing the sacrament of the alter, and Extremunction, Died penitently.

1234.—William Marshall gave battle to the rest of the Englishmen of Ireland, where William himself was slaine[5] and Geffry March was taken. Phelym o'Connor, King of Conaught with his forces came to Meath, burnt Ballelogh-luaha and Ardnurcher with many other townes.

1235.—The English of Ireland went with theire forces to Connaught, until they came to the abbye of Boylle, where they encamped within the wales of the said abby, tooke all the goods that they could finger, as well as holy vestments, challices, as alsoe the habits of the monks, and stripped the ffryers and monkes very irreverently[6] of their habitts in the midst of theire Cloister, tooke also a great prey from Cormack

---

[1] *Bonagaluie*.—*i.e.* the end of the Galway river.

[2] *K^n Moan* —The barony of Raphoe, Co Donegal

[3] *Castle of K*.—Properly C. na Caillighe, the Hag's Castle, on an artificial island in Lough Mask

[4] *Charles*.—He was the son of Cathal Gall, *i.e* the Englishman.

[5] *Slaine* —See Gilbert's *Viceroys*, p. 95, and for a more detailed account, Matthew Paris' *Hist. Angl.*, ad ann 1234

[6] *Irreverently* — The *Annals F. M.* add 'The English chiefs however were disgusted at this, and sent back everything they could find, and paid for what they could not find' in 275. See also the *Annals of Ulster*, 1 323.

mᶜDermott, which was then generally called the prey of preyes. The carrick of Logh Ke was taken by the said English army, and a strong ward was put therein. Cormack mᶜArt o'Melaghlen was taken in Athlone by Morish ffitzgerald.

1236.—The castle of Loghriagh was made by m'William Burk. The castle of Ardmach was made by the lord Deputy mᶜMorish.[1] The said Deputy had a meeting with Felym o'Connor at Moy-ney-myne,[2] and being there mett, the Deputie with all his forces of horse and ffoot, rushed on Phelym to kill him and his people, which ffelym seeing, betook himself to the swiftness of his feet, and soe held on untill he came to Seysye. Bryen MᶜTerlagh o'Connor was then established in the possession of the five cantredes of land belonging to the king of Connaught, who preyed the province and destroyed it without respect of spirituall or temporall lord. Phelym o'Connor with an army came to Connaught again and marched on untill he came to John's-house, tooke all the spoiles of the town and Ilands thereof, and left nothing that they could take or see, from the doore of the castle forth. ffelym's camp lay at the market cross of the towne, many of the meaner sort of ffelym's army were Drownded in the pudle of that towne, he left much of the small cattle of the said prey. Hugh o'Malone bushopp of Clonuicknos, died amongst the monckes of Kilbeggan. The castle of Ullemme Wanagh[3] was founded.

1237.—ffelym o'Connor came againe with another armie to Connaught, gaue an ouerthrow to Bryan mᶜTerlagh o'Connor, to Connor mᶜCormack, and to the rout of Munstermen and to the sonns of Rory o'Connor, where many of the meanest of them were killed. Alsoe Phelym made a prey, in reuenge of his Dealing, upon the said Cormack, and Connor mᶜCormac, that he tooke all their own spoyles, and

---

[1] *m'Morish.* — 2nd baron of Offaly See *The Earls of Kildare*, p. 11.

[2] *Moy-ney-myne.*—On the east side of the river Suck, in the parish of Taghboy, Co. Roscommon.

[3] *U Wanagh.*—In the townland of Onagh and barony of Athlone. See O'Donovan's note, *Annals F M*, III. 413.

goods and their followers, and left them nothing to sustaine themselves, that they were like to perrish for famine. Cormack the next day fled to the Boyle, and his son to the Deputy's house that then dwelt at Ryndowne alias John's House. Felym soon after tooke Logh Ke¹ and Logharuagh,² and other places, and killed many of his enemies took upon him of Connaught again and banished all his enemies out of the province. Donace o'ffurie³ primate of Ardmach died in England, as he was comeing from the pope, with great honour and spirituall glory from the pope.

1238 —m^cGillemorie, a good chieftaine of Ulster, was killed by some of the people of Hugh Delacie, earl of Ulster, as he was going to the earles house, whereupon Donnslewe the king of Ulster's son, Melaghlen prince of Kinell owen, and all the chieftains of Ulster took armes and banished the said earle of Ulster out of the whole province. The earle of Ulster assembled together all the English of Ireland, and went the second tyme to Ulster, where he possessed himself of all the lands again in the three months of harvest, and banished Maglaghlen from thence into Connaught. o'Neale the Redd tooke the superiority and principalitie of Tyreowne, afterwards.

1239.—Cormack m^cArt o'Melaughlen the prince that most anoyed and hindered the English in his owen time, and next successor of the kingdom of Meath, if he had lived and were suffer'd by the English, Died quietly in his bed, without fight or Dissention, in Inisdowginn, upon the river of Suck. Geffrey o'Dalie an excellent poet died in pilgrimadge in Sruhir. Mac Morish the Deputie took a great prey from Dromkliew and all Criok Carbry.⁴ Walter Delacie repaired to the king of England, the earl of Ulster's sone was killed by the Ulstermen, and twenty eight men in shirts of maile with him.

---

¹ *L. Ke*—M'Dermott's dwelling, in a small island in the lake.
² *Logharuagh.*—L. Arrow, between Roscommon and Sligo.
³ *D. o'ffurie.*—He was translated from the See of Clogher to Armagh in 1227. See Ware's *Bishops*, p. 15.
⁴ *C. Carbry.*—Now the barony of Carbury in North Sligo

1240.—ffelym o'Connor went into England, because the English of Ireland refused to yeeld him any justice; the king graunted him the five Cantreds, which himself had, and returned in safety. William Delacie[1] lord of Meath, the onely sone of Walter Delacie, and his wife died in own week, some say they were poysoned. There arose great Discention in Ulster this year. Richard Tuite with a company of 3000 souldiers went to assist him.

1241.—Walter Delacie, the bountifullest Englishman for horses, cloaths, mony & goold, that ever came before his tyme into this kingdome, Died[2] in England of a wound. A Scottishman that was primate[3] of Ardmach came to Ireland this yeare. The great church of ffryers Minors, in Athlone was consecrated by this primate. Donell o'Donnell prince of Tyre Conel, Died. Gillernewe o'fferall, chieftaine of the Anallye, was killed by the English, and Donell succeeded him in this place.

1242.—Donnogh Carbreagh o'Bryan died, who was prince of Thomond, and alsoe Terlagh, sone of the said Donnogh Carbreagh, died the same yeare whoe succeeded as prince.

1243.—Teige mᶜHugh mᶜCahall Crouderg o'Connor had his eyes put out by Cahall o'Reyly, & Cowchonoght o'Relly. The Barrons of Ireland went to Bourdeaux to meet with the king of England, in which voyage Richard mᶜWilliam Burk died. Rory mᶜHugh mᶜCahall Croudearg was drowned upon the Synen at Athliag. Connor mᶜHugh mᶜCahall Croudearg, Died.

1244.—Phelym o'Connor with great forces went to be revenged (for theire sinister Dealings) on Teige o'Relly and the brenie-men, and made havocke of all they could

---

[1] *W. Delacie.*—He was only son of Walter, whom he predeceased by one year.

[2] *Died.*—He left two daughters coheiresses; the elder, Margery, married John De Verdon, the younger, Mabel, Geoffry De Genneville. The palatinate of Meath was divided between them. See Butler's *Trim*, p. 26.

[3] *Primate.*—The author's mistake in calling him a Scotchman arises from the similarity of the two words *almaineach*, a German, and *albanach*, a Scot. He was a Dominican, named Albert of Cologne. See *Hib. Dom.*, p. 458. A notice of him is given in Ware's *Bishops*, p. 63.

meett withall in that contrey without any respect to either sex or age whatsoever, they killed both men and beasts without any remorse at last they came to the Corre,[1] where there was a tymber house of Couples, into which Magnus m^cMortagh, and Connor m^cCormack entred, & immediatly there arose a great blast of winde, which fell downe the house, whereof one couple fell on the said Magnus, and did put the top of his head through his braines to his very neck, and caused his neck to sink into his breast, was strucken dead; this is the end of this man that escaped narrowly out of many dangers before, lost his life in this manner by a blast of Winde miserably. Donnogh More o'Daily chief of Ireland for poetry died: Donnogh o'Connor[2] Bushop of Oylfyn Died.

1245.—The Castle of Sligo was founded this yeare by m^cMorrish m^cGerrald. Conor Roe m^cMurtagh Mouneagh was killed as he was parting a fray between 4 of his owne people.

1246.—Donell o'fflanagan abbott of Cong Died. Phelym o'Connor & all the nobility & barrons of Ireland went to Wales to aid the King of England for recouery of that Contry, whether the Inhabitants would or noe.

1247.—Melaghlen o'Donell prince of Tyreconell, m^cSowarley, & Gille-Monelagh o'Boylle, with others of the chiefest & principallest of Tyre Conell were killed[3] at Bealaseanay by Morish ffitzgerald. William Burke sherrif of Connaught, & m^cElligott were killed by Donnogh m^cAnmchy m^cDonnogh m^cGillepatrick. William Burk Died in England.

1248.—Mahon m^cDermott, the son of Magnus m^cMurtagh (whome I mentioned before) burnt the Castle of Tyren-more[4] and tooke alsoe the Constable thereof. Dermott m^cMagnus was killed by the english of o'Maille.[5] Teige m^cConnor Roe

---

[1] *Corre*—Ath-na-Corie, a ford on the Yellow River, which flows into Lough Allen, Co. Leitrim.

[2] *D. o'Connor.*—Ware says he held the See about twelve years. *Bishops*, p. 628

[3] *Killed.*—See *Annals F. M.*, III. 319.

[4] *Tyren-more.*—It is called the castle of Mac Henry, *i. e.* Piers Power. *Ibid.* ad ann.

[5] *o'Maille.*—*i. e.* Umhall, the

was killed by the m^cCasdellies. John Tyrell with the principallest of his People was alsoe killed by Gillernew o'fferall.

1249.—Pierce Power, David Drew, & others of the household family of m^cGerald, were killed by Hugh o'Connor. Gerodin Bermingham was alsoe killed in revenge thereof. The Deputy of Ireland assembled together all the English of Meath and Leinster & with them came to Athlone, from thence to Sile Moray m^cMorice was of the other side with all the forces of the English of Conaught and Mounster, both armeys met at Oylfin, Destroying & Spoyleing all Sile morey to that place from whence they sent for Terlaugh m^cHugh m^cCahall Croudearg, who being come was by them made King of Conaught insteed of ffelym m^cCahall Croudearg, they afterwards preyed and spoyled the lands of Brenie and made alsoe many great hurts in that Contry and conwayed theire preyes with them, remayned twenty nights in Sile-morey ruineing and Destroying that Contry, they took with them the preys and spoyles of Logh Ke Carrick & theire Ilands, the Deputy returned to Meath, m^cMorrice to Sliggoe, and Terlaugh o'Conor was left in Connaught to Ward and Defend Sile-morey. The nobility of Conaught went to Athenrie to prey and spoyle the towne on the day of our Lady the Blessed Virgin Mary in the midst of harvest, there were a great armye with Terlaugh m^cHugh, and Hugh m^cHugh, the sherrife of Connaught with many englishmen were in the said towne before them, the Sherrif and Englishmen desired them in honour of the blessed Virgin Mary whose day then was, to forbeare with them that day, which the Irish Nobility refused to give any respect, either in honor of the Blessed Virgin, or holly Rood, they assaulted the towne against the will of the said Terlaugh, which Jordan De extra[1] the Sherrife and englishmen seeing, they rushed forth to meet with the said Irishmen, where the Virgin Mary

---

territory of the O'Malleys, now the baronies of Murrisk and Burrishoole, in the west of Mayo.

[1] *De extra.*—*i.e.* De Exeter. He was the founder of this family in Ireland. They settled in Gallen, Co Mayo. After a time they took the surname of MacJordan. Campion says, in his time (1571), 'they were very wild Irish.' See Introd.

wrought miraculously against the said nobillity: When the Irish Nobility saw the Englishmen and horsmen well apoynted with harnish, armes, and shirtes of maile made towards them, they were daunted and affrighted of at theire sight and were presently Discomfitted. Hugh m'Hugh o'Connor was killed in that presence. Dermott Roe m'Cormak o'Melaghlen, the two sonnes of o'Kelly, Bryan & Dery m'Manus, Carrick & Tiuall m'Neale o'Connor, Brithgalagh m'Keigan the sons of Dermott Backagh o'Connor, the two sons of Laughlen o'Connor, Daniel m'Cormack m'Dermoda, ffinanagh m'Branann, and Cocomowan m'Cassurley with many more were killed in that place. Donnagh m'Anmchey m'Donnogh m'Gillepatrick the best head of a company that ever Descended of Ossery of the race of Colman m'Patrick Keigh or Scanlan m'Kinfoyle Donne, both for manhood, valour, and bounty, was killed by the Englishmen of the forgie as he Deserved of the English Divers tymes before, for he killed, preyed and burnt many an Englishman before that day. Donnough was the third Ireishman that warred against the Englishmen after theire first footing in this Land, vidzt. Connor o'Melaghlin, Connor of the Castle m'Coghlan and this Donnogh m'Anmchy, for the Sone of Anmchye in his owne persone did use to goe to take vew of the Englishmens towns and ffortes in the Habbitt of a poore man, Carpender, Turner or other Tradsman.

1251.—Clarus Archi-Diaconus olfin vir providus et Discretus, qui carnem suam jejunijs & orationibus macerabatt, qui pauperes et orphanos defendebat, qui patientiam et coronam observabat, qui persecutionem a multis propter justitiam patiebatur, venerabilis fundato(r) locorum fraternitatis Sanctæ trinitatis per totam hiberniam et specialiter fundator¹ Monasterii Sanctæ trinitatis apud logh Ke, vir

---

to *Top. Poems*, p. 23. Frequent mention of the family is made in the *Annals of Multifarnham*.

¹ *Fundator*.—There were nine monasteries of the Premonstratensian Order in Ireland. He was founder of four of them. See *Hib Dom.*, p 737.

locum sepulturæ ibidem elegit, et in Christo requievit Sabbato Penthecostes Dominice Cujus Animæ propitietur Deus Omnipotens in Cœlo cui ipse seruuit in seculo. In Cujus honore ecclesiam Deryndoyne & Monasterium Sanctæ trinitatis apud Logh oghter, ecclesiam sanctæ trinitatis apud Athmoye, Ecclesiam sanctæ trinitatis apud Killrusse ædificavit.

There was great thunder and Lightning this yeare that it killed much of the Cattle of the Kingdome. Thomas Miles Cardin had his eyes put out and his tongue alsoe. There was a great convocation of the Clergie of Connaught this yeare.

1252.—The Castle of Koyle-usge[1] was built by m{c}Gerald. The Castle of Moycoua[2] was also made by him.

1253.—Owen o'Heyne, Prince of ffiaghragh Aynie, Died.

1254.—Moylebride o'Moylefomore, Died. Moylefinien o'Beollaun archdeane of Drumklewe, Died.

1255.—Thomas m{c}Dermoda, archdeane of Moylorge and Arteagh, Died.

1256.—Flan o'fflynn[3] arch Bushop of Twaime died in Bristow. Rory o'Gara, prince of Shew Louth, was killd by David Cushen.

1257—Cahall m{c}Hugh m{c}Cahall Croudearge had his eyes put out by Hugh o'Connor. Morice m{c}Gerrald (in this history called m{c}Gerald) Died. ffelym o'Connor founded and built a house for the ffryars of St. Dominickes order[4] in Roscommon. The great Deane[5] of London elected to be arch Bishop of Twayme.

1258.—Walter o'Salerna, Deane[5] of London and arch Bishop of Twayme, Died. m{c}Sawarle[6] brought a great fleet with him from the Ilands of Scotland, went about Ireland

---

[1] *Koyle-usge.*—Between Warrenpoint and Newry, Co. Down The castle is still standing

[2] *Moycoua*—Donaghmore, in the barony of Upper Iveagh, Co. Down.

[3] *F o'fflynn.*—He held this See from 1256. See Ware's *Bishops*, p. 605.

[4] *Order.*—Its history is given in Hib. Dom., p 258.

[5] *Deane.*—He is called by some the Dean of St Paul's. He held the See for one year only, and never saw his diocese. Ware's *Bishops*, p 606

[6] *M{c} Sawarle*—One of the M'Donnells of Scotland Somhairle was a family name of theirs

of the West, where they robbed a merchants ship of all the goods therein, as Wine, Cloth, Brasse, and Irons. Jordan de exetra, then Sherif of Conaught pursued him at sea with a great fleet of Englishmen. m'Sawarle landed upon an Iland in the sea and did put his ships at anchor and seeing the Sherrif with his people make towards them m'Sawarle Girted himselfe with his armour and harnish of steele, & soe did all the Company that were with him out of hand. Whereupon the Sherriff landed in the Island, where he was well served by m'Sawarle, the Sherrif himself was Instantly Killed with Sr Pierce Caward[1] a worthy Knight with many others, the English after receaveing this great loss returned, & m'Sawarle alsoe returned with the happy success of a rich Booty to his owen contry. Hugh m'ffelym and Teige o'Brian had a meeting with Bryan o'Neale at the Castle of Koile Uske, where peace was concluded between them and agreed that Brian o'Neale should be King of the Irish of Ireland, whereupon Hugh m'ffelym yealded Hostages to Bryan, alsoe the Cheefest of the o'Bryans and Mointir Rellys from Kells to Drumklewe yeelded hostages to Hugh o'Connor.

1259.—Thomas m'Terlagh o'Melaghlen o'Conor came from Roome this yeare, where he receaved the order of Bushup[2] and brought his Pallium with many other profitts to the Church.

1260.—Hugh o'Connor went to the north to assist Bryan o'Neale against the English with a great Company of Cannaughtmen where the said Bryan with the forces of Tyre owne and Hugh o'Conor with theire complices went to give battle to the English. In which battle Bryan o'Neale named the King of the Irish of Ireland was killed with those insueing of the Irish nobility, vidzt. Donell o'Kerry, Dermott Maglahlen, Magnus o'Cahan, Kyan o'Kinnerge, Downsleyve Macana, Hugh o'Cahan, Murtagh o'Cahan, Conor o'Duff-

---

[1] *Caward*—In the *Annals F M.* he is called Agabard.
[2] *Bushup*.—Archbishop of Tuam.

He held the See from 1259 to 1279. See Ware's *Bishops*, p. 607, and *Annals F M*, iii. 431.

dirma, and Hugh his sonne, Awley o'Garmley, Cownley o'Hanlan & 15 of the Cheefest of the famlie of the o'Cahanes. There were alsoe slaine of the Connaughtmen these ensueing persons, vidzt. Cahall m'Tiernan o'Conor, Gillechrist m'Connor m'Cormack, Donell m'Dermoda, Moyleronye m'Donogh, Cahall m'Donogh m'Murtagh, Hugh m'Murtagh ffinn, Teige m'Cahall m'Bryan m'Moyledownye, Dermott m'Teige m'Moreyey m'Tomalty o'Moileronie, Connor m'Gillearrie, Teige m'Keyne o'Garie, Gilleberie o'Keyne, and Charles the Bushop o'Mories sonne with many others of the Noble and Ignoble sort. This battle is called the Battle of Dawne-da-leathglasse, and Bryan o'Neale is since called Bryan chatha an Dwynn, which is as much to say in English as Brian of the battle of Downe. John Deuerdin came over into Ireland this yeare. Abraham o'Conallie[1] arch Bushop of Ardmach Died. Robyn Lawlesse Died on Easter Day.

1261.—ffelym o'Connor from the north with a great armye with him from Tyre Connell, came first to the Brenie, & from thence to the Land of Imanye, and Banished Terlaugh o'Connor out of all Connaught, that Terlaugh was Driven to make his repaire againe to the English to partake with them and to shelter himselfe from the violence of ffelym o'Connor. ffelym gathered all the goods and cattle of his people and followers, and brought them downe over the Mount called Sliewe Siesie, the English sent him messengers that they would be content to receave him into theire favour and friendships againe, and alsoe restore him into the possession of the Kingdome of Connaught, which he was ready to accept, and soe was reconsiled with the English as aforesaid. Carbry o'Melaghlen, a worthy prince for manhood, bounty, and many other good parts was treacherously killed by David Roche in Athboye in the territory of ffearkeall. Clarus m'Moylynn o'Moilchonry brought the white Cannons of the order of premonstra neare Christmas from trinity Island in

---

[1] *A. o'Conallie.*—Or O'Connellan. He held the See from 1247 to 1260. See Ware's *Bishops*, p. 67.

logh Ke to Trinity Iland upon Logh Oghter in the Brenie and were there lisiensed of Cahall o'Relly, who granted the place after this manner: In puram et perpetuam Elimozinam, in honore sanctæ trinitatis et idcirco Clarus hoc fecitt in Domino, qui monstratenses gaudant consimili privilegio cum monachis ita quod ad ullum alium ordinem transire possunt 1261 vell verius 1248. Gerald Suckagh¹ Died this yeare. o'Reignie killed his owne landlord m°Coghlan, for which cause Richard Tute caused o'Reignie to be hanged, drawne, and quartered for the fact.

1262.—King Henery of England sent new coyned mony to this Kingdome. There was a great drought this yeare in the earth & a very hott summer.

1263.—David m°Kelly² arch Bushop of Cashell, Died. Helen, o'Madden's daughter and wife of Teige o'Kelly, Died. Ebdon, king of Denmark, Died in the Ilands of Arcades, as he was in his jorney to come to Ireland. Moilekieran o'Malone, abott of Clonuicknos, Died.

1264—m°William Burk built a castle in Athengail³ in Coran this yeare. Art m°Cormack m°Art o'Melaghlen made great wair upon the english of Meath & made great slaughter upon them at the river of Brosnach,⁴ where he that was not killed of them was Drowned in that River. Donn Magwyer killed Mortagh m°Donnell o'Harty and burnt his followers. There arose great Discention and strife in England betweene the king of England and the king of Wales, where his nobillity and earles forsooke king Henery and his sone edward. In the end there was a battle fought betweene them, wherein king Henry and his sone Edward were taken Captives, Alsoe John Deverden was taken, and an Infinite number slain. They of Delvin m°Coghlan took a great prey from those of Sile-anmchye and alsoe killed the five sones of o'Madden in

---

¹ *G. Suckagh.*—*i. e.* the merry, Sir G. Fitz Gerald.

² *D. m°Kelly*—He held the See from 1238 to 1252. The Dominican priory of Cashel was founded by him. *Ibid.*, p. 472.

³ *Athengail.*—The name is now obsolete

⁴ *Brosnach.*— Now the Brosna, which rises in Westmeath, and falls into the Shannon at Shannon Harbour.

pursuit thereof. The Lord Deputy of Ireland, earle of Ulster, mᶜGerald and the english nobility of Ireland had a meeting with ffelym o'Connor and with Hugh his sone in Athlone: the English nobillity seeing the great multitude of people following ffelym and his sone were struck with great feare, whereupon they advised with themselves if it were better for them to be in peace with ffelym and his sone then in continual Dissention, which was accordingly accepted of phelym and concluded by them. Alsoe there arose Dissention between mᶜWilliam Burk, the earle of Ulster and mᶜGerrald this yeare, that the most part of the kingdome was brought to utter ruine by reason of theire warres against one another, in soe much that the said earle took all the Castles of m'Gerrald in Conaught into his owne hands, burnt and destroyed all his manors. Art o'Melaghlin burnt all the Castles and street-townes in Delvin mᶜCoghlan, Brawnye, and Calrie, banished the Englishmen out of them all, and tooke hostages for himselfe of the chiefest of the said Contryes, and alsoe burnt Baile-logh-twaha too. The Deputy of Ireland, John Cowgan, and Theobald Buttler were taken prisoners by mᶜGerald within a hallowed church. The Castles of Lough Measga[1] and Ardrahan[2] were taken by mᶜWilliam in his owne hands.

1265.—ffelymn mᶜCahall Crovderg o'Conor king of Connaught, defender of his owne province and friends everywhere, a Destroyer and Banisher of his enemies where he could find them, one full of Bounty and prowess and magnanimity both in English and Irish, Died penitently and was buried in the abby[3] of the ffryers preachers of Roscomon which himself before graunted to the order in honour of God and S. Dominick, after whose death his sone Hugh o'Conor (a valorous and sturdie man) tooke upon him the name of King of Connaught and Immediately made his first and

---

[1] *L. Measga.*—Now L. Mask, in the south of Co. Mayo.

[2] *Ardrahan.*—Fifteen miles S.E. of Galway

[3] *Abby.*—It was founded in 1255. There was an older abbey here, founded by S. Coman about the middle of the sixth century.

Regall prey upon the Contry of Affalie, made great burnings and other outrages in that Country, from thence turned to Athlone, where he put out the eyes of Cahall m{{c}}Teige o'Connor, who soone after the looseing of his eyes Died

1266.—Mahon o'Cullen, Prince of the Cloenglasse,[1] was killed with a stabb of a knife by his own wife for Jealousie. The castle of Teadoconna[2] was broken this yeare and all Conuackne wasted. Donell o'Hara, prince of Lwyne, was killed as he was burning Ardnarea (Athenrie) upon the Englishmen. Manie castles were burnt in Kilfiaghragh and their cornes destroyed this yeare. An Italian was made Bishop of Clonfert[3] and went over to Roome to the Pope againe. There arose great warrs in England between the king and Simon Sufforne.

1268.—Melaghlen m{{c}}Coghlan was killed at Kill-bileaghan[4] by Richard Tuite. fferall o'Molloy, prince of ffearkeall, was Deseatfully and treacherously slaine by the English of Athboye. Conor o'Brien, Prince of Thomond, was killed by Dermott m{{c}}Mortagh and his sone John Dowloghlen o'Loughlynn and Thomas o'Beollann, with many others were there killed on Tuseday before Whitsunday in Corcomroe in the Camp called the Siwdayne,[5] the sonne of Murtagh was afterwards taken and maymed in prison with Bryan Roe in revenge of his fathers death in Muckenagh.[6] There was an englishman made abbott of the abby of Cnockmoy. Enos o'Dalye arch-Poet of Ireland Died. Morice Roe m{{c}}Gerald was Drowned in the sea comeing from England to this kingdome, and a shipfull of passengers being his owen people were Drowned alsoe.

1269 —Hobert or Robert Suforne or Stafford[7] came over

---

[1] *Cloenglasse.* — In the barony of Upper Connello, Co. Limerick.

[2] *Teadoconna.* — Tyaquin, eight miles north of Athenry, Co Galway The castle is still standing.

[3] *Clonfert* —He was bishop of this See till 1296, when he was transferred to Benevento in Italy Ware's *Bishops*, p. 639.

[4] *Kill-bileaghan.*—The name is now obsolete.

[5] *Siwdayne.* — In the parish of Drumcreehy, north Burren

[6] *Muckenagh.* — Perhaps Muckiniss, near Ballyvaughan, Co. Clare.

[7] *Stafford.* — Robert De Ufford, who was Deputy from 1268 to 1282, except for some short intervals.

from England as Deputy of this kingdome, apointed by the king of England for the reformation of the Lawes, customs, and statutes of this land, and made his first voyage with his forces to Connaught and by the help of the English forces of Ireland he built a Castle[1] at Roscomon : the opportunity & occation of building of the said castle was, because Hugh o'Connor king of Connaught fell sick of a grieveous disease suposed to be Irrecoverable. Christina, o'Neaghtans Daughter, the wife of Dermott Myeagh m^cDermoda, a right exceeding beautifull woman, well limmed, bountifull in bestowing, chast of her body, of ingenious and wittie deliverie of her mind, Devout in her prayers, and finallie she was Inferior to none of her tyme for any good parts requisite in a noble Gentlewoman and charitable towards the Order of Grey Monks, died with good penance. Hugh o'fflynn a good musitian Died.

1270.—Sligeach was burnt by o'Donnell & Tire Connell, and m^cBreallye of the karne was killed of that jorney. There arose great dissention and Warrs betweene the king of Conaught and Walter Burk earle of Ulster, in soe much that all the English and Irish of the kingdom could not seperate them or keep them from anoying each other, the earle procured the Lord Deputy with all the English forces of Ireland to come to Conaught, came to Roscomon the first night, from thence to Portlick,[2] where they encamped, the next day they advised that the earle of Ulster with the most part of the forces should goe eastward of the river of Synen, to the place on the River called the foord of Conells Weare.[3] As for Hugh o'Conor king of Conaught he was redy prepared with the few company he had before the English at Moyne Issye.[4] The Lord Deputy remained of the west of the river of Synen

---

[1] *Castle*.—Still standing, one of the finest of the Anglo-Norman buildings. See an account of it in the *Journal R. S. A. I.* for 1891, p 546.

[2] *Portlick*.—Near Jamestown, Co. Roscommon. The name is now obsolete.

[3] *C. Weare*.—Near Carrick-on-Shannon. Now obsolete.

[4] *M. Issye*.—A level tract on the east side of the Shannon, in the barony of Leitrim. See *Annals F. M*, iii. 307.

at the ffurney.¹ After the earle had passed to Atheora Conell as aforesaid, was assaulted by a few of o'Connors people in the woods of Conuackne,² where a few of the English armye were killed The Englishmen never made residence or any stay untill they came to Moyn Issye, which was the place where o'Conor encamped, where the English did likewise encamp that night. The Englishmen advised the earle to make peace with Hugh o'Connor, and to yeeld his brother William Oge mcWilliam More mcWilliam the Conquerour in hostage to o'Conor during the tyme he should remaine in the earles house concluding the said peace, which was accordingly condescended and don: as soone as William came to o'Connors house he was taken, & alsoe John Delphin and his sone were killed. When Tydeings came to the eares of the earle how his brother was thus taken, he the next morning tooke his jorny to Athan-Kip,³ where o'Connor the second night behaved himselfe as a fierce and frowarde Lyon about his prey, without sleeping or taking any rest, that he did not suffer his enemies to take refection or rest all this Tyme, and the next day soone in the morning gott up & he tooke him to his armes. The Englishmen the same morning came to the said ffoord called Athan-Kip, where they were overtaken by Terlaugh o'Bryan, the earle returned upon him and killed the said Terlaugh without the help of any other in that place. The Conaughtmen pursued the Englishmen and made theere hindermost part to rune and breake upon their vaunt-guard or foremost, in such sort and foule discomfiture that in that Instant 9 of their chiefest were killed upon the bogg about Rickard ne Koylle⁴ and John Buttler, who were killed over and above the said Knights. It is unknowne how many were slaine in that Conflict, save onely that a 100 Horses with theire sadles and other furnitures with a 100

---

¹ *ffurney.*—No name like this is given in the Ordnance Survey list.

² *Conuackne.*—C. Magh Rein, in Co. Leitrim See p. 228, *antea.*

³ *Athan-Kip*—A ford near Carrick-on-Shannon The name is obsolete

⁴ *R. ne Koylle*—i.e. of the wood. He seems to have been a brother of the Earl of Ulster.

shirts of maile were left after these things were thus done. o'Connor killed William Oge the earles Brother that was given him before in Hostage, because the earle killed Terlaugh o'Bryan that came to assist o'Connor against the earle; o'Connor immediately tooke and brake downe to the earth the Castles of Athengaille, the Castle of Sliew-Louth,[1] and the Castle of Kilcolman,[2] alsoe he burnt Roscomon, Rwyn-dwyne als Teadoyn and Vllemanagh;[3] Brian Roe o'Bryan made a retraite on the Englishmen, tooke great spoyles from them & tooke the Castle of Athdacara.[4] Edward prince of England, the king of Englands sone, went to the holy land to recouer itt. Lewis the ffrench King Died

1271.—Walter Burk earle of Ulster and Lord of the English of Conaught, Died in the Castle of Galway of one weekes sickness after good pennance and was entred in Rath Cashell.[5] Thomas mᶜMorice died in the castle of Logh-Measka, Nicoll mᶜJohn Verdon, lord of the Contry of Uriell, was killed by Geffry o'fferall and by those of the Analye. The Castle of Logh-temple,[6] the Castle of Sligagh and Athleag were broken Downe by Hugh o'Connor this yeare.

1272.—Henery Buttler lord of the territory of o'Mailey and Hodge Mebricke were killed by Cathal mᶜConor Roe and some of the Irish nobility of Conaught. The Castle of Roscomon was broken down by Hugh o'Connor. James Dowdall[7] Deputy of Ireland was killed by o'Brian and some Conaughtmen. All Meath was burnt to Granard by Hugh o'Connor; Athlone was also burnt, and the bridge thereof fallen downe. Richard Tute the worthyest barron in all Ireland died.

1273.—Maurice mᶜGerald with great forces went to Thomond & tooke hostages of the o'Bryens and subdued the

---

[1] *S. Louth.*—In the barony of Costelloe, Co Mayo

[2] *Kilcolman.*—In same district.

[3] *Vllemanagh.*—In the barony of Athlone, Co Roscommon. It belonged to the Mac Keogh family.

[4] *Athdacara.* — Perhaps Clare Castle, Co. Clare.

[5] *Rath Cashell.*—This name is not given in the Ordnance Survey list of townlands.

[6] *L.-temple.* — Templehouse, in the barony of Leyny, Co Sligo

[7] *Dowdall.*—Lord Audley, who was killed by a fall from his horse. He was Deputy for two years only.

whole contry. Geffry Genuille came as Deputy from England from the King this yeare.

1274.—Teige m‘Keruell Boy o'Daly chefe poet of Hugh o'Conor for poetry Died. Gillernew o'fferall chieftaine of the Analie died, and was entred in the abby of Boyle. Hugh m‘ffelym o'Connor king of Conaught for 9 years died, the 5th of the Nones of May on Thursday, that is to say upon the feast day of the Invention of the Crosse, this is the king that wasted and destroyed Conaught upon the English, this is he that razed and broke downe their houses and Castles, made them eaven with the earth, & gave themselves many over-throwes and conflicts, this is hee that tooke the hostages of o'Mbraym and Tireconell, this is he that spoyled and Defended from other spoyles the province of Conaught, and finally this is he that most was feared of the English of all the kings of Conaught that were before his tyme, and was with great reverence buried with the monkes in the abby of Boyle, after whose death Owne m‘Rory m‘Hugh m‘Cahall Croudearg was ordayned king of Conaught, who raigned not long, but ¼ of a yeare, when he was killed treacherously by his owne kinsman or Brother Rory m‘Terlaugh o'Connor in the Church of fryers preachers of Roscomon. After him succeeded Hugh m‘Cahall Dall o'Connor as king of that province, whoe did not raigne as long as his predecessor, though his predecessors were short. Hugh m‘Cahall raigned but a fortnight, when he was killed by one Thomas m‘Oreaghty & o'Beyrne, after him succeeded as king of Conaught Teige m‘Terlaugh m‘Cahall the same yeare Conaught sustayned great loss this yeare which is the death of 3 kings successively, vidzt. Hugh m‘ffelym, Owen m‘Rory and Hugh m‘Cahall Doylle.

1275 —Art m‘Cormack o'Melaghlen was hurt by o'Molloy and by those of Kineleagh, and the 2 sones of Mahonn Magawley were alsoe killed by them. Carbry o'Scopa,[1] first

---

[1] *C o'Scopa*—He held the See of Raphoe from 1266 to this year. He was present at the General Council held at Lyons in 1274 under Pope Gregory X. See De Burgo, *Hib. Dom*., p. 461.

a frier of the Order of Preachers and afterwards Bishop of Rathbothe, Died. John de Verdon and 13 knights were poysoned together in England.

1276.—A base sone was presented to ffelym m^cCahall Croudearg o'Connor after the death of the said ffelym a long space who was called Hugh Moyneagh, soe called because he was nourished and brought up in Mounster, and came to Conaught from thence, and as soone as he came and was knowen to be the sone of ffelym, Silemory & Clann Moyleronye accepted of him and had him in great accoumpt and reverence. There arose great contention and warrs betweene the lord Deputy of Ireland and m^cMurrogh[1] king of Leinster. m^cMurrogh gave a great overthrow to the Deputy & killed many of his army and wounded himself grievously. m^cMurrogh alsoe took Hostages of the Englishmen and caused them to eat theire horses in Gleann[2] for famine.

1277.—The earle of Clare his sonne tooke Brian Roe o'Brian[3] prisoner very deceiptfully after they had sworne to each other all the oaths in Mounster, as bells, relickes of saints and Bachalls to be true to one another for ever, and not endomage each other; alsoe after they became sworne Goships, & for confirmation of this theire indissoluble bond of friendship perpetually, they drew part of the blood of each other, which they put in a vessell and mingled it together: after all which protestations the said Brian was taken as aforesaid and bound to a sterne steeds & so was tortured to death by the said earles sone. Hugh Moyneagh m^cffelym fell downe the Castle of Roscomon by the help of Donell o'Donell and Conaughtmen. Conor m^cDonell Bregagh o'Melaghlen, he that most warred with englishmen in his owen tyme, a second Guairy for bounty, and a Lyon for strength, and a tyger for ficreness in tyme of enterprisers

---

[1] *m^cMurrogh.* — *i e.* Mortagh. See p. 254, *postea.* The *Annals F. M.* say, by mistake, this defeat of the English took place in Ulidia. iii 425.

[2] *Gleann* — Glenmalure, Co. Wicklow.

[3] *o'Brian.* — He and Turlough O'Brian were then contending for the sovereignty of Thomond.

and onsets, & one hoped to be King of Ireland if he were suffered by the English, Died penitently at Kilbeggan.

1278.—Hugh Moyneagh m^cffelym was ordayned and made king of Connaught Donogh m^cBrian Roe o'Brian gave the overthrow of Coinche[1] to Thomas De Clare (the earle before mentioned) & burned the Church of Coynche, over the heads of the said earle and his people, where infinite numbers of people were both slaine and killed therein, and escaped narrowly himself (for which escape my author saith) that himself was sorry for.

1279.—Murrogh o'Melaghlen was killed by Donell Melaghlin, whereupon Robert o'Neaghton brother of the said Murrogh challenged him to a single combatt of hand to hand, when the said Donell answered, and killed Robert alsoe.

1280.—John Tuite was killed by his sone David and by the sons of Gillekewgyn (the excommunicate) o'Kenedy, the sone was taken. King Edward sent new mony into Ireland which was weighed with the ould mony, every house in Ireland had his weights to weigh these monys. There arose some disagreement between Hugh Moyneagh m^cffelym m^cCahall Croudearg king of Conaught and the sons of Murtagh Mayneagh o'Conor, whoe killed Hugh Moyneagh m^cKoyll-an-daingin, tooke Melaghlen m^cManus o'Conor prisoner, and was ransomed by o'Donell for the number of 400 Cowes & 20 horses, and alsoe installed king of Conaught. Cahall m^cConnor Roe m^cMortagh Moyneagh m^cTerlagh More o'Conor.

1281.—This yeare was fought between o'Neale and o'Donnell the battle of Disert-da-crich,[2] which was given between Hugh Boyl m^cDonell oge m^cHugh surnamed the fatt m^cHugh was called the Lasye-a..ed youth; and all the English of Ulster of the one side. Donell o'Donell

---

[1] *Coinche*.—Quin, three miles S E. of Ennis, Co. Clare. The church mentioned here is not that of the abbey, which was not founded till later, but the more ancient church close by, which was dedicated to St. Finghin.

[2] *Disert-da-crich*.—Now Desertcreaght, ten miles north of Dungannon, Co. Tyrone.

king of Tyreconell, ffermanagh, & Uriell with the most part of the Irish of Connaught and Ulster and Brenie-men of the other side. Tireconell was Discomfitted, Donell o'Donell slaine, the best Irishman for bounty, prowes, worthyness and many other perfections that lived in his Tyme, and was buried in the church of Derye after he had all things fallen out with him fortunately until that day of his death. These were slaine with him, Moyleronye o'Boyell chieftaine of the Twathas,¹ owen mᶜMelaghlen o'Donell, Ceallagh o'Boyle, the best chieftaine for liberallity and hospitallity in his age, Gillechriost mᶜGlanchie chieftaine of Dartrye, Donell mᶜGillefinnen chieftaine of Mointir Peadaghan,² Annyleas o'Boylle and Dowgall his sone, Enna Garmley the kingly chieftaine of Kynell-Moan, Cormack mᶜenirlegynn o'Donell, chieftaine of the Country of ffanad, Gillecomye Moyledownye prince of Lwyrg,³ Cormack mᶜCormack o'Donell, Gillemenag mᶜDalredockar, Melaghlen mᶜo'Boylle, Anyleas mᶜMortagh mᶜDonell, Loghlinn mᶜMurtagh o'Donell, fflathuertagh mᶜBwyeghann, Magnus mᶜCoynne, Gillenenewe o'Heoghagan, Murtagh o'fflaherty, Murtagh mac Enulty, with many others noblemens sones and theire Inferiors, which here are omitted to be recoumpted There was a field fought betweene the Barretts⁴ of the one side and the Cusacks of the other side, where the Barretts were vanquished. William Barrett and Addam ffleming with many others were slaine. There were two Irishmen of Cusacks side that surpassed the Company of both sides for prowess, manhood, dexterity of handleing of armes, hardiness and all other poynts of activity, named **Faithleagh o'Dowdy** and **Faithleagh o'Boyle**

1282.—King Henery the 3ᵈ Died this yeare at Westminster, and his sone Edward the first began his raigne,

---

¹ *Twathas.* — Three districts in the barony of Kilmacrenan, Co. Donegal, which belonged to the M'Swinys.

² *M Peadaghan* —A territory in the barony of Magherabey, Co. Fermanagh

³ *Lwyrg* —Now a barony in the north of the same county.

⁴ *Barretts* — An account of the Barretts of Tirawley will be found in the *Tribes of Hy Fiachrach*, p. 325. They and the Cusacks were of Welsh descent.

surnamed Edward Longshanks. The Bushop of Meath[1] Died & was buried in Molingare. Phillip De la Rochell was changed with Theobald Butler for a piece of a Contry. Mortagh m^cMurtagh & Art his brother of Leinster were killed by the English of Beere-Hauen,[2] this Murtagh was king of Leinster. Faithleagh m^cMoylronye o'Doudye (before spoken of) prince of the contry of o'ffiaghragh Moye, one of great prowess and bounty & of great & continual discention with the English & all foriners in Defence of his Contry, was killed by Adam Cusack att Beere-Hauen.

1283.—Lazarina, daughter of Cahal Croudearg Died. Art m^cCormack o'Melaghlen surnamed Art ne gaislean, the greatest warriour in Ireland in his tyme against the Englishmen, and he that killed most of the English and Irish, and alsoe he that broke downe 27 Castles both great and small in the course of his warrs, and he that gave many overthrowes to the English and Irish, Died with penance, after whose death his sone Carbry succeeded him in his place and was constituted king of Meath. Died Arlache, Daughter of Cahall Croudearg & abbess. Hugh Boye o'Neale king of Aileagh was killed. Cahall m^cTeige o'Kelly Died and was buried in Clonvicknose.

1284.—Symon the exeter[3] was killed by Bryan o'fflyn at fertgedye.[4] Donnogh m^cBryan Roe o'Bryan was killed by Terlagh o'Bryan, after giving these securities Mahon o'Loughlen and Kenedie m^cBrian Aharly,[5] and was killed himselfe at that Instant by the hands of Donagh o'Bryan himself. Morice m^cNeale o'Conor first a fryer of the order of Preachers and afterwards Bushop[6] of Oylfynn, Died.

1285.—Hugh m^cHugh o'Conor, and flann o'Melaghlen

---

[1] *B. of Meath.*—Hugh De Tachmon. See Ware's *Bishops*, p. 143.

[2] *Beere-Hauen* —They were slain at Wicklow or Arklow, according to Clynn's *Annals*.

[3] *The exeter.*—De Exeter. See p. 239, *antea*.

[4] *Fertgedye.*—Now obsolete.

[5] *Aharly.*—Of Aherloe, a beautiful valley lying along the north side of the Galtee range, Co. Tipperary. A branch of the O'Briens were lords of this district.

[6] *Bushop.*—He occupied the See of Elphin for eighteen years. See *Hib Dom.*, p. 460

with other noble youths in theire companys tooke a great prey from William Crocke, where they were pursued and quite Discomfitted, in soe much that above 20 of them were killed and Drowned together with Bryan m^{c}Donell Bregagh o'Melaghlen, a youth then of the age of 15 yeares. Theobald Buttler with his forces accompanied with the forces of o'Kellye, of Elye o'Karoll, of Ormond, of Arye,[1] of Ohnie o'Mulryan,[2] of Sile-anmchye, and Clanwilliam[3] of the Burkes came to Delvin m'Coghlan to take the spoyles of that Contry and to destroy and subvert itself by their powers. Carbry o'Melaghlen King of the Irish of Meath, heareing thereof with such few forces as he on a suddaine could make up, came to defend the Contry from them, and gave them the onsett at temclene o'Doynne (now called Lomclene[4] o'fflatrye) where there were killed at the suddaine Sir William de la Rochelle knight with many others, with Murrogh m^{c}Cormack o'Kelly & Divers of the cheefest of the said Theobalds armye slaine besides many captives that were taken as Sire Hobert Donn m'William Burk knight, with 4 other principall Englishmen with him. Theobald Buttler Died at beere-Hauen. m'Gerald, Geffry Genuill & Bermingham made up a great armye with the forces of Meath and marched to the Contry of Affalye where they seized upon a great prey of Cowes. Where the Inhabitants of the said Contry assembled together theire forces and went to the streights & passages of the Contry to defend them and sent to Carbry o'Melaghlen king of Meath, Cloyn Colman, and the Irishrie of Meath, to come to ayd them against the said armye their adversarys, who came with a well apointed armye of soldiers and mett the Englishmen in the field, the Irishrie of Meath and Inhabitants of Affalie stricking stifly to theire heade and chief man Carbry o'Melaghlen, made fiercely and corageously towards the battle of the english and gaue a great overthrow to them, took

---

[1] *Arye.*—See p. 168, *antea.*
[2] *o'Mulryan.*—This tribe inhabited the district to the south of the above, called Uaithne, now Owney.
[3] *Clanwilliam.*—Now a barony in the south-west of Co. Tipperary.
[4] *Lomclene.*—Now Lumploon, near Croghan, King's Co.

mᶜGerrald prisoner & Sir Adam Pettit knight and about 3 score knights and free houlders with a great slaughter of the inferiour sort. There was a great snow this yeare which continued from Christmas to St. Bridgets day. Gillessa mᶜTiernann chiefe of Teallagh Donnoghaa,¹ Died.

1286.—Finola ny Melaghlen arch abbess of Meath, Died. Cahall o'Madden prince of sile anmchie Died. There was such scarsity of victuals and corne in the spring tyme and summer of this Yeare, that a hoop or Cronocke was sould for 4 shillings, & there was alsoe a Murren of Cowes the same spring. The earle of Ulster repaired with great forces to Conaught, comitted great outrages in that province, and espetially in the abbyes and church lands, and notwithstanding their unruliness the earle had the victory of his enemies every where in that jorney, and tooke hostages of o'Neale and o'Donell; Deposed Donell mᶜBryan o'Neale of his principallity and gave the rule, government, & chief name of Ulster to Neale Kulanagh o'Neale. Morice ffitzgerald surnamed the bald, Died this yeare.

1287.—Dermott Myegh mᶜDermott mᶜMorice mᶜCahall mᶜDermott Cheife of the Mulronies, and eldest and worthyest man of his owen name, Died. fflorence o'Gibbolan arch Deane of Oylfyn, a man of wonderful knowledge, Learning, and great philosophy, Died. Thomas De Clare Died.

1288.—There were fifteen ecclesiasticall men both abbotts and priests Drowned this Yeare coming from Roome upon the Coasts of Ireland. Terlagh mᶜOwen mᶜRory tooke a House upon Manus mᶜConor Roe, burnt the house over his head, and afterwards Manus escaped safe against the will of the said Terlaugh the house belonging to fflann o'Donellan arch Poett (for Irish poetry) of Conaught. Donell Bregagh was killed with the privity of Carbry o'Melaghlen by Melaghlen o'Melaghlen.

1289.—John Santford² Deputy of Ireland and archbushop of Dublin, Manus o'Conor king of Conaught, Donell o'Kelly,

---

¹ *T. Donnoghaa.* — Now Tully-hunco, a barony in the east of Co Cavan.

² *Santford.*—He was Deputy for

prince of Imanie, and Syacus o'Kelly Tanist of Imanie, marched with all theire forces to Athlone, from thence to Bailelogh-Lwaha, from thence to Killcoursey, and from thence to Athmaynie, where they were mett by Carbry o'Melaghlen, o'Molloy, Mageoghegan, and Neale Roe ffox, and not suffered to march furder over, untill they were driven to Returne back againe to Kilcoursey. The English and Irish of the Deputies party advised themselves for avoyding of danger to pass over at Moyne-ne-Bynne.[1] In the meane time Carbry o'Melaghlen, o'Molloy, maGeoghegan and Neale roe ffox with others theire partakers gave the said army the onsett, wherein Carbry o'Melaghlen behaved himselfe with such Lyonlike force, valour, and courage that he might be well compared to Hector, & soe did his partakers behave themselves with the like valour. Where in the end the English army were discomfitted. Syacus o'Kelly, a worthy man both for bounty and manhood, was slaine. Richard Tute a noble and honorable Barron and Meyler Persye with many others were slaine therein.

1290.—Carbry m^{c}Art o'Melaghlen of the Irishrie of Meath was slaine by David m^{c}Coghlan. Dauid himself was the first that struck him, his brother Gille Keewgin m^{c}Coghlan with 16 others of the familie of the m^{c}Coghlans did in like manner strike him, the said David being a Gossip to the said Carbry before, for which cause the earle of Ulster spoyled and destroyed the said m^{c}Coghlan and his Contry, though o'Melaghlen was in the wrong first. Murrogh o'Melaghlen sone of the said Carbry succeded him in his place. This David m^{c}Coghlan (as I take him) was the auncestor of the Slioght Donell who was sone of Donell himself and father of ffynyne and Donogh of whome the 2 scepts of Slioght ffynyne and Slioght Donnogh descended. His brother Gillekewgin is auncestor of the scept of Leackagh, his other brother Rosse was auncestor of the scept of Clandownye, and ffynyn of the scept of Boynnean.

---

three years, and Archbishop of Dublin from 1284 to 1294. See Ware's *Bishops*, p. 325.

[1] *M.-ne-Bynne.*—Now obsolete.

Here there are certaine years missing in mine ould Booke. I will begin with such years as I can meet withall.

1299 —Alexander m^cDonnell (of the m^cDonells) the best man for bounty and hospitallity in Scotland was killed by Alexander m^cDonell with a great slaughter of his people with him. Morice o'Hogan,[1] Bushop of Killaloe died. S^{ir} John Delamere Knight, the best, worthyest, powerfillest & bountifillest Knight of all Meath, was killed by Geffrey o'fferall in pursuit and defence of his owne prey. The ffamilies of Dalamares, Ledwitches, ffraynes and Cabyes are of the remnant of the Danes that remaine in this Kingdome. The Tartars and Armenians gave a battle to the Soldan of Babilon and Sarazens upon the day of the Nativity of our Lady, where the Soldan and Sarazens were overthrone and an infinite number of them slaine & alsoe the holy land recovered and possessed by the Christian Kings.

1300.—Theobald Buttler, a noble Barron, died. John Prendergrasse was slaine by the sone of ffiaghra o'fflynn. The Castle of Athlean Corann alias Ballymote[2] was founded by the red earle this yeare. Addam Stonton,[3] Lord of Beara,[4] died.

1301.—ffelym m^cCarhy young prince of Desmond, died. Lady Finola, the daughter of ffelym o'Connor & abbess of Killcrewnat,[5] died. Cormack m^cCormack o'Melaghlenn was killed by the sonne of Art o'Melaghlen, who was his owne Cozen German, his fathers brothers sone. Gilleissa m^cffirvissy chiefe chronicler of Tirefiaghragh, wonderfull well skilled in histories, poetry, computation, and many other sciences, died. Cahall o'Moiledwyne the King of Conaughts steward died. The King of England with m^cGerrald, the Lord Bremingham

---

[1] *o'Hogan.* — He held this See from 1281 to 1298. Ware's *Bishops*, p. 592.

[2] *Ballymote.*—In the barony of Corran, Co Sligo. A part of the castle is still standing.

[3] *Stonton.*—This family, of English descent, afterwards took the name of M'Evilly. See Introd. to *Top Poems*, p 32.

[4] *Beara.* — Properly Keara, or Carra, now a barony of Co. Mayo.

[5] *Killcrewnat* — Now Killcrevanty, three miles N W of Tuam. Some remains of this convent still exist.

with all the forces of the English of Ireland save only the Earle of Ulster, went to Scotland to conquer the said Kingdome, where they continued for a fortnight before Lamas untill alhollandtide, and made noe Intire Conquest thereof.

1302.—Donell Roe m°Carthie, the eldest of age, the worthyest for hospitallity, the bountifullest for bestowing of guifts, and the hardiest for prowess and manhood of all Irishmen after good penance died. Miles[1] grandchild of the Earle of Leinster, and Bushop of Limberick, died. Stephen o'Brogann,[2] archbishop of Cashel, died. Down Magwyer, prince of Fermanagh, the best of all Ireland for hospitallity, liberallity and prowes, died. Great comparisons have been made between this Down Magwyer and Donell Roe m°Carthye before mentioned for their bountyes and hospitallityes, which Down Magwyer by the judgment of a certaine learned poet (which remained for a long time in the houses of the said Down and Donell, Covertly and in the habitt of a Carrough[3] or common gamster to know which of them surpassed the other), was accounpted to surpas or excell Donell in all good parts, as by this Irish verse made by the said Poet you may know.

Donn ṁaguiḋiṙ maḋ ṙé ṙin mo ḋeaṙmumain in óuṫaiġ
Ṁó ṙá ġó ḋolaiḋ ḋuinn. aċṫ ciḋ mo ḋoman Ḋomnaill.

which is as much as to say in english, as notwithstanding Desmond and the lands of Donell m°Carthie be far greater than the lands of Down Magwyer, yett Down eatayneth in his house twise as many as Donell doth. William o'ffineann[4] Bushop of Clonvicknosse and before Abbott of Killbegann, died.

---

[1] *Miles.*—He is probably the same who is called by Ware Gerald De Mareshal. *Bishops*, p. 506. He was bishop of Limerick from 1270 to 1301.

[2] *S. o'Brogann.*—A native of Ulster, who, from being Archdeacon of Glendalough, was promoted to this See. He held it from 1291 to 1302. *Ibid.*, p. 475.

[3] *Carrough* —'A kind of people that wander up and down to gentlemen's houses, living only upon cards and dice.' See Spenser's *View of the State of Ireland*, p. 117. From the Irish *carach*, tricky, deceitful.

[4] *W. o'ffinnean.* — He held the See from 1298 to 1300. Ware's *Bishops*, p 172.

1303.—Nicoll m^cMoyle Issa[1] archbushop of Ardmach, the devoutest in his prayers, the greatest housekeeper and bountifullest churchman in Ireland, died. Terlaugh o'Donell, prince of Tyreconell, was killed by his own brother Hugh o'Donell with these ensuing men, vidzt. Mortagh Maglaghlen, Donell o'Cahan, Donogh m^cMeannman, Hugh m^cMeannman, sone of fferlegin o'Donell, Neale m^cDonell o'Boyle, o'Heossye and his sone and his brother Addam, Adam Cendall, with many other English and Irishmen. The king of England with a great army went into Scotland with a great fleet both of the English and Irish of Ireland, took many cities in Scotland, and took the Kingdome. Theobald Burke, the redd Earles Brother, died at Carrickfergus upon Christmas night, returning from the said voyage. Donell oge m^cCarthie Prince of Desmond, died. Morice m^cWilliam Galda maGeoghegan died the 4th of the nones of June. Manus m^cGranell chieftain of Tellagh-aagh[2] died.

1304.—The Countess, wife of the Red Earle, died, and Walter Burke heire of the Red Earle alsoe the same yeare. William Oge m^cWilliam Galda Mageoghegan died the prides of the Ides of October this yeare.

1305.—Mortagh o'Connor of Offalie, Mullmorey his brother, and Callagh o'Connor with 29 of the chiefest of theire familie were treacherously killed by Pierce Bremingham within the Castle of Carrick Feorais.[3] Terlagh m^cBryan Roe o'Bryan died. Hugh Oge o'fferall alsoe died. The Castle of Inisowne[4] was founded and built by the Red Earle this yeare.

1306.—Terlaugh o'Bryan, Prince of Thomond, a renowned and famous housekeeper, a fortunat man in all his successes, and the best of his owne tyme, Died. Whose sone Donnough m^cTerlaugh o'Brian succeeded him in his place immediately.

---

[1] *N. m^cMoyle Issa.*—He held the primacy from 1272 to 1303. 'He was an inveterate enemy to such Englishmen as were promoted to bishopricks in this kingdom.' Ware's *Bishops*, p. 69.

[2] *Tellagh-aagh* Now Tullyhaw, Co. Cavan.

[3] *C. Feorais.* — Castle Carbury, Co. Kildare. A portion of it is still standing.

[4] *Inisowne.*—Greencastle, on the western shore of Lough Foyle near its mouth.

Robert Bruise was crowned king of Scotland against the king of Englands will. Ser William Prendergrass, a noble & worthy knight, died. Nicoll o'Dorchy a priest, and a virgin from his birth, was killed by the black horse of the Barretts without any occation, and whosoever sayeth one paternoster for his Soule hee shall have plenary indulgence of his sines as he sayeth it.

1307.—Donough Moyneagh o'Kelly, prince of Imanie, a common housekeeper for all Ireland in generall, a very bountifull man, died penitently, and Teige his sonne immediately died. Laurence o'Laghtnann[1] abbot of Easroe, abbot of Cnockmoy, and at last Bushop of Killmacdwagh, died. The Englishmen of Roscommon were all killed by Donogh Moyneagh o'Kelly before his death at Athaskragh, when Phillip Moyntir, John Moyntir, and Mathew Drew with 70 other persons were taken and killed, also the sherrif of Roscomon, Dermott Gall mᶜDermott, and Cormack mᶜKehernie were by him sett at libertie, and concluded peace with him for the burning of the towne by Edmond Buttler then Deputy of Ireland. Edward the Great King of England, Wales, and Scotland, Duke of Gascoignes and Lord of Ireland, died in the 35th yeare of his raigne and in the 66th yeare of his age. After whose death the Crowne of England, Wales, Ireland, and Scotland was given to Edward, his sonne, surnamed of Carnarvon. Donnogh o'Flanagan,[2] abbot of Boyle for the space of 5 years, and Bushop of Olynfin for 3 years and ½, a famous man for hospitallity, devotion, and many good parts belonging to his function throughout all Europe, one that never refused any one whatever, neither for meat or cloathes, one that maintained, protested and made peace between the inhabitants of the province of Connaught, one full of wisdome and good delivery to maintaine any thing he took in hand, one charitable and freeharted towards all men, died

---

[1] *o'Lachtnann*—He was Bishop of Kilmacduagh from 1290 to 1306. See Ware's *Bishops*, p. 648. Another of this name was Bishop of Elphin a few years later.

[2] *o'Flanagan*.—'A man of great reputation for his wisdom, hospitality, and other virtues.' *Ibid.*, p. 630.

penitently of 5 weekes sickness the 10th of the Calends of June. Carolus mᶜAnliahanye was elected to the Bushoprick of Oylfin of the one part and was abbot of Logh Ke, who received his orders at Armagh, and enjoyed the profit of the Bishoprick. William Bremingham, archbushop of Connaught, did elect Molussy Magaoy[1] of the other side to be bushop of the said place who resided in Roome for 3 years, and at last came. Melaghlen o'Garmley, arch-chieftaine of Kinell-Moan, died.

1308 —King Edward the first died this yeare in Burrogh upsands in the marches of Scotland. Molrony mᶜDermoda tooke a great prey from the sons of Donell o'Connor in the land of Krith Carbrye in Connaught. Bryan o'Dowdy and the English of Lwyne and Tirefiaghragh tooke another prey from the said sons of Donell o'Connor, after that they agreed and delivered hostages for securityes of the peace before. After all which preyes and spoyles taken, the sonnes of Donell aforesaid came to the Mount of Sliew-da-ene,[2] and took with them thither but their horses, armour, &c., and stood, the said Englishmen of the lands of Lwyney and Tyrefiaghragh hearing of theire being there, assembled theire forces and followed them to the said mount, the sons of Donnell and mᶜDonough retraited upon them, where they gave them an overthrow, and put them to flight, and pursued them to a place called Leack-eassa-Dara,[3] where they killed Thomas mᶜWalter constable of the castle of Bona-finne, with his brother and divers others. Piers Gaveston,[4] a great favorite (or the king's Minion) of the king of Englands came to this kingdome this yeare & soone after his comeing killed o'Dempsye. A Thunder bolt came from heaven and lighted upon the abbye of the ffryers of Roscomon & broke down the said abby uppon St. Steephens night in Christmas holy

---

[1] *Magaoy* —He is called Malachy mac Aedha by Ware, *Bishops*, p 631, and mac Hugh in these Annals *ad ann* 1312

[2] *Sliew-da-ene.*—In the barony of Tirrerell, Co Sligo.

[3] *Leack-eassa-Dara.*—i e. the flat rock, at Ballysadare, Co Sligo.

[4] *P. Gaveston.*—He was Deputy for one year only.

dayes. The Easter of this yeare was in the month of March and there was a great murren of cattle therein A° 1308.

1309.—Hugh mᶜOwen mᶜRory mᶜHugh mᶜCahall Croudearg o'Connor king of Conaught and one for birth, prowes, liberaility, and many other noble parts, worthy to be king of a kingdome, was killed by Hugh Breifneagh mᶜCahall Roe o'Conor in Killcloghan,[1] in the teritory of the Brenie, with these ensuing persons that were killed at the said place with him, vidzt. Connor mᶜDermoda, Dermoid Roe mᶜTeige mᶜAndrias, Dermott mᶜCahall, Carragh mᶜDermoda, Hugh mᶜMurtagh mᶜTeige mᶜMoleronye, Dermott oge o'Helye, who was a modest, liberall, and great housekeeper, Moyledownye the Gillowe-Glasse, Gillernew chief Brehon of Conaught, ffogartagh o'Dowalgie of the househould men of Tomaltagh mᶜDermott with many others, with the loss of 200 more of them. After which Deed Hugh Brenagh came to his house where the three Twaithies, that is the three thirds of the province, came to congratulate him. In the meane time Moyleronye mᶜDermoda a prince of Moylorge with the assemblyes and forces of his allies and friends of all partes, came to the midst of Sile Moreye to maintaine the principallity & name of king of Conaught for his owne fostersone ffelym o'Connor: sent his messengers to all his friends and all of the English and Irish, that they should come to assist him in that Interprise, & William Burk with his brothers and kinsmen came accordingly and there encamped in the midst of the province with theire said manie forces, fearing the inhabitants should joyne with Hugh brefnagh (the aforesaid kingkiller) to make him king of the province. The said Moyleronie tooke himself to the revenewes & profits belonging to the king of Conaught, together with such Jeweles & principall as belonged to the place, and made the Inhabitants take theire oathes never to yeeld to any other but to ffelym (the said Moilronyes foster sonne) whereupon William Burke returned to Oylfinn. Hugh Brenagh went to Meath to meet

---

[1] *Killcloghan* —O'Donovan suggests Killclogha, in the barony of Clankee, Co Cavan.

with the Earles, and in his absence the Inhabitants of the province came upon the land of oghter-Tyre,[1] took a great prey, which they consumed in theire camp of Oughter-Tyre aforesaid.

1310.—Tany More o'Mullronye, chief chronicler of Sile Morye, Died in the spring of this yeare. Hugh Beifneagh made a great prey called the prey of Toytyn or fire upon Moylronie mᶜDermott in Clogher, where Donogh mᶜDonogh mᶜDermott was taken captive and his wife (o'fflanagans daughter) was killed; women, children & many others were also there killed, and encamped at Oghterhyrie, before mᶜDermott and the Inhabitants of Sile Morey, which when William Burk heard he encamped at Killomatt[2] in the sight of the said Hugh Breifneagh. While they were thus encamped before each other Hugh Breifnagh sent privie message to his Brother Rory mᶜCahall that he should goe then in the absence of William Burk to his castle of Bonafinne, which he did accordingly prey, and spoyled the towne and castle of Bonafinne aforesaid & converted all they could find therein to theire owne uses. Hugh Brefnagh staid there with his Bwannaghtmen and theire Chiefe head Jonock[3] mᶜVuellen,[4] & when this Johnock with hyred bwannaght men saw Hugh Breifnagh all alone, after the sending of the most part of all his forces with his Brother, to take the spoyles of Bonafinne aforesaid, being provoked thereunto by William Burk, who promised him a certaine stipend for killing the said Hugh Brefnagh, who accordingly getting the said opportunity killed the said Hugh Brefnagh according his promise to William Burk before made. When Tydeings came thereof to William Burke, Molronye mᶜDermoda, and Sile Morye of theire camp at Killomatt, they Immediately sent theire forces to take the preyes and spoyles of the followers and

---

[1] *O-Tyre*—The northern part of the barony of Boyle, Co. Roscommon.

[2] *Killomatt.*—In the same barony.

[3] *Jonock.*—*i.e.* John og, young John.

[4] *mᶜVuellen.*—McQuillin, a Welsh family which settled in north Antrim about the time of the Anglo-Norman invasion. See *ad ann.* 1404, *postea*.

people that belonged to Hugh Breifnagh ; William Burke himself came to the middst of the Contry and cessed m'Vuellen with his route of 200 men upon them, soe as there was not a Town in Silemorrey without a continuall Bwannye,[1] noe nor parrish without oppression, nor noe good man without great wrong don him during the rule and government of William Burk after the death of Hugh Breifnagh When Mollronye m'Dermott saw how his fostersonne ffelym sett naught by, and the revenewes which of Right belonged to him, taken by William Burk, and that the Englishmen exercised theire Captivities and Imprisonments upon the Irishmen to weaken and bring them Loe, who conjectured that if Molronye were cutt off, that there would be noe resistance in Connaught, and that the whole province should be theires without contradiction, hee determined with himself to promote the said ffelym to be king of Conawght, and thus he resolved to doe, whether they would or noe. Whereupon they brought the said ffelym with them to Carnefreeigh[2] (where they then used to create theire kings) and there made him king of Conaught after the manner before used in his predecessors Tyme. hee was enstalled King with as great solemnity, Ceremonies[3] and other customes theretofore practized as any one of his auncestors since the Tyme of his Auncestor Bryan[4] m'Eachye Moymean some tyme king of Conaught. Alsoe the said Molronye made a magnifitient and great feast in honour thereof, with the assembly and presence of all the nobility of Conaught such as none other of his auncestors or predecessors kings of Conaught ever before him was heard or read in bookes to have made. The Castle of Sligeagh was repaired and made by the earles this yeare. Twenty Tunnes of wine was putt ashore at

---

[1] *Bwannye.*—*i. e.* buanacht, the money and food which the soldiers were entitled to receive for their support.

[2] *Carnefreeigh.*—Carnfree, in the barony and county of Roscommon, a little to the south of the village of Tulsk. See *Annals F. M.*, iii. 221.

[3] *Ceremonies.*—For a detailed account of the manner of inauguration of the Irish kings, see *Tribes, &c., of Hy Fiachrach*, p. 439.

[4] *Bryan.*—See the Genealogical Table, *ibid.*, p. 477.

Moykednie[1] this yeare. Joan, Daughter of o'Connor of Affalie and wife to Mortagh Mageoghegan, chieftaine of Kinnaleagh, Died. fferall m‍cMortagh More Mageoghegan was killed by these of the Annalie, which was the first cause of enemye betweene Kinaleagh, and those of the Analie. Geffry o'fferall with the forces of the Annalie came to Donouer in Kinaleagh, to take the preyes and spoyles of that Contry, but the Natives and Inhabitants of the Contry soe well behaved themselves against them in Defence of theire contry and goods, that they killed Donell m‍cHugh oge o'fferall, Hugh m‍cMoyle Issa, and Geffry mac Mortagh.

1311.—Mortagh more Congolagh m‍cGeoghegan chieftaine of Kinaleagh and the race of ffiagh m‍cNeale was killed. Jordan De Exeter repaired to Moylerge, to take the prey of that Contry, which he tooke and brought with him, and killed Teige o'Hanly Chieftaine of Kinell Dowhy[2] in pursuite thereof Donell o'Bryen Chieftaine of Tyre Bryan, Died. Moyle Issa o'Daly,[3] a Wonderfull good housekeeper and an excellent Poett, died. m‍cWilliam Burk with a great armye went into Mounster to encounter with Clare,[4] where they encountered and gave battle, wherein Clare was discomfitted and quite overthrone: but William Burk followed the flying persons of the discomfitted side, was taken, and though he was taken, yet he gave no overthrowe to his enemies and gained the field with honour. Butt by the way this much I gather out of this history, whome I take to be an authentick author and worthy prelate of the Church, that would tell nothing but truth, that there raigned more Disscentions, strifes, warres, and Debates betweene the Englishmen themselves in the beginning of the Conquest of this kingdome than between the Irishmen, as by perusing the warres betweene the Lasies of Meath, John Coursy earl of Ulster, William Marshall

---

[1] *Moykednie.*—The plain between the rivers Drowse and Erne.

[2] *K. Dowhy.* Their territory extended along the west bank of the Shannon from Caranadoe Bridge to Drumdaff.

[3] *o'Daly* — See the historical sketch of the family of O'Daly, prefixed to O'Daly's *Tribes of Ireland*

[4] *Clare* —The battle took place at Bunratty, Co Clare, on the feast of the Ascension.

and the English of Meath and Mounster: mac Gerrald, the Burkes, Buttlers and Cogann may appear. There arose great Warrs in Thomond this yeare Donnough mʻne Marie and the Inhabitants of the cantred of o'Gassine encountred & gave battle to o'Bryen and all his Mounstermen, where Donnogh himself with the vehement power of o'Bryen and Mounster-men together with the most part of the chiefest of his partakers and followers with many others of the other side were slaine. Donogh o'Bryen, king of Thomond and a man worthy of the monarchy of a kingdome, was treacherously slaine by Murrogh mᶜMahon o'Bryen. Sean-oge mᶜVuellen was killed in a fray at Ballen-tobher bride[1] by the same gallowglasses where withall he killed Hugh Brenagh beforesaid My author prayeth God to reward him that killed him, for murdering Hugh Breneagh as before is rescited: Dermott Cleragh king of Mounster was Deposed of his kingdome, and Murtagh o'Bryan was constituted in his place. Bryan maGeoghegan prince of Uriell, Died

1312.—The Templers[2] were Destroyed throughout all christendom this yeare. William Bremingham[3] archBushop of Twayme the 2nd day of the Moone before the 10th Indiction, Died. Benedict o'Brackan,[4] Bushop of Lwynie, Died. Mollassie mʻHugh[5] Bushop of Oylfyn was elected archBushop of Twayme. Pierse Gaueston was killed, the King's minion. Dervorgill, daughter of Manus o'Connor king of Conaught, Died. The feast of Easter this yeare was in the month of March.

1313.—Pope Clement rested in our Lord God. Dermot Cleareagh o'Bryan, king of Mounster, Died. Robert Bruce,

---

[1] *B. bride* —Ten miles north-west of the town of Roscommon. A considerable part of it is still standing. See the *Journal R. S. A. I.* for 1889, p. 24 It has its name from St. Brigid's well close by.

[2] *Templers.*—For an account of their suppression in Ireland, see Gilbert's *Viceroys*, p. 125, and Grace's *Annals*, p. 51.

[3] *Bremingham.*—He held the See of Tuam from 1289 to 1311. See Ware's *Bishops*, p 608.

[4] *o'Brackan* —He seems to have held the See from 1297 to 1311. *Ibid*, p. 659.

[5] *M mᶜHugh.*—He was Bishop of Elphin from 1311 to 1313, and Archbishop of Tuam from the latter date to 1348. *Ibid.*, p. 611.

king of Scotland, came upon the coasts of Ireland this yeare. The ffrench king died.

1314 —Neale o'Donell Died. There was a battle fought by Robert Bruce king of Scotland aganst the Englishmen, where the said Robertt in defence of his Kingdome killed an infinite number of earls, knights and nobles of england, with a great slaughter of theire Inferiours at a place called Scrubleith[1] in Scotland, where the earle of Glocester (who then was next the king of England for nobility and greatness of Revenues) was killed. Neale m^cBryan o'Neale a Prince both famous for riches & good government, and that did beare greatest sway in Ireland, Died. Roalue m^cMahon was killed by his owen brother.

1315.—Edward m^cRobert Bruce, earle of Carick and brother of king Robert, king of Scotland, Landed with a fleet of 300 ships in the north[2] of Ulster: at whose comeing all the Inhabitants of Ireland both English and Irish were stricken with great terrour, that it made the Lands and Inhabitants of Ireland to shake for feare. Immediately after his arrival hee burnt the Towns of Downdealgan, Athfirdia[3] and Rathmore,[4] Harryed and spoyled all Ulster in Generall, tooke theire hostages, collected the revenewes of that province to himself, and made the Ulstermen to consent and acknowledge him as theire king, and Delivered him the Regallities belonging to the king, and gave him the name of king of Ireland. When Richard Burk, earl of Ulster, heard that Edward Bruce was thus arrived, and that he usurped the name of king and exercised the fore-recited Tyranyes, he out of all partes gathered a great armye with him to Roscomon, from thence he marched on to Athlone, through the Borders of Meath and Moybrey accompanied with ffelym o'Connor king of Conaught. Theire army consisted of twenty Cohorts, the English army

---

[1] *Scrubleith* —Sterling. Bruce's army extended from Bannockburn to this place.

[2] *North.* — At Olderfleet, near Larne, Co. Antrim.

[3] *Athfirdia.*—Ardee, in Co. Louth.

[4] *Rathmore.*—Two miles north of Athboy, Co. Meath. The castle and church are still standing, close to the Hill of Ward.

never spared neither spirituall nor Temporall land in every
place where they came without respect of saint or shrine or
sacred place, from the river of Synen of the south to Cowle-
Ryan[1] of the north and Inisown. As this great army was
thus marching on spoyleing and Destroying all places on
their way, they saw Edward Butler, then Deputy of Ireland,
likewise marching on towards them with 30 cohorts of well
appoynted souldiers armed at all poynts, at whose sight the
earle was somwhat angrye, alledging that himselfe was of
suffitient power to expell Bruce and his Scottishmen out of
the kingdome, and desired and advised the Deputy not to
joyne with himselfe, and that he needed not his assistance.
The earle that night encamped at Athfirdia neare the mount
called Sliew Brey, and Edward Bruce with his Scottish and
Ulstermen at Inis Kaeyne,[2] the earle the next daye followed
him and encamped in the town of Louth. William Burk, to
take some advantage of Bruce, skirmished with him where
there were a few killed on either side. As for Edward Bruce
and his armye by the procurement of o'Neal and Ulstermen he
tooke his jorneye to Coulerayne of the ninth and to the
borders of Inisowne, and fell down and broke the bridge of
Cowlerayne to stop the earles passage over the river of Banne,
whome the earle followed until he came to the said River and
from thence through Ulster, where he marched, houlding on
their course of spoyleing and Destroying all places where
they came, not spareing church or chaple, in soe much that
they did not leave neither field of corn undestroyed nor towne
unransacked, nor unfrequented place (were it never so little
nor soe desert) unsearched and unburnt, and consumed to
meere ashes the very churches that lay in their way unto the
bare stones, the encounter of which army on both sides of the
river of Banne was soe inconvenient that neither partye could
hinder or offend the other; for they were severed from each
other by the deep, spatious, and smooth-running waters or
river. Nevertheless they had daily shooting of arrows of both

---

[1] *Cowle-Ryan.* — Coleraine, in Co. Derry.

[2] *Inis Kaeyne.*—Inniskeen, seven miles west of Dundalk.

sides of the river. Edward Bruce hearing of the great fame of ffelym o'Conor king of Conaught that then was with the red earle, he sent him privie message that he would give him the province of Conaught at his Disposition, and to adheare to himselfe, and alsoe to return from the earle to Defend his owne province, to which offer the said ffelym listned and acknowledged to accept of him. In the mean tyme Rory m'Cahall Roe o'Connor seeing himself to have his opportunity in the absence of ffelym and his nobles, that went to him in the jorney of Ulster, he alsoe made his repaire to Edward Bruce with whome he had secret Communication, and Promissed the said Edward to Banish all Englishmen out of Conaught if Edward would be pleased to accept of his owne service. Edward authorised him to warr against Englishmen and not to meddle with the lands of ffelym, but having received that favour of Bruce, hee did not onely warre upon Englishmen, but alsoe upon ffelym and his partakers, and saught all meanes to get the kingdome of Conaught into his owen hands and immediately assembled together Breny-men & great Companies of Gallowglasses and Conaught men, and made towards the middle part of Sile-morey, where first of all he burnt the street towne of Sligeagh, Athklean Coran, the castle of Killcolman, the towne of Tobber Bride[1]; Downoman with the Castle, Roscomon, Ryndowne als Teadoyn ard Athlone together with all the houses that lay in his way between these places. After committing of which great exploytts, he desired m^cDermoda to give him the duties due upon him, belonging to the king of Connaught and alsoe to yield him obedience which m^cDermoda absolutely denied, and with all refused to give him hostages, but he received hostages and pledges of the rest of the whole province, Incontinently went to Carne-fro-aigh, where he was Invested king of Connaught by the 12 Chieftaines of Sile Morie, 12 cowarbbs, and other spirituall that were accustomed to use the Ceremonies at the tyme of the Investure of the king, remained for a tyme amonst Sile-Morey preying and Destroy-

---

[1] *Tobber Bride.*—Ballintober. See p. 267, *antea.*

ing such of that country as he suposed to stick to Phelym, and that would not yield him allegiance, and alsoe the chiefest cause of his residence there was Tarrieing for the returne of ffelym and his forces from the north. In the meane tyme ffelym o'Conor thinking with himself that Rory would usurp the rule of Conaught in his absence, he spoke to the red earle & tould him how Rory would warre against him in Conaught and seeke to get the whole government and rule of that province into his own hands by this oportunity he had in theire absence. Whereupon he intended to depart from the earle to defend his lands in Conaught who in his jorny through Ulster and Uriel had not one dayes rest, but continuall assaults and skirmishes untill he came to Granard and to a place called Killenenamas[1] & to the people of his uncle, his mothers brother Shane o'fferrall after great slaughter and Losses of his people, & flight of some of them with theere goods. After his return he advised with his princes and chiefs that were with him in that tumultious jorny, and in those places Rory o'Conor did constitute others of his one side, that they and every of them should returne to their places, and take and hould them of Rory. During the tyme they should contend together for the preheminence, with condition that if he had overcome Rory they should hold of him as they did before, & as for his owne fosterfather m^cDermott of Moylorg, seeing it is thought that Rory would not agree with him for any reasonable conditions of peace, hee was content hee should remaine with himself dureing his warrs until he had seen the end and Issue thereof.

The redd earle and Englishmen seeing ffelym and his Conaught men gave them noe assistance aganst theire enemies, and alsoe saw them Depart in that manner, they returned back againe from Cowlerayne to the Castle of Conyre, whome the Scottish and Ulstermen seeing followed them, & as they were at the poynt to meet and give battle, at the first onset William Burk with some of his knights were taken, with the 2 sons of m^caMiles, the red-earle himselfe tooke his flight and was

---

[1] *Killenenamas.*—'Coillnanamus, the people of John O'Ferall.' *Annals of Loch Ce*, I. 569.

chased from thence to Connaught; after whose comeing into the province his allyes and friends both of the English and Irish flocked to his house, in hopes to be relieved by him from the oppression of Rory o'Connor; these ensueing persons were the chiefest men of note that had Recourse to him, ffelym o'Conor king of Conaught, Mortagh o'Bryan Prince of Thomond, Mulronye m^cDermott Prince of Moylorg, Gilbert o'Kelly, prince of Imanie, who all were banished out of theire possessions. When they were thus mett and Mulrony m^cDermott saw soe many exiled noblemen together in one house, hee recomitted with himseef, was abashed, and said that he could never after be reconed amongst soe many or that number of Deposed chieftaines, but would repaire to teige o'Kelly, by whose Intercession he thought to come in favour & creditt with Rory and gett his owen againe, which accordingly was don, upon yeelding of Hostages by the said Mulrony to Rory o'Connor, for keeping his allegiance & fidelity to him.

Hugh Ballagh o'Connor was treacherously killed by Cahall m^cDonell o'Connor; Hugh m^cArtt and Dermott m^cSymon ne Troye, were in like manner killed by him in revenge of his father that before was killed by the said Dermott. Donell the next day tooke a great prey from the sons of Murtagh, where Magnus m^cMagnus and Donell his brother were killed in pursuit thereof, and Tomaltagh m^cDonogh was taken captive, after comitting of which exploytes they tooke part and partaketh with the English for theire owne defence. When newes came to the eares of ffelym o'Conor of these things, he with a few of his trustyest friends went to the sons of Donell o'Conor, viz. to Rory, Magnus, Cahall, Mortagh, Donogh, John, & Teige, and after some conference had, they with the help of their kinsmen and such others as joyned with them, preyed Bryan o'Dowoye, took another prey from Arteach of Dermott Gall, killed many of his people and burnt his haggards and corne together with theire houses, and alsoe tooke another prey from the sons of Cahall o'fflanagan which they tooke in theere way to the weare called Kara-Kowla-

Kwirk;[1] they could not drive the prey by reason the great moysture of the bog because the feet of the Cattle waded soe deep in the meere, and also being pursued by a great company in soe much that all the forces of the sones of Cahall and that parts did overtake them, with Mahon mᶜGranell chieftaine of Moynter-eolas, with his kinsmen and followers; mᶜDermott hearing of the clamorous noyse of the Drivers, and such as were about the said pray comeing to Kara aforesaid, he followed them to Kowlevakar,[2] & seeing the prey stayed & like to be kept by the owners, he did not well like of, but had rather theire prey should be taken by ffelym and his adherents; whereupon he Immediately assisted ffelym notwithstanding the great multitudes that were against him, and upon the sudaine Conor Roe mᶜHugh Breifne was killed, Mahon mᶜGranell chieftaine of Momtyr-eolas, o'Mullmyay chief of Moyntier-Keruellan,[3] & Discomfitted these that withheld the prey from ffelym, tooke the prey himselfe without restitution to the owners, came that night to the abby of Boylle, the next day over Segasse north-easterly, from thence to Kowle o'fflyn,[4] to the Koran & soe to the contry of Lwynie, where ffelym expected his comeing. When Rory o'Conor heard that Mulronye mᶜDermott had done these great exployts & that he had joyned in company with his fosterson felym, he caused to be assembled from all partes his forces, and with them encamped that night at Ballymore o'fflynn, made little respect of the reverence due to the Church of easse-da-chonne,[5] preyed the monks of the abby of Boyle: Tomaltagh mᶜMorgiessa mᶜDonogh with all his forces and Dependents went to assist ffelym. Dermott Gall went to Crwaghan the king's palace. Teige o'Kelly went to assist Rory, and there followed his promis of allegiance upon Mulronye mᶜDermott, & being soe

---

[1] *K.-Kwirk.* — *i. e.* the weir of Kuil Cuire, now obsolete.

[2] *Kowlevakar.*—Culbhathar. *Annals of Loch Cé*, I. 573.

[3] *M.-Keruellan.*—A tribe in the barony and county of Leitrim.

[4] *K. o'fflyn.* — Now Coolavin, a district in the south of Co. Sligo.

[5] *E.-da-chonne.*—Called also Eas mᶜNeirc, from St. Machona, son of Erc, patron of the place. It is a short distance to the north of Boyle, and is now known as Assylyn. See *Annals F. M.*, iii. 162.

joyned together, they pursued ffelym and Mulronye to Letter Loyny¹ and to the borders of the mount of Sliew-gawe² and also to the place called Glann-fahrowe³ where Infinite number of cowes, garrons, and sheep were killed by them, striping gentlewomen that could make noe resistence of theire cloathes to theire nakid skins; Destroyed and killed without remorse children & Little ones of that jorney. There was not soe much hurt done in them parts before in any man's memory without profitt to the doers thereof. Mulronye mᶜDermott hearing that Dermott Gall sat in the priviledge seat of his auncestors of Carick of Logh Ke, and with Honour conwayed to Crwaghan to enjoy the principallity belonging to himselfe as his right, and that he made havock & killed all his cowes att Glann-fahrowe (as before is specified) he with his houschould and such others as he had in readiness for the purpose marked towards Carrick, turned his back to Kara and Synen and the 3 Kerryes,⁴ vidzt the Lower Kerry, Kerry May, and Kerry Artie, with theire Cattle; it is thought that in these dayes there was not such an assault given or such a prey taken by any man whatsoever, for they made all the province to shake for theire feare. The wife of Dermott Gall was taken prisoner at once with the said prey, together with a few other gentlewomen. Dermott Gall after that day never enjoyed any happy Day, besaught Restitution, & upon refusal preyed Moylorg, tooke all the cowes and horses they could meet, notwithstanding Dermott had warning before, which did not avayle him, although he had a great assembly of people before them, and left Moylurg wast and void of cattle, there was noe respect of temporall or church land in that country, theire cattle, corne, & other things were snacht eaven from the very alters, and Delivered over to the gallowglasses for their wages.

---

¹ *L Loyny.* — The territory of Luigne. *Annals of Loch Cé*, 1. 575

² *Sliew-gawe* — Now the Ox Mountains, forming the boundary between the counties of Mayo and Sligo.

³ *G.-fahrowe,*—Now Glenfarne, in the barony of Drumahaire, Co. Leitrim.

⁴ *Kerryes* —Some of the Carraigi, driven from south Munster, settled near Castlerea and in the barony of Costello. See *Annals F.M*, III 238.

The towne of Dunmore was burnt by Rory o'Connor, Eoghroym[1] o'Manie was burnt by the said Rory and the Castle thereof ffallen Downe. The Cantred of Moynmoy was wasted and Destroyed by Teig o'Kelly, ffelym o'Connor, m^{c}Dermott, Tomaltagh m^{c}Donogh, & the sons of Donell o'Conor partaketth with the English of Ighter Conaught, & after they accorded peace with them, they Destroyed Tyrenna,[2] Tyreneaghtynn, Moyntyr Kreghan[3] and the Demeasne of Donmore called Convakney. Richard Burk earle of Ulster called the red-earle remayned this yeare without force or power in any the parts of Ireland. Then raigned many Diseases generally throughout the whole kingdome, a great loss of the Inhabitants, great scarcity of victualls, great slaughter of people, and in Summer ugly and fowle weather. Hugh o'Donell prince of Tyre Conell came to the lands of Carbrye in Conaught and Destroyed all that contry by the advice of his wife the Daughter of Magnus o'Connor, & came herself with a great route of gallowglasses and tooke all the spoyles of the Churches of Dromkliew without respect of church or churchmen of that place. The castle of Sligeagh was taken and fallen down by o'Donnell of that jorny.

1316. Hugh o'Donnell prince of Tyreconell aforesaid gathered together all the forces of Tyreconell & with them again came to the Country of Carbrey aforesaid, and went to the Castle of m^{c}Connor where Rory m^{c}Donell severed himself from his owne kinsmen & accorded with o'Donnell, & yeelded him chiefryes and rents of Crich Carbry. Dervorgill, Daughter of Magnus o'Conor (o'Donells wife) retayned a great company of gallowglasses to whome she gave a consideration of mony for killing Rory m^{c}Donell o'Conor, who killed him accordingly after all the oathes of Tyreconnell passed between them for theire concordance and securities to each other, & afterwards they of Tyreconnell took great preyes of the contry of Carbrye.

---

[1] *Eoghroym.* — Now Aughrim, near Ballinasloe, Co. Galway, in the ancient territory of Hy Many.

[2] *Tyrenna.*—Terran, in the barony of Longford, Co. Galway.

[3] *M. Kreghan.* — Perhaps M. Checharain. See *Tribes, &c., of Hy Many,* p. 40.

Phelym o'Conor tooke a prey from the sons of ffailge, killed Richard himself, and made a great slaughter of his people. After all these things ffelym gathered together a huge armye both of Irish & Englishmen, amongst whom the lord Bermingham, Mulrony m^{c}Dermott, the sones of Donell o'Conor, & other noblemen (which for brivity's sake I omitt) are nott to be forgotten, to give Battle to Rory m^{c}Cahall Roe o'Connor who tooke the kingdome of Conaught before of the said ffelym, being soe accompanied they marched on towards Sile Morey, which beeing tould to Rory o'Connor king of Conaught, as then sitting att the top of ffie Ikie[1] of Connaught in Clynn Convoy[2] watching the proceedings of ffelym & his partakers, where he encamped and being soe sett the said Phelym and his foster father Mullronye m^{c}Dermoda with theire squadrons well sett in battle aray fiersely make towards him, ffelym himself & his foster father Mulronye in the foremer rank, together with the most part of the English of Conaught, espetially of that part of the prouince following them & Drawing to a place in his presence called Togher-Mone-Koyne.[3] The Conaught men with theire king Rory m^{c}Cahall o'Connor mett them in the same place, where king Rory and his army by the multiplicity of hands and armes against him, was quite overthrone & Discomfitted, king Rory himself (a man of wonderful prowess, a destroyer of foriners and an expeller of them out of all Ireland) was killed, alsoe Dermott Gall m^{c}Dermott prince of Moylorg, Cormack m^{c}Kehearne, prince of Kerry, Gillecriost m^{c}Dermoda, Dermot m^{c}fferall m^{c}Dermoda, Cennegan m^{c}Cennegan, Donell m^{c}Cennegan, Donogh m^{c}Rory with one hundred gallowglasses & divers others were killed: Dermott & Donell o'Boyle & alsoe Roback Bremingham of the other side were hurt. This battle was given the 7th of the calends of March the yeare of our Lord 1316. ffelym o'Conor afterwards tooke all the preys and

---

[1] *ffie Ikie.* — Mullach Fidhig, to the west of the river Suck, in the barony of Ballymoe, Co Galway.

[2] *C. Convoy* — Now locally called Clanconoo.

[3] *Togher-Mone-Koyne* — In the parish of Templetogher, barony of Ballymoe, Co. Galway.

spoyles of all that belonged to Rory o'Connor, or that partaketh with him before, and tooke himselfe the Government & name of king of Conaught as before he had which extends from Easroe in Ulster to Eaghtge, tooke Hostages for the preservation of allegiance of the Brenye men, Constituted Uloyge o'Roirk as theire king, alsoe he tooke the Hostages of the o'Kellyes, o'Maddins, o'Dermoddaes, o'haras, o'Dowdies, and after setling himselfe prepared an army, with whome hee went to banish the English of Conaught, Immediately burnt the towne of Athlone, killed Stephen Dexeter therein, Miles Cogan, William Prendergrasse, & John Stanton, knights, & alsoe William Lawless, with a great slaughter of their people; he burnt all the Contry from the place called Castle Corran to Roua,[1] tooke all theire spoyles & preyes, returned to his house with a rich booty of his enemies and fortunate success of his affaires. King ffelym haveing thus returned to his house made noe long stay, but went to Meelick to meet with those of Mounster and Leathmoy, where he burnt and fell downe the Castle, at first Murtagh o'Bryan prince of Thomond came to his house, & all the families of the o'Brians face to face, with whome he went to Roscommon to fall the Castle thereof to the earth. ffelym o'Conor heareing of the returne of William Burke to Conaught from Scotland, he proclaimed that all his people from all partes where they were, with such as would joyn with them would gather together to banish William Burk from out of Conaught, at whose command all the Irishrie of Conaught from Easroe to Sliew Veghty or eighty were obedient & came to that place of meeting. Donnogh o'Bryan prince of Thomond, o'Melaghlan king of Meath, o'Roirk king of the Breifnie, o'fferall chieftaine of the Annallie, called Convackne, Teige o'Kelly king of Imanie, with many others of the Nobility of Ireland, came to this assembly and marched towards Athenrie to meet with William Burk, the Lord Bremingham and others the english of the province of Conaught, where

---

[1] *Roua.*—Now the Robe, which flows into the eastern side of Lough Mask.

they met and gave battle in a place near the town ; in which Battle the Irishmen were Discomfitted & quite overthrowne ; ffelym o'Connor king of Conaught was therein killed ; alsoe Teige o'Kelly, king of Imanie, and 28 of the Chiefest of that familie. Magnus m⸰Donell o'Connor tanist of all Conaught, Artt o'Hara, prince of Lwynie, Melaghlen Carragh o'Dowdye, Conor Oge o'Dowdye, Murtagh m⸰Connor o'Dowdye, Dermot m⸰Dermott Tanist of Moylorg, Murtagh m⸰Taghleagh m⸰Dermoda, Mortagh m⸰Dermoda m⸰fferall, Molronye Oge m⸰Magnusa, John m⸰Murogh o'Madden, Donell o'Boylle, Donell m⸰Hugh o'Conchennan prince of the o'Dermotts & his brother Mortagh, Murrogh o'Madden, Donnell o'Boylle, Donnogh o'Molloye of fferkeall with his people, the sone of Murrogh o'Manon & 100 of his people, Neale ffox prince of Teaffa men with his people, fferall m⸰John Galda[1] o'fferall, William m⸰Hugh oge o'fferall, Thomas m⸰Auley o'fferall, five of the familie of the m⸰Donoghs, viz. Tomaltagh, Murrogh, Murtagh, Conor Mortagh & Melaghlen m⸰Donogh, John m⸰Kiegan o'Connor's chiefe judg, Conor & Gillernew the sons of Dalere-Docker o'Deuelyn, the man called far Iomchar-ne-honchen,[2] Thomas o'Conollan of the kings guard ; all which Persons with many others of Mounster, Meath, & Conaught which were Tedious to resite were slaine in that battle as a certaine Irish Poett pitifully in an Irish verse[3] said :

Móṗ mac ṗíġ nac aḃṗaim a ainm, do maṗḃa iṗ an móṗ maiúni

Do ḟlúaġ mive iṗ múman. Tṗuaġ léim eṗoiṫi in caṫuġaḋ.

This battle was given upon the day of St. Lawrence the Martyre, ffelym o'Conor being then but of the age of 23 years, in the 5th year of whose raigne Rory m⸰Cahall Roe

---

[1] *Galda.*—*i. e.* the foreigner ; a term of reproach addressed to one who was the friend of the English, or adopted their habits.

[2] *I.-honchen.*—*i.e.* the man who carried the leopard, the standard-bearer of the O'Connors, whose arms were a leopard. See the Appendix to Keating's *H. of Ireland*, ed. 1726.

[3] *Verse.*—'The mighty son of a king, his name I will not mention, was slain in the great fight of the host of Meath and Munster. Sorrow is in my heart for that battle.'

o'Connor (before mentioned) deposed him for one ¼ yeare, who being killed as before is declared, ffelym succeeded him for another ¼ yeare untill he was slaine at Athenrye aforesaid. Rory surnamed Rory na ffidh[1] mᶜDonogh mᶜOwne mᶜRory succeeded next as king of Conaught. William Burke with a great armye came to Silemorye, where all the families and scepts of this contry agreed to make peace with William, but mᶜDermott onely; whereupon William Burk marched to mᶜDermotts Contry of Moylorg, tooke all the preyes and spoyles of that Country from a place called Athenkip, and from Vaghter-herye,[2] alsoe burnt & destroyed the whole contry, & returned from thence without skirmish or any loss worthy of note. Rory na ffidh mᶜDonaugh the king of Conaught (before mentioned) was deposed of his principallity by Mulronye mᶜDermoda after he had raigned a quarter and a ¼ king of Conaught. The Lady Dervorgill or Dervorg, Daughter of Magnus o'Connor K. of Conaught & wife of Hugh o'Donell, Died.

1317. Terlaugh mᶜHugh mᶜOwen was constituted king of Conaught by Conaught men this yeare, Robert bruce king of Scotland this yeare came to Ireland with a great army of Gallowglasses to assist his brother Edward Bruce to conquer & bring in subjection this kingdome & to banish all Englishmen here-hence. Meyler Dexeter Lord of Athleathan[3] was killed by Cahall mᶜDonell o'Conor, & by Donell mᶜTeige surnamed Donell of Irros at a place called the Mehannagh neare Dromkliew & 14 men were killed with him. The castle of Ath-ele in Korann in the province of Conaught was fallen downe this yeare. Donogh o'Bryan, prince of Thomond, was killed. Melaghlen Carragh mᶜDermoda, Tanist and next to succeed in Moylorg, Magnus o'fflanagan successor or Tanist of Clan Cahall were killed by Gilbert mᶜCosdealaye[4]

---

[1] *Na ffidh* — Of the Fews, O'Naughten's country, in Roscommon, where perhaps he was fostered.

[2] *Vaghter-herye.*—U. Tire. See p. 453, *antea.*

[3] *Athleathan.* — *i e.* Athcliath, Ballymote.

[4] *mᶜCosdealaye.* — Or Costello, who, according to some, are descended from the second son, Gilbert de Angulo.

and Conor mᶜCowarba Coman o'Connor with many others.
The overthrow of Kilmore was given upon mᶜRory & breifnie
men, where 150 Gallowglasses belonging to mᶜRory were
killed, & the sone of Hugh Breifnagh o'Connor was taken
Captive, the 2 sones of Neale o'Roirk, Conor Boye mᶜTyernan
cheiftaine of Teallay Donoghoe were killed, Mahon mᶜTyernan,
Gilleroe mᶜAnarchinny, Nicoll mᵉen Maister and many others
of that familie were alsoe killed. Moyle Issa Roe mᶜKiegan[1]
the best learned in Ireland in the brehon law in Irish called
ꝑenecuꝑ, Died, this fenechus or brehon law is none other
then the sivil Law, which the Brehons had to themselves in
an obscure & unknown language, which none could understand except those that studied in the open schooles they
had, whereof some were judges and others were admitted to
plead as barresters, & for theire fees costs & all receaved the
11th part of the thing in demand of the party of whome it was
ordered, the Loozer paid noe costs. The brehons of Ireland
were divided into several tribes and families as the mᶜKiegans,
o'Deorans, o'Brisleans, & mᶜTholies, every contry had his
peculiar Brehan Dwelling within itselfe, that had power to
Decide the cases of that Contry & to maintaine theire controversies against theire neibor-contries; by which they held
theire Lands of the lord of the Contry where they dwelt;
this was before the Lawes of England wer of full force in this
Contry or land, and before the kingdome was devided into
shieres. Randolph mᶜGranell chieftaine of Moyntir-eolas was
Deposed of his chieftainship by the people of his owne Contry,
& the Captainery given over by them to Geoffry mᶜGranell
as more worthy thereof. There was great scarcity of victuals
in & throughout the realme of Ireland this yeare.

1318. o'Keruell gave a great overthrow to Englishmen
in the Contry of Elye where Addam March[2] with many other
English-men were slaine. Molronye mᵒDermoda, prince of

---

[1] *mᶜKiegan.*—Or Mac Egan. This family was long famed as ollamhs, and practised this profession in several parts of Ireland, as may be seen in the *Annals F. M.*

[2] *A. March.*—He is called Adam Mares in the *Annals F. M.* Grace says 200 of the English were slain.

Moylorg gathered together a great army consisting of the ensuing noblemen, vidz^t Terlaugh o'Connor, king of Conaught, Ularg o'Roirk, prince of the Brenye, Conor o'Kelly, prince of Imanie, and Tomaltagh m^{c}Donaugh, prince of Tyre-ayl-lealla, marched towards Cahall m^{c}Donell o'Connor, who dwelt at ffasagh-Koylle.[1] Cahall offered them great guiftes & bribes, and not to come to him, which they refused, & marched towards the midst of the place where he encamped, which he seeing & haveing none other remedy, he tooke hart anew, & with a Coragious stomack without daunting, he issued from out house, made fiercely towards the place he saw his enemys aproch, and gave them a valorous onsett, killed Conor o'Kelly, prince of Imanie at the first, and Bryan m^{c}Terlaugh o'Conor, tanist or next successor of the kingdome of Conaught, Bryan m^{c}Magnus, Cahall m^{c}Gillecriost, & manie others of the noble and ignoble sort were killed therein; and immediately afterwards tooke a great prey from m^{c}Dermoda, tooke the government and name of king of Conaught to himselfe, & Deposed Terlaugh o'Conor thereof, & for his defence partaketh with William Burke & the English of Conaught. John o'Neals sone, that is to say, the son of Donell o'Neall, was killed by Hugh O'Neale in the town of Derry, the said Hugh & Divers others were killed & drowned the same day, Richard De Clare Died. Edward Bruce Destroyer of all Ireland in Generall both English and Irish, was killed[2] by the English in maine battle by their valour at Dondalke the 14th of the Month of October In anno 1318 together with m^{c}Rory[3] king of the islands and m^{c}Donnell prince of the Irish of Scotland with many other Scotish men. Edward Bruce seeing the English encamp befre his face and feareing his brother Robert Bruce king of Scotland (that came to this kingdome for his assistance) would acquire and get the glory of that victory which he mad himselfe believe he would get of the English which

---

[1] *ffasagh-Koylle.*—In the barony of Carbury, Co. Sligo.
[2] *Killed*—At Faughart, near Dundalk, by Mapas Bermingham, who commanded the English army, was rewarded with the earldom of Louth and the barony of Ardee
[3] *m^{c}Rory*—Lord of the Hebrides.

he was sure he was able to overthrow without the assistance of his said Brother, he rashly gave them the assault, & was therein slaine himselfe as is declared to the great joy & comfort of the whole kingdome in generall, for there was not a better deed, that redounded better or more for the good of the kingdome since the creation of the world and since the banishment of Fine ffomores[1] out of this land, done Ireland then the killing of Edward Bruce, for there raigned Scarcity of Victuals, breach of promisses, ill performance of covenants, & the loss of men and women throughout the whole realme for the space of three yeares and a half that he bore sway. In soe much that men did commonly eat one another for want of sustenance during his tyme. John o'fferall was killed by his owne sone with an arrow Geoffrey m'Gillernew o'fferall chieftaine of the Analye, in the 36th year of his captainery, Died. There was such snow this yeare that there was not soe great seen for many yeares before.

1319.—Heenry m'Encrossan,[2] Bushop of Rathboth, Died. Thomas m'Cormack o'Donell was elected to succeed him in that Bushoprick. The Bushops of Derry, Clogher, & Clonfert, Died this yeare. Donell o'Neale prince of Tyreowne was banished by the o'Neales of Clonhuge Boy,[3] & Englishmen out of his territoryes, & was also Treacherously & most deceatfully dealt withall by these of Fermanagh, took great preyes of him, & after all which miseryes sustayned, he was againe restored to his owne place, and enjoyed his contry & principallitye. Bryan m'Donell o'Neale was killed by the o'Neales of Clanna Boye.

1320.—Cahal o'Conor & Mulronye m'Dermot had a meeting where a friendly atonement was agreed and concluded between them; whereupon Mulronye upon some occations of his left the contry. The said Cahall contrary to his late

---

[1] *F. ffomores.* — *i e.* the Fomorians. See p 14, *antea*.
[2] *m'Encrossan* —He was Bishop of Raphoe from 1306 to 1319.
[3] *C. Boy.* — *i e.* Clandeboy, an extensive territory to the east of Lough Neagh, in the counties of Down and Antrim. The name is taken from their ancestor Aodh Buidhe, who died in 1283.

agreement tooke his advantage by the opportunity he had in his absence, & met him at a place called Tarawnagh,[1] whome he Instantly took prisoner, & alsoe Granie, Daughter of m^{c}Magnus & wife of the said Mulrony, whom he found staying for a boote to pass over into the Iland of Carrick-locha-ke, tooke the spoyles and preyes of the whole Contry: alsoe he tooke prisoner Moyle Issa Donn m^{c}Kiagan, and his sone, & Tomaltagh m^{c}Donnogh, Lord of the Territory called Tyreallealla in Connaught Hugh m^{c}Teige o'Connor, a young man of great worth and expectation, and one suffitient for birth, Composition of Body and Liberallity to be a king was killed by m^{c}Martyn, who was killed in reveng thereof. Mahon m^{c}Donell Connaghtagh o'Bryan Tanist and next successor of Mounster was killed by those of Kilkollen this yeare. More Daughter of o'Boylle and wife to o'fferall, Died.

1321.—The Lady Granye, Daughter of Magnus and wife of Mulronye. m^{c}Dermoda, died. Rory na ffidh (of whom mention was made before) was deceiptfully killed by Cahall m^{c}Hugh m^{c}Owen o'Connor. The Carrick of Logh-ke was broken Down and raced by Cahall m^{c}Donell o'Connor, king of Conaught, there was a great murren of Cowes throughout all Ireland that the like was never seene before. Magnus o'Hanlon, prince of the orhir[2] was blinded by his owne brother, & mightylye oppressed by Neale m^{c}Conally o'Hanlon upon Wensday the weeke before Easter. Neale o'Hanlon, Prince of orhyr, was treacherously killed by the English of Dundalk. Andrew Bremingham & the Englishmen of Meath gave a great overthrow to the noble youth of Affalye.

1322.—There arose great wars betweene the king of England and his nobles. Mathew o'Hohie[3] Bushop of Ardagh, Died. Gilbert o'Kelly, Prince of Imanie, Died. Mulronye m^{c}Dermoda, prince of Moylorg, was taken by Connor m'Teige o'Connor, & by the Howshould men of Cahal o'Conor at

---

[1] *Tarawnagh.* — Mullagh Daramhnach. *Annals F. M.*, ad ann. The name is now obsolete

[2] *Orhir.* — Now the baronies of Upper and Lower Orior, in the east of Co. Armagh

[3] *o'Hohie.*—He occupied this See from 1290 to 1322.

Cloncumasge.[1] Richard Bremingham[2] lord of Athenrye, Died. William (the hore) sonne of William more Burk, Died. Bryan o'Bryan gave a great overthrow to the Englishmen. Gillernew mᶜGeffry mᶜGillernew tooke the Captainery of the Analye this yeare.

1323.—Carbry surnamed Carbry an scregann[3] & Melaghlen king of Meath, was killed; Mulronye MaGeoghegan, Died. Johnyn o'fferall was killed by the sons of Johnyn o'fferall. o'Hara was killed by the Convachan[4] the same yeare.

1324.—William Burk mᶜWilliam Died. Cahall mᶜDonell king of Conaught, was killed by Terlaugh mᶜHugh mᶜOwen, who was held to be the hardiest and supstantiallest Irishman of his time. Melaghlen mᶜTerlaugh o'Donnell & Gillechriost oge, mᶜDonogh with many others were killed at once with him, in the Contry of Tyrebryan the 7 of the Calends of September, after he had raigned king of Conaught 6 yeares and a ½ against the wills of Irish & English, after whose death Terlaugh o'Conor succeeded in the kingdome of Connaught. The murren of Cowes continued still in Ireland and was called the Moyle Dawine. Gillecriost o'Byrne, Died.

1325.—Donell mᶜBryan o'Neale king of Ulster, Died. Cownley mᶜDonell mᶜBryan o'Neale was killed by his owne nephes, the Sons of Neale mᶜBryan o'Neale. The murren of Cowes continued still.

1326.—Richard Burk earle of Ulster & lord of Conaught, the choyce Englishman of all Ireland Died[5] this yeare a little before Lammas day. There grew great wars betweene the king of England and the ffrench king this yeare. Lawrence o'Laghtnann[6] Bushop of Oylfyn, Died. Melrasion o'ffinsneaghty was elected to that Bushoprick. Imer

---

[1] *Cloncumasge.*—Now obsolete.
[2] *Bremingham.*—Fourth baron. See Archdall's *Peerage*, iii. 35.
[3] *Scregann*—i. e. of the rocky land.
[4] *Convachan.*—The inhabitants of Ballycroy, Co. Mayo, now anglicised Conway.
[5] *Died.*—Shortly before he retired to the monastery of Athassel, near Cashel, founded by his great-grandfather, and was buried there. Archdall's *Peerage*, i. 121.
[6] *o'Laghtnann.*—He occupied the See from 1313 to 1325. See Ware's *Bishops*, p. 631.

Magranell, chieftaine of Moyntyr eolas, was killed by his owne Brothers. Nicoll o'Heyne, Died.

1327.—There arose great wars between the king of England and his queen, the french kings Daughter, where at last the king was Deposed of his crown, & given to his owne sone Edward by the advice of the Councell of England. King Edward the 2ᵈ was pressed to death by pressing a great table on his belly this yeare with many other tortures in the Castle of Berckley, and was entred in Glocesster. Gormphley, the Daughter of mᶜDermoda, first married to Magnus mᶜDonell o'Connor, tanist of Connaught for a time, afterwards married to Conor Kelly, prince of Imanie, & lastly to ffarall o'Hara, the best woman for liberallity, manners, and hospitallity of her scept, Died after good penance. Edward king of England after he was Deposed of his crown and kingdome died. There raigned a Disease called the pied-pox or little pox[1] in Ireland in general & tooke away many persons both great and small: Melaghlen mᶜDonell mᶜTeige mᶜConnor, died of the same Disease. fferall mᶜUlarg o'Royrke Died. Cullen o'Dempsy, Died.

1328.—Melaghlen o'Reyly lord of Moynter-Mulmerry, was taken & hurt by the English of Meath, & was ransomed by yeelding prisoners for him; & afterwards Died of the hurt he receaved in his owne house. There was great thunder and Lightning this yeare, that it Destroyed a great deale of the Corns of the kingdome, that they grew whitish by reson they lost theire supstance. There was a Generall Disease throughout all Ireland called the murrene continued for the space of three or 4 days & brought Divers eauen to the poynt of death. The Earl of Ulster the Donne Earle, grandchild[2] to the red earle, called William Burk, Sʳ John Burks sonne, came to Ireland this yeare. John Bremingham, earle of

---

[1] *Little Pox.* — Called in Irish galar breac, *i.e.* the speckled disease. It is now mentioned for the first time in the Irish Annals.

[2] *Grandchild.* — His father was John, who died at Galway in 1313. His mother was Elizabeth, third daughter of the Earl of Gloucester, and granddaughter of Edward I. See Archdall's *Peerage*, i. 123.

Louth, the best earle for worthyness, bounty, prowess & valour of his hands, was treacherously killed by his owen people, the English of Uriell, & alsoe killed at once with him many good and worthy Englishmen and Irishmen. Mollrony m{c}Keruell, chief mutition of the kingdome & his brother Gillekeigh were killed in that Company; of whome it is reported that noe man in any age eauer heard, or shall hereafter heare a better Tympanist. Morish o'Gibellan master of art, one exceedingly well learned in the ould & new law, siuill and canon, a cuning and skilfull philosopher, an excellent poet in Irish & an excellent eloquent & exact speaker of the speech which in Irish is called ogham, in sume one that was well seen in many other good sciences; he was a Cannon & singer in Twayme, Olfin, Aghaconary,[1] Killalye, ednagh Downe,[2] & Clonfert, he was officiall & common Judg of the whole Diocesses & ended his dayes this yeare. Thomas o'Meallie[3] Bushop of eanagh downe Died in Roome in the Pope's Court. William Burk earle of Ulster assembled together a great army Consisting of these noble personages following with theire forces, vizdt. Terlaugh o'Connor king of Conaught, Murtagh o'Bryan king of Mounster, against Bryan Bane[4] o'Bryan. Bryan Bane gaue an ouerthrow to o'Bryan where Conor o'Bryan was killed, who was a young man of great expectation, bounty, comlyness of personage, & suffitient to gouern a Monarchy & with him 80 persons more were killed. There was a Generall Meeting at a place called Ath-kynn-logha-teohy[5] between Walter m{c}William Burk, Gilbert m{c}Cosdeally of the one side, & Mulrony m{c}Dermoda, Tomaltagh his son, Donell m{c}Donogh, & Clan Mulronye or that familie of the other side, whereupon some Distastfull speeches passed between them; from words they fell to bloes of armes; in the end William was owerthrone, Bryan m{c}teige

---

[1] *Aghaconary*—Achonry, in Co Mayo.
[2] *E Downe*—Anadowne, on the east side of Lough Corrib
[3] *Thomas o' Meallie*—See Ware's *Bishops*, p. 605
[4] *B. Bane.*—*i. e.* the white or fair.
[5] *A. teohy*—L Techet, now Lough Gara, a little to the south of Boyle.

m^cDonogh was slayn by his owne brother in reuenge of Bryan m^cDonell m^cDonogh that he killed before. Donogh Gall m^cDonogh o'Conor was killed by hugh m^cTeige m^cMelaghlen m^cMagnus o'Connor.

1329.—Teige m^cTerlaugh o'Connor, Prince of Conaught, was wilfully murdered by Dermott o'Graie. Cahall m^cDonell o'Royrk young prince & next to succeed in the territory of Brenye, was killed by the sonns of John o'fferall & the English of Meath treacherously with some of his people. Mortagh m^cDonnell o'Connor lord of the territory of Carbrye, & one worthy the Kingdome of Conaught, Died. Walter m^cWilliam Burk called m^cWilliam procured the Banishment of Cahall m^cHugh m^cOwen o'Connor out of the fewes & the territory of o'Manye of the o'Kellyes. There arose great dissention between Terlaugh o'Connor king of Conaught & the family of Clan Mulronye whereof ensued great Damages & losses. Tomaltagh m^cDermoda (Mulrony of whom often mention heretofore is made his sonne) tooke the preyes & spoyles of Dermott o'fflanagan, chieftaine of Clan Cahall. An Daughter of fferall o'Kelly & wife to Tomaltagh m^cDermode Died the third day before Christmas. Sr Dabuke Don m^cWilliam Burke a good and wealthy knight died.

1330.—Prince Magnus son of Hugh Breifnach o'Conor was killed by Cahall m^cHugh o'Connor in a place called ferannedaragh,[1] & Symon m^cAnfalgye alsoe. Terlaugh o'Conor king of Conaught gaue an assault to Walter m^cWilliam Burke at a place called Leackinoy[2] in Moylorg, & from thence chased him to Carhaly age fad,[3] & Gilbert m^cCosdeally with a great Company came to assist m^cWilliam, & alsoe tomaltagh m^cDermott came to relieve him too; & being met & joyned together, retracted upon o'Conor to Ath-digert-nwan,[4] & there about that foord killed a few of his people, with Donagh m^cDonell mac Mahon & the sone of Gillecougan,

---

[1] *F daragh.*—Now obsolete.
[2] *Leackmoy*—Now Legmoy, near Carrick-on-Shannon.
[3] *C. fad.* — Perhaps Knockacharta, in the parish of Killurin, Co. Roscommon.
[4] *A. nwan.*—Now Easternsnow, in the barony of Boyle.

with others that for prolixity sake I omitt here to name, & soe o'Conor escaped valorously & came to the twathies, whome mcWilliam followed & encamped at Killomat in his presence, whereupon mcWilliam assembled all the forces of the English and Irish of Conaught with Intent to take kingdome and name of king of Conaught to himselfe. macDermott & o'Conor came to a friendly agreement and peace was concluded between them. o'Roirk with his forces came to ffianatha[1] where he was Discomfitted by the english of that town, Prince Art o'Roirk with many others of his people were killed. Terlaugh o'Conor King of Conaught was killed by Walter mcWilliam Burk as he was comeing from the earle of Ulster's house.

1331.—Mulronye mcDermoda, prince of the territory of Moylorg, forsooke his Government and principallity, entred into religion in the Order of Gray Monks in the abby of Boylle, & within a short time after Died; after whose death his son Tomaltagh the 6 of May succeeded him in his place. Walter Burk (called mcWilliam) with a great army repayred to Moylorg, where he burnt, preyed, and destroyed all places in that contry, save onely Churches and Church lands, which he rescued and had in great respect ; but Tomaltagh mcDermot & his forces could not well brooke that mcWilliam should enjoy any rest in that contry and therefore they suddenly betook themselves to theire armes which they then held to be theire best & rediest friend in tyme of need, and gave them the onset, but mcWilliam and his people taking theire hart anew gaue a fresh encounter to Tomaltagh, chased him and his people, killed divers of them, which Tomaltagh did not leave unrevenged, for he could not digest that so many of his people were killed and that they should escape without rendering an account of soe many heads of theires too for entring soe bouldly into his territory. Meyler Mageoghegan Died this yeare the 3d of the Calends of January.

1332.—Walter mcWilliam Burk was taken by the earle of

---

[1] *ffianatha.*—Now Finae, in the barony of Half Fowre, Co Westmeath.

Ulster called the Donne earle, and was conveyed prisoner to New Castle[1] in Inisowen, In the prison of which castle he remayned prisoner untill he died of ffamine. Ballioll made a massacre of all the nobility of Scotland this yeare. The english earles sone[2] gaue an ouerthrow at a place called Bearna-an-mile[3] to mcWilliam Burk & tomaltagh mcDermott, where many of mcWilliam's people were killed. William Galda mcMortagh more Mageoghegan chieftaine of the Contry of Kineleagh died in the month of November.

1333.—William Burk earle of Ulster was killed by the English[4] of Ulster, for which cause the king of England caused the said Englishmen to be hanged, drawn and quartered. Hugh o'Donell king of Tireconell & fermanagh, one that tooke hostages of the teritory of Carbry & Sligeach and Brenie, one Deputed to be next successor of the kingdome of Ulster, the best man in Ireland for bounty, prowess, magnanimity, rule, and good government, and in summe he that most killed of the English and Irish that were his enemies, Died this yeare after he had ouercome the world & devill, & alsoe after he had raigned fortunatly in the principallity of Tyreconell 50 yeares, & after he had entred religion in the habitt of a Gray monk, receaving the sacraments of penance and extremunction, after whose death his sone Conor o'Donell was Constituted to succeed him in his place, betweene whome & Art his brother there grew debate for the succession; but Conor Immediately took Art prisoner & killed him at Instant. Tomaltagh mcDonogh lord of the territory of Tireaillealla, a principal man for manhood, bounty, constancy of promis, & honest & playne dealing, Died. ffelym o'Donell, the worthyest prince for birth, the fayrest for Composition of body, & one of Greatest expectation of the whole Kingdome in Generall, Died this yeare. Cahall

---

[1] *New Castle* —Called also Greencastle. See p. 260, *antea*
[2] *Sone* —The son of the Earl of Ulster
[3] *B mile* —Now obsolete

[4] *English*.—By Robert De Mandeville, who was instigated thereto by his brother's wife, to revenge the imprisonment of her brother Walter De Burgo.

m^cDermott Gall killed Gilber m^cCasdeally in the midst of his owne house treacherously.

1334—Johnock m^cMurtagh maGeoghegan, chieftaine of Kinaleagh m^cNeale Died the 14 of the Calends of January. Teige m^cCahall m^cDonell o'Conor Died. Donogh m^cConsnawa chief of Moyntir-Kenay, Died. There was a great army of Conaughtmen as well of the English as Irish gone to Mounster against m^cnaMarra of whom they had power and yeelded them hostages. Some of the said army burnt a church wherein 180 persons with 2 priests were altogether burnt & turned to ashes.

1335.—The Lady ffynola o'Bryan's daughter & wife of Terlaugh o'Connor, Died. The earle of Ulster's son tooke John o'Hary & alsoe took the spoyles of the most part of his people. The sonns of Donell o'Connor tooke a prey from the sons of Garalt Succach & killed m^cMorrish himselfe. This is m^cMorish of the preyes; he is of the Geraldins. falsam. The family of Clan Morrish tooke another preye in reveng thereof from the sone of o'Donell. Edmund Burk destroyed & wasted all the west of Conaught called iarthar Conaught, he killed many & committed great burnings, tooke great preyes, & committed many other vile outrages upon the earles sonne & upon the families of Clan Richard this yeare, & at last they grew to friendly accord of peace. There was such great snow in the Spring of this yeare that the most part of the small foule of Ireland died.

1336.—Tomaltagh m^cDermott prince of Moylorg, one that slaughtered many of his one full of bounty & charity, one true & constant in his purposes & promises & respected the best of his owen quallity, Died the 9th of the Calends of June on trinity Night, & was with great reuerence buried in the abby of Boylle, he Died in his house of Carrick, after whose death his sone Connor succeeded him in the principallity of that territory. Theobald Burk, sone of Ulick, Died. Meyler m^cJordan Dexeter, Died. Owen o'Madden gaue an overthrow to the burkes of Clan Richard, where 66 of them were killed. Dermott offlanagan, cheeftaine of Clan Kaell,

Died. ffelym o'Conor & the sons of Dermott Gall tooke a great prey from the familie of mᶜCosdallyes & killed Madiuck mᶜWaltrinn in pursuit of the said prey. Edmund mᶜWilliam Burk tooke a prey from the Inhabitants of Clan Kahill & also tooke the spoyles of Connor offlanagan in pursuit of that prey; they of the Contry tooke mᶜen Mile. Connor mᶜDermoda prince of Moylurg, hugh mᶜffelym mᶜHugh o'Connor & the household menye of o'Connor together with the families of Clan Donogh & o'Connors of Carbry (now called the teritory of Sliggo) with Cormack mᶜRory o'Connor, repayred to take the preys & spoyles of Tirefiaghragh, came to Mullagh-Rathe, from whome all the cowes of the Contry fled; notwithstanding they returned not empty handed, for they had some moueables, Garrans, & a few horses, & committed slaughter in the Contry, returned safe & sound without bloodshed or loss of any of themselves. Terlaugh o'Conor King of Conaught, with all the forces of Twathes & Clancahall with Moylorge, went to Arteagh,[1] tooke Castlemore[2] of mᶜCosdeally, & afterwards broke downe the same; the ward of which castle came forth upon mᶜDermot's protection, whose lives he saved accordingly.

1337.—William Burk the earle of Ulsters sone, accorded and made peace with Bryan Bane o'Bryan; where it was agreed of both sides that as much lands as Bryan Bane wasted of the Demeasne of William Burkes should be held by Bryan Bane for the valuable rent thereof. Hugh Reawar (als fat) o'Neale accorded and grew to articles of peace with these of Uriell and fermanagh. Terlaugh o'Conor King of Conaught encamped at Athliag for prevention of Edmund Burk. John offallawon chieftaine of Clannfwadagh Died. Donogh mᶜMurtagh more maGeoghegan, chieftaine of the Contry of Kinaleagh, was killed by the o'Conors of Affalie.

---

[1] *Arteagh.*—A district in the west of Co. Roscommon, adjoining the barony of Coolavin.

[2] *Castlemore.*—A short distance to the south-east of Ballaghadereen, Co. Mayo.

Loway o'Daly,[1] Bushop of Clonvicknos, Died. Mathew o'Higgen an excellent Irish Poet & good housekeeper, Died. Teige and Melaghten the 2 sons of Heber maGranell and Cahall were killed by theire owne Brothers the other sons of the said Heber, Cosmor & Tomaltagh, by the help of William MaGeoghegan and the youth of theire Contry in pursuit of a prey Magnus and Cahall were killed alsoe by them the same day, & constituted Teige magranell chieftaine in the said Teige his steed. Donell Roe o'Malye and his sone Cormack were killed by the sons of Ebrick[2] with the help of other Englishmen upon St. Stephens night.

1338.—Rory Magwyer prince of ffermanagh and Logheirnye, one that bestoed most of gould, Silver, cattle, & other guifts upon poets & bards & others of theire kind in Ireland Died. Edmund Burk,[3] the earle of Ulsters sonne, was taken by the other Edmund Burk & did put a stone abut his neck, & afterwards threw him into the poole of logh measka, wherof ensued the Confusion & destruction of the English of Conaught & of theire owne family of Burkes; which did enable terlaugh o'Connor to take the superiority & power of Conaught, and banished Edmund m*c*Burk from out of all Conaught, and Destroyed the spirituall and temporall lands of all the west of Connaught; Edmund Burk assembled a fleet of ships, barkes, & boates, betooke himselfe with them to the Ilands of the seas a long tyme in exile. The Contrys of Lwyny & Coran were wasted & Destroyed, & afterwards posessed by theire ould natives of the Irish after they banished thereout the English. The most part of the sheep of Ireland perrished this yeare. There arose great ware between the king of England and the french king this yeare.

1339.—Edmund Burk with his ships were banished into

---

[1] *o'Daly.*—He died in 1337. Nothing further is known of him. See Monahan's *Diocese of Ardagh*, p. 95.

[2] *Ebrick.*—Merrick, a Welsh family, settled in Mayo. See *Tribes, &c., of Hy Feachrach*, p. 331.

[3] *E Burk.*—Called na feisoge, i. e. of the beard. He was fourth son of the Red Earl, and ancestor of the Lords of Castleconnell and Brittas.

Ulster. The Daughter of terlaugh o'Bryan late wife to the earle of Ulsters sone was taken to wife by terlaugh o'Conor, & put away his owne wife, the lady Deruaile, Hugh o'Donnells Daughter. There arose great Discention, wars & Debats between the English and Irish of Meath this yeare. All the corne of Ireland was Destroyed whereupon ensued a Generall famine in this kingdome. fferall Moyneagh o'Dowgenan founded the Church of Kilronann.

1340.—There arose a great strife between the o'Kellyes of Imanie, between Teige m^{c}Teige o'Kelly & William Donogh Moyneagh o'Kelly. Terlaugh o'Conor king of Conaught graunted the principallity, name, and chiefe rule of the o'Kellyes to Teige o'Kelly, who by vertue of the said graunt posessed the same, & banished William thereout, whome they all followed in pursuite, he retraited upon them, & killed Donnough m^{c}Hugh o'Kelly, & alsoe tooke Captive Teige himself, & at his taking Teige was hurt grievously, of which hurt Teige Died afterwards. Melaghlen o'Gormley Chieftaine of Kinelmoan Died. Hugh m^{c}ffelym o'Connor was taken by Terlaugh o'Connor king of Conaught, and committed to the Castle of Roscomon, to be safely kept; for which cause there grew great debate between the king of Conaught & m^{c}Dermott. m^{c}Dermott in a skirmish between him & the said king chased him into the Castle of Ballenmote, which saued the king's life, and afterwards they grew to a composition of peace. Connor o'Donnell with the forces of Tyre Conell came to Conaught. m^{c}William Burk gave an ouerthrow to the familie of the Geraldines of m^{c}Morish where Morish m^{c}Johnock Roe, with many others were killed.

1341.—The Castle of Roscomon was taken by Terlaugh o'Conor king of Conaught, was betrayed & yeelded ouer to the said Terlaugh by Hugh m^{c}ffelym o'Connor before mentioned that was prisoner therein. John magmahon prince of Uriell was banished out of his country.

1342.—Morish maGeoghegan Died. Conor Roe maGeoghegan chieftaine of Kinaleagh was killed. Terlaugh o'Connor king of Conaught, & Connor m^{c}Dermott prince of

Moylorg, fell to great contentions and debates amongst themselves. Edmund Burk partaked with Conor mᶜDermott against the king of Conaught with hugh mᶜffelym o'Conor, Donogh o'Bryan chiefe of tire Bryan. O'Bryan chased king Conor into the Contry of Oylfynn, where some of his gallowglasses were killed together with their Constable & head mᶜRory. This was done upon an occation of king Terlaugh's comeing to o'Bryans contry to Distraine for a prey that o'Bryan tooke before from Hobert Burk; wherefore ensued great & comon calamities throughout the whole province, espetially of Clan Murtagh.[1] Hugh mᶜHugh Breifneagh, Cahall mᶜHugh Breifnie, & Teigne mᶜRory entred in Rebellion & spoyled the most part of the Corne of the Contry or province. o'Connor procured William Burk to be treacherously killed & Thomas Burk by mᶜMorish in an assembly Thomas had: alsoe Johnynn Burk was in like manner killed. mᶜDermott & his princes that partak with him gaue a great ouerthrow to Terlaugh king of Connaught at the foord of Athslissen,[2] where Dermot mᶜBryan o fferall the best & chiefest man of the Annalie for all respects, & his sone, together with mᶜHobert Burk, Con mᶜDonough Duffe o'Kelly were killed. John Magmahon a nobleman of great excellency & magnifisience, prince of the territory of Uriell, was killed with Divers of his Gallowglasses, as he was taking a prey from Hugh mᶜRoylph[3] mᶜMahon, & others of them were drowned. Donell o'Docherty chieftaine of Ardmire[4] and a very good man, Died, after whose death his sone John o'Docherty succeeded him. Sile Morey & the most part of all Conaught opposed themselves and rebelled against Terlaugh mᶜHugh mᶜOwen o'Connor, king of Conaught, espetially these ensuing, viz: Edmond Burk, Conor mᶜDermoda, prince of Moylorg with his kinsmen & followers;

---

[1] *C Murtagh* —The O'Finaghtys, who inhabited the district on the east side of the river Suck, in Co. Roscommon. See *Annals F M.*, iii. 237.

[2] *Athslissen.*—Now Belaslishen, a ford on the river Uain, near Elphin.

[3] *mᶜRoylph.*—i. e. Ralph, or Rudolph.

[4] *Ardmire* — A territory lying west of Kinel Enda, in the direction of Lough Finn.

Hugh mᶜHugh Brefnagh, with all the Inhabitants of the Brenye and Analye, Hugh mᶜffelym mᶜHugh mᶜOwen, who being joyned together in one Confederacy banished Terlaugh o'Connor out of the whole Contry, deposed him; whereupon he aduised with the best he had to come to mᶜDermott's house, whereof Clann Murtagh haueing had intelligence thereof, lay priuily in ambush in his way as he was passing with 4 or 5 horsmen in his Company in the dark of the night to mᶜDermotts house, escaped narrowly by the force of valorous and hardy hand, grievously wounded Cahall mᶜHugh Breifnagh (one of these that lay in the ambuish) whereof mᶜDermott had noe notice untill o'Connor was ferried over into mᶜDermott's house of Carrick, where being come mᶜDermott heard the cries & lamentations made for the hurting of Cahall. Nevertheless he kept o'Connor with him for the space of a seven night useing him in his house with sure reverence as befitted him, giueing liberty to such of his friends and allies to haue access to him to convers with him; at last when mᶜDermott being Lycensed to come to an agreement of peace with him, he sent him with safe Conduct to the Castle of Roscomonn where he left him. Hugh mᶜHugh Breifnach o'Connor was constituted king of Conaught by mᶜWilliam Burke & Conaughtmen the first Munday of winter, & alsoe Hugh mᶜffelym was made tanist of Connaught. The territory of Tyrealleaíla was granted to fferall mᶜDermott, Teige mᶜTomaltagh mᶜDonnogh deposed thereof & banished by Connor mᶜDermoda, whereupon Teige Joyned with Terlaugh o'Connor.

1343.—Terlaugh o'Connor was againe restored to his kingdome, alsoe peace was concluded between him & mᶜDermott. Slainy, o'Bryans Daughter, & wife to Terlaugh o'Connor king of Conaught, being his owne mother's sister, Died. Shee was before married to the earle of Ulsters son. Ulick[1] mᶜUlick mᶜRickard mᶜUlick surnamed Ulick Leith[2] chiefe of all the English race in Ireland for bounty & prowess, Died. The Breminghams and Burkes of Clanricard

---

[1] *Ulick.*—A family name of the Burkes, contracted from William og, young William.
[2] *Leith.*—*i. e.* liath, the grey.

gave a great overthrow to the familie of o'Kelly & Inhabitants of Imanie, where Connor Kearruagh o'Kelly with 11 princes sonns of that familie were slayne. Connor m^cDermoda prince of Moylorg, the fountaine and well spring of all goodness of the familie of Clan Mulronye & the sone of Teige m^cCahall m^cConnor, Died in his house on saturday, 7 dayes before All hollantide, and was buried in the abby of Boylle, In whose place succeeded his owne sone as prince of Moylorg named fferall m^cConnor.

1344.—Art more m^cCormack o'Melaghlin king of Meath was killed by Cormack Ballagh o'Melaghlen & tooke the principallity of Meath to himselfe. Hugh m^cRoylf Mag Mahon prince of Uriell, Died, after whose death succeeded in his place Murrogh m^cBryan (of the Chalices of the Mass) Mag Mahon as prince of that territory, who within a week after died. Alsoe Magnus mac Eoghie m^cRoylph succeeded next after Murrogh.

1345.—Terlaugh o'Connor of Conaught, after he had raigned 21 years, was killed by the shott of an arrow in ffiedorow[1] in Moyntir-eolas, being purposely gone thither to assist Teige maGranell against Clan Murtagh at Lougharynn,[2] whome the said clan Murtagh & the rest of the inhabitants of Moyntir Eolas pursued to ffiedorow, & there at a place called gurtynnaspideog[3] was killed by an arrow as aforesaid. There was not a greater exploit don with an arrow since Neale of the 9 Hostages was killed[4] by Eochy m^cEnna Kinsealagh at the Tyrrhean seas, in whose place Hugh m^cTerlaugh was constituted king of Conaught.

1346.—Thomas m^cCarlen Prince of o'Neahagh[5] in Ulster was hanged by the English. Owen o'Madden prince of Sile Anmchy, Died, & his sone Murrogh o'Madden succeeded him in his place. Henry m^cHugh Boy o'Neale Died.

---

[1] *ffiedorow.*—Now Fedaro, in the barony of Mohill, Co. Leitrim.
[2] *L. arynn.*—Near the town of Mohill.
[3] *G. spidcog.*—i.e. the field of the redbreast. The name is now obsolete.
[4] *Killed.*—See p. 64, *antea*.
[5] *o'Neahagh*—The inhabitants of the barony of Iveagh, in the western part of Co. Down

1347.—Neale Garwe o'Donell was killed by Magnus Meawlagh[1] o'Donell treacherously. There grew great Discention between fferall m^cDermott & Rory m^cCahall m^cDonnell, whereupon m^cCahall burnt m^cDermott's chiefe towne: m^cDermott assembled all his friends and allies of Conaught and followed m^cCahall to Ballen Mote, burnt all that towne & Castle, and tooke all the prisoners within the Castle together with o'Roirks sone & returned safely to theire owne houses, without anger or pursuit.

1348.—The earle of Ulsters grand child came to Conaught, tooke a prey, was overtaken by m^cWilliam Burk and his sone, who gaue a great overthrowe to the said earles Grandchild, tooke him prisoner, & alsoe killed & tooke Captives many of the Burkes. There was a Generall plague in Moylorg and all Ireland in generall, whereof the earle of Ulsters Grandchild Died. Also Mathew m^cCahall o'Roirk Died of it. Murtagh Riaganagh[2] magenes was killed by his brothers.

1350.—Hugh m^cHugh Breifnagh o'Connor was killed by Hugh o'Royrck at Moyengalty.[3] Hugh m^cTerlaugh o'Connor was Deposed of his kingdome by m^cWilliam and Conaughtmen, and Hugh m^cffelym o'Connor was by them put in his place. Enos o'Heogussie Died, and Enos o'Daly the best Learned in Ireland in Irish poetry Died. Cowchogry more MaGeoghegan chieftaine of the Contry of Kinaleagh, Died.

1351.—Hugh m^cTerlaugh o'Conor came to the province of Conaught againe. The Inhabitants in generall yeelded him Hostages for keeping of theire faith & allegiance to him, & banished Hugh m^cffelym o'Conor out of the whole province for the space of a yeare. Hugh o'Royrck was taken by m^cPhillipin m^cWilliam Burk as he was returning from the pilgrimage of Crwagh Patrick, for which cause fferall m^cDermott prince of Moylorg entred in rebellion whereby afterwards all Conaught fell to Generall Dissention &

---

[1] *Meawlagh.*—*i.e.* treacherous, deceitful.
[2] *Riaganagh.*—*i.e.* the hangman.
[3] *Moyengalty.*—O'D. conjectures Moy, now Newtowngore, in the barony of Carigallen, Co. Leitrim.

mᶜDermott's Contry Destroyed & brought to utter ruin. William o'Donogh Moyneagh o'Kelly inuited all the Irish Poets, Brehons, bards, harpers, Gamesters or common kearoghs, Jesters, & others of theire kind of Ireland to his house upon Christmas this yeare, where euery one of them was well used dureing Christmas holy Dayes, & gaue contentment to each of them at the tyme of theire Departure, soe as euery one was well pleased and extolled William for his bounty, one of which assembly composed certaine Irish verses[1] in commendation of William and his house which began thus:

ꝼɩlɩo eɾeann ᵹo haoinꞇeac &c.

1352.—Hugh mᶜTerlaugh o'Conor tooke upon him the name of king of Conaught in spight of such of the English and Irish race as opposed against him. Hugh o'Roirck prince of Breme was killed by Cahall mᶜHugh Breifnagh o'Connor and Clan Murtagh, and a great slaughter of the Gallowglasses belonging to the families of the mᶜSwynies was also made. Dabuck Dillon sonne of Ulick of the Contry of Vriell, Chiefe head of all the Kearne of Conaught, Died. Hugh mᶜTerlaugh againe was deposed of his principallity of Conaught, & convayed out of the Contry of mᶜBranan. The Lady Gormphley, o'Donells Daughter, & wife to o'Neale, Died. Mathew mᶜGillernew o'fferall cheeftaine of the Annalye Died.

1353.—Rory o'More prince of the territory of Lease, Died. The Lady Deruorgill, o'Conor's Daughter, Died. John o'ffynsneachty[2] Bushop of Oylfyn, Died. o'Laghtna[3] Bushop of Twayme & Conaught Died. mᶜMurrogh[4] of Leinster was put to death by the English, for which cause there ensued great wars in Ireland. Bryan mᶜHugh More o'Neale, &

---

[1] *Verses.*—This poem, the author of which is not known, will be found among the Irish MSS. in the R. I. Academy, 23. L. 17, fol. 97 b.

[2] *O'ffynsneachty.*—He was Bishop of Elphin from 1326 to 1354. See Ware's *Bishops*, p. 631.

[3] *o'Laghtna.*—He is not mentioned by Ware.

[4] *mᶜMurrogh.*—'He was torn asunder by foreigners, through which a great war occurred between the foreigners and Gaeidhil.' *Annals of Loch Ce*, ii. 11.

Brother to Neale oge, Died. The o'Neales of Clannaboy with the help of the English of Dondalk gaue a great overthrow to Hew o'Neale and mad a great slaughter of them. Hobert Burk Died this yeare.

1355.—Morish ffitzthomas, earle of Desmond,[1] & deputy of Ireland died this yeare Donell sone of John fferall chieftaine of the Annalie, Died, and was entred in the abbey of Lethra The English of the west of Conaught gaue an overthrow to mᶜWilliam & killed Divers of his people. Richard the younger killed many of the Househould menye of mᶜWilliam, that is to say of Edmund Burk, & of these of sile Anmchie, where stephen mac Jordan, Henery mᶜPhilippin with 16 of the chiefest Gentlemen of the familie of o'Maddens were slayn. Edmund mᶜWilliam mᶜRichard Burk was killed by these of sile Anmchy; the Irish of Leinster killed many of the English of Dublin.[2] The king of England gaue a battle to the ffrench king where the ffrench king and his sone were taken Captives, theere army discomfitted, and an Infinite number of them slayne. The Bushops sea of Tuayme was burnt by Cahall oge & by mᶜWilliam Burk. One sheep had tenn lambs this yeare. fferall mᶜfferall mᶜMurtagh more mageoghegan Chieftaine of the Contry of Kinaleagh, Died.

1356.—Hugh mᶜTerlaugh o'Conor king of Conaught was killed by Donogh Cairragh o'Kelly & by the scept called clan Barde[3] by the procurement of the o'Kellys, because he forceably took away the Daughter of Johnyn Burk being formerly the wife of o'Kelly. Hugh mac ffelym o'Conor after the death of Hugh mᶜTerlaugh tooke the whole principallity of Conaught. Geready Tyrrell was put to death upon the green of Dublin & was there hanged, drawn, & quartered by the English.

1357.—The Earl of Desmond[4] was drowned pasing over.

---

[1] *E. of Desmond.*—The first Earl. He was appointed Deputy the preceding year.

[2] *Dublin.*—Our annals make no mention of this defeat.

[3] *C. Barde.*—The tribe-name of a sept in the cantred of Sodhen in Hy Many, called also Mac Ward.

[4] *E. o'Desmond.*—Maurice Oge, the second Earl. Archdall says he died suddenly at Castlemaine in Kerry. *Peerage,* i. 64.

John o'Donell killed Phelym o'Donell & his sone being Captives. The 2 Cahalls were agreed and brought to a Composition of peace, vidzt. Cahall m⁰Hugh Breifnagh, & Cahall oge m⁰Cahall m⁰Donell. Magnus m⁰Mahon, prince of Uriell, died. Mathew m⁰Thomas o'Roirck cheefe man for hardiness & valour of his hands of the Brenye, Died. Downesleyve m⁰Caruell an excellent musitian, Died.

1358.—Hugh o'Neale gaue a great ouerthrow to these of Uriell & ffermanagh, where Hugh m⁰Caba & Bushop Dowdyes sones were killed. There was a great shower of haile in the summer tyme of this yeare in the teritory of Carbry; every stone thereof was noe less than a Crabb. o'More of the Contry of Lease, gaue a great Discomfiture[1] to the English of Dublin, where were killed of them 240 persons. Bryan mac Cauill[2] or Rathmoyle Bushop of Uriell, Died. Semnickin m⁰Vuell Died, alsoe the sone of Andrew Bremingham, Died.

1359.—Connor m⁰Carthy, king of Desmond, Died. Cahall oge o'Connor gaue an overthrow to the Inhabitants of Tyreconell at Belaseannye, where John o'Dochorty chieftaine of Ardmire, & terlaugh m⁰Swynie were taken, and a great many of others slaine besides. Mathew maGawran next successor of Teallaghaagh was hurt in the same place, from thence was convayed to his house, & died of the wound. The said Cahall went to the lands of o'Gormley, where Cahall (surnamed the Deaf) o'Roirck was killed by Melaghlen o'Gormley. Henry m⁰Ullick m⁰Richard burk, Died.

1360.—The king of Englands sone[3] came to Ireland this yeare. Many great burnings were committed in the kingdome this yeare, as Roscommon, Dowinis, Sligeach, the abby of Lisgauall,[4] ffynagha,[5] & Dromlyas.[6] Dermot o'Bryan was deposed by his owne nephew. Sʳ. Robert Savage died.

---

[1] *Discomfiture.*—None of our Annals gives further details.

[2] *macCauill.* He was Bishop of Clogher from 1356 to 1361.

[3] *Sone.*—Lionel, Duke of Clarence, third son of Edward III.

[4] *Lisgauall.*—Now Lisgool, on the west bank of Lough Erne, a little south of Enniskillen.

[5] *ffynagha.*—Fenagh, near Ballinamore, Co. Leitrim.

[6] *Dromlyas.*—Now Drumlease, in the barony of Dromahaire, Co Leitrim

1361.—Artt m^cMurrogh,[1] king of Leinster, & Donell Riauagh[2] his next successor or tanist being sinisterly taken by the king of Englands sone in his house, Died prisoner with him. Sr Edmund Burk Died. The kings game[3] was used generally throughout Ireland. Richard Savage Died thereof, Redmond Burk of The Monye-More, Died. Walter Stonton Died.

1362.—Owen ffinn o'Conor, the king of Conaughts sone Died. Cahall oge and the sone of ffelym o'Conor tooke the Castle of Ballentobbar. Hugh m^cffelym o'Conor, king of Conaught, and Cahall oge o'Conor marched with theire forces to Meath, burnt & destroyed all places where they came to the hills of Cnockaisde[4] in Kinealeagh, of that Jorny they burnt 14 churches & the church of Kilkenny in Machairy chuirknye, comitted many outrages upon the English of Meath, & were soe many that it were hard to recount them, Returned at last to theire houses in safetye. Cormack Ballagh o'Mellaghlen king of meath, Died. Cahall oge o'Connor the hardiest, & man of Greatest valour of any noble man of his tyme, Died of the plague at Sligeagh the third of November. Cowchoghry m^cDermott maGeoghagan & Morrish m^cMurtagh Mageoghegan Died. Magnus (surnamed Eoganagh) o'Donell Died this yeare.

1363.—Hugh maGwyer, Prince of ffermanagh, Died. Beuynn Daughter of maGeoghegan the read, Died.

1364.—Hugh o'Neale king of Ulster, the best king of any province in his tyme that liued, died after good pennance as a good Christyan. Margarett, Daughter of Walter Burk, & wife of Hugh m^cffelym king of Conaught, died. Dermott

---

[1] *A. m^cMurrogh.* — Art Mac Murchada, king of Leinster and Domhnall Riabhach, royal heir of Leinster, were taken prisoners by the son of the king of the Saxons perdolum, and they died with him, *i. e.* while in his power. *Annals of Loch Ce,* ii. 23.

[2] *Riauagh* — *i. e.* the swarthy.

[3] *Kings game.* — Probably the Black Death, which prevailed throughout Europe at this time. The origin of the Irish name is not known. See the Census for 1851, pt. v. p. 88.

[4] *Cnockaisde* — Now Knockshee-gowna, seven miles south of Birr, in King's Co.

o'Bryan king of Thomond Died. Dermott o'Skyngin[1] an excellent chronicler & Brian o'Broyn a good Tympanist, Died.

1365.—Rory m^cDonell o'Neale was killed by Melaghlen m^cengyrr m^cCathmoyle by the shot of an arow. ffelym m^cAn-enny[2] in English called the bountifull, sone of Donell o'Connor of Corcomroe, Died. Bryan m^cHugh magMahon tooke upon him the principallity of the Contry of Uriell, tooke to wife the Daughter of Sawarle m^cEoin Duff m^cDonnell archconstable & head of the Gallowglasses of Ulster, was procured to put away the Daughter of o'Kelly that was formerly married to him. Not long after Sawarle Invited his said sone in law to his house, & being conuayed to an Inner Roome therein, as though to pass the tyme in conversation & drinking of wine, was filthyly taken by his said ffather in law and comitted to a strong place on a logh to be kept,[3] for which cause Sawarle was banished from out the whole Contry. Cowchonoght o'Relly entred in religion this yeare, & Philip o'Relly was ordayned in the principallity in his steed. Robert Barrett[4] son of Wattin Died. The king of Englands sone departed out of Ireland this yeare.

1366.—Cahall m^cHugh Breifnie & his sone Magnus oge were killed by Philip maGwyer prince of Fermanagh; afterwards tooke great preyes from Clann Murtagh. They of ffermanagh & the familie of the o'Roirkes concluded peace with one another (afterwards Cormack Donne m^cCarhye prince of the Carbryes & of o'Neahagh[5] of Munster was treacherously killed by his nephew Donell, sone of Donell of the Donells

---

[1] *o'Skyngin.*—He was the hereditary Ollamh of the O'Donnells. See *Tribes, &c., of Hy Fiachrach*, p. 77.

[2] *m^cAn-enny*—i e *daonachdach*, the generous.

[3] *Kept.*—From the *Annals F. M.* and the *Annals of Ulster* it would seem that Sawarle was seized by McMahon, bound hand and foot, and thrown into a lake.

[4] *Barrett.*—This family is of Welsh descent, and having settled in Tirawley, a branch migrated also a little to the north of the city of Cork, and has given its name to a barony there. See *Tribes, &c., of Hy Fiachbrach*, p. 325.

[5] *o'Neahagh.*—Ivahagh, the territory of the O'Mahonys, extending from Balledehob to Dunmanus bay, in the south-west of Co. Cork.

maCarthy. Donell o'Neale mad a great preparation & assemblyes to warre against Neale o'Neale. o'Neale banished mᶜCathmoyle out of his Contry. Randolph mᶜ Alexander chief of the mᶜDonells came out of the Isles to assist Neale o'Neale in that warr, where the 2 sonnes of the mᶜDonells mett, that is to say Randolph of the one side, & his kinsmen the other mᶜDonells of the other side Terlaugh & his sone Allexander. Randolph sent Allexander his sone & heire and Terlaugh mᶜDonell to his kinsmen desireing them in regard they were his kinsmen & he chiefe of the house they were of, that they would be pleased to desist from contending against him, they little regarding his Intreatys made fiercely towards the foord where they saw Randolph stand, which was answered the like courage & fierceness by Randolph & his company, at last, the sone of Randolph was killed & allexander mᶜDonell was taken by Randolphs company whome the Company would kill in reuenge of Randolphs sonne, but that they were not suffered by Randolph himselfe, who worthily said to them that were soe Intended to kill Allexander, that he would not loose his sone & kinsman both together & that hee thought the killing of his sone sufitient loss & not to suffer his owne men to kill his kinsman too. Alsoe there was a great slaughter of Donell o'Neale's people in that presence.

1367.—Cowchonaght o'Relly prince of the Brenie who before entred in religion & resigned his principallity to another, Died. The Lady Dervorgill, Daughter of Mulronye More mᶜDermott, some tyme prince of Moylorg, Died. shee was wife of Ualgarck o'Rork. Melaghten mᶜGeffry fitzPatrick[1] of Ossery was sincerely killed by the English.

1368.—Hugh mᶜffelym o'Connor king of Conaught a prince both hardy & venterous, worthy to be compared to Loway Lawady[2] for prowess and manhood in all his attempts as well

---

[1] *Fitz Patrick.*—This family is usually called in the Irish Annals Mac Giollapatraic. They are descended from Conla, son of Breasal Breac, of the same stock as Cathair Mor. See Keating's *H. of Ireland*, p. 243.

[2] *L. Lawady.*—See *Ibid.*, p. 93.

against the English as Irish that were against him, after 12 yeares raigning as king of Conaught, Died with good penance at Roscomon. The territory called Krich-Karbry was after his death divided into 2 parts, whereof one part was allotted to Donell mᶜMurtagh, & the other part to the sone of Manus o'Conor. ffcrall mᶜDermoda prince of Moylorg, Died. Dermott mᶜCormack Done maCarthye was taken by mᶜCarthy of the Carbryes, & Delivered over to the English who executed him to a death of great tortures. David o'twahall was killed by the English of Dublin. William Saxanagh, sone of Sʳ Redmund Burk, heere of the mᶜWilliams, Died of the little pox at Innis Kwa,[1] alsoe Thomas mᶜfferall mᶜDermott tanist of Moylorg, Died of the same disease. Lysagh mᶜDavid o'More, Died. Teige mᶜMagnus mᶜCahall was Deceiptfully taken by the King of Conaught in his house of Ard-an-Killen,[2] being brought thither to the kings house by Cormack mᶜDonogh upon his security, of which villannous Dealing that ould Irish proverb grew by comparcing thereof to any wicked Actt, the takeing of macManus is noe wors, he was within a little while after worse used, for he was given over to Donell mᶜMurtagh o'Connor, whoe vilely did put him to death in the Castle of sligagh, whereof ensued great contentions & Generall Discords throughout all Connaught, espetially between o'Connor mᶜWilliam and mᶜDermott. Rory mᶜJohnock mᶜMurtagh maGeoghegan a very bountiful worthy & hardy man without doubt, Died upon the 5ᵗʰ of the kalends of June this Yeare. Though mine authority maketh this great account of this Rory that he extolleth him beyond reason, yet his Issue now & for a long tyme past are of the meanest of theire owen name.

1372.—mᶜWilliam Burk Died, after receaving the sacraments of extream-unction & penance, after whose death his sone Thomas succeeded him in his place. Geffry mᶜGillernew o'fferall tanist of the Annalie, Died.

---

[1] *I. Kwa* —Now Inishcoe, a townland extending from the western side into Lough Con, Co. Mayo

[2] *A. Killen* —A townland in the barony and county of Roscommon.

1373.—Teige o'Roirck, prince of the Brenie, Died. Tigernan o'Roirck succeeded him in his place. Cowafnie o'Connor of affalie his sone, a very worthy & excellent young man, Died. Rwaraghan o'Hawaile o'Hanlons chief poet, Eoyn o'Ronow Magenos his chiefe man for poetry, Died. Hugh o'Toole, prince of o'Male[1] was killed by the English. Daluagh mᶜMelaghlen o'Bryan a prince his sone, & a good man, was hurt by his owne spurs and thereof Died. Connor o'Reachann a good Chronicler, Died. Keallagh mᶜCrowttynn,[2] chiefe poet of Thomond, died. Bevin the Daughter of Donell o'Doyne and wife to o'Dempsy, Died.

1377.—Walter, sone of Sʳ David Burk, Died. mᶜNemara and they of the Contry of Clan Kullan[3] gaue a great overthrow to those of Clan Rickard, where Theobald mᶜUllick, head of the great kearne, o'Heynes[4] three sonns, & many of the Chiefest of Clan Rickard were killed. Bushop Kelly[5] Bushop of Clonfert, Died. There grew great Dissentions and Discord between Rory o'Connor & mᶜDermott, soe as all the teritory ot Moylorg was altogether wasted, spoyled, & brought to utter ruine, the Inhabitants killed, theire houses and buildings burnt & consumed to ashes, theire corne destroyed, and theire Cattle preyed. At last they came to a composition of peace. Rory gave full satisfaction of his Losses & damages sustained to mᶜDermott for condescending to that agreement before it was concluded. The field of Roscomon was fought between Rory o'Connor & William Burk & Melaghlen o'Kelly Prince of Imanie, where Richard Burk, Donell mᶜCahall oge o'Connor, Teige oge mᶜTeige

---

[1] *o'Male.*—Imaile, in the western part of Co. Wicklow. The O'Tooles took possession of it after being driven from their original territory, the southern half of Co. Kildare.

[2] *mᶜCrowttynn.* — Now Curtin. They were the hereditary Ollamhs of Thomond

[3] *C. Kullan.* — The portion of Clare lying east of the Fergus.

[4] *o'Heynes.*—They were chiefs of Hy Fiachrach Aidhne. O'Donovan gives their pedigree at length in *Tribes, &c., of Hy Fiachrach*, p. 398.

[5] *Kelly.*—He was Bishop of Clonfert from 1347 to 1377.

o'Kelly, o'Mannynn, a good housekeeper, m‘Donell, gallowglasses, and the sone of Neale Kam with many others were slaine. Edward the third king of England Died. ffaghtna m‘David o'More prince of the territory of Lease, Died. Donogh m‘William (surnamed the faire) o'Kervell, prince of the Country of Elie, Died. The Castle of Lisardawla[1] in the Annalye was built by John o'fferall this yeare.

Here endeth the raign of Edward the 3^d.

1378.—Terlaugh m‘Swyne head & cheefe of all the Gallowglasses of Conaught, Died. Walter m‘William Burk Died.

1379.—Phillip m‘Nicoll Dalton lord of the barrony of Rath-Con-Rath in Westmeath, Died. David o'Doyn[2] chieftaine of the Contry of Iriagann,[3] was killed by the sone of Caroll o'Donne. Henry o'Neale gave an overthrow to those of ffermanagh, where Teige maGwyer with many of them were killed & Donell m‘Gormgall m‘Tygernan. Cowmara m‘Nemara was wilfully killed by his owne brother. Bushop ffaltagh[4] Bushop of Meath, Died. Richard o'Dowagan, chronicler by profession, Died.

1380.—Terlaugh o'Donell gaue an assault to o'Donell, killed himself & his sonne, & afterwards tooke great preyes & bootyes from the Inhabitants of Tyreconell. m‘William Burk the Inferiour,[5] gaue an overthrow to Richard oge m‘William the Superior, in the towne of Athleahan, where Jordan De exeter lord of Athleahan aforesaid & John De exeter were killed. Art oge mac Geralt Kauanagh Died. Art Magenos prince of the Neohagh was taken by the

---

[1] *Lisardawla*.—A townland, three miles east of the town of Longford.

[2] *o'Doyn*.— Now Dunne. The head of this clan is the family of Dunn of Brittas, near Mountmellick, the pedigree of which is given in the *Annals F. M*, iv 958.

[3] *Iriagann*.—Now included in the barony of Tinnehinch, in the northwest of Queen's Co.

[4] *ffaltagh*—Stephen De Valle, or Wall. He was Bishop of Meath from 1369 to 1379. Ware's *Bishops*, p. 147.

[5] *Inferiour*.—After the death of William, third Earl of Ulster, the descendants of William Fitzadelm De Burgo in Connaght took the name of Mac William Uachtar and Mac W. Iochtar, *i e.* upper and lower.

English. Art m‵Gerald m‵Thomas fflynn, of the m‵Murroghs of Leinster, was killed by Art m‵Murrogh, king of Leinster. Kien o'Karuell tanist of the Contry of Elye was killed with an arrow by Hugh o'Molloy. There was a field fought between Henry o'Neale & Conor o'Donell, wherein Conor was quite ouerthrown & many of his people slaine therein. After which discomfiture Terlaugh o'Donell took upon him the principallity of TyreConell. The Lord Mortimer with great forces went to the province of Ulster, where he destroyed many townes both spirituall & temperall, & espetially the Urnie,[1] Downaghmore,[2] Aregall[3] & Clogher. The Lady ffynola, o'Kellyes Daughter & m‵William Burke's wife, Died. Hugh m‵Murtagh Moyneagh maGeoghegan, Died upon the prides of the callends of October. Donell m‵David maGeoghegan, Died in the Ides of September

1381.—o'Doyne was killed by those of ffearkeall as he was Takeing theire preey. S`r` Edmund Mortimer[4] lord of all the englishmen of Ireland, died. The Castle of Athleahan[5] was fallen by Clan m‵Donogh & the Iron grate thereof was conwayed to Ballenmote. Rory o'Connor tooke the spoyles & preyed the sons of ffelym o'Connor, banished themselves & tooke of them the castle of Ballintober. o'Connor & the sons of Hugh o'Connor went to the west part of Meath to take the preyes and spoyles of the Inhabitants of that Contry, were mett by the English collonyes of them parts, being assembled before them they took great preyes, but they were soone brought to a restitution by the English. Alsoe o'Connor was taken and conuayed prisoner to the towne of trymme & John Redy o'Connor surnamed the sone of Meaghtoige, chiefe head of the Gallowglasses, was killed. The Castle of Athlone was taken by the earle & the sone of

---

[1] *Urnie.* — Near Lifford, Co. Donegal

[2] *Downaghmore.* — Near Castlefin, in the same county

[3] *Aregall* —Near Augher, in the barony of Clogher, Co Tyrone.

[4] *Mortimer* — Son-in-law of Lionel, Duke of Clarence. He died a few months after he was appointed Deputy, and was succeeded by his son Roger.

[5] *Athleahan.*—Now Ballylahan, near Foxford, Co. Mayo, erected by the De Exeters.

o'ffox was killed therein. Madame Sawe,[1] the daughter of Ullick Burk and o'Connors wife, Died. Dowcouley, Daughter of o'Connor of Affalie & wife to Donell mᶜTheobald o'Molloy, whoe was auncestor of the scept of Balle-ath-boy, died. Owen ffox tanist of ffoxes country was killed by the Daltons. Hugh mᶜMortagh Moyneagh maGeoghegan was killed by Meyler mᶜTheobald o'Molloy, as they were fighting a horsback the prides of the Calends of October.

1382.—Lawrence Tute was killed by the sons of John o'fferall, Murrogh and Donell : fferall Roe mᶜDonagh mᶜMortagh more maGeoghegan chieftaine of the Contry of Kinaleagh, the first of May in the yeare aforesaid was killed by these of ferkeall in a place called Kill-mona[2] easterly of Rath-Hugh mᶜBrick : fferall o'Molloy & mᶜTheobald made this assault and Meyler Mantyn was he that killed him. This fferall Roe is the auncestor of the scept of Newtowne called Slioght fferall : his brother Dermott the auncestor of those of Moy-Cashell called Slioght Hugh Boy : theire other Brother, Wᵐ Galda was the auncestor of the scept of Comninstown ; theire Brother Johnock auncestor of those of Clone called Slioght mᶜShane, and Cowchogry, theire other brother, head of the scept of Lismayne called Slioght Cowchogrye of the little head, &c. Hugh o'Connor was ransomed from the English of Meath. Rory o'Connor tooke all the chieftaines of Connaught in an assembly he had, vidzt. Jmer o'Hanly, o'Byrne, o'Kehernie, &c.

1383.—The Englishmen of the County of Weixford killed Art MᶜThomas MᶜMorroghow, tanist & next in succession in the kingdome of Leinster. Art Magenos prince of Iveagh of Ulster, a noble and bountifull man, Died prisoner at Trymm of the plague. Muragh (na Rathnie ats of the fearn) o'Bryan, Died of the plague, this Infection was Generally euery where in the kingdome this yeare. The Ladyes More, Daughter of Murrogh o'Madden, and wife of mᶜWilliam Burk of

---

[1] *Sawe.*—i.e Sabh, a very common female name in former times. It is latinized Sabia.

[2] *Kill-mona.*—In the parish of Rahugh, barony of Moycashel, Co. Westmeath.

The Annals of Clonmacnoise. 309

Clann Rickard, and Joane, the earle of Ormonde's daughter and wife to Teige o'Conell, prince of the Contry of Elie, died of the same Disease. Hugh oge o'Neale, a nobleman worthy to govern a monarchy for birth, manhood, & other good quallityes was killed by Revellyn Savage. Henery Sauadg Died. Dermott o'Dempsy prince of Klyn-Malierie was killed by the English. Murrogh o'Bryan o'Kennedy, Died of the plague. Don magmahon of the neck, prince of Corckovaiskin, died alsoe of the plague. Owen m^cDonogh m^cRory o'Kelly Died of the plague aforesaid. m^cLondrous[1] of Athboy & the ffentagh[2] of Tymonna, died thereof. The Daughter of Teig o'Bryan, o'Kennedy's wife, and Onora daughter of Ullick Burk, o'Meaghayres wife, died of the said Infection. m^cGillepatrick prince of Ossery and the sonne of Keallagh ffitzpatrick tanist of Ossery, Died thereof. St Patricks day & the sunday of the Resurrection were upon one day this year. 22 marty pasch.

1384.—Rory m^cTerlaugh o'Conor king of Conaught, died of the plague upon the night of St Katherne the Virgin in winter, after he had raigned king of Conaught quitly for the space of 16 years and one quarter as the Chronicler and poet Moylynn o'Mulchonry recounteth, numbering the kings of Conaught in his verses.[3] After whose death there grew great discord between the o'Connors for the succession. o'Kelly, they of Clan Rickard, Donell m^cMurtagh o'Connor, and the family of Clan Donogh joyned together to make Terlaugh oge m^cHugh m^cTerlaugh (nephew to the former king) king of Conaught : m^cDermott of Moylorg, the sons of Mortagh Moyneagh o'Connor and the Chieftains of Sile Morey, combined together to make Terlaugh Roe m^cHugh m^cffelym o'Connor king of Conaught, whereby ensued generall Warrs in and throughout the whole province of Conaught

---

[1] *m^cLondrous* — Loundres was lord of Athboy in Westmeath. The name of this family occurs frequently in the Irish annals

[2] *ffentagh*—i. e. ffont of Taghmon, in the barony of Shelmaliere W., Co. Wexford.

[3] *Verses.*—Of this poem, beginning Fuaip Ruaöpi, &c., the author is said by some to be Donough O'M.

between the said 2 elected kings and theire partakers, the one spoyleing, burning, and destroying the friends and allies of the other: So as the Inhabitants of Connaught sustayned Intollerable losses and Irrecoverable damages through theire discordance. The one of the said kings is auncestor of o'Connor Donne, the other of o'Connor Roe, and thus began these 2 names. Paule m^cTeige Cowarb or substitute of Clonvicknos Died. William sone of Sir Redmund Burk, Died. Mortagh o'Connor prince of Affalye died in his decrepitt & ould age. Thomas Magdorchy, chieftaine of the Contry of Kinell Loghan[1] was killed by his owen knife as he was shoeing a horse. Cowchonaught o'fferall lord of the Contry of Mochrea,[2] Died. Hugh o'Kelly, and fferaagh o'Kelly, Died of the plague in one week. Richard m^cMadiuck m^cThomynn Barett, a man of exceeding good housekeeping, and one that deserved to be well commended of the Rhymers, Poetts, and such others in Ireland for his Liberallity towards them, Died after good penance. John Burk died of the plague this yeare.

1385.—Artt, sone of Art (surnamed the great) O'Melaghlin, Died. m^cDonogh and o'Royrck with theire forces and Gallowglasses repayred to the Contry of Moylorg where they burnt m^cDermotts one Chiefe dwelling house and the whole teritory besides, and alsoe killed in pursuit the sone of John o'Hara, and his other brother taken. The sones of ffelym o'Connor assaulted Magoreaghty,[3] burnt the town, killed his people, and tooke himselfe captive. David m^cEdmond m^cHobert was taken by Hugh o'Connor and died prisoner with him in Ballentobbar. ffelym Cleragh o'Connor and Connor oge m^cDermoda with theire forces repayred to the Contry of Tireaillealla; the Inhabitants being warned of theire comeing were well set and ready in theire way before them, gaue the assault to each other egerly, many Cowes and sheep were killed at first with theire arrowes, and were

---

[1] *K. Loghan.*—In the parish of Ballinamore, Co Leitrim.

[2] *Mochrea*—Now Moytra, in the barony of Longford, Co Longford.

[3] *Magoreaghty.*—Mac Aireachtaigh, chief of Calry.

answered at by the horsmen of the watch. Cahall Cairbreagh mᶜDonogh was killed in that presence. Conor mᶜDermott was taken and phelym o'Connor was wounded. Mortagh and Cormack mᶜRory, Teige mᶜDermott & Cahall mᶜDermott with theire forces joyned together, made an Inrode upon maGranell Roe, and upon Hugh o'Connor, tooke them both prisoners and Conwayed them to be safely kept to the Carrick of Logh ke. o'Connor Roe mᶜDermott the sonns of Mortagh o'Connor and the chieftaines of Conaught made an Inrode upon Edmund mᶜWilliam o'Kelly, burnt his towne, brought much to ruine therein, and alsoe killed William Boy o'Neachtyn. The Inhabitants of the Brenye and they of Tyreallealla repayred to meet o'Conor Donn, burnt the Contry of Corckaglan and did cut theire fields of green corne. mᶜWilliam Burk burnt the Contry of Tirefiaghragh, marched with his forces from thence to Sligeagh, where he killed maDiuck the bald, and tooke certaine prisoners. The Country of Tireawley was throughly burnt by Donell mᶜMurtagh, killed the Inhabitants, tooke certaine captives, and brought with them the spoyles of that Contry. Murrogh o'Connor prince of the Territory of Offalye and the Inhabitants of Kinaleagh and fferkeall gaue a great overthrow to the English of Meath at Clogher Croghan,[1] where one Chambers and his sonne and Nugent of Meath with many others were killed. Tanaye o'Mulchonry, chiefe chronicler of all Conaught, one that was in great favour with the Inhabitants in Generall, Died in his owen house after long and good pennance at Lammas, and was buried in Cloncorphye.[2] The Conaughtmen after all the aforesaid losses of burning and spoyleing of all sides, came to an atonement of peace. The Contryes of Syle Morey were diuided between the 2 o'Connors, Hugh o'Conor and Connor

---

[1] *C. Croghan.*—A little to the south-east of the hill of Croghan, King's Co. O'Connor Faly had a castle here.

[2] *Cloncorphye.* — Kilbarry, ten miles south-east of Strokestown, Co. Roscommon. It was founded by St. Berach, who lived towards the end of the sixth century. His feast is on February 15th.

mᶜDermoda that were prisoners were sett at Liberty. The Lady Dervorgill, Cahall oge o'Connor's daughter and wife to o'Connor Roe, Died.

1386.—Carbry mᶜBryan mᶜMurragh offerall, lord of the Calye of the Annalye, Died. The Lady Anye, Daughter to Teige mᶜDonogh, and wife to Tygernan o'Royrck, died in Twayme Seancha,[1] adjoining Loch fin-moye, and was entred in the abbey of Sligeach. Neale mᶜCowchogrye oge Mageoghegan was killed by the Daltons the 17th of the Calends of May. He was a very good successor of a Contry. o'Connor Roe with his forces of Conaught, such as he could command, repayred to assist mᶜWilliam Burk against Donell mᶜMurtagh and the family of mᶜDonogh, tooke great preyes from Tirefiaghragh, and from thence they went to Clan Rickard to prey the contry, where they were overtaken by infinite and huge forces of o'Bryans, that came to aid mᶜWilliam of Clanrickard against them. o'Connor Roe notwithstanding theire forces retracted upon them, gaue them an overthrow, killed at that Instant Conor mᶜTeige mᶜConnor o'Bryan and diuers others.

1387.—Sawe, Daughter of Hugh o'Neale and wife to Eayne mᶜBissix, a Lady that far surpassed all the Ladyes of Clanna Neales in all good partes requisit in a Noble matron, Died. Rory o'Kyenan chiefe Chronicler of the territory of Uriell, died. Conor mᶜBryan Carragh o'Neale, was killed by the english of Srade-bally.[2]

1388.—Shane Roe o'Twahaile, prince of O'Morie in Leinster a man of wonderfull prowes and bounty, and one that went farr beyond all others of his kind in these and many other good parts, was killed by a churrell of his one house, the Churle afterwards was killed by him immediately. o'Connor Roe tooke great preyes from o'Connor Donn, whereof ensued great Warrs in Connaught. Cowchoigry

---

[1] *T. Seancha* — Now Toomonaghan, in the parish of Carrigallen, Co. Leitrim.

[2] *Srade-bally.* — S. B. Dundealgainn, the ancient name of Dundalk. The name is still retained in Street-town, which is a part of Dundalk.

o'Molloy prince of ffearkall died the 7th of the Calends of March. The o'Royrcks and mᶜDonoghs prepared to warr against one another this yeare.

1389 —Morish (the Bald) o'Connor of Affalye was killed with an arrow by one of the o'Kellyes of Ley in Clanmaliere. o'Roircke entertayned the sons of Cahall oge with theire forces to maintayne the said Warrs against the mᶜDonnoghs, whereby the Dissention was out of hand increased. Owen o'Roirck and the sons of Cahall made an Inrode to the Castle Anorer,[1] were overtaken by the horsemen of Moyntir Elye, chased them, killed Magnus o'Helye and o'Helye's sonn, and at last o'Roirck and the sons of Cahal tooke o'Heyly's prey, and in the time of the Dissention before it was ended killed Murtagh o'Hely. After these losses sustayned by the mᶜDonoghs and o'Roircks, the heat of theire warrs begat the child of peace, and soe it was concluded firmly of both sides. Alsoe peace was agreed upon and concluded between mᶜDonogh and mᶜDermott; and Murrogh mᶜDermott (that before was prisoner) was enlarged. Donell mac Mortagh tooke the preyes and spoyles of Tire Conell. Neale oge o'Neale, sone of Neale more mᶜHugh, was taken prisoner by the English this yeare.

1390.—There was great dissentions between o'Roirck, o'Relly, & the o'fferalls, the MaGranells; Tomaltagh mᶜDonnogh and the sonnes of Murtagh came to Conaught upon heareing of the said warres, by the procurement of Donell mᶜMurtagh and Donell mᶜDonogh. Magnus o'Roirck remayned prisoner with o'Relly in the Island of Loghoghter, from whence he went to the castle of Loghskwyre,[2] where being betrayed to the sonns of Murtagh, they killed him as hee was leaving the Coytt. o'Roirck and o'Reilye came to certaine articles of agreement, and at last peace was firmly concluded between them, but before this peace was thoroughly Concluded o'Roirck gave great guifts to o'Relly for consenting

---

[1] *C. Anorer.*—Caislean an Ubhair, now Castleore, in the barony of Tirerrill, Co. Sligo.

[2] *Loghskwyre* — A little to the north-west of the village of Keshcarrigan, Co. Leitrim.

to theese agreements and for banishing his enemies from out of his territoryes; for performance of these articles Owen o'Roirck mᶜCahall Reagh was given as a faithfull pledge. The sons of Murtagh and Teallagh Donogh with theire forces made an Inrode upon o'Roirck at a place called ffie ffinoigh;[1] and the Mount called Sliew Corrann[2] and Keann-Kwachar, o'Roirck hearing thereof being at ffye Gaiule,[3] brought his preyes and people with him to a place called Barre[4] and from thence he assaulted the said parties his adversaries, ouerthrew them, killed many of their people and Cattle, and held on his course of killing them from Belagh Derg[5] to the top of the place called Tullagh Brefnagh; Thomas mᶜMahon o'Relly, died the harvest ensuing. Shane o'Relly receaved the principallity and name of Prince of the Brenye.

1391.—Dermott MaGeoghegan, sonne of Donogh mᶜMurtagh more MaGeoghegan, chieftaine of the Contry of Kinaleagh and Race of ffiagha mᶜNeale of the 9 Hostages, Died in the pride of the Ides of January. o'Roirck & o'Relly continued in theire atonement of peace. o'Roirck with a few of his houshold menye repayred to the towne of Drumleahan[6] to meet with o'Relly, was Intercepted by 65 persons of Clan Murtagh in his passage. o'Roirck seeing them to stand in his way, and seeing himself without other remedy, hee tooke hart anew, gave them the onset valiantly, which Shane More Magmahon thinking to prevent them ofered o'Roirck a blow of a Launce, which o'Roirck accepted and made towards the said Shane with wonderfull Courage, whome at first he runed through with his launce. This Shane was sone of a woman that could weave, which of all trades is of greatest reproach

---

[1] *ffie ffinoigh.*—i. e. o'Finnock's wood. Now obsolete.

[2] *S. Corrann*—A hill in the southeast of Co. Sligo, which gives its name to the barony of Corran.

[3] *ffye Gaiule*—Glean G., in the *Annals F. M.*, a valley lying between Slieve-an-ierin and Quilca, in the barony of Tullyhaw, Co. Cavan.

[4] *Barre.*—Beal-atha-Dairi. Now obsolete.

[5] *B. Derg.*—In *Annals F. M.* it is called Bealathadoire Dubhain. Both names are now obsolete.

[6] *Drumleahan.* — Drumlane, in the barony of Loughtee, Co. Cavan. A monastery was founded here about the middle of the sixth century.

amongst the Irishrye, espetially the sons and husbands of such tradeswomen, and therefore Shane Mor was nicknamed the weaueing woman's sone. o'Roirck gaue another blow to Donogh mᶜHugh an Cleitty,[1] and presently killed him, made a fortunate escape without loss of any of his people, after killing four kernes of his enemies Donell mᶜCarthy, prince of Desmond, died penetently.

1392.—Gregory o'Mahon[2] ArchBushop of Conaught, Died. Henery Ainrey[3] in English the Contentious, sone of Neale More, tanist and next successor of the principallity of Ulster, after his brother Neale oge o'Neale's death, (if he had lived), and one worthy the Government of a monarchy, the Bountifullest and greatest giuer of guifts of the race of the 9 Hostages, and one of a rare and wonderfull freenes of hart in graunting all manner of things that came to his hands at all Tymes, Died a good Death upon St. Brandon's day in summer. The Countes of Desmond, Daughter of the earle of Desmond, a noble bountifull and surpassing Charitable Lady, Died. Donell o'Dempsey, Died. o'Connor Donn with the forces of the most part of Conaught repaired to the Contry of Imanie, burnt the whole territory Cahall mᶜHugh o'Roirck being disorderly and unadvisedly left in the hindermost part of o'Connor Donns company, was taken by o'Connor Roes company of the Advers party and killed many others of them. Terlaugh o'Donell tooke prisoner Donell mac Henry o'Neale, and alsoe the same day tooke great prey and spoyles from himself and his people.

1393.—Hugh mᶜConnor mᶜDermott Prince of Moylorg, a man compleat with all good parts befitting a nobleman, after good pennance and receaueing the sacraments of the Holy Church, Died, & Immediately after his death his sonne Cahall mᶜDermott was drowned upon Logh Dorry.[4] Molronie

---

[1] *Cleitty.*—*i e.* of the weaver's quill

[2] *o'Mahon.*—He was archbishop for one year only, having been deprived of the See by Pope Urban VI

[3] *Ainrey*—*i. e.* aimhreach, contentious; by antiphrasis, for he was of a very peaceful disposition See Colton's *Visitation*, p 51, and *Annals F M.*, ad ann

[4] *L. Dorry.*—Inisterry, in Loch Ce *Annals of Loch Ce,* ii. 76

m⁽fferall macDermada was made prince of Moylorg by the force and power of Tomaltagh m⁽Donnogh. The sons of Hugh m⁽Dermott made an assault upon m⁽Dermott at Clone o'Connen[1] in the strands of Logh-Deakar,[2] where they mett each other fiercely; the sons of Hugh were discomfitted, Tomaltagh Duff m⁽Dermott was slaine; Connor m⁽Dermoda & Rory m⁽Dermoda, the 2 sons of Hugh m⁽Dermoda were taken, fferall m⁽Donnogh Reavagh was alsoe taken therein, escaped narrowly afterwards, and many others were taken Captives besides. Morish Kam m⁽Rory MaGeoghegan Died the 9th of November, and Bryan m⁽William oge MaGeoghegan died the 6 of the nones of October.

1394 —Bryan m⁽Caba Constable or head of the Gallow-glasses of the Contry of Uriell, died. The earle of March ariued in Ireland of a purpose to get his rents of the Inhabitants of the Kingdome. Meyler of Exeter or Dexetra, lord of Ath-leahan was wilfully killed by the sons of John Dexetra. Thomas o'Dempsy was killed by the English.

1395.—Donell m⁽Murtagh o'Connor Lord of the Territory of Carbye and Sligeach, and supreame lord from the Mountaine Downe, died in the castle of Sligeagh a week before Christmas. Hugh m⁽Cahall oge o'Connor, and sone of the Daughter of Terlaugh o'Connor, Died. Philip MaGwyer prince of ffermanagh died after he vanquished the Devill and the world, and Gilleduff maGwyer (named Thomas) was Constituted in his place. Cowlagh More, Daughter of Cahall m⁽Donell o'Connor nick-named the port and haven of the three enemyes, because she was married to three Husbands that were professed enemyes to one another, first to o'Donell, secondly to Hugh o'Roirck, and thirdly & lastly to Cahall m⁽Hugh Brefnagh o'Connor, and dyed this yeare. The lady Owna, Daughter of Teige m⁽Magnus o'Connor and wife to MaGwyer, Died.

1396.—David m⁽Theobald m⁽Ullick, died. Conor m⁽Owen

---

[1] *C. o' Connen.*—In the parish of Kilnamanagh, in the barony of Boyle.

[2] *L. Deaker.*—*i e* L. Techet; now L. Gara, in the barony of Coolavin, Co. Sligo.

o'Molloy with a certaine Company tooke shipping and
repayred to get themselves some spoyles at seas, which they
accordingly gott, and filled their ship with all such stuff as
they could find, and at last the whole company shipp and all
were unfortunately drowned, but one man onely that escaped
by some hard shift; Connor Roe fought the field of Crega,[1]
with o'Connor Donn, where o'Connor Donn was overthrone,
together with Hugh o'Connor, Con mᶜBrannan, and Hugh
o'Hanly chieftaine of Kynell-Dowha, that partaketh with
o'Connor Donn, also Conn mᶜBranan, John o'Teige, and the
sone of John o'Hanlay with others were slaine in the said
field.

1397.—o'Connor Roe with all the forces of his kinsmen
the sons of ffelym o'Connor mᶜWilliam Burk, the sone of Sr.
Edward Albanagh[2] the sons of Cahall oge o'Connor, the
sons of Hugh mᶜDermoda, the inhabitants of the territory of
Imanye, with theire Gallowglasses and marched with all the
said forces to o'Conor Donns mansion house of Curragh
Kinetty[3] upon the playnes of Moyne Je, o'Connor Don himself
was not then at home, but was in Clan-Mackneoyne,[4] the
said forces being come to the said towne as aforesaid mad
towards the Company, & did let fly sharp-poynted arrows or
Darts, that they made them stick fast in the bodyes of theire
enemyes, & at last o'Connor Roe & the sonns of ffelym
o'Connor overthrew theire adversaryes in that presence,
killed mᶜDonogh, one of great note and respect in Conaught,
& alsoe killed Hugh Keige o'Connor tanist of the province,
with these ensuing persons vidzt. Dermott mᶜDonogh Tanist
of the Contry of Tirealleallla, Dermott mᶜDonogh mᶜGilla
Criost, the 2 sons of Rory mᶜMulrony mᶜDonagh ffynn
mᶜDonogh, Art mᶜCahall Cleragh, Cowafnie mᶜCowafnie,
mᶜSwyney head of the Gallowglasses of Ighter Conaught, his

---

[1] *Crega* —Perhaps Creggains, in the barony of Ballymoe, Co. Galway.

[2] *Albanagh.*—He was second son of Sir William, called Liagh (see p 284, *antea*), and ancestor of the Earls of Mayo. Archdall's *Peerage*, i. 127.

[3] *C. Kinetty.*—Now Kinnety, near the town of Roscommon.

[4] *C. Mackneoyne.*—Now a barony in the east of Co. Galway.

2 brothers Donnslieue & Conor macSwynie, with divers others of the noble & ignoble sort, it were impossible to recount the spoyles of horses, armes, Cowes, Cloathes, & other things they found that day This exployt was done upon the first lady day[1] in harvest. o'Connor Donn upon hearing of these Tydeings came to o'Kellys Contry, his adversaryes encamped with theire rich Bootyes & great prizes about Leytrim which o'Connor Don assaulted & skirmished withall; in the end recovered a great part of the Cattle that were taken by them, & gaue them a Discomfiture; this is the third day after the first prey & slaughter. ffelym m^cCahall oge & Dowgall m^cDonell Galda repayred to o'Donells house, to whom they related in particular the said exploits, whereupon Donell without delay caused to be assembled the Inhabitants, such as were apoynted to bear armes & repayred with the sons of Cahall aforesaid to the territory of Carbry; the Inhabitants of that Contry finding themselves unable to resist the power of o'Donnell fled into their holts & places of greatest force in theire lands, to secure themselves, theire goods & chattles from the Invincible armies (as they tooke them). o'Donell's forces made noe stay untill they came to a place called the fair of Tireaylealla, where they burnt many houses & cornes, & tooke the spoyles of Cormac m^cRory. Mulrony m^cDonnogh prince of the Contry of Tiralealla, o'Dowdy & o'Hara yeelded Hostages to o'Donell & to the sons of Cahall oge o'Connor, as pledges of their fidelity, & faithfully promised never thenceforward to contradict him nor oppose themselves against him in any matter soever, afterwards o'Donell returned to his house. The sonns of Cahall, the family of Moynter Dornynn,[2] & m^cDonell with his Gallowglasses repayred to the teritory of Carbry, where they rested that night, dividing the teritory amongst themselves. At which tyme Murtagh backagh[3] m^cDonell was at fasagh killed, with such of the family of the clan Swynies in

---

[1] *Lady day.* — August 15th, the feast of the Assumption of the B. V. M.

[2] *M. Dornynn.*—This name is often anglicised Cuffe.

[3] *Backagh.*—i e. the lame.

his company as returned alive out of the great overthrow before mentioned, about Donell mᶜSwynie, o'Hara, the lower of the race of ffiauertagh o'Rwairke, with whome the next morning he tooke his jorney to the foot of the place called Brenoge, adjoining to the town of Lissondoill;[1] Clan Cahall sent theire squadrons of horse between him and Sligeagh, who could not come near him to Indomage him being compassed of the one side, where he encamped, with Brenoge aforesaid, of the other side with the seas; but at last they skirmished with each other; in the end whereof o'Donell & the sons of Cahall were discomfited, Marcus mᶜDonell & his sone Dowgall mᶜDonell, Eoyn mᶜTihie,[2] with many others of theire gallowglasses were slaine, alsoe they tooke great preys from the sons of Cahall oge & banished themselves ouer the River of Earny,[3] who were left there with great sadness, griefe, & sorrow, that a little before were full of mirth, joy, & pleasure, the case being soe altered with them. These things thus fell out on our Lady day in harvest or thereabouts. Neale More mᶜHugh o'Neale monarch of the province of Ulster, after Confession of his sins to a Ghostly father, and receipt of the sacraments, died. After whose death his sone Neale oge succeeded him in his place & principallity. Dermott mᶜImer o'Beyrne being sick of an ague in his house, & being conuayed from thence in a little litter to the house of Murrogh mᶜThomas, where being arrived lept out of the litter or Coitt into the watter & was unfortunately drowned, & afterwards entred in the church of Kill-more-ne-synna[4] in the month of July.

1398.—The Lord Garrett earle of Desmond, a nobleman of Wonderfull Bounty, Mirth, cheerfullness in conversation, easie of access, charitable in his deeds, a witty & Ingenious composer of Irish poetry, a learned & profound Chronicler,

---

[1] *Lissondoill.*— Now Lissadill, eight miles north of Sligo, on Drumcliff Bay.

[2] *E. mᶜTihie*—Perhaps one of the mᶜShechys of Munster, who were gallowglasses of the Earls of Desmond.

[3] *Earny*—The Erne.

[4] *K.-ne-synna.*— In the district called Tuarune, Co. Roscommon.

and in fine one of the English nobility that had Irish learning & professors thereof in greatest reuerence of all the English of Ireland, died penitently after receipt of the sacraments of the Holy Church in due forme. Alsoe the Earle of Kildare was taken by Callogh m^cMurrogh o'Connor, & the horsemen of Affalye & yeelded ouer to his father Murrogh o'Connor, prince of Affalye, to be kept his prisoner untill he had been ransomed; & the third mischance that befell the Geraldins this yeare, was Sr John earle of Desmond was unluckily drowned in the riuer of Suire. David o'Dowgennan Cowarb of the Virgin st. Lassar, m^cDermott's chiefe Chronicler and his great favourite, a Common housekeeper for all comers of Ireland in generall, a reverent attendant of a Nobleman, afoot or a horsback, & one that never refused any man whatsoever for any thing he had in his power untill his death, Died in his house and was entred in the church of Kilronan. o'Broyne[1] & o'Twahall fought against the Englishmen where they killed the young earle of March[2] with many other Englishmen. Neale oge o'Neale brought a great army to tyre-Conell, destroyed all places to Easroe, tooke the spoyles of the abby of that towne & at last some of o'Donell's people encountred with them, where some were killed. Hugh m^cfferall o'Roirck was taken by those of Tireowen. Neale oge & his forces returned home without any loss & in safety. Thomas Burk Lord of the English of Conaught, and Terlaugh Roe o'Conor lord of the Irish of Conaught accompanied with ffelym m^cCahall oge o'Conor and his brothers, Rory o'Dowdy with his forces, mac Dermott, teige o'Hara with his assemblyes repayred to the Contry of Tyrealealla, wasted & destroyed all that Contry, both spirituall & temporall lands, Islands of loghs, together with all theire holts & places of fortification · Connor oge m^cHugh m^cDermott departed from the said forces, & went to Moylorg. Molronye m^cfferall m^cDermott prince of Moylorg went that night to the abby of Boyle, tooke all the victualls

---

[1] *o'Broyne.*—O'Byrne of Wicklow.
[2] *E. of March*—He was killed, June 10th, at Kells, in Ossory. He was then Lord Deputy.

he could find there, which he caused to be sent to the Carrick of Logh Ke, whose tract Conor mᶜDermott found, he followed Eaghdroym[1] of Hugh in the Contry of Tyre Bryan, they having entred the Church of Eachdroym aforesaid, he burnt the church over theire heads, killed Connor mᶜfferall mᶜDermott therein, tooke Mulronye himselfe, killed many of his people, & beraued them of all theire horses & armours: Mortagh mᶜDonell o'Connor with all his forces went to the territory of Tire-Hugh of Easroe to hinder o'Donell, they could find noe good bootyes therein, att theire returne were pursued by Hugh o'Dornine, with all his horsemen did sett upon them at Bel-athà-seanna, Hugh himselfe fell from his horse, and was not sufered to mount his horse againe, the Multitudes thronged upon him, & killed him. John mᶜJohnyn Roe was alsoe killed in that pursuit. The Island of Logharuagh was taken by Rory mᶜHugh mᶜDermott, next successor of the Contry of Moylorg. It is unknowen what store of good things they found therein and tooke from thence. Muriogh Bane, sone of John mᶜDonnell o'ferall the best Chieftaines sone in his tyme of Ireland, Died in November, & was buried in the abby of Lohra, where his father & grandfather were alsoe entred. Morish mᶜPierce Dalton was killed by Murtagh oge maGeoghegan & by Bryan o'Connor of Afahes sonne. Glean-da-logha was burnt by the English of Ireland in the summer time this yeare. Donell o'Nollan was killed by the English. Walter mᶜDauid Burk was killed by the English of Mounster. Geralt o'Broyn, prince of o'ffiolan, Died. Thomas mᶜCahall mᶜMurrogh o'fferall was killed by the English of Meath in a place called Koyliin Crowbagh. This Thomas deposed his elder Brother John o'fferall of the Captaineship of the Annalie, though he ought not to presume to depose his elder Brother by birth. Macarthy gave a great overthrow to the family of the o'Sulevans, killed o'Sulevan the Bald & the 2 sons of o'Sullevan the great, Owen and Connor o'Sullevan Bearrie, with many others Murtagh oge Magenos was killed by his Brothers.

---

[1] *Eaghdroym*.—Aughrim, in the parish of Roscommon.

mcWilliam Burk & the sonns of Cahall oge assaulted the Castle of Sligeagh, burnt the whole towne, tooke the spoyles thereof, & ransacked it altogether. King Richard king of England ariued in Ireland this yeare, by whome Art mcMurochow, king of Leinster was mightely weakened & brought low. mcMurrogh upon an Inrode he made was overtaken by the English of Leinsh & Meath, where many of the English armye & the retained kearne of mcMorrogh were killed with the sonns of Donogh o'Doyne, Karoll & Owen, with theire Chiefest people: alsoe William mcKaroll FitzPatrick was killed there; the daughter of Bryan o'fferall & wife of o'ffox, died. ffinola daughter of Cahall o'Madden, Died. There was a great plague generally throughout all Ireland this yeare.

1399.—Bryan o'Bryan, prince of Thomond, one numbered amongst the best princes of Ireland, after good penance, died. Alsoe Terlaugh o'Bryan another of great fame & name, well nigh equall to the said Bryan, Died. Terlaugh mcMolmorie mcSwynie, lord of the Contry of ffanaid, died. Cownley mcNeale o'Neale a great Benefactor of the Professors of Irish poetry & musick, died. ffelym mcCahire o'Connor, Tanist of Affalie, died. John mcBryan mcMorogh o'fferall chieftaine of the Analie (to whome succeeded Donell mcJohn o'fferall) died. Henry (the Quick) sonne of Wattin Lord of the Contry of Tire awley, died. Dermott mcHugh mcffelym tanist of the province of Conaught, died. mcHeoghae[1] chiefe poet of the Contry or rather familye of the mcMurroghs of Leinster, Died a good death. Colton[2] Lord primate of Ardmach, died. Teige o'Keruell Prince of the Contry of Elye was taken by the Earle of Ormond. The raigne of King Richard the 2d ended this yeare.

1400.—Hugh o'Molloy, prince of the territory of ffearcall, died the 17th of the Calends of ffebruary. Laighneagh mcfferall Roe mcDonogh maGeoghegan died in the ides of

---

[1] *mcHeoghae.*—Now Mac Keogh 'He was chief protector of the men of Erin.' *Annals of Loch Cé*, ii. 37.

[2] *Colton*—He was Primate from 1382 to 1404. We have an account of his Visitation made in 1397, edited by Reeves.

September. Richard Bremingham with others were treacherously killed in the house of the lord Bushop of Meath. Donogh ffox lord of the Contry of Moyntir agan als foxes Contry & of right prince of the Contryes of Teaffa, died. Dermott m⁰Bryan, the 2 sonnes of Caharnagh, sonne of ffox, died in the Calends of August. The Castle of Donoman was taken by the sone of the abbott o'Connor. Hobert m⁰Edmund m⁰Hobert Burk was killed therein, & the sone of Edmund o'Kelly that was prisoner in the same castle was set at liberty. Gregory sonne of Tanay o'Mulchonry, chiefe chronicler of Sile Morey by profession & a very authentick author in many knowledges was killed with a blow of a lance by the hands of William Garve m⁰David in the Conflict of Donoman aforesaid by chaunce-medle, for which cause the offender was driuen to pay 126 cowes in satisfaction or eirrick of them. Rory m⁰Art Magenos prince of o'Neahagh of Ulster was killed by the sons of Conuley o'Neale & by Cathvarr Magenos. Shane m⁰Ulgarge m⁰Hugh o'Roirck a proper towardly & well disposed young man, was killed by Clan Casdealive with an arrow. Donell m⁰Theobald o'Molloy surnamed m⁰Theobald Tanist & next successor of the principallity of ffearkeall (if he had liued) was killed at Allon[1] by the English of Leinster. The king of England's sonne[2] came to Ireland this yeare. Teige o'Keruell escaped out of prison from the English of Belaghgawran.[3] Morish the earle of Desmond's sone, died of the plague this yeare. Richard m⁰en Miley, lord of the Stontons, was killed by Ullick Burk.

1403.—o'Connor Donn & Murtagh Backagh m⁰Donell lord of Sligeagh & the territory thereof, with theire forces repayred to the lands of Owen m⁰Murrogh o'Madden; which Contry they possessed themselves of, & from thence they went to Clanricarde to assist Ullick m⁰Rickard Burk against the o'Kellyes of Imanie, from thence they returned to theire houses without any loss or accidental mischance. Soon after

---

[1] *Allon* —Allen, in Co. Kildare.
[2] *Sonne.*—Thomas, Duke of Lancaster, son of Henry IV.
[3] *Belaghgawran.*—Now Gowran, in Co. Kilkenny, which gives its name to a barony.

Murtagh Bachach m^{c}Donell m^{c}Murtagh, lord of Ighter-Conaught yeelded death her due, after he lived fortunately having had good success in all his Interprises against his enemies, died the fryday next after the feast-day of St Michaell the Archangel. Mortagh Garve o'Seaghnosy tanist of Tirefiaghragh-ayne, was killed by those of Imanie. John Boy, the grandchild of Johynnin Burk, was killed by the o'Kellyes of Clannvickneoyn & by the sons of Hobert Dalton. Connor m^{c}Hugh m^{c}Dermoda a man compleat with all goodness and perfection, prince of the contry of Moylorg, died. Bryan m^{c}Bryan o'Neale king of Ulster died.

1404.—Thomas Barrett[1] Bushop of Oylfyn a very reuerend & noble prelate, & full of all good quallities belonging to his function, Died in the spring of this yeare & was entred in Derrie of Lough Conn,[2] the families of Barrets, Cusacks & m^{c}Wellens of the roote[3] are Welsh, & came from Wales to this land. Connor oge m Hugh m^{c}Dermott prince of Moylorg, a desperate and hardy man of his hands, Died between Michaelmas & alhollantide, & Teige m^{c}Hugh m^{c}Dermott was established in his place at Holantide: I doe not know whether this be the Connor mentioned in the presedent yeare, if he be, Impute the fault to mine author & not to me. Cormack m^{c}Dermott was killed in an hostinge in Clanricarde by some of the horsemen of Clan Rickard in September of this yeare. Moylorg sustayned great losses thereby, Connor & Cormack. The Daughter of o'Connor of Affalye & wife to Gillepatrick o'More, Died. Donell mac Henry o'Neale was Invested king of Ulster this yeare. There raigned many diseases in Ireland this yeare, and amongst the rest the kingdome abounded with feavors. The earle of Ormond,[4] head of

---

[1] *Barrett.*—He was bishop of this See from 1372 to 1404.

[2] *D. of L Conn*—Now Errew, where there are remains of an ancient church, the patron of which is St. Tighearran.

[3] *Roote.*—The northern portion of Co. Antrim. The name Route is a corruption of the ancient name Dalriada. See Keating's *H. of Ireland*, p 249.

[4] *Earle of Ormond.*—James, the third earl, who built Gowran castle, and resided there until he purchased the castle of Kilkenny in 1391. See Archdall's *Peerage*, iv. 9

the chivalrie of Ireland, died. ffelym o'Twahall prince of Morie in Leinster, died. Keruell o'Daly, chief composer of Ireland, dane of the Contry of Corcomroe, died ffinyn mᶜOwen mᶜCarthye Died. Andrew Barrett was killed by mᶜMurrogh. Owen mᶜConnor mᶜCahall o'Conor of Affalye was killed by the earle of Kildare. The Lady Nwaly, daughter of Donell mᶜMurtagh o'Connor & wife to o'fferall mᶜCormack mᶜDonogh, died. William o'Deoran chiefe professor of the Brehon law with the mᶜMorroghs of Leinster, died. fferall mᶜTheobald o'Molloy died. Rory mᶜHugh mᶜDermada, tooke upon him the principallity of Moylorg, the Contry & profits were diuided in twoo moyetyes between him & the sons of fferall mᶜDermoda, that lived before in exile.

1405.—Richard Butler (surnamed hard foot) was killed by ffaghtna o'More. There arose great dissention & warrs between mᶜMurrogh[1] of Leinster & the English whereof ensued the burning wasting & destroying of the County of Kildare, Catherlagh & Disertdermott Richard or Risdard maGranell, chieftaine of Moyntir-eolas, died at Christmas by takeing a surfeit of aqua vitae, to him aqua mortis Dermott mᶜDonogh o'Connor Kerry was killed by mᶜMorrish of Kerry. Donell oge o'Roirck, died. Miles Dalton was killed by Dalton himself chiefe of that name. New castle[2] alṣ Castle neva o'ffinnaghan was broken down by the family of the o'Broynes this yeare.

1406.—Leyseach o'Mollan, Tanist of ffohertye, & Hugh o'Twahaile tanist of Imaile, & also Bran o'Broyne Tanist of ffoylan, Thomas mᶜThomas mᶜMurrogh, died all of the plague this yeare. Mullronye mᶜTeige mᶜDonogh, prince of tyre Aylealla, after good penance, died in his owne house, & was buried in the abby of Boyle. Murrogh o'Connor prince of Affalye, with his sons & kinsmen & alsoe with the help of the 2 sonns of the king of Connaught, Cahall Duff & Teige o'Connor, with their followers and dependants, whome

---

[1] *mᶜMurrogh.*—Art, son of Art.
[2] *New castle.* — A little to the south-east of Newtown Mount Kennedy, Co. Wicklow.

the said Murrogh Intertained, as well to offend the English of Meath as alsoe to defend himselfe & his contry from them, gave a great overthrow to the abbott o'Connors sonne & his retayned kearne of Conaught, the said abbots son with his route of kearne went to a place in the upper parts of Gesill, called Clon-Imorrosa,[1] to the towne of one Gilleboye mᶜMoyle Corra (from whence it had been better for themselves to have staid) for they were ouertaken there by Cahall mᶜMurrogh o'Connor with Cahall o'Connor & the number of 6 horsemen only, who finding the said Conaught men spoyling the said Gilleboy of all his goods & amongst other things one of the said kearnes tooke a great cauldron that Callagh before lent to the said Gilleboy to brew withall, which Gilleboy seeing one of the kearnes carry out from out of his house in presence of Callogh that lent it, said to Callogh: Callogh, there is your cauldron, take it, & discharge me of my lone, which Callogh willingly accepted, saying, I take it as suffitient satisfaction of you, & sudainely one of Callogh's people flung a stone & hit the cauldron; at the great sound thereof the kearne broke out of theire places, & fled as fast as they could, where at last the abbott's sone was killed upon the bogg adjoining to the towne, & of theire men & kearne they lost no less than 300 persons between that place & Clonanie[2] in Keigh-na-Kedagh, in Affalye, being hotly pursued by the inhabitants of Affalie to that place; besides the loss of theire men, they alsoe lost one of the Relickes of St. Patrick, which before remayned at Elfynn until it was lost by them that day, which was counted by them to be the chiefest Relick of all Conaught. This Discomfiture was given on Saturday the 16th day of July this yeare. Brian o'Connor that lost Affalie by his attainder was descended of the said o'Connor Lynally, vidzt. Bryan was son of Cahire, who was sonne of Conn, who was sone of Callogh, who was son of the said Murrogh. Terlaugh oge mᶜHugh mᶜTerlaugh that raigned 22 years Joyntly king of Conaught

---

[1] *C.-Imorrosa.*—The name is now obsolete.

[2] *Clonanie.* — Near the hill of Croghan.

with o'Connor Roe, was killed by Cahall Duff o'Connor Roes sonne & by John mᵉHobert mᵉEdmund mᵉHobert mᵉDavid Burk (who was sone of Benavon Daughter of ffelym o'Connor) in the house of Rickard mᵉShane mᵉEdmund mᵉHobert, called the Kregan adjoyning to ffie Ike in the Contry of Clyn Convay; Terlaugh o'Connor was the 3rd king of Conaught that was slaine in Clan Convoy, vidzt. Connor mᶜRory mᶜTerlaugh More, Rory mᶜCahall mᶜConor Roe mᶜMurtagh Moyneagh, who was sonne of Terlaugh monarch of Ireland; & lastly Terlaugh oge o'Connor, as before I have declared.

1407.—Cahall o'Connor, sone of o'Connor of Affalye was killed by the family of the Berminghams. Mortagh o'Kelly[1] archBushop of Conaught, a learned & wittie prelate, Died in Twayme at Michaelmas. Mulmorey o'Dempsey prince of Clanmalierie, Died. There was foule & badd weather this yeare and a great murren of cattle. The English of Ireland with Scroope[2] the king's deputy gaue an overthrow to the Irish of Mounster, by whome Teige o'Keruell, prince of the territory of Elye was slaine. This Teige was deseruedly a man of great accoumpt & fame with the professors of poetry and musick of Ireland and Scotland, for his Liberallity extended towards them & every of them in generall. The overthrow of Killeachye[3] was given this yeare by o'Connor Roe & by the sonn of Melaghlen o'Kelly & by Rory mᶜDermot prince of Moylorg, to mᶜWilliam Burk of Clanricarde & to Cahall mᶜRory o'Connor, whoe was called king instead of Terlaugh o'Connor Donne, that was killed by Cahall Duffe (as before is Declared) the forces of mᶜWilliam & Cahall mᶜRory were putt to flight, themselves both were taken, & many of theire people slaine & taken therein. The Castle[4] of Tobber Tulske

---

[1] *o'Kelly.*—He occupied this See from 1394 to 1407.

[2] *Scroope.*—He was Deputy of Thomas of Lancaster in 1401 and in 1407. He died at Castledermot. See Gilbert's *Viceroys*, pp. 296, 300.

[3] *Killeachye.*—Perhaps Killiagh-an, in the parish of St. John, barony of Athlone.

[4] *Castle.*—Built by O'Connor in 1406. About forty years after a house was founded here for Dominicans by the M'Dowells. See *Hib. Dom.*, p. 315.

was taken & broken down before by Bryan m⁰Donell m⁰Murtagh and by the familie of the m⁰Donnoghs, & Cahall m⁰Rory was by them conwayed to Carnefroighe to be created king of Conaught Conuak o'fferall died of a sudaine & unprovided death.

1408.—Prince Thomas[1] the king of England's sone came to Ireland this yeare. The kings sone with his forces marched to the province of Leinster, and Hodgin Tute, a man of great worth, was lost of that hoasting. Awley maGawley, chieftaine of Calrie, died & was entred at Athlone. There was a generall plague this yeare in Meath whereof Scroop a noble knight that suplyed the roome of the kings Deputy in this realme, died. Cahall mac Kehernye, Conor ffynn m⁰Kehernie were all killed by Clann Murtagh in revenge of the killing of Magnus m⁰Murtagh m⁰Cahall that was killed by that scept of Clann Kehernie before. Magnus Magawran was killed by Boyhanagh m⁰Gille Roe by a throw of a staf of a hedge. Cormack o'Maylle was killed by his owen brother, & the race of Cahall o'fferall killed his sonne & tooke his Castle too.

Here endeth this Booke ffebruary 9th, 84.

I Leaue the few leaues unto ritten herein to make an Index of the things of note comprised in the Booke, which if the seriousness of your affairs will not suffer yourselfe to take in hand, when you shall peruse the same, & shall please to Returne it unto me, I will at my better leasure make an end therof: & soe I rest the last of June 1627.

Y^{rs} C. M. G.

---

[1] *Prince Thomas.*—Of Lancaster He landed at Carlingford on September 30th, a week atter, he came to Dublin and arrested the Earl of Kildare. See Gilbert's *Viceroys*, p. 294.

Index.

₊ *The Figures in this List refer to the pages of the Volume.*

Aaron, 19, 20.
Abbot and king, 143.
Abel, anchorite, 204.
—— of Athomna, 119.
Abraham, 10, 12, 13.
Acathlon, 101, 102.
Achabo, 75, 97, 99, 110, 145, 150.
Achroym o'Maynye, 119, 275, 321.
Achy Conn, 84.
—— Forcha, 74.
Acoranen, 99.
Acorns, 136, 176
Adalstan, 149
Adalvleih, 146.
Adam, 10, 11, 12, 21, 210.
Adamar, 45.
Adawnanus, 110-112, 114, 133, 158.
Adfiath, b. of Armagh, 127.
Adrean, pope, 179.
Adulf mʳEtulfe, 149.
Adyrchreach, 184.
Aeneas, 21.
Aeremon, 28.
Aestulapius, 18.
Affalie, 81, 152, 182, 186, 192, 195, 202, 205, 228, 246, 255, 260, 283, 291, 305, 308, 320, 326.
—— princes of, 29, 98, 119, 120, 126, 129, 139, 143, 144, 147, 151, 154, 157, 167, 168, 180, 183-185, 192, 231, 232, 266, 310, 311, 313, 321, 322, 324, 325, 327.
Affrick, a. of Kildare, 117, 135.
Africa, 12.
Agabo. *See* Achabo.

Agamemnon, 14, 21.
Agapicus, pope, 78.
Agatho, pope, 106.
Aghaconary, 286.
Agnamayne foltchoeyn, 211.
Agnomoynfin, 210.
Ahagh, k. of S., 115.
—— mᶜConlay, 84.
Aharly, 254
Aidan, 212.
—— abbot, 108.
—— anchorite, 98.
—— b. of Lindisfarn, 104.
—— b. of Mayo, 122.
—— Glasse, 210.
—— k. of Scotland, 91, 96-98, 101.
—— mᶜGawran, 74, 90, 91, 97, 98,
—— mᶜReaghtay, 143.
—— o'Connuaye, 132.
—— o'Fighragh, 88.
—— of Rahin, 127.
—— St., 104, 122.
Aihgean, a. of Tirdaglasse, 105.
Aihleagh mᶜDurgrean, 61.
Ailby, princess, 47.
Aileagh, 24, 151, 188.
—— princes of, 73, 142, 145, 151, 155, 157, 165, 180, 185, 233, 254.
Ailfinn. *See* Oylfinn.
Aillealla Cassaicklagh, 210.
—— Fynn, 211.
Aillill, a. of Armagh, 76, 78.
—— brother of Hugh O., 128.
—— Eaghie G , 73.
—— Flanneassa, 107.
—— grandson of H. Slaine, 105.

330   *Index.*

Ailhll, k. of Munster, 111.
— k. of Ossory, 101.
— m‹Colman, 103.
— m‹Conill Graint, 113.
— m‹Dongaile, 110.
— m‹Donogh, 105, 128.
— m‹Feray, 113.
— m‹H. Royne, 103.
— m‹Owen, 144.
— Molt, 71, 72, 79, 83, 171.
— o'Donchowe, 120, 121.
— the harper, 102.
Ailve, St., 77, 127.
— Seanchwa o'N., 79.
Ailwan o'Lugdadan, 124.
Ainmire m‹Sedna, 80, 88–90, 172.
— o'Kahallaine, 154.
Ainwith, 115.
Alba longa, 21.
Albanagh, Sir E., 317.
Albord Roe, 133.
Alchon, 114.
Aldergoid, 34, 212.
Alduston, 151.
Alea, 18.
Aleran the witty, 107.
Alexandria, 49.
Alfrith, 112.
Algenan, 115.
Algna, b. of Ardbreachan, 124.
Algnio m‹Gnoy, 120.
Aliter, a. of C., 97.
Allayde, 210.
Alleluia, 70.
Allgot, 133.
Allie, 142.
Allon, 62, 77, 112, 113, 323.
Almayne, 204.
Almon, 109.
Aloa Neide, 211.
Alpinn, k. of the Picts, 123.
— k. of Scotland, 115.
Alps, 65.
Altades, 14.
Altiodorensis, 70, 71.
Altyre Duff earle, 134.
Aludon, 148.
Alvie, 42.
Amintas, 14.
An, dr. of O'Kelly, 287.

Anacletus, 49.
Anais, 44.
Analie, 122, 196, 249, 266, 277, 294, 295, 306, 312, 321.
— chiefs of, 196, 237, 250, 277, 282, 284, 298, 299, 304, 312, 321, 322.
Anastasius, emperor, 75, 111.
— monk, 98, 99.
— pope, 73, 74.
Ancha, St., 159.
Anchon, 114.
Anchorites, 98, 111, 117, 124, 128–131, 137–142, 147, 150, 160, 168, 169, 173, 174, 176, 177, 179, 204.
Anckell, 48.
Andagha, 18.
Andrew, St., 49.
Anfceally, 123.
Anfrith, 102.
Angine, 107.
Anlon, 124.
Anlwan, 211.
Anmcha, 101.
Anmcharad m‹Concharad, 113.
Anmine, k. of I., 88.
Anoroit m‹Rwaragh, 145.
Anthony, St., 63.
Antioch, 49.
Antrim, Earl of, 209.
Anye, w. of o'Royrek, 312.
Anyn, 14.
Apollo, 18.
Aqua vitæ, 325.
Ar, fier, &c., 124.
Aralius, 14.
Arannan, Fynian, 109.
Araye, 46.
Arbatus, 43.
Arcades. *See* Orcades.
Archaa, 210.
Ardagh, 73, 183, 283.
Ard-an-Killen, 304.
Ardanmaith, 31.
Ardbrackan, 124, 131, 156, 174, 192, 195, 214, 223.
Ardcorran, 71.
Ardfahie, 103.
Ardgall, 116.
— m‹Connell, 76.

Ardkarna, 76.
Ardlaura, 30.
Ardleyren, 11.
Ardmagh, 10. 38, 65, 108, 113–115, 124, 126, 132, 138, 140, 142, 145, 147, 150, 158, 160, 163, 164, 170, 180, 181, 204, 220, 235, 262.
—— abbots of, 75, 76, 78, 100, 112, 122, 127, 129, 131, 132, 135, 136, 139, 143, 150.
—— bishops, primates of, 65, 72, 90, 105, 110, 136, 140, 141, 150, 163, 171, 185, 189, 190, 197, 201, 236, 237, 243, 260, 322.
Ardmire, 294, 300.
Ardnarea, 246.
Ardnurcher, 217, 222, 226, 232, 234.
Ardrahan, 245.
Ardstrathy, b. of, 99.
Ardtibra, 79.
Ardvron o'Kelly, 120.
Areaghtach mᶜAnfie, 154.
Aregall, 307.
Argamoyne, 121.
Argedgryne, 46.
Argedrosse, 28, 29.
Argedwar, 38, 213.
Arick mᶜBrith, 151.
Arie, 168, 255.
Aristotle, 60.
Arius, 106.
—— k. of Assyria, 14.
Ark of Noah, 12.
Arlache, dr. of O'Connor, 254.
Armagh. *See* Ardmagh.
Armarkes, 14.
Armenians, 258.
Aron, 170.
Arraghtagh o'Fielan, 127.
Art Enear, 59, 209.
—— Imleagh, 36, 212.
—— Kir, 76.
—— mᶜHugh, 212.
—— mᶜLowaye, 37, 38, 212.
—— ne Mangye, 212.
Artchall, 111.
Arteagh, 216, 230, 241, 272, 291.
Arthur, son of k. Aidan, 96.
Artry, 213.

Artry, k. of C., 132, 133.
—— k. of M., 115, 127.
—— mᶜCahall, 127.
—— mᶜConnor, 132.
Arye (Ara), 255.
Ascanius, 21.
Ascatades, 14.
Asia, 12.
Assyria, 13–16, 27, 28.
Assyrians, 12, 25, 43.
Athankip, 248, 279.
Athantrostan, 55, 56.
Athaskragh, 261.
Athboy, 227, 243, 246, 309.
Athbrea, 61.
Athcora Conell, 248.
Athdacara, 249.
Athdalaragh, 217, 220.
Ath-da-feart, 130.
Athdara, 71.
Ath-disert-nwan, 287.
Ath-ele, 279.
Athengail, 244, 249.
Athenrie, 239, 246, 277, 279.
—— lord of, 284.
Athfirdia, 152, 181, 268, 269.
Athgoan, 102.
Athkleyh Mearye, 58.
Athkynnloghateohy, 286.
Athlayen, 56.
Athlean Corann, 258, 270.
Athleathan, 279, 306, 307, 316.
Athliag, 165, 191, 229, 233, 237, 249, 291.
Athlone, 147, 165, 184, 191, 193, 204, 205, 223, 224, 228, 230, 231, 235, 237, 239, 245, 246, 249, 257, 268, 270, 277, 307, 328.
Athmaynie, 257.
Athmoye, 241.
Athmoyne, 203.
Athomna, 119.
Athrosda, 56.
Athrumni, 118.
Athronny, 222.
Athseany, 116.
Athslissen, 294.
Athy, 56.
Aughrim. *See* Achroym o'M.
Augusta, b. of, 106.

Augustine, St., 90.
— b. of Beanchor, 124.
Aurea, 76.
Auxilius, St., 69, 71.
Avall Kehernie, 194.
Avirgin, 23, 28, 29, 203.
Awargin mᶜKynaye, 154.
— o'Morrey, 175, 187.
Awfer, 148.
Awgary mᶜT., 158.
Awirgin, 213.
Awley, 142, 154, 163.
— Cwaran, 151.
— ffroit, 151.
— Keanchyreagh, 150.
— k. of Denmark, 134.
— k. of Munster, 81.
— k. of York, 156.
— mᶜGodfrey, 150–152.
— mᶜIllulfe, 158.
— mᶜMoielan, 181.
— mᶜSitricke, 159.
— p. of o'Manie, 127.
— p. of the Danes, 141, 150, 154, 163, 170.
— son of Imer, 158.
Awus, 133.
Ayne, 77, 167.
Aynmyre. See Ainmire.
Aydan, 89.
— k. of Scotland, 101.
— mᶜFinn, 62.

Baath, 20.
Babylon, 10, 258.
Bachall, 140, 190, 201, 251.
Backlaure, 85.
Baghlayhes, 89.
Baile-locha-lwaha, 221, 234, 245, 257.
Baleus, 14.
— secundus, 14.
— tertius, 14.
Balla, 75, 102.
Balle-athboy, 308.
Ballenmote, 258, 293, 297, 307.
Ballentobber, 301, 307, 310.
— bride, 267.
Ballinechowrry, 228.
Balholl, 289.

Ballymore O'Flynn, 273.
Ballymote. See Ballenmote.
Bangor in England, 108.
— in I. See Beanchor.
Bann, the, 13, 115, 269.
Banncha, 43.
Banva, 18, 26.
Bard, 42.
Barde of Boyne, the, 150.
Bards, 42, 292, 298.
Barnard, St., 205.
Barney, 89.
Barons, the, 237.
Barre, 314.
Barrett, Andrew, 325.
— Richard, 310.
— Robert, 302.
— Thomas, b. of Elphin, 324.
— Wattin, 302.
— William, 253.
Barretts, 253, 261, 324.
Barrow, the, 15, 44.
Bartholeme, 13, 14.
Battle Abbey, 179.
Beaaghah, 39.
Beag mᶜBrinyn, 103
— mᶜConley, 122.
— mᶜDonnewan, 155.
— mᶜFergus, 106.
— mᶜKwawagh, 97.
Beagan Reymynn, 109.
Beagbrwich, 108.
Beagny, St., 98.
Beagvarchye, 101.
Beaha, 39.
Bealaghatha, 90.
Bealaghbricke, 124.
— conglaissy, 15
— monie ne Sirrhidye, 226.
Bealaseany, 238, 300, 321.
Bealayleaghta, 157.
Beallaghmowna, 144.
Bealykervell, 220.
Beanchor, 75, 84, 98, 99, 118, 129, 131, 142
— abbots of, 75, 97-99, 103, 106–110, 118, 124, 127, 129, 147, 149.
Beann Artgaile, 206.
Beanrye. See Dinrye.
Beara, 258.

Bearagh, 108.
Bearba. *See* Barrow.
Bearna-an-mile, 289.
Bearngal mᶜGeye, 35
Bearry, Breassail of, 123
Beckett, T., 207
Bede, 10, 78, 103, 112, 116.
Beere-Hauen, 254, 255.
Befaile, 128.
Beg mᶜDe, 83, 84
Beighrenne, 131
Beisson, 133
Beladoyn, 122.
Belagh Derg, 314.
Belaghgawran, 323.
Belanaha, 90.
Bel-atha-seanna, 321.
Belfada, 193.
Bells, 83, 87, 130, 197, 218, 251
Belochus, 14.
Belopares, 14.
Benavon, dr. of o'Connor, 327.
Benedictus, monk, 77.
—— pope, 89.
Benignus, 72.
Beogawyne, 210.
Beoheaghty, 210.
Beoy, 81
—— b. of Ardkarna, 76.
Berchann, 79
Berckley Castle, 285.
Bernith, 111.
Bethe, 11
Beuynn, dr. of MaGeoghegan, 301
Bevin, dr. of o'Doyne, 305
Bicor, 100
Bile Tanna, 29.
Billus, 22, 210.
Birmingham. *See* Bremingham.
Birr, 85, 88, 120, 132, 138, 148, 222, 227.
Biscaie, 23
Bithinia, 106.
Bithlynn, 158
Blacaire mᶜGodfrey, 152, 154
—— mᶜImer, 154.
Blaheaghty, 210.
Blathmach, 212
—— mᶜAidan, 104
—— k of I., 101, 106, 107, 172.

Blathmach, k. of Teaffa, 107
—— k of Ulster, 101.
—— mᶜFlaynn, 132
—— o'Mardivoe, 130.
Blayd, 211.
Blefeth, 79
Blood, showers of, 110, 112, 141
—— of two mingled, 251.
Boban of St. Kevin, 197.
Boganie, 107.
Bohine, a of Byrre, 148.
—— St., 10, 78, 81, 90, 97.
Bohyn, a. of Bangor, 107.
Bolgagh, 109.
Bonafinne, castle of, 262, 264.
Bonagalme, castle of, 234.
Bonifacius, pope, 77, 78.
Books, 8, 60, 61, 94-96, 130, 139, 215, 218, 220, 258.
Borbeasse, 39.
Boren, Roaring boys of, 89.
Borohua, 54, 55, 57, 109, 111, 222
Bourdeaux, 237.
Bowgna, 150.
Bowyne, 113.
Boy Connell, 83, 186
Boyan, 88.
Boydan, k. of I, 172.
—— mᶜAinmire, 80.
Boyhan, b. of Inisbofinne, 112.
—— mᶜCarill, k. of U, 89.
—— mᶜAnynnea, 88, 90.
Boyhin mᶜBroynn, 76.
Boyhinn, St., 76, 78, 81, 90, 97.
Boyle, river, 236.
—— abbey of, 234, 250, 261, 273, 288, 290, 296, 320, 325.
Boyne, the, 15, 58, 60, 61, 77, 136, 139.
Boynnean, sept of, 257.
Boyvinn, 133.
Bran, 115.
—— Beag mᶜMurchowe, 117.
—— Brick, 117.
—— k. of L, 101, 115, 127
—— mᶜColman, 149
—— mᶜConell, 110.
—— mᶜFoylan, 136, 137.
—— nephew of Foylan, 110
—— son of Kynadon, 124.

Branchowe, 115.
Brandon, b. of Armagh, 72
—— St., of Byrre, 85, 88, 218.
—— cowarbs of, 214, 224.
—— laws of, 118.
—— of Clonfert, 85, 89, 315.
Branduffe mᶜEaghagh, 91, 97.
Branyn mᶜMoyle Oghtray, 108
—— son of Moylefohorty, 108.
Brasse, 39.
Bratha, 210.
Brawnie, 125, 131, 138, 147, 176, 182, 186, 200, 245
Brayn, St., 117.
Breaghmhaine. See Brawnie.
Breasall, son of Deine, 76
Breasry, 36, 37, 212.
Breassall, 212.
—— Bodivo, 46.
—— Brick, 213.
—— Concalagh, 175
—— mᶜColgan, 119.
—— of Bearry, 123.
—— son of k. Fineaghty, 110.
Breasse, 17, 18, 209.
Breathnagh, D., 222.
Breawie, 38, 43.
Bregghtra, 111.
Brehon law, 280, 325.
Brehons, 263, 280, 298, 325.
Breifne. See Brenie
Bremyngham, Andrew, 255, 258, 276, 277, 283, 300.
—— E of Louth, 285.
—— Gerodin, 239
—— John, 285.
—— Lord, 258, 276, 277.
—— Meyler, 217, 219, 221, 226.
—— Pierce, 260.
—— Richard, 284, 323.
—— Roback, 276.
—— William, 262, 267.
Bremynghams, 295, 327
—— country of the, 163, 181
Brenaynn mᶜBriwyn, 89.
Brenie, the, 192, 197, 234, 239, 243, 244, 263, 289, 311.
—— kings of, 129, 144, 179, 182, 193, 196, 201, 277, 281, 287, 298, 300, 303 305, 314.

Brenie, men of, 144, 179, 189, 195, 237, 253, 263, 270, 277, 280, 295.
Brenoge, 319.
Brenyes, the, 122.
Breowen, 23, 210.
Bressall mᶜAngne, 140.
Bretton, Sir W., 207
Brey, 42, 51, 102, 125, 136, 156, 174, 175.
—— princes of, 102, 146, 156, 228
Breyuick Teige, 203
Brian Borowe, 7, 8, 69, 88, 116, 133, 135, 154, 157, 158, 162-172, 174, 178, 206, 211.
—— mᶜKennedy. See Brian Borowe.
—— son of Eochy M., 64, 265.
Bricke, 91.
Brickny, a of Lohra, 139.
Bridges, 165, 191, 193, 205, 207, 223, 227.
Bridgett, St., 69, 76, 92, 96, 120, 205, 256.
Brigantia, 23.
Bristow, 241.
Britain, 74, 127.
Britanie, 68, 107, 110, 127.
Britons, 46, 70, 72, 89, 99, 103, 109, 110, 111, 119.
—— kings of the, 99, 101, 102, 110, 144, 145, 152.
Brittan the Bald, 14.
Broen mᶜMoylemorrey, 154, 169.
Brogaine of Tchille, 113.
Brosnagh, the, 29, 244.
Broydan mᶜCarill, 72.
Broycoll, 230
Broyn, b. of Cuill-iro, 75
Bruce, E., 268-270, 279, 281, 282.
—— R., 261, 267, 268, 279, 281
Brudeus, 114, 116
Brught, 134.
Bruno, St, 91
Brutus, 47, 68
Brwader, 166.
Brwidy mᶜMilcon, k. of Picts, 71, 88, 89
Brwyne da Dearg, 48
Bryan Borowe. See Brian B.
Duff mᶜM, 101

Index. 335

Bryan macCauill, 300.
— o'Neill, 242.
— son of Aidan, 96.
— son of Eochy M., 64, 265.
Burke, Dabuke, 287.
— David m^{c}E., 310.
— David m^{c}T., 316.
— Sir David, 305.
— Edmond, 290, 291, 292, 294, 299.
— Edmond m^{c}W., 291, 299.
— Edmond, son of the Earl, 292.
— Sir Edmond, 301.
— Sir Edward Albanach, 317.
— Henry m^{c}U , 300.
— Hobert, 294, 299.
— Sir Hobert Donn, 255.
— Hobert m^{c}E., 323.
— John, 310.
— Sir John, 285.
— John Boy, 324.
— John m^{c}Hobert, 327.
— Johnyn, 294, 299, 324.
— m^{c}Hobert, 294, 327.
— m^{c}Philippin, 297.
— m^{c}William, 235, 244, 245, 266, 284, 287, 288, 289, 293, 295, 297, 299, 304, 307, 308, 311, 312, 317, 322, 327.
— m^{c}William the Inferior, 306.
— m^{c}W. the Superior, 306.
— Redmond, 301.
— Sir Redmond, 304, 310.
— Richard, 305.
— Richard, E. of Ulster, 258, 268, 271, 275, 284.
— Richard m^{c}Shane, 327.
— Richard m^{c}William, 237, 305, 306.
— Richard ne Koylle, 248.
— Richard Oge, 306.
— Richard the Red E., 258-260, 270, 271, 275, 284.
— the younger, 299.
— Theobald, br. of the R. E., 260.
— Theobald, son of U , 290, 305.
— Thomas, 294, 320.
— Thomas, son of m^{c}W., 304.
— Ulick, 290, 308, 309, 323.

Burke, Ulick m^{c}R., 323.
— Ulick m^{c}U., 295.
— Walter, E. of U., 247 249, 301.
— Walter m^{c}David, 305, 321.
— Walter m^{c}W., 286-288, 306.
— Walter, son of the Red E., 260.
— William, 217, 263-6, 269, 271, 277, 279, 281, 294, 305.
— William, E. of U., 289.
— William Fitzadelm, 216-220, 229, 233, 234.
— William m^{c}W., 284.
— William More, 284.
— William of Clanricarde, 327.
— William Oge m^{c}W., 248, 249.
— William Saxanagh, 304.
— William, sheriff of C., 238.
— William, son of Sir R., 310.
— William, the Dun E , 285, 286, 289, 290, 295, 297.
— William, the Earl's son, 291.
— William the Hore, 284, 288, 295.
Burkes, the, 255, 267, 292, 295, 297.
— of Clanricarde, 290, 295.
Burrogh upsands, 262.
Butler, Edmond, 261.
— Edward, 269.
— Henry, 249.
— John, 248.
— Richard hardfoot, 325.
— Theobald, 245, 254, 255, 258.
Butlers, the, 267.
Bwaise, the, 13.
Bwannaght men, 264.
Bwannye, 265.
Bwilg Lwatha, 100.
Byrre. *See* Birr.

Cabyes, the, 258.
Caeman, 84.
Caffie m^{c}Fergossa, 84.
Caffye o'Kelly, 120.
Cahal, k. of Connaught, 101, 115, 119.
— k. of Munster, 97.
— k. of o'Keansealy, 120.
— m^{c}Aillella, 140.

Cahal mᶜCahal, 193.
—— mᶜConnor, 144, 147.
—— mᶜDonell, 168.
—— mᶜDunlinge, 130.
—— mᶜFynguyne, 117.
—— mᶜHugh, 100, 211.
—— mᶜMoregan, 183.
—— mᶜMoresse, 137
—— mᶜMorgissa, 116.
—— mᶜRagally, 109
—— Moynmoyne, 119.
Cahallan mᶜCarbry, 143.
Caharnagh, 323
—— of o'Cassine, 170.
Cahassagh, c. of St. Kevyn, 177.
—— k. of Picts, 109.
—— k. of Ulster, 101.
—— mᶜDonell B., 110
—— mᶜLorkynic, 107.
—— mᶜMoyledoyn, 109
—— of Killitte, 130.
Cahire, 29.
Cahire more, 57, 58
Cailkine, 105.
Cainan, 11, 21
Cainneagh, St., 94.
Caisee, 213
Caiss Kedcoyngnyc, 212.
Calae, 229
Calah, 123.
Calathros, battle of, 109.
Calcedon, 70, 106
Calye, 312
Calistinc See Celestine.
Calitigernus, 112.
Calixtus, 61.
Calletin, 48.
Calloes. See Collas
Calrie, 125, 154, 178, 182, 189, 245, 328.
Canfrith, 97.
Canneagh of Aghaboe, 75, 97.
Canon, son of Gartnaitt, 110
Canon law, 286.
Canons, the white, 243
Canterbury, b of, 207.
—— abbey of, 207
Cantred, 16, 237.
Canute, 192
Caolinsge. See Keyle Usge.

Capacyront, 19.
Carbrey Losckleahan, 211.
Carbrey, in C., 182, 275, 287, 289, 291, 300, 316, 318.
—— in L., 163, 181, 182, 200.
—— in M., 302, 304.
Carbry an Scregann, 284.
—— Crom, 137.
—— Kinncatt, 49, 50.
—— Liffeachair, 41, 60-63, 209.
—— k. of Munster, 89.
—— mᶜCahall, anchorite, 168.
—— mᶜCahall, k. of L., 73, 139.
—— mᶜCriowhan, 89.
—— mᶜFiagha, 91.
—— mᶜLoygnen, 123.
—— mᶜNeale, 73, 74, 78, 171.
—— mᶜOwgany, 42.
—— Nia, 76.
—— o'Scopa, b of Rathboy, 250.
—— race of, 107, 108, 113.
Carcall, 115
Cardin, Thomas, 241.
Carhaly age fad, 287
Carhayne, 209.
Carhinn mᶜCorlvoy, 70.
Carhyn finn, 211
Carlan, b. of Armagh, 90.
Carleil (Carlegion), 99.
Carnarvon, 261
Carne Anlwayne, 36
Carneagh, St , 77.
Carneferagh, 100.
Carneferiy, 32, 137
Carnefiagha, 51, 122.
Carnefraoigh, 265, 270, 328
Carolus mᶜA , b. of Oylfyn, 262
Carpreach the swift, 204
Carrey, 42.
Carrick, Earl of, 268.
Carrick of Logh Ce, 217, 235, 239, 274, 283, 290, 295, 311, 321.
Carrickfeorais, 260
Carrickfergus, 223, 260
Carrough, 259, 298.
Carthusians, 91
Cashel, 7, 46, 75, 112, 130, 140, 143, 144, 145, 150-152, 154, 156 158, 175, 182, 185, 188, 191, 202, 244, 259

Index. 337

Cashel, psalter of, 8.
Cassclochie, 212.
Casse, 211.
Cassina, Mount, 77.
Cassius, 47.
Cassyne, 211.
Castle Anorer, 313.
—— Cnock, 115.
—— Corran, 277.
—— m^cCoghlan, 240
—— More m^cCosdeally, 291.
—— of the Obber, 217
Catherlagh, co of, 325.
Cathnia, a. of Duleek, 30.
—— o'Gwary, 127.
Cathwaye, 209, 213.
Cato, 60.
Cavan, co., 122.
Caward, Sir Pierce, 242.
Cayluoth m^cCrouvarie, 63.
Cayneagh, 148
Ceallagh, a. of C., 117.
—— Cwalann, 112.
—— k. of Connaught, 101.
—— k. of Ireland, 101, 103, 172.
—— k. of Leinster, 101, 112, 115
—— k. of Ossory, 101.
—— k. of Scotland, 101, 151.
—— m^cBran, k. of Leinster, 133, 135, 136.
—— m^cComaski, 142
—— m^cDungaill, 129
—— m^cFogorty, 146.
—— m^cFynnaghty, 136.
—— m^cGwayre, 107.
—— m^cKervill, 144.
—— m^cMoyle Cova, 105.
—— m^cSarayne, 105.
—— Murchow, 123.
—— p. of Scotland, 151.
—— primate, 189, 190.
—— son of Donell B., 104.
Ceallagh, dr. of D., 14.
—— St, 160
Ceallaghan of Cashel, 150–152, 154, 156.
Ceanfoyle, k. of Connaught, 101.
—— k of Ireland, 101, 172.
—— k. of Munster, 115.
—— k of Ossory, 81.

Ceanfoyle m^cBlathmack, 108.
—— m^cColgan, 104, 109.
—— m^cLorcan, 149.
—— m^cRwamann, 131.
—— the wise, 109.
Ceannath, k. of the Picts, 89
Cearmna finn, 32.
Cearnaghann m^cDowlegenn, 145.
Celeagher Moyornogh, b. of C , 179.
Celestine, pope, 65, 106.
Cenay m^cLachtren, 102.
Cendall, Adam, 260.
Cerall, k. of U., 71.
Cervall m^cFinnaghty, 132.
Cervell m^cMoregan, 144, 145.
Cesarea, 11, 12.
—— dr. of the k. of France, 42
Chahir, 28.
Cham, 12, 14.
Chambers, 311.
Characters, Irish, 9.
Charles, the sword of, 163.
Charles the Great, 130.
Cheapstowe, 207, 208
Chess-tables, 153.
Children, wonderful, 143, 188.
Christina, dr of o'Neaghtan, 247.
Chroniclers, 5, 7, 8, 10, 21, 99, 112, 306, 143, 145, 178, 206, 258, 264, 302, 305, 306, 309, 311, 312, 319, 320, 323.
Chus, son of Cham, 14.
Ciaran, St. *See* Queran.
Cinay m^cArtragh, 133
Cinnfoyle m^cColgann, 109.
Clan Barde, 299
—— Cahall, 279, 287, 290, 291, 319.
—— Casdealive, 323.
—— Colman, 51, 88, 121, 125, 162, 172, 175, 255.
—— Conall, 279, 287, 290, 291, 319.
—— Conwaye, 255, 276, 327.
—— Cullen, 305
—— Donnogh, 291, 307, 309.
—— Downye, 257.
—— Kehernie, 328.
—— Kelly, 223
—— Kullan *See* C. Cullen
—— Mackneoyne, 317, 324.

Clan mcDonogh, 307, 328.
—— Morrish, 290.
—— Mortagh, 294-296, 298, 302, 314, 328.
—— Mulronie, 251, 286, 287, 296.
—— Richard. *See* Clanrickard.
—— Swynies, 318.
Clanmaliere, 192, 203, 309, 313, 327.
Clanna boye, 282, 299.
—— Milead, 19, 28, 65.
—— Neale, 141, 171, 312.
—— Nevie, 3, 14, 15, 65
—— Rowry, 41, 45, 58, 81, 105, 157.
Clannfwadagh, 291.
Clanrickard, 290, 295, 305, 309, 312, 323, 324, 327.
Clanvickneoyn, 324.
Clanwilliam, 255.
Claravall, 205.
Clare, Earl of, 251, 266.
Clare Athmonie, 227.
Clarence, Duke of, 300.
Claringneagh, 79.
—— pilgrim, 112.
Clarus, archd. of Elphin, 240, 243, 244.
Clehra, 47.
Cleitagh, 60, 77, 127.
Clement, pope, 52, 267.
Cleragh, Art mcC., 317.
Cleufoile the wise, 109.
Cliah, battle of, 48.
Clieu Maile, 42.
Clifford, Symon, 233.
Cloenglasse, 246.
Clogher, 111, 149, 264, 307
—— bishops of, 138, 182.
—— Croghan, 311.
Clonanie, 326.
Clonard, 81, 84, 93, 138, 151, 156, 170, 176, 177, 180, 195, 199, 200, 214
—— abbots of, 105, 107, 114, 118, 120, 123, 127, 135, 142, 143, 148, 149
—— bishops of, 90, 116, 123
Clonbayren, 123, 127, 130, 231.
Clonbronye, 117, 124, 126, 129, 189

Clonconor, 126.
Clonconric, 196
—— Tomayne, 137.
Cloncork, 42.
Cloncorphye, 311.
Cloncowardy, 139
Cloncuiffyne, 125.
Cloncumasge, 284.
Cloncury, 91.
Clondalkan, 124, 135, 142, 144, 178.
Clondewer, 140.
Clone, 104, 145, 178, 189, 190, 308. *See* Clonvicknose.
—— o'Connen, 316.
Cloneawynn, 184.
Cloneois, 112, 123, 129, 138, 149, 225.
Cloneyneagh, 98, 122, 138, 139.
Clonfada Boghan, 89.
Clonfert Brandon, 85, 89, 139, 158, 195, 213, 218, 220, 286.
—— abbots of, 85, 89, 100, 114, 119, 121, 126.
—— bishops of, 89, 213, 246, 282, 305.
—— Molwa, 89, 124, 127.
Clonfiachna, 10.
Clonfinlogh, 192.
Clonhughe Boy, 282
Clon-Imorrosa, 326.
Clonkwaise, 31.
Clonmore Moye, 136.
—— of Moyoge, 136.
Clontarf, 116, 133, 166, 167
Clonvey, 143.
Clonvicknose, 10, 79, 81, 82, 83, 88, 99, 102, 104, 114, 119-121, 126, 127, 135-139, 144, 145, 147, 150, 152, 154, 156-158, 160, 161, 163, 169, 170, 174, 175, 176, 177-182, 185, 186, 188-190, 194, 196, 200, 203, 204, 214, 216, 219-221, 227, 230, 232, 233, 254, 310.
—— abbots of, 79, 89, 90, 97, 99, 100, 102, 104, 107, 109, 110, 113, 116, 117, 119, 120, 123, 127, 136, 139, 142, 148, 154, 156, 198, 213, 233, 244, 310.
—— bishops of, 152, 156, 165, 176, 179, 189, 227, 235, 259, 292.

Index. 339

Cloone, 145.
Clowne Baryn. *See* Clonbayren.
Cluan mor Maedog. *See* Clonmore.
Clynn Conway. *See* Clan C.
Cnessy, 75
Cnockany, 38.
Cnocksaide, 301.
Cnockmoye, 218, 246, 261.
Coaches, 36.
Coarban, b. of Fearta C , 74.
Cobfath, 145.
Cogan, Miles, 214, 277.
Cogann, 267.
Coghlan, Terence, 7.
Cogrich, 189.
Cohorts, Irish, 61.
Coinche, battle of, 252.
Coining in C , 214.
Coinre, a. of, 123.
Colen mᶜCeally, 148
Coleraine. *See* Cowlerayne.
Colga, 102.
—— mᶜConnagann, 143.
—— mᶜDonell, 89.
—— mocloihe, 76
Colgan Dolene, 98.
—— mᶜFalve, 109.
Colla da Krioch, 63.
—— Meann, 63.
—— Wais, 63, 209.
Collas, the three, 41, 62.
Collawyn, 35
Colleges, Irish, 8, 9
Colman, a. of Beanchor, 109
—— a. of Clonmacnoise, 109, 123.
—— ancestor of o'M , 43, 125.
—— Beag, 88, 89, 90, 124
—— b. of Inisboffin, 108, 109.
—— Boy mᶜVihelly, 105.
—— Casse, 107.
—— Conelleie, 144
—— Eala mᶜWihealla, 81, 98, 104, 156.
—— k of I., 97.
—— k. of L., 81.
—— k. of Ossory, 81.
—— mᶜAllealla, 148.
—— mᶜCobheye, 97.
—— mᶜMoyle Patrick, 155.

Colman mᶜPatrick, 240
—— more, 84, 88, 100, 124, 125.
—— of Glandalogha, 105.
—— of Lynnealae, 81.
—— of the Welshmen, 119
—— Rimheadha, 97, 98, 172.
—— Stellan, 100.
—— Wamagh, 113.
Colmana, s. of St. Patrick, 70.
Colp, 23.
Colteberia, 23.
Colton, primate, 322.
Columb, a., 108.
—— mᶜCriowhan, 81, 84.
—— mᶜFoylgussa, 127.
—— of Inis Kealtra, 84.
—— a. of Imleagh, 165.
Columban mᶜLardan, 100.
Columbkille, St., 10, 76, 78, 81-83, 88-96, 112, 119, 129, 130, 132, 148, 160, 164, 171, 175, 178, 181, 201, 205.
—— families of, 130.
—— relics of, 132.
—— rules of, 119.
—— shrine of, 175.
Colvan, a Dane, 160.
Coman the religious, 118.
—— bishop, 109.
—— St., 127.
Comar, battle of, 29.
Comaskagh mᶜCahaill, 132.
—— mᶜEnos, 136.
Comet, 109, 169, 179.
Commor, battle of, 32.
Comninstown, 308.
Comsowe mᶜDyrero, 139
Comyn, a. and b. of Armagh, 105.
—— b. of Indrym, 105.
—— foda, 91, 105.
—— mᶜColman, 90.
—— mᶜLyvren, 90.
—— o'Mooney, 118.
—— of Moyorne, 111.
—— the white, 108.
Comynie, a of C., 107.
Comynye, 108.
Conackine, b. of, 228
Conallagh mᶜConyng, 113.
Conall Chowe, 98.

Conard Keare, 100.
Conarey More, 166.
Conary Kew, 59.
—— k of I , 48, 49.
—— mᶜEdersgell, 48.
Conawill mᶜGillearrie, 159.
Conchayune, 105.
Conchongeall, 130.
Concumba, 114
Conell, a of Twaym Greny, 119.
—— ancestor of the E. of Tyrconnell, 43, 126, 127.
—— clogagh, 106.
—— Collawragh, 45.
—— Criowhan, 64, 72, 88, 172.
—— Cronndawna, 105
—— Gulban, 64, 76, 107, 172.
—— Guthbinn, 98.
—— Kearnagh, 49, 213
—— k of C., 57, 58.
—— k. of I., 101, 172
—— k of Scotland, 101, 115.
—— Loybrey, 98.
—— mᶜCowgall, 80, 89
—— mᶜCronnmoyle, 126.
—— mᶜDonnogh, 109.
—— mᶜEaghy, 211.
—— mᶜMoyle Duff, 100
—— mᶜNeale, 51, 92, 96
—— mᶜSwyne, k. of the D , 111.
—— mᶜSwynie, k. of M , 102
—— Meann, 113.
—— of Killskry, 142
—— son of Cowhagh k., 43
—— son of Coylerotha, 213
—— son of H. Slane, 104.
Conell's Weare, 247.
Cong, 218-220, 238
Congall, a. of Bangor, 75, 131
—— a of Slane, 129
—— Ceanmayor, 112
—— Clairingneagh, 46
—— Keannfoda, 108
—— Keyle, 103
—— k. of I., 101, 103, 172
—— k. of M., 110
—— k. of Scotland, 101
—— k. of U., 97, 101
—— Kymnajor, 101
—— mᶜMoyle Duff, 100

Congall, prince of Brey, 102.
Congallach, 116, 151, 152, 154-157
—— mᶜConnor, 168
—— mᶜConyng, 113.
—— mᶜMoylemilii, 151, 152, 154, 172.
—— mᶜMoylemorrey, 169
Congus, 114.
Conleas, a. of C., 113
Conley Crwackelgay, 210.
—— Keywe, 45.
Conly, b. of Kildare, 75
—— p. of Moyteaffa, 117, 124.
—— son of Artkir, 76
—— son of Conn C., 58, 59.
Conn Cedcahagh, 57-59, 61, 76, 166, 209.
—— house of, 46.
—— na mbocht, 99, 136, 180, 184.
Connaghtagh, 111.
Connall Chowe, 98.
—— kear, 97, 101.
—— k of Scotland, 80, 97.
Connannann, 149.
Connaught, 9, 12, 13, 15-17, 28, 30,
40, 43, 46-48, 51, 54, 64, 78, 81.
83-85, 97, 104, 111, 114, 118, 127,
132, 136, 138, 139, 143, 147-151,
154, 160, 162-164, 167, 168, 170,
171, 173, 177, 179, 182, 186-188,
192-194, 196-199, 202, 203, 204,
207, 213, 215-220, 223-225, 229,
231, 232, 235, 236, 238, 239, 241-
243, 245, 247-251, 253, 256, 261-
263, 265, 270-272, 277, 278, 281,
288, 290, 292-294, 297-299, 304-
306, 308-313, 315, 322, 326,
327.
—— kings of, 15, 28, 47, 57, 60, 72,
74, 79, 81, 83, 97, 101, 103, 109,
114, 115, 117, 119, 121-123, 126,
132, 133, 135, 137, 139, 142-144,
158, 160, 178, 182-185, 196, 198,
201-203, 206, 207, 215, 217-219,
221, 224, 227, 229-236, 239, 241,
243, 245, 247, 250, 252, 256, 258,
263, 265, 267, 268, 270, 271, 276,
278, 279, 281, 283, 284, 286, 287,
291, 293-299, 301, 304, 309, 322,
325 328.

Index. 341

Connaught, men of, 51, 54, 56, 77, 78, 132, 137, 143, 145, 149, 169, 181, 191, 221, 230, 243, 248, 251, 253, 270, 276, 290, 295, 297, 311, 320, 326.
—— rough third of, 122, 132.
Connell Clogagh, 106.
—— Eahtwar, 211.
—— k. of I , 172.
Connery, b. of, 79.
Connor, 212.
—— Auraroe, 49
—— k of I., 172.
—— mᶜD , k. of I , 115
—— mᶜDonnogh, k. of Meath, 128, 130, 131, 141
—— mᶜD o'Melaghlin, 133, 156.
—— mᶜKervell, 162, 163.
—— mᶜMoylekeyne, 151.
—— mᶜTeige, 116.
—— Moyle mᶜFuhie, 44.
—— o'Melaghlin, 132, 133, 135, 146.
—— son of Breassall, 212.
—— son of k. Donnogh, 128
—— son of k Faghtna, 47
—— son of Locheny, 115.
Conn's half *See* Leah Coyne.
Connraih mᶜDuffdaleah, 129.
Conolagh mᶜComyn, 123, 124.
—— mᶜConoy, 124.
Conquest of Ireland, 3, 43.
Conrado, emperor, 173, 194, 204.
Conrey (Connor), 75, 88, 105, 133, 157.
Conrie (in Meath), 120, 142.
Conry mᶜE , 48.
Constantine, emperor, 90, 103, 106
—— king, 106.
—— k. of Scotland, 115, 156, 163.
Constantinople, 76, 106.
Conulf, k of Saxons, 131.
Convackne, 228, 246, 248, 275, 277, 284.
Convall o'Locheny, 116
Convallo (Convoyle), 31, 32, 212.
—— k of Scotland, 72.
Convocation of the clergy, 203, 213, 241.
Convocation at Taragh, 124.

Conyng Begeglach, 37.
—— b of Eochie, 37.
—— grandson of Hugh S , 106, 126.
—— mᶜAwley, 117.
—— mᶜDon Cwan, 167
—— mᶜFewer, 14
—— mᶜKnoyle, 106, 109.
—— mᶜNeale G., 151
—— o'Daynt, 105.
Conynge mᶜFinn, 37.
Conyng's tower, 14.
Conyre, castle of, 271.
Coran *See* Corran
Corck, a. of Kildare, 115.
Corck mᶜFergus, 81.
Corckaghlan, 231, 311.
Corckbaeskynn, 129, 141, 167, 309.
Corcke, 211.
Corckymore (Cork), 138
Corcomroe, 30, 117, 175, 246, 302, 325.
Corcran Cleireagh, 173, 174, 176
Cork, 109, 131, 138, 144, 145, 182, 190.
—— island of, 131.
Corkelaye, 37.
Corkes, the two, 193.
Cormac, a. of C., 120, 142.
—— b. of Athdrumni, 118.
—— Cass, 211
—— Inderny, 74
—— Keigh, 78.
—— mᶜAllella, 112.
—— mᶜArt, 60.
—— mᶜCahallaine, 157
—— mᶜConn na mboght, 184, 188
—— mᶜCriowhan, 91.
—— mᶜCuilenann, 144, 145.
—— mᶜCuillenann, b. of Lismore, 147
—— mᶜEnos, 76.
—— mᶜMooney, 150.
—— mᶜo'Cuillennann, 145.
—— Mainisdreach, 185.
—— o'Haielealla, 155.
—— o'Liahan, 142.
Cormack, 91, 209
Corn, 169, 285, 293.

Cornan, a of Bangor, 110.
—— mᶜEahagh T , 88.
Cornie Conell, battle of, 103.
Corran, 42, 88, 100, 111, 173, 244, 273, 277, 279, 292.
Corre, 238.
Cosedge, a. of Louth, 120.
Cosgragh mᶜConnor, 48.
—— of Tehille, 142.
Cosmy, 169
Cossar, 133.
Cosse Warce, 151.
Costry Hemer, 134.
Couhagh, a. of Sayer, 130.
Councils, general, 106.
Courcy, Sir John. *See* De Courcy.
Cowarbs, 74, 107, 120, 148, 149, 157, 160, 163-165, 169, 171, 177, 178, 186, 188, 192, 195, 196, 197, 200, 201, 204, 205, 213, 214, 220, 224, 270, 310, 320.
Cowchongalt, 143
Cowchoullen, 48.
Cowchoylle mᶜDowleyn, 170
Cowcorb mᶜMoycorb, 55
Cowdaylye mᶜK , 167.
Cowdenagh mᶜF., 113.
Cowgall, a of Bangor, 94, 97, 131, 169
—— bishop, 99.
—— cowarbs of, 157, 169.
—— mᶜDawangort, 78.
—— pilgrim, 149.
Cowgan, John, 245.
—— mᶜCuthenna, 107.
—— Mather, 107.
Cowhagh, a. of Disert D., 181.
—— Koew, 211.
—— Koylebrey, 42-44, 210.
—— Minn, 42.
—— p. of Kildare, 180.
Cowkearky, 101
Cowkowran, 101.
Cowlagh more, dr. of o'Connor, 316.
Cowle Cahire, 29.
— Conery, 83.
— Innsyn, 88.
— Keallan, 102.
—— Lwachra, 217.

Cowleannan mᶜConnor, 175.
Cowlerayne, 269, 271.
Cownge of St. Fechin. *See* Cong.
Cowry mᶜDary, 47.
Coygenus of Glendalocha, 99.
Coylevotha, 213.
Coynrey, 142.
Credy, castle of, 114.
Credyn, 17.
Creg, 116.
Crega, 317.
Cregg, 116.
Crewhan, 71
Crewlasragh, 145
Cridan of Indroym, 103.
Crienna, 58, 59
Criohann, k. of I., 49, 64.
—— K. of M., 72
Criok Carbry, 236, 262, 275, 304.
Crioslagh, 133
Criowhann Cosgragh, 45.
—— Enna mᶜSeny, 102.
—— k. of Ireland, 64.
—— k of Leinster, 97.
—— k. of Munster, 72.
—— mᶜBriwyn, 84.
—— mᶜCarbry, 91.
—— mcEnna, 69, 73.
—— mᶜLoway, 49
—— mᶜNeale, 76.
—— Nia Nare, 209.
—— Skeihuell, 28.
Critan, a. of Beanchor, 108.
Crocke, W., 255.
Croinnis, 171.
Cronan Beag, 110.
—— b. of Indroym, 103.
—— mᶜOloye, 102.
—— mᶜSilny, 107
—— mᶜTygernye, 88
—— of Moyville, 104.
Cronmoyle, 67.
—— b. of Kildare, 149
—— mᶜColgann, 116
Crossan Fyn, 196.
Crossanaght, 196
Crosse na Skeaptra, 178
Crosses, the three at C., 175.
Crouantyne, 133
Crowhan mᶜBriwyn, 84.

Crown of Ireland, 3, 43, 46, 52, 68, 74, 161, 179.
Cruachan, 30, 46, 57, 273, 274.
Cruagh Patrick, 297
Cruinneachan, 93.
Crwyn Bagroye, 213.
Cuill-iro, 75.
Cumascach, 120.
Curaw, 97.
Curr cluana, 204.
Curragh Kinetty, 317.
Cusack, Adam, 254.
Cusacks, 253, 324.
Cushen, David, 241.
Cwan, k. of Munster, 104.
—— mᶜConnell, 104.
—— o'Lochan, 173, 174.
Cwanagh mᶜCailcin, 103.
—— mᶜEigny, 123
—— p. of Mackwaises, 103.
Cwangus, a. of Leihmore, 119
Cwillen mᶜEtigen, 164.
Cwircke, 211
Cwirckny, 125, 182
Cwymka mᶜCathmoa, 73.
Cymboye, 40
Cynath, 172
—— mᶜAwalgie, 189.
—— son of Malcolme, 163.
Cynay mᶜConying, 136.
—— mᶜCorbry, 150.
Cyndealvan mᶜMoyleron, 148.

Dachra Lwachra, 105.
Dachwa mᶜDavid, 117
Dahye mᶜFiachragh, 64, 171
Da Inver, 113.
Dairmhagh   *See* Dorowe
Daiwinis (Devenish), 105, 137, 143
Dalagh mᶜMortaugh, 142
Dalasse MacWinge, 103.
Dalgaisse, 155, 158, 159, 196, 201, 202.
Dalnary, 54, 141, 144, 149, 157, 213
—— kings of, 63, 66, 91, 100.
Dalriada, 14, 89, 90, 100, 101, 114-116, 123, 124, 127, 160.
—— kings of, 89, 103, 108, 133, 160.

Dalton, Hubert, 324
—— Miles, 325
—— Morish, 321
—— Philip, 306
Daltons, 308, 312, 325
Dalviagha, 50.
Damasus, pope, 106.
Dan, tribe of, 21
Danes, 3, 7, 116, 127-167, 170, 171, 174, 175, 178-181, 183, 187, 188, 190, 192-196, 202, 205, 214, 258.
Daniel, a. of Gleandalogha, 142.
—— k. of Leinster, 115.
—— mᶜLurckan, 162
—— mᶜTwahallain, 106
—— of Kingary, 105.
Darchill mᶜC., 109.
Dardany, 75.
Darearca, 75.
Darensie, 131
Dartry, 30, 253
Darynna, 53
Dauinis, 137, 300
David Breathnagh, 222
—— k. of Israel, 22.
—— mᶜCarill, 90.
—— mᶜConell, k. of U., 80
—— mᶜKellaye, a. of Cashel, 244
—— mᶜMoyle Colme, 204
—— St., of Inverdoyle, 103
—— St , of Kilmoney, 91.
David's, b. of St., 207
Dawangart, k. of Scotland, 72, 88.
—— mᶜDonnell, 108
—— mᶜNissie, 74.
—— son of Aidan, 96.
Dawdachrich, 117.
Dawinis, 143, 147, 300.
Dawyn mᶜD , 89
De Captionibus Hiberniæ, 3.
De Clare, Richard, 281
—— Thomas, 252, 256.
De Courcy, John, 92, 214, 216, 217, 220, 266
De Exeter, John, 306, 316.
—— Jordan, 239, 242, 266, 306.
—— Meyler, 279, 290, 316
—— Stephen, 277.
—— Symon, 254.
De la Grosse, R., 207, 214.

344 Index.

De la Rochelle, P., 254.
—— Sir W., 255.
De Lacy, Hugh, 216, 217, 220, 221, 223, 228.
—— Hugh the younger, 217, 220, 229, 236.
—— Robert, 221.
—— Walter, 223, 229, 236, 237.
—— William, 228, 229, 223, 234, 237.
Dea, 37.
Dealvoye, 18.
Deane of London, the, 241.
Dearky, b., 106.
Deatha, 210.
Dedimus O'Foirvhen, 147.
Deilginis, 115.
Deine, 76.
Deirg, 211.
Deirghyne, 211.
Deirgne Mogoroge, 170
Dela mᶜLoich, 15.
Delamere, Sir J , 258
Delameres, 258.
Delna, battle of, 76.
Delphin, John, 248.
Deluge, the, 10, 12.
Delvin, 117, 170, 182, 186, 192, 219, 225, 226, 229.
—— Beathra, 132, 133, 136, 165, 178, 184, 194.
—— mᶜCoghlan, 176, 178, 227, 244, 245, 255.
—— More, 187, 205.
—— Nwagat, 120, 130.
Deman, 72.
—— mᶜCarill, 84, 89
Dempster, T , 96.
Denmark, 134, 148, 151, 166, 192, 244.
Deputy, 222-225, 230-233, 236, 239, 245, 247, 249-251, 256, 257, 261, 269, 299, 327, 328.
Dercylus, 27.
Derghine, k. of M., 55.
Derie places, 177.
Derills, 114.
Dermot, a. of Fernes, 142.
—— a. of Hy, 132.
—— chief, 131.
—— Duffe mᶜD., 121.

Dermot, k. of C., 116.
—— k. of I., 72, 101, 172.
—— mᶜClothny, 123.
—— mᶜConyng, 136
—— mᶜDermott, 142
—— MᶜEbergell, 142.
—— mᶜHugh S., 102, 103, 106, 107, 126, 131.
—— mᶜKervall, k. of O., 149.
—— mᶜKervell, k. of I., 78-91, 103, 106, 124, 172.
—— mᶜMagnus, 238.
—— mᶜMorrogh, 192-199, 201, 202, 205-8.
—— mᶜMoylenemo, 176-180.
—— mᶜNeale, 132
—— mᶜSymon ne T., 272.
—— mᶜTeige, 187.
—— mᶜThorpa, 156.
—— mᶜTomalty, 135.
—— o'Laghtna, 165.
—— o'Moyletelcha, 169.
—— primate of Armagh, 140.
—— Roe, 263
Derrie of Lough Con, 324.
Derry, 94. 135, 164, 188, 253, 281, 282.
Dervail, dr. of mᶜD., 214.
—— dr. of M. mᶜD., 303.
—— dr. of o'Donnell, 293.
—— dr. of o'Melaghlin, 214.
Dervorgill, dr. of o'C., 267, 275, 298.
—— dr. of o'Melaghlin, 199, 206, 214.
—— q. of I., 49, 187.
—— wife of o'Connor Roe, 312.
—— wife of o'Donnell, 275, 279.
Derycalgie. See Derry.
Derye, 253.
Derymelly, 130.
Deryndoyne, 241.
Desert Dermott. See Dysert D.
Desies, in Munster, 42, 108, 152, 167, 222.
—— kings of, 108, 111, 147, 167.
Desmond, 199, 202, 259, 300, 315.
—— countess of, 315.
—— earls of, 299, 315, 319, 320, 323.

Index. 345

Desmond, princes of, 123, 129, 233, 258, 260, 300, 315
Devenish. *See* Daiwinis.
Deverden, John, 243, 244, 251
—— Nicoll, 249
Deyne, 210.
Dicolla mᶜMenedi, 119.
Dieaghladhrye, 210.
Dihorba mᶜDimaine, 38, 39, 40.
Dillon, Dabuck, 298.
—— Ulick, 298.
Dimma, b., 106.
Dinngall mᶜFerall, 139
Dinrye, 44.
Diocletian, 77.
Dionitius, 77.
Dirry. *See* Derry.
Diseases, 123, 126, 198, 275, 285, 324.
Disert-da-crich, 252.
Dochat, St., 137
Dochonna, St., 128.
Docus, b , 72.
Dolor gentilium, 156
Dombarr, earl of, 167.
Domdahoile, 143.
Dominick, St., 241, 245.
Domitian, 50.
Don, 23, 25.
Donall, k of Picts, 106.
Donaskiagh, 88, 171
Donawley, 142, 144.
Doncearmna, 28, 32.
Donchann mᶜMoyletoyly, 139
Doncowole Sirville, 35.
Doncwan mᶜFlanagan, 146.
Doneagha mᶜO., 110.
Donel Break, 104, 109, 110.
—— br. of k. D., 147
—— God, 174
—— k. of I , 80, 88, 89, 90, 97, 102, 105, 115-119, 121, 122, 172
—— k of Meath, 185.
—— k. of S., 97, 106, 115.
—— Kloen, 158, 159, 160.
—— mᶜCahall, 101, 148, 168.
—— mᶜCeallay, 114.
—— mᶜDermott, 167.
—— mᶜDonnogh, 187.
—— mᶜDuff Davercann, 168

Donel mᶜEarcka, 79, 83, 97.
—— mᶜEvin mᶜC., 167
—— mᶜFlathnia, 126
—— mᶜFlynn, 146, 147, 150, 155.
—— mᶜFynn, 155.
—— mᶜHugh, k. of Ireland, 100, 101, 103, 107.
—— mᶜHugh, k. of the north, 123, 128.
—— mᶜHugh, p. of Aileagh, 145.
—— mᶜLorckan, 160.
—— mᶜMoregan, 143.
—— mᶜMoylemoray, 157.
—— mᶜMurtagh, 157
—— mᶜSeanchan, 175.
—— mᶜTiernan, 182
—— mᶜTuloge, 170.
—— mᶜTwahallan, 106.
—— o'Cannan, 163.
—— o'Neale, k. of I., 157, 158, 172.
—— of Meath, 119.
—— son of k. Hugh, 145.
—— son of mᶜEarka, 79, 83, 97
—— son of Neale, 145.
Dongalie, 144
Dongall mᶜDereth, 122
Dongolman, ford of, 205
Dongomer, Robert, 225
Donkearmna *See* Doncearmna
Donkware, 129.
Donlaith, 152.
Donleith glasse, 152.
Donleo, 191, 218.
Donmore, 200, 202, 232, 275.
Donnaganis, 155.
Donne Sgyath, 171.
Donnell, 212
—— Ballagh, 209.
Donnogh, b of C., 152.
—— k of Connaught, 115, 122.
—— k. of Ireland, 115, 123, 126, 127, 128, 148, 172.
—— k. of Moybrey, 175.
—— k. of Munster, 115
—— k of Scotland, 97, 101
—— k. of Taragh, 128.
—— k. of Ulster, 97.
—— mᶜAllene, 123.
—— mᶜBrenan, 149.

346 *Index*

Donnogh mᶜBryan B , 3, 168, 170, 173, 174, 175, 177, 179
—— mᶜCeallaghan, 158.
—— mᶜDonnell, 115.
—— mᶜDonnell, k. of L., 164.
—— mᶜDonnell, k. of M., 155.
—— mᶜDonnell o'M., 155
—— mᶜDonnell Reawar, 184.
—— mᶜDowlen, k. of L., 176.
—— mᶜDuff D., 143.
—— mᶜFlynn, k. of I., 146, 147, 150.
—— mᶜFlynn o'M , 146.
—— mᶜGillemocholmocke, 193.
—— mᶜHugh, 315.
—— mᶜMelaghlin, 152.
—— mᶜMoyledwyn, 143.
—— mᶜNeale, 147, 148, 149.
—— mᶜRory, 276.
—— mᶜSolowann, 139.
—— nephew of Ronan, 108
—— son of Donnell, 121, 122.
—— son of Hugh S , 104, 105
Donnslewie, 236.
Donoman, castle of, 270, 323.
Donouer, 266.
Donowan mᶜDowlen, 168.
Donsoghlyn, 69.
Donsovarke, 28, 32, 36, 148.
Dontaise, 186.
Donum Dei, b. of Meath, 231
Doors of the nobility, 85.
Dorowe, 91, 95, 96, 121, 132, 135, 149, 155, 170, 176, 178, 180, 182, 186, 193, 196, 200, 205, 227, 233.
—— abbots of, 127, 130, 136.
Dorymlehan, 32.
Dowangart, 96.
Dowchowley, dr of k. of C., 183.
—— dr. of o'C , 308.
—— q. of I., 214.
Dowdaleah, 127.
Dowdall, James, 249
Dowdavorean, 157.
Dowdy, b., 300.
Dowen *See* Downpatrick.
Dowgean, 133, 158.
Dowgill, 180
Dowhagh, 157.
Dowhowly, 187.
Dowinis, 300.

Dowleeke, 73, 130, 142, 147, 148, 156
Dowlen mᶜCarbry, 145.
—— mᶜTwahall, 168.
Dowhh mᶜSealvay, 149
Dowlitter, priest of Armagh, 147.
Dowlittye, a. of Finglasse, 124, 127
Dowmreaght, 115
Down. *See* Downpatrick.
Downacha mᶜL , 148
Downagh, k. of I., 154.
—— mᶜE., 156.
—— of Disert, k., 157.
Downaghmore, 307.
Downaghmoyen, 133.
Downaghpatrick, 156, 163.
Downan, archb. of Dublin, 181, 188.
Downdealgan, 268.
Downedaleathglasse, 214, 220, 243.
Downoman, 270.
Downpatrick, 92, 156, 243.
Downsoghlin, 174.
Downsy, q. of I , 102.
Dowrancha, 28.
Dowslany, 174.
Dragons, 116, 118.
Dregtus, 108.
Dreivne, 76.
Drew, David, 239.
—— Matthew, 261.
Driwymkoylinn, 141.
Drocheda, 15.
Dromadery, 114.
Drombrey, 76.
Dromcleive, 149, 236, 241, 242, 275, 279
Dromdeargye, 75.
Dromkehaire, 90.
Dromkleichy, 84.
Dromleahglaissy, 90, 214
Dromlyas, 300.
Drom mᶜEircke, 89
Dromrahie, 155.
Dromrovay, 120.
Drost, 112.
Drostus, 109.
Drought, 118, 152, 244
Droym mᶜAwley, 133.

Index. 347

Droymbethy, 28.
Droymtınyn, 28.
Drumleahan, 314.
Drust, k. of Picts, 113, 114.
—— mᶜErb, k of Picts, 71
Dublin, 58, 59, 63, 68, 124, 137, 138, 140, 142, 144, 146–148, 150–154, 156, 158–161, 163–165, 168, 170, 175, 180, 181, 183, 185, 186, 192, 193, 201, 205, 213, 214, 222, 223, 225, 227, 256, 299, 300, 304.
Duchna of Balla, 102.
Duffagh, a. of Armagh, 75.
—— father of St B., 76.
—— mᶜMoyletoylye, 142.
—— mᶜTagaine, 163.
Duffcomar, 62.
Duffdamver mᶜConolay, 114.
Duffdakrick mᶜD., 113.
Duffdalehe, 164.
Duffdavorean, a of Fower, 117.
—— a. of Clonard, 127.
Duff Doyne, 108, 145.
Duffe, 213.
Duffeinreaght, k. of C., 122.
—— mᶜFergus, 124.
Duffelaghtna, 115.
Duffslat o'Freana, 84.
Duleek. See Dowleeke.
Dunatt, 116.
Dunbolge, 97.
Duncha mᶜOrckdy, 110.
Dunchus, archb of Dublin, 186.
Dundalk, 281, 283, 299.
Dungall, k. of Ossory, 115.
—— k. of Scotland, 115
—— son of Sealuy, 116
Dunlen, k. of Leinster, 115.
—— k. of Ossory, 115
Dunmasse (Dunamaise), 139.
Dunmore, 193, 275.
Dunstan, St., 160.
Durlesse, 164
Durrowe. See Dorowe.
Dwagh Dalta Dea, 37, 46, 47, 211.
—— Finn, 212.
—— Galy, 69
—— Layer, 38
—— mᶜFiaghy, 38.
—— Teangowa, 72, 74.

Dyan Kight, 17.
Dyeing, 32.
Dyman Ara, 130.
Dymma, b. of Conrye, 105.
Dymsach, 120.
Dyrath, 110.
Dyrry. See Derry
Dysert Dermott, 139, 143, 181, 325.
—— Kieran, 156, 157.

Eacha mᶜNeyrck, 119.
Eachie Bo. See Achabo
Eachroyme See Achroym O'M.
Eachye Gairve, 211.
—— mᶜArdgar, 159.
—— mᶜDawny, 167.
—— Seolmoy, 42.
Eaghagh Finn, 96.
—— Foltleahan, 210.
—— mᶜBlathmack, 105.
Eaghdroym See Achroym O'M.
Eaght, dr. of o'Connor, 221.
Eaghtge. See Sliew E.
Eaghye, 211.
—— Baliderg, 211
—— Bwagaye, 210.
—— Gairve, 211.
—— Warcheasse, 212
Eahagh, 209.
—— Boye, 101
—— Cova, 213.
—— Finn, 96
—— mᶜBreassall, 118.
Ealgagh o'Moyleoyer, 117.
Ean, 29
Earck, b. of Slane, 75
Earl, the Red. See Burke
Earlahy, b. of Armagh, 72
Earny, the river of, 319.
Earthquake, 67. 72, 75, 107, 109.
Easawyn Eawna, 210.
Easroe, 15, 39, 137, 187, 188, 196, 230, 261, 277, 320, 321.
Easse-da-chonne, 273.
Easter, feast of, 99.
Eastmeath, 51, 185.
Eave, dr. of mᶜMurrogh, 208.
Eawyn-Vacha, 31, 38, 41, 44, 46, 89, 131

Ebdon, k. of Denmark, 244.
Ebrick, the sons of, 292.
Ebricke mcIr, 28, 32, 213.
Echtgen, 89
Echtygerne mcM., 213.
Eclipse, 141, 173.
Edenburrogh, 149.
Edersgel More, 48.
Edgen o'Mathgna, 113.
Ednagh Downe, 286.
Edulfe, 145.
Edward I., k. of E., 27, 244, 249, 252, 253, 261, 262.
—— II , 285
—— III., 285, 300, 301, 306.
—— k of the Saxons, 148.
Egbricht, 114.
Egechar, a. of Lynally, 142.
Egertagh, 175.
Eghtgie. *See* Sliew E.
Eghtigerne mcBroyne, 176.
—— mcFlanncha, 147.
—— son of Kennedy, 155.
Eghtigin, b., 120.
Egypt, 10, 19, 22, 23, 44.
Egyptians, 19-22.
Ehan mcUga, 28, 29.
Eighneach mcColgan, 113.
Eihine Wahagh, 73.
—— d. of k. Hugh, 146.
—— dr. of o'Swarte, 169.
—— m. of St. Columbkill, 92.
—— queen of I , 156.
—— queen of Leinster, 127.
Eihnie, the, 29
Eihyn, dr. of k Eochy F., 47.
Eilny mcScannaile, 110.
Eirck, 209.
Eirrick, 323.
Eithreoile, 210.
Elbrig, 126.
Eldeaa, 212.
Elie, 89, 118
—— o'Karoll, 169, 173, 178, 193, 196, 255, 280.
—— princes of, 121, 170, 220, 280, 306, 307, 309, 322, 327.
Elim Olfinsneachty, 36.
Elly, k. of the Saxons, 101.
Elphines, k. of the Picts, 114.

Elpin of Glassnayen, 120.
Elym mcConragh, 50
Emptor, 68.
England, 27, 43, 68, 70, 90, 91, 92, 96, 104, 111, 116, 120, 121, 127, 128, 151, 160, 171, 179, 184, 192, 194, 206, 214-216, 219, 220, 222-224, 228-230, 236, 237, 240, 244, 246, 247, 249-251, 259, 260, 285.
—— kings of, 27, 70, 120, 121, 128, 151, 185, 192, 204, 219, 223, 224, 228, 237, 238, 244, 246, 249, 250, 253, 258, 260, 261, 268, 283, 284, 289, 292, 299, 300, 302, 306, 322, 323.
English, 3, 8, 9, 69, 171, 208, 214, 216, 217, 219-223, 228, 229, 231, 233, 236-8, 240, 242-249, 251, 252, 254, 255, 257, 261-263, 265, 266, 268, 270-272, 275-277, 279-282, 284-290, 292, 293, 296, 298-301, 303-309, 311, 313, 320, 321-323, 325-327.
Enna Argheagh, 33.
—— Ayneagh, 45, 210.
—— Derig, 212.
—— mcCathfie, 71.
—— Moneheoyn, 211.
—— o'Loingsye, 90.
—— son of Neale, 64.
—— the Red, 37.
Enoch, son of Jareth, 11, 20.
Enos, *alias* mcNisie, 75.
—— a Pict, 114.
—— br. of Moriegh, 137.
—— G., 213.
—— Gaybwaifeagh, 61
—— k. of Munster, 71.
—— k. of Picts, 114, 119.
—— k. of Scotland, 72, 115, 120.
—— mcAngussa, 149
—— mcCarrhie Calman, 165, 169.
—— mcColman, 98, 100
—— mcConloingsie, 156.
—— mcDonnogh, 154.
—— mcFlaynn, 145
—— mcFergos, 116, 120.
—— mcMoylebryde, 156.
—— m'Naofreigh, 69, 73.
—— Magawley, 91.

Index. 349

Enos of Ulster, 107.
—— Ollow, 44.
—— Olmoye, 33.
—— o'Moyledorie, 157.
—— son of Eochy F., 76.
—— son of Seth, 11, 21.
—— Twyrmeagh, 45, 210, 211.
Enoy mᶜEloysie, 83, 89.
Enuotha, 210.
Eoanan mᶜTwahallam, 105.
Eochagann, 115.
Eochy Altleahan, 45.
—— Ancheann, 53.
—— Bway, 41.
—— Boye, 97.
—— Dowlen, 41, 63, 209.
—— Edgohach, 32.
—— Eigeann, 31.
—— Fewerglass, 32, 33, 212.
—— Feyleagh, 47, 48, 209.
—— Fiemoyne, 37.
—— Finn, 55, 56, 59, 76, 96.
—— Gunnall, 60.
—— Gwyneagh, 73.
—— Jarlaly, 107.
—— k. of I., 80, 88, 172.
—— k. of Munster, 72
—— k. of Scotland, 101, 115.
—— mᶜConley, 72.
—— mᶜEirck, 16, 17.
—— mᶜEnna Kinsealy, 64, 296.
—— mᶜLughta, 47, 203.
—— mᶜMorey, 71
—— mᶜOillealla, 38.
—— mᶜOwgany, 42.
—— Moymean, 63, 64.
—— Moiuo, 33.
—— Oireaw, 48.
—— Ophagh, 36.
—— Tyrncharna, 72.
Eoganaght, 150.
—— of Cashel, 175, 182, 202.
—— of Loghlein, 167, 189.
Eogawyne, 210.
Eogroym o'Manie. *See* Achroym.
Eolbeck, 114
Ephesus, 52, 106
Ephraim, tribe of, 21.
Erard mᶜCoyssie, 161, 162.
Erck, 72.

Ere, q. of the Tuatha de D., 18, 23, 26.
Ere, son of Heber, 28, 30.
Eremon, k. of S., 115.
Erick, 198.
Ernagh mᶜEhinn, 122.
Ernany mᶜCressine, 102.
—— mᶜF., 101.
Esker Riada, 58.
Essre, son of Gathelus, 20, 210.
Etayn mᶜElly, 100.
Ethelbald, 120.
Ethelfrith, 97, 99, 102, 108.
Ethrial, 31.
Etigen, 174
Ettymon, k. of the Saxons, 154.
Etwynn, battle of, 101.
Eudoxius, 106
Eugenell, q. of I., 128.
Eugenius III., pope, 204.
Euphalus, 27.
Europe, 12, 130, 204.
Eusebius, 10.
Eustaces, 30.
Eutices, 126.
Eutitian heretics, 75.
Euticianus, b. of Rome, 61.
Evlyne, battle of, 77.
Excommunication, 130, 202, 218, 222, 224.
Extreme Unction, 171, 208, 224, 234, 289, 304.

Faailt, 200.
Faghtna Fahagh, 47, 48, 101.
—— Lector, 174.
—— mᶜFolaghtaine, 114.
Fachtnagh, a. of Fower, 124.
Fagarthach, 101.
Failan mᶜColman, 102.
Failge, sons of, 276.
—— Richard, 276
Failve, a of Hy, 108, 109.
—— father of St. Manchan, 107.
—— Flannfivay, 100
—— Flaynn, 100, 102.
—— Ilchoraye, 212.
—— k. of M., 97.
—— mᶜEahagh, 101.
Fair of Tailten, 146, 148.

Fair of Tireaylealla, 318
Fallawyn, Flann, 231.
Faltagh, b. of Meath, 306.
Famine, 111, 121, 122, 219, 293
Fanaid, 83, 253, 322.
Far iomchar ne honchen, 278
Farannan, p. of Armagh, 140.
Farcha, battle of, 140.
Farnoy, 194.
Fartalo, 89.
Faruley, 124.
Fasagh, 318.
—— Koylle, 281.
Fasteus, 20.
Fatha, 133.
Fathye, 213.
Faylann, k. of L., 97.
Feagna, 28.
Feann, k. of Ossory, 101.
Fear, 137.
Fearaagh, 116.
Fearadagh mᶜRossa, 72.
Fearagh, 32.
—— mᶜTwahallan, 110.
Fearbill, 186.
Fearchair mᶜD., 97.
Fearcorb, 44, 45, 211.
Fear-Dacrich, 122.
Feardownagh o'Mooney, 156
Fearga, 72
Feargna, 30.
Fearkiall. See Ferkeall.
Fearlio, 120.
Fearna. See Fernes.
Fearnmoy, 167
Fearnoy, 191
Fearny, 103.
Fearta Coarban, 74.
Feartullagh, 121, 168, 170, 198
Fearty Nevie, 165
Feawyne, battle of, 101.
Fechin, St , 107, 165, 178, 197, 201, 218, 219, 220, 224
Fehyn, p. of Armagh, 141
Feirst, battle of, 107.
Feis Taragh, 34, 52, 59, 71, 72
Feldova, 111.
Felimie, 212
Felix, pope, 72, 73, 77.
Felym, k. of Ireland, 76.

Felym, k. of M., 71, 81, 115.
—— mᶜCriowhan, 130-138, 140.
—— mᶜTygerny, 91.
—— Reaghtwar, 54, 55, 57, 59, 76, 96, 209.
Fenechus, 280.
Fentagh of Tymonna, the, 309.
Feoir. See Nore.
Feragh Feaghtnagh, 50.
—— mᶜDwagh, 89
—— son of Sealuy, 116.
Ferall, k. of Connaught, 101.
—— k. of Ireland, 113, 115, 121.
—— k. of Scotland, 101.
—— mᶜAnmcha, 128.
—— mᶜConyng, 165.
—— mᶜEahagh Leawna, 113.
—— mᶜElay, 123
—— mᶜLorckan, 160.
—— o'Haylyeaghty, 113
—— o'Royrck, 158, 167.
Feranan, 25.
Ferannedaragh, 287.
Feray Finnaghtny, 209
Ferdonagh, 114.
Ferdoronagh, 140
Ferdownagh mᶜF., 149.
Fergall, k. of O., 115.
—— mᶜM., 101, 112.
Fergus, 116
—— b. of Dromleaglaissy, 90.
—— br of Connell, 92.
—— Ceannada, 76.
—— Dowdedagh, 60.
—— Fortawyle, 45.
—— G., 213.
—— Glutt, 117.
—— Keruel, 72, 88
—— k. of Connaught, 115, 139.
—— k. of Dalriada, 115
—— k. of Ireland, 80, 88, 89, 172.
—— k. of Scotland, 26, 27, 72, 115.
—— k of Spain's son, 59.
—— Knoy, 42
—— Leahdearg, 14.
—— mᶜCahall, 124.
—— mᶜCanyne, 60.
—— mᶜEarcka, 79, 83.
—— mᶜEothy, 116
—— mᶜKeallay, 118, 119

Fergus mᶜMoynaye, 117.
—— mᶜNellyne, 89, 90.
—— more mᶜEarcka, 74.
—— o'Heoaine, 113.
—— Reyne, 42
—— son of Aidan, 212.
—— son of Eochy Moymean, 64.
—— son of k. Donell, 105.
—— son of k. of I., 26.
—— son of mᶜEarcka, 79.
—— son of Neale, 92.
—— son of Owgany, 42.
—— son of Ragally, 105.
Fergussa, 209.
Ferith mᶜFoholan, 104.
Ferkeall, 51, 59, 157, 169, 184, 186, 191, 196, 199, 225, 226, 228, 233, 243, 307, 308, 311.
—— princes of, 147, 148, 157, 170, 180, 193, 246, 278, 313, 322, 323.
Fermanagh, 216, 253, 259, 282, 289, 291, 292, 300, 301, 302, 306, 316.
Fernes, 130, 136, 138, 207.
—— abbots of, 100, 105, 106, 119, 124, 143.
—— bishops of, 110, 112, 229.
Ferone, 28, 30.
Ferrus Mersey, 226.
Fertas Camsa, 188.
Fertgedye, 254.
Fertullagh. *See* Feartullagh.
Fevin, battle of, 70.
Fewes, the, 287.
Fiacha, 213
—— Araye, 213
—— Finawnus, 213.
—— Finn, 50.
—— Finnolay, 50.
—— Fionnsgohagh, 33.
—— Firvara, 45.
—— Keannan, 16.
—— Lawrynne, 32.
—— mᶜNeill, 51, 64, 74, 75, 91, 314.
—— o'Huiday, 84.
—— Scraptine, 62, 63.
—— Swyn, 59.
Fiachra Ayney, 78, 241.
—— Cassan, 50.

Fiachra mᶜBoydon, 89.
—— mᶜCahell, 126.
—— mᶜGarvan, 118.
—— o'Macnya 119.
—— son of Eochy M., 64.
Fiachras, 120.
Fiagh mᵃNeale, 266.
Fiagha, 35, 213.
—— Finsgothy, 33, 213.
—— Keannann, 16.
—— k of Ossory, 115.
—— mᶜDelvoye, 18, 24.
—— Tolgaye, 210.
Fiaghna, k. of O., 115.
—— k. of S., 97, 115.
—— k. of U., 97, 127, 143
—— mᶜBoydan, 96, 97, 100
—— mᶜDemaine, 100.
—— mᶜHeremon, 115.
—— mᶜHugh Royne, 118.
Fianatha, 288
Fiangalach o'Moyleaghlin, 117.
Fie Finoigh, 314.
—— Gaiule, 314.
—— Ike, 276, 327.
Fiedorow, 296.
Fiegann mᶜTorvie, 136.
Fighna, k. of U., 127.
Figinty, 104.
Fihellagh mᶜFlyn, 110
Finaghtye *See* Fineaghty.
Finan, a. of Cloneis, 123.
Finchaa, 213.
Finchar, 147.
Fine, a. of Kildare, 129.
Fine fomores. *See* Fomoraghes
Fineaghty, k. of I., 54, 101, 108-110, 172.
—— son of O. Fodla, 35.
Fingall, 134, 159, 194.
Finglas, 128, 142.
Fingonie o'Molloy, 147.
Fingvyne, k. of M., 111.
Finian. *See* Fynian.
Finn mᶜBaicke, 44.
—— mᶜBraha, 37.
—— mᶜCoyle, 61, 62.
Finn, the, 13.
Finnawla, k. of L. 109.
Finnawragh, 174.

Finnell mᶜRosse, 47.
Finnie, 103.
Finnin mᶜFiachra, 99.
Finnya mᵉWiheulla, 84.
Finola, dr of o'Connor, 258.
—— dr. of o'Kelly, 307.
—— dr. of o'Madden, 322.
—— ny Melaghlen, 256.
—— w. of o'Connor, 290.
Finsneaghty, 108–110.
—— mᶜKeallay, 129.
Fintan, 11, 12.
—— mᶜIntrewe, 99
—— of Tymonna, 102.
—— St., of Clonenagh, 98.
Finnyn's well, 99
Fire, mount of, 204.
Firvolge, 3, 14–17.
Fitzgerald. Garrett, 319.
—— Gerald Suckagh, 244, 290.
—— Sir John, 320.
—— mᶜGerald, 241, 245, 255, 256, 258, 267.
—— mᶜMorish, 235, 236, 238, 239, 241, 290, 294.
—— Morish, 208, 235, 238.
—— Morish Fitzt., 299.
—— Morish mᶜG, 241, 249.
—— Morish mᶜJ. Roe, 293.
—— Morish Roe, 246.
—— Morish, son of E. of D., 323.
—— Morish the bald, 256.
—— Thomas Fitzmorris, 223, 249.
Fitzpatrick, Keallagh, 309.
—— Melaghlen, 303.
—— William, 322.
Fitzstephen, R., 206, 207, 214.
Fitz Urse, Sir R., 207.
Fivagh, 120
Flaihvertagh mᶜL , 101.
Flaithnia mᶜK., 129.
Flaithvertagh, k. of Cashel, 145.
—— mᶜConnor, 157.
—— mᶜLoyngsy, 101, 121, 172.
—— O'Kannan, 163.
—— son of Mortagh mᶜN , 155.
Flann, a. and b., 126.
—— Feaula, 112.
—— Feorna, 117
—— Follawyn, 231.

Flann, k. of I., 172.
—— k. of Munster, 128.
—— lector, 178.
—— mᶜConying, 142.
—— mᶜFlynn, 154.
—— mᶜMoyleroyrie, 140.
—— mᶜMoylescaghlyn, 116, 143–147, 155.
—— mᶜMoylescaghlyn God, 177.
—— mᶜRogellye, 113.
—— mᶜTyrnie, 144.
—— o'Colla, a. of C., 114.
—— o'Congoghe, 119.
—— o'Fagan, 170.
—— o'Konoly, 117.
—— o'Moylemihie, 158.
Flann, q. of Aileagh, 151.
Flannagan mᶜAlchon, 156.
—— o'Riagan, 147.
Flanngearg, 111.
Flangus mᶜLoyngsy, 131.
Flathry, k. of C , 116.
—— mᶜDonnell, 123
Flathy, k. of C., 123.
Flayhenn, 184.
Fleets, Danish, 136, 185, 194.
Fleming, Adam, 253
Flodricus, emperor, 138.
Foala. *See* Fodhla
Fobhair. *See* Fower.
Fobreagh, 75.
Fobrie. *See* Fower
Focas, emperor, 98.
Fodhla, 18, 26.
Fogartagh, 172.
—— Finn, 179.
—— mᶜKelly, 145.
—— p. of Elye, 120.
Fohagh mʳConell, 84.
Fohartagh macNeale, 113.
—— mᶜSwyny, 144.
Foharte, 117, 194.
Fohertye, 325.
Fohertyes, 56, 221.
Foilge Merrye, 75.
Folinn mʳConan, 99
Folla, 210.
Follawyn mʳConchongailt, 122.
Folorg, 112.
Folva Foda, a. of C , 99

Fomaltagh, k. of S., 115.
Fomoraghes, 14, 15, 17, 31, 32, 36, 282.
Fomore, 213.
Foradruyn, 103.
Forannan, a. of Armagh, 136, 139.
—— a. of Clonard, 118.
—— a. of Kildare, 111.
—— bishop, 122.
—— primate, 140.
Forbasach mcAileala, 117
—— mcMoyle Tola, 123.
—— p. of Bowyne, 113.
Ford of Conell's Weare, 247.
—— of the two virtues, 130.
Fordroyne, 162.
Forgie, the, 240.
Foriron, a. of C., 110
Forolve, 149.
Fortulfe Asalftand, 149.
Fostering, 41.
Fothy Argheagh, 62.
—— Cairpreagh, 62.
Fothyes, 62.
Fower (Fore), 83, 107, 117, 119, 122, 124, 126, 132, 142, 215
Fox. *See* o'Fox.
—— Connor, 231.
—— Donogh, 323.
—— Neale, k. of Teaffa, 234, 278.
—— Neale Roe, 257.
—— Owen, tanist, 308.
—— sons of, 323.
Foxes' country, 62, 125, 183, 198, 200, 308, 323.
Foylan, k. of Leinster, 101, 103, 110.
—— k. of Ossory, 101, 105, 115.
—— mcColman, 100, 107
—— mcMoreay, 148, 152.
—— o'Broyn, k. of L., 116.
Foylcha, 97
Foylchor o'Moylower, 110.
Foyldio, 42
Foyliow, a of Hy, 112.
Foyngen, 16
Foyrie *See* Fower.
France, 63, 68, 123, 207
—— kings of, 42, 105, 130, 138, 175, 194, 207, 228, 249, 268, 284, 285, 292, 299

Fraynes, family of, 258
Freawynn, 74, 102.
Frenchmen, 68, 185.
Friars Minors, 237.
—— Preachers, 241, 245, 250, 251, 254, 262.
Frost, 90, 91, 131, 157.
Fruits, abundance of, 120.
Fulartagh, b. of Clonard, 123.
Fulmann, 28.
Furney, the, 248.
Furseus, a. of Eacha mcN., 119.
—— a. of Leakyn, 119.
Fursie, St., 100, 105, 123.
Fwadagh, king of C., 97.
Fyher, d. of k. Twahall, 53.
Fynagha, 300.
Fynaghty, k. of C., 116.
—— k. of L., 115.
Fynan, a of Clonard, 81, 93, 163, 195.
—— a. of Cloneis, 123.
—— a. of Moybile, 93
Fynglass. *See* Finglas
Fynian Arannan, 109.
—— mcRivea, b , 105
—— St., 163.
Fynn, a Dane, 133
—— son of Roynie Roe, 209.
Fynnachan mcCosgray, 131.
Fynnaghty Fleagh, 108.
Fynnawragh, 174.
Fynnban, a of Clonbronay, 129
Fynncha, k. of o'Keansly, 73.
Fynnorey, 203.
Fynnya mcWihealla, 84.
Fynola. *See* Finola.
Fynore, 132.
Fyntan macIntrewe, 99.
—— St., of Clonenagh, 98.
—— St., of Tymonna, 102.
Fyr, 64.

Galar breac, 285.
Galen, 54.
Galey, 151.
Gallen, 9, 131
Gallenges, 131, 151, 181, 182.
Gallo, 22, 23, 25.

Gallowglasses, 263, 267, 270, 275, 276, 279, 280, 294, 298, 302, 306, 307, 310, 316-319.
Galway, 249.
Gann, 15, 16.
Gara mcDownay, 175.
Garalt, 114.
Gargoris, 22.
Garmly, Enna, 253.
Garnayt, 97, 106, 108, 109.
Garuan, St., 131.
Garvey, 81.
Gascoignes, 261
Gathelus, 19, 20, 210.
Gathly, 33.
Gauls, 46.
Gaveston, Piers, 262, 267.
Gawra, 60.
—— Liffe, 88.
Gawran, k. of Scotland, 72, 88.
—— son of Dawangart, 72.
Geanann, 15, 16.
Gearr an choggan, 174.
Gearrgeala, 174.
Gebeachan, 151.
Gelasius, pope, 73.
Genuille, Geffry, 250, 255.
George, St., 62.
Gerald Suckagh, 244, 290.
Geraldines, 290, 320
—— of mcMorish, 293.
Geran mcDichosta, 142.
German, 93
Germanus Altiodorensis, 70, 71.
Geshil, 28, 126, 326.
Geveannagh mcDowagan, 167.
Geye Ollogagh, 35.
Giallcha mcO., 36, 210.
Gillacolme o'Hugh, 168.
—— o'Kannan, 163.
Gillapatrick mcDonnogh, 164, 178.
Gillchaa, 213.
Gilleadawnayne, 209
Gilleboy mcMoylecurra, 326.
Gillebride, 209.
Gillebrwitte, 179.
Gillecougan, 190, 287.
Gillefin mcGillawallachan, 188
Gillekevyn mcKenneye, 160.
Gillemocholmoge, 192.

Gillenesally mcGillekevin, 175.
Gillepatrick, poet, 190.
Gillernew, brehon, 263.
—— mcConn ne mboght, 10.
—— mcGeoffry, 284.
Gillopatricke, k. of O., 178.
Gioga, 213.
Gittrick, k. of Dublin, 163.
Glandibar, a. of L. Broyne, 122.
Glan-fahrowe, 274.
Glassnayen, 120.
Gleandalogha, 82, 99, 105, 109, 126, 130, 136, 142, 149, 159, 168, 170, 321.
Gleanmannye, 164.
Gleann, 251.
Gleann Sawasge, 46.
Glen Iarn mcA. *See* Glun I.
Glocester, 285.
—— E of, 268.
Gluniarn mcAwley, 159, 160.
Gnahnat, 110.
Godfrey, 148, 149.
—— chief of the Danes, 155.
—— k. of the Danes, 150, 185.
—— mcAwley, 157.
—— mcSittrick, 156.
—— of Dublin, 185, 186.
—— o'Himar, 147.
—— son of Cathwaye, 210.
—— son of Harold, 160.
Goisdean, 28.
Goivnean, 78.
Gold, 32, 34, 118, 161, 187.
Golden calf, 60.
Goldsmith, 32.
Goll Cuana, 190.
Gordianus, 91.
Gorman, 10.
—— anchorite, 177.
—— of Louth, 120.
Gorman, dr. of mcFlynn, 122.
Gormgall mcDinaye, 129.
Gormon, a pilgrim, 99.
Gormphlath, 130.
—— q. of I., 182
Gormphly, dr. of k. Flann, 145, 155.
—— dr. of o'Donnell, 298.
—— wife of o'Connor, 285.
—— wife of K. Neale, 145, 153.

Index. 355

Gortann, 93.
Goshlyn, 134.
Gotman, a Dane, 133
Gowrann, 142.
Goyheynie o'More, 142
Granard, 249, 271.
Grane, battle of, 73.
Granie, dr. of o'Connor, 283.
Granie, battle of, 73.
Gratian, prince, 106.
Greallaghtollye, 110.
Greally da Phill, 80
Grecians, 12-15, 18, 21.
Greece, 13, 14, 16, 18, 156.
Gregory, pope, 78, 89, 91, 98.
—— St., 77, 219.
Greman, archb. of Dublin, 201
Grey monks, the, 247, 288, 289.
Griffin a herald, 133.
—— p. of Wales, 207.
Gromflath, a. of Clonbarren, 130.
Gurten Cowle Luachra, 217, 232.
—— na Spideog, 296.
Gwaire, a. of Glendalough, 130.
—— k. of C., 100, 101, 106, 196, 201, 251.

Hail, 171.
Harold, a Dane, 148, 177.
—— k of E , 179.
—— k. of Inisgall, 160.
—— o'Hymer, 151.
Head of Eochie m^cL , 203
Heber the white, 5, 6, 21, 23, 28-33, 36, 209, 211-213.
—— Glasse, 210
—— Glunyenn, 210.
—— Swift, 210.
Heber, w. of Cowchoullen, 48.
Helen, dr. of o'Madden, 244.
Hellen, w of Menelaus, 18.
Henery, k of Britons, 110.
Henrick m^cDavid, k. of S., 200.
—— m^cWillelan, 194.
Henry Beauclerck, 184, 215.
—— I , of England, 184, 215
—— II , of England, 43, 179, 207, 208, 215

Henry III , of England, 229, 244, 253
—— IV., of England, 3.
—— II., E of Germany, 173.
—— the quick, 322
—— the younger, 224.
Heraclius, emperor, 98, 99, 103.
Heragh Feura, 23.
Herald m^cAwley, 164.
Herapolis, 49
Heremon, 5, 21, 23, 27-30, 33, 36-38, 43, 45, 50, 209, 210.
—— m^cKennedy, 146.
Herenan, 5, 23.
Herod, 10.
Hillarius, anchorite, 129.
—— pope, 71, 72.
Himer, 146, 149.
Hingest, 70.
Historia Magna, 3.
Hoa Deck, 151.
Hodibeis, 105.
Hoell m^cCahall, 155
Holy Evangelists, 73.
—— Land, 249, 258.
Honey, 22, 112, 121
Honorius, pope, 99
Hormista, pope, 75, 76.
Howard, W , 226.
Howth, 124.
Hugh Allen, 101, 115, 117, 172
—— Balb, 115
—— Balire, k. of C., 117.
—— Beannan, 99, 106.
—— Bethra, 105
—— Boy, 98.
—— Brecke, 88.
—— br. of Moriertagh, 137.
—— Duffe, a. of Kildare, 103.
—— Duff m^cSwynie, 80, 88, 91.
—— Finleith, 115, 116, 141, 171, 172
—— Fortawill, 83.
—— Fynn, 123.
—— Gwary, 85-88.
—— Koew, 211.
—— k. of Connaught, 81
—— k. of Leinster, 81.
—— k. of Munster, 81
—— k of Teaffa, 156.

356 *Index.*

Hugh mᶜAichie, 156.
— mᶜAinmireagh, 80, 89, 90, 94, 97, 98, 107, 172.
— mᶜArt, 272.
— mᶜBrenyn, 88, 91, 95.
— mᶜBrick, 91.
— mᶜColgan, 117.
— mᶜConnor, 143.
— mᶜDluhye, 110.
— mᶜDuffe, 139.
— mᶜEahagh, 137.
— mᶜEoghagan, 146.
— mᶜFlinn, 146
— mᶜFlynn, 122
— mᶜGawran, 80
— mᶜMoriegh, 137.
— mᶜNeale, 141, 146.
— mᶜNeghtigerne, 160.
— Mundearg, 127.
— o'Dowdy, 160.
— of Glendalogha, 130.
— Ordan, 172.
— Ornye, 97, 98, 115, 127-130, 135, 172.
— Roe macBayorne, 38, 39.
— Rone, 98.
— Royne, 101.
— St., 91.
— Slaine, 43, 51, 88, 95, 97, 98, 102-105, 110, 123-126, 131, 172, 186.
— son of Neale F., 130.
Hugh. *See* Hy.
Hurling, 57
Hushe, 141, 142.
Hy, 89, 91, 97, 102, 104, 105, 108, 109, 111, 129, 132, 141, 159, 174
Hy Fidhgeinte, 104.
Hymer mᶜCarhon, 200.
— of Dublin, 163
— of Waterford, 164.
— son of Harold, 177.

Iaranngle of Athye, 210.
Iaranngleo Fathay, 210.
Iarthar Connaught, 130, 196, 215, 218, 290
Ibrywyn, 175.
Ice, 152, 174
Icova, 117.

Idris, 102
Idiona, 48
Idval mᶜAnoroit, 152.
Ife (Eva), dr. of D. mᶜMorrogh, 208.
— dr. of Fox, 233.
— dr. of Owgany, 42.
Ighdonn, 32.
Ighter Connaught, 187, 275, 317, 324.
Ilaiheawil mᶜD., 113.
Illan mᶜDowlan, 73, 74, 76
Imacwais, 126.
Imaile, 305, 325.
Imaine, 78, 85, 127, 130, 176, 243, 287, 293, 296, 315, 317, 324
— princes of, 98, 100, 104, 110, 112, 119, 167, 181, 257, 261, 272, 277, 278, 281, 283, 285, 305.
Imar, 133, 151.
Imer, 133
Imleagh, 122, 124, 165.
— Iver, 105, 127, 150.
Imokuylle, 214
Inamar, 211.
Indiction, 69, 267
Indreaghtach mᶜConnor, 147.
Indroym, 73, 103, 105, 109.
Inenen, 174.
Inis Angin, 79, 184
— bofyn, 108, 109, 112, 169, 184
— Cahie, 158.
— Clothran, 113, 169, 184
— Doicble, 131.
— Dowginn, 236
— Eany, 202
— Gall, 160, 193
— Kaeyne, 269.
— Kealtra, 84, 137.
— Keyndea, 149
— Kihlean, 18
— Koynedea, 126.
— Kwa, 304
— Moghty, 152, 174
— Moryc, 119, 128, 129
— Owen, 115, 188, 260, 269, 289
— Patrick, 177.
Inne, battle of, 74.
Inneoyn, 205.
Innocentius III., pope, 228.
Inreaghtagh, br. of Donnogh, 128.

Inreaghtagh, k. of C., 101.
—— mᶜCahallaine, 149.
Interpreters, the 70, 12.
Inver Colpe, 15.
—— doile, 103.
—— ne marke, 137.
Invers, the two, 78.
Ionamar, 46.
Iorna Siorgalye, 210.
Ire, 23, 25, 29, 30, 209, 213.
Ireland, colonies in, 11-21.
—— divisions of, 13, 15, 16.
—— kings of, 1, 3, 16-18, 26, 39, 41-51, 54-56, 58-65, 69, 71-80, 85-88, 90, 97, 101-103, 107, 108, 110, 113, 115-117, 121-126, 128, 130, 133, 135-137, 139-141, 143-148, 151-169, 171-173, 176, 177, 179, 180, 200, 201, 203-206, 214, 230, 242, 251-253, 268.
—— queens of, 18, 26, 27, 39, 67, 102, 128, 145, 149, 153, 155, 156, 160, 170, 182, 187, 190, 214.
Ireland, a hill, 71.
Irero, 44, 45.
—— Arda, 212
Irgaliach o'Conyng, 111.
Iriagann, 306.
Iriell, 30, 31.
—— Glunwar, 49 213.
Irish-Scottishmen, 63.
—— tongue, 8, 9.
Irros, 279.
Iserninus, b., 72.
Isill kieran, 180, 184
Isiodorus, 99.
Island of St. Patrick, 128.
Islands, the, 151, 186.
Isle of Man, 74, 89.
Israel, 22.
Israelites, 19, 20, 21.
Ita, 46.
Italy, 139.
Ithus, 23, 24, 28, 30, 58.
Iveagh, 84, 118, 308
—— viscount of, 30, 212.
Iver of Waterford, 159.
—— b, 74.
Iwayre mᶜMoylegann, 154.
Iwulfe, k. of S., 157.

Jacob, legate, 229.
James Zebedius, St., 65.
Japhet, 12, 20.
Jareth, 11, 20.
Jarvanel, 14.
Jerusalem, 22, 99
Jesters, 298.
Jesus Christ, birth of, 47.
—— crucified, 48.
Jewels, 190.
Jews, 19, 22.
Joan, dr. of E. of Ormond, 309.
—— dr. of o'Connor, 266.
Johannes Cassianus, 69
—— pope, 76, 89
John, k. of E., 223, 224, 227, 229
—— St., 52, 135, 204.
—— the monk, 90
John's House. *See* Rindown.
—— town, 216.
Jordan de Exeter, 239, 242, 266.
Joseph, archb. of Armagh, 150.
—— o'Kearny, a. of C., 127.
—— of Rossemore, 138.
Judea, 22.
Juffrie mᶜIwer, 143.
Julius Cæsar, 44, 46, 47.
—— pope, 106.
Justinian, 106, 109.
Justinianus, 77.
Justinus, senior, 75.
—— the younger, 108.

Kaharnagh Shennagh, 183, 187
Kallen, 140.
Kallye castle, 234.
Kara, 274.
—— Kowla-Kwirk, 272.
Karne, the, 247.
—— Itolarge, 156.
Karvell, k. of O., 115.
Katherine, St., 309.
Kauanagh, Art oge, 306
Kawagh, the, 126
Keallagh mᶜAilealla, 141.
—— mᶜKervel, 144
Keanfoily, 101.
Keankoylean, 214.
Kean-Kwacher, 314.

358 *Index.*

Keansealies, 132.
Keara, 83, 258
Kearmad Milvoyle, 18
Kearmna, 32.
Kearmott mᶜCahassy, 141.
Kearnaghan, 190.
Kearnagh Sota, 107.
Kearoghs, 298.
Kearvall mᶜMoregan, 145, 153.
Keassar, 11, 12.
Keassra, 12
Kchernagh mᶜComasgage, 130.
Kehernie, b. of, 186.
Keigh-na-Kedagh, 326.
Keilachar macConn, 10
Kells, 35, 95, 124, 129, 147, 156, 163, 169, 178, 180, 181, 205, 242.
Kelly, b of Clonfert, 305
Kenaleagh, 160
Kenedy. *See* Kinnitty.
Kennedy mᶜGoyhinn, 144.
—— mᶜLorcan, 152, 154, 155, 167, 211.
Kennedyes, 154.
Kenneth mᶜAlpin, 145.
Kennety. *See* Kinnitty.
Kenny mᶜConnor, 147.
—— mᶜCosgray, 138.
—— St. *See* Canneagh.
Keowan, a of Lyndwachill, 139.
Kerne, 188, 298, 315, 322, 326.
Kerry, 144, 276.
—— Artie, 274.
—— lower, 274
—— Luachra, 146, 167.
—— May, 274.
Kerryes, the three, 274.
Kervall mᶜLorckan, 160.
—— mᶜMoregan, 145.
Kevin, St., 82, 99, 160, 177, 186, 197
Keybann Brick, 77.
Keyle Usge, 139, 224
Keylke, 197
Keyly mᶜScannall, 149
Keyman mᶜDalye, 142
Keyndea, 149
Keyneachar, 155.
Keyuanagh, 206

Keyvin. *See* Kevin.
Kieran, St. *See* Queran.
Kilbeggan, 226, 229, 235, 252, 259.
Kilclare, 227
Kilcolman, 249, 270.
Kildare, 114, 120, 123, 129, 133, 135, 136, 148, 149, 158, 164, 169, 170, 180, 182, 325.
—— abbesses of, 110, 115, 129, 136, 145, 146, 158, 169, 180, 193.
—— abbots of, 103, 111, 126, 132, 139, 141, 147.
—— bishops of, 75, 136, 138, 141, 145, 159
—— earls of, 320, 325.
Kilfiaghragh, 246.
Kilgarad, 114
Kilkenny, 124
—— (Co Westm), 156, 189, 301.
Kilcollen. *See* Killcullen.
Kill, 75.
Kill Bryan, 90, 220.
Kill O'Milchon, 206.
Killalga, 120, 143.
Killalaye, 286.
Killaloe, 169, 178, 192, 222, 228, 258.
Killare, 222.
Killbileaghan, 246.
Killcloghan, 263
Killcoursey, 183, 257.
Killcrewnatt, 258
Killcullen, 84, 126, 151, 155, 283
Killdrownan, 176
Kille, battle of, 31
Killeachie, 84, 130, 136, 140, 143, 156, 182, 327.
Killenenamas, 271.
Killeneoene, 220.
Killeneoyne, 220.
Killin, b of Fernes, 112
Killitte, 130
Killmayne, 152.
Killmona, 308.
Killmore, 225, 280
—— ne Synna, 319.
Killnamanagh, 126, 140.
Killomat, 264, 288.
Killosny, battle of, 73.
Killrusse, 241

Index. 359

Killskry, 142, 156.
Killsleyve, 105
Kilmacduagh, 261.
Kilmaynham, 126.
Kilmcoyne, 220.
Kilmoney, 91.
—— battle of, 157.
Kilmore, 280.
Kilnegrann, 225-226.
Kilronann, 293, 320.
Kimboyc mᶜFintan, 37-41.
Kinaleagh, 51, 74, 75, 81, 112, 117,
  152, 189, 193, 221, 222, 229, 250,
  266, 289, 290, 291, 293, 297, 299,
  301, 308, 311, 314.
Kinclare, 226
Kincora, 88, 169, 178.
Kincorbadan, 106.
Kineann, St., 73
Kinell Dowhy, 266, 317.
—— Feray, 101
—— Loghan, 310.
—— Moan, 234, 253, 262, 293.
—— owen, 236.
—— vikearka, 101.
Kingary, 105.
King's game, 301.
Kings of Ireland *See* Ireland
Kinneigh, 145.
Kinnitty, 139, 143, 222, 227.
Kinsealagh, Eochy, 296.
Kirkynn, battle of, 96
Kisarme, 36
Kleynlogh, 78
Kliagh, 77.
Khew, 32.
Kloen, 167
Kloynolagh, 190.
Klynkelly. *See* Clan K
Knockmoy. *See* Cnockmoy
Konolagh, 115
Koran. *See* Corran
Kowle o'fflynn, 273.
Kowlevakar, 273
Koyle, M mᶜD., 221.
Koyle Usge, castle of, 241, 242.
Koyllin Crowbagh, 321.
Kregan, the, 327
Krith Carbryc, 262.
Kwaillie Kyannaghty, 202

Kwalann, 28, 192.
—— k. of L., 97.
Kwasan, 182.
Kyannaght, 78, 106, 117, 137.
Kyerway, 63, 143.
Kymboye, 38, 39, 41.
Kynadon, 124.
Kynalagh. *See* Kinaleagh
Kynay mᶜColme, 158.
Kyndealgan, 113
Kynell. *See* Kinell.
Kynfoyle, 108.
Kynnaghty, 106.
Kynnailve, 74.
Kynnayc mᶜCumusky, 127.
Kynneagh, 77.
Kynnetty. *See* Kinnitty
Kynoy, k. of L., 128
Kynoye macIrgally, 113
Kyntire, 109.
Kyonnaghta, 36.
Kyrb, 213.

Labdon, 21.
Laestheness, 25, 28
Lagerie, k. of I., 65, 66, 68, 69, 71,
  103, 148, 169, 171, 178, 187, 190,
  201
Lagery Lorck, 42, 43, 44.
Laghtna, 211.
Laharna, 42.
Lahra, 42.
Lahry, 115.
Laighnen, k of C , 101.
Lambert, b. of Kilmayne, 152
Lamech, 11, 20.
Lampades, 14, 77.
Lampares, 15.
Lamprides, 14.
Lann, 144.
Laoighis. *See* Lease.
Lareagh Bryne, 122, 127.
Lasies, the, 266.
Lassar, St., 320
Lathreagh Broyne *See* Lareagh
  Bryne.
Laughlen, 13.
Lauthus, 12, 29, 30, 58, 171
Lawfynn, 210

Lawgire mcLowagh, 36.
Lawless, Robyn, 243.
—— William, 277.
Lawra Lwirck, 210.
Lawrence, St., 278.
Lawry Longseach, 43, 44.
Lawrynne, 33.
Laws. *See* Rules.
Layene, 11.
Laygery, p. of Desmond, 129.
Laygnen, k. of C., 101.
—— mcDoneanny, 118.
Laygneyn, 212.
Layne, 30.
Layny, *à quo* Laigean, 44.
Lazarina, 254.
Leackagh mcCoghlan, 257
Leackan, 154.
Leack-cassa-dara, 262.
Leackmoy, 287.
Leack Riada, 56.
Leackyn, 119.
Leagery, son of Neale, 65.
Leahayegh mcConcarad, 113.
Leah Coyne, 58, 118, 144, 147, 176, 180, 200.
Leah Moye, 58, 176, 177, 187, 194, 277.
Leahtairve, battle of, 101.
Lease, 56, 192, 193, 202, 203, 222.
—— princes of, 144, 175, 187, 203, 298, 300, 306.
Leases, the seven, 56.
Leathlovar, 115.
Leavelin, p of Wales, 173.
Lecale, 149.
Ledwitches, 258.
Legate, 201, 213, 214, 229.
Leh Con. *See* Leah Coyne.
—— Moye. *See* Leah Moye.
Leheid-mynd, 100.
Lehra *See* Lohra.
Leigh Olav, 175.
Leighlin, 103, 122, 141, 151, 189
Leih, a of, 138.
Leihcale, 152.
Leihmanchan, 104, 107, 176, 220.
Leihmore, 84, 89, 119, 150.
Leihrie, battle of, 91.

Leinster, 15, 16, 29, 43, 53, 55, 57, 61, 62, 65, 76, 82, 100, 103, 112, 117, 128, 129, 136, 138, 142, 151, 160, 164, 168, 178, 180, 181, 184, 188, 191, 194, 199, 201-203, 205-207, 213, 216, 221, 222, 225, 226, 228, 239, 259, 298, 299, 303, 308, 322, 323, 325, 328.
—— earl of, 259.
—— kings of, 28, 43, 44, 47, 53, 56, 64-66, 69, 76, 81, 91, 97, 101, 102, 103, 107, 109, 110-112, 114-117, 119, 120, 123, 127-130, 132, 133, 136, 137, 139, 143-145, 147, 148, 151-155, 157-160, 164-166, 168-170, 176, 184, 185, 191-193, 195, 196, 202, 205, 251, 254, 301, 307, 308, 322, 325.
—— queens of, 103, 119, 146, 308.
Leinstermen, 51, 53, 55, 63, 71, 73, 74, 77, 79, 88, 97, 104, 105, 108-111, 113, 116, 123, 124, 127, 132, 142, 144, 151, 153, 154, 157, 158, 163, 167, 174, 178, 181, 185, 195, 206, 231.
Leith Manchan *See* Leihmanchan,
Leithmore, 104
Leitter Crannagh, 198.
Leo, pope, 70, 71, 106, 109, 112.
Leprosy, 89, 95, 109
Lergus mcCronenn, b. of K., 143
—— o'Fiachayn, 126.
Lerveanvan, 127.
Lethra. *See* Lohra.
Letter Loyny, 274
Lewis, k. of France, 249.
Ley, 158, 313
Leyhmore Mochoevoy, 143.
Leythlyn, 203.
Leyvanchan. *See* Leihmanchan.
Leytrym (now Tara), 27.
—— co., 122, 318.
Leyunie Wanic, 226.
Liahmore, 152
Liavanchan *See* Leihmanchan.
Liber, a. of Eachybo, 99.
Liffie, 13, 32, 42, 71, 102, 132, 136, 156.
Ligach, dr. of k Flann, 147.
Lightning, 48, 65, 151, 171, 241, 285.

Limerick, 15, 139, 143, 147, 149, 150, 151, 158 168, 176, 179, 190, 202, 217, 219, 221, 222, 259
Lindisfarn, 104.
Linneally, 117.
Lir, 133.
Lisan Tosgely, 200
Lisardawla, 306.
Liseagh leanmore, 55.
Liseanabbeye, 194, 221.
Lisgauall, 300.
Lismore, 91, 98, 102, 124, 133, 145, 147, 156, 157, 173, 176, 190.
Lismoyne, 203, 227, 308.
Lissondoil, 319.
Loasthenes, 27.
Loch, 211.
Lochan Dalmanna, 98.
Lochne mean, a. of Kildare, 111.
Lochyne, 103, 115.
Logh. *See* Lough.
Loghanmoye, 31.
Loghne, 129.
Loghtemple, 249.
Loghtere, 124
Lohra, abbey of, 85, 86, 105, **127**, 139, 157, 299, 321.
—— castle of, **222**.
Loicheach, 129
Lomclene o'Doyne, 255.
—— o'Flatrye, 255.
Lomhwhile, b. of Kildare, 126.
London, 241.
Longe, a. of C., 104.
Longford, 122, 125.
Longseagh, a. of Armagh, 132.
—— mᶜFlaithverty, 119.
Longshanks, Edward, 254.
Lorcan mᶜCahaill, 141.
—— mᶜDonogh, 147, 152.
—— mᶜFoylan, 151.
—— mᶜLaghtna, 211.
Lothar, 209.
Lothra. *See* Lohra.
Lough Arvagh, 236, 321.
—— Arynn, 296.
—— Baye, 21
—— Bway, 21.
—— Carman, 138.
—— Colgan, 179.

Lough Cwan, 148, 150, 152.
—— da Keigh, 21.
—— Deakar, 316.
—— Deirke, 12.
—— Dorry, 315.
—— Eiruscan, 149.
—— Erne, 33, 137, 149, 150, 292.
—— Finlogh, 13.
—— Finmeay, 21, 312.
—— Forareawan, 13.
—— Foyle, 32.
—— Gagawar, 109, 142.
—— Gawney, 149.
—— Grayne, 21.
—— Innil, 157, 162, 171, 198.
—— Ke, 235, 236, 239, 240, 244, 262.
—— Keylan, 181.
—— Kirre, 145.
—— Kymy, 21.
—— Kynne, 162.
—— Lein, 167.
—— Levin, 185.
—— Loygeachan, castle of, 230
—— Luymnin, 13.
—— Measga, 245, 249, 292.
—— Meilge, 44.
—— Neaagh, 109, 129, 137, 138, 149
—— Oghter, 241, 244, 313.
—— Riagh, 21, 128, 235.
—— Rie, 118, 120, 139, 147, 149, 150, 156, 182, 184, 216, 217, 229, 232
—— Rowrie, 147.
—— Skwyre, 313.
—— Sileann, 32.
—— Temple, 249.
—— Treahan, 102.
Loughs, 13, 21, 29.
Louth, 78, 106, 120, 133, 136, 138, 160, 181, 269, 286.
Louthus, 27, 28.
Loway, 31, 36, 66, 213.
—— Iardonn, 212.
—— Keyhleann, 18.
—— Lawady, 304.
—— Lawdearg, 212.
—— Laye, 38.
—— Loyney, 42, 211.

362   *Index.*

Loway Lwange, 46.
—— Lysie, 55, 56, 57.
—— mᶜConn, 59, 60.
—— mᶜEnna, 37, 38.
—— mᶜEochye, 37
—— mᶜIonamar, 46.
—— mᶜLaygerie, 72, 73, 74, 171.
—— mᶜOwgany, 42
—— myonn, 211
—— priest of C., 83
—— Shrewderg, 49, 209
Lowna, St., 83.
Lowy of Lismore, 91.
Loyney, 42
Loynseagh, 101, 111, 172
—— mᶜEnos, 110
Loyre Lere, 118.
Lucall, 99
Lucritt, a of C , 119.
Lugedus, b of Connery, 79
Lupus, b , 70
Lusk, 73, 116, 126, 144, 148, 194
Luynie (Lwyne), 223, 232, 262, 273, 278, 292.
—— b. of, 267.
—— in Meath, 183, 185, 218.
—— of Tara, 61, 173
—— p of, 223, 246
Lwacherdea, battle of, 32, 42.
Lwachra, battle of, 78.
Lwyegh. *See* Louay
Lwyne, 30
Lwyrg, 253
Lya Fail, 26.
Lye, the, 13.
Lymbrick. *See* Limerick.
Lyncoln, 91.
Lynndwachill, 138, 139.
Lynnealla, 123, 142
Lynnlere, 149
Lynnrosa, 139.
Lynsoleagh, 139.

Macabees, 10.
mᶜAgenann, 185.
mᵉaMiles, 271.
mᶜAnarchinny, G., 280.
Macana, Downsleyve, 242.
mᶜAn-enny, F., 302.

mᶜAnfalgye, S., 287.
mac Anliahanaye, C., 262.
mᶜAreaghty, D., 230, 233.
Macarhon, 29.
—— G., 221.
Macartan, 30.
Macarthie. *See* mᶜCarthy.
mᶜArtt, Hugh, 272.
mᶜBeachy mᶜMorreaye, 167.
mᶜBissex, Eayne, 312.
mᶜBranan, 298
—— Con, 317
—— E., 231.
—— F., 240.
mᶜBrayn, 176.
mᶜBreallye, 247
mᶜBrian, 30.
—— Dermott, 323.
mᶜBrian Aharly, 30.
—— K , 254
mᶜBrogaroann, 166.
mᶜBwyeghann, F., 253
mᶜCaba, Bryan, 316.
—— Hugh, 300
mᶜCahall, Cahall, 193.
—— Dermot, 263.
mᶜCaharnie, C., 231.
mᶜCaille, 73.
mᶜCarlen, T., 296.
mᶜCarthy, 30, 58, 191, 199, 202, 217, 321.
—— Connor, k. of Desmond, 300.
—— Cormack, 191, 193, 199, 202.
—— Cormack Donne, 302.
—— Cormack, k. of C., 194.
—— Dermott mᶜC., 198.
—— Dermott, k. of D., 233.
—— Dermott mᶜC D , 304
—— Donell, 302, 315.
—— Donell Oge, 260.
—— Donell Roe, 259.
—— Donogh, 192, 196.
—— Felym, 258.
—— Finyn mᶜOwen, 325
—— of the Carbryes, 304.
mᶜCaruell, D., 300.
mᶜCasdellies. *See* mᶜCosdeallies.
mᶜCassurley, C., 240.
mᶜCathmoyle, M., 302, 303.
mᶜCauill, B., b. of Uriell, 300.

mᶜCennegan, C., 276.
—— D., 276.
mᶜCoghlan, 30, 136, 165, 186, 244, 257.
—— Connor, 192.
—— Connor of the Castle, 240.
—— country of, 136, 165.
—— David, 257.
—— Donell, 257.
—— Donnogh, 257.
—— Donslevie, 226.
—— Fynyne, 257.
—— Gillechrist, 226.
—— Gillekewgin, 257.
—— Gillernew, 225.
—— Hugh, 184.
—— Melaghlen, 229, 246.
—— Melaghlen, p. of Delvin, 226.
—— Randalphe, 214.
—— Rory, 229.
—— Rosse, 257.
—— Slioght Donnell, 257.
—— Slioght Donnogh, 257.
—— Slioght Fynyn, 257.
mᶜConcornye, M., 185
mᶜConn na mboght, 99.
—— Cormack, 184, 188.
—— Moylekyeran, 180.
mᶜConnor, 275.
mᶜConrye, p. of Delvin, 192.
mᶜConsnawa, D., 290.
mᶜCorb, 44.
mᶜCormack, C., 235, 238.
—— G., 243.
mᶜCorthean, 187.
mᶜCosdeallie, G., 224, 225, 279, 286, 287, 290.
mᶜCosdeallies, 239, 291
mᶜCossie, Erard, 161, 162.
mᶜCowfanie, C., 317.
mᶜCoynne, Magnus, 253.
mᶜCrowttynn, K., 305.
mᶜDalredockar, G., 253.
mᶜDavid, William Garve, 323.
mᶜDermoda. *See* mᶜDermott.
mᶜDermott, 217, 270, 271, 273, 275, 279, 281, 285, 293-295, 304, 305, 309, 310, 313, 320.
—— Cahall, 289, 311, 315.
—— Cahall mᶜC., 217

mᶜDermott, Carragh, 263.
—— Connor, 263, 290, 291, 294-296.
—— Connor mᶜHugh, 324.
—— Connor Oge, 310, 311, 316, 320, 321, 324
—— Connor, p. of Moylurg, 291, 293-296.
—— Cormack, 235, 236, 324.
—— Daniel, 240.
—— Dermott, 278.
—— Dermott Gall, 261, 272-274, 276, 290, 291.
—— Dermott mᶜCahall C., 263.
—— Dermott mᶜFerrall, 276.
—— Dermott Myeagh, 247, 256.
—— Dermott, t of Moylurg, 278.
—— Donnell, 167, 243.
—— Donnell mᶜCormack, 240
—— Donnagh mᶜD , 264.
—— Ferall, 295-297, 304, 325.
—— Ferall mᶜConnor, 296.
—— Gillecriost, 276.
—— Hugh, 316, 317.
—— Hugh mᶜC., 315.
—— Hugh mᶜM., 263.
—— Mahon, 238.
—— Melaghlen, 279.
—— Mulrony, 262-265, 272-274, 276, 279, 280, 282, 283, 286, 288
—— Mulrony mᶜF., 315, 316, 320, 321.
—— Mulrony mor, 303.
—— Murrogh, 313.
—— Murtagh, 278.
—— Rory, 316, 327.
—— Rory mᶜHugh, 321, 325.
—— Teige, 311.
—— Teige mᶜC., 296.
—— Teige mᶜHugh, 324.
—— Thomas, 241.
—— Thomas mᶜF , 304.
—— Tomaltagh, 263, 286-290.
—— Tomaltagh Duff, 316.
mᶜDermott's church, 188.
mᶜDonnagann, R , 168.
mᶜDonnell 29, 63, 209, 258, 306.
—— Alexander, 209, 258, 303.
—— Anyleas, 253.
—— Connor, 232.

mᶜDonnell, Donnell, 209.
— Donnell Ballagh, 209.
— Dowgall, 318, 319.
— Enos the Great, 209.
— Enos the Younger, 209.
— Eoyn, 209.
— Eoyn Kahanay, 209.
— Eoyn More, 209.
— Malcolme, 156.
— Marcus, 319.
— Murtagh B , 318, 323, 324.
— Randolph, 209, 303.
— prince of the I. of S., 281
— Sawarle, 209, 302.
— Terlaugh, 303.
mᶜDonough, 262, 310, 312, 313, 317, 328.
— Brian mᶜD., 286.
— Brian mᶜT., 286.
— Cahall Cairbreagh, 311
— Conor, 278.
— Cormack, 304, 318.
— Dermott, 317.
— Dermott mᶜG., 317.
— Donnell, 286, 313.
— Ferall, 316, 325.
— Gillechriost oge, 284.
— k. of C., 101.
— lord of Tir A., 283.
— Melaghlin, 278.
— Moyleronye, 243, 318.
— Mulrony mᶜT., 325.
— Murrogh, 278.
— Murtagh, 278, 313.
— O'Ferrall mᶜC., 325.
— Rory mᶜM., 317.
— Teige, 295, 312.
— Tomaltagh, 272, 275, 278, 281, 283, 289, 290, 295, 313, 316.
— Tomaltagh mᶜM., 273.
mᶜDowell, 202.
mᶜDowlen, D., k. of L., 176.
mᶜDownay, Gara, 175.
mᶜEarcka, 83.
Macedonius, heresy of, 106.
mᶜEgan, 63.
Maceilgi, 148.
mᶜElligott, 238.
mᶜEncrossan, b. of Raphoe, 282.
mᶜ en Maister, N., 280.

mᶜ en Mile, 291
— R , 323.
mᶜEnulty, M., 253.
mᶜErcka, 79.
mᶜFaylan, T., 147.
mᶜFevis, 33.
mᶜFinbarr, 182.
mᶜFirvissy, G., 258
mᶜFlathnia, D , 126.
mᶜFlynn, Donell, 184.
— Odor, 178.
mᶜFoylan, 167, 176.
mᶜGallgoyle, T., 223.
mᶜGawran, 89.
mᶜGeoghegan. See maGeoghegan.
mᶜGerald. See Fitz Gerald.
mᶜGillearrie, Conawill, 159.
— Connor, 243.
mᶜGillecriost, Cahall, 281.
— Dermot mᶜD., 317.
mᶜGillefinnen, Donell, 253.
mᶜGillemorie, 236.
mᶜGillepatrick, 29, 309.
— Donnell C , 225
— Donnogh, 175.
— D., k. of Ossory, 176, 206.
— D. mᶜAnmchy, 238, 240.
— D. mᶜDonnell, 184.
— Keallagh, 309.
— k. of Ossory, 176, 184, 309.
— Teige, 175, 187.
mᶜGilleroe, Boyhanagh, 328.
mᶜGlanchie, G., 253.
mᶜGodfrey, 150
mᶜGoill, p. of Elie, 220.
mᶜGranell, Geoffrey, 220.
— Mahon, 273
— Manus, 260.
— Randolph, 280.
mᶜGrenie, 18, 26.
mᶜGwyer. See Maguire.
Macha Mongroe, 38-42.
Machaire Cuirenie, 156, 301.
Machenie, b. of Leighlynn, 141.
mᶜHeoghae, 322
mᶜHobert, David, 310.
mᶜHugh, M , b of Oylfyn, 267.
mᶜInrwise O'Keowan, 186.
mᶜJohnyn, John, 321.
mᶜJordan Dexeter, Meyler, 290.

mᶜJordan Dexeter, Stephen, 299
mᶜKeallagh, D , 160.
mᶜKeght, 26.
mᶜKehearne, Cormack, 276.
mᶜKehernie, Cahall, 328.
—— Connor Fynn, 328.
—— Cormack, 261.
mᶜKelly, David, b. of Cashel, 244.
mᶜKerwell, Gillekeigh, 286.
—— Mulrony, 286.
—— p of Elie, 170.
mᶜKiegan, 29, 280.
—— Brithgalagh, 240.
—— John, 278
—— Moyle Issa D., 283.
—— Moyle Issa R., 280.
mᶜKight, 18.
mᶜKinnedy H., 146.
mᶜKoyll, 18
mᶜKoyll-an-daingin, 252.
Mackwaises, 103.
mᶜLasre, a. of Armagh, 100.
—— a. of Beanchor, 103
—— of Inismorye, 128.
mᶜLaughlin, 64, 187, 188
mᶜLeanna, a. of Imleagh I., 150.
mᶜLiag, 169.
mᶜLondrous, 309.
mᶜLoughlin, 29.
—— Donell, 185.
—— Mortagh mᶜN., 199, 201-205, 215.
mᶜMagnus, 283.
—— Bryan, 281.
—— Magnus, 272.
—— Molronye Oge, 278.
mᶜMahon, 29, 30, 63, 189, 325.
—— Bryan mᶜH., 302.
—— Don, 309
—— Donagh mᶜD., 287.
—— Donagh mᶜH., 315.
—— Hugh mᶜR , 294, 296.
—— John, 293, 294
—— land of, 189, 225.
—— Magnus, 296, 300
—— Murrogh mᶜB., 296.
—— Roalve, 268.
—— Shane More, 314, 315.
mᶜMartyn, 283.
mᶜMeannman, D., 260.

mᶜMeannman, H., 26.
mᶜMeran, 232.
mᶜMoleronye, H., 263.
mᶜMordever, T , 120.
mᶜMoregan, Cahall, 183.
—— Cearvell, 144.
mᶜMoriey O'Morgan, 120.
mᶜMorish of the preys, 290, 294.
—— of Kerry, 325.
—— the Deputy, 236, 238, 239.
mᶜMoyle Corra, G., 326.
mᶜMoyledownye, T., 243.
mᶜMurchow, Bran B , 117.
mᶜMurrogh, 29, 57, 251, 298, 307, 322, 325.
—— Art, 254.
—— Art, k. of L., 301, 307, 322, 325
—— Art mᶜG., 307.
—— Art mᶜThomas, 308
—— Dermot, 192-196, 198, 199, 201, 202, 205-208.
—— Donell Riauagh, 301.
—— Mortagh, 254.
—— Morris, 231.
—— Mulmorrey, k. of L , 166.
—— Murtagh, k. of L., 254.
—— Thomas mᶜT, 325.
mᶜMurtagh, Cahall, 248.
—— Magnus, 238.
mᶜMurtagh finn, H., 243.
Macnemara, 30, 290, 305.
—— Cowmara, 306.
—— Donnogh, 267.
mᶜNeochy of Ulster, 173
mᶜNideferty, 118.
mᶜNissie, a. of C , 90.
—— b. of Conrye, 75.
—— cowarb of, 156.
mᶜNya mᶜCormack, 23.
mᶜo'Boyle, M., 253.
Macoghlan. *See* mᶜCoghlan.
mᶜO'Kelly, 117
mᶜOtyr, 193.
mᶜOyreaghty, Donn, 230.
—— Thomas, 250.
mᶜPhilippin, Henry, 299.
mᶜQuoill, 26.
mᶜRandalphe mᶜMorey, 191.
mᶜRannell. *See* Magrannell.

maCrathe, 30
m'Rowry, 280, 294.
—— Cormack, 311, 318.
—— Donagh, 276
—— k. of the islands, 281.
—— Murtagh, 311.
mᶜRwaragh, k. of Brittans, 144.
mᶜSawarlie, 238, 241, 242.
mᶜSwynie, 64, 298, 317
—— Conor, 318.
—— Donell, 319.
—— Donnslieve, 318.
—— Hugh, 90
—— Terlagh, 300, 306.
—— Terlagh mᶜM., 322.
mᶜTayle, 84
mᶜTeige, Paule, 310.
mᶜTholies, 280.
mᶜThomas, Murrogh, 319.
mᶜTiernan, Conor Boye, 280.
—— Donell, 182.
—— Donell mᶜG., 306.
—— Gillessa, 256.
—— Mahon, 280.
mᶜTihie, Eoyn, 319.
mᶜTornayn, M., 148.
mᶜTygernan. *See* mᶜTiernan.
mᶜTyre, 214.
mᶜVihelly, a. of Clonard, 105.
mᶜVuellen, Jonock, 264, 265, 267.
—— Semnickin, 300.
mᶜVuellens, 324
mᶜWailtrin, Madiuck, 291.
mᶜWalter, Thomas, 262.
mᶜWilliam. *See* Burke.
Madadan, k. of Scotland, 115.
Madiuck mᶜWaltrinn, 291.
—— the bald, 311.
Magaoy, Molussy, 262.
Magawley, 29 64.
—— Awley, 328.
—— Gillesynata, 182.
—— Mahonn, 250.
Magawran, Magnus, 328.
—— Mathew, 300
Magdorchy, T., 310.
Magenis, 30, 45.
—— Art, 212, 306, 308.
—— Art ne Mangye, 312.
—— Arthur, 212.

Magenis, Cathvarr, 323.
—— Donell More, 212.
—— Donell Oge, 212.
—— Eachmyle, 212.
—— Enos, 212.
—— Enos More, 212.
—— Enos Oge, 212.
—— Eoyn, 305.
—— Flathvertagh, 212.
—— Gillecolme, 212.
—— Hugh, 212.
—— Hugh Reawar, 212.
—— Mortagh Riaganagh, 212, 297.
—— Murtagh Oge, 321.
—— Rory, 212.
—— Rory mᶜArt, 323.
—— Viscount of Ivehaghe, 212.
Mageoghegan, 29, 51, 64, 257, 301.
—— Bryan, 267.
—— Bryan mᶜW., 316.
—— Connell, 7, 9, 328.
—— Conor Roe, 293.
—— country of, 51.
—— Cowchoghry mᶜD., 301.
—— Cowchoghry More, 297.
—— Dermott, 314.
—— Donell mᶜD., 307.
—— Donogh, 230.
—— Donough mᶜM., 291, 314.
—— Ferall mᶜD , 308.
—— Ferall mᶜF., 299.
—— Ferall mᶜM , 266
—— Ferall Roe, 308.
—— Hugh mᶜM , 307, 308.
—— Johnock mᶜM., 290.
—— Laighneagh, 322.
—— Meyler, 288.
—— Morish, 293.
—— Morish Kam, 316.
—— Morish mᶜM., 301.
—— Morish mᶜW., 260.
—— Mortagh, 266.
—— Mortagh More, 266.
—— Mortagh Oge, 321.
—— Mulronye, 284.
—— Neale mᶜC., 312.
—— Rowry, 304.
—— the Red, 301.
—— William Galda, 289, 292, 308.
—— William Oge, 260.

Magic art, 16, 25, 49, 99.
Magicians, 26, 39, 57, 66, 67.
Maglaghlen, C., 189.
—— D., 242.
—— M., 260.
Maglannchye, 30
Magmahon. *See* mᶜMahon.
Magog, 20.
Magopoc mᶜIlawa, 105.
Magoreachty, 310.
Magrannell, 30, 313.
—— Cahall, 292.
—— Cosmor, 292.
—— Heber, 292.
—— Imer, 285.
—— Magnus, 292.
—— Melaghten, 292.
—— Richard, 325.
—— Roe, 311.
—— Teige, 292, 296.
—— Tomaltagh, 292.
Magwire, 29, 63, 316.
—— Donn, 244, 259.
—— Gilleduff, 316
—— Hugh, 301.
—— Philip, 302, 316.
—— Rory, 292.
—— Teige, 306.
—— Thomas, 316.
Mahon, 211.
Mail, shirts of, 166.
Mainemarye, 30.
Malale, 11, 20.
Malcolme, k. of Scotland, 156, 163, 185.
—— mᶜD., k. of Wales, 163.
Male mᶜRochrye, 54, 59
Malone, abbot of, 218.
Mamemoye, 42.
Mamillius, 14.
Man, the Isle of, 74, 89.
Mancaleus, 14.
Manchan, St, 107.
Manchinus, a. of Menadrochatt, 104.
Maney mᶜKervil, 78.
Manichees, 106.
Manic, a. of Indroym, 109.
—— mᶜNeale N., 64, 69, 125, 146.

Mantan, 66.
Mantua, 44.
Mantyn, Myler, 308.
Manue, 21.
Manye, 213.
Maolgarbh, the, 160.
Marcan mᶜDawayn, 104.
Marcellinus, 75, 78.
March, Adam, 280.
—— Geffrey, 221, 223, 226, 227, 228, 230, 232, 234.
—— William, 231.
March, the Earl of, 316, 320.
Margaret, dr. of W. Burke, 301.
—— q. of S., 185.
Mark the Evangelist, St., 49.
Marka, 42.
Marshal, W., 221, 230, 234, 266.
Martha, a. of Kildare, 120.
Martian, emperor, 71, 106.
Martyn, pope, 103
—— St, 63, 64, 110, 150.
Mary Magdalen, 50.
Mass, 120.
Mathew, k. of U., 152.
—— mᶜHugh, 150.
—— mᶜHugh M, 156.
—— mᶜMoriey, 137.
Mayessel, 31.
Mayfea, 42
Mayle, 213.
Mayneann, b. of Clonfert, 89.
Mayo of the Saxons, 9, 114, 122, 126, 219, 220.
Mayochus (Maedog), St., of Ferns, 100.
Mayowne, 13.
Meades. *See* Medes.
Meaghtoige, 307.
Meargaye, 209.
Meath, 16, 38, 42, 43, 51, 62, 98, 118–120, 122, 125, 128, 138, 139, 144, 146, 151, 154, 157, 162, 165, 174, 177, 178, 180, 184, 186, 187, 189–193, 199, 201, 202, 204, 213, 217, 218, 220–223, 226, 228, 229, 231, 233, 234, 237, 239, 244, 249, 254, 255, 256, 258, 263, 266, 268, 278, 283, 285, 287, 293, 301, 306, 307, 311, 321–323.

Meath, kings of, 51, 102, 104, 121, 122, 128, 139, 141, 154, 155, 157, 167, 173-175, 180-185, 187, 189, 191, 192, 194, 196, 198, 200, 201, 204-206, 216, 254, 255, 277, 284, 296, 301.
Meathmen, 56, 122, 132, 168, 175, 178, 181, 198, 221.
Meaths. See Medes.
Meaw Crwachan, 47.
Mebricke, Hodge, 249.
Medes, 12, 43.
Meelick. See Milick.
Mehannagh, the, 279
Meilge Mollthye, 210.
Melaghlin, Donnell, 252.
—— God, 174.
—— k. of Meath, 284.
—— m^{c}Dermott, 194.
—— m^{c}Donnell, 285.
—— p. of Kinell Owen, 236.
Melge, 44.
Meliola, 22.
Menadrochatt, 104.
Menelaus, 18.
Mercorius, pope, 78.
Merlin, 79, 94.
Methusalem, 11, 20.
Meyler, 216, 219, 221, 222, 225, 226, 228.
—— Robert, 225
Michael, St , 324.
Miles, b. of Limerick, 259.
—— Cogan, 277.
Miletus, of Spain, 3, 5, 12, 18, 21, 22, 23, 25, 26, 30, 65, 209, 210, 212, 213.
Milick, 218, 219, 220, 233, 277.
Militus, 90.
Mill of Oran, 104.
Mitreus, 16, 27.
Moa Nwadad, 211.
Moacorb, 211.
Mocheus of Indroym, 73, 78, 103.
Mochevogus, St., 104.
Mochrea, 310.
Mocht, St., 120.
Mochuda, St., 102.
Mochwa, a. of Beanchor, 108.
—— m^{c}Lowaine, St., 105.

Mocolmocke, St , 163.
Moe Corb, 211.
Moeyne, 210.
Moghrea, 125.
Mogorne, 137, 193.
Mogornn, 123
Moilmarie, 145.
Molemorey m^{c}Moylemoye, 170.
Molen Oran, 104.
Moling Luachra, St., 54, 108, 111.
Molingar, 90, 104, 254.
Moll, k. of E., 121.
Mollengare. See Molingar.
Molloye, p. of Ferkeall, 170
Monann m^{c}Cormacke, 123.
Moneagh Mwindearge, 69.
Money, coined in C , 214.
—— new, 244, 252.
—— shower of, 112.
Moneyderg, 88
Mongan m^{c}Fiaghna, 100, 201.
Mongayne, 212.
Mongfinn, 64.
Moniagh, a. of Clonfert, 127.
Montyr See Moyntir.
Monyemore, 301.
Moon, the, 108, 110, 119
Moonagh, a of Lothra, 157.
—— m^{c}Cormick, 157.
—— m^{c}Shiel, 147.
Mooreheyvmye, 42, 111.
Moran, b of Clochar, 138.
More, dr. of Kervell, 146.
—— dr. of m^{c}Kelly, 160.
—— dr. of O'Boyle, 283.
—— dr. of O'Brien, 183, 229.
—— dr. of O'Madden, 308.
—— queen of Meath, 196.
—— queen of Munster, 102.
—— wife of Cathal C., 229.
Morea, 13.
Moreagh Tyreagh, 63.
Morean, a of Kildare, 132, 146, 158.
—— dr of K. Congallagh, 158.
—— dr of Swart, 146.
Moreay Muchna, 211.
Morgeall, dr. of k. Flann, 148.
Morgeis, 128.
—— m^{c}Conell, 113.

Index. 369

Morican, b of, 218.
Morie, b of, 228.
—— in Leinster, 325
Moriegh Balgragh, 37
—— br. of Cearr an C , 174.
—— Kewe, 71
—— k of C., 101.
—— k of I., 37.
—— k. of L., 101, 115.
—— k. of Scotland, 115.
—— mᶜBroyne, 129, 143.
—— mᶜB., k. of L., 143.
—— mᶜC , a of Kildare, 126.
—— mᶜD., b. of Meath, 128
—— mᶜEahagh, 137.
—— mᶜInreaghty, 114.
—— mᶜRiuaragh, 129, 132.
—— Madadan, 115.
—— Male, 42.
—— of Moye Je, 111.
—— O'Nwaat, 182.
—— Ultagh, 169
Moriertagh mᶜEarcka, 73–77.
—— mᶜNeale, 149, 150.
—— mᶜTiernie, 146.
—— na Gochall C., 153, 154.
—— O'Brian, 184
—— son of k. Donnell, 122
Morisk, 43.
Mortagh mᶜBraine, 130.
—— mᶜDongaile, 129.
—— mᶜEarcka, 72, 73, 74.
—— mᶜLiag, 169.
—— of the Leather C., 153, 154.
—— O'Neale, 144, 172.
—— son of Neale G., 148, 151–153, 155.
Mortality in I., 79, 83, 106, 107, 109, 186.
Mortcan of Kildare, 132.
Mortimer, Lord, 307.
—— Sir Edmund, 307.
Morville, Sir Hugh, 207.
Mothlae mᶜD mᶜF., 167.
Movie Clarineagh, 92, 93.
—— mᶜWiheally, 101.
Mowlua, St., 84.
Mownemon, 33, 34.
Moy, 114.
Moy Je, 214.

Moyalve, battle of, 77.
Moyargedrosse, 42.
Moybile, 93, 99.
Moybrey, 109, 111, 122–125, 131, 132, 136, 138, 142, 143, 146, 147, 154, 165, 173–175, 189, 268.
Moycashel, sept of, 308.
Moychey, St. of Louth, 78.
Moycoua, 241.
Moydan, 114.
Moydwine, 154.
Moye, the, 13.
Moye Ife, 43, 213.
Moye of the E. *See* Mayo.
Moye oge, 186.
Moyeayre, 159.
Moyelly, 31, 62.
Moyene, 210
Moyengalty, 297.
Moyenoye, 150.
Moyeochter, battle of, 91.
Moyerayney, 149.
Moyfarcha, 202.
Moyfea, 73.
Moygullen, 111.
Moyhrea, 111.
Moyith, 107.
Moykednie, 266.
Moyldeyn, 115.
Moyle (Mel), St., 73.
Moyleawa mᶜB , 97.
Moylebarryn, 145.
Moylebresaile mᶜM , 107.
Moylebressal, 100, 115.
Moylebryde O'Mothlann, 103.
—— O'Moylefin, 177
Moylecahy, k. of C., 81.
Moylecalgie, 100.
Moylechraich mᶜD., 126.
Moyle Clarineagh, 92
Moylecloiche mᶜConnor, 145.
Moylecomarb, a of Glendalough, 126.
Moyleconoge, 136
Moylecova, a of Armagh, 143.
—— k of I., 97–99, 172.
—— k. of M., 34, 101.
—— k. of U., 101
—— Moylecryvie mᶜToylegen, 146.
Moyle Dawine, 284.

Moyledihriv, St., 138.
Moyledor, a of Dawinis, 143.
Moyledownye, 253, 263
Moyldoye mᶜFenin, 107.
—— mᶜSwyne, 104.
Moyledoyer, b., 109
Moyledoyne mᶜColman, 103.
—— mᶜScan, 107.
Moyledoynn, 100.
Moyledwynn, 106.
—— mᶜHugh, p. of Aileagh, 142
—— mᶜHugh A., 126.
—— mᶜHugh B., 120.
—— mᶜMorgissa, 137.
—— son of Moynagh, 108.
Moylefihre, 101.
Moylefithry, 113.
Moylefohorty, 108.
—— k. of M., 157
Moylegarow, the, 123, 160.
Moylegula, k. of M., 115
Moyle Imorchor, 119.
Moyleissa, a Dane, 151
—— king and poet, 196.
—— mᶜHugh, archb of Tuam, 267.
—— primate of A., 185.
Moylekeigh mᶜSeannoile, 101, 107,
Moylekevyn, a. of Tymochwa, 149.
Moylckyeran mᶜCon ne mboght, 180.
—— mᶜRonane, 142.
—— O'Maney, 160.
Moylelonge, 108.
Moylemartan O'Skellan, 151.
Moylemary, Q of I., 190.
Moylemihie, 152.
Moylemihil, mᶜF., 146.
Moylemorey, 143.
—— mᶜMoylemoye, 170.
—— son of Cosse Warce, 151.
Moylemorie mᶜScanlan, primate, 163.
Moylemoye, br. of Brian B , 158
—— mᶜDowgille, 165.
Moylena, 59, 170, 184.
Moyleowa mᶜBoydan, 98.
—— mᶜEnos, 102
—— mᶜForanany, 102.
—— mᶜTayhill, 122.
Moylepatrick, a. of Armagh, 150.

Moylepoile, b. of C., 165.
—— mᶜAileall, 147.
Moylerge. See Moylorge.
Moyleronye, k. of Ulster, 180.
—— mᶜDonogh, 139.
—— mᶜRoen, 177.
Moylerrwayn, a. of Disert, 143
—— Tawlaghty, 127
Moyleseaghlyn, k. of I., 88, 115.
—— mᶜConnor, 183
—— mᶜDonnell, 116, 159–165, 167–169, 171–173
—— mᶜMoyleronye, 140, 141, 148, 174.
—— mᶜMoyleroye, 140.
—— mᶜMoylerwanie, 172.
—— mᶜNeale, 143.
—— More, 88.
Moyletola, a. of Laragh B., 127.
Moyleyghen, 122.
Moylorge, 150, 218, 230, 241, 266, 274, 279, 287, 288, 297, 305, 310, 320, 321.
—— princes of, 263, 271, 272, 276, 278, 279, 281, 283, 288, 291, 294, 296, 303–305, 309, 315, 316, 320, 321, 324, 325, 327.
Moylyn, William, 227.
Moymoriske, 43.
Moymucroyve, battle of, 59.
Moymwaye, 31.
Moynagh mᶜBwyhy, 104.
—— mᶜColman, 122.
—— mᶜFinyn, 106
—— mᶜSachaday, 139.
Moynarb, 42.
Moyne, dr. of Conn C., 58.
Moyne, son of Heremon, 30.
—— son of Owgany, 42.
Moyne Corrie, 228.
Moyne Je, 317.
Moyne Issyc, 247, 248.
Moyne Koysse Blaie, 120.
Moyneailve, 42.
Moynebrokan, battle of, 155.
Moynealta, 13
Moynemore, battle of, 199.
Moynemoye, 42, 218, 275.
Moyne-ne-Bynne, 257.
Moynevillan, 175.

Index. 371

Moyneymyne, 235, 257.
Moyngall mᶜBreacan, 149.
Moynid Krewe, 114.
Moynie, 30.
Moyniss, 35, 131.
Moynithe, 24, 107, 139.
Moynmoye, 90, 275.
Moynod, 58.
Moynoye, 164, 218, 230.
Moyntir Dornynn, 318.
—— Elye, 313.
—— Eolas, 273, 280, 285, 296, 325.
—— Gorman, 99, 136.
—— Hagan, 183, 188, 200, 323.
—— Kenay, 188, 219, 290.
—— Keruellan, 273.
—— Keyndelan, 148.
—— Kreghan, 275.
—— Kyergie, 203.
—— Luss, 191.
—— Milchon, 219.
—— Moyleynna, 200.
—— Mulmerry, 285.
—— Peadaghan, 253.
—— Relly, 242.
—— Rodan, 193.
—— Swanym, 191.
—— Thlaman, 183.
Moyntir, John, 261.
—— Philip, 261.
Moyorne, 111.
Moyrched, 31.
Moyreyne, 149.
Moyroth, 100.
Moysainue, 42.
Moyses, 19, 20.
Moytar, 42.
Moyteaffa, 124, 125.
Moytoyrey, 17.
Moyty, 92.
Moyvile, 98, 104, 156.
Moyvora, 180.
Muckenagh, 246.
Mucksnawe, 133.
Mugron mᶜEnos, 139.
Muinter. *See* Moyntir.
Mullagh Rathe, 291.
Mullamaisden, 55.
Mulmorry O'Hargedy, 79.
—— mᶜM., k. of L., 166.

Mulmorry, p. of Kerry L., 144.
—— p. of Rathlin, 144.
Mulmoye (Mulloye), k. of M., 157.
Mulromes, 256
Munster, 15, 16, 28, 33, 34, 38, 42, 46, 47, 55, 56, 96, 102, 113, 126, 127, 130, 140, 141, 146, 151, 155, 163, 165, 181, 183–185, 188, 191-193, 194, 198, 199, 202-204, 217, 221, 223, 225, 226, 229, 239, 251, 267, 277, 278, 283, 290, 302, 321, 327.
—— kings of, 28, 47, 55, 58, 69, 71–73, 81, 89, 91, 97, 100, 102, 104, 106, 107, 109–112, 115, 117, 120, 127, 128, 130, 131, 138, 140, 144, 152, 156, 157, 175, 192, 203, 226, 267.
—— men of, 31, 38, 41, 51, 55, 56, 112, 123, 127, 130, 132, 141, 144, 150-152, 156-158, 162, 163, 165, 169, 172, 177, 181, 182, 184–186, 199, 235, 267, 283.
Murcha mᶜMoyledynn, 131.
Murgaill mᶜNynnea, 122.
Murgeall mᶜReaghtaioratt, 123.
Muries, k. of C., 116.
Murrain, 46, 111, 123, 160, 256, 263, 283, 284, 285, 327.
Murrogh, k. of C., 116.
—— mᶜBrayn, 112, 114.
—— mᶜFerall mᶜM., 117.
—— mᶜFlynn O'M., 51, 180.
—— mᶜMoyledwynn, 131.
—— mᶜThomas, 319.
—— of Ulster, 135.
—— p. of Leinster, 178.
—— son of Brian B., 167.
—— son of k. Dermot, 178, 180.
—— son of k. Donnell, 122.
Murtagh Bacagh mᶜD., 324.
—— mᶜNeale, 151.
—— sons of, 314.
Muskerry, p. of, 162.
Musicians, 247, 300.
Mwynemon, 212.
Mynn Beaireann, a. of Achabo, 110.

Naas, 53, 153.
Nadarcha, 124.

Nahie mᶜFiaghra, 70.
Narb, 42.
Nardo, 84.
Nare, 209.
Narhirs, the, 113.
Narne, 42
Ne Troye, Dermott mᶜS., 272.
Neaghtin, k. of Picts, 112, 114.
—— mᶜDerilly, 114.
—— Seachnassach, 112.
Neale Caille, 135–140, 172.
—— Frossagh, 112, 115, 121, 123, 172.
—— Glunduff, 115, 116, 145, 146, 153, 155, 172.
—— Kam, 306.
—— k of Meath, 122.
—— mᶜEochie, 179.
—— mᶜEochie M., 64.
—— mᶜFenius, 19, 20.
—— mᶜFerall, 151.
—— mᶜHugh, 131, 145.
—— o'Coyne, 167.
—— of the 9 H., 51, 64, 65, 75, 76, 78, 88, 166, 171, 296, 314, 315.
—— Tolairy, 156.
Nealgussa, 209.
Nean, bishop, 78.
Neathagh, 118.
Nector, 106.
Nemon, of Lismore, 98.
Neohagh, the, 306.
Nero, 90.
Nestorius, 106.
Nevie, 14.
Newae, 17.
Newcastle o'Finnaghan, 325.
—— in I. Owen, 289.
Newman O'Seanchin, 168.
Newtowne, 308.
Nevy mʳSrawgynn, 59.
Nia mʳCormack, 113.
—— mᶜSedawyn, 45, 211.
Nibroth, 14.
Nicene Council, 106.
Nicene seas, 234.
Nicicorus, 23.
Nicoll m'Moyle Issa, 260.
Ninnvaille, 210.
Nisan the leper, 84.

Niva macOirck, 113.
Noeh, 11, 12, 14, 20.
—— mᶜDaniell, 108.
Nobber. *See* Obber.
Norannagh, 197.
Nore, the, 15, 28
Normandy, 184, 215.
Normans, 7, 139, 143, 151, 154, 179.
Norwich, b. of, 222–224.
Nowafinnfaile, 36.
Noygiallach, 64.
Noyman of Iniscahie, 158.
Nuada Noaght, 48.
Nugent of Meath, 311.
Nwa, b. of Glendalogha, 149.
Nwadad, 210.
—— Delawe, 212.
—— fyn Fayle, 210.
Nwadat mᶜSegenye, 140.
Nwaly, dr. of o'Connor, 325.
Ny Melaghlin, Finola, 256.
Nynny mᶜDivagh, 79.

Oak near Kells, 95.
Oa Meith, 133.
Oaths, 52, 71, 196, 201, 203, 204, 275.
Obber, castle of the, 217.
O'Bearrga, Cowdoly, 174.
O'Beollan, Moylefinien, 241.
—— Thomas, 246.
O'Beyrne, 250.
—— Dermott mᶜI., 319
—— Murrogh mᶜT., 319.
O'Bichollye, G., 220.
O'Boyle, 29, 283.
—— Annyless, 253.
—— arch. of Armagh, 189.
—— Ceallagh, 253.
—— Dermott, 276.
—— Donnell, 276, 278.
—— Dowgall, 253
—— Faithleagh, 253
—— Gille-Monelagh, 238.
—— Melaghlen, 253.
—— Moyleronye, 253.
—— Neale mᶜD., 260
O'Boysgne, 61.

Index. 373

O'Brackan, B., 267.
O'Brennan, 64.
O'Brien. *See* O'Bryen.
O'Brisleans, 280.
O'Briwynes, 120
O'Brogann, S., arch. of Cashel, 259.
O'Brothloghann, M , 183.
O'Broyan, 57.
O'Broyen, T., p. of Lwynie, 218.
O'Broyn, B., a tympanist, 302.
—— Geralt, 321.
O'Broyne, 29, 320, 325.
—— Bran, 325.
—— Donnogh, 160.
—— Faylan, 116
—— Moriegh, 120
—— Tiege, 218.
O'Bryan, Donogh, 294.
—— Mortogh, 232.
O'Bryen, 30, 58, 191, 199, 219, 242, 249, 250, 267, 277, 290, 295, 312.
—— Bryen, 211, 284.
—— Bryen Bane, 286, 291.
—— Bryen m^{c}T , 198.
—— Bryen, p of T., 322.
—— Bryen Roe, 246, 249, 251.
—— Conell, 194.
—— Connor, 190–194, 196, 211, 286.
—— Connor m^{c}Dermott, 192.
—— Connor m^{c}Donnell, 198, 203.
—— Connor m^{c}Teige, 312.
—— Connor ne Suidyne, 211
—— Connor, p. of Eoghanachts, 182.
—— Connor, p of T., 246.
—— Connor Roe, 216
—— Daluagh, 305.
—— Dermott, 211, 300, 302.
—— Dermott Cleragh, 267.
—— Donnell, 202, 206.
—— Donnell Mor, 211.
—— Donnogh, 211, 254, 267.
—— Donnogh Carbreagh, 211, 223, 225, 233, 237.
—— Donnogh, k. of Thomond, 267.
—— Donnogh m^{c}B. Roe, 252, 254.
—— Donnogh m^{c}T., 260.
—— Donnogh of Tirebryan, 294.

O'Bryen, Donnogh, p. of Thomond, 277, 279.
—— Henry, 211.
—— Kennedy, 183.
—— Mahon, 211.
—— Mahon m^{c}D., 283.
—— Mahon, son of Murtagh, 190.
—— Moriertagh, k. of I., 184–188, 211.
—— Moriertagh m^{c}B., 222.
—— Morrogh m^{c}M. 267.
—— Murrogh na Rathine, 308.
—— Morrogh, p. of I , 179
—— Murtagh, 202, 216, 222, 225, 229
—— Murtagh, k. of Dublin, 181, 182.
—— Murtagh, k. of I , 186–190.
—— Murtagh, k. of M., 196, 202, 204, 267, 277, 286.
—— Murtagh m^{c}Connor, 199.
—— Murtagh of Lwyne, 232.
—— Murtagh, prince, 211, 222, 226.
—— Murtagh, p. of T , 272, 277.
—— Murtagh, son of Terlaugh, 182.
—— Teig, 180, 187, 199.
—— Teig, k. of T., 196, 242, 309.
—— Teig, son of Terlagh, 183, 211.
—— Terlagh, 211.
—— Terlagh, 179, 254, 260.
—— Terlagh, k. of I., 180–184, 187, 190–192, 198, 199, 203.
—— Terlagh, k. of M , 179, 192, 193, 199, 201, 202, 260, 293.
—— Terlagh m^{c}B. Roe, 260
—— Terlagh, p. of Thomond, 260, 322.
—— Terlagh, son of Don Carb., 237, 248, 249.
O'Bruyns of Brenie, 205.
O'Byrne, 29, 308.
—— Gillecriost, 284.
O'Cahall, Gillemochoynne, 229.
O'Cahan, 29, 64, 243.
—— Donnell, 260.
—— Hugh, 242.
—— Magnus, 242.

374   *Index.*

O'Cahan, Murtagh, 242.
O'Caharnie (Fox), 183.
—— Kynath, 183.
—— Melaghlen m^cN., 230.
—— Teig, 183.
O'Cahassie, Kyeran, 183.
O'Cananann, Moylecolumb, 157
O'Cannann, 154.
—— Donnell, 163.
—— Flathvertagh, 163.
—— Gillicholme, 163.
—— Rowrie, 155, 163.
—— p. of Tirconnell, 164.
O'Carhie, M., poet, 179
O'Carmackan, Finn, 223
O'Carmeady, C. b. of Clonfert, 213.
O'Carroll, 309.
O'Carry Calma, M., 170.
O'Cassine, 170.
Ockie, battle of, 72, 119.
O'Clocan, cowarb of Kells, 205.
O'Clohogan, 180
O'Clowan, Gillaenos, 198
O'Coffie, 30
O'Colgan, 29.
O'Conallie, arch of Armagh, 243.
O'Conchennan, D., 278
—— M , 278.
O'Connell, p. of, 175
—— T., 309.
O'Connor, 105.
O'Connor of Affalie, 29, 57, 183, 184, 185, 228, 266, 268, 291, 308, 324, 327.
—— Brian, 236, 321.
—— Cahall, 327.
—— Cahire, 326.
—— Callogh, 260, 320, 326.
—— Conn, 326.
—— Connor, 185
—— Cowafnie, 305.
—— daughter of, 266, 324.
—— Donnogh, 192.
—— Felim m^cCahire, 322
—— m^cCahall, 325
—— Melaghlin, 232.
—— Morish the bald, 312.
—— Morrogh, 311, 320, 325, 326.
—— Mortagh, 180, 260, 310.
—— Mullmorey, 231, 260.

O'Connor, Owen m^cC., 325
O'Connor of Carbrey, 291.
—— Donnell, 304, 309, 316, 325.
—— Mortagh, 287.
O'Connor of Connaught, 64, 222, 298, 309.
—— Brian m^cMagnus, 281.
—— Bryan m^cTerlagh, 235, 281
—— Cahall, 165, 272, 273, 281, 282.
—— Cahall Carragh, 215, 216, 217.
—— Cahall Crovdearg, 215-219, 223-5, 229, 230, 251, 254.
—— Cahall Duff, 325-327
—— Cahall m^cC. Roe, 249.
—— Cahall m^cC. Roe, k. of C., 252.
—— Cahall m^cDermott G., 289.
—— Cahall m^cDonnell, 272, 279, 281-283, 316
—— Cahall m^cD., k of C , 283, 284.
—— Cahall m^cHugh, 182
—— Cahall m^cHugh B., 294, 295, 298, 300, 302, 316.
—— Cahall m^cHugh m^cC , 241
—— Cahall m^cHugh m^cO., 283, 287.
—— Cahall m^cMurrogh, 326.
—— Cahall m^cRory, 327, 328.
—— Cahall m^cTeige, 246.
—— Cahall m^cTiernan, 243.
—— Cahall of C., 165
—— Cahall oge, 299-301, 312, 313, 317-319, 322.
—— Carrick, 240.
—— Charles, 234
—— Connor, 197.
—— Connor m^cC., 235, 238.
—— Connor m^cCowarba C., 280.
—— Connor m^cHugh, 237
—— Connor m^cRory, 327
—— Connor m^cTeige, 283
—— Connor m^cTerlagh, 194, 198.
—— Connor Meanmoye, 217, 218.
—— Connor Roe m^cH. B., 273.
—— Connor Roe m^cM., 238.
—— Connor, son of Terlagh, 197.
—— Cormack, 235, 236.
—— Cormack m^cRory, 291, 318.
—— Dermott Backagh, 240

Index. 375

O'Connor, Dermott Gall, 272.
—— Dermott mᶜHugh, 322.
—— Dermott mᶜMagnus, 238
—— Dermot Roe, 263
—— Donn, 29, 310, 311, 312, 315, 317, 318, 323, 327.
—— Donnell, 262, 272, 275, 276, 290.
—— Donnell mᶜC., 305.
—— Donnell mᶜMurtagh, 304, 309, 311-313, 325.
—— Donnell of Irros, 279.
—— Donnell, p of C , 182
—— Donnell, son of k Terlaugh, 198.
—— Donogh, b of Aylfynn, 238.
—— Donogh Gall, 287
—— Donogh mᶜRory, 276.
—— Donogh More, 234.
—— Donogh, son of D , 272.
—— Eaght, dr. of Rowrie, 221
—— Felym, 232-239, 241, 243, 245, 258
—— Felym Cleragh, 310, 311.
—— Felym, k. of C., 263, 265, 268, 270-279, 291, 301, 307, 310, 311, 317, 327.
—— Felym mᶜCathal oge, 317, 318, 320
—— Felym, son of Cathal C., 239, 251
—— Hugh, 177, 179.
—— Hugh Ballagh, 272.
—— Hugh Breifnach, 263-265, 267, 280, 287.
—— Hugh Dall, 219.
—— Hugh Keige, 317.
—— Hugh, k of C., 178.
—— Hugh mᶜC., k. of C., 230-233.
—— Hugh mᶜC. Dall, k. of C., 250.
—— Hugh mᶜC Oge, 316.
—— Hugh mᶜFelym, k. of C., 239, 241, 242, 245, 247-250.
—— Hugh mᶜF mᶜH., 291, 293-295, 297, 301, 303, 307, 308, 310, 311.
—— Hugh mᶜHugh, 239, 240, 254.
—— Hugh mᶜHugh B , 294, 295, 297.

O'Connor, Hugh mᶜOwen, 263
—— Hugh mᶜRory, 204, 232, 234.
—— Hugh mᶜTeige, 283, 287.
—— Hugh mᶜT., k. of C., 142.
—— Hugh mᶜTerlaugh, 297-299
—— Hugh Moyneagh, 234, 251, 252.
—— Hugh, son of Terlaugh, 195.
—— John, 272.
—— John Redy, 307.
—— Laughlen, 240.
—— Magnus, 272, 275, 278, 279, 285, 287.
—— Magnus mᶜMurtagh, 238.
—— Magnus Oge, 302.
—— Mahon mᶜC., 231.
—— Manus, 267, 304.
—— Manus mᶜC. Roe, 256.
—— Melaghlen mᶜC. C., 226
—— Melaghlen mᶜD., 285
—— Melaghlen mᶜH , 232.
—— Melaghlen mᶜM , 252.
—— Moreis, 231.
—— Morice, b of Oylfin, 254
—— Morrogh, k. of Meath, 193
—— Mortagh, 272, 311.
—— Mortagh mᶜD., 321.
—— Mortagh Moyneagh, 224, 252, 309, 311
—— Owen Finn, 301.
—— Owen mᶜRory, 250.
—— Prince Magnus, 287.
—— Prince Teig, 178
—— Ranelt, dr. of R. O'Connor, 225.
—— Roderick, 206.
—— Roe, 29, 310-312, 315, 317, 327.
—— Roe mᶜDermott, 311.
—— Rory, 190, 225, 230, 305, 307.
—— Rory, k. of C , 183-185, 201-206, 221, 230, 232, 235.
—— Rory, k. of I., 3, 201, 206, 207, 214, 230, 231.
—— Rory mᶜCahall, 264, 275, 276, 327.
—— Rory mᶜCahall Roe, 270-273, 275-278.
—— Rory mᶜD., 275.
—— Rory mᶜHugh, 237.

O'Connor, Rory mᶜTerlagh, 196-198, 206, 250, 309.
—— Rory na Fidh, 279, 283
—— Teige, 325.
—— Teige mᶜCahall, 290
—— Teige mᶜConnor M., 217.
—— Teige mᶜConnor Roe, 238.
—— Teige mᶜDonnell, 272
—— Teige mᶜGilleroe, 231.
—— Teige mᶜHugh, 178.
—— Teige mᶜHugh mᶜC., 237.
—— Teige mᶜMagnus, 304, 316.
—— Teige mᶜRory, 294
—— Teige mᶜTerlagh, 198.
—— Teige mᶜT., p of C., 287.
—— Teige mᶜT. mᶜC., 250.
—— Terlaugh, 230, 243.
—— Terlaugh, k. of C., 281, 284, 286-288, 290-296, 316
—— Terlaugh, k. of I., 190-200.
—— Terlagh mᶜC. C., 227.
—— Terlagh mᶜHugh, 239.
—— Terlagh mᶜH. mᶜO., 279, 284, 294
—— Terlagh mᶜOwen, 256.
—— Terlagh mᶜRory, 189, 232.
—— Terlagh Oge mᶜH. mᶜT., 309, 326, 327.
—— Terlagh Roe mᶜH. mᶜF , 309, 320
—— the abbot, 326.
—— Thomas, archb. of T., 242.
—— Tiuall mᶜNeale, 240.
—— Tomaltagh, b of Moye Ife, 213.
O'Connor of Corcomroe, 30, 175.
—— Donnell, 302
—— Felim mᶜAn-enny, 302.
O'Connor of Kerry, 30, 179.
—— Dermot, 325
O'Connor of Lynally, 326.
—— Donnell, 302.
O'Connor of Sligo, 29, 291.
—— Cahall oge. 301
—— Donnell mᶜMurtagh, 304, 316.
—— Manus, 304
O'Conollan, Th , 278
O'Conway, 200.
O'Conynges, 102
O'Coyne, Neale, 167.

Octlarge mᶜFogith, 104.
O'Cullen, Mahon, 246.
O'Daly, arch poet, 195.
—— Cowchonnought, 191.
—— Donnogh More, 238.
—— Enos, 246, 297.
—— Geffrey, 236.
—— Keruell, 325.
—— Loway, b of C., 292.
—— Melaghlen, 232.
—— Moyle Issa, 266.
—— Teige, 250.
O'Dea, 30.
O'Dempsey, 29, 57, 262, 305.
—— Cowlen, 225, 231.
—— Cullen, 232, 285.
—— Dermot, 309.
—— Donnell, 315
—— Donogh, 227.
—— Finn, 227.
—— Hugh, 203
—— Melaghlen, 228.
—— Mulmorey, 327.
—— Thomas, 316.
O'Deoran, 280.
—— W., 325.
O'Dermoddaes, 277.
O'Dermott, Cahal, 217.
O'Dermotts, 278.
O'Deuclyn, Connor, 278.
—— Dalere-Docker, 278
—— Gillernew, 278
O'Docherty, 29, 64
—— Donell, 294.
—— John, 294, 300.
O'Donelan, F , 256.
O'Dongaly, M , 184.
O'Donnell, 29, 64, 76, 107, 247, 252, 256, 290, 306, 316, 318-321
—— Art, 289.
—— Connor, 289, 293, 307.
—— Cormack mᶜC., 253.
—— Cormack mᶜE , 253
—— Donnell, 233, 237, 251-253
—— Donnell, p of Tirec., 237.
—— Felym, 289.
—— Ferlegin, 260.
—— Gormphley, dr. of, 298.
—— Hugh, 260, 275, 279, 289, 293.
—— Hugh Boyl, 252.

O'Donnell, John, 300.
—— Loghlinn, 253
—— Magnus Eoghanach, 301
—— Magnus Meawlagh, 297.
—— Melaghlen, 284
—— Melaghlen, p. of T., 238.
—— Molmory, 184.
—— Neale, 268
—— Neale Garwe, 297.
—— Owen, 253
—— Phelym, 300
—— p. of Durlesse, 164.
—— Terlagh, p. of Tirec., 260, 306, 307, 315.
—— Thomas, b of Raphoe, 282.
O'Donnoyle, 29.
O'Donsynay, M., 146.
Odor mᶜFlynn, 178.
O'Dorchy, N., 261.
O'Dornine, Hugh, 321.
O'Dowagan, Richard, 306
O'Dowalgie, Fogartagh, 263.
O'Dowdie, 64, 277, 318
—— Bryan, 262.
—— Conor oge, 278
—— Faithleagh, 253, 254.
—— Hugh, 160
—— Melaghlen, C , 278.
—— Mortagh. 278.
—— Rory, 320
O'Dowgennan, 64.
—— David, 320.
—— Ferall, 293.
O'Dowgin, Conyn, 184.
O'Dowlen, 57.
O'Dowley, Gillechrist, 168.
O'Dowlies, 121
O'Dowlyn, k. of Fertullagh, 198.
O'Dowoye, Bryan, 272.
O'Doyne, 29, 57, 305, 307.
—— Caroll, 306.
—— David, 306.
—— Donell, 305.
—— Donogh, 322.
—— Donnogh, k. of Moybrey, 173, 175
—— Karoll, 322.
—— Owen, 322.
O'Duffdirma, C., 242.
—— H., 243

O'Duffie, C., archb. of C , 213, 216.
—— D., archb. of C , 194.
—— Moriegh, archb. of C., 194, 196, 197.
Oeny, 186.
O'Fagan, Flann, 170
O'Fallawyn, Dermot, 190
—— John, 291.
O'Falie. *See* Affalie.
O'Faylan, p of L., 192
O'Fearghusa, 64.
O'Feilan, 29, 192, 205, 321.
—— Arraghtagh, 127
O'Ferrall, 30, 45, 167, 177, 191, 232, 277, 313.
—— Bryan, 322.
—— Cahall, race of, 328.
—— Carbry, 312.
—— Conuak, 328.
—— Cowchonaught, 310
—— Dermot, 294.
—— Donell, 299.
—— Donell, chief of Anallye, 237.
—— Donell Duff, 186
—— Donell mᶜHugh, 266.
—— Donell mᶜJohn, 308, 322.
—— Ferall mᶜJ Galda, 278.
—— Geffrey, 249, 258, 266
—— Geffrey mᶜG., 282, 304.
—— Geffrey mᶜMortogh, 266.
—— Gillernew, 237, 239, 250.
—— Gillernew mᶜG , 284.
—— Hugh mᶜM., 266.
—— Hugh Oge, 260.
—— John, 282, 287, 299, 306, 308, 321
—— John mᶜBryan, 322.
—— John mᶜDonell, 321
—— Johnyn, 284.
—— Matthew, 298
—— Morrogh, 308.
—— Morrogh Bane, 321.
—— Morrogh mᶜG., 196.
—— Shane, 271.
—— Thomas mᶜA., 278.
—— Thomas mᶜC , 321.
—— William mᶜHugh, 278.
Offrick mᶜAlfrithe, 101.

378   Index.

O'Fiachras, 120.
O'Fiaghragh Ayney, 78, 220.
—— Moye, 230, 251.
—— prince of, 241.
O'Fielan. See O'Feilan.
O'Finallan, 30.
—— M., k of Delvin, 205.
O'Fineann, W., b. of C., 259.
O'Finsneaghty, J., 298.
—— Melrasion, 284.
O'Fiolan, p. of, 321.
O'Flaherty, Murtagh, 253.
—— Moyleguley, 215
O'Flannagan, Cahall, 272, 273.
—— Connor, 291.
—— Dermott, 287, 290.
—— Donell, 238.
—— Donnogh, b. of Oylfin, 261.
—— Eoghye, 10, 12.
—— Magnus, 279.
O'Flannagan's daughter, 264.
O'Flathverty, 179.
—— F., 185.
—— M , 215.
—— Rory, 218.
O'Flattyhe, G , 184
—— Hugh, 184, 194.
O'Flynn, 30, 64.
—— Bryan, 254.
—— Fiaghra, 258.
—— Flann, arch. of Tuam, 241.
—— Gillenewe, 193.
—— Hugh, 247.
O'Fogarty, F., 185.
O'Fohertie, 182.
O'Foirvhen, D , a. of C., 147.
O'Forga, 178, 240.
O'Foylan, 57, 195.
—— of the Desies, 222.
—— p. of L., 192.
—— tanist of, 325.
O'Fox, 29, 64, 187, 230, 231, 233,
   308, 322, 323. See Fox
O'Furie, primate of Armagh, 236
O'Gair, A., 176.
O'Gara, Rory, 241.
O'Garie, D., 287.
—— T., 243.
O'Garmley. See O'Gormley.
O'Gartie, 30.

O'Gassine, 267.
O'Gawyn, battle of, 106.
O'Gerans, 182
Ogham, 286.
Oghterard, 185
Oghtertyre, 264.
O'Giarans. See O'Gerans.
O'Gibbelan, Florence, 256.
—— Morish, 286.
Ognie, earl of, 207.
O'Gormley, 197, 300.
—— Awley, 243.
—— Enna, 253.
—— Melaghlen, 293, 300.
—— Melaghlin, chief, 262.
—— Neale, 197, 234.
O'Gwary, C., 127.
O'Haillealla, 117.
—— Cormac, 155.
O'Hanlon, 305.
—— Cownley, 243.
—— Magnus, 283.
—— Neale, p of Orhir, 283.
O'Hanly, Hugh, 317.
—— Imer, 308.
—— John, 317.
—— Teige, 266.
O'Hanvye, p. of Fearbill, 186
O'Hara, 277, 284, 318, 319
—— Art, p, of Lwynie, 278.
—— Connor God, 223.
—— Donell, 246.
—— Farall, 285.
—— John, 310.
—— Teige, 320.
O'Hargedy, M., 79.
O'Harie, 30.
—— John, 290.
—— Morrogh, 194
—— Taighleagh, 194.
O'Harlagh, 30.
O'Hart, p of E Teaffa, 187.
O'Harty, Mortagh, 244.
O'Hawaile, R , poet, 305.
O'Haylyeaghty, F., 113.
O'Heignye, p of Fermanagh, 216,
   225.
O'Heiraisscol, 30.
O'Helye, Dermot, 263
—— Magnus, 313.

Index. 379

O'Helye, Murtagh, 313.
O'Heoaine, F., 115.
O'Heoghaa, 207.
—— D., k. of U., 185.
—— G., k. of U., 191.
—— R., k. of U., 216.
O'Heogussie, Enos, 297.
O'Heossye, Adam, 260.
O'Heredin, 29.
O'Heyne, N., 285.
—— Owen, 241.
O'Hiffernan, 30.
O'Higgin, Matthew, 292.
Ohinbeg, 112.
Ohinmore, 112.
Ohnie Mulrian, 255.
O'Hogan, b. of Killaloe, 238.
—— Swynie, 128.
O'Hoyne, M., p. of Ayny, 167.
O'Hugh, G., p. of Teaffa, 168.
—— Hugh, 193.
O'Hughtann, D., 163.
Oicke, battle of, 73.
Oilill Anye, 43.
—— k. of C., 72.
—— k. of Ossory, 101.
—— m^{c}Ross, 47.
—— Molt, 71, 72, 171.
—— Molt Invanna, 83.
—— son of Art, 38.
—— son of Conlye, 45.
Oillealla Olcheoyn, 210.
Oisle, 151.
O'Kahallaine, A., 154.
O'Kaharnie, Kynath, 183
—— Moriegh, 218.
—— T Sheannagh, 183.
O'Kananann, F., 164.
O'Kannanann, R. m^{c}Neale, 163.
O'Karuell, Kien, 307.
—— p. of Loghlein, 189.
O'Keally, Gillekoewgyn, 228.
O'Keansellye, king of, 73, 120, 150, 158, 168.
O'Keansellyes, 129, 132, 160, 184.
O'Kearney, J., a. of C., 127.
O'Kehernie, b. of Ferns, 186.
—— chief, 308
O'Kelly of Brey, 29, 43, 51, 125, 129, 136, 156, 228.

O'Kelly of Imaine, 29, 63, 97, 120, 130, 194, 195, 240, 255, 277, 287, 293, 296, 299, 302, 307, 309, 318, 323, 324.
—— Ardvron, 120.
—— Bryan, 240.
—— Caffye, 120.
—— Cahall m^{c}Teige, 254.
—— Cathrannah, 120.
—— Con m^{c}Donough, 294.
—— Connor, 181.
—— Connor Kearruagh, 296.
—— Connor, p. of Imaine, 281, 285.
—— Dery, 240.
—— Donell, p. of Imaine, 256.
—— Donnogh C., 299
—— Donnogh m^{c}Hugh, 293.
—— Donnogh Moyneagh, 261.
—— Donnogh, prince, 181
—— Edmund, 323.
—— Edmund m^{c}W., 311.
—— Feraagh, 310.
—— Ferall, 287.
—— Gilbert, 272, 283.
—— Hugh, 310.
—— Melaghlen, prince, 305, 327.
—— Morrogh m^{c}C., 255.
—— Morrogh m^{c}M., 221.
—— Morrogh O'B., 309.
—— Moylekieran, 220.
—— Murtagh, archb. of C., 327.
—— Owen m^{c}D., 309.
—— Soirvrechagh, 196.
—— Syacus, tanist, 257.
—— Teige, 244, 261, 272, 273, 275, 277, 278.
—— Teige m^{c}Teige, 293.
—— Teige Oge m^{c}T., 305.
—— Teige, p. of I., 167, 194, 277.
—— William, 298.
—— William O'D, 293
O'Kellyes of Ley, 313.
O'Kendalan, C., 201.
O'Kennedy, 30, 309.
—— Gillekewgyn, 252.
—— Murrogh o'B., 309.
O'Kenny, Sayrgus, 138.
O'Keoghie, k. of Ulster, 202.
O'Kerry, Donell, 242.

O'Kervell, 30, 58, 280.
—— b. of Uriell, 213.
—— Donnell, 232.
—— Donnogh, k. of Uriell, 201, 202, 205, 215.
—— Donnogh mᶜW., 306.
—— Kien, t. of Elye, 307.
—— Teige, p. of Eli, 322, 323, 327.
O'Keyne, Gilleherie, 243.
O'Keyrgie, Gillemorie, 182
O'Kierga, Gillegot, 200.
O'Kiergie, Gillepatrick, 181.
—— Rory, 227.
O'Killen, Cormack, 189.
O'Kindelan, Donnell, 169.
O'Kinnerge, Kyan, 242.
O'Kinsealyes. *See* O'Keansellyes.
O'Koewan, M., 186.
O'Konolley, M., 163.
O'Konoly, D., 162.
—— Flann, 117.
O'Konoyle, Hugh, 185.
O'Koyn, Glaisden, 186.
O'Krychan, p. of Fearnoy, 191.
O'Kwanna, M., 187.
O'Kyenan, Rory, 312.
O'Kyergie, Carbrey, 203.
—— Hugh, 165.
—— Moyleronye, 163.
—— Ulgarg, 165
O'Laghtna, b. of Tuam, 298.
—— D., p. of Teaffa, 165.
O'Laghtnann, a of Assaroe, 261.
—— L., b. of Oylfinn, 284.
O'Layhen, p. of Uriell, 182.
Olchover, k. of Cashel, 140.
—— k. of Munster, 115.
—— mᶜEyrck, 128.
Oleagh Neyde, 24.
O'Leihlovar, p of Dalnary, 144.
O'Leygachan, Cowley, 221.
—— Hugulat, 216.
O'Liahan, 168.
—— C., 142.
Olleal, 35.
Ollowe Fodla, 34, 35, 213.
O'Lochan, Cwan, 173, 174.
O'Locheny, C., 116.
O'Loogan, Seannan, 173.

Olorb, the, 62.
O'Loughlynn, Dermot, 246.
—— John, 246.
—— Mahon, 254.
O'Loyngsie, F., 188, 189.
O'Macnya, F., 119.
O'MacWais, 103, 145, 189.
O'Madden, 29, 63, 244, 277, 299.
—— Cahall, 256, 322.
—— Finola, 322.
—— Helen, 244.
—— John, 278.
—— Murrogh, 278.
—— Murrogh, p., 296, 308.
—— Owen, 290, 296.
—— Owen mᶜM., 323.
O'Mahon, 58.
—— Gregory, archb. of C., 315.
—— k. of U., 179.
O'Maille, Cormack, 292, 328.
—— Donnell Roe, 292.
—— territory of, 238, 249.
—— Thomas, b. of E. Downe, 286.
O'Male. *See* Imaile.
O'Malone, Cahall, 221.
—— Hugh, 200, 235.
—— Moilekieran, 244.
O'Manchan, Brehawe, 186.
O'Manie *See* Imaine.
O'Mannynn, 306.
O'Manon, Murrogh, 278.
O'Mayne. *See* Imayne.
O'Mayney, M., 160.
O'Meaghayre, 309.
O'Mealie *See* O'Maille.
O'Melaghlen, 29, 43, 51, 64, 72, 121, 122, 128, 130, 140, 144, 172, 184, 195, 277
—— Art, 214, 221
—— Art mᶜC., 244, 245, 250, 254, 258.
—— Art More, 296, 310.
—— Art na Gaislean, 254.
—— Art, son of Art, 310.
—— Art, son of Murrogh, 192, 221.
—— Bryan, 255.
—— Carbry, 243, 255, 256, 257.

Index. 381

O'Melaghlen, Carbry, k. of M., 254-257.
—— Carbry mᶜArt, 257.
—— Conn, 176.
—— Connor, 51, 176-178, 180, 187, 189, 240.
—— Connor, grandson of D., 192.
—— Connor, k of I., 133, 135.
—— Connor, k. of Meath, 180, 192.
—— Connor mᶜDonnell, 156.
—— Connor mᶜD. Bregagh, 251.
—— Connor mᶜKeruell, 163.
—— Connor mᶜM., 186, 187, 193.
—— Connor, prince, 146, 194.
—— Connor, p of Tara, 178
—— Cormack Ballagh, 296, 301.
—— Cormack mᶜArt, 225, 226, 228, 232, 235, 236.
—— Cormack mᶜC., 258.
—— Dermott, k. of Meath, 202-204, 206.
—— Dermott mᶜD., 200
—— Dermott Roe, 240.
—— Donnell, 189, 225, 226, 252.
—— Donnell Bregach, 226, 233, 256.
—— Donnell mᶜD., 225, 226.
—— Donnell mᶜFlynn, 147, 182, 184, 185, 190.
—— Donnell mᶜen Gott, 189.
—— Donnell mᶜHugh B, 173.
—— Donnell mᶜM., 194, 196, 198.
—— Donnell, p of Aileagh, 180
—— Donnogh, k. of Meath, 149, 151, 189, 192, 200, 216.
—— Donnogh mᶜD., k. of Meath, 201-205, 209.
—— Donnogh mᶜD, p. of Taragh, 155.
—— Donnogh mᶜF, 146-149, 184.
—— Donnogh mᶜM, 186, 187, 189, 198, 200, 205, 216.
—— Donnogh ne Maliagh, 232.
—— Flann, 176, 254.
—— Flayhenn, 184
—— Henry, 231.
—— Hugh mᶜFlynn, 146.
—— Kearnaghan, 182.
—— Melaghlen, 221, 256.

O'Melaghlen, Melaghlin Beg, 221, 227.
—— Melaghlin mᶜC., 181, 183.
—— Melaghlin mᶜM, 229
—— Melaghlin mᶜMorrogh, 198, 199, 204, 205.
—— Melaghlin mᶜM., k. of M., 204, 205.
—— Melaghlin Oge, 228.
—— Morrogh, 252, 257.
—— Morrogh, k. of M., 190-197, 199, 200, 214.
—— Morrogh, k. of T., 192.
—— Morrogh mᶜC., 180, 181, 183.
—— Morrogh mᶜFlynn, 51, 180.
—— Mortagh, 198.
—— Mortagh mᶜFlynn, 181.
—— Mortagh mᶜMelaghlen, 221.
—— Moylerwame God, 158.
—— Moyleseachlin mᶜC., 183.
—— Moyleseachlin mᶜC, 182, 183.
—— Moyleseachlin mᶜM., 191.
—— Moyleseachlin more, 200
—— Murtagh, 221, 232.
—— Roen, 175.
—— Tailty, dr. of, 190.
—— the knight, 232.
O'Molchonry. *See* O'Mulchonry.
O'Mollan, Leyseach, 325.
O'Molloye, 29, 51, 64, 250, 257.
—— Albyn, b. of Fernes, 229.
—— Conor mᶜOwen, 316.
—— Cowchoigry, 313.
—— Dermott, 308.
—— Donnell mᶜT., 308, 323.
—— Donnogh, k of Fearcall, 191.
—— Ferall mᶜTheobald, 308, 325.
—— Ferall, p. of Fearcall, 246.
—— Ferall, the son of, 193.
—— Fingonie, 147.
—— Gillebryde, 180.
—— Gillecolume, 232.
—— Hugh. 307, 322.
—— Meyler mᶜTheobald, 308.
—— Morrogh, 228.
—— Mortagh, 191.
—— Mowgroyn, 157.
—— Rory, 193
O'Mooney, Comynge, 118.
—— Feardownagh, 156.

O'Mooney, Moyle Kovay, 123.
—— Moynagh, 126
—— Moyneagh of Loghtere, 124.
O'More, 30, 45, 57, 232, 300.
—— Collogh, 10, 14, 25.
—— Denis, b. of Oylfin, 233.
—— Faghtna, 325.
—— Faghtna mᶜD., 306.
—— Gillepatrick, 324.
—— Goyheynie, 142.
—— Lysagh, 304.
—— mᶜRath, 203.
—— Rory, p. of Lease, 298.
O'Morey, 167.
O'Morie, C., 243.
O'Morie, prince of, 312.
O'Moriean, M., b. of C., 227.
O'Morrey, A., 175, 187.
—— C., 185, 243.
O'Moylechonrie. See O'Mulchonry.
O'Moyledory, 29, 173.
—— Enos, 157.
—— Hugh, 162.
—— Molrony, 175.
—— Neale, 178.
—— p. of Tyrconnell, 157, 162, 168, 178.
O'Moyledowyne, b. of C., 189.
—— Cahall, 258.
—— Gillecomye, 253.
O'Moylefin, M , 177.
O'Moylefomer, 213.
O'Moylefomore, M., 241.
O'Moylemihie, F., 158.
—— G., 179.
O'Moyleoyer, E., 117.
O'Moylcoyne, M., a. of C., 233.
O'Moyleronie, Dermott mᶜC., 223.
—— Dermott mᶜT., 243.
—— mᶜRoen, 177.
—— Tany, 264.
O'Moylerwayne, K. mᶜD., 217.
O'Moyletelcha, D., 169.
O'Mulchonry, 64.
—— Clarus, 240, 243.
—— Gregory, 323.
—— Moylynn, 10, 309.
—— Tanaige, 10, 311.
O'Mullana, 29.
O'Mullmyay, 273.

O'Mulloye. See O'Molloye.
O'Mullronye. See O'Moyleronie.
O'Mynnachan, 189.
Onagh, a. of Lismore, 124.
O'Naillealla, Seanchwa, 79.
Onchowe, 149.
O'Neaghten, 29, 63.
—— Christina, 246.
—— Robert, 252.
—— William Boy, 311.
O'Neaghagh, of Munster, 302.
—— of Nardo, 84.
—— of Ulster, 150, 173, 296, 306, 323.
O'Neale of Tyrone, 29, 54, 88, 91, 92, 95, 100, 112, 113, 116, 117, 124, 131, 137, 141, 167, 168, 201, 216, 221, 223-225, 252, 256, 269, 282.
—— Bryan, 242, 243.
—— Bryan mᶜB., 324.
—— Bryan mᶜD., 282.
—— Bryan mᶜHugh, 298.
—— Conor mᶜBryan, 312.
—— Connley, 323.
—— Cownley mᶜD., 284.
—— Cownley mᶜNeale, 322.
—— Donnell, 281, 282, 303.
—— Donnell, k. of I., 157, 158.
—— Donnell mᶜBryan, 256, 284.
—— Donnell mᶜHenry, 315, 324.
—— Donnell, p. of Tireowne, 282.
—— Flaithvertagh, 174.
—— Henry, 306, 307.
—— Henry Ainrey, 315.
—— Henry mᶜHugh Boy, 296.
—— Hugh, 164, 281.
—— Hugh Boye, 254.
—— Hugh Boyle mᶜD., 252.
—— Hugh, k. of Aileagh, 230, 233.
—— Hugh, k. of U., 299, 300, 301, 312.
—— Hugh Oge, 309.
—— Hugh, p. of Tirone, 164, 165.
—— Hugh Reawar, 291.
—— John, 281.
—— Murtagh, 144.
—— Neale, 303.
—— Neale Kulanagh, 256.

Index. 383

O'Neale of Tyrone, Neal mᶜB., 268, 284.
—— Neal More mᶜH., 313, 315, 319.
—— Neale Oge, 299, 313, 315, 319, 320.
—— of Clan Hugh Boye, 282, 299.
—— of Moybrey, 142.
—— of the north, 29, 64, 113, 131, 141, 201.
—— of the south, 113, 138.
—— of the west, 29, 64, 95, 113, 159.
—— Rory, 302.
—— the Red, 236.
O'Nolan, 29, 57, 167.
—— Donnell, 321.
—— Eochy, 194.
Onora, dr. of U. Burke, 309.
O'Nosyn, H., archb. of C., 203.
'Nwaat, M., 182.
Ophaly. *See* Affalie
Oran, 104.
Orb, 42.
Orba, 28, 30.
Orcades, 113, 166, 244.
O'Reachann, Connor, 305.
Orear Anoghlae, 141.
O'Reignie, 244
O'Reilly, 29, 64, 103, 313, 314.
—— Cahall, 233, 237, 244.
—— Cowchonoght, 237, 302, 303.
—— Godfrey, 205.
—— Melaghlen, 285.
—— Philip, 302.
—— Shane, 314
—— Teige, 237.
—— Thomas, 314.
Orestes, 77
Orhanagh, b. of Kildare, 138.
Orhir, the, 283.
O'Riagan, Flanagan, 147.
—— Mahon, 174.
Oriell. *See* Uriell.
Orlaith, 179.
Orlath, q. of I., 152.
Ormond, 193, 199, 255.
—— Earl of, 309, 322, 324.
Orney, 42.
O'Ronow, Ceallach, 182.

O'Ronow, Eoyn, 305.
O'Royrck, 29, 64, 168, 173, 177, 186, 195, 277, 288, 302, 310, 313, 314.
—— Art, 170, 183.
—— Art, prince, 288.
—— Cahall mᶜDonnell, 287.
—— Cahall mᶜHugh, 315.
—— Cahall the Deaf, 300.
—— Donnell Oge, 325.
—— Donnogh, son of K., 182, 183.
—— Ferall, 167.
—— Ferall, k. of C., 168.
—— Ferall mᶜUlarg, 285.
—— Flavertagh, 319.
—— Hugh, 316.
—— Hugh, k. of Delvin B., 178.
—— Hugh mᶜArt, 179.
—— Hugh mᶜFerall, 320.
—— Hugh, p. of Brenie, 297, 298.
—— king of Breffnie, 277.
—— Koyleagh, 182.
—— Magnus, 313.
—— Matthew mᶜC., 297.
—— Matthew mᶜT., 300.
—— Neale, 165, 280.
—— Owen, 313, 314.
—— Shane, 323.
—— son of, 297.
—— Teige, 305.
—— Tiernan, 191, 196, 198, 200-206.
—— Tigernan, p. of Brenie, 305, 312.
—— Ularg, 281, 303.
—— Uloyge, 277.
Orpheus, 18
O'Rwadan, b., 213.
O'Salerna, b. of Twayme, 241.
O'Scopa, b. of Rathbothe, 250.
O'Seaghnoseye, 64.
—— Gillenenew, 229.
—— Mortagh Garve, 324.
Osfa, k. of E., 128.
O'Sheanchin, N., 168
O'Sheile, 29.
O'Skellan, M., 151
O'Skyngin, Dermott, 302.
O'Sleivtyne, Hugh, 111.

Osrith, 112.
Ossill, a Dane, 134.
Ossory, 89, 109, 110, 117, 144, 148, 149, 151, 152, 157, 170, 174, 175, 176, 181, 185, 188, 192, 193, 194, 201, 202, 203, 207, 240, 309.
—— kings of, 69, 81, 89, 91, 97, 101, 103, 105, 109, 115, 117, 128, 139, 144, 148, 149, 164, 176, 178, 184, 206, 303, 309.
Ossve, battle of, 104.
Ossve, k. of Saxons, 105, 108, 109, 112.
Ossyn mᶜFinn, 62.
Ossyny Foda, 105.
Osu, battle of, 103.
O'Suarte, 169.
O'Sullevan, 321.
—— Bearrie, 321.
—— Connor, 321.
—— More, 321.
—— Owen, 321.
—— Philip, 25.
—— the bald, 321.
Oswald, 102, 103.
O'Swany of Rahin, 118, 119, 191.
O'Teige, John, 317.
Othlyn, plains of, 151
Othna more, 105, 112
O'Tigernie, T., 129.
O'Toole. *See* O'Twahall.
Ottyre Earle, 134.
O'Twahall, 29, 194, 320.
—— David, 305.
—— Felim, 325.
—— Hugh, p. of O'Male, 305.
—— Hugh, t. of Imaile, 325.
—— Lorcan, archb. of Dublin, 213, 214.
—— Lorcan, p. of Leinster, 228.
—— Murrogh, 192.
—— Owgarie, 194.
—— Phelim, p. of Morie, 325.
—— Shane Roe, 312.
Ouchawe mᶜSarann, 106.
Ova, battle of, 98.
Owa, battle of, 180.
Owen, 43, 46.
—— Bell, k. of C., 79.

Owen, b. of Ardstrathy, 99.
—— Britt, b. of Kildare, 141.
—— house of, 43, 46.
—— k. of M., 72.
—— k. of Scotland, 115.
—— Kymboye, 115.
—— mᶜCorcrann, 84.
—— mᶜNeale, 131, 172.
—— mᶜTorvey, 136.
—— Manisdreagh, 132, 135.
—— More, 58, 59.
—— son of Nial, 64, 126, 127.
Owgaire mᶜA., k. of L., 170.
Owgany More, 41–43, 210.
Owna, dr. of O'Connor, 316.
Owran, 217.
Oycke, 121.
Oylfyn, 217, 220, 239, 240, 256, 263, 286, 294, 326.
—— bishops of, 233, 238, 254, 261, 262, 267, 284, 298, 324, 326.

Palladius, 65.
Pallium, 242.
Panmas, 15, 16.
Pantha, 103, 104, 105, 108, 110.
Papinon, Cardinal, 199.
Pariena, 105.
Paris of Troy, 18.
Parthia, 22.
Paschal Cycle, 77.
Patrick mᶜIver, 159.
—— St., 3, 20, 63, 65–70, 73, 74, 78, 89, 92, 107, 116, 122, 127, 128, 131, 136, 145, 148, 171, 197, 204, 307, 309, 326.
—— cowarbs of, 74, 136, 150, 164, 224.
—— Island of, 128.
Paul, St , 49, 224.
Paule mᶜTeige, 310.
Pelagian heresy, 70.
Pelagius, pope, 84, 89.
Persia, 99.
Persye, Meyler, 257.
Pestilence, 83, 129
Peter, St., 49, 224, 228.
Pettit, Sir Adam, 256.
—— William, 225.

Index. 385

Pharao, 19, 20, 22.
Philip 4th, of Spain, 25.
—— St , 49.
Philippicus, 111.
Philippus, 111.
Phrygia, 49.
Phylistines, 21.
Physicians, 82.
Pictland, 26, 65, 74, 108, 120, 141
Picts, 25, 26, 70, 88, 101, 107, 111, 114, 115, 119.
—— kings of, 71, 74, 88, 89, 97, 101-107, 109, 110, 113, 114, 116, 120, 123.
Pilgrimages, 110, 120, 136, 149, 159, 160, 175, 179, 226, 229, 236, 297.
Pillars of lightning, 154.
Placida, 70.
Plagues, 177, 186, 297, 301, 308-310, 322, 323, 325, 328.
Plunketts, 30.
Poetry, 34, 39, 51, 61, 150, 250, 256, 258, 297, 319.
Poets, 34, 39, 44, 58, 143, 149, 150, 161, 169, 173, 179, 182, 190, 191, 195, 196, 198, 238, 246, 250, 256, 258, 266, 286, 292, 297, 298, 305, 309, 310, 322, 325, 327.
Poison, 64
Pompeius, 44.
Pontus, 109
Popes, 51, 52, 61, 65, 69-78, 84, 89, 91, 98, 99, 103, 104, 106, 112, 123, 179, 199, 204, 213, 222, 224, 229, 236, 246, 267, 286
Portlick, 147, 247.
Port-na-tri-namhad, 316.
Portugall, 22.
Pox, the pied, 109, 156, 285, 304.
Power, Pierce, 239.
—— William, 216.
Powers, 30.
Preachers, order of, 254.
Premonstra, order of, 243, 244.
Prendergasse, John, 258.
—— William, 271, 277.
—— Sir William, 261.
Priam, 21.
Princely Institutions, 60.

Prophecies, 62, 74, 80, 83, 84, 92, 124, 138, 143, 148.
Psalms of David, 87.
Psalter of Cashel, 8.

Queran, of Beladoyn, 122.
—— St. of C., 75, 79-83, 89, 93, 94, 99, 104, 113, 118, 122, 127, 133, 140, 147, 161, 163, 169-171, 176, 177, 181, 182, 184, 190, 197, 200, 201, 206, 214, 217, 224.
—— cowarbs of, 160, 171, 188, 189, 192, 195, 200, 201, 204, 213, 224.
—— of Dawinis, 147.
—— of Kells, 178
—— of Tymonna, 125, 126.
Race of Bowyne, 113.
—— Carbry, 107, 108, 113.
—— Carbry Crom, 137.
—— Carbry mᶜNeale, 171.
—— Conell Criowhan, 172.
—— Connell Gulban, 126, 127, 172
—— Dahye mᶜF., 171
—— Dalgaisse, 158.
—— Fiagh mᶜN., 266.
—— Gartnayt, 108.
—— Hugh Slane, 124-126, 131, 172.
—— Icova, 117.
—— k. Dahye, 171.
—— k. Lagerie, 148, 169, 178, 187, 190, 201.
—— Manie mᶜNeale, 64, 69, 125, 146.
—— Owen, 43, 46, 126, 127, 131, 172.
Rachrann, 102, 122, 127.
Ragainn, 111.
Ragall, 97.
Ragally, 105.
—— mᶜTreadagh, 103.
Rahin, 102, 118, 119, 127, 191, 196, 220. 221, 226, 233.
Ranalt, dr of O'Ferall, 232.
Randolph, e. of Antrim, 209.
—— a Dane, 153, 163.
—— mᶜAwley, 159.

Randolph mᶜDonnell, 209.
—— mᶜHymer, 168.
—— mᶜMorey, 191.
—— the Dane, 152.
Ranell O'Hemer, 134.
Ranelt, dr. of O'Connor, 225.
Rathangan, 129.
Rathbeg, 88.
Rathbehie, 28, 29.
Rathbothe, 95, 251, 282
Rathbrendon, 196.
Rathcashell, 249.
Rathconrath, 306.
Ratheyney, 151.
Rathgwayne, 223.
Rath-Hugh mᶜBrick, 308.
Rathkrae, 184.
Rathlin, 144, 177.
Rathlowrie, 133.
Rathmore, 109, 268.
Rathmoyeanye, 126.
Rathmoyle, 300.
Rathonie, 28.
Rathouth, 207.
Raths, 15, 28, 31.
Rattynie, 158.
Ravenna, 70, 72.
Rawaghan, 198.
Raymond de la Grosse, 207, 214.
Red Daughter, the, 134.
Reaghlawra, a. of Leih, 138.
Reaghtaury, 156.
Red Earl, the, 258, 260, 270, 271, 275
—— Sea, 19, 20.
—— Shanks. *See* Dalriada.
Relics, 94, 108, 139, 155, 197, 251.
—— of St. Adawnanus, 114, 133.
—— of St. Columkille, 132.
—— of St. Dochonna, 128.
—— of St. Patrick, 127, 326.
Renan, k. of Leinster, 97.
Reyne, 42.
Rhymes, 39.
Riched, 158.
Richard I , k. of E., 216.
—— II , k. of E., 322.
—— k. of France, 175.
—— mᶜen Miley, 323.
—— ne Koylle, 248.

Richard Strongbow, 207.
Rie, the, 124.
Rigallan mᶜConyng, 101.
Rindown, 25, 204, 216, 232, 235, 236, 249, 270.
Rings, 34.
Rional, 16.
Roadanus, a. of Lorha, 85–88.
Robert Moylann, 136.
—— the curtois, 184.
Rocean, 31.
Roch mᶜMaffias, 31.
Roche, David, 243.
Rochnia, a. of C , 126
Rochoeyne, 212.
Rochork mᶜGollann, 31.
Rochry, 213.
Rodanus. *See* Roadanus.
Roen, p. of Meath, 175.
Roheaghty, 210, 212.
—— k. of I., 33, 36.
—— Rithdearg, 41, 42, 211.
Roirck. *See* O'Royrck.
Romans, 12, 44, 46, 84, 89, 91, 103.
Rome, 3, 44, 49, 50, 54, 61, 65, 69, 174, 179, 228, 242, 246, 256, 262, 286.
Ronan, a. of C., 139.
—— mᶜBeraye, 107, 108.
—— mᶜColman, 100.
Rood, the holy, 239.
Rory, son of Dela, 15, 16.
—— k. of L., 115.
Roscommon, 123, 129, 220, 241, 245, 247, 249, 250, 251, 261, 262, 268, 270, 277, 293, 295, 300, 304, 305.
Roscrea, 143, 147, 149, 202.
Rose de Hoileagh, 15.
Ross, 46.
Rossawyn glass, 212.
Rosse, 213.
Rosseglassie, 231.
Rossemide, 206.
Rossemore, 138.
Roua, 277.
Rouartagh mᶜMooney, 126.
Rouaye Connell, 128, 204.
Rovartagh, 142.
Rowanus. *See* Roadanus.

Rowrie, 213
—— mᶜSitrick, 45, 46.
—— son of Bartoleme, 13.
Royndown. *See* Rindown
Roynie Roe, 209.
Ruadhan. *See* Roadanus.
Rubinn, 113.
Rules of St Aidan, 122.
—— of St. Ailve, 127.
—— of St Brandon, 118.
—— of St Columkille, 119.
—— of St Coman, 127.
—— of St. O'Swany, 118.
—— of St. Patrick, 116, 122, 131, 132.
—— of St. Queran, 118, 122, 127.
—— of St. Sagnus, 120.
Rurhagh, 13.
Rwabehy, 193.
Rwadan, b. of Lusk, 144.
Rwaragh, battle of, 123.
Rwarck, k. of L., 115.
Ryndowne. *See* Rindown.

Sabinianus, pope, 98.
Sagnus, St., 120.
Saithne, 183.
Salamon, 209.
Salmons, 178.
Sam, 12
Samias Nimas, 14
Sampson, 21.
Sanctuaries, 131.
Sane, k of E., 192.
Santford, John, Deputy, 256.
Sanv, 42.
Saracens, 258.
Sarad, 58
Saran, a. of Beanchor, 118.
—— mᶜCridan, 106.
Saraynne, 212.
Sattynn, battle of, 100.
Sauall, church of, 170.
Savage, Henry, 309.
—— Revellyn, 309.
—— Richard, 301.
—— Sir Robert, 300.
Savia, 23.
Saw, 58.

Sawarle, 209.
Sawe, dr. of Burke, 308.
—— dr. of O'Neale, 312
Sawhyn, of Clonbrony, 117.
Sawthurst, 84.
Saxolve, 137.
Saxons, 9, 70, 72, 97, 100, 101, 102, 105, 108, 109, 111, 112, 131, 141, 142, 145, 146, 148, 149, 151, 152, 154, 179.
Saxony, 194.
Sayer, 89, 118, 130, 138, 142, 156.
Sayrbrey, a. of C , 127.
Sayrgus O'Cahaille, 124.
—— O'Kenny, 136.
Sayuer, the, 13.
Scanlagh mᶜClonbayren, 119.
Scanlan, a. of Louth, 106.
—— k. of M , 72.
—— mᶜKinley, 97.
—— more mᶜKynfoyle, 103, 240.
Scannall, a. of Kilkenny, 124.
—— b. of Kildare, 143.
—— mᶜGorman, 147.
Scannlan mᶜCahall, 167.
Scathyne, a. of Durrow, 155
Schools, 7, 8.
Scithia, 19, 22, 23.
Scota, 22, 23
Scotland, 26, 27, 29, 43, 46, 50, 63, 71, 72, 78, 80, 82, 88, 90-94, 96, 128, 132, 149, 151, 159, 167, 241, 258, 259, 260, 261, 262, 277, 281, 289, 327.
—— kings of, 26, 45, 50, 69, 74, 80, 88, 90, 96-98, 101, 111, 115, 120, 145, 156-158, 163, 185, 187, 200, 204, 261, 268, 279, 281.
—— men of, 68, 88, 149, 163, 237, 269, 271, 281.
Scribes, 113, 114, 122, 124, 126, 128, 129, 132, 136, 138, 139, 140-142, 147, 149, 150, 169.
Scroope, 327, 328.
Scrubleith, 268.
Sdarne, 14.
Seachnall, 69.
Seachnassagh, k. of I , 101, 108, 172.
—— mᶜArueay, 109.

Seachnassagh of Dorowe, 149.
—— p. of Imaine, 112.
—— son of Blathmack, 107.
Seaga, 28
Seaisse, 74, 273.
Sealuy, 116
Seanagh Garve, 100.
Seanchan, a of Imleach, 122, 124
—— mᶜColman, 91.
Seang Rifflar, 23.
Seangan mᶜDela, 15, 16.
Secundinus, 69, 70.
Sedna Art, 33, 213.
—— Anerie, 37, 212.
Sedragh mᶜSobarchinn, 124.
Segain mᶜIlkwid, 106.
Segasse, 273.
Segeni, a. of Hy, 102, 104.
Segine, b. of Armagh, 110.
Seirgall o'Daingne, 124
Semiramis, 13, 14.
Senagh, b. of Clonard, 90.
Seolmoy, 42.
Sept of Balle-Athboy, 308.
—— of Boynnean, 257.
—— Clandownye, 257.
—— Colman, 51.
—— Clone, 308.
—— Comninstown, 308.
—— Donogh, 257.
—— Finyne, 257.
—— Firbolgs, 15, 16.
—— Fomores, 15, 282.
—— Heber, 5, 29-33, 36, 209, 210, 212, 213.
—— Heremon, 5, 29-31, 33, 35-38, 43, 45, 50, 209.
—— Hugh Slane, 51, 172.
—— Ire, 29, 30.
—— Lauthus, 29, 30, 58.
—— Leackagh, 257.
—— Lismayne, 308.
—— Louay, 57.
—— Moycashell, 308.
—— Newtowne, 308
—— O'Neals, 54.
—— O'Roirck, 191.
—— Tuatha de Danaan, 17.
—— Ulster, 35.
Septs, 8, 29, 54, 63, 64, 125.

Sergeants, 85, 148.
Sesibutus, 99.
Seth, 11, 21.
Sevdan, a. of Kildare, 115.
Severinus, pope, 99.
Seysye, 235.
Shannon, the, 93, 120, 130, 137, 158, 159, 165, 184, 191, 194, 196, 204, 229, 237, 247, 269, 274.
Sheriffs, 238, 239, 242, 261
Shiell mᶜFeray, 132.
Showers of blood, &c., 112, 121, 170.
Shrines, 94, 158, 175, 197.
Silagh, 22.
Sile Anmcha, 175, 188, 192, 202, 219, 244, 255, 256, 296, 299.
—— Daly, 142.
—— Dluhy, 102.
—— Morraye, 111, 187, 194, 239, 251, 263-265, 270, 276, 279, 294, 309, 311, 323.
—— Moyleroyne, 193
—— Ronan, 189, 203, 221
—— Sawa, 58.
Silelawe, 213
Sillan, a. of Moibille, 99.
—— b. of Daiwinis, 105.
Sillane mᶜComyn, 98.
Silver, 32.
—— shower of, 121.
Silverius, pope, 78.
Simyrgwill, 210.
Simplicius, pope, 72.
Sinagh of I. Clothrann, 113.
Sincheall mᶜKean, 84.
Sineall, b. of Moyville, 98.
Siorna mᶜDeyn, 35, 36.
Siracusa, 78.
Sirelaw, 37, 213.
Sithfrey, 151.
Sithmath, 123.
Sitrick, 146, 151, 169, 192, 213
—— mᶜAwley, 164, 169, 175.
—— mᶜConvaye, 189
—— O'Hymer, 148, 170.
Sixtus, pope, 65.
Siwdayne, battle of, 246.
Slaine, 75, 119, 122, 126, 129, 155.
Slainy, dr. of O'Bryan, 295.

Index. 389

Slane, a. of Louth, 120.
—— son of Dela mᶜL , 15, 16.
Slane. *See* Slaine
Slanoll, 35.
Slaynge, son of Bartheleme, 13
Sleawyn, 73, 98.
Slieve Beacha, 150.
—— Beth, 11.
—— Bleanne, 178.
—— Bloome, 138, 198.
—— Brey, 269.
—— Corrann, 314
—— -da-ene, 262
—— Eachtge, 277.
—— Fwagde, 124, 131, 174.
—— Gawe, 274
—— Gowlyn, 75
—— Grot, 173
—— Kava, 96
—— Louth, 241, 249
—— Mairge, 207.
—— Mis, 37.
—— Seysie, 233, 243.
—— Twa, 63, 99
Sligeach (Sligo), 79, 239, 247, 270, 289, 291, 300, 301, 311, 312, 316, 319, 323.
—— castle, 238, 249, 265, 275, 304, 316, 322.
—— river, 13
Slioght Cowchogrye, 308.
—— Donell, 257.
—— Donnogh, 257.
—— Ferall, 308
—— Fynyne, 257
—— Hugh Boy, 308.
—— mᶜShane, 308
Smerhie, 227.
Smeyrtire, 63
Smergol, 32.
Snamhe da en, 218
Sneriagall, a. of C., 126.
Snow, great, 35, 36, 118, 157, 173, 256, 282, 290.
Soldan, the, 258.
Solomon, 10, 22
Solomon's temple, 190
Sorares, 20.
Soige, 28.
—— mᶜDuff, 31.

Sosarinus, 16.
Souarge, 28.
Sovarke, 32
Spain, 3, 5, 21, 22, 23, 25, 59
Spaniards, 23, 59.
Spartus, 14.
Sphereus, 14.
Srade-bally, 312.
Srue, 20, 210.
Sruhir, 236.
Staff of Jesus, 197, 201.
Stafford, Hobert, 246.
Stanton. *See* Stonton.
Star, bright, 99.
Stephen, k of E., 215.
—— St., 179, 262, 292.
Stonton, Adam, 258.
—— John, 277.
—— Walter, 301.
Stontons, Lord of the, 323.
Strathkaron, battle of, 110.
Strongbow, Richard, 207.
Suanus, St , of Rahin, 119, 221.
Suck, the, 29, 120, 130, 236.
Sufforne, S., 246.
Suir, the, 15, 320.
Sun, eclipses of, 141, 173.
—— sworn by, 171.
Suns, two, 144.
Swanchean, 133.
Swamou, the, 97.
Swarleagh, a. of Clonard, 142.
—— b. of Fower, 119.
Swart, 146, 169.
Sweep of Fanaid, the, 83.
Sword of Charles, 163.
—— of St Finnan, 195.
Swords, 170, 192.
Swyne, 209.
—— a. of Clonfert, 121.
—— a. of Lynnlere, 149.
—— mᶜColman, 97, 103.
—— mᶜCwoihre, 105.
—— mᶜFarny, a. of Armagh, 132.
—— mᶜKonolaye, 113.
—— Mean, 97, 99, 172.
Swynie mᶜDuff D , 143
—— mᶜMoyleowa, 109.
—— O'Hogan, 178
Swynies, the, 318.

Swynshed, 229.
Sye, battle of, 77.
Symedes, 22.
Symmachus, pope, 74, 75.
Symon Breachus, 37, 210.
—— mcAnfalgye, 287.
—— Magus, 49.
Syn, 42.
Synan, the. *See* Shannon.
Synods, 106, 124, 201, 224 228.
Syonan, 112.
Syvre, the. *See* Suir.

Taburna, 68.
Tahamore, 134.
Tailten, 26, 108, 146, 148, 164.
Tailty, dr. of o'Melaghlin, 190.
Tain bo Cwailgne, 48.
Tall, 211.
Talo, battle of, 89.
Talorg mcCougusa, 115.
Talorgan mcFergus, 119.
Tamberlane, 135
Tanaised Abbot, 147.
Tandy mcGwyer, 157.
Tanist, 224, 257, 278, 279, 281, 283, 285, 295, 300, 304, 308, 309, 315, 317, 322–325.
Tanning, 95
Tantanes, 27.
Tara, 16, 26, 27, 34, 35, 42, 45, 47, 52, 56, 59, 61, 64, 66, 71, 72, 80, 86-88, 108, 124, 128, 130, 138, 159, 165
—— kings of, 54, 90, 122, 133, 144, 148, 155, 162, 169, 176-178, 189, 192, 200.
Tarawnagh, 283.
Targets, silver, 33.
Tarileus, 27.
Tarry, 42.
Tartars, 258.
Tauorne, 210.
Taw Caissi, 71.
Tawnye, p of, 113
Taylchoynne, 174.
Tea, 27.
Teadochonna, 246.
Teadoyne. *See* Rindown.

Teaffa, 31, 69, 111, 138, 146, 174, 180-183, 189, 191, 192, 201, 203–205.
—— kings of, 84, 88, 89, 91, 95, 107, 117, 122, 136, 155, 156, 165, 168, 183, 187, 189, 231, 234, 278, 323.
Teag mcMordevor, 120
Teagasg Ri, 60.
Teagh Eoin *See* Rindown.
Teallaghaagh, 260, 300.
—— Donnoghaa, 256, 280, 314.
Teamur, 27,
Teanmay, 31.
Tehille, 113, 118, 142, 143.
Teig, son of Brian B., 168, 173, 179
—— br. of Flathvertagh, 157.
—— mcFaylan, 147
Temclene o'Doynne, 255.
Templars, 267.
Templevickinloyhe, 81.
Terence, gr. son of Brian B., 167, 211.
Termon lands, 133, 140, 160, 178, 182, 224
Testaments transcribed, 95.
Thayde, 210.
Theodorus, b. of Brittaine, 110.
—— heretic, 106.
—— pope, 103.
Theodosius, emperor, 65, 106.
Thineus, 27.
Thomas, a. of Beanchor, 127.
—— son of k of E., 328.
Thomond, 58, 168, 170, 181, 191, 199, 202, 249, 267, 305
—— the earl of, 211.
—— princes of, 196, 222, 237, 246, 260, 267, 272, 277, 279, 302.
Thracia, 18
Thunder, great, 116, 128, 171, 241, 285.
Thunderbolt, 74, 75, 191, 262.
Tiberius Cæsar, 48.
Tibreydultan, 223
Tigernach of Derymelly, 130.
Tigernwas, 31, 210
Tinnie, bridge of, 227.
Tionoye, 115.

Index. 391

Tiprady, k. of C., 115.
—— mᶜCalgie, 97.
—— mᶜTeige, 126.
—— Tyreagh, 59, 213.
Tire Ailealla, 281, 283, 289, 295, 310, 311, 317, 318, 320, 325.
—— Awley, 311, 322
—— Bryan, 205, 266, 284, 294, 321.
—— Connell, 43, 76, 82, 92, 119, 142, 154, 155, 157, 162-165, 168, 172, 178, 232, 237, 238, 243, 247, 250, 253, 260, 275, 289, 293, 300, 306, 307, 313, 320.
—— Daglasse, 105, 138, 139, 149, 198.
—— Dalogha, 192.
—— Fiaghragh, 258, 262, 291, 311, 312.
—— Fiaghragh Aidhne, 216, 324
—— Hugh, 321.
—— Owen, 29, 43, 141, 165, 172, 197, 202, 220, 230, 236, 242, 320.
—— —— princes of, 164, 236, 282.
Tirewirb, 211.
Tirrhian sea, 42.
Tobber Bride, 270.
—— Tulske, 327.
Togher-Mone-Koyne, 276
Toighigh O'Tigernie, 129.
Tola mᶜD., b. of Clonard, 116
Tolorchan mᶜAnfrith, 105.
Tolorg, 114.
Tor, 133
Torbagh, a. of Armagh, 129.
Torbert O'Duffe, 133
Torlan, 146.
Tormair mᶜAlchi, 148.
Tormyn mᶜKeile, 134.
Tortan, battle of, 79
Torvearan mᶜGallgoyle, 223.
Tory, church of, 100.
Toymnercke, 104
Toytin, prey of, 264.
Tracy, Sir W., 207.
Trajan, emperor, 52.
Tredath, 201
Tree in Moyeayre, 159.
Treoide, 122.

Trevan, 133.
Triagharney, 42.
Triah, 42.
Tribute, 134
Trim, 131, 190, 228, 307, 308.
Trinity I. in L Ke, 240, 243
—— in L. Oghter, 241, 244
Trinity, order of the, 240.
Trogy, bog of, 36.
Trojan war, 18.
Trojans, 18.
Troy, 18, 21.
Tryme. *See* Trim.
Tuite, David, 252.
—— Hodgin, 328.
—— John, 252.
—— Lawrence, 308.
—— Richard, 224, 237, 244, 246, 249, 257.
Tulanes, 27.
Tullagh Brefnagh, 314.
Tullean, 156
Turgesius, 133, 139.
Turkill, 133.
Turks, 134
Turren (Tours), 63, 64
Tuylelaidh, a. of Kildare, 143.
Twachar, b. of Kildare, 136
Twagarta, a of Keyndea, 149.
Twahal, k. of L., 115
—— mᶜAwgaire, 157.
—— mᶜFeraye, 133.
—— mᶜMorgan, 106
—— mᶜMoyle Rowa, 163.
—— mᶜOenganann, 148
—— Moylegarve, 72, 78-80, 171
—— Teachtwar, 16, 50, 52, 54, 209.
Twaliah, q. of L, 119
Twaime (Tuam), 217, 220, 224, 230, 241, 267, 286, 298, 299, 327.
—— Grenie, 119, 127.
—— Seancha, 312.
Twamsnawa, k. of O., 97, 101, 109.
Twatha de Danann, 3, 16, 17, 21, 25, 26, 27, 65.
Twathas, the, 253, 263, 288, 291.
Twenoc, a of Ferns, 106.
Twilleliah, a of Cloncuiffne, 125.

Tygernwas, 31, 210.
Tymnen of Kilgarad, 114.
Tymochwa, 149
Tymoling, 149.
Tymonna, 102, 125, 130, 132, 309.
Tympanist, 286, 302.
Tyre. *See* Tire.
Tyrenmore, castle of, 238
Tyreneaghtynn, 275.
Tyrenna, 275.
Tyrone. *See* Tireowen.
Tyrrell, Geready, 299.
—— John, 239.
—— Sir Walter, 215.
Tyrrhian sea, 42, 64, 296.

Uaisle, dr. of Swynie, 103.
Uaran, 220.
Ugaine Mor, 41–43, 210.
Ulgarg o'Kyerga, 165
Ullemanagh, 249.
Ullemine Wanagh, 235.
Ulster, 15, 16, 28, 32–41, 43, 46–48, 50, 54, 63, 66, 70, 73, 80, 83, 84, 107, 115, 118, 125, 130, 131, 133, 139, 150, 168, 169, 173, 177, 187–189, 202, 217, 220, 223, 226, 229, 236, 237, 253, 268–271, 277, 289, 293, 296, 302, 307, 308.
—— countess of, 260.
—— earls of, 229, 236, 245, 247–249, 256, 257, 259, 266, 268, 284, 285, 286, 288, 289, 290, 291, 292, 295, 297.
—— kings of, 34, 37, 41, 44, 47–49, 54, 55, 69, 72, 84, 89, 90, 97, 101, 108, 118, 127, 135, 137, 143, 146, 152, 159, 179, 180, 185, 191, 202, 216, 236, 284, 301, 319, 324.
Ulstermen, 50, 56, 74, 89, 90, 107, 111, 127, 132, 153, 164, 177, 181, 189, 214, 236, 269, 271.
Ultan mᶜDicholla, 109.
—— mᶜErnany, 106.
—— mᶜIchonga, 107.
—— St., 105.
Un mᶜUga, 28, 29.
Unonn, 189.
Upercroossann, 116.

Uriell, 54, 163, 189, 191, 195, 206, 213, 271, 286, 291, 298, 300, 312, 316.
—— bishops of, 213, 300.
—— princes of, 97, 146, 182, 201, 205, 215, 249, 253, 267, 293, 294, 296, 300, 302.
Urnie, the, 307.
Usneagh, 38, 75, 192.
Utices, 107.
Uwlfie, 143.

Vaghan more, 48.
Vaghter-herye, 279.
Valentinian, 70.
Varde eallae, 216.
Venemous beasts, 19.
Verdon. *See* De Verden.
Vertiger, 70.
Vespation, 50
Via Salaria, 78.
Victor, the angel, 63
Vigilius, pope, 78, 84, 106.
Vinianus, 89
Virgil, 44.
—— a. of Tyrdaglass, 149
Vitalianus, pope, 104.

Wales, 9, 48, 96, 109, 238, 324.
—— kings of, 85, 86, 155, 163, 173, 180, 204, 207, 244, 261.
Wallagh, 39.
Wallaghan mᶜCahall, 144.
Walter English, 134
—— O'Salerna, 241.
Wasbagh, 133.
Waterford, 15, 145, 148, 159, 164, 168, 170, 190, 194, 196.
—— bishop of, 222.
Wattin, of Tireawley, 322.
Weaving, 314.
Wells, sacred, 99.
Welshmen, 8, 9, 14, 68, 100, 107, 119, 131, 141, 206, 214, 324.
Westmeath, 38, 51, 73, 74, 102, 182, 190, 191, 195, 198, 306.
Westminster, 27, 253.

Index

Wexford, 138, 150, 308.
Whale, 118.
Wheat, showers of, 121, 170
Wicklow, 66
William March, 231.
—— Marshall, 230, 234
—— Rufus, 184, 215.
—— the Conqueror, 179, 184, 215.
—— the Conqueror (Burke), 248
Wind, boisterous, 67, 91, 109, 160, 162, 196, 229.

Wind, sworn by, 71
Wine, kyve of, 77.
Wirgrean, sons of, 61
Witchraft, 25, 117.
Wolf speaking, 110.

Xistus, pope, 09

York, 92, 142, 152, 154, 156.

THE END.

Lightning Source UK Ltd.
Milton Keynes UK
UKHW020239040820
367650UK00011B/286